REEDS

NAUTICAL COMPANION

THE HANDBOOK TO COMPLEMENT REED'S ALMANACS

NORTH AMERICAN EDITION

Editor: John J. Kettlewell
Assistant Editor: Leslie Kettlewell

Editorial Team:
Jean Fowler, M.R.I.N.
Thomas B. Stableford, Master Mariner, M.R.I,N.
Lt. Cdr. Harry J. Baker, R.D., R.N.R., M.R.I.N.
Robin Ekblom, F.R.I.C.S.
Arthur Somers, C.ENG., M.I.E.E.
Roger Taylor
Kathleen Karny
Catherine Degnon

THOMAS REED
PUBLICATIONS INC

LONDON BOSTON

NAUTICAL PUBLISHERS SINCE 1782

122 Lewis Wharf
Boston MA 02110
U.S.A.
Tel: (617) 248 0084 Fax: (617) 248 5855

First Edition 1993

ISBN 0-947637-58-3
ISSN 0968 4387

Printed in Great Britain by BPCC Wheatons Ltd, Exeter

Contents

Acknowledgements

Flag information is provided and authenticated by the Flag Institute, Chester, England.

Inmarsat and GMDSS information compiled by the International Maritime Satellite Organisation, London, England,

'Fast Boat Navigation' and 'Dealing with Hull Leaks' written by Kim Hollamby.

State of Sea Photographs:
Force 0,1,2,5,6,7,8,11,12 are reproduced with permission of H.M. Stationary Office.
Force 3 (R. Palmer), Force 4, (P. J. Weaver), Force 9 (O. R. Bates), Force 10 (J. Hodkinson).

Cloud photographs are reproduced with permission of R. K. Pilsbury.

International Code Flags are reproduced with permission of the Controller, H. M. Stationary Office.

Color Buoyage Illustrations are reproduced with the permission of the United States Coast Guard.

Information on marine ropes is provided by New England Ropes.

LEGAL NOTES

The Story of Reed''s Almanac . . .

IT HAS BEEN called the Yachtsman's Bible, the Sailor's Vade Mecum, even the Navigator's ABC. It has done service in countless thousands of ships, yachts and small craft in peace and war. It has saved lives, and brought children into the world. It is *Reed's Nautical Almanac*, known universally as plain *Reed's*, and it owes its existence to the inspired dedication of one man.

In June 1931 a young ex-Merchant Navy officer came to the Sunderland office of Thomas Reed & Co with a proposal for the managing director, Harold Brunton-Reed.

Founded in 1782, Reed's were reputed to be the oldest nautical publishers in the world. In 1859, they had produced the first textbook for officers taking the new Masters' and Mates' certificates. Their *Reed's Seamanship,* first published in the 1830s, had sold more than 100,000 copies. How, asked the young man, would they like a chance to publish something even more successful?

At the time Reed's were finding business difficult. The depression had hit publishing hard, if not quite as hard as it had hit the firm's shipyard neighbors on the banks of the River Weir. Their largest regular job was the annual printing of the Christmas catalogue for a local department store. So Brunton-Reed listened to his visitor with interest.

One of the youngest Merchant Navy officers ever to hold a Master's certificate, O. M. Watts had left the sea in 1927. For a time he eked out a precarious living delivering yachts and teaching yachtsmen navigation, supplemented by work editing *Pearson's Nautical Almanac.* While working on the almanac – and using it on his deliveries all around Britain – Watts became convinced that he could improve on the model, with an almanac designed specifically for the yachts, fishing boats and small commercial vessels operating in the treacherous waters around the British Isles.

Watt's idea was that he should compile, and Reed's should publish, a standard reference so comprehensive that it would have a place on every yacht and merchant ship's chart table. In one volume it would assemble all the knowledge a navigator would need to con a vessel in Home Trade Waters. But best of all, as far as Reed's were concerned, was Watts' assertion that its buyers would willingly come back for a replacement every year.

Pearson's was sold in 1931, giving Watts the incentive to take his idea further. First he needed to find a publisher. He had used Reed's before to print his own technical publications, and with their reputation and background felt they would be an ideal choice. Full of confidence, he made the long journey from his home in London to Sunderland.

Brunton-Reed was enthusiastic, even more so when he heard that *Pearson's* would not be published the following year, giving the proposed new title a clear run. Publisher and editor shook hands – as Watts described it, "the only agreement we ever made" – and Watts returned to London to compile the first issue of the new almanac for publication by January 1, 1932.

Often working until two in the morning, Watts spent the next six months compiling his almanac. With his declared intention of comprehensive coverage of Home Trade Waters, he had to draw up a complete list of lights and buoys for British and Continental ports from Brest to the Elbe, including Denmark, the Faeroes and Iceland. He had to prepare the tidal data for countless ports, calculate course and distances from port to port, and write whole sections on maritime law, signalling and pilotage.

The first ediion of *Reed's Home Trade Nautical Almanac and Tide Tables*, as the book was called, was published in the first week of January 1932. A measure of the effort that went into the production is that even the first edition ran to 990 pages.

Sales of the new almanac were everything Watts and Brunton-Reed had hoped for, although Harold's son Kenneth was later to claim that it took twenty years for the almanac to show a profit. Watts immediately began work on the second edition, his enthusiasm bolstered by scores of letters of appreciation from professional seamen and yachtsmen alike.

Many of the letters offered helpful observations and suggestions for other useful sections and tables, which Watts was able to incorporate into the second and subsequent editions. The second edition saw the introduction of a full-color guide to the International Code of Signals, followed over the next five years by further additions such as tidal stream charts of the Pentland Firth and the Solent, Sun and Star GHA tables, and a section on first-aid at sea. Never too proud to listen to feedback, even when *Reed's* had earned itself the status of navigator's Bible, Watts carefully considered every suggestion for improvement and, if it was practical, adopted it. As a glance through the pages of this edition will show, his policy of continuous improvement is maintained even today.

During the thirties Watts opened a chandlery in Albemarle Street, off London's Piccadilly, where he continued to compile and edit successive editions of *Reed's* from an office in the back of the shop. As the war clouds began to gather over Europe, Albemarle Street was the logical site for his next venture; a sea school where yachtsmen could be taught what they would need to know to serve in the Royal Naval Volunteer Reserve in the coming conflict.

This symbiotic relationship with amateurs who were shortly to become professionals enabled Watts to remain in close touch with the needs of the contemporary navigator and to fine-tune his book to suit the conditions. When war finally broke out, the *Reed's Almanac* that had been a convenience for sailors became a lifeline for the professional, and Watts was acutely aware of the awesome responsibility he now bore.

As the bombs fell on London during the Blitz, Watts continued to work on the next year's Almanac. In the preface to the 10th edition, he wrote: "No new features have been introduced into *Reed's Almanac* for 1941 for the main reason that the majority of the pages have been prepared in London during night after night of incessant bombing and gunfire, which has made it a physical impossibility . . . We in London are glad to bear many of the horrors of modern warfare so that some at least may be lifted from the shoulders of our seafarers – Royal and Merchant Navy men both".

Reed's finest hour came in 1944, when the government ordered 3000 extra copies of the almanac for use in vessels involved in the Normandy D-Day landings.

After the war, as yachtsmen began once more to roam the seas, those who had served in the Royal and Merchant Navies naturally continued to use the almanac that had seen them through the hostilities. *Reed's* was now what Watts had promised Harold Brunton-Reed it would be: as essential an item of chartroom equipment as a pair of compasses, and aboard many boats the only reference apart from charts and pilots that any navigator ever used.

What was it that made *Reed's* so indispensable? Murray Sayle, reporting to the *Sunday Times* from an OSTAR yacht in mid-Atlantic in 1972, gives a clue:

"Apart from being a quarry of hard-won sea lore, *Reed's* is composed in a unique literary form, half prose, half verse, like some early Norseman's saga. 'Worm and parcel with the lay, turn and serve the other way' is advice which must have comforted many a lonely sailor on a night watch. I turned idly to Section XIX, the most riveting of all Reed's 1240 pages, 'Weather Forecasting by a single observer'. I had just drawn a blanket up to my chin when a couplet leapt from page five: 'At sea with low and falling glass, soundly sleeps a careless ass.' In three seconds I was out of my berth, flashlight in hand, tapping the barometer."

Every year produced new features or improvements, culled from reader's suggestions or dreamt up by Watts' fertile imagination. One of the more extraordinary additions was a section on childbirth at sea, commissioned from a doctor friend. "We never thought it would be used," said Watts. But he had reckoned without pregnant yachtswoman Rosie Swale. As she and her husband set off from Southampton for Italy in their 30ft catamaran, Mrs. Swale told a newspaper reporter: "We are putting our faith in good old *Reed's Nautical Almanac* It has loads of information on the subject, including this wonderful advice to keep calm, unhurried and let nature take its course." Six months later, the joke became reality when husband Colin had to deliver Rosie's 12lb baby off Fiumicino, Italy.

O. M. Watts continued to edit *Reed's* until 1981, always from the office in Albemarle Street. On his retirement he was succeeded as Editor by Jean Fowler, who had been working for Thomas Reed Publications for more than twenty years and was able to take over the reins without in any way compromising the accuracy and usability for which *Reed's* was famous.

The change of ownership has made it possible to make significant improvements to *Reed's Almanac* to bring it truly up-to-date. The use of modern desktop publishing technology has enabled the editors to improve the layout and to introduce color within the main body of the Almanac without affecting publishing lead times. This ensures that the information remains as current as it has always been.

Foreign editions and expanded coverage are another part of the story. But the most obvious change, perhaps, is the separation of the almanac into two publications. It might surprise readers to know that this is not the first time that *Reed's* has been a two-volume reference book. In 1942, recognising the value of the Almanac to seamen, the Government was reluctant to put obstacles in the way of publication; but with paper – like everything else imported – then in short supply, the book's customary 1100-plus pages could not be maintained. The company therefore published a slimmed-down version of 250 pages containing only the information that changed annually: Sun, Moon, Stars and the Tide Tables. Readers were asked to keep their 1941 editions as a companion volume to be used in conjunction with the 1942 volume.

More recently, in 1975, 'J.L.D.' wrote in the Journal of the Honourable Company of Master Mariners: "In spite of the Publishers' note 'Less Bulk – More Pages' Reed's still seems to me a bit bulky, and I wonder if thought has ever been given to publishing it in two parts. A yachtsman friend whose opinion I value suggested that all the permanent information such as conversion tables, distance tables, navigation and the like need only be published, say, once in five years and the ephemeris, tide tables, etc, every year. This would reduce the bulk very considerably and the two smaller books would be easier to handle than one large one."

Well, J.L.D., we have done it. We hope you approve.

NAVIGATION RULES – INLAND

1

Page

INTRODUCTION

The Inland Rules in this book replace the old Inland Rules, Western Rivers Rules, Great Lakes Rules, their respective pilot rules and interpretive rules, and parts of the Motorboat Act of 1940. Many of the old navigation rules were originally enacted in the last century. Occasionally, provisions were added to cope with the increasing complexities of water transportation. Eventually, the navigation rules for United States inland waterways became such a confusing patchwork of requirements that in the 1960's several attempts were made to revise and simplify them. These attempts were not successful.

Following the signing of the Convention on the International Regulations for Preventing Collisions at Sea, 1972, a new effort was made to unify and update the various inland navigation rules. This effort culminated in the enactment of the Inland Navigational Rules Act of 1980. This legislation sets out Rules 1 through 38 – the main body of the Rules. The five Annexes were published as regulations. It is important to note that with the exception of Annex V to the Inland Rules, the International and Inland Rules and Annexes are very similar in both content and format.

The effective date for the Inland Navigation Rules was December 24, 1981, except for the Great Lakes where the effective date was March 1, 1983.

PART A – GENERAL

Rule 1 *Application*

(a) These Rules apply to all vessels upon the inland waters of the United States and to vessels of the United States on the Canadian waters of the Great Lakes to the extent that there is no conflict with Canadian law.

(b) (i) These Rules constitute special rules made by an appropriate authority within the meaning of Rule 1(b) of the International Regulations.

(ii) All vessels complying with the construction and equipmentrequirements of the International Regulations are considered to be incompliance with these Rules.

(c) Nothing in these Rules shall interfere with the operation of any special rules made by the Secretary of the Navy with respect to additional station or signal lights and shapes or whistle signals for ships of war and vessels proceeding under convoy, or by the Secretary with respect to additional station or signal lights and shapes for fishing vessels engaged in fishing as a fleet. These additional station or signal lights and shapes or whistle signals shall, so far as possible, be such that they cannot be mistaken for any light, shape, or signal authorized elsewhere under these Rules. Notice of such special rules shall be published in the Federal Register and, after the effective date specified in such notice, they shall have effect as if they were a part of these Rules.

(d) Vessel traffic service regulations may be in effect in certain areas.

(e) Whenever the Secretary determines that a vessel or class of vessels of special construction or purpose cannot comply fully with the provisions of any of these Rules with respect to the number, position, range, or arc of visibility of lights or shapes, as well as to the disposition and characteristics of sound-signaling appliances, the vessel shall comply with such other provisions in regard to the number, position, range, or arc of visibility of lights or shapes, as well as to the disposition and characteristics of sound-signaling appliances, as the Secretary shall have determined to be the closest possible compliance with these Rules .The Secretary may issue a certificate of alternative compliance for a vessel or class of vessels specifying the closest possible compliance with these Rules The Secretary of the Navy shall make these determinations and issue certificates of alternative compliance for vessels of the Navy.

(f) The Secretary may accept a certificate of alternative compliance issued by a contracting party to the International Regulations if he determines that the alternative compliance standards of the contracting party are substantially same as those of the United States.

Rule 2 *Responsibility*

(a) Nothing in these Rules shall exonerate any vessel, or the owner, master, or crew thereof, from the consequences of any neglect to comply with these Rules or of the neglect of any precaution which may be required by the ordinary practice of seamen, or by the special circumstances of the case.

(b) In construing and complying with these Rules due regard shall be had to all dangers of navigation and collision and to any special circumstances, including the limitations of the vessels involved, which may make a departure from these Rules necessary to avoid immediate danger.

Rule 3 *General Definitions*

For the purpose of these Rules and this Act, except where the context otherwise it requires:

(a) The word "vessel" includes every description of water craft, including nondisplacement craft and seaplanes, used or capable of being used as a means of transportation on water;

(b) The term "power-driven vessel" means any vessel propelled by machinery;

(c) The term "sailing vessel" means any vessel under sail provided that propelling machinery if fitted, is not being used;

(d) The term "vessel engaged in fishing" means any vessel fishing with nets, lines, trawls, or other fishing apparatus which restricts maneuverability, but does not include a vessel fishing with trolling lines or other fishing apparatus which does not restrict maneuverability;

(e) The word "seaplane" includes any aircraft designed to maneuver on the water;

(f) The term "vessel not under command" means a vessel which through some exceptional circumstances is unable to maneuver as required by these Rules and is therefore unable to keep out of the way of another vessel;

(g) The term "vessel restricted in her ability to maneuver" means a vessel which from the nature of her work is restricted in her ability to maneuver as required by these Rules and is therefore unable to keep out of the way of another vessel; vessels restricted in their ability to maneuver include, but are not limited to:

(i) a vessel engaged in laying, servicing, or picking up a navigation mark, submarine cable, or pipeline;

(ii) a vessel engaged in dredging, surveying, or underwater operations;

(iii) a vessel engaged in replenishment or transferring persons, provisions, or cargo while underway;

(iv) a vessel engaged in the launching or recovery of aircraft;

(v) a vessel engaged in mineclearance operations; and

(vi) a vessel engaged in a towing operation such as severely restricts the towing vessel and her tow in their ability to deviate from their course.

(h) The word "underway" means that a vessel is not at anchor, or made fast to the shore or aground;

(i) The words "length" and "breadth" of a vessel mean her length overall and ,greatest breadth;

(j) Vessels shall be deemed to be in sight of one another only when one can be observed visually from the other;

The term "restricted visibility" means any condition in which visibility is restricted by fog, mist, falling snow, heavy rainstorms, sandstorms, or any other similar causes;

(j) "Western Rivers" means the Mississippi River, its tributaries, South Pass, and Southwest Pass, to the navigational demarcation lines dividing the high seas from harbors, rivers, and other inland waters of the United States, and the Port Allen-Morgan City Alternate Route, and that part of the Atchafalaya River above its junction with the Port Allen-Morgan City Alternate Route including the Old River and the Red River;

(m) "Great Lakes" means the Great Lakes and their connecting and tributary waters including the Calumet River as far as the Thomas J. O'Brien Lock and Controlling Works (between mile 326 and 327), the Chicago River as far as the east side of the Ashland Avenue Bridge (between mile 321 and 322), and the Saint Lawrence River as far east as the lower exit of Saint Lambert Lock;

(n) "Secretary" means the Secretary of the department in which the Coast Guard is operating;

(o) "Inland Waters" means the navigable waters of the United States shoreward of the navigational demarcation lines dividing the high seas from harbors, rivers and other inland waters of the United States and the waters of the Great Lakes on the United States side of the International Boundary;

(p) "Inland Rules" or,"Rules" mean the Inland Navigational Rules and the annexes thereto, which govern the conduct of vessels and specify the lights; shapes, and sound signals that apply on inland waters; and

(q) "International Regulations" means the International Regulations for Preventing Collisions at Sea, 1972, including annexes currently in force for the United States.

PART B – STEERING AND SAILING RULES

SUBPART I —CONDUCT OF VESSELS IN ANY CONDITION OF VISIBILITY.

Rule 4 *Application*

Rules in this subpart apply in any condition of visibility.

Rule 5 *Look-out*

Every vessel shall at all times maintain a proper look-out by sight and hearing as well as by all available means appropriate in the prevailing circumstances and conditions so as to make a full appraisal of the situation and of the risk of collision.

Rule 6 *Safe Speed*

Every vessel shall at all times proceed at a safe speed so that she can take proper and effective action to avoid collision and be stopped within a distance appropriate to the prevailing circumstances and conditions.

In determining a safe speed the following factors shall be among those taken into account:

(a) By all vessels:

(i) the state of visibility

(ii) the traffic density including concentration of fishing vessels or any other vessels;

(iii) the maneuverability of the vessel with special reference to stopping distance and turning ability in the prevailing conditions;

(iv) at night the presence of background light such as from shore lights or from back scatter of her own lights;

(v) the state of wind, sea, and current, and the proximity of navigational hazards;

(vi) the draft in relation to the available depth of water.

(b) Additionally, by vessels with operational radar;

(i) the characteristics, efficiency and limitations of the radar equipment;

(ii) any constraints imposed by the radar range scale in use;

(iii) the effect on radar detection of the sea state, weather, and other sources of interference;

(iv) the possibility that small vessels, ice and other floating objects may not be detected by radar at an adequate range;

(v) the number, location, and movement of vessels detected by radar; and

(vi) the more exact assessment of the visibility that may be possible when radar is used to determine the range of vessels or other objects in the vicinity.

Rule 7 *Risk of Collision*

(a) Every vessel shall use all available means appropriate to the prevailing circumstances and conditions to determine if risk of collision exists. If there is any doubt such risk shall be deemed to exist.

(b) Proper use shall be made of radar equipment if fitted and operational, including long-range scanning to obtain early warning of risk of collision and radar plotting or equivalent systematic observation of detected objects.

(c) Assumptions shall not be made on the basis of scanty information, especially scanty radar information.

(d) In determining if risk of collision exists the following considerations shall be among those taken into account:

(i) such risk shall be deemed to exist if the compass bearing of an approaching vessel does not appreciably change; and

(ii) such risk may sometimes exist even when an appreciable bearing change is evident, particularly when approaching a very large vessel or a tow or when approaching a vessel at close range.

Rule 8 *Action To Avoid Collision*

(a) Any action taken to avoid collision shall, if the circumstances of the case admit, be positive, made in ample time and with due regard to the observation of good seamanship.

(b) Any alteration of course or speed to avoid collision shall, if the circumstances of the case admit, be large enough to be readily apparent to another vessel observing visually or by radar; a succession of small alterations of course or speed should be avoided.

(c) If there is sufficient sea room, alteration of course alone may be the most effective action to avoid a close-quarters situation provided that it is made in good time, is substantial and does not result in another close-quarters situation.

(d) Action taken to avoid collision with another vessel shall be such as to result in passing at a safe distance. The effectiveness of the action shall be carefully checked until the other vessel is finally past and clear.

(e) If necessary to avoid collision or allow more time to assess the situation, a vessel shall slacken her speed or take all way off by stopping or reversing her means of propulsion.

(f) (i) A vessel which, by any of these rules, is required not to impede the passage or safe passage of another vessel shall, when required by the circumstances of the case, take early action to allow sufficient sea room for the safe passage of the other vessel.

(ii) A vessel required not to impede the passage or safe passage of another vessel is not relieved of this obligation if approaching the other vessel so as to involve risk of collision and shall, when taking action, have full regard to the action which may be required by the rules of this part.

(iii) A vessel the passage of which is not to be impeded remains fully obliged to comply with the rules of this part when the two vessels are approaching one another so as to involve risk of collision.

Rule 9 *Narrow Channels*

(a) (i) A vessel proceeding along the course of a narrow channel or fairway shall keep as near to the outer limit of the channel or fairway which lies on her starboard side as is safe and practicable.

(ii) Notwithstanding paragraph (a)(i) and Rule 14(a), a power-driven vessel operating in narrow channels or fairways on the Great Lakes, Western Rivers, or waters specified by the Secretary, and proceeding downbound with a following current shall have the right-of-way over an up-bound vessel, shall propose the manner and place of passage, and shall initiate the maneuvering signals prescribed by Rule 34(a)(i), as appropriate. The vessel proceeding upbound against the current shall hold as necessary to permit safe passing.

(b) A vessel of less than 20 meters in length or a sailing vessel shall not impede the passage of a vessel that can safely navigate only within a narrow channel or fairway.

(c) A vessel engaged in fishing shall not impede the passage of any other vessel navigating within a narrow channel or fairway.

(d) A vessel shall not cross a narrow channel or fairway if such crossing impedes the passage of a vessel which can safely navigate only within that channel or fairway. The latter vessel shall use the danger signal prescribed in Rule 34(d) if in doubt as to the intention of the crossing vessel.

(e) (i) In a narrow channel or fairway when overtaking, the vessel intending to overtake shall indicate her intention by sounding the appropriate signal prescribed in Rule 34(c) and take steps to permit safe passing. The overtaken vessel, if in agreement, shall sound the same signal. If in doubt she shall sound the danger signal prescribed in Rule 34(d).

(ii) This Rule does not relieve the over-taking vessel of her obligation under Rule 13.

(f) A vessel nearing a bend or an area of a narrow channel or fairway where other vessels may be obscured by an intervening obstruction shall navigate with particular alertness and caution and shall sound the appropriate signal prescribed in Rule 34(e).

(g) Every vessel shall, if the circumstances of the case admit, avoid anchoring in a narrow channel.

Rule 10 Vessel *Traffic Services*

Each vessel required by regulation to participate in a vessel traffic service shall comply with the applicable regulations.

SUBPART II – CONDUCT OF VESSELS IN SIGHT OF ONE ANOTHER

Rule 11 *Application*

Rules in this subpart apply to vessels in sight of one another.

Rule 12 *Sailing Vessels*

(a) When two sailing vessels are approaching one another, so as to involve risk of collision, one of them shall keep out of the way of the other as follows:

(i) when each has the wind on a different side, the vessel which has the wind on the port side shall keep out of the way of the other;

(ii) when both have the wind on the same side, the vessel which is to windward shall keep out of the way of the vessel which is to leeward; and

(iii) if a vessel with the wind on the port side sees a vessel to windward and cannot determine with certainty whether the other vessel has the wind on the port or on the starboard side, she shall keep out of the way of the other.

(b) For the purpose of this Rule the windward side shall be deemed to be the side opposite to that on which the mainsail is carried or, in the case of a square-rigged vessel, the side opposite to that on which the largest fore-and-aft sail is carried.

Rule 13 *Overtaking*

(a) Notwithstanding anything contained in Rules 4 through 18, any vessel overtaking any other shall keep out of the way of the vessel being overtaken.

(b) A vessel shall be deemed to be overtaking when coming up with another vessel from a direction more than 22.5 degrees abaft her beam; that is, in such a position with reference to the vessel she is overtaking, that at night she would be able to see only the sternlight of that vessel but neither of her sidelights.

(c) When a vessel is in any doubt as to whether she is overtaking another, she shall assume that this is the case and act accordingly.

(d) Any subsequent alteration of the bearing between the two vessels shall not make the overtaking vessel a crossing vessel within the meaning of these Rules or relieve her of the duty of keeping clear of the overtaken vessel until she is finally past and clear.

Rule 14 *Head-on Situation*

(a) Unless otherwise agreed, when two power-driven vessels are meeting on reciprocal or nearly reciprocal courses so as to involve risk of collision each shall alter her course to starboard so that each shall pass on the port side of the other.

(b) Such a situation shall be deemed to exist when a vessel sees the other ahead or nearly ahead and by night she could see the masthead lights of the other in a line or nearly in a line or both sidelights and by day she observes the corresponding aspect of the other vessel.

(c) When a vessel is in any doubt as to whether such a situation exists she shall assume that it does exist and act accordingly.

(d) Notwithstanding paragraph (a) of this Rule, a power-driven vessel operating on the Great Lakes, Western Rivers, or waters specified by the Secretary, and proceeding downbound with a following current shall have the right-of-way over an upbound vessel, shall propose the manner of passage, and shall initiate the maneuvering signals prescribed by Rule 34(a)(i), as appropriate.

Rule 15 *Crossing Situation*

(a) When two power-driven vessels are crossing so as to involve risk of collision; the vessel which has the other on her starboard side shall keep out of the way and shall, if the circumstances of the case admit, avoid crossing ahead of the other vessel.

(b) Notwithstanding paragraph (a), on the Great Lakes, Western Rivers, or specified by the Secretary, a vessel crossing a river shall keep out of the way of a power-driven vessel ascending or descending the river.

Rule 16 *Action by Give-Way Vessel*

Every vessel which is directed to keep out of the way of another vessel shall, so far as possible, take early and substantial action to keep well clear.

Rule 17 *Action by Stand-on Vessel*

(a) (i) Where one of two vessels is to keep out of the way, the other shall keep her course and speed.

(ii) The latter vessel may, however, take action to avoid collision by her maneuver alone, as soon as it becomes apparent to her that the vessel required to keep out of the way is not taking appropriate action in compliance with these Rules.

(b) When, from any cause, the vessel required to keep her course and speed finds herself so close that collision cannot be avoided by the action of the give-way vessel alone, she shall take such action as will best aid to avoid collision.

(c) A power-driven vessel which takes action in a crossing situation in accordance with subparagraph (a)(ii) of this Rule to avoid collision with another power-driven vessel shall, if the circumstances of the case admit, not alter course to port for a vessel on her own port side.

(d) This Rule does not relieve the give-way vessel of her obligation to keep out of the way.

Rule 18 *Responsibilities Between Vessels*

Except where Rules 9, 10, and 13 otherwise require:

(a) A power-driven vessel underway shall keep out of the way of:

(i) a vessel not under command;

(ii) a vessel restricted in her ability to maneuver;

(iii) a vessel engaged in fishing; and

(iv) a sailing vessel.

(b) A sailing vessel underway shall keep out of the way of:

(i) a vessel not under command;

(ii) a vessel restricted in her ability to maneuver; and

(iii) a vessel engaged in fishing.

(c) A vessel engaged in fishing when underway shall, so far as possible, keep of the way of;

(i) a vessel not under command, and

(ii) a vessel restricted in her abiiity to maneuver.

(d) A seaplane on the water shall, in general, keep well clear of all vessels, and avoid impeding their navigation. In circumstances, however, where risK collision exists, she shall comply with the Rules of this Part.

SUBPART III – CONDUCT OF VESSELS IN RESTRICTED VISIBILITY

Rule 19 *Conduct of Vessels in Restricted Visibility*

(a) This Rule applies to vessels not in sight of one another when navigating in or near an area of restricted visibility.

(b) Every vessel shall proceed at a safe speed adapted to the prevailing circumstances and conditions of restricted visibility. A power-driven vessel shall have her engines ready for immediate maneuver,

(c) Every vessel shall have due regard to the prevailing circumstances and conditions of restricted visibility when complying with Rules 4 through 10.

(d) A vessel which detects by radar alone the presence of another vessel shall determine if a close-quarters situation is developing or risk of collision exists. If so, she shall take avoiding action in ample time, provided that when such action consists of an alteration of course, so far as possible the following shall be avoided:

(i) an alteration of course to port for a vessel forward of the beam, other than for a vessel being overtaken; and

(ii) an alteration of course toward a vessel abeam or abaft the beam.

(e) Except where it has been determined that a risk of collision does not exist, every vessel which hears apparently forward of her beam the fog signal of another vessel, or which cannot avoid a close-quarters situation with another vessel forward of her beam, shall reduce her speed to the minimum at which she can be kept on course. She shall if necessary take all her way off and, in any event, navigate with extreme caution until danger of collision is over.

PART C – LIGHTS AND SHAPES

Rule 20 *Application*

(a) Rules in this Part shall be complied with in all weathers.

(b) The Rules concerning lights shall be complied with from sunset to sunrise, and during such times no other lights shall be exhibited, except such lights as cannot be mistaken for the lights specified in these Rules or do not impair their visibility or distinctive character, or interfere with the keeping of a proper lookout.

(c) The lights prescribed by these Rules shall, if carried, also be exhibited from sunrise to sunset in restricted visibility and may be exhibited in all other circumstances when it is deemed necessary

(d) The Rules concerning shapes shall be complied with by day

(e) The lights and shapes specified in these Rules shall comply with the provisions of Annex I of these Rules.

Rule 21 *Definitions*

(a) "Masthead light" means a white light placed over the fore and aft centerline of the vessel showing an unbroken light over an arc of the horizon of 225 degrees and so fixed as to show the light from right ahead to 22. 5 degrees abaft the beam on either side of the vessel, except that on a vessel of less than 12 meters in length the masthead light shall be placed as nearly as practicable to the fore and aft centerline of the vessel.

(b) "Sidelights" mean a green light on the starboard side and a red light on the port side each showing an unbroken light over an arc of the horizon of 112.5 degrees and so fixed as to show the light from right ahead to 22.5 degrees abaft the beam on its respective side. On a vessel of less than 20 meters in length the side lights may be combined in one lantern carried on the fore and aft centerline of the vessel, except that on a vessel of less than 12 meters in length the sidelights when combined in one lantern shall be placed as nearly as practicable to the fore and aft centerline of the vessel.

(c) "Sternlight" means a white light placed as nearly as practicable at the stern showing an unbroken light over an arc of the horizon of 135 degrees and so fixed as to show the light 67.5 degrees from right aft on each side of the vessel.

(d) "Towing light" means a yellow light having the same characteristics as the "sternlight" defined in paragraph (c) of this Rule.

(e) "All-round light" means a light showing an unbroken light over an arc of this horizon of 360 degrees.

(f) "Flashing light" means a light flashing at regular intervals at a frequency of 120 flashes or more per minute.

(g) "Special flashing light" means a yellow light flashing at regular intervals at a frequency of 50 to 70 flashes per minute, placed as far forward and as nearly as practicable on the fore and aft centerline of the tow and showing an unbroken light over an arc of the horizon of not less than 180 degrees nor more than 225 degree and so fixed as to show the light from right ahead to abeam and no more than 22·5 degrees abaft the beam on either side of the vessel.

Rule 22 *Visibility of Lights*

The lights prescribed in these Rules shall have an intensity as specified in Annex 1 to these Rules, so as to be visible at the following minimum ranges:

(a) In a vessel of 50 meters or more in length:
a masthead light, 6 miles;
a sidelight, 3 miles;
a sternlight, 3 miles;
a towing light, 3 miles;
a white, red, green or yellow all-round light, 3 miles; and a special flashing light, 2 miles.

(b) In a vessel of 12 meters or more in length but less than 50 meters in length:

(a) masthead light, 5 miles; except that where the length of the vessel is less than 20 meters, 3 miles;
a sidelight, 2 miles;
a sternlight, 2 miles;
a towing light, 2 miles;
a white, red, green or yellow all-round light, 2 miles; and a special flashing light, 2 light, 2 miles.

(b) In a vessel of less than 12 meters in length:
a masthead light, 2 miles;
a sidelight, 1 mile;
a sternlight, 2 miles;
a towing light, 2 miles;
a white, red, green or yellow all-round light, 2 miles; and a special flashing light, 2 miles.

(c) In an inconspicuous, partly submerged vessel or object being towed:
a white all-round light, 3 miles.

Rule 23 *Power-Driven Vessels Underway*

(a) A power-driven vessel underway shall exhibit:

(i) a masthead light forward; except that a vessel of less than 20 meters in length need not exhibit this light forward of amidships but shall exhibit it as far forward as is practicable;

(ii) a second masthead light abaft of and higher than the forward one; except that a vessel of less than 50 meters in length shall not be obliged to exhibit such light but may do so:

(iii) sidelights; and

(iv) a sternlight;

(b) An air-cushion vessel when operating in the nondisplacement mode shall, in addition to the lights prescribed in paragraph (a) of this Rule, exhibit an all-round flashing yellow light where it can best be seen.

(c) A power-driven vessel of less than 12 meters in length may, in lieu of the lights prescribed in paragraph (a) of this Rule, exhibit an all-round white light and I sidelights.

(d) A power-driven vessel when operating on the Great Lakes may carry an all round white light in lieu of the second masthead light and sternlight prescribed in paragraph (a) of this Rule. The light shall be carried in the position of the second masthead light and be visible at the same minimum range.

Rule 24 *Towing and Pushing*

(a) A power-driven vessel when towing astern shall exhibit: (i) instead of the light prescribed either in Rule 23 (a)(i) or 23(a)(ii), two masthead lights in a vertical line. When the length of the tow, measuring from the stern of the towing vessel to the after end of the tow exceeds 200 meters, three such lights in a vertical line;

(ii) sidelights;

(iii) a sternlight;

(iv) a towing light in a vertical line above the sternlight; and

(v) when the length of the tow exceeds 200 meters, a diamond shape where it can best be seen.

(b) When a pushing vessel and a vessel being pushed ahead are rigidly connected in a composite unit they shall be regarded as a power-driven vessel and exhibit the lights prescribed in Rule 23

(c) A power-driven vessel when pushing ahead or towing alongside, except as required by paragraphs (b) and (i) of this Rule, shall exhibit:

(i) instead of the light prescribed either in Rule 23(a)(i) or 23(a)(ii), two 'masthead lights in a vertical line;

(ii) sidelights; and

(iii) two towing lights in a vertical line.

(d) A power-driven vessel to which paragraphs (a) or (c) of this Rule apply shall also comply with Rule 23(a)(i) and 23(a)(ii).

(e) A vessel or object other than those referred to in paragraph (g) of this Rule being towed shall exhibit:

(i) sidelights;

(ii) a sternlight; and

(iii) when the length of the tow exceeds 200 meters, a diamond shape where it can best be seen.

(f) Provided that any number of vessels being towed alongside or pushed in a group shall be lighted as one vessel:

(i) a vessel being pushed ahead, not being part of a composite unit shall, exhibit at the forward end sidelights, and a special flashing light; and

(ii) a vessel being towed alongside shall exhibit a sternlight and at the forward end sidelights.

(g) An inconspicuous, partly submerged vessel or object being towed shall, exhibit:

(i) if it is less than 25 meters in breadth, one all-round white light at or near each end;

(ii) if it is 25 meters or more in breadth, four all-round white lights to mark its length and breadth;

(iii) if it exceeds 100 meters in length, additional all-round white lights between the lights prescribed in subparagraphs (i) and (ii) so that the distance between the lights shall not exceed 100 meters: Provided, That any vessels or objects being towed alongside each other shall be lighted as one vessel or object;

(iv) a diamond shape at or near the aftermost extremity of the last vessel or object being towed; and

(v) the towing vessel may direct a searchlight in the direction of the tow to indicate its presence to an approaching vessel.

(h) Where from any sufficient cause it is impracticable for a vessel or object being towed to exhibit the lights prescribed in paragraph (e) or (g) of this Rule, all possible measures shall be taken to light the vessel or object towed or at least to indicate the presence of the unlighted vessel or object

(i) Notwithstanding paragraph (c), on the Western Rivers (except below the Huey P. Long Bridge on the Mississippi River) and on waters specified by the Secretary, a power-driven vessel when pushing ahead or towing alongside, except as paragraph (b) applies, shall exhibit:

(ii) sidelights; and

(iii) two towing lights in a vertical line.

(j) Where from any sufficient cause it is impracticable for a vessel not normally engaged in towing operations to display the lights prescribed by paragraph (a), (c) or (i) of this Rule, such vessel shall not be required to exhibit those lights when engaged in towing another vessel in distress or otherwise in need of assistance. All possible measures shall be taken to indicate the nature of the relationship between the towing vessel and the vessel being assisted. The searchlight authorized by Rule 36 may be used to illuminate the tow.

Rule 25 *Sailing Vessels Underway and Vessels Under Oars*

(a) A sailing vessel underway shall exhibit:

(i) sidelights; and

(ii) a sternlight.

(b) In a sailing vessel of less than 20 meters in length the lights prescribed in paragraph (a) of this Rule may be combined in one lantern carried at or near the top of the mast where it can best be seen.

(c) A sailing vessel underway may, in addition to the lights prescribed in paragraph (a) of this Rule, exhibit at or near the top of the mast, where they can best be seen, two all-round lights in a vertical line, the upper being red and the lower green, but these lights shall not be exhibited in conjunction with the combined lantern permitted by paragraph (b) of this Rule.

(d) (i) A sailing vessel of less than 7 meters in length shall, if practicable, exhibit the lights prescribed in paragraph (a) or (b) of this Rule, but if she does not, she shall have ready at hand an electric torch or lighted lantern showing a white light which shall be exhibited in sufficient time to prevent collision.

(ii) A vessel under oars may exhibit the lights prescribed in this Rule for sailing vessels, but if she does not, she shall have ready at hand an electric torch or lighted lantern showing a white light which shall be exhibited in sufficient time to prevent collision.

(e) A vessel proceeding under sail when also being propelled by machinery shall exhibit forward where it can best be seen a conical shape, apex downward. A vessel of less than 12 meters in length is not required to exhibit this shape, but it may do so.

Rule 26 *Fishing Vessels*

(a) A vessel engaged in fishing, whether underway or at anchor, shall exhibit only . the lights and shapes prescribed in this Rule.

(b) A vessel when engaged in trawling, by which is meant the dragging through the water of a dredge net or other apparatus used as a fishing appliance, shall exhibit:

(i) two all-round lights in a vertical line, the upper being green and the lower white, or a shape consisting of two cones with their apexes together in a vertical line one above the other; a vessel of less than 20 meters in length may instead of this shape exhibit a basket;

(ii) a masthead light abaft of and higher than the all-round green light; a vessel of less than 50 meters in length shall not be obliged to exhibit such a light but may do so; and

(iii) when making way through the water, in addition to the lights prescribed in this paragraph, sidelights and a sternlight.

(c) A vessel engaged in fishing, other than trawling, shall exhibit:

(i) two all-round lights in a vertical line, the upper being red and the lower' white, or a shape consisting of two cones with apexes together in a vertjcal ' line one above the other; a vessel of less than 20 meters in length may instead of this shape exhibit a basket;

(ii) when there is outlying gear extending more than 150 meters horizontally from the vessel, an all-round white light or a cone apex upward in the direction of the gear; and

(iii) when making way through the water, in addition to the lights prescribed; in this paragraph, sidelights and a sternlight.

(d) A vessel engaged in fishing in close proximity to other vessels engaged in fishing may exhibit the additional signals described in Annex II to these Rules.

(e) A vessel when not engaged in fishing shall not exhibit the lights or shapes prescribed in this Rule, but only those prescribed for a vessel of her length,

Rule 27 *Vessels Nor Under Command or Restricfed in Their Ability To Maneuver*

(a) A vessel not under command shall exhibit:

(i) two all-round red lights in a vertical line where they can best be seen-;

(ii) two balls or similar shapes in a vertical line where they can best be seen; and (iii) when making way through the water, in addition to the lights prescribed~ in this paragraph, sidelights and a sternlight.

(b) A vessel restricted in her ability to maneuver, except a vessel engaged in' mineclearance operations, shall exhibit:

(i) three all-round lights in a vertical line where they can best be seen. The. highest and lowest of these lights shall be red and the middle light shall be white;

(ii) three shapes in a vertical line where they can best be seen. The highest and lowest of these shapes shall be balls and the middle one a diamond;

(iii) when making way through the water, masthead lights, sidelights and a sternlight, in addition to the lights prescribed in subparagraphs (b)(i); and

(iv) when at anchor, in addition to the lights or shapes prescribed in subparagraphs (b) (i) and (ii), the light, lights or shapes prescribed in Rule 30.

(c) A vessel engaged in a towing operation which severely restricts the towing vessel and her tow in their ability to deviate from their course shall, in addition to the lights or shapes prescribed in subparagraphs (b)(i) and (ii) of this Rule, exhibit the lights or shape prescribed in Rule 24.

(d) A vessel engaged in dredging or underwater operations, when restricted in her ability to maneuver, shall exhibit the lights, and shapes prescribed in 1 subparagraphs (b)(i), (ii), and (iii) of this Rule and shall in addition, when an obstruction exists, exhibit:

(i) two all-round red lights or two balls in a vertical line to indicate the side on which the obstruction exists;

(ii) two all-round green lights or two diamonds in a vertical line to indicate the side on which another vessel may pass; and

(iii) when at anchor, the lights or shape prescribed by this paragraph instead of the lights or shapes prescribed in Rule 30 for anchored vessels-

(e) Whenever the size of a vessel engaged in diving operations makes it impracticable to exhibit all lights and shapes prescribed in paragraph (d) of this — the following shall instead be exhibited:

(i)Three all-round lights in a vertical line where they can best be seen. The highest and lowest of these lights shall be red and the middle light shall be white.

(ii) A rigid replica of the international Code flag "A" not less than 1 meter in height. Measures shall be taken to insure its all-round visibility.

(f) A vessel engaged in mineclearance operations shall, in addition to the lights prescribed for a power-driven vessel in Rule 23, or to the lights or shape prescribed for a vessel at anchor in Rule 30, as appropriate, exhibit three all-round green lights or three balls. One of these lights or shapes shall be exhibited near the foremast head and one at each end of the fore yard. These lights or shapes indicate that it is dangerous for another vessel to approach within 1,000 meters of the mineclearance vessel.

(g) A vessel of less than 12 meters in length, except when engaged in diving operations is not required to exhibit the lights or shapes prescribed in this Rule.

(h) The signals prescribed in this Rule are not signals of vessels in distress and requiring assistance. Such signals are contained in Annex IV to these Rules.

Rule 28 (Reserved)

Rule 29 Pilot Vessels

(a) A vessel engaged on pilotage duty shall exhibit:

(i) at or near the masthead, two all-round lights in a vertical line, the upper being white and the lower red;

(ii) when underway, in addition, sidelights and a sternlight; and

(iii) when at anchor, in addition to the lights prescribed in subparagraph (i), the anchor light, lights, or shape prescribed in Rule 30 for anchored vessels.

(b) A pilot vessel when not engaged on pilotage duty shall exhibit the lights or shapes prescribed for a vessel of her length.

Rule 30 *Anchored Vessels and Vessels Aground*

(a) A vessel at anchor shall exhibit where it can best be seen:

(i) in the fore part, an all-round white light or one ball; and

(ii) at or near the stern and at a lower level than the light prescribed in subparagraph (i), an all-round white light.

(b) A vessel of less than 50 meters in length may exhibit an all-round white light where it can best be seen instead of the lights prescribed in paragraph (a) of this Rule.

(c) A vessel at anchor may, and a vessel of 100 meters or more in length shall, also use the available working or equivalent lights to illuminate her decks.

(d) A vessel aground shall exhibit the lights prescribed in paragraph (a) or (b) of this Rule and in addition, if practicable, where they can best be seen:

(i) two all-round red lights in a vertical line; and

(ii) three balls in a vertical line.

(e) A vessel of less than 7 meters in length, when at anchor, not in or near a narrow channel, fairway, anchorage, or where other vessels normally navigate, shall not be required to exhibit the lights or shapes prescribed in paragraphs (a) and (b) of this Rule.

(f) A vessel of less than 12 meters in length when aground shall not be required to exhibit the lights or shapes prescribed in subparagraphs (d)(i) and (ii) of this Rule.

(g) A vessel of less than 20 meters in length, when at anchor in a special anchorage area designated by the Secretary, shall not be required to exhibit the anchor lights and shapes required by this Rule.

Rule 31 *Seaplanes*

Where it is impracticable for a seaplane to exhibit lights and shapes characteristics or in the positions prescribed in the Rules of this Part she sh exhibit lights and shapes as closely similar in characteristics and position as possible.

PART D – SOUND AND LIGHT SIGNALS

Rule 32 *Definitions*

(a) The word "whistle" means any sound signaling appliance capable of producing the prescribed blasts and which complies with specifications in Annex 111 to these Rules.

(b) The term "short blast" means a blast of about 1 second duration.

(c) The term "prolonged blast" means a blast of from 4 to 6 seconds duration.

Rule 33 *Equipment for Sound Signals*

(a) A vessel of 12 meters or more in length shall be provided with a whistle and a, bell and a vessel of 100 meters or more in length shall, in addition, be provided with a gong, the tone and sound of which cannot be confused with that of the bell. The whistle, bell and gong shall comply with the specifications in Annex III to these Rules. The bell or gong or both may be replaced by other equipment having the same respective sound characteristics, provided that manual sounding of the prescribed signals shall always be possible.

(b) A vessel of less than 12 meters in length shall not be obliged to carry the sound signaling appliances prescribed in paragraph (a) of this Rule but if she does not, she shall be provided with some other means of making an efficient sound signal.

Rule 34 *Maneuvering and Warning Signals*

(a) When power-driven vessels are in sight of one another and meeting or crossing at a distance within half a mile of each other, each vessel underway when maneuvering as authorized or required by these Rules:

(i) shall indicate that maneuver by the following signals on her whistle: one short blast to mean "I intend to leave you on my port side"; two short blasts to mean "I intend to leave you on my starboard side"; and three short blasts to mean "I am operating astern propulsion".

(ii) upon hearing the one or two blast signal of the other shall, if in agreement, sound the same whistle signal and take the steps necessary to effect a safe passing. If, however, from any cause the vessel doubts the safety of the proposed maneuver, she shall sound the danger signal specified in paragraph (d) of this Rule and each vessel shall take appropriate precautionary action until a safe passing agreement is made.

(b) A vessel may supplement the whistle signals prescribed in paragraph (a) of this Rule by light signals:

(i) These signals shall have the following significance: one flash to mean "I intend to leave you on my port side"; two flashes to mean "I intend to leave you on my starboard side"; three flashes to mean "I am operating astern propulsion";

(ii) The duration of each flash shall be about 1 second; and

(iii) The light used for this signal shall, if fitted, be one all-round white or yellow light, visible at a minimum range of 2 miles, synchronized with the whistle and shall comply with the provisions of Annex I to these Rules.

(c) When in sight of one another:

(i) a power-driven vessel intending to overtake another power-driven vessel shall indicate her intention by the following signals on her whistle: one short blast to mean "I intend to overtake you on your starboard side"; two short blasts to mean "I intend to overtake you on your port side"; and

(ii) the power-driven vessel about to be overtaken shall, if in agreement, sound a similar sound signal. If in doubt she shall sound the danger signal prescribed in paragraph (d).

(d) When vessels in sight of one another are approaching each other and from any cause either vessel fails to understand the intentions or actions of the other, or is in doubt whether sufficient action is being taken by the other to avoid collision, the vessel in doubt shall immediately indicate such doubt by giving at least five short and rapid blasts on the whistle. This signal may be supplemented by a light signal of at least five short and rapid flashes.

(e) A vessel nearing a bend or an area of a channel or fairway where other vessels may be obscured by an intervening obstruction shall sound one prolonged blast. This signal shall be answered with a prolonged blast by any approaching vessel that may be within hearing around the bend or behind the intervening obstruction.

(f) If whistles are fitted on a vessel at a distance apart of more than 100 meters, one whistle only shall be used for giving maneuvering and warning signals.

(g) When a power-driven vessel is leaving a dock or berth, she shall sound one prolonged blast.

(h) A vessel that reaches agreement with another vessel in a meeting, crossing, or overtaking situation by using the radiotelephone as prescribed by the Bridge-to-Bridge Radiotelephone Act (85 Stat. 165; 33 U.S.C. 1207), is not obliged to sound the whistle signals prescribed by this Rule, but may do so. If agreement is not reached, then whistle signals shall be exchanged in a timely manner and shall prevail.

Rule 35 *Sound Signals in Restricted Visibility*

In or near an area of restricted visibility, whether by day or night, the signals prescribed in this Rule shall be used as follows:

(a) A power-driven vessel making way through the water shall sound at intervals of not more than 2 minutes one prolonged blast.

(b) A power-driven vessel underway but stopped and making no way through the water shall sound at intervals of not more than 2 minutes two prolonged blasts in succession with an interval of about 2 seconds between them.

(c) A vessel not under command; a vessel restricted in her ability to maneuver, whether underway or at anchor; a sailing vessel; a vessel engaged in fishing, whether underway or at anchor; and a vessel engaged in towing or pushing another vessel shall, instead of the signals prescribed in paragraphs (a) or (b) of this Rule, sound at intervals of not more than 2 minutes, three blasts in succession; namely, one prolonged followed by two short blasts.

(d) A vessel towed or if more than one vessel is towed the last vessel of the tovv if manned, shall at intervals of not more than 2 minutes sound four blasts ir succession; namely, one prolonged followed by three short blasts. When practicable, this signal shall be made immediately after the signal made by the towing vessel.

(e) When a pushing vessel and a vessel being pushed ahead are rigidly connected in a composite unit they shall be regarded as a power-driven vessel and shall give the signals prescribed in paragraphs (a) or (b) of this Rule.

(f) A vessel at anchor shall at intervals of not more than 1 minute ring the bell rapidly for about 5 seconds. In a vessel of 100 meters or more in length the bell shall be sounded in the forepart of the vessel and immediately after the ringing of the bell the gong shall be sounded rapidly for about 5 seconds in the after part of the vessel. A vessel at anchor may in addition sound three blasts in succession namely, one short, one prolonged and one short blast, to give warning of her position and of the possibility of collision to an approaching vessel.

(g) A vessel aground shall give the bell signal and if required the gong signal prescribed in paragraph (f) of this Rule and shall, in addition, give three separate and distinct strokes on the bell immediately before and after the rapid ringing of the bell. A vessel aground may in addition sound an appropriate whistle signal.

(h) A vessel of less than 12 meters in length shall not be obliged to give the above-mentioned signals but, if she does not, shall make some other efficient sound signal at intervals of not more than 2 minutes.

(i) A pilot vessel when engaged on pilotage duty may in addition to the signals prescribed in paragraphs (a), (b) or (f) of this Rule sound an identity signal consisting of four short blasts.

(j) The following vessels shall not be required to sound signals as prescribed in paragraph (f) of this Rule when anchored in a special anchorage area designated by the Secretary:

(i) a vessel of less than 20 meters in length; and

(ii) a barge, canal boat, scow, or other nondescript craft.

Rule 36 *Signals To Attract Attention*

If necessary to attract the attention of another vessel, any vessel may make light or sound signals that cannot be mistaken for any signal authorized elsewhere in these Rules, or may direct the beam of her searchlight in the direction of the danger, in such a way as not to embarrass any vessel.

Rule 37 *Distress Signals*

When a vessel is in distress and requires assistance she shall use or exhibit the signals described in Annex IV to these Rules.

PART E—EXEMPTIONS

Rule 38 *Exemptions*

Any vessel or class of vessels, the keel of which is laid or which is at a corresponding stage of construction before the date of enactment of this Act provided that she complies with the requirements of:

(a) The Act of June 7, 1897 (30 Stat. 96), as amended (33 U.S.C. 154-232) for vesselS navigating the waters subject to that statute;

(b) Section 4233 of the Revised Statutes (33 U.S.C. 301-356) for vessels navigating the waters subject to that statute;

(c) The Act of February 8, 1895 (28 Stat. 645), as amended (33 U.S.C. 241-295) for vessels navigating the waters subject to that statute, or

(d) Sections 3, 4, and 5 of the Act of April 25, 1940 (54 Stat. 163)t as amended (46 U.S.C. 526 b, c, and d) for motorboats navigating the waters subject to that statute; shall be exempted from compliance with the technical Annexes to these rules as follows:

(i) the installation of lights with ranges prescribed in Rule 22, until 4 years after the effective date of these Rules, except that vessels of less than 20 meters In length are permanently exempt;

(ii) the installation of lights with color specifications as prescribed in Annex to these Rules, until 4 years after the effective date of these Rulest except that vessels of less than 20 meters in length are permanently exempt;

(iii) the repositioning of lights as a result of conversion to metric units and rounding off measurement figures, are permanently exempt; and

(iv) the horizontal repositioning of masthead lights prescribed by Annex I to these rules:

(1) on vessels of less than 150 meters in length, permanent exemption.

(2) on vessels of 150 meters or more in length, until 9 years after the effective date of these Rules

(v) the restructuring or repositioning of all lights to meet the prescriptions of Annex I to these Rules, until 9 years after the effective date of these Rules;

(vi) power-driven vessels of 12 meters or more but less than 20 meters in length are permanently exempt from the provisions of Rule 23(a)(i) and 23 (a)(iv) provided that, in place of these lights, the vessel exhibits a white light aft visible all round the horizon; and

(vii) the requirements for sound signal appliances prescribed in Annex III to these Rules, until 9 years after the effective date of these Rules.

ANNEX I

POSITIONING AND TECHNICAL DETAILS OF LIGHTS AND SHAPES

§ 84.01 Definitions.

(a) The term "height above the hull" means height above the uppermost continuous deck. This height shall be measured from the position vertically beneath the location of the light.

(b) The term "practical cut-off" means, for vessels 20 meters or more in length, 12.5 per cent of the minimum luminous intensity (Table 84.15(b)) corresponding to the greatest range of visibility for which the requirements of Annex I are met.

(c) The term "Rule" or "Rules" means the Inland Navigation Rules contained in Sec. 2 of the Inland Navigational Rules Act of 1980 (Pub. L. 96-591, 94 Stat 3415, 33 U.S.C. 2001, December 24, 1980) as amended.

§ 84.03 Vertical positioning and spacing of lights.

(a) On a power-driven vessel of 20 meters or more in length the masthead lights shall be placed as follows:

(1) The forward masthead light, or if only one masthead light is carried, then that light, at a height above the hull of not less than 5 meters, and, if the breadth of the vessel exceeds 5 meters, then at a height above the hull not less than such breadth, so however that the light need not be placed at a greater height above the hull than 8 meters;

(2) When two masthead lights are carried the after one shall be at least 2 meters vertically higher than the forward one.

(b) The vertical separation of the masthead lights of power-driven vessels shall be such that in all normal conditions of trim the after light will be seen over and separate from the forward light at a distance of 1,000 meters from the stem when viewed from water level.

(c) The masthead light of a power-driven vessel of 12 meters but less than 20 meters in length shall be placed at a height above the gunwale of not less than 2.5 meters.

(d) The masthead light, or the all-round light described in Rule 23(c), of a powerdriven vessel of less than 12 meters in length shall be carried at least one meter higher than the sidelights.

(e) One of the two or three masthead lights prescribed for a power-driven vessel when engaged in towing or pushing another vessel shall be placed in the same position as either the forward masthead light or the after masthead light, provided that the lowest after masthead light shall be at least 2 meters vertically higher than the highest forward masthead light.

(f) (1) The masthead light or lights prescribed in Rule 23(a) shall be so placed as to be above and clear of all other lights and obstructions except as described in paragraph (f)(2) of this section.

(2) When it is impracticable to carry the all-round lights prescribed in Rule 27(b)(i) below the masthead lights, they may be carried above the after masthead light(s) or vertically in between the forward masthead light(s) and after masthead light(s), provided that in the latter case the requirement of § 84.05(d) shall be complied with.

(g) The sidelights of a power-driven vessel shall be placed at least one meter lower than the forward masthead light. They shall not be so low as to be interfered with bv deck liqhts.

(h) (Reserved)

(i) When the Rules prescribe two or three lights to be carried in a vertical line, they shall be spaced as follows:

(1) On a vessel of 20 meters in length or more such lights shall be spaced not less than 1 meter apart, and the lowest of these lights shall, except where a towing light is required, be placed at a height of not less than 4 meters above the hull;

(2) On a vessel of less than 20 meters in length such lights shall be spaced not less than 1 meter apart and the lowest of these lights shall, except where a towing light is required, be placed at a height of not less than 2 meters above the gunwale;

(3) When three lights are carried they shall be equally spaced.

(j) The lower of the two all-round lights prescribed for a vessel when engaged in fishing shall be at a height above the sidelights not less than twice the distance between the two vertical lights.

(k) The forward anchor light prescribed in Rule 30(a)(i), when two are carried, shall not be less than 4.5 meters above the after one. On a vessel of 50 meters or more in length this forward anchor light shall be placed at a height of not less than 6 meters above the hull;

§ 84.05 Horizontal positioning and spacing of lights.

(a) Except as specified in paragraph (b) of this section, when two masthead lights are prescribed for a power-driven vessel, the horizontal distance between them shall not be less than one quarter of the length of the vessel but need not be more than 50 meters. The forward light shall be placed not more than one half of the length of the vessel from the stem.

(b) On power-driven vessels 50 meters but less than 60 meters in length operated on the Western Rivers and those waters specified in § 89.25, the horizontal distance between masthead lights shall not be less than 10 meters.

(c) On a power-driven vessel of 20 meters or more in length the sidelights shall not be placed in front of the forward masthead lights. They shall be placed at or near the side of the vessel.

(d) When the lights prescribed in Rule 27(b)(i) are placed vertically between the forward masthead light(s) and the after masthead light(s) these all-round lights shall be placed at a horizontal distance of not less than 2 meters from the fore and aft centerline of the vessel in the athwartship direction.

§ 84.07 Details of location of direction-indicating lights for fishing vessels, dredgers and vessels engaged in underwater operations.

(a) The light indicating the direction of the outlying gear from a vessel engaged in fishing as prescribed in Rule 26(c)(ii) shall be placed at a horizontal distance of not less than 2 meters and not more than 6 meters away from the two all-round red and white lights. This light shall be placed not higher than the all-round white light prescribed in Rule 26(c)(i) and not lower than the sidelights.

(b) The lights and shapes on a vessel engaged in dredging or underwater operations to indicate the obstructed side and/or the side on which it is safe to pass, as prescribed in Rule 27(d)(i) and (ii), shall be placed at the maximum practical horizontal distance, but in no case less than 2 meters, from the lights or shapes prescribed in Rule 27(b)(i) and (ii). In no case shall the upper of these lights or shapes be at a greater height than the lower of the three lights or shapes prescribed in Rule 27(b)(i) and (ii).

§ 84.09 Screens.

(a) The sidelights of vessels of 20 meters or more in length shall be fitted with mat black inboard screens and meet the requirements of § 84.17. On vessels of less than 20 meters in length, the sidelights, if necessary to meet the requirement of § 84.17, shall be fitted with mat black inboard screens. With a combined lantern, using a single vertical filament and a very narrow division between the green and red sections, external screens need not be fitted.

(b) On power-driven vessels less than 12 meters in length constructed afterJuly 31, 1983, the masthead light, or the all-round light described in Rule 23(c) shall be screened to prevent direct illumination of the vessel forward of the operator's position.

§ 84.11 Shapes.

(a) Shapes shall be black and of the following sizes:

(1) A ball shall have a diameter of not less than 0.6 meter;

(2) A cone shall have a base diameter of not less than 0.6 meter and a height equal to its diameter;

(3) A diamond shape shall consist of two cones (as defined in paragraph (a)(2) of this section) having a common base.

(b) The vertical distance between shapes shall be at least 1.5 meters.

(c) In a vessel of less than 20 meters in length shapes of lesser dimensions but commensurate with the size of the vessel may be used and the distance apart may be correspondingly reduced.

§ 84.13 Color specification of lights.

(a) The chromaticity of all navigation lights shall conform to the following standards, which lie within the boundaries of the area of the diagram specified for each color by the International Commission on Illumination (CIE), in the "Colors of Light Signals", which is incorporated by reference. It is Publication CIE No. 2.2. (TC-1.6), 1975, and is available from the Illumination Engineering Society, 345 East 47th Street, New York, NY 10017. It is also available for inspection at the Office of the Federal Register, Room 8401, 1100 L Street N.W., Washington, D.C. 20408. This incorporation by reference was approved by the Director of the Federal Register.

(b) The boundaries of the area for each colour are given by indicating the coordinates, which are as follows:

(1) *White:*

x	0.525	0.525	0.452	0.310	0.310	0.443
y	0.382	0.440	0.440	0.348	0.283	0.382

(2) *Green:*

x	0.028	0.009	0.300	0.203
y	0.385	0.723	0.511	0.356

(3) *Red:*

x	0.680	0.660	0.735	0.721
y	0.320	0.320	0.265	0.259

(4) *Yellow:*

x	0.612	0.618	0.575	0.575
y	0.382	0.382	0.425	0.406

§ 84.15 Intensity of lights.

a) The minimum luminous intensity of lights shall be calculated by using the formula:

$L = 3.43 \times 10^6 \times T \times D^2 \times K^{-D}$

where L is luminous intensity in candelas under service conditions,

T is threshold factor 2 x 10-7 lux,

D is range of visibility (luminous range) of the light in nautical miles,

K is atmospheric transmissivity. For prescribed lights the value of K shall be 0.8, corresponding to a meteorological visibility of approximately 13 nautical miles.

(b) A selection of figures derived from the formula is given in Table 84.15(b).

Table 84.15(b)

Range of visibility (luminous range) in nautical miles D	Minimum luminous intensity of light in candelas for K = 0.8 L
1	0.9
2	4.3
3	12
4	27
5	52
6	94

§ 84.17 Horizontal sectors.

(a) (1) In the forward direction, sidelights as fitted on the vessel shall show the minimum required intensities. The intensities shall decrease to reach practical cut-off between 1 and 3 degrees outside the prescribed sectors.

(2) For sternlights and masthead lights and at 22.5 degrees abaft the beam for sidelights, the minimum required intensities shall be maintained over the arc of the horizon up to 5 degrees within the limits of the sectors prescribed in Rule 21. From 5 degrees within the prescribed sectors the intensity may decrease by 50 percent up to the prescribed limits; it shall decrease steadily to reach practical cut-off at not more than 5 degrees outside the prescribed sectors.

(b) All-round lights shall be so located as not to be obscured by masts, topmasts or structures within angular sectors of more than 6 degrees, except anchor lights prescribed in Rule 30, which need not be placed at an impracticable height above the hull, and the all-round white light described in Rule 23(d), which may not be obscured at all.

§ 84.19 Vertical sectors.

(a) The vertical sectors of electric lights as fitted, with the exception of lights on sailing vessels underway and on unmanned barges, shall ensure that:

(1) At least the required minimum intensity is maintained at all angles from 5 degrees above to 5 degrees below the horizontal;

(2) At least 60 percent of the required minimum intensity is maintained from 7.5 degrees above to 7.5 degrees below the horizontal.

(b) In the case of sailing vessels underway the vertical sectors of electric lights. as fitted shall ensure that:

(1) At least the required minimum intensity is maintained at all anglesfrom 5 degrees above to 5 degrees below the horizontal;

(2) At least 50 percent of the required minimum intensity is maintained from 25 degrees above to 25 degrees below the horizontal.

(c) In the case of unmanned barges the minimum required intensity of electric lights as fitted shall be maintained on the horizontal.

(d) In the case of lights other than electric lights these specifications shall be met as closely as possible.

§ 84.21 Intensity of non-electric lights.

Non-electric lights shall so far as practicable comply with the minimum intensities, as specified in the Table given in § 84.15.

§ 84.23 Maneuvering light.

Notwithstanding the provisions of § 84.03(f), the maneuvering light described in Rule 34(b) shall be placed approximately in the same fore and aft vertical plane as the masthead light or lights and, where practicable, at a minimum height of one-half meter vertically above the forward masthead light, provided that it shall be carried not less than one-half meter vertically above or below the after masthead light. On a vessel where only one masthead light is carried the maneuvering light, if fitted, shall be carried where it can best be seen, not less than one-half meter vertically apart from the masthead light.

§ 84.25 Approval. (Reserved)

ANNEX II

ADDITIONAL SIGNALS FOR FISHING VESSELS FISHING IN CLOSE PROXIMITY

§ 85.1 General.

The lights mentioned herein shall, if exhibited in pursuance of Rule 26(d), be placed where they can best be seen. They shall be at least 0.9 meter apart but at a lower level than lights prescribed in Rule 26(b)(i) and (c)(i) contained in the Inland Navigational Rules Act of 1980. The lights shall be visible all around the horizon at a distance of at least 1 mile but at a lesser distance than the lights prescribed by these Rules for fishing vessels.

§ 85.3 Signals for trawlers.

(a) Vessels when engaged in trawling, whether using demersal or pelagic gear may exhibit:

(1) When shooting their nets: two white lights in a vertical line;

(2) When hauling their nets: one white light over one red light in a vertical line;

(3) When the net has come fast upon an obstruction: two red lights in a vertical line.

(b) Each vessel engaged in pair trawling may exhibit:

(1) By night, a searchlight directed forward and in the direction of the other vessel of the pair;

(2) When shooting or hauling their nets or when their nets have come fast upon an obstruction, the lights prescribed in paragraph (a) above.

§ 85.5 Signals for purse seiners.

Vessels engaged in fishing with purse seine gear may exhibit two yellow lights in a vertical line. These lights shall flash alternately every second and with equal light and occultation duration. These lights may be exhibited only when the vessel is hampered by its fishing gear.

ANNEX III

TECHNICAL DETAILS OF SOUND SIGNAL APPLIANCES

Subpart A—Whistles

§ 86.01 Frequencies and range of audibility.

The fundamental frequency of the signal shall lie within the range 70-525 Hz. The range of audibility of the signal from a whistle shall be determined by those frequencies, which may include the fundamental and/or one or more higher frequencies, which lie within the frequency ranges and provide the sound pressure levels specified in § 86.05.

Table 86.05

Length of vessel in meters	*Fundamental frequency range (Hz)*	*For measured frequencies (Hz)*	*1/3 - octave band level at 1 meter in dB referred to 2 x 10^{-5}N/m²*	*Audibility range in nautical miles*
200 or more	70-200	130-180 180-250 250-1200	145 143 140	2
75 but less than 200	130-350	130-180 180-250 250-1200	140 138 134	1.5
20 but less than 75	250-525	250-450 450-800 800-1600	130 125 121	1.0
12 but less than 20	250-525	250-450 450-800 800-2100	120 115 111	0.5

§ 86.03 Limits of fundamental frequencies.

To ensure a wide variety of whistle characteristics, the fundamental frequency of a whistle shall be between the following limits:

(a) 70-200 Hz, for a vessel 200 meters or more in length;

(b) 130-350 Hz, for a vessel 75 meters but less than 200 meters in length;

(c) 250-525 Hz, for a vessel less than 75 meters in length.

§ 86.05 Sound signal intensity and range of audibility.

A whistle on a vessel shall provide, in the direction of the forward axis of the whistle and at a distance of 1 meter from it, a sound pressure level in at least one ⅓ - octave band of not less than the appropriate figure given in Table 86.05 within the following frequency ranges (± 1 per cent):

(a) 130-1200 Hz, for a vessel 75 meters or more in length;

b) 250-1600 Hz, for a vessel 20 meters but less than 75 meters in length

(c) 250-2100 Hz, for a vessel 12 meters but less than 20 meters in length.

NOTE: The range of audibility in the table above is for information and is approximately the range at which a whistle may usually be heard on its forward axis in conditions of still air on board a vessel having average background noise level at the listening posts (taken to be 68 dB in the octave band centered on 250 Hz and 63 dB in the octave band centered on 500 Hz).

In practice the range at which a whistle may be heard is extremely variable and depends critically on weather conditions; the values given can be regarded as typical but under conditions of strong wind or high ambient noise level at the listening post the range may be much reduced.

§ 86.07 Directional properties.

The sound pressure level of a directional whistle shall be not more than 4 dB below the sound pressure level specified in § 86.05 in any direction in the horizontal plane within ±45 degrees of the forward axis. The sound pressure level of the whistle at any other direction in the horizontal plane shall not be more than 10 dB less than the sound pressure level specified for the forward axis, so that the range of audibility in any direction will be at least half the range required on the forward axis. The sound pressure level shall be measured in that one-third octave band which determines the audibility range.

§ 86.09 Positioning of whistles.

(a) When a directional whistle is to be used as the only whistle on the vessel and is permanently installed, it shall be installed with its forward axis directed forward.

(b) A whistle shall be placed as high as practicable on a vessel, in order to reduce interception of the emitted sound by obstructions and also to minimize hearing damage risk to personnel. The sound pressure level of the vessel's own signal at listening posts shall not exceed 110 dB (A) and so far as practicable should not exceed 100 dB (A).

§ 86.11 Fitting of more than one whistle.

If whistles are fitted at a distance apart of more than 100 meters, they shall not be sounded simultaneously.

§ 86 13 Combined whistle systems.

(a) A combined whistle system is a number of whistles (sound emitting sources) operated together. For the purposes of the Rules a combined whistle system is to be regarded as a single whistle.

(b) The whistles of a combined system shall:

(1) Be located at a distance apart of not more than 100 meters;

(2) Be sounded simultaneously;

(3) Each have a fundamental frequency different from those of the others by at least 10 Hz, and;

(4) Have a tonal characteristic appropriate for the length of vessel which shall be evidenced by at least two-thirds of the whistles in the combined system having fundamental frequencies falling within the limits prescribed ir § 86.03, or if there are only two whistles in the combined system, by the higher fundamental frequency falling within the limits prescribed in § 86.03

NOTE: If due to the presence of obstructions the sound field of a single whistle or of one of the whistles referred to in § 86.11 is likely to have a zone of greatly reduced signal level, a combined whistle system should be fitted so as to overcome this reduction.

§ 86.15 Towing vessel whistles.

A power-driven vessel normally engaged in pushing ahead or towing alongside. may, at all times, use a whistle whose characteristic falls within the limits prescribed by § 86.03 for the longest customary composite length of the vessel and its tow.

Subpart B – Bell or gong.

§ 86.21 Intensity of signal.

A bell or gong, or other device having similar sound characteristics shall produce a sound pressure level of not less than 110 dB at 1 meter.

§ 86.23 Construction.

Bells and gongs shall be made of corrosion-resistant material and designed to give a clear tone. The diameter of the mouth of the bell shall be not less than 300 mm for vessels of more than 20 meters in length, and shall be not less than 200 mm for vessels of 12 to 20 meters in length. The mass of the striker shall be not less than 3 per cent of the mass of the bell. The striker shall be capable of manual operation .

NOTE: When practicable, a power-driven bell striker is recommended to ensure constant force.

Subpart C—Approval.

§ 86.31 Approval. (Reserved)

ANNEX IV

DISTRESS SIGNALS

§ 87.1 Need of assistance.

The following signals, used or exhibited either together or separately, indicate distress and need of assistance:

(a) A gun or other explosive signal fired at intervals of about a minute;

(b) A continuous sounding with any fog-signaling apparatus;

(c) Rockets or shells, throwing red stars fired one at a time at short intervals;

(d) A signal made by radiotelegraphy or by any other signaling ,method consisting of the group . . . – – – . . . (SOS) in the Morse Code.

(e) A signal sent by radiotelephony consisting of the spoken word "Mayday";

(f) The International Code Signal of distress indicated by N.C.;

(g) A signal consisting of a square flag having above or below it a ball or anything resembling a ball;

(h) Flames on the vessel (as from a burning tar barrel, oil barrel, etc.);

(i) A rocket parachute flare or a hand flare showing a red light;

(j) A smoke signal giving off orange-coloured smoke;

(k) Slowly and repeatedly raising and lowering arms outstretched to each side; .

(l) The radiotelegraph alarm signal;

(m) The radiotelephone alarm signal;

(n) Signals transmitted by emergency position-indicating radio beacons;

(o) Signals transmitted by radiocommunication systems.

(p) A high intensity white light flashing at regular intervals from 50 to 70 times per minute.

§ 87.3 Exclusive use.

The use or exhibition of any of the foregoing signals except for the purpose of indicating distress and need of assistance and the use of other signals which may be confused with any of the above signals is prohibited.

§ 87.5 Supplemental signals.

Attention is drawn to the relevant sections of the Interrlational Code of Signals the Merchant Ship Search and Rescue Manual, the International Telecommunication Union Regulations and the following signals:

(a) A piece of orange-colored canvas with either a black square and circle or other appropriate symbol (for identification from the air);

(b) A dye marker;

ANNEX V

PILOT RULES

§ 88.01 Purpose and applicability.

This Part applies to all vessels operating on United States inland waters and to United States vessels operating on the Canadian waters of the Great Lakes to the extent there is no conflict with Canadian law.

§ 88.03 Definitions.

The terms used in this part have the same meaning as defined in the Inland Navigational Rules Act of 1980.

§ 88.05 Copy of Rules.

After January 1, 1983, the operator of each self-propelled vessel 12 meters or more in length shall carry on board and maintain for ready reference a copy of the Inland Navigation Rules.

§ 88.09 Temporary exemption from light and shape requirements when operating under bridges.

A vessel's navigation lights and shapes may be lowered if necessary to pass under a bridge.

§ 88.11 Law enforcement vessels.

(a) Law enforcement vessels may display a flashing blue light when engaged in direct law enforcement or public safety activities. This light must be located so that it does not interfere with the visibility of the vessel's navigation lights.

(b) The blue light described in this section may be displayed by law enforcement vessels of the United States and the States and their political subdivisions.

§ 88.12 Public Safety Activites.

(a) Vessels engaged in government sanctioned public safety activities, and commercial vessels performing similar functions, may display an alternately flashing red and yellow light signal. This identification light signal must be located so that it does not interfere with the visibility of the vessel's navigation lights. The identification light signal may be used only as an identification signal and conveys no special privilege. Vessels using the identification light signal during public safety activities must abide by the Inland Navigation Rules, and must not presume that the light or the exigency gives them precedence or right of way.

(b) Public safety activities include but are not limited to patrolling marine parades, regattas, or special water celebrations; traffic control; salvage; firefighting; medical assistance; assisting disabled vessels; and search and rescue.

§ 88.13 Lights on barges at bank or dock.

(a) The following barges shall display at night and, if practicable, in period of restricted visibility the lights described in paragraph (b) of this section:

(1) Every barge projecting into a buoyed or restricted channel.

(2) Every barge so moored that it reduces the available navigable width of any channel to less than 80 meters.

(3) Barges moored in groups more than two barges wide or to a maximum width of over 25 meters.

(4) Every barge not moored parallel to the bank or dock.

(b) Barges described in paragraph (a) shall carry two unobstructed white lights of an intensity to be visible for at least one mile on a clear dark night, and arranged as follows:

(1) On a single moored barge, lights shall be placed on the two corners farthest from the bank or dock.

(2) On barges moored in group formation, a light shall be placed on each of the upstream and downstream ends of the group, on the corners farthest from the bank or dock.

(3) Any barge in a group, projecting from the main body of the group toward the channel, shall be lighted as a single barge.

(c) Barges moored in any slip or slough which is used primarily for mooring purposes are exempt from the lighting requirements of this section.

(d) Barges moored in well-illuminated areas are exempt from the light requirements of this section. These areas are as follows:

Chicago Sanitary Ship Canal

(1) Mile 293.2 to 293.9
(3) Mile 295.2 to 296.1
(5) Mile 297.5 to 297.8
(7) Mile 298 to 298.2
(9) Mile 298.6 to 298.8
(11) Mile 299.3 to 299.4
(13) Mile 299.8 to 300.5
(15) Mile 303 to 303.2
(17) Mile 303.7 to 303.9
(19) Mile 305.7 to 305.8
(21) Mile 310.7 to 310.9
(23) Mile 311 to 311.2
(25) Mile 312.5 to 312.6
(27) Mile 313.8 to 314.2
(29) Mile 314.6
(31) Mile 314.8 to 315.3
(33) Mile 315.7 to 316

(35) Mile 316.8
(37) Mile 316.85 to 317.05
(39) Mile 317.5
(41) Mile 318.4 to 318.9
(43) Mile 318.7 to 318.8
(45) Mile 320 to 320.3
(47) Mile 320.6
(49) Mile 322.3 to 322.4
(51) Mile 322.8
(53) Mile 322.9 to 327.2

Calumet Sag Channel
(61) Mile 3 1 6. 5

Little Calumet River
(71) Mile 32 1. 2
(73) Mile 322.3

Calumet River
(81) Mile 328.5 to 328.7
(83) Mile 329.2 to 329.4
(85) Mile 330, west bank to 330.2
(87) Mile 331.4 to 331.6
(89) Mile 332.2 to 332.4
(91) Mile 332.6 to 332.8

Cumberland River
(101) Mile 126.8
(103) Mile 191

§ 88.15 Lights on dredge pipelines.

Dredge pipelines that are floating or supported on trestles shall display the following lights at night and in periods of restricted visibility.

(a) One row of yellow lights. The lights must be:

(1) Flashing 50 to 70 times per minute;

(2) Visible all around the horizon;

(3) Visible for at least 2 miles on a clear dark night;

(4) Not less than 1 and not more than 3.5 meters above the water;

(5) Approximately equally spaced, and

(6) Not more than 10 meters apart where the pipeline crosses a navigable channel. Where the pipeline does not cross a navigable channel the lights must be sufficient in number to clearly show the pipeline's length and course.

(b) Two red lights at each end of the pipeline, including the ends in a channel where the pipeline is separated to allow vessels to pass (whether open or closed). The lights must be:

(1) Visible all around the horizon, and

(2) Visible for at least 2 miles on a clear dark night, and

(3) One meter apart in a vertical line with the lower light at the same height above the water as the flashing yellow light.

NOTE: SEE CHAPTER 4, BOATING REGULATIONS, FOR THE VESSEL BRIDGE-TO-BRIDGE RADIOTELEPHONE REGULATIONS.

Navigation Rules – International

2

RECOGNITION OF LIGHTS AND SHAPES
(Complete details in Collision Regulations)
LIGHTS

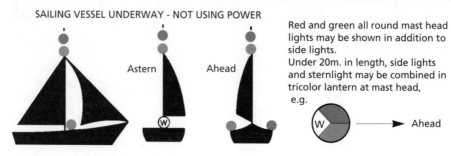

SAILING VESSEL UNDERWAY - NOT USING POWER

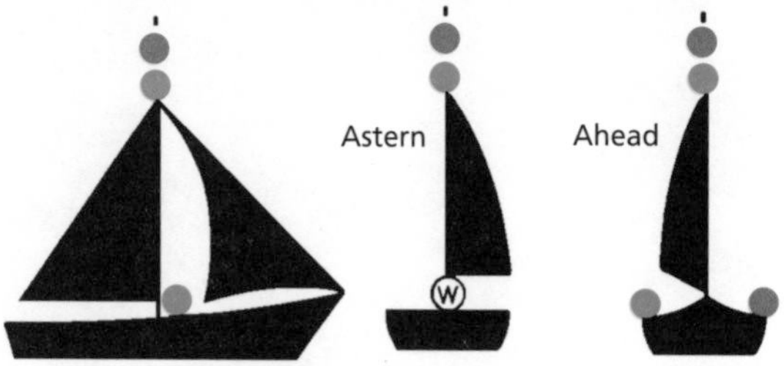

Red and green all round mast head lights may be shown in addition to side lights.
Under 20m. in length, side lights and sternlight may be combined in tricolor lantern at mast head, e.g.

Under 7m. in length, if not practicable to exhibit these lights, vessel shall have a white light ready to display to avoid collision.

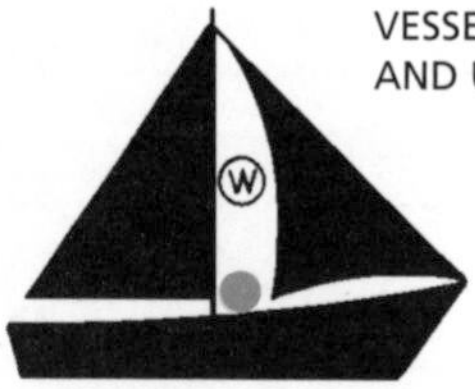

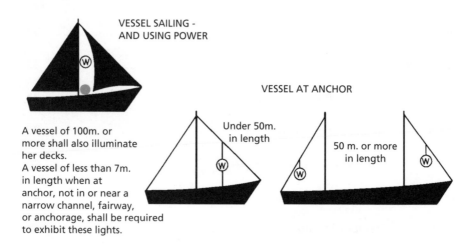

VESSEL SAILING - AND USING POWER

VESSEL AT ANCHOR

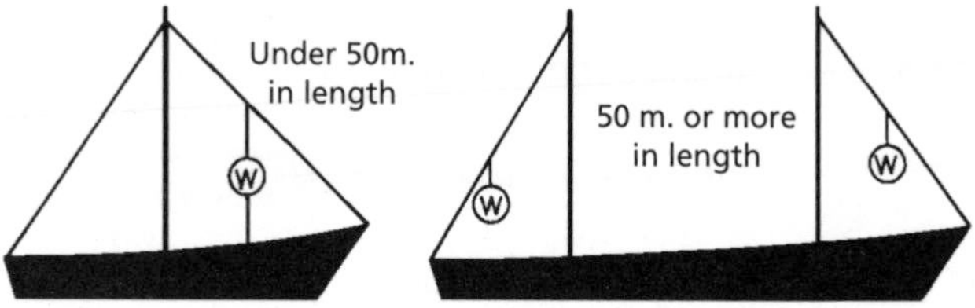

A vessel of 100m. or more shall also illuminate her decks.
A vessel of less than 7m. in length when at anchor, not in or near a narrow channel, fairway, or anchorage, shall be required to exhibit these lights.

POWER DRIVEN VESSEL UNDERWAY

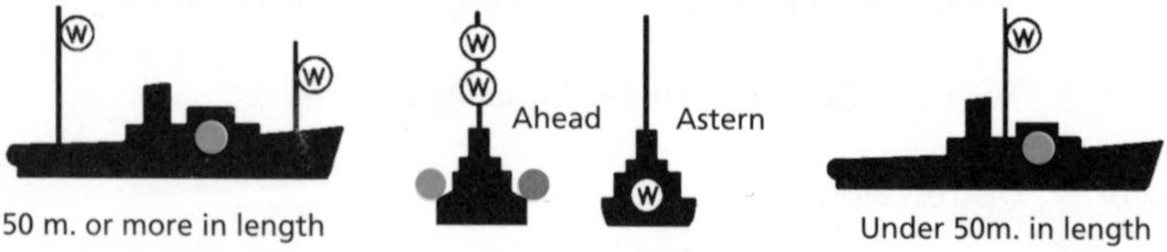

Under 12m. may exhibit all round white light and side lights.

Less than 7m. and maximum speed not exceeding 7 knots an all round white light may be shown, and if practicable side lights.

HOVERCRAFT

Normal lights as for power driven vessels and when in non-displacement mode an all round flashing yellow light.

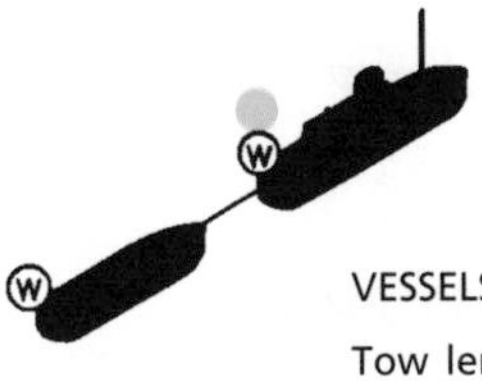

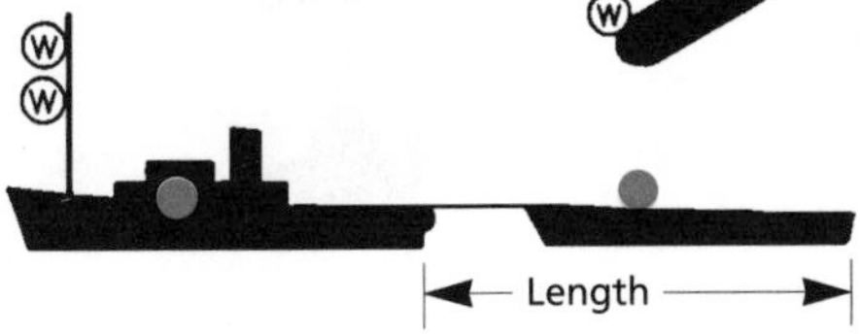

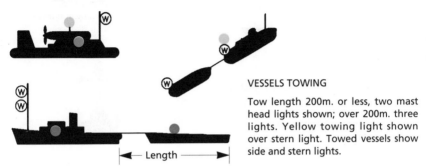

VESSELS TOWING

Tow length 200m. or less, two mast head lights shown; over 200m. three lights. Yellow towing light shown over stern light. Towed vessels show side and stern lights.

VESSEL ENGAGED IN UNDERWATER OPERATIONS

When making way also shows mast head, stern and side lights.
When at anchor does <u>NOT</u> show anchor light.

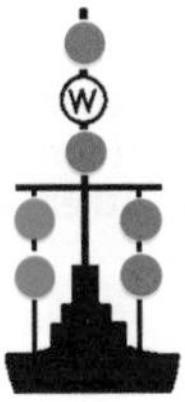

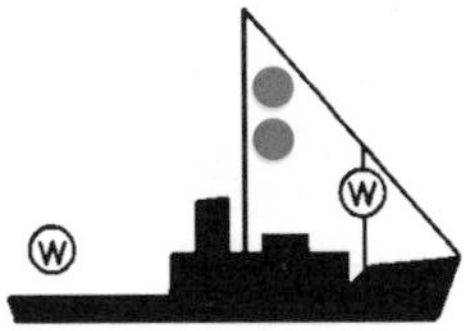

VESSEL AGROUND

Two all round red lights and anchor light(s).

A vessel of less than 12m. in length shall not be required to exhibit these lights.

VESSELS RESTRICTED IN ABILITY TO MANOEUVRE

Shows 3 all round lights, red over white over red.
When making way shows mast head, stern and side lights.
When at anchor shows an anchor light.

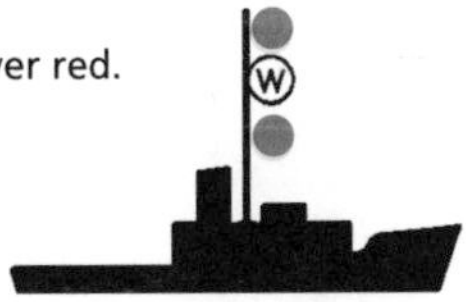

PILOT VESSEL ON DUTY

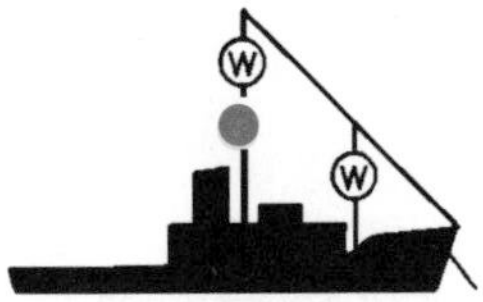

Anchored

2 all round lights, white over red.
When underway shows stern and side lights instead of anchor light.

Underway, from astern

Underway, from ahead

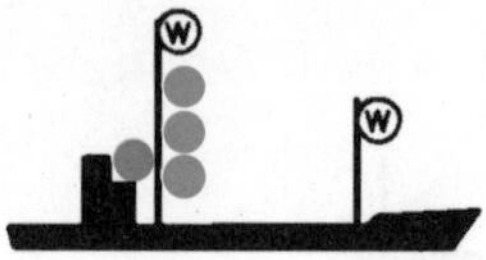

VESSEL CONSTRAINED BY HER DRAUGHT

Three all round red lights,
with normal navigation lights.

VESSEL ENGAGED IN MINESWEEPING

Three all round green lights,
with normal navigation lights.

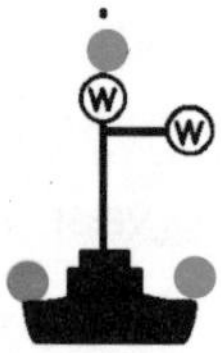

VESSEL FISHING, OTHER THAN TRAWLING

Two all round lights red over white with one all round white light in direction of gear if it extends more than 150m. horizontally.

Each vessel engaged in "pair trawling" may direct a searchlight forward and in direction of other vessel.

VESSEL TRAWLING

Two all round lights green over white,
with normal navigation lights.
Mast head light optional under 50m.

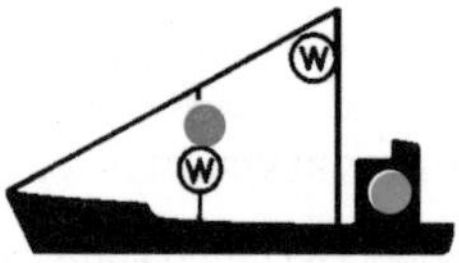

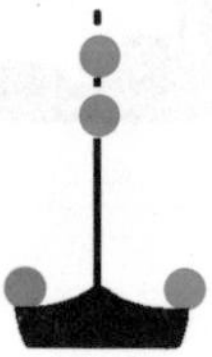

VESSEL NOT UNDER COMMAND

Two all round red lights and when making way stern and side lights.

REMEMBER

A sailing vessel when using its engine - with or without sails - is a powr driven vessel within the meaning of the Rules and must act accordingly, showing the appropiate shapes and lights.
Therefore a tricolor lantern may be used when under power

DAYMARKS

VESSEL SAILING AND USING POWER

Black cone, point down.

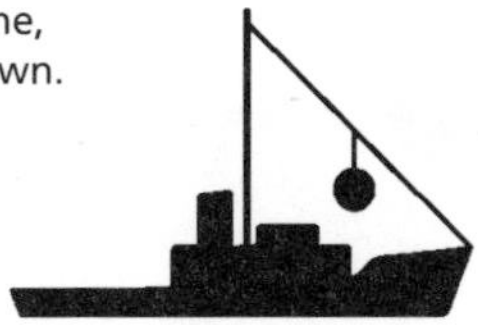

VESSEL AT ANCHOR

Black ball.

Vessel of less than 7m. in length when at anchor, not in or near a narrow channel, fairway or anchorage, shall not be required to exhibit the ball.

VESSEL TOWING

If length ot tow exceeds 200m. a black diamond shape to be exhibited on each vessel.

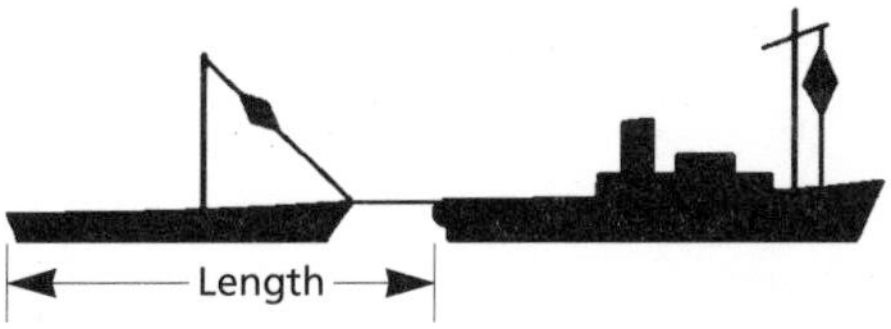

VESSEL RESTRICTED IN ABILITY TO MANOEUVRE

Black ball over black diamond over black ball

VESSEL ENGAGED IN UNDERWATER OPERATIONS

Two black balls on the side of the obstruction.

Two black diamonds on side on which vessels may pass.

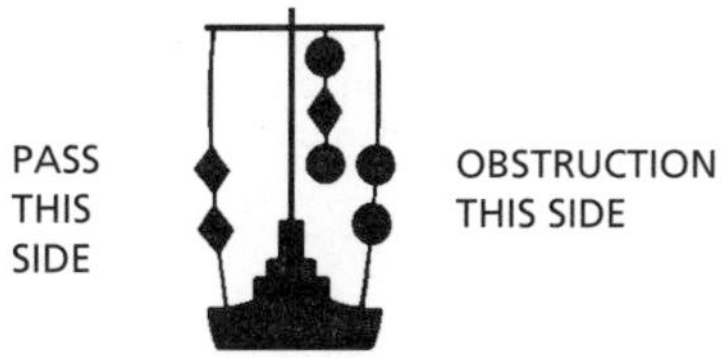

If vessel is too small to exhibit above shapes a rigid replica of code flag A shall be flown. White and blue.

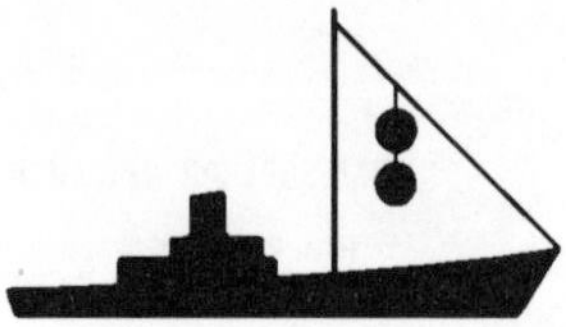

VESSEL NOT UNDER COMAND

Two black balls

VESSEL ENGAGED IN MINESWEEPING

Three black balls

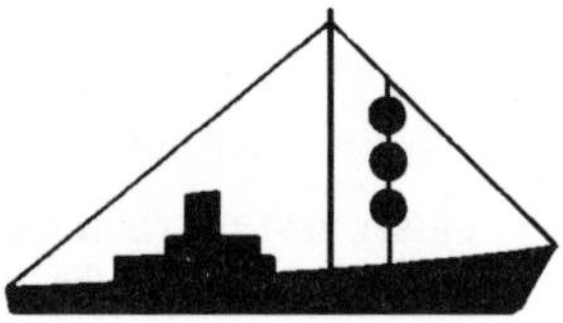

VESSEL AGROUND

Three black balls to be exhibited.
Not required for vessel under 12m.

VESSEL ENGAGED IN FISHING

Two black cones, points together.
May be replaced by basket if under 20m.

If outlying gear extends more tham 150m. horizontally, a black cone point up is shown in direction of gear, e.g.

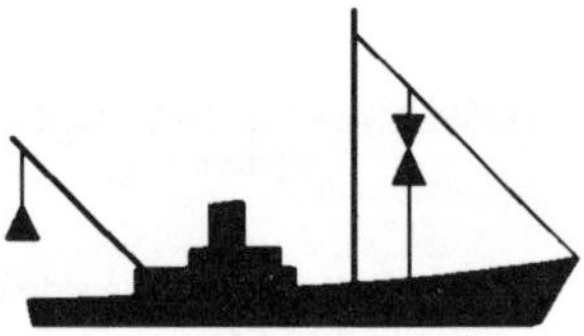

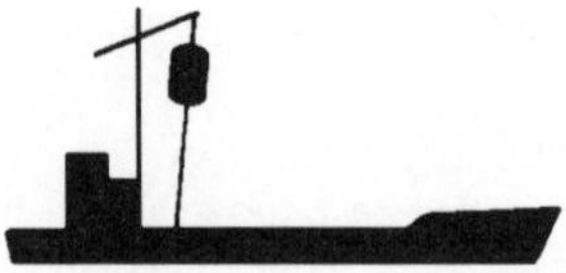

VESSEL CONSTRAINED BY HER DRAUGHT

A black cylinder

Introduction. Explanatory notes are added to individual rules in the Steering and Sailing Rules Section, while general comments only are made in parts C (Lights and Shapes) and part D (Sound and Light Signals). These notes are intended for the less experienced skippers of small craft.

Itt is important for anyone going to sea to fully understand the rules, and the ability to recognise lights and shapes and understand sound signals is vital. It should never be necessary in an emergency to consult a book to identify a particular group of lights or a signal.

As a matter of interest the newcomer to sailing may consider it odd to refer to arcs of lights in half degrees, when steering to half a degree is impracticable e.g. "the stern light shall be visible 22½° abaft the beam". Originally magnetic compasses were marked in 32 cardinal points thus each point equated to 11¼°. Whilst the use of degrees became universal the old arcs of visibility were retained, thus "2 points abaft the beam" became 22½° abaft the beam" in the modern nomenclature.

INTERNATIONAL REGULATIONS FOR PREVENTING COLLISIONS AT SEA.

PART A – GENERAL

Rule 1 *Application*

(a) These Rules shall apply to all vessels upon the high seas and in all waters connected therewith navigable by seagoing vessels.

(b) Nothing in these Rules shall interfere with the operation of special rules made by an appropriate authority for roadsteads, harbours, rivers, lakes or inland waterways connected with the high seas and navigable by seagoing vessels. Such special rules shall conform as closely as possible to these rules.

(c) Nothing in these Rules shall interfere with the operation of special rules made by the Government of any State with respect to additional station or signal lights, shapes or whistle signals for ships of war and vessels proceeding under convoy, or with respect to additional station or signal lights, or shapes for fishing vessels engaged in fishing as a fleet. These additional station or signal lights, shapes or whistle signals shall, so far as possible, be such that they cannot be mistaken for any light, shape or signal authorised elsewhere under these Rules.

(d) Traffic separation schemes may be adopted by the Organization for the purpose of these Rules.

(e) Whenever the Government concerned shall have determined that a vessel of special construction or purpose cannot comply fully with the provisions of any of these Rules with respect to the number, position, range or arc of visibility of lights or shapes, as well as to the disposition and characteristics of sound-signalling appliances, such vessel shall comply with such other provisions in regard to the number, position, range or arc of visibility of lights or shapes, as well as to the disposition and characteristics of sound-signalling appliances, as her Government shall have determined to be the closest possible compliance with these Rules in respect of that vessel.

Rule 2 *Responsibility*

(a) Nothing in these Rules shall exonerate any vessel, or the owner, master or crew thereof, from the consequences of any neglect to comply with these Rules or of the neglect of any precaution which may be required by the ordinary practice of seamen, or by the special circumstances of the case.

(b) In construing and complying with these Rules due regard shall be had to all dangers of navigation and collision and to any special circumstances, including the limitations of the vessels involved, which may make a departure from these Rules necessary to avoid immediate danger.

NOTE TO RULE 2 It must be remembered that rules do not give absolute right of way to any vessel. Right of way is conferred by one vessel to another by an alteration of course and speed, but both vessels have responsibility to avoid a collision. In certain circumstances the "give way" vessel may be unable to take avoiding action and then the "stand on" vessel is required to take the necessary action.

Rule 3 *General Definitions*

For the purpose of these Rules, except where the context otherwise requires:

(a) The word "vessel" includes every description of water craft including non-displacement craft and seaplanes, used or capable of being used as a means of transportation on water.

(b) The term "power-driven vessel" means any vessel propelled by machinery.

(c) The term "sailing vessel" means any vessel under sail provided that propelling machinery, if fitted, is not being used.

(d) The term "vessel engaged in fishing" means any vessel fishing with nets, lines, trawls or other fishing apparatus which restrict maneuverability, but does not include a vessel fishing with trolling lines or other fishing apparatus which do not restrict maneuverability.

(e) The word "seaplane" includes any aircraft designed to maneuver on the water.

(f) The term "vessel not under command" means a vessel which through some exceptional circumstance is unable to maneuver as required by these Rules and is therefore unable to keep out of the way of another vessel.

(g) The term"vessel restricted in her ability to maneuver" means a vessel which from the nature of her work is restricted in her ability to maneuver as required by these Rules and is therefore unable to keep out of the way of another vessel.
The term "vessels restricted in their ability to maneuver" shall include but not be limited to:

(i) a vessel engaged in laying, servicing or picking up a navigation mark, submarine cable or pipeline;

(ii) a vessel engaged in dredging, surveying or underwater operations;

(iii) a vessel engaged in replenishment or transferring persons, provisions or cargo while underway;

(iv) a vessel engaged in the launching or recovery of aircraft;

(v) a vessel engaged in mine clearance operations;

(vi) a vessel engaged in a towing operation such as severely restricts the towing vessel and her tow in their ability to deviate from their course.

(h) The term "vessel constrained by her draft" means a power-driven vessel which because of her draft in relation to the available depth and width of navigable water is severely restricted in her ability to deviate from the course she is following.

(i) The word "underway" means that a vessel is not at anchor, or made fast to the shore, or aground.

(j) The words "length" and "breadth" of a vessel mean her length overall and greatest breadth.

(k) Vessels shall be deemed to be in sight of one another only when one can be observed visually from the other.

(l) The term "restricted visibility" means any condition in which visibility is restricted by fog, mist, falling snow, heavy rainstorms, sandstorms or any other similar causes.

NOTE TO RULE 3 A useful explanation of various terms which occur in the rules and should be known and understood by those in charge of any seagoing vessel.

PART B – STEERING AND SAILING RULES

SECTION I – CONDUCT OF VESSELS IN ANY CONDITION OF VISIBILITY.

Rule 4 ***Application***

Rules in this Section apply in any condition of visibility.

Rule 5 ***Lookout***

Every vessel shall at all times maintain a proper lookout by sight and hearing as well as by all available means appropriate in the prevailing circumstances and conditions so as to make a full appraisal of the situation and of the risk of collision.

NOTE TO RULE 5 Keeping a proper lookout at all times is one of the most important duties of any vessel. It is particularly difficult in a sailing yacht with a long footed headsail especially when heeled but it is vital to keep a good lookout to lee-ward in these circumstances. Watch-keeping at night also presents problems insofar as the lights on the vessel are con-cerned. Chart table lights and any internal lights visible to the helmsman should be red which reduces night vision by a relat-ively small amount. Deck lights for sail changing at night constitute a real diffic-ulty for the lookout both at the time and for a short while afterwards. In conditions of poor visibility a good listening watch is also important – it cannot be kept from inside a closed wheelhouse.

Rule 6 ***Safe Speed.***

Every vessel shall at all times proceed at a safe speed so that she can take proper and effective action to avoid collision and be stopped within a distance appropriate to the prevailing circumstances and conditions.

In determining a safe speed the following factors shall be among those taken into account:

(a) By all vessels:

(i) the state of visibility;

(ii) the traffic density including concentrations of fishing vessels or any other vessels;

(iii) the maneuverability of the vessel with special reference to stopping distance and turning ability in the prevailing conditions;

(iv) at night the presence of background light such as from shore lights or from back scatter of her own lights;

(v) the draft in relation to the available depth of water.

(b) Additonally, by vessels with operational radar:

(i) the characteristics, efficiency and limitations of the radar equipment;

(ii) any constraints imposed by the radar range scale in use;

(iii) the effect on radar detection of the sea state, weather and other sources of interference;

(iv) the possibility that small vessels, ice and other floating objects may not be detected by radar at an adequate range.

(v) the number, location and movement of vessels detected by radar.

(vi) the more exact assessment of the visibility that may be possible when radar is used to determine the range of vessels or other objects in the vicinity.

NOTE TO RULE 6 This rule refers to a "safe speed" i.e. not necessarily high speed. High speed in a sailing yacht is rarely a contributory factor in a collision situation but slow speed may be. The essence of the Rule is to have complete control and maneuverability at all times. A sailing yacht carrying a spinnaker at night in a congested traffic situation would not be conforming to the spirit of this Rule, she should be sailing more slowly under plain sail but with complete maneuverability. For the fast motor yacht high speed in a tight situation may be a danger as it effectively reduces "thinking time".

Rule 7 ***Risk of Collision***

(a) Every vessel shall use all available means appropriate to the prevailing circumstances and conditions to determine if risk of collision exists. If there is any doubt such risk shall be deemed to exist.

(b) Proper use shall be made of radar equipment if fitted and operational, including long-range scanning to obtain early warning of risk of collision and radar plotting or equivalent systematic observation of detected objects.

(c) Assumptions shall not be made on the basis of scanty information, especially scanty radar information.

(d) In determining if risk of collision exists the following considerations shall be among those taken into account:

(i) such risk shall be deemed to exist if the compass bearing of an approaching vessel does not appreciably change;

(ii) such risk may sometimes exist even when an appreciable bearing change is evident, particularly when approaching a very large vessel or a tow or when approaching a vessel at close range.

NOTE TO RULE 7 In the situation of an approaching or crossing vessel the first step is to take a compass bearing of the vessel and repeat it at suitable intervals. If the bearing does not change, risk of collision exists. Note that it is the compass bearing, not the relative bearing that is crucial.

Rule 8 ***Action to avoid a Collision***

(a) Any action taken to avoid collision shall, if the circumstances of the case admit, be positive, made in ample time and with due regard to the observance of good seamanship.

(b) Any alteration of course and/or speed to avoid collision shall, if the circumstances of the case admit, be large enough to be readily apparent to another vessel observing visually or by radar; a succession of small alterations of course and/or speed should be avoided.

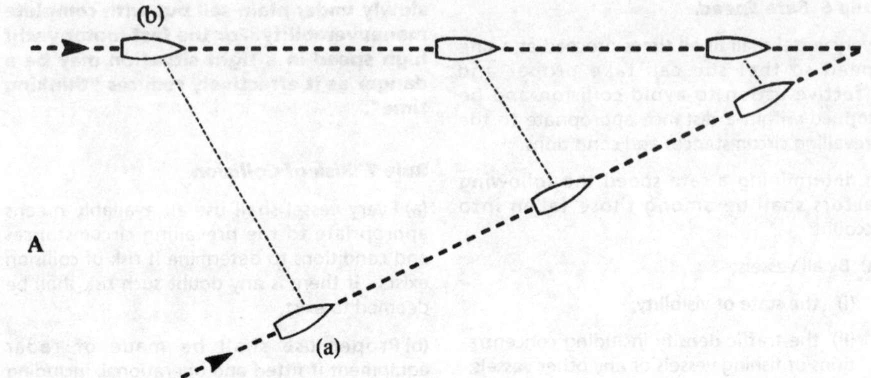

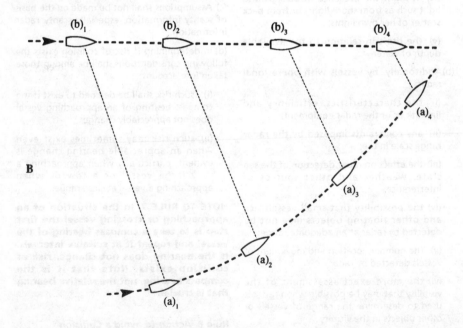

In A. the compass bearing of (a) relative to (b) is constant and therefore risk of collision exists. In this particular case the relative bearing of (a) to (b) is also constant

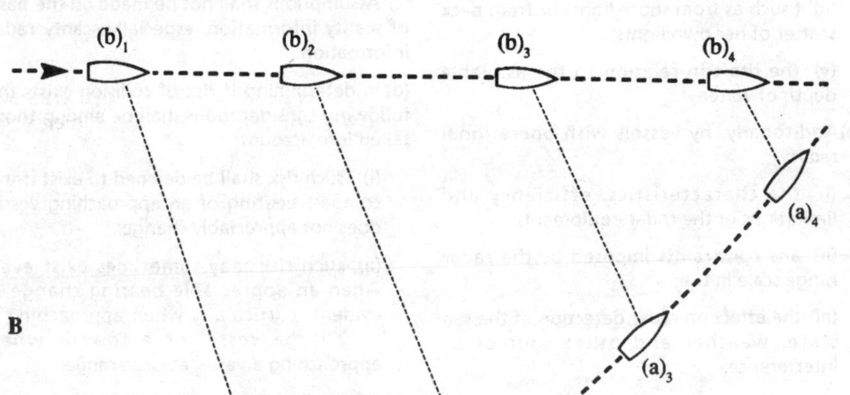

In B. the relative bearing of $(b)_1$ from $(a)_1$ is abaft the beam. At $(a)_2$ the bearing is approximately abeam and at $(a)_3$ and $(a)_4$ is moving ahead of the beam. The compass bearing however, remains constant and therefore risk of collision exists.

(c) If there is sufficient sea room, alteration of course alone may be the most effective action to avoid a close-quarters situation provided that it is made in good time, is substantial and does not result in another close-quarters situation.

(d) Action taken to avoid collision with another vessel shall be such as to result in passing at a safe distance. The effectiveness of the action shall be carefully checked until the other vessel is finally past and clear.

(e) If necessary to avoid collision or allow more time to assess the situation, a vessel shall slacken her speed to take all way off by stopping or reversing her means of propulsion.

(f) (i) A vessel which, by any of these rules, is required not to impede the passage or safe passage of another vessel shall, when required by the circumstances of the case, take early action to allow sufficient sea room for the safe passage of the other vessel.

(ii) A vessel required not to impede the passage or safe passage of another vessel is not relieved of this obligation if approaching the other vessel so as to involve risk of collision and shall, when taking action, have full regard to the action which may be required by the rules of this part.

(iii) A vessel the passage of which is not to be impeded remains fully obliged to comply with the rules of this part when the two vessels are approaching one another so as to involve risk of collision.

NOTE TO RULE 8 Action to avoid collision must be taken in good time and in such a manner that the "stand on" vessel is left in no doubt that the "give way" vessel is taking avoiding action. In the case of the "give way" vessel being a small yacht any alteration in speed is unlikely to be obvious from any distance. The action therefore must be to alter the profile of the yacht by a marked change of course. Rule 8(f) draws attention to the importance of small vessels navigating in traffic separation schemes not to impede vessels moving in the lane.

Rule 9 *Narrow Channels*

(a) A vessel proceeding along the course of a narrow channel or fairway shall keep as near to the outer limit of the channel or fairway which lies on her starboard side as is safe and practicable.

(b) A vessel of less than 20 meters in length or a sailing vessel shall not impede the passage of a vessel which can safely navigate only within a narrow channel or fairway.

(c) A vessel engaged in fishing shall not impede the passage of any other vessel navigating within a narrow channel or fairway.

(d) A vessel shall not cross a narrow channel or fairway if such crossing impedes the passage of a vessel which can safely navigate only within such channel or fairway.The latter vessel may use the sound signal prescribed in Rule 34(d) if in doubt as to the intention of the crossing vessel.

(e) (i) In a narrow channel or fairway when overtaking can take place only if the vessel to be overtaken has to take action to permit safe passing, the vessel intending to overtake shall indicate her intention by sounding the appropriate signal prescribed in Rule 34(c)(i). The vessel to be overtaken shall, if in agreement, sound the appropriate signal prescribed in Rule 34(c)(ii) and take steps to permit safe passing. If in doubt she may sound the signals prescribed in Rule 34(d).

(ii) This Rule does not relieve the overtaking vessel of her obligation under Rule 13.

(f) A vessel nearing a bend or an area of a narrow channel or fairway where other vessels may be obscured by an intervening obstruction shall navigate with particular alertness and caution and shall sound the appropriate signal prescribed in Rule 34(e).

(g) Any vessel shall, if the circumstances of the case admit, avoid anchoring in a narrow channel.

NOTE TO RULE 9 On occasion doubt may arise whether one is in a "narrow channel" – usually it is obvious, but if not, any channel which has port and starboard hand buoys will be regarded as a narrow channel by ocean-going vessels. Hence all other vessels should have regard to the requirements of this rule when in such a channel. It is important to note that 9(a) refers to "a vessel", hence a sailing yacht is also required to keep as near as possible to the starboard side of the channel and avoid impeding the passage of a vessel which can only navigate with safety in a narrow channel.

Rule 10 *Traffic Separation Schemes*

(a) This Rule applies to traffic separation schemes adopted by the Organization and does not relieve any vessel of her obligation under any other rule.

(b) A vessel using a traffic separation scheme shall:

(i) proceed in the appropriate traffic lane in the general direction of traffic flow for that lane;

(ii) so far as practicable keep clear of a traffic separation line or separation zone;

(iii) normally join or leave a traffic lane at the termination of the lane, but when joining or leaving from either side shall do so at as small an angle to the general direction of traffic flow as practicable.

(c) A vessel shall so far as practicable avoid crossing traffic lanes, but if obliged to do so shall cross on a heading as nearly as practicable at right angles to the general direction of traffic flow.

(d) (i) A vessel shall not use an inshore traffic zone when she can safely use the appropriate traffic lane within the adjacent traffic separation scheme. However, vessels of less than 20 meters in length, sailing vessels and vessels engaged in fishing may use the inshore traffic zone.

(ii) Notwithstanding sub-paragraph (d)(i) a vessel may use an inshore traffic zone when en route to or from a port, offshore installation or structure, pilot station or any other place situated within the inshore traffic zone, or to avoid immediate danger.

(e) A vessel other than a crossing vessel or a vessel joining or leaving a lane, shall not normally enter a separation zone or cross a separation line except:

(i) in cases of emergency to avoid immediate danger;

(ii) to engage in fishing within a separation zone.

(f) A vessel navigating in areas near the terminations of traffic separation schemes shall do so with particular caution.

(g) A vessel shall so far as practicable avoid anchoring in a traffic separation scheme or in areas near its terminations.

(h) A vessel not using a traffic separation scheme shall avoid it by as wide a margin as is practicable.

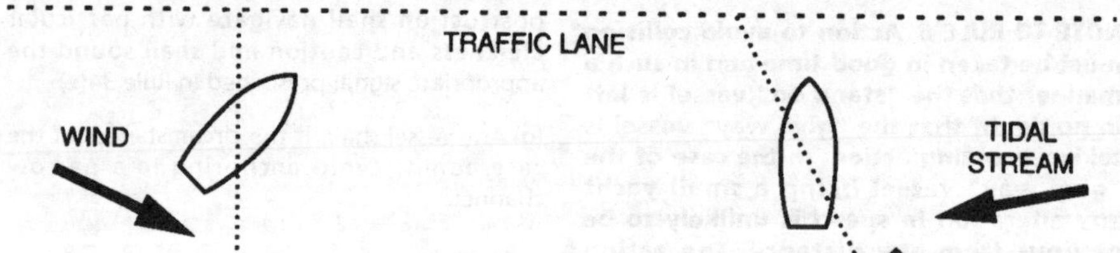

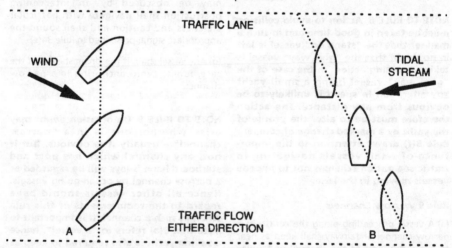

In the sketch, Yacht A is counteracting the effect of the tidal stream to make her track at 90° to the lane, but her profile to vessels in the lane is considerably reduced. This has two results. Firstly, her time in crossing the lane is much increased and secondly, her reduced profile means that she is less visible, both visually and on radar screens, than if she presented a full profile. The action taken by Yacht A is incorrect.

Yacht B is correctly presenting her full profile in the lane and is not attempting to counteract the tidal stream. Although her track is longer than that of Yacht A she will cross in less time. This is the correct procedure.

In the case of having to cross against a head wind and motoring is not practicable, a yacht should sail close hauled on that tack which makes her heading as close as possible to 90° to the lane.

(i) A vessel engaged in fishing shall not impede the passage of any vessel following a traffic lane.

(j) A vessel of less than 20 meters in length or a sailing vessel shall not impede the safe passage of a power-driven vessel following a traffic lane.

(k) A vessel restricted in her ability to maneuver when engaged in an operation for the maintenance of safety of navigation in a traffic separation scheme is exempted from complying with this Rule to the extent necessary to carry out the operation.

(l) A vessel restricted in her ability to maneuver when engaged in an operation for the laying, servicing or picking up of a submarine cable, within a traffic separation scheme, is exempted from complying with this Rule to the extent necessary to carry out the operation.

NOTE TO RULE 10 This is an extremely important rule and there are two aspects of it which are particularly important to sailing vessels.

Firstly, all crossing vessels must cross on a heading as nearly as practicable at right angles to the lane, thereby presenting a full profile to vessels using the lane.

Secondly, a sailing vessel is required "not to impede the safe passage of a power-driven vessel following a traffic lane".

This means that the sailing vessel shall achieve maximum speed and hence maneuverability. The aim should be to cross as quickly as possible which means using the engine when necessary and not trying to counteract any sideways effect of the tidal stream.

SECTION II – CONDUCT OF VESSELS IN SIGHT OF ONE ANOTHER

Rule 11 *Application*

Rules in this Section apply to vessels in sight of one another.

Rule 12 *Sailing Vessels*

(a) When two sailing vessels are approaching one another, so as to avoid risk of collision, one of them shall keep out of the way of the other as follows:

(i) when each has the wind on a different side, the vessel which has the wind on the port side shall keep out of the way of the other;

(ii) when both have the wind on the same side, the vessel which is to windward shall keep out of the way of the vessel which is to leeward;

(iii) if a vessel with the wind on the port side sees a vessel to windward and cannot determine with certainty whether the other vessel has the wind on the port or on the starboard side, she shall keep out of the way of the other.

(b) For the purposes of this Rule the windward side shall be deemed to be the side opposite to that on which the mainsail is carried or, in the case of a square-rigged vessel, the side opposite to that on which the largest fore-and-aft sail is carried.

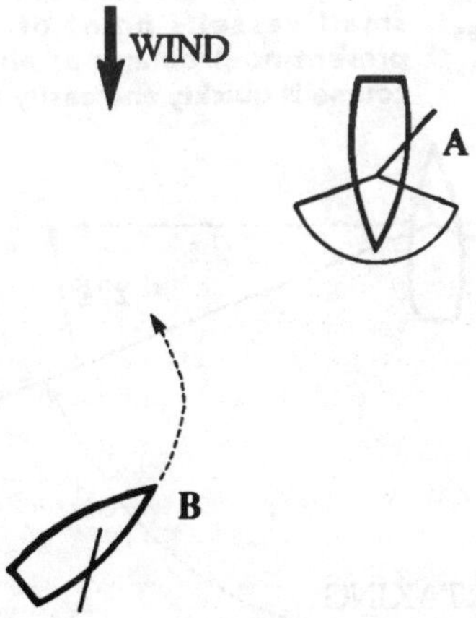

When B is in doubt about A's tack, it is the responsibility of B to keep clear.

NOTE TO RULE 12 (a)(i) and (a)(ii) are quite clear and are well known but (a)(iii) must be fully understood. A yacht close hauled on the port tack approaching a yacht running free and unable to determine her tack must keep clear. The windward boat may be carrying a spinnaker which makes it difficult to determine her tack and in any case at night quite impossible. In these circumstances it is the duty of the close hauled port tack vessel to keep clear.

Rule 13 ***Overtaking***

(a) Notwithstanding anything contained in the Rules of Part B, Sections I and II any vessel overtaking any other shall keep out of the way of the vessel being overtaken.

(b) A vessel shall be deemed to be overtaking when coming up with another vessel from a direction more than 22.5 degrees abaft her beam, that is, in such a position with reference to the vessel she is overtaking, that at night she would be able to see only the sternlight of that vessel but neither of her sidelights.

(c) When a vessel is in any doubt as to whether she is overtaking another, she shall assume that this is the case and act accordingly.

(d) Any subsequent alteration of the bearing between the two vessels shall not make the overtaking vessel a crossing vessel within the meaning of these Rules or relieve her of the duty of keeping clear of the overtaken vessel until she is finally past and clear.

NOTE TO RULE 13 It is important to note the final sentence of this rule, i.e. that the overtaking vessel shall keep clear until she is "past and clear". This applies equally to sailing yachts as well as power-driven craft.

Rule 14 ***Head-on Situation***

(a) When two power-driven vessels are meeting on reciprocal or nearly reciprocal courses so as to involve risk of collision each shall alter her course to starboard so that each shall pass on the port side of the other.

(b) Such a situation shall be deemed to exist when a vessel sees the other ahead or nearly ahead and by night she could see the masthead lights of the other in a line or nearly in a line and/or both sidelights and by day she observes the corresponding aspect of the other vessel.

(c) When a vessel is in any doubt as to whether such a situation exists she shall assume that it does exist and act accordingly.

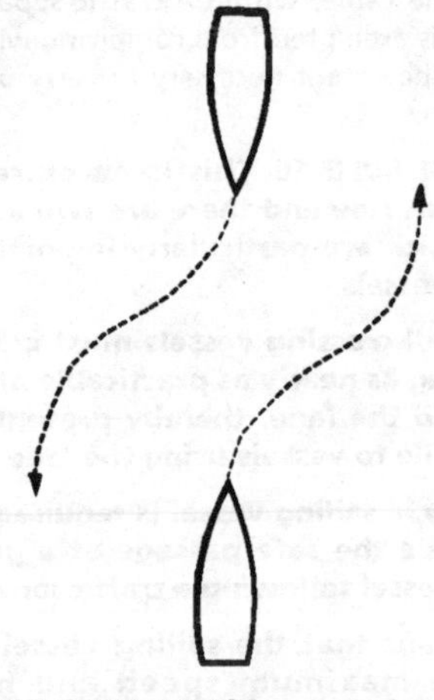

NOTE TO RULE 14 This very simple rule may cause problems for large vessels on nearly reciprocal courses but from the small vessel's point of view should present no problems as an alteration of course is quickly and easily made.

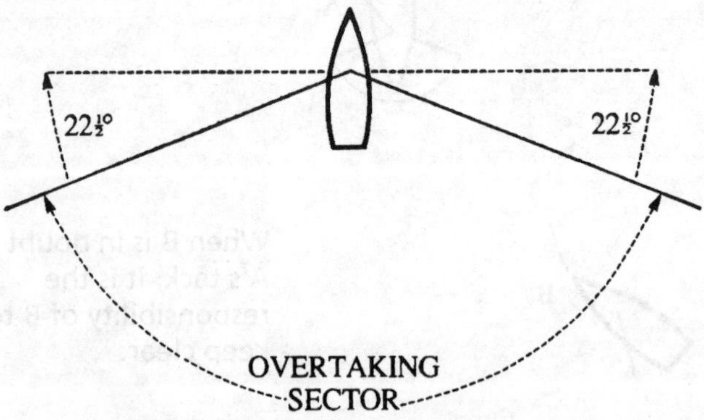

Rule 15 ***Crossing Situation***

When two power-driven vessels are crossing so as to involve risk of collision, the vessel which has the other on her own starboard side shall keep out of the way and shall, if the circumstances of the case admit, avoid crossing ahead of the other vessel.

NOTE TO RULE 15 The normally correct action for A is to alter course to starboard and pass under B's stern.

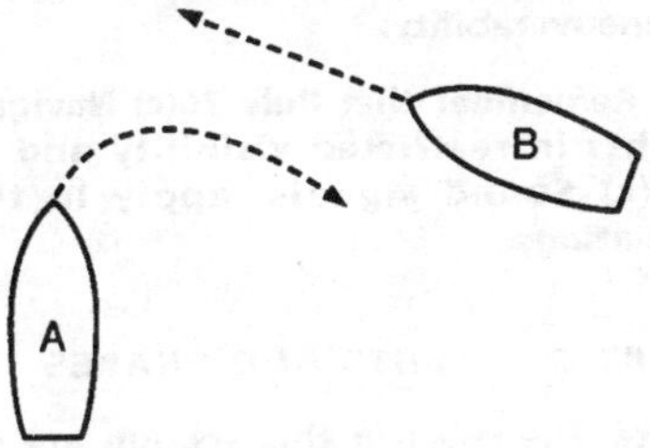

Rule 16 ***Action by Give-way Vessel***

Every vessel which is directed to keep out of the way of another vessel shall, so far as possible, take early and substantial action to keep well clear.

Rule 17 ***Action by Stand-on Vessel***

(a) (i) Where one of two vessels is to keep out of the way the other shall keep her course and speed.

(ii) The latter vessel may however take action to avoid collision by her maneuver alone, as soon as it becomes apparent to her that the vessel required to keep out of the way is not taking appropriate action in compliance with these Rules.

(b) When, from any cause, the vessel required to keep her course and speed finds herself so close that collision cannot be avoided by the action of the give-way vessel alone, she shall take such action as will best aid to avoid collision.

(c) A power-driven vessel which takes action in a crossing situation in accordance with sub-paragraph (a)(ii) of this Rule to avoid collision with another power-driven vessel shall, if the circumstances of the case admit, not alter course to port for a vessel on her own port side.

(d) This Rule does not relieve the give-way vessel of her obligation to keep out of the way.

NOTE TO RULE 17 This is an important rule as it requires the "stand on" vessel to take avoiding action if it appears that the "give way" vessel is not acting in accordance with the rules.

This may pose problems for a small vessel meeting a large ship, particularly at night; the small vessel may well have right of way according to the rules but would be foolish to "stand on" as she may not be visible to the large ship.

The sensible course of action for the small vessel in this situation is to turn completely away from the large ship.

Rule 18 ***Responsibilities between Vessels***

Except where Rules 9, 10 and 13 otherwise require:

(a) A power-driven vessel underway shall keep out of the way of:

(i) a vessel not under command;

(ii) a vessel restricted in her ability to maneuver;

(iii) a vessel engaged in fishing;

(iv) a sailing vessel.

(b) A sailing vessel underway shall keep out of the way of:

(i) a vessel not under command;

(ii) a vessel restricted in her ability to maneuver;

(iii) a vessel engaged in fishing;

(c) A vessel engaged in fishing when underway shall, so far as possible, keep out of the way of:

(i) a vessel not under command;

(ii) a vessel restricted in her ability to maneuver.

(d) (i) Any vessel other than a vessel not under command or a vessel restricted in her ability to maneuver shall, if the circumstances of the case admit, avoid impeding the safe passage of a vessel constrained by her draft, exhibiting the signals in Rule 28.

(ii) A vessel constrained by her draft shall navigate with particular caution having full regard to her special condition.

(e) A seaplane on the water shall, in general keep well clear of all vessels and avoid impeding their navigation. In circumstances, however, where risk of collision exists, she shall comply with the Rules of this Part.

NOTE TO RULE 18 Basically this rule very sensibly means that the more maneuverable vessel shall keep out of the way of the less maneuverable one.

SECTION III – CONDUCT OF VESSELS IN RESTRICTED VISIBILITY

Rule 19 *Conduct of Vessels in Restricted Visibility*

(a) This Rule applies to vessels not in sight of one another when navigating in or near an area of restricted visibility.

(b) Every vessel shall proceed at a safe speed adapted to the prevailing circumstances and conditions of restricted visibility. A power-driven vessel shall have her engines ready for im-mediate maneuver.

(c) Every vessel shall have due regard to the prevailing circumstances and conditions of restricted visibility when complying with the Rules of Section I of this Part.

(d) A vessel which detects by radar alone the presence of another vessel shall determine if a close-quarters situation is developing and/or risk of collision exists. If so, she shall take avoiding action in ample time, provided that when such action consists of an alteration of course, so far as possible the following shall be avoided:

(i) an alteration of course to port for a vessel forward of the beam, other than for a vessel being overtaken;

(ii) an alteration of course towards a vessel abeam or abaft the beam.

(e) Except where it has been determined that a risk of collision does not exist, every vessel which hears apparently forward of her beam the fog signal of another vessel, or which cannot avoid a close-quarters situation with another vessel forward of her beam, shall reduce her speed to the minimum at which she can be kept on her course. She shall if necessary take all her way off and in any event navigate with extreme caution until danger of collision is over.

NOTE TO RULE 19 It is obviously impossible to lay down a rule where there are so many imponderables. From the yachts-man's point of view the following points are vital.

(a) Have a radar reflector of proven efficiency mounted as high as possible.

(b) Keep a good lookout, both visual and aural. If underway with an auxiliary going, a lookout should be well forward away from the sound of the engine.

(c) Keep clear of shipping lanes and if possible move into water too shallow for larger vessels.

(d) Be ready for immediate action.

(e) If under sail ensure that sails set and speed are suitable for complete maneuverability.

(f) Remember that Rule 20(c) Navigation lights in restricted visibility and Rule 35(c) Sound signals, apply in these situations.

PART C – LIGHTS AND SHAPES

Note The rules in this section are clear and explicit and need no classification. However, one important rule which is regrettably not always observed by small vessels is the use of the correct signals when anchored (Rule 30). It is not necessarily obvious to a large vessel whether a small yacht is anchored if she is not displaying the correct signals.

Rule 20 *Application*

(a) Rules in this Part shall be complied with in all weathers.

(b) The Rules concerning lights shall be complied with from sunset to sunrise, and during such times no other lights shall be exhibited, except such lights as cannot be mistaken for the lights specified in these Rules or do not impair their visibility or distinctive character, or interfere with the keeping of a proper look-out.

(c) The lights prescribed by these Rules shall, if carried, also be exhibited from sunrise to sunset in restricted visibility and may be exhibited in all other circumstances when it is deemed necessary.

(d) The Rules concerning shapes shall be complied with by day.

(e) The lights and shapes specified in these Rules shall comply with the provisions of Annex I to these Regulations.

Rule 21 ***Definitions***

(a) "Masthead light" means a white light placed over the fore and aft centerline of the vessel showing an unbroken light over an arc of the horizon of 225 degrees and so fixed as to show the light from right ahead to 22.5 degrees abaft the beam on either side of the vessel.

(b) "Sidelights" means a green light on the starboard side and a red light on the port side each showing an unbroken light over an arc of the horizon of 112.5 degrees and so fixed as to show the light from right ahead to 22.5 degrees abaft the beam on its respective side. In a vessel of less than 20 meters in length the sidelights may be combined in one lantern carried on the fore and aft centerline of the vessel.

(c) "Sternlight" means a white light placed as nearly as practicable at the stern showing an unbroken light over an arc of the horizon of 135 degrees and so fixed as to show the light 67.5 degrees from right aft on each side of the vessel.

(d) "Towing light" means a yellow light having the same characteristics as the "sternlight" defined in paragraph (c) of this Rule.

(e) "All-round light" means a light showing an unbroken light over an arc of the horizon of 360 degrees.

(f) "Flashing light" means a light flashing at regular intervals at a frequency of 120 flashes or more per minute.

Rule 22 ***Visibility of Lights***

The lights prescribed in these Rules shall have an intensity as specified in Section 8 of Annex I to these Regulations so as to be visible at the following minimum ranges.

(a) In vessels of 50 meters or more in length:
a masthead light, 6 miles;
a sidelight, 3 miles;
a sternlight, 3 miles;
a towing light, 3 miles;
a white, red, green or yellow all-round light, 3 miles.

(b) In vessels of 12 meters or more in length but less than 50 meters in length:
a masthead light, 5 miles; except that where the length of the vessel is less than 20 meters, 3 miles;
a sidelight, 2 miles;
a sternlight, 2 miles;
a towing light, 2 miles;
a white, red, green or yellow all-round light, 2 miles.

(c) In vessels of less than 12 meters in length:
a masthead light, 2 miles;
a sidelight, 1 mile
a sternlight, 2 miles;
a towing light, 2 miles;
a white, red, green or yellow all-round light, 2 miles.

(d) In inconspicuous, partly submerged vessels or objects being towed:
a white all-round light, 3 miles.

Rule 23 ***Power-driven Vessels underway***

(a) A power-driven vessel underway shall exhibit:

(i) a masthead light forward;

(ii) a second masthead light abaft of and higher than the forward one; except that a vessel of less than 50 meters in length shall not be obliged to exhibit such light but may do so;

(iii) sidelights;

(iv) a sternlight.

(b) An air-cushion vessel when operating in the non-displacement mode shall, in addition to the lights prescribed in paragraph (a) of this Rule, exhibit an all-round flashing yellow light.

(c) (i) A power-driven vessel of less than 12 meters in length may, in lieu of the lights prescribed in paragraph (a) of this Rule, exhibit an all-round white light and sidelights;

(ii) a power-driven vessel of less than 7 meters in length whose maximum speed does not exceed 7 knots may in lieu of the lights prescribed in paragraph (a) of this Rule exhibit an all-round white light and shall if practicable, also exhibit sidelights;

(iii) the masthead light or all-round white light on a power-driven vessel of less than 12 meters in length may be displaced from the fore and aft centerline of the vessel if centerline fitting is not practicable, provided that the sidelights are combined in one lantern which shall be carried on the fore and aft centerline of the vessel or located as nearly as practicable in the same fore and aft line as the masthead light or the all-round white light.

Rule 24 ***Towing and Pushing***

(a) A power-driven vessel when towing shall exhibit:

(i) instead of the light prescribed in Rule 23 (a)(i) or (a)(ii), two masthead lights in a vertical line. When the length of the tow, measuring from the stern of the towing vessel to the after end of the tow exceeds 200 meters, three such lights in a vertical line;

(ii) sidelights;

(iii) a sternlight;

(iv) a towing light in a vertical line above the sternlight;

(v) when the length of the tow exceeds 200 meters, a diamond shape where it can best be seen.

(b) when a pushing vessel and a vessel being pushed ahead are rigidly connected in a composite unit they shall be regarded as a power-driven vessel and exhibit the lights prescribed in Rule 23.

(c) A power-driven vessel when pushing ahead or towing alongside, except in the case of a composite unit, shall exhibit:

(i) instead of the light prescribed in Rule 23(a)(i) or (a)(ii), two masthead lights in a vertical line;

(ii) sidelights;

(iii) a sternlight.

(d) A power-driven vessel to which paragraphs (a) or (c) of this Rule apply shall also comply with Rule 23(a)(ii).

(e) A vessel or object being towed, other than those mentioned in paragraph (g) of this Rule, shall exhibit:

(i) sidelights;

(ii) a sternlight;

(iii) when the length of the tow exceeds 200 meters, a diamond shape where it can best be seen.

(f) Provided that any number of vessels being towed alongside or pushed in a group shall be lighted as one vessel:

(i) a vessel being pushed ahead, not being part of a composite unit, shall exhibit at the forward end, sidelights;

(ii) a vessel being towed alongside shall exhibit a sternlight and at the forward end, sidelights.

(g) An inconspicuous, partly submerged vessel or object, or combination of such vessels or objects being towed, shall exhibit:

(i) if it is less than 25 meters in breadth, one all-round white light at or near the forward end and one at or near the after end except that dracones need not exhibit a light at or near the forward end;

(ii) if it is 25 meters or more in breadth, two additional all-round white lights at or near the extremities of its breadth;

(iii) if it exceeds 100 meters in length, additional all-round white lights between the lights prescribed in sub-paragraphs (i) and (ii) so that the distance between thelights shall not exceed 100 meters;

(iv) a diamond shape near the aftermost extremity of the last vessel or object being towed and if the length of the tow exceeds 200 meters an additional diamond shape where it can best be seen and located as far forward as is practicable.

(h) Where from any sufficient cause it is impracticable for a vessel or object being towed to exhibit the lights or shapes prescribed in paragraph (e) or (g) of this Rule, all possible measures shall be taken to light the vessel or object towed or at least to indicate the presence of such vessel or object.

(i) Where from any sufficient cause it is impracticable for a vessel not normally engaged in towing operations to display the lights prescribed in paragraph (a) or (c) of this Rule, such vessel shall not be required to exhibit those lights when engaged in towing another vessel in distress or otherwise in need of assistance. All possible measures shall be taken to indicate the nature of the relationship between the towing vessel and the vessel being towed as authorised by Rule 36, in particular by illuminating the towline.

Rule 25 ***Sailing Vessels underway and Vessels under Oars***

(a) A sailing vessel underway shall exhibit:

(i) sidelights;

(ii) a sternlight.

(b) In a sailing vessel of less than 20 meters in length the lights prescribed in paragraph (a) of this Rule may be combined in one lantern carried at or near the top of the mast where it can best be seen.

(c) A sailing vessel underway may, in addition to the lights prescribed in paragraph (a) of this Rule, exhibit at or near the top of the mast, where they can best be seen, two all round lights in a vertical line, the upper being red and the lower green, but these lights shall not be exhibited in conjunction with the combined lantern permitted by paragraph (b) of this Rule.

(d) (i) A sailing vessel of less than 7 meters in length shall, if practicable, exhibit the lights prescribed in paragraph (a) or (b) of this Rule, but if she does not, she shall have ready at hand an flashlight or lighted lantern showing a white light which shall be exhibited in sufficient time to prevent collision.

(ii) A vessel under oars may exhibit the lights prescribed in this Rule for sailing vessels, but if she does not, she shall have ready at hand an flashlight or lighted lantern showing a white light which shall be exhibited in sufficient time to prevent collision.

(e) A vessel proceeding under sail when also being propelled by machinery shall exhibit forward where it can best be seen a conical shape, apex downwards.

Rule 26 ***Fishing Vessels***

(a) A vessel engaged in fishing, whether underway or at anchor, shall exhibit only the lights and shapes prescribed in this Rule.

(b) A vessel when engaged in trawling, by which is meant the dragging through the water of a dredge net or other apparatus used as a fishing appliance, shall exhibit:

(i) two all-round lights in a vertical line, the upper being green and the lower white, or a shape consisting of two cones with their apexes together in a vertical line one above the other; a vessel of less than 20 meters in length may instead of this shape exhibit a basket;

(ii) a masthead light abaft of and higher than the all-round green light; a vessel of less than 50 meters in length shall not be obliged to exhibit such a light but may do so;

(iii) when making way through the water, in addition to the lights prescribed in this paragraph, sidelights and a sternlight.

(c) A vessel engaged in fishing, other than trawling, shall exhibit:

(i) two all-round lights in a vertical line, the upper being red and the lower white, or a shape consisting of two cones with their apexes together in a vertical line one above the other; a vessel of less than 20 meters in length may instead of this shape exhibit a basket;

(ii) when there is outlying gear extending more than 150 meters horizontally from the vessel; an all-round white light or a cone apex upwards in the direction of the gear;

(iii) when making way through the water, inaddition to the lights prescribed in this paragraph, side lights and a sternlight.

(d) A vessel engaged in fishing in close proximity to other vessels engaged in fishing may exhibit the additional signals described in Annex II to these Regulations.

(e) A vessel when not engaged in fishing shall not exhibit the lights or shapes prescribed in this Rule, but only those prescribed for a vessel of her length.

Rule 27 ***Vessels not under command or restricted in their ability to maneuver***

(a) A vessel not under command shall exhibit:

(i) two all-round red lights in a vertical line where they can best be seen:

(ii) two balls or similar shapes in a vertical line where they can best be seen;

(iii) when making way through the water, in addition to the lights prescribed in this paragraph, sidelights and a sternlight.

(b) A vessel restricted in her ability to maneuver, except a vessel engaged in mine clearance operations, shall exhibit:

(i) three all-round lights in a vertical line where they can best be seen. The highest and lowest of these lights shall be red and the middle light shall be white;

(ii) three shapes in a vertical line where they can best be seen . The highest and lowest of these shapes shall be balls and the middle one a diamond;

(iii) when making way through the water, a masthead light or lights, sidelights and a sternlight, in addition to the lights prescribed in sub-paragraph (i);

(iv) when at anchor, in addition to the lights or shapes prescribed in sub-paragraphs (i) and (ii), the light, lights or shape prescribed in Rule 30.

(c) A power-driven vessel engaged in a towing operation such as severely restricts the towing vessel and her tow in their ability to deviate from their course shall, in addition to the lights or shapes prescribed in Rule 24(a), exhibit the lights or shapes prescribed in sub-paragraphs (b)(i) and (ii) of this Rule.

(d) A vessel engaged in dredging or underwater operations, when restricted in her ability to maneuver, shall exhibit the lights and shapes prescribed in sub-paragraphs (b)(i), (ii) and (iii) of this Rule and shall in addition, when an obstruction exists, exhibit:

(i) two all-round red lights or two balls in a vertical line to indicate the side on which the obstruction exists;

(ii) two all-round green lights or two diamonds in a vertical line to indicate the side on which another vessel may pass;

(iii) when at anchor, the lights or shapes prescribed in this paragraph instead of the lights or shape prescribed in Rule 30.

(e) Whenever the size of a vessel engaged in diving operations makes it impracticable to exhibit all lights and shapes prescribed in paragraph (d) of this Rule, the following shall be exhibited:

(i) three all-round lights in a vertical line where they can best be seen. The highest and lowest of these lights shall be red and the middle light shall be white;

(ii) a rigid replica of the International Code flag 'A' not less than 1 meter in height. Measures shall be taken to ensure its all-round visibility.

(f) A vessel engaged in mine clearance operations shall, in addition to the lights prescribed for a power-driven vessel in Rule 23 or to the lights or shape prescribed for a vessel at anchor in Rule 30 as appropriate, exhibit three all-round green lights or three balls. One of these lights or shapes shall be exhibited near the foremast head and one at each end of the fore yard. These lights or shapes indicate that it is dangerous for another vessel to approach within 1,000 meters of the mine clearance vessel.

(g) Vessels of less than 12 meters in length, except those engaged in diving operations, shall not be required to exhibit the lights and shapes prescribed in this Rule.

(h) The signals prescribed in this Rule are not signals of vessels in distress and requiring assistance. Such signals are contained in Annex IV to these Regulations.

Rule 28 *Vessels constrained by their draft*

A vessel constrained by her draft may, in addition to the lights prescribed for power-driven vessels in Rule 23, exhibit where they can best be seen three all-round red lights in a vertical line, or a cylinder.

Rule 29 *Pilot Vessels*

(a) A vessel engaged on pilotage duty shall exhibit:

(i) at or near the masthead, two all-round lights in a vertical line, the upper being white and the lower red;

(ii) when underway, in addition, sidelights and a sternlight;

(iii) when at anchor, in addition to the lights prescribed in sub-paragraph (i), the light, lights or shape prescribed in Rule 30 for vessels at anchor.

(b) A pilot vessel when not engaged on pilotage duty shall exhibit the lights or shapes prescribed for a similar vessel of her length.

Rule 30 *Anchored Vessels and Vessels aground*

(a) A vessel at anchor shall exhibit where it can best be seen:

(i) in the fore part, an all-round white light or one ball;

(ii) at or near the stern and at a lower level than the light prescribed in sub-paragraph (i), an all-round white light.

(b) A vessel of less than 50 meters in length may exhibit an all-round white light where it can best be seen instead of the lights prescribed in paragraph (a) of this Rule.

(c) A vessel at anchor may, and a vessel of 100 meters and more in length shall, also use the available working or equivalent lights to illumi-nate her decks.

(d) A vessel aground shall exhibit the lights prescribed in paragraph (a) or (b) of this Rule and in addition, where they can best be seen:

(i) two all-round red lights in a vertical line;

(ii) three balls in a vertical line.

(e) A vessel of less than 7 meters in length, when at anchor, not in or near a narrow channel, fairway or anchorage, or where other vessels normally navigate, shall not be required to exhibit the lights or shape prescribed in paragraphs (a) and (b) of this Rule.

(f) A vessel of less than 12 meters in length, when aground, shall not be required to exhibit the lights or shapes prescribed in subparagraphs (d)(i) and (ii) of this Rule.

Rule 31 ***Seaplanes***

Where it is impracticable for a seaplane to exhibit lights and shapes of the characteristics or in the positions prescribed in the Rules of this Part she shall exhibit lights and shapes as closely similar in characteristics and position as is possible.

PART D – SOUND AND LIGHT SIGNALS

Note The rules are clear and explicit and, from the yachtsman's point of view the most important aspects are, firstly to have the most effective fog signal that can be used on board and secondly to carry a supply of white flares or a flare gun with white cartridges. At night or in fog it is important and reassuring to make one's presence known in a close quarters situation.

A point to note in sound Signals is Rule 34 – 3 short blasts – "I am operating astern propulsion". In the case of a large vessel she may carry her way for an appreciable time after putting the engines astern. This can appear confusing and should not be overlooked.

Rule 32 ***Definitions***

(a) The word "whistle" means any sound signalling appliance capable of producing the prescribed blasts and which complies with the specifications in Annex III to these Regulations.

(b) The term "short blast" means a blast of about one secons's durationn.

(c) The term "prolonged blast" means a blast of from four to six seconds duration.

Rule 33 ***Equipment for Sound Signals***

(a) A vessel of 12 meters or more in length shall be provided with a whistle and a bell and a vessel of 100 meters or more in length shall, in addition, be provided with a gong, the tone and sound of which cannot be confused with that of the bell. The whistle, bell and gong shall comply with the specifications in Annex III to these Regulations. The bell or gong or both may be replaced by other equipment having the same respective sound characteristics, provided that manual sounding of the prescribed signals shall always be possible.

(b) a vessel of less than 12 meters in length shall not be obliged to carry the sound signalling appliances prescribed in paragraph (a) of this Rule but if she does not, she shall be provided with some other means of making an efficient sound signal.

Rule 34 ***Maneuvering and Warning Signals***

(a) when vessels are in sight of one another, a power-driven vessel underway, when maneuvering as authorised or required by these Rules, shall indicate that maneuver by the following signals on her whistle:

one short blast to mean "I am altering my course to starboard"

two short blasts to mean "I am altering my course to port";

three short blasts to mean "I am operatingastern propulsion".

(b) Any vessel may supplement the whistle signals prescribed in paragraph (a) of this Rule by light signals, repeated as appropriate, while the maneuver is being carried out:

(i) these light signals shall have the following significance:

One flash to mean "I am altering my course to starboard"

two flashes to mean "I am altering my course to port"

three flashes to mean "I am operating astern propulsion";

(ii) the duration of each flash shall be about one second, the interval between flashes shall be about one second, and the interval between successive signals shall be no less than ten seconds;

(iii) the light used for this signal shall if fitted, be an all-round white light, visible at a minimum range of 5 miles and shall comply with the provisions of Annex I to these Regulations.

(c) When in sight of one another in a narrow channel or fairway:

(i) a vessel intending to overtake another shall in compliance with Rule 9(e)(i) indicate her intention by the following signals on her whistle:

two prolonged blasts followed by one short blast to mean "I intend to overtakeyou on your starboard side";

two prolonged blasts followed by two short blasts to mean "I intend to overtake you on your port side";

(ii) the vessel about to be overtaken when acting in accordance with Rule 9(e)(i) shall indicate her agreement by the following signal on her whistle:

One prolonged, one short, one prolonged and one short blast, in that order.

(d) When vessels in sight of one another are approaching each other and from any cause either vessel fails to understand the intentions or actions of the other, or is in doubt whether sufficient action is being taken by the other to avoid collision, the vessel in doubt shall immediately indicate such doubt by giving at least five short and rapid blasts on the whistle. Such signal may be supplemented by a light signal of at least five short and rapid flashes.

(e) A vessel nearing a bend or an area of a channel or fairway where other vessels may be obscured by an intervening obstruction shall sound one prolonged blast. Such signal shall be answered with a prolonged blast by any approaching vessel that may be within hearing around the bend or behind the intervening obstruction.

(f) If whistles are fitted on a vessel at a distance apart of more than 100 meters, one whistle only shall be used for giving manoeuvring and warning signals.

Rule 35 *Sound signals in restricted visibility*

In or near an area of restricted visibility, whether by day or night, the signals prescribed in this Rule shall be used as follows.

(a) A power-driven vessel making way through the water shall sound at intervals of not more than 2 minutes one prolonged blast.

(b) A power-driven vessel underway but stopped and making no way through the water shall sound at intervals of not more than 2 minutes two prolonged blasts in succession with an interval of about 2 seconds between them.

(c) A vessel not under command, a vessel restricted in her ability to maneuver, a vessel constrained by her draft, a sailing vessel, a vessel engaged in fishing and a vessel engaged in towing or pushing another vessel shall, instead of the signals prescribed in paragraphs (a) or (b) of this Rule, sound at intervals of not more than 2 minutes three blasts in succession, namely one prolonged followed by two short blasts.

(d) A vessel engaged in fishing, when at anchor, and a vessel restricted in her ability to maneuver when carrying out her work at anchor, shall instead of the signals prescribed in paragraph (g) of this Rule sound the signal prescribed in paragraph (c) of this Rule.

(e) A vessel towed or if more than one vessel is towed the last vessel of the tow, if manned, shall at intervals of not more than 2 minutes sound four blasts in succession, namely one prolonged followed by three short blasts. When practicable, this signal shall be made immediately after the signal made by the towing vessel.

(f) When a pushing vessel and a vessel being pushed ahead are rigidly connected in a composite unit they shall be regarded as a power-driven vessel and shall give the signals prescribed in paragraphs (a) or (b) of this Rule.

(g) A vessel at anchor shall at intervals of not more than one minute ring the bell rapidly for about five seconds. In a vessel of 100 meters or more in length the bell shall be sounded in the forepart of the vessel and immediately after the ringing of the bell the gong shall be sounded rapidly for about five seconds in the afterpart of the vessel. A vessel at anchor may in addition sound three blasts in succession, namely one short, one prolonged and one short blast to give warning of her position and of the possibility of collision to an approaching vessel.

(h) A vessel aground shall give the bell signal and if required the gong signal prescribed in paragraph (g) of this Rule and shall, in addition, give three separate and distinct strokes on the bell immediately before and after the rapid ringing of the bell. A vessel aground may in addition sound an appropriate whistle signal.

(i) A vessel of less than 12 meters in length shall not be obliged to give the above mentioned signals but, if she does not, shall make some other efficient sound signal at intervals of not more than 2 minutes.

(j) A pilot vessel when engaged on pilotage duty may in addition to the signals prescribed in paragraphs (a), (b) or (g) of this Rule sound an identity signal consisting of four short blasts.

Rule 36 ***Signals to attract attention***

If necessary to attract the attention of another vessel any vessel may make light or sound signals that cannot be mistaken for any signal authorized elsewhere in these Rules, or may direct the beam of her searchlight in the direction of the danger, in such a way as not to embarrass any vessel. Any light to attract the attention of another vessel shall be such that it cannot be mistaken for any aid to navigation. For the purpose of this Rule the use of high intensity intermittent or revolving lights, such as strobe lights, shall be avoided.

Rule 37 ***Distress Signals***

When a vessel is in distress and requires assistance she shall use or exhibit the signals described in Annex IV to these Regulations.

PART E – EXEMPTIONS

Rule 38 ***Exemptions.***

Any vessel (or class of vessels) provided that she complies with the requirements of the International Regulations for Preventing Collisions at Sea, 1960, the keel of which is laid or which is at a corresponding stage of construction before the entry into force of these Regulations may be exempted from compliance therewith as follows:

(a) The installation of lights with ranges prescribed in Rule 22, until four years after the date of entry into force of these Regulations.

(b) The installation of lights with color specifications as prescribed in Section 7 of Annex I to these Regulations, until four years after the date of entry into force of these Regulations.

(c) The repositioning of lights as a result of conversion from Imperial to metric units and rounding off measurement figures, permanent exemption.

(d) (i) The repositioning of masthead lights on vessels of less than 150 meters in length, resulting from the prescriptions of Section 3(a) of Annex I to these Regulations, permanent exemption.

(ii) The repositioning of masthead lights on vessels of 150 meters or more in length, resulting from the prescriptions of Section 3(a) of Annex I to these Regulations, until nine years after the date of entry into force of these Regulations.

(e) The repositioning of masthead lights resulting from the prescriptions of Section 2(b) of Annex I to these Regulations, until nine years after the date of entry into force of these Regulations.

(f) The repositioning of sidelights resulting from the prescriptions of Sections 2(g) and 3(b) of Annex I to these Regulations, until nine years after the date of entry into force of these Regulations.

(g) The requirements for sound signal appliances prescribed in Annex III to these Regulations, until nine years after the date of entry into force of these Regulations.

(h) The repositioning of all-round lights resulting from the prescription of Section 9(b) of Annex I to these Regulations, permanent exemption.

ANNEX I

POSITIONING AND TECHNICAL DETAILS OF LIGHTS AND SHAPES

1. Definition

The term "height above the hull" means height above the uppermost continuous deck. This height shall be measured from the position vertically beneath the location of the light.

2. Vertical positioning and spacing of lights

(a) On a power-driven vessel of 20 meters or more in length the masthead lights shall be placed as follows:

(i) the forward masthead light, or if only one masthead light is carried, then that light, at a height above the hull of not less than 6 meters, and, if the breadth of the vessel exceeds 6 meters, then at a height above the hull not less than such breadth, so however that the light need not be placed at a greater height above the hull than 12 meters;

(ii) when two masthead lights are carried the after one shall be at least 4.5 meters vertically higher than the forward one.

(b) The vertical separation of masthead lights of power-driven vessels shall be such that in all normal conditions of trim the after light will be seen over and separate from the forward light at a distance of 1,000 meters from the stem when viewed from sea level.

(c) The masthead light of a power-driven vessel of 12 meters but less than 20 meters in length shall be placed at a height above the gunwale of not less than 2.5 meters.

(d) A power-driven vessel of less than 12 meters in length may carry the uppermost light at a height of less than 2.5 meters above the gunwale. When however a masthead light is carried in addition to sidelights and a sternlight or the all-round light prescribed in Rule 23(c)(i) is carried in addition to sidelights, then such masthead light or all-round light shall be carried at least one metre higher than the sidelights.

(e) One of the two or three masthead lights prescribed for a power-driven vessel when engaged in towing or pushing another vessel shall be placed in the same position as either the forward masthead light or the after masthead light; provided that, if carried on the aftermast, the lowest after masthead light shall be at least 4.5 meters vertically higher than the forward masthead light.

(f) (i) The masthead light or lights prescribed in Rule 23(a) shall be so placed as to be above and clear of all other lights and obstructions except as described in sub-paragraph(ii).

(ii) When it is impracticable to carry the all-round lights prescribed by Rule 27(b)(i) or Rule 28 below the masthead lights, they may be carried above the after masthead light(s), or vertically in between the forward masthead light(s) and after masthead light(s)provided that in the latter case the requirement of Section 3(c) of this Annex shall be complied with.

(g) The sidelights of a power-driven vessel shall be placed at a height above the hull not greater than three quarters of that of the forward masthead light. They shall not be so low as to be interfered with by deck lights.

(h) The sidelights, if in a combined lantern and carried on a power-driven vessel of less than 20 meters in length, shall be placed not less than one metre below the masthead light.

(i) When the Rules prescribe two or three lights to be carried in a vertical line, they shall be spaced as follows:

(i) on a vessel of 20 meters in length or more such lights shall be spaced not less than 2 meters apart, and the lowest of these lights shall, except where a towing light is required, be placed at a height of not less than 4 meters above the hull;

(ii) on a vessel of less than 20 meters in length such lights shall be spaced not less than 1 meter apart and the lowest of these lights shall, except where a towing light is required, be placed at a height of notless than 2 meters above the gunwale;

(iii) when three lights are carried they shall be equally spaced.

(j) The lower of the two all-round lights prescribed for a vessel when engaged in fishing shall be at a height above the sidelights not less than twice the distance between the two vertical lights.

(k) The forward anchor light prescribed in Rule 30(a)(i), when two are carried, shall not be less than 4.5 meters above the after one. On a vessel of 50 meters or more in length this forward anchor light shall be placed at a height of not less than 6 meters above the hull.

3. Horizontal position and spacing of lights

(a) When two masthead lights are prescribed for a power-driven vessel, the horizontal distance between them shall not be less than one half of the length of the vessel but need not be more than 100 meters. The forward light shall be placed not more than one quarter of the length of the vessel from the stern.

(b) On a power-driven vessel of 20 meters or more in length the sidelights shall not be placed in front of the forward masthead lights. They shall be placed at or near the side of the vessel.

(c) When the lights prescribed in Rule 27(b)(i) or Rule 28 are placed vertically between the forward masthead light(s) and the after masthead light(s) these all-round lights shall be placed at a horizontal distance of not less than 2 meters from the fore and aft centerline of the vessel in the athwartship direction.

4. Details of location of direction – indicating lights for fishing vessels, dredgers and vessels engaged in underwater operations

(a) The light indicating the direction of the outlying gear from a vessel engaged in fishing as prescribed in Rule 26(c)(ii) shall be placed at a horizontal distance of not less than 2 meters and not more than 6 meters away from the two all-round red and white lights. This light shall be placed not higher than the all-round white light prescribed in Rule 26(c)(i) and not lower than the sidelights.

(b) The lights and shapes on a vessel engaged in dredging or underwater operations to indicate the obstructed side and/or the side on which it is safe to pass, as prescribed in Rule 27(d)(i) and (ii), shall be placed at the maximum practical horizontal distance, but in no case less than 2 meters, from the lights or shapes prescribed in Rule 27(b)(i) and (ii). In no case shall the upper of these lights or shapes be at a greater height than the lower of the three lights or shapes prescribed in Rule 27(b)(i) and (ii).

5. Screens for sidelights

The sidelights of vessels of 20 meters or more in length shall be fitted with inboard screens painted matt black, and meeting the requirements of Section 9 of this Annex. On vessels of less than 20 meters in length the sidelights, if necessary to meet the requirements of Section 9 of this Annex, shall be fitted with inboard matt black screens. With a combined lantern, using a single vertical filament and a very narrow division between the green and red sections, external screens need not be fitted.

6. Shapes

(a) Shapes shall be black and of the following sizes:

(i) a ball shall have a diameter of not less than 0.6 meter;

(ii) a cone shall have a base diameter of not less than 0.6 meter and a height equal to its diameter;

(iii) a cylinder shall have a diameter of at least 0.6 meter and a height of twice its diameter;

(iv) a diamond shape shall consist of two cones as defined in (ii) above having a common base.

(b) The vertical distance between shapes shall be at least 1.5 meters.

(c) In a vessel of less than 20 meters in length shapes of lesser dimensions but commensurate with the size of the vessel may be used and the distance apart may be correspondingly reduced.

7. Color specification of lights

The chromaticity of all navigation lights shall conform to the following standards, which lie within the boundaries of the area of the diagram specified for each color by the International Commission on Illumination (CIE).

The boundaries of the area for each color are given by indicating the corner co-ordinates, which are shown at foot of page.

8. Intensity of lights

(a) The minimum luminous intensity of lights shall be calculated by using the formula:

$$L = 3.43 \times 10^6 \times T \times D^2 \times K^{-D}$$

(i)	*White*						
	x	0.525	0.525	0.452	0.310	0.310	0.443
	y	0.382	0.440	0.440	0.348	0.283	0.382
(ii)	*Green*						
	x	0.028	0.009	0.300	0.203		
	y	0.385	0.723	0.511	0.356		
(iii)	*Red*						
	x	0.680	0.660	0.735	0.721		
	y	0.320	0.320	0.265	0.259		
(iv)	*Yellow*						
	x	0.612	0.618	0.575	0.575		
	y	0.382	0.382	0.425	0.406		

Where:

L is luminous intensity in candelas under service conditions,

T is threshold factor 2 x 10^{-7} lux,

D is range of visibility (luminous range) of the light in nautical miles.

K is atmospheric transmissivity. For prescribed lights the value of K shall be 0.8, corresponding to a meteorological visibility of approxi-mately 13 nautical miles.

(b) A selection of figures derived from the formula is given below.

9. Horizontal sectors

(a) (i) in the forward direction, sidelights as fitted on the vessel shall show the minimum required intensities. The intensities shall decrease to reach practical cut off between 1 degree and 3 degrees outside the prescribed sectors.

(ii) for sternlights and masthead lights and at 22.5 degrees abaft the beam for sidelights, the minimum required intensities shall be maintained over the arc of the horizon up to 5 degrees within the limits of the sectors prescribed in Rule 21. From 5 degrees within the prescribed sectors the intensity may decrease by 50 per cent up to the prescribed limits; it shall decrease steadily to reach practical cut-off at not more than 5 degrees outside the prescribed sectors.

(b) All-round lights shall be so located as not to be obscured by masts, topmasts or structures within angular sectors of more than 6 degrees, except anchor lights prescribed in Rule 30, which need not be placed at an impracticable height above the hull.

10. Vertical sectors

(a) The vertical sectors of electric lights as fitted, with the exception of lights on sailing vessels underway shall ensure that:

(i) at least the required minimum intensity is maintained at all angles from 5 degrees above to 5 degrees below the horizontal;

(ii) at least 60 per cent of the required minimum intensity is maintained from 7.5 degrees above to 7.5 degrees below the horizontal.

(b) In the case of sailing vessels underway the vertical sectors of electric lights as fitted shall ensure that:

(i) at least the required minimum intensity is maintained at all angles from 5 degrees above to 5 degrees below the horizontal;

(ii) at least 50 per cent of the required minimum intensity is maintained from 25 degrees above to 25 degrees below the horizontal.

(c) In the case of lights other than electric these specifications shall be met as closely as possible.

11. Intensity of non-electric lights

Non-electric lights shall so far as practicable comply with the minimum intensities, as specified in the Table given in Section 8 of this Annex.

12. Maneuvering light

Notwithstanding the provisions of paragraph 2(f) of this Annex the maneuvering light

Range of Visibility (luminous range) of light in nautical Miles D	Luminous Intensity of light in candelas for K = 0.8 L
1	0.9
2	4.3
3	12
4	27
5	52
6	94

Note: The maximum luminous intesity of navigation light should be limited to avoid undue glare. This shall not be achieved by a variable control of the luminous intensity.

described in Rule 34(b) shall be placed in the same fore and aft vertical plane as the masthead light or lights and, where practicable, at a minimum height of 2 meters vertically above the forward masthead light, provided that it shall be carried not less than 2 meters vertically above or below the after masthead light. On a vessel where only one masthead light is carried the maneuvering light, if fitted, shall be carried where it can best be seen, not less than 2 meters vertically apart from the masthead light.

13. Approval

The construction of lights and shapes and the installation of lights on board the vessel shall be to the satisfaction of the appropriate authority of the State whose flag the vessel is entitled to fly.

ANNEX II

ADDITIONAL SIGNALS FOR FISHING VESSELS FISHING IN CLOSE PROXIMITY

1. General

The lights mentioned herein shall, if exhibited in pursuance of Rule 26(d), be placed where they can best be seen. They shall be at least 0.9 meter apart but at a lower level than lights prescribed in Rule 26(b)(i) and (c)(i). The lights shall be visible all round the horizon at a distance of at least 1 mile but at a lesser distance than the lights prescribed by these Rules for fishing vessels.

2. Signals for trawlers

(a) Vessels when engaged in trawling, whether using demersal or pelagic gear, may exhibit:

(i) when shooting their nets: two white lights in a vertical line;

(ii) when hauling their nets: one white light over one red light in a vertical line;

(iii) when the net has come fast upon an obstruction: two red lights in a vertical line.

(b) Each vessel engaged in pair trawling may exhibit:

(i) by night, a searchlight directed forward and in the direction of the other vessel of the pair;

(ii) when shooting or hauling their nets or when their nets have come fast upon an obstruction, the lights prescribed in 2(a) above.

3. Signals for purse seiners

Vessels engaged in fishing with purse seine gear may exhibit two yellow lights in a vertical line. These lights shall flash alternatively every second and with equal light and occultation duration. These lights may be exhibited only when the vessel is hampered by its fishing gear.

ANNEX III

TECHNICAL DETAILS OF SOUND SIGNAL APPLIANCES

1. Whistles

(a) *Frequencies and range of audibility*

The fundamental frequency of the signal shall lie within the range 70-700 Hz.

The range of audibility of the signal from a whistle shall be determined by those frequencies, which may include the fundamental and/or one or more higher frequencies, which lie within the range 180-700 Hz (±1 per cent) and which provide the sound pressure levels specified in paragraph 1(c) below.

(b) *Limits of fundamental frequencies*

To ensure a wide variety of whistle characteristics, the fundamental frequency of a whistle shall be between the following limits:

(i) 70-200 Hz, for a vessel 200 meters or more in length;

(ii) 130-350 Hz, for a vessel 75 meters but less than 200 meters in length;

(iii) 250-700 Hz, for a vessel less than 75 meters in length.

(c) *Sound signal intensity and range of audibility*

A whistle fitted in a vessel shall provide, in the direction of maximum intensity of the whistle and at a distance of 1 meter from it, a sound pressure level in at least one ⅓ octave band within the range of frequencies 180-700 Hz (±1 per cent) of not less than the appropriate figure given in the table overleaf.

The range of audibility in the table is for information and is approximately the range at which a whistle may be heard on its forward axis with 90 per cent probability in conditions of still air on board a vessel having average back-ground noise level at the listening posts (taken to be 68 dB in the octave band centered on 250 Hz and 63 dB in the octave band centered on 500 Hz).

In practice the range at which a whistle may be heard is extremely variable and depends critically on weather conditions; the values given can be regarded as typical but under conditions of strong wind or high ambient noise level at the listening post the range may be reduced.

(d) *Directional properties*

The sound pressure level of a directional whistle shall be not more than 4 dB below the prescribed sound pressure level on the axis at any direction in the horizontal plane within ± 45 degrees of the axis. The sound pressure level at any other direction in the horizontal plane shall be not more than 10 dB below the prescribed sound pressure level on the axis, so that the range in any direction will be at least half the range on the forward axis. The sound pressure level shall be measured in that ⅓ octave band which determines the audibility range.

(e) *Positioning of whistles*

When a directional whistle is to be used as the only whistle on a vessel, it shall be installed with its maximum intensity directed straight ahead. A whistle shall be placed as high as practicable on a vessel, in order to reduce interception of the emitted sound by obstructions and also to minimise hearing damage risk to personnel. The sound pressure level of the vessel's own signal at listening posts shall not exceed 110 dB (A) and so far as practicable should not exceed 100 dB(A).

(f) *Fitting of more than one whistle*

If whistles are fitted at a distance apart of more than 100 meters, it shall be so arranged that they are not sounded simultaneously.

(g) *Combined whistle systems*

If due to the presence of obstructions the sound field of a single whistle or of one of the whistles referred to in paragraph 1(f) above is likely to have a zone of greatly reduced signal level, it is recommended that a combined whistle system be fitted so as to overcome this reduction. For the purposes of the Rules a combined whistle system is to be regarded as a single whistle. The whistles of a combined system shall be located at a distance apart of not more than 100 meters and arranged to be sounded simultaneously. The frequency of any one whistle shall differ from those of the others by at least 10 Hz.

2. Bell or gong

(a) *Intensity of signal*

A bell or gong, or other device having similar sound characteristics shall produce a sound pressure level of not less than 110 dB at a distance of 1 meter from it.

(b) *Construction*

Bells and gongs shall be made of corrosion-resistant material and designed to give a clear tone. The diameter of the mouth of the bell shall be not less than 300 mm for vessels of 20 meters or more in length, and shall be not less than 200 mm for vessels of 12 meters or more but of less than 20 meters in length. Where practicable, a power-driven bell striker is recommended to ensure constant force but manual operation shall be possible. The mass of the striker shall be not less than 3 per cent of the mass of the bell.

3. Approval

The construction of sound signal appliances, their performance and their installation on board the vessel shall be to the satisfaction of the appropriate authority of the State whose flag the vessel is entitled to fly.

Length of vessel in meters	⅓ octave band level at 1 meter in dB referred to 2×10^{-5} N/m²	Audibility range in nautical miles
200 or more	143	2
75 but less than 200	138	1.5
20 but less than 75	130	1
Less than 20	120	0.5

ANNEX IV

DISTRESS SIGNALS

1. The following signals, used or exhibited either together or separately, indicate distress and need of assistance:

(a) a gun or other explosive signal fired at intervals of about a minute;

(b) continuous sounding with any fog signalling apparatus;

(c) rockets or shells, throwing red stars fired one at a time at short intervals;

(d) a signal made by radiotelegraphy or by other signalling method consisting of the group • • • — — — • • • (SOS) in the Morse Code;

(e) a signal sent by radiotelephony consisting of the spoken word "Mayday";

(f) the International Code Signal of distress indicated by N.C.;

(g) a signal consisting of a square flag having above or below it a ball or anything resembling a ball;

(h) flames on the vessel (as from a burning tar barrel, oil barrel, etc.);

(i) a rocket parachute flare or a hand flare showing a red light;

(j) a smoke signal giving off orange-colored smoke;

(k) slowly and repeatedly raising and lowering arms outstretched to each side;

(l) the radiotelegraph alarm signal;

(m) the radiotelephone alarm signal;

(n) signals transmitted by emergency position-indicating radio beacons;

(o) approved signals transmitted by radio communication systems.

2. The use or exhibition of any of the foregoing signals except for the purpose of indicating distress and need of assistance and the use of other signals which may be confused with any of the above signals is prohibited.

3. Attention is drawn to the relevant sections of the International Code of Signals, the Merchant Ship Search and Rescue Manual and the following signals:

(a) a piece of orange colored canvas with either a black square and circle or other appropriate symbol (for identification from the air);

(b) a dye marker.

Aids to Navigation

3

Page

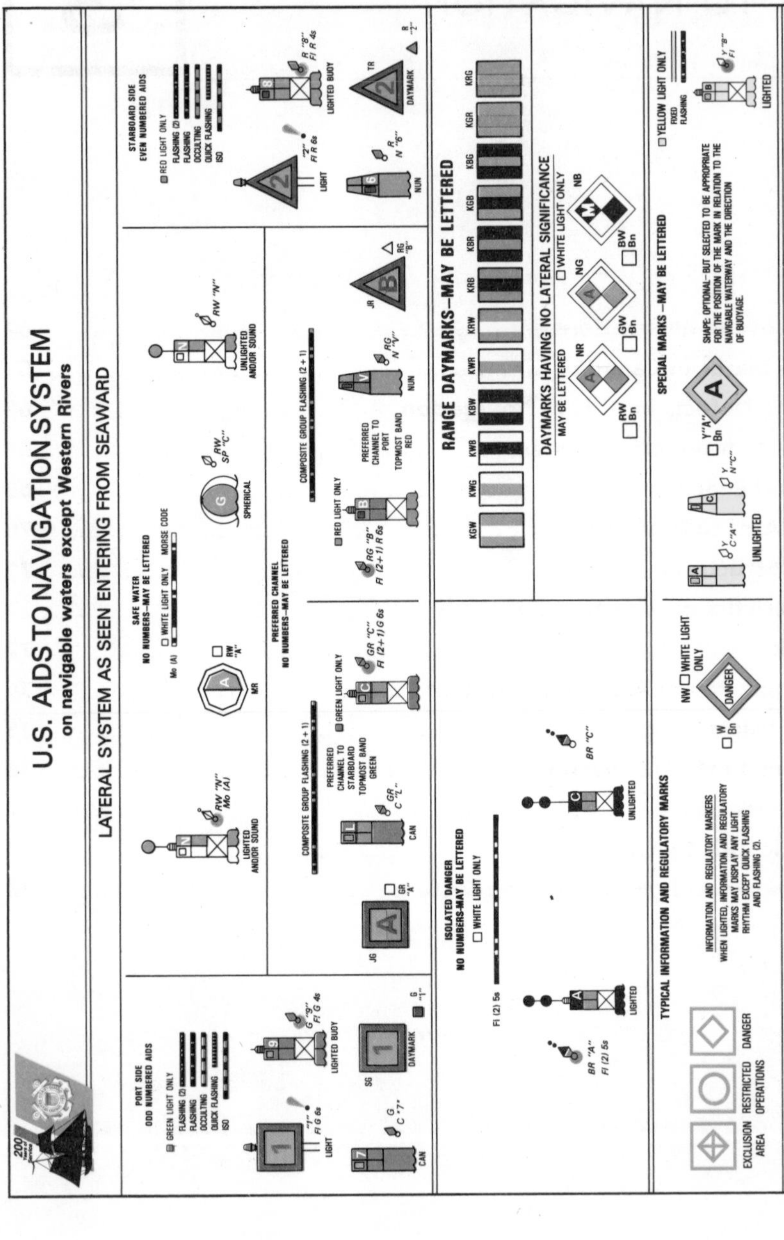

Aids to navigation marking the Intracoastal Waterway (ICW) display unique yellow symbols to distinguish them from aids marking other waters. Yellow triangles △ indicate aids should be passed by keeping them on the starboard (right) hand of the vessel. Yellow squares □ indicate aids should be passed by keeping them on the port (left) hand of the vessel. A yellow horizontal band ▭ provides no lateral information, but simply identifies aids as marking the ICW.

Plate 1

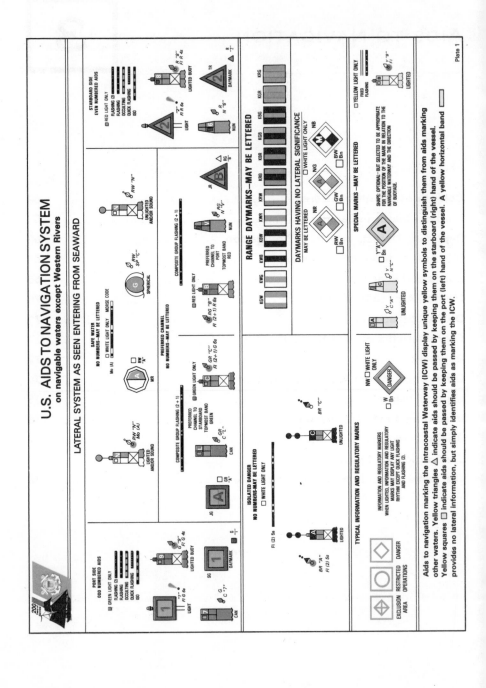

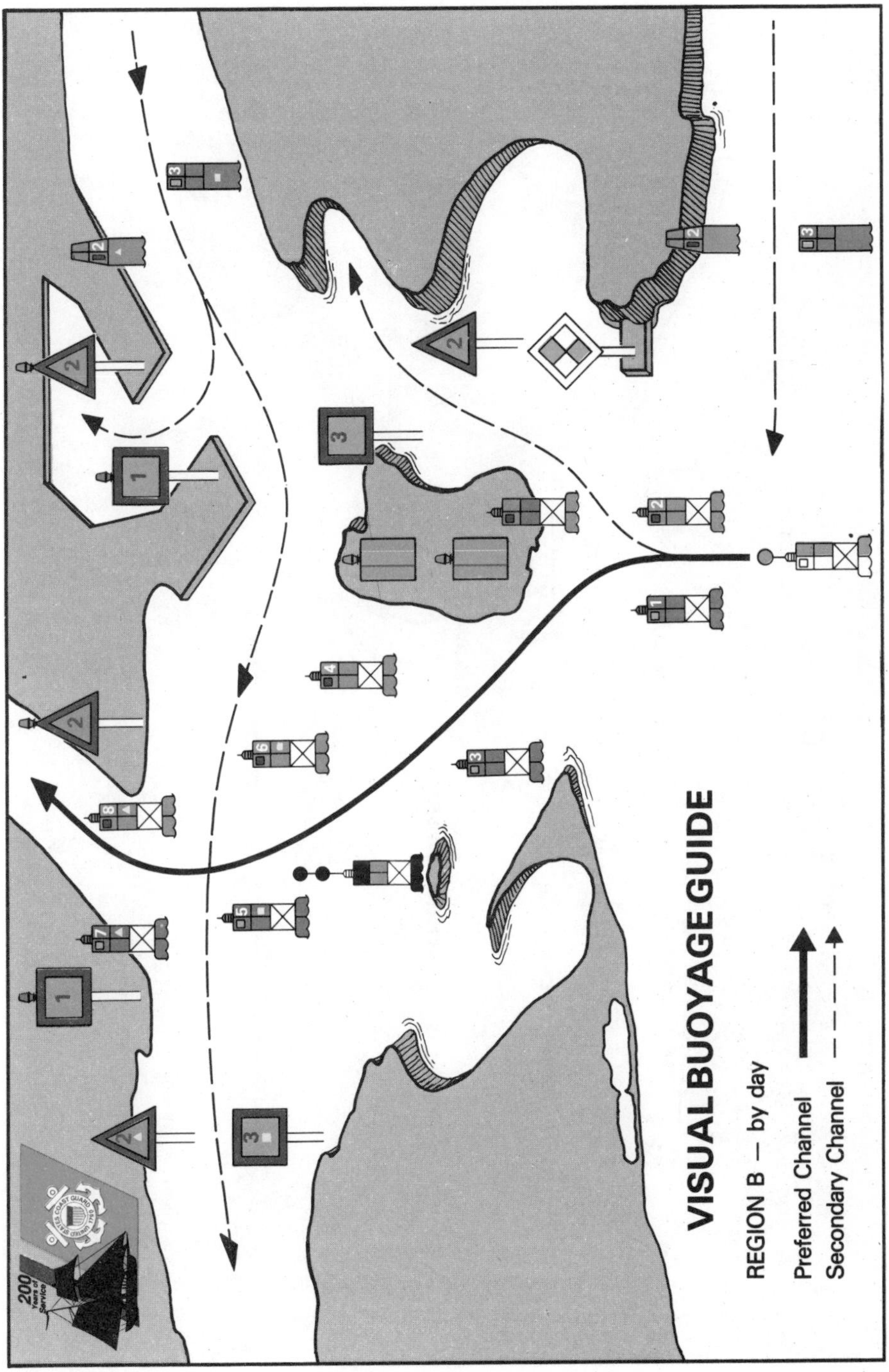
VISUAL BUOYAGE GUIDE
REGION B — by day
Preferred Channel
Secondary Channel
200 Years of Service

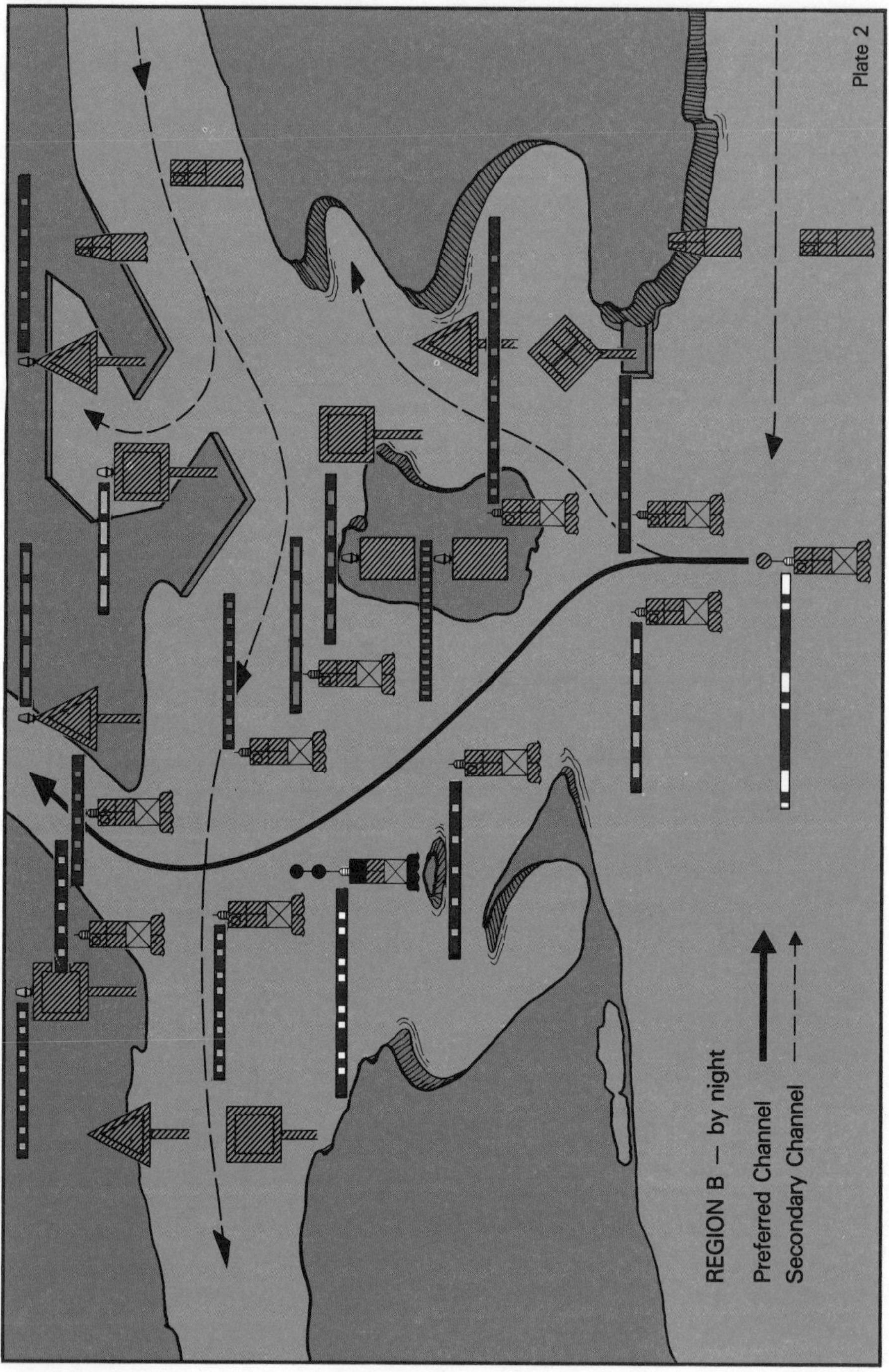
Plate 2
REGION B — by night
Preferred Channel
Secondary Channel

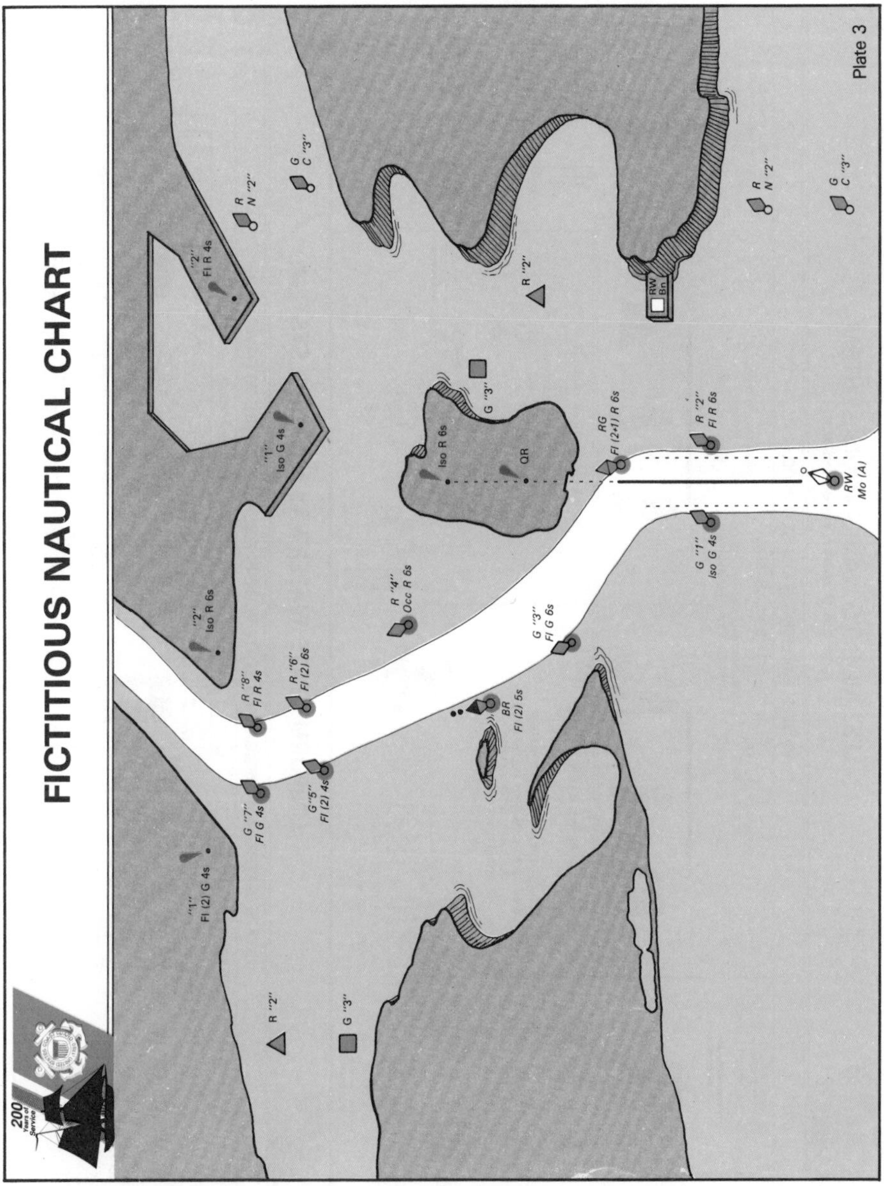
FICTITIOUS NAUTICAL CHART
200 Years of Service
Plate 3
"1" Fl (2) G 4s
G "7" Fl G 4s
G "5" Fl (2) 4s
R "8" Fl R 4s
R "6" Fl (2) 6s
"2" Iso R 6s
BR Fl (2) 5s
R "4" Occ R 6s
G "3" Fl G 6s
"1" Iso G 4s
"2" Fl R 4s
R N "2"
G C "3"
Iso R 6s
QR
G "3"
RG Fl (2+1) R 6s
R "2" Fl R 6s
G "1" Iso G 4s
RW Mo (A)
R "2"
RW Bn
R "2"
G "3"

3

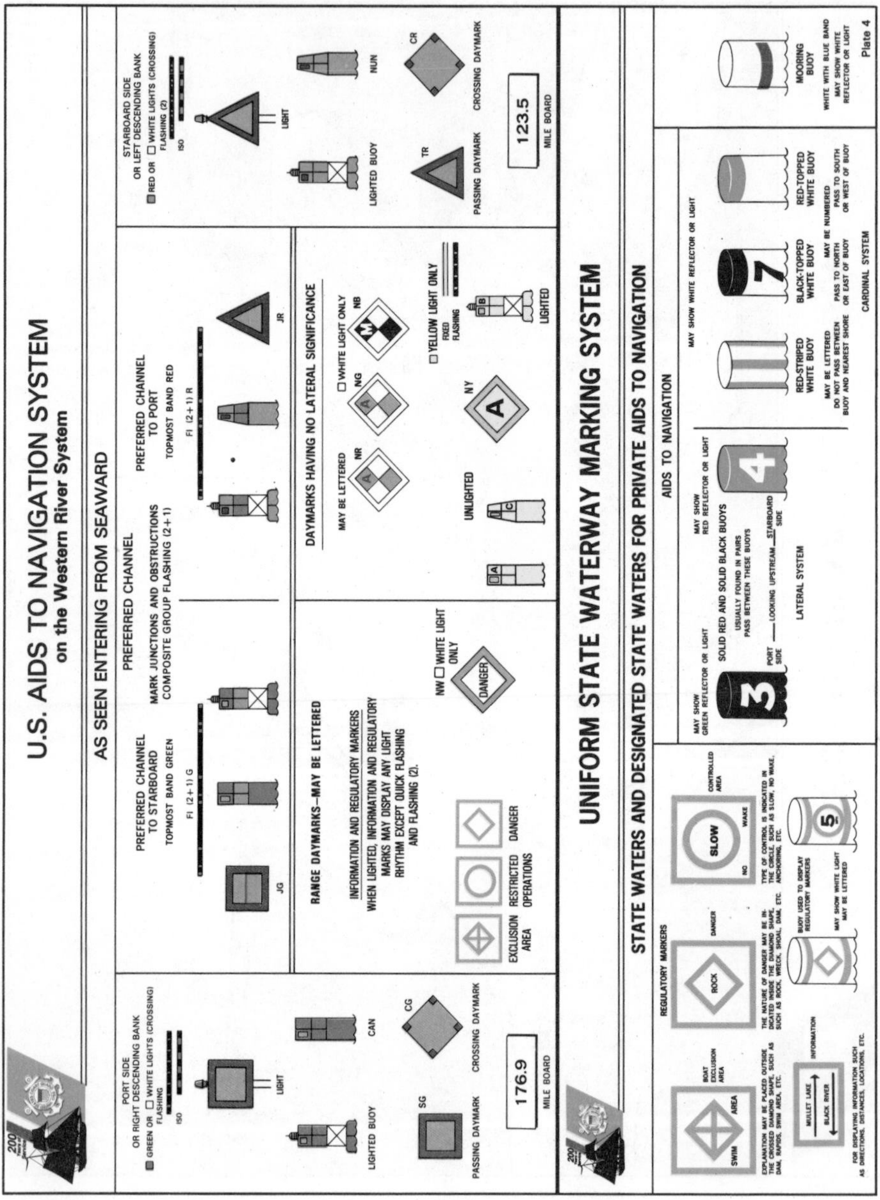
U.S. AIDS TO NAVIGATION SYSTEM
on the Western River System
AS SEEN ENTERING FROM SEAWARD
PORT SIDE
OR RIGHT DESCENDING BANK
GREEN OR WHITE LIGHTS (CROSSING)
FLASHING
ISO
LIGHT
LIGHTED BUOY
CAN
SG
CG
PASSING DAYMARK
CROSSING DAYMARK
176.9
MILE BOARD
PREFERRED CHANNEL
MARK JUNCTIONS AND OBSTRUCTIONS
COMPOSITE GROUP FLASHING (2+1)
PREFERRED CHANNEL TO STARBOARD
TOPMOST BAND GREEN
Fl (2+1) G
JG
PREFERRED CHANNEL TO PORT
TOPMOST BAND RED
Fl (2+1) R
JR
STARBOARD SIDE
OR LEFT DESCENDING BANK
RED OR WHITE LIGHTS (CROSSING)
FLASHING (2)
ISO
LIGHT
LIGHTED BUOY
NUN
TR
CR
PASSING DAYMARK
CROSSING DAYMARK
123.5
MILE BOARD
RANGE DAYMARKS—MAY BE LETTERED
INFORMATION AND REGULATORY MARKERS
WHEN LIGHTED, INFORMATION AND REGULATORY MARKS MAY DISPLAY ANY LIGHT RHYTHM EXCEPT QUICK FLASHING AND FLASHING (2).
NW WHITE LIGHT ONLY
DANGER
EXCLUSION AREA
RESTRICTED OPERATIONS
DANGER
DAYMARKS HAVING NO LATERAL SIGNIFICANCE
MAY BE LETTERED
NR
NG
WHITE LIGHT ONLY
NB
NY
UNLIGHTED
YELLOW LIGHT ONLY
FIXED
FLASHING
LIGHTED
UNIFORM STATE WATERWAY MARKING SYSTEM
STATE WATERS AND DESIGNATED STATE WATERS FOR PRIVATE AIDS TO NAVIGATION
REGULATORY MARKERS
SWIM AREA
BOAT EXCLUSION AREA
EXPLANATION MAY BE PLACED OUTSIDE THE CROSSED DIAMOND SHAPE, SUCH AS DAM, RAPIDS, SWIM AREA, ETC.
ROCK
DANGER
THE NATURE OF DANGER MAY BE INDICATED INSIDE THE DIAMOND SHAPE, SUCH AS ROCK, WRECK, SHOAL, DAM, ETC.
SLOW
NO WAKE
CONTROLLED AREA
TYPE OF CONTROL IS INDICATED IN THE CIRCLE, SUCH AS SLOW, NO WAKE, ANCHORING, ETC.
MULLET LAKE
BLACK RIVER
INFORMATION
FOR DISPLAYING INFORMATION SUCH AS DIRECTIONS, DISTANCES, LOCATIONS, ETC.
BUOY USED TO DISPLAY REGULATORY MARKERS
MAY SHOW WHITE LIGHT
MAY BE LETTERED
AIDS TO NAVIGATION
MAY SHOW GREEN REFLECTOR OR LIGHT
MAY SHOW RED REFLECTOR OR LIGHT
SOLID RED AND SOLID BLACK BUOYS
USUALLY FOUND IN PAIRS
PASS BETWEEN THESE BUOYS
PORT SIDE —— LOOKING UPSTREAM —— STARBOARD SIDE
LATERAL SYSTEM
MAY SHOW WHITE REFLECTOR OR LIGHT
RED-STRIPED WHITE BUOY
MAY BE LETTERED
DO NOT PASS BETWEEN BUOY AND NEAREST SHORE
BLACK-TOPPED WHITE BUOY
PASS TO NORTH OR EAST OF BUOY
MAY BE NUMBERED
RED-TOPPED WHITE BUOY
PASS TO SOUTH OR WEST OF BUOY
CARDINAL SYSTEM
MOORING BUOY
WHITE WITH BLUE BAND
MAY SHOW WHITE REFLECTOR OR LIGHT
Plate 4

CARDINAL MARKS IN CANADA

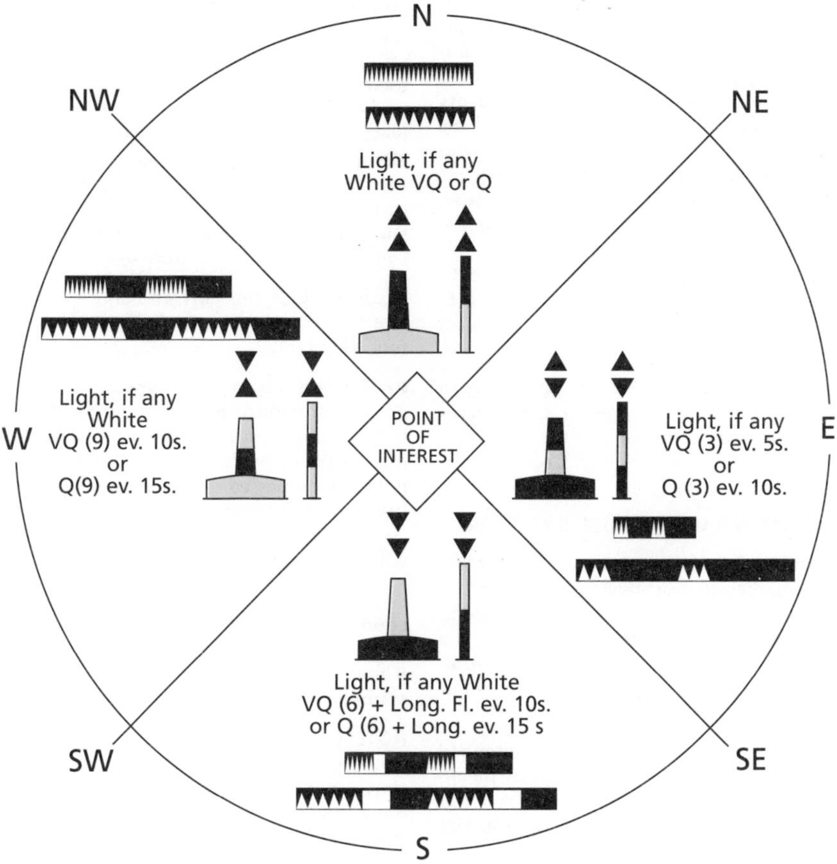

REPORTING DEFECTS IN AIDS TO NAVIGATION

Mariners should realize the Coast Guard cannot keep the thousands of aids to navigation comprising the U.S. Aids to Navigation System under simultaneous and continuous observation and that it is impossible to maintain every aid to navigation operating properly and on its assigned position at all times. Therefore, for the safety of all mariners, any person who discovers an aid to navigation that is either off station or exhibiting characteristics other than those listed in the Light Lists should promptly notify the nearest Coast Guard unit. Radio messages should be prefixed "COAST GUARD" and transmitted directly to one of the U.S. Government radio stations listed in Reed's Nautical Almanac.

Recommendations and requests pertaining to aids to navigation and to report aids to navigation that are no longer needed should be mailed to the Coast Guard district concerned.

AIDS TO NAVIGATION SYSTEM

The waters of the United States and its territories are marked to assist navigation by the U.S. Aids to Navigation System. This system encompasses buoys and beacons, conforming to the International Association of Lighthouse Authorities (IALA) buoyage guidelines, and other short range aids to navigation.

The U.S. Aids to Navigation System is intended for use with nautical charts. The exact meaning of a particular aid to navigation may not be clear to the mariner unless the appropriate nautical chart is consulted. Additional, important information supplementing that shown on charts is contained in the Light List, Coast Pilots, Sailing Directions,and Reed's.

TYPES OF MARKS

Lateral marks are buoys or beacons that indicate the port and starboard sides of a route to be followed, and are used in conjunction with a "conventional direction of buoyage".

Generally, lateral aids to navigation indicate on which side of the aid to navigation a vessel should pass, when navigable channels are entered from seaward and a vessel proceeds in the conventional direction of buoyage. Since all channels do not lead from seaward, certain assumptions must be made so the system can be consistently applied. In the absence of a route leading from seaward, the conventional direction of buoyage generally follows a clockwise direction around land masses.

Virtually all U.S. lateral marks are located in IALA Region B and follow the traditional 3R rule of "red, right, returning". In U.S. waters, returning from seaward and proceeding toward the head of navigation is generally considered as moving southerly along the Atlantic coast, westerly along the Gulf coast and northerly along the Pacific coast. In the Great Lakes, the conventional direction of buoyage is generally considered westerly and northerly, except on Lake Michigan, where southerly movement is considered as returning from sea.

A summary of the port and starboard hand lateral mark characteristics is contained in the following table.

Preferred channel marks are aids to navigation which mark channel junctions or bifurcations and often mark wrecks or obstructions. Preferred channel marks may normally be passed on either side by a vessel, but indicate to the mariner the preferred channel. Preferred channel marks are colored with red and green bands.

At a point where a channel divides, when proceeding in the "conventional direction of buoyage", a preferred channel in IALA Region B may be indicated by a modified port or starboard lateral mark as follows:

NOTE: U.S. lateral aids to navigation at certain Pacific islands are located within Region A and thus exhibit opposite color significance. Port hand marks are red with square or cylindrical shapes while starboard hand marks are green with triangular or conical shapes.

CAUTION: It may not always be possible to pass on either side of preferred channel aids to navigation. The appropriate nautical chart should always be consulted.

Non-lateral marks have no lateral significance but may be used to supplement the lateral aids to navigation specified above. Occasionally, daybeacons or minor lights outside of the normal channel will not have lateral significance since they do not define limits to navigable waters. These aids to navigation will utilize diamond-shaped dayboards and are divided into four diamond-shaped sectors. The side sectors of these dayboards are colored white, and the top and bottom sectors are colored black, red, or green as the situation dictates.

Safe water marks are used to mark fairways, mid-channels, and offshore approach points, and have unobstructed water on all sides. They can also be used by the mariner transiting offshore waters to identify the proximity of an intended landfall. Safe water marks are red and white striped and have a red spherical topmark to further aid in identification. If lighted, they display a white light with the characteristic Morse code "A".

Isolated danger marks are erected on, or moored above or near, an isolated danger, which has navigable water all around it. These marks should not be approached closely without special caution. These marks are scheduled for introduction in 1991. Isolated danger marks are colored with black and red bands, and if lighted, display a group flashing (2) white light. A topmark consisting of two black spheres, one above the other, is fitted for both lighted and unlighted marks.

Special marks are not intended to assist in navigation, but rather to alert the mariner to a special feature or area. The feature should be described in a nautical document such as a chart, Light List, Coast Pilot or Notice to Mariner. Some areas which may be marked by these aids to navigation are spoil areas, pipelines, traffic separation schemes, jetties, or military exercise areas. Special marks are yellow in color and, if lighted, display a yellow light.

Information and regulatory marks are used to alert the mariner to various warnings or regulatory matters. These marks have orange geometric shapes against a white background. The Preferred channel meanings associated with the orange shapes are as follows;

1) An open-faced diamond signifies danger.

2) A diamond shape having a cross centered within indicates that vessels are excluded from the marked area.

3) A circular shape indicates that certain operating restrictions are in effect within the marked area.

4) A square or rectangular shape will contain directions or instructions lettered within the shape.

BUOYS AND BEACONS

The IALA maritime buoyage guidelines apply to buoys and beacons that indicate the lateral limits of navigable channels, obstructions and other dangers such as wrecks, and other areas or features of importance to the mariner. This system provides five types of marks: lateral marks, safe water marks, special marks, isolated danger marks and cardinal marks, (Cardinal marks are not presently used in the United States.) Each type of mark is differentiated from other types by distinctive

Characteristic	*Port Hand Marks*	*Starboard Hand Marks*
Color	Green	Red
Shape (buoys)	Cylindrical (can) or pillar	Conical (nun) or pillar
Dayboard or Topmark when fitted)	Green square or cylinder	Red triangle or cone, point upward
Light Color (when fitted)	Green	Red
Reflector Color	Green	Red
Numbers	Odd	Even

Characteristic	*Preferred channel to starboard*	*Preferred channel to port*
Color	Green with one broad red band	Red with one broad green band
Shape (buoys)	Cylindrical (can) or pillar	Conical (nun) or pillar
Dayboard	Green square, lower half red	Red triangle, lower half green
Topmark (when fitted)	Green square or cylinder	Red triangular cone
Light (when fitted)		
Color	Green	Red
Rhythm	Composite group flashing (2+1)	Composite group flashing (2+1)
Reflector Color	Green	Red

colors, shapes and light rhythms. Examples are provided on the enclosed color illustrations.

Buoys are floating aids to navigation used extensively throughout U.S, waters, They are moored to the seabed by concrete sinkers with chain or synthetic rope moorings of various lengths connected to the buoy body.

Buoy positions represented on nautical charts are approximate positions only, due to the practical limitations of positioning and maintaining buoys and their sinkers in precise geographical locations. Buoy positions are normally verified during periodic maintenance visits. Between visits, atmospheric and sea conditions, seabed slope and composition, and collisions or other accidents may cause buoys to shift from their charted locations, or cause buoys to be sunk or capsized.

Buoy moorings vary in length. The mooring lengths define a "watch circle", and buoys can be expected to move within this circle. Actual watch circles do not coincide with the symbols representing them on charts.

CAUTION: Mariners attempting to pass a buoy close aboard risk collision with a yawing buoy or with the obstruction which the buoy marks. Mariners must not rely on buoys alone for determining their positions due to factors limiting buoy reliability. Prudent mariners will use bearings or angles from fixed aids to navigation and shore objects, soundings and various methods of electronic navigation to positively fix their position.

Beacons are aids to navigation which are permanently fixed to the earth's surface. These structures range from lighthouses to small unlighted daybeacons, and exhibit a daymark to make these aids to navigation readily visible and easily identifiable against background conditions. The daymark conveys to the mariner, during daylight hours, the same significance as does the aid to navigation's light at night.

CAUTION: Vessels should not pass fixed aids to navigation close aboard due to the danger of collision with rip-rap or structure foundations, or with the obstruction or danger being marked.

LIGHTED AIDS TO NAVIGATION

Most lighted aids to navigation are equipped with controls which automatically cause the light to operate during darkness and to be extinguished during daylight. These devices are not of equal sensitivity, therefore all lights do not come on or go off at the same time. (Mariners should ensure correct identification of aids to navigation during twilight periods when some lighted aids to navigation are lit while others are not.)

The lighting apparatus is serviced at periodic intervals to assure reliable operation, but there is always the possibility of a light being extinguished or operating improperly.

The condition of the atmosphere has a considerable effect upon the distance at which lights can be seen. Sometimes lights are obscured by fog, haze, dust, smoke, or precipitation which may be present at the light, or between the light and the observer, and which is possibly unknown by the observer. Atmospheric refraction may cause a light to be seen farther than under ordinary circumstances. A light of low intensity will be easily obscured by unfavorable conditions of the atmosphere and little dependence can be placed on it being seen. For this reason, the intensity of a light should always be considered when expecting to sight it in thick weather. Haze and distance may reduce the apparent duration of the flash of a light. In some conditions of the atmosphere, white lights may have a reddish hue.

Lights placed at high elevations are more frequently obscured by clouds, mist, and fog than those lights located at or near sea level.

In regions where ice conditions prevail in the winter, the lantern panes of unattended lights may become covered with ice or snow, which will greatly reduce the visibility of the lights and may also cause colored lights to appear white.

The increasing use of brilliant shore lights for advertising, illuminating bridges, and other purposes, may cause marine navigational lights, particularly those in densely inhabited areas, to be outshone and difficult to distinguish from the background lighting, Mariners are requested to report such cases in order that steps may be taken to improve the conditions.

The "loom"(glow) of a powerful light is often seen beyond the limit of visibility of the actual rays of the light. The loom may sometimes appear sufficiently sharp enough to obtain a bearing.

At short distances, some flashing lights may show a faint continuous light between flashes.

The distance of an observer from a light cannot be estimated by its apparent intensity. Always check the characteristics of lights so powerful lights, visible in the distance, are not mistaken for nearby lights (such as those on lighted buoys) showing similar characteristics of low intensity.

If lights are not sighted within a reasonable time after prediction, a dangerous situation may exist requiring prompt resolution or action in order to ensure the safety of the vessel.

The apparent characteristic of a complex light may change with the distance of the observer. For example, a light which actually displays a characteristic of fixed white varied by flashes of alternating white and red (the rhythms having a decreasing range of visibility in the order: flashing white, flashing red, fixed white) may, when first sighted in clear weather, show as a simple flashing white light. As the vessel draws nearer, the red flash will become visible and the characteristics will apparently be alternating flashing white and red. Later, the fixed white light will be seen between the flashes and the true characteristic of the light will finally be recognized - fixed white, alternating flashing white and red (F W Al WR).

If a vessel has considerable vertical motion due to pitching in heavy seas, a light sighted on the horizon may alternately appear and disappear. This may lead the unwary to assign a false characteristic and hence, to err in its identification. The true characteristic will be evident after the distance has been sufficiently decreased or by increasing the height of eye of the observer.

Similarly, the effects of wave motion on lighted buoys may produce the appearance of incorrect light phase characteristics when certain flashes occur, but are not viewed by the mariner. In addition, buoy motion can reduce the distance at which buoy lights are detected.

Sectors of colored glass are placed in the lanterns of some lights in order to produce a system of light sectors of different colors. In general, red sectors are used to mark shoals or to warn the mariner of other obstructions to navigation or of nearby land. Such lights provide approximate bearing information since observers may note the change of color as they cross the boundary between sectors. These boundaries are indicated in Reed's and by dotted lines on charts. These bearings, as all bearings referring to lights, are given in true degrees from 000° to 359°, as observed from a vessel toward the light. Altering course on the changing sectors of a light or using the boundaries between light sectors to determine the bearing for any purpose is not recommended. Be guided instead by the correct compass bearing to the light and do not rely on being able to accurately observe the point at which the color changes, This is difficult to determine because the edges of a colored sector cannot be cut off sharply. On either side of the line of demarcation between white, red, or green sectors, there is always a small arc of uncertain color, Moreover, when haze or smoke are present in the intervening atmosphere, a white sector might have a reddish hue.

The area in which a light can be observed is normally an arc with the light as the center and the range of visibility as the radius. However, on some bearings the range may be reduced by obstructions. In such cases, the obstructed arc might differ with height of eye and distance. When a light is cut off by adjoining land and the arc of visibility is given, the bearing on which the light disappears may vary with the distance of the vessel from which observed and with the height of eye. When the light is cut off by a sloping hill or point of land, the light may be seen over a wider arc by a vessel farther away than by one closer to the light.

The arc drawn on charts around a light is not intended to give information as to the distance at which it can be seen, but solely to indicate, in the case of lights which do not show equally in all directions, the bearings between which the variation of visibility or obstruction of the light occurs.

OIL WELL STRUCTURES

Oil well structures in navigable waters are not listed in the Light List. The structures are shown on the appropriate nautical charts. Information concerning the location and characteristics of those structures which display lights and sound signals not located in obstruction areas are published in Local and/or Weekly Notices to Mariners.

In general, during the nighttime, a series of white lights are displayed extending from the platform to the top of the derrick when drilling operations are in progress. At other times, structures are usually marked with one or more fixed or quick flashing white or red lights, visible for at least one nautical mile

3

during clear weather. Obstructions which are a part of the appurtenances to the main structure, such as mooring piles, anchor and mooring buoys, etc., normally are not lighted. In addition, some of the structures are equipped with sound signals (bell, siren, whistle, or horn). When operating, bells sound one stroke every 15 seconds, while sirens, whistles, or horns sound a single two-second blast every 20 seconds.

CHARACTERISTICS OF AIDS TO NAVIGATION

LIGHT COLORS

Only aids to navigation with green or red lights have lateral significance. When proceeding in the conventional direction of buoyage, the mariner in Region B, may see the following lighted aids to navigation:

Green lights on aids to navigation mark port sides of channels and locations of wrecks or obstructions which must be passed by keeping these lighted aids to navigation on the port hand of a vessel. Green lights are also used on preferred channel marks where the preferred channel is to starboard (i.e., aid to navigation left to port when proceeding in the conventional direction of buoyage).

Red lights on aids to navigation mark starboard sides of channels and locations of wrecks or obstructions which must be passed by keeping these lighted aids to navigation on the starboard hand of a vessel. Red lights are also used on preferred channel marks where the preferred channel is to port (i,e., aid to navigation left to starboard when proceeding in the conventional direction of buoyage).

White and yellow lights have no lateral significance. The purpose of aids to navigation exhibiting white or yellow lights may be determined by the shapes, colors, letters, and light rhythms.

Most aids to navigation are fitted with retroreflective material to increase their visibility in darkness. Red or green retroreflective material is used on lateral aids to navigation which, if lighted, will display lights of the same color.

LIGHT RHYTHMS

Light rhythms have no lateral significance. Aids to navigation with lateral significance exhibit flashing, quick, occulting or isophase light rhythms. Ordinarily, flashing lights (frequency not exceeding 30 flashes per minute) will be used.

Preferred channel marks exhibit a composite group-flashing light rhythm of two flashes followed by a single flash.

Safe water marks show a white Morse code "A" rhythm (a short flash followed by a long flash).

Isolated danger marks show a white flashing (2) rhythm (two flashes repeated regularly).

Special marks show yellow lights and exhibit a flashing or fixed rhythm; however, a flashing rhythm is preferred.

Information and regulatory marks, when lighted, display a white light with any light rhythm; except quick flashing, flashing (2) and Morse code "A".

For situations where lights require a distinct cautionary significance, as at sharp turns, sudden channel constrictions, wrecks or obstructions, a quick flashing light rhythm will be used.

DAYMARKS

The first letter of the daymark listing indicates it's basic purpose.

S=Square. Used to mark the port (left) side of channels when entering from seaward.

T=Triangle. Used to mark the starboard (right) side of channels when entering from seaward.

J=Junction. May be a square or a triangle. Used to mark channel junctions or bifurcations in the channel. May be used to mark wrecks, or other obstructions, which may be passed on either side. The color of the top band has lateral significance for the preferred channel.

M=Safe Water. Octagonal. Used to mark the fairway, or middle of the channel.

K=Range. Rectangular. When the front and rear daymarks are aligned on the same bearing, you are on the azimuth of the range this usually marks safe water.

N=No lateral significance. Diamond or rectangular shaped. Used for special purposes as a warning, distance or location marker.

Additional information after a - :

-I=Intracoastal Waterway. A yellow reflective strip will be oriented horizontally on the daymark.

-SY=Intracoastal Waterway. A yellow reflective square will be on the daymark. This indicates a port hand marker. This may appear on a red triangular daymark, in places where the Intracoastal Waterway coincides with another channel's markings

-TY=Intracoastal Waterway. A yellow reflective triangle will be on the daymark. This indicates a starboard hand marker. This may appear on a green square daymark, in places where the Intracoastal Waterway coincides with another channel.

These abbreviations are combined in the list of aids to navigation. The following list gives many of the major designations:

SG=Square green daymark with a green reflective border.

SG-I=Square green daymark with a green reflective border, and a yellow reflective horizontal strip.

SG-SY=Square green daymark with a green reflective border, and a yellow reflective square.

SG-TY=Square green daymark with a green reflective border, and a yellow reflective triangle

SR=Square red daymark with a red reflective border.

TG=Triangular green daymark with a green reflective border.

TR=Triangular red daymark with a red reflective border.

TR-I=Triangular red daymark with a red reflective border, and a yellow reflective horizontal strip.

TR-SY=Triangular red daymark with a red reflective border, and a yellow reflective square.

TR-TY=Triangular red daymark with a red reflective border, and a yellow reflective triangle.

JG=Daymark with horizontal bands of green and red, green band topmost, with a green reflective border.

JG-I=Daymark with horizontal bands of green and red, green band topmost, with a green reflective border, and a yellow reflective horizontal strip.

JG-SY=Daymark with horizontal bands of green and red, green band topmost, with a green reflective border, and a yellow reflective square.

JG-TY=Daymark with horizontal bands of green and red, green band topmost, with a green reflective border, and a yellow reflective triangle.

JR=Daymark with horizontal bands of green and red, red band topmost, with a red reflective border.

JR-I=Daymark with horizontal bands of green and red, red band topmost, with a red reflective border, with a yellow horizontal strip.

JR-SY=Triangular daymark with horizontal bands of green and red, red band topmost, with a red reflective border, and a yellow reflective square.

JR-TY=Triangular daymark with horizontal bands of green and red, red band topmost, with a red reflective border, and a yellow reflective triangle.

MR=Octagonal daymark with stripes of white and red, with a white reflective border.

MR-I=Octagonal daymark with stripes of white and red, with a white reflective border and a yellow reflective horizontal strip.

CG=Diamond shaped green daymark bearing small green diamond shaped reflectors at each corner.

CR=Diamond shaped red daymark bearing small red diamond shaped reflectors at each corner.

KBG=Rectangular black daymark bearing a central green stripe.

KBG-I=Rectangular black daymark bearing a central green stripe and a yellow reflective horizontal strip.

KBR=Rectangular black daymark bearing a central red stripe.

KBR-I=Rectangular black daymark bearing a central red stripe and a yellow reflective horizontal strip.

KBW=Rectangular black daymark bearing a central white stripe.

KBW-I=Rectangular black daymark bearing a central white stripe and a yellow reflective horizontal strip.

KGB=Rectangular green daymark bearing a central black stripe.

KGB-I=Rectangular green daymark bearing a central black stripe and a yellow reflective horizontal strip.

KGR=Rectangular green daymark bearing a central red stripe.

KGR-I=Rectangular green daymark bearing a central red stripe and a yellow reflective horizontal strip.

KGW=Rectangular green daymark bearing a central white stripe.

KGW-I=Rectangular green daymark bearing a central white stripe and a yellow reflective horizontal strip.

KRB=Rectangular red daymark bearing a central black stripe.

KRB-I=Rectangular red daymark bearing a central black stripe and a yellow reflective horizontal strip.

KRG=Rectangular red daymark bearing a central green stripe.

KRG-I=Rectangular red daymark bearing a central green stripe and a yellow reflective horizontal strip.

KRW=Rectangular red daymark bearing a central white stripe.

KRW-I=Rectangular red daymark bearing a central white stripe and a yellow reflective horizontal strip.

KWB=Rectangular white daymark bearing a central black stripe.

KWB-I=Rectangular white daymark bearing a central black stripe and a yellow reflective horizontal strip.

KWG=Rectangular white daymark bearing a central green stripe.

KWG-I=Rectangular white daymark bearing a central green stripe and a yellow reflective horizontal strip.

KWR=Rectangular white daymark bearing a central red stripe.

KWR-I=Rectangular white daymark bearing a central red stripe and a yellow reflective horizontal strip.

NB=Diamond shaped daymark divided into four diamond shaped colored sectors, with the sectors at the side corners white, and the sectors at the top and bottom corners black, with a white reflective border.

NG=Diamond shaped daymark divided into four diamond shaped colored sectors, with the sectors at the side corners white, and the sectors at the top and bottom corners green, with a white reflective border.

NR=Diamond shaped daymark divided into four diamond shaped colored sectors, with the sectors at the side corners white, and the sectors at the top and bottom corners red, with a white reflective border.

NW=Diamond shaped white daymark with an orange reflective border and black letters describing the information, or regulatory nature, of the mark.

ND=Rectangular white mileage marker with black numerals indicating the mile number.

NL=Rectangular white location marker with an orange reflective border and black letters indicating the location.

NY=Diamond shaped yellow daymark with a yellow reflective border.

OTHER SHORT RANGE AIDS TO NAVIGATION

Lighthouses are placed on shore or on marine sites and most often do not show lateral markings. They assist the mariner in determining his position or safe course, or warn of obstructions or dangers to navigation. Lighthouses with no lateral significance usually exhibit a white light.

Occasionally, lighthouses use sectored lights to mark shoals or warn mariners of other dangers. Lights so equipped show one color from most directions and a different color or colors over definite arcs of the horizon as indicated on the appropriate nautical chart. These sectors provide approximate bearing information and the observer should note a change of color as the boundary between the sectors is crossed. Since sector bearings are not precise, they should be considered as a warning only, and used in conjunction with a nautical chart.

Large navigational buoys (LNBs) were developed to replace lightships and are placed at points where it is impractical to build lighthouses. The unmanned LNBs are 40 feet in diameter with light towers approximately 40 feet above the water. LNBs are equipped with lights, sound signals, radiobeacons, and racons. The traditional red color of LNBs has no lateral significance, but is intended to improve visibility.

Seasonal aids to navigation are placed into service or changed at specified times of the

LIGHT CHARACTERISTICS

Abb.	Old Abb		Period shown
F		FIXED a continuous steady light	
		OCCULTING total duration of light more than dark and total eclipse at regular intervals	
Oc.	Occ.	SINGLE OCCULTING steady light with eclipse regularly repeated.	
Oc.(2)	Gp.Occ.(2)	GROUP OCCULTING two or more eclipses in a group, regularly repeated	
Oc.(2+3)	Gp.Occ.(2+3)	COMPOSITE GROUP OCCULTING in which successive groups in a period have different number of eclipses.	
Iso.		ISOPHASE a light where duration of light and darkness are equal.	
		FLASHING single flash at regular interals. Duration of light less than dark.	
Fl.		SINGLE FLASHING light in which flash is regularly repeated at less than 50 flashes per minute	
L.Fl.		LONG FLASHING a flash of 2 or more seconds, regularly repeated	
Fl.(3)	Gp.Fl.(3)	GROUP FLASHING successive groups, specified in number, regularly repeated.	
Fl.(2+1)	Gp.Fl. (2+1)	COMPOSITE GROUP FLASHING in which successive groups in a period have different number of flashes	
		QUICK usually 50 or 60 flashes per minute	
Q.	Qk.Fl.	CONTINUOUS QUICK in which a flash is regularly repeated	
Q.(3)	Qk.Fl.(3)	GROUP QUICK in which a specified group of flashes is regularly repeated.	
IQ	Int.Qk.Fl.	INTERUPTED QUICK sequence of flashes interrupted by regularly repeated eclipses of constant and long duration.	
		VERY QUICK usually either 100 or 120 flashes per minute	
VQ.	Q.Qk.Fl.	CONTINOUS VERY QUICK flash is regularly repeated.	
VQ.	V.Qk.(3)	GROUP VERY QUICK specified group of flashes regularly repeated.	
IVQ.	Int.V.Qk.Fl.	INTERRUPTED VERY QUICK FLASH in groups with total eclipse at regular intervals of constant and long duration.	
		VERY QUICK usually either 100 or 120 flashes per minute.	
U.Q.		CONTINOUS ULTRA QUICK in which flash is regularly repeated.	
IUQ.		INTERRUPTED ULTRA QUICK in groups with total eclipse at intervals of long duration.	
Mo.(K)		MORSE CODE in which appearances of light of two clearly different durations are grouped to represent a character(s) in the Morse code.	
F.Fl.		FIXING AND FLASHING steady light with one brilliant flash at regular intervals.	
Al.WR.	Alt.WR.	ALTERNATING a light which alters in color in successive flashing.	

year, The dates shown in the Light List are approximate and may vary due to adverse weather or other conditions.

Ranges are non-lateral aids to navigation systems employing dual beacons which when the structures appear to be in line, assist the mariner in maintaining a safe course. The appropriate nautical chart must be consulted when using ranges to determine whether the range marks the centerline of the navigable channel and also what section of the range may be safely traversed. Ranges display rectangular dayboards of various colors and are generally, but not always lighted. When lighted, ranges may display lights of any color.

Sound signal is a generic term used to describe aids to navigation that produce an audible signal designed to assist the mariner in fog or other periods of reduced visibility. These aids to navigation can be activated by several means (i.e. manually, remotely, or fog detector). In cases where a fog detector is in use, there may be a delay in the automatic activation of the signal. Additionally, fog detectors may not be capable of detecting patchy fog conditions. Sound signals are distinguished by their tone and phase characteristics.

Tones are determined by the devices producing the sound, e.g, diaphones, diaphragm horns, sirens, whistles, bells, and gongs.

Phase characteristics are defined by the signal's sound pattern, i.e., the number of blasts and silent periods per minute and their durations. Sound signals sounded from fixed structures generally produce a specific number of blasts and silent periods each minute when operating. Buoy sound signals are generally activated by the motion of the sea and therefore do not emit a regular signal characteristic. It is common, in fact, for a buoy to produce no sound signal when seas are calm. Mariners are reminded that buoy positions are not always reliable.

The characteristic of a sound signal can be located in the Light List. Unless it is specifically stated that a sound signal "Operates continuously", or the signal is a bell, gong, or whistle on a buoy, it can be assumed that the sound signal only operates during times of fog, reduced visibility, or adverse weather.

An emergency sound signal is sounded at some locations when the main and stand-by signals are inoperative.

CAUTION: Mariners should not rely on sound signals to determine their position, Distance cannot be accurately determined by sound intensity. Occasionally, sound signals may not be heard in areas close to their location. Signals may not sound in cases where fog exists close to, but not at, the location of the sound signal.

VARIATIONS TO THE U.S.SYSTEM

Intracoastal Waterway aids to navigation: The Intracoastal Waterway runs parallel to the Atlantic and Gulf coasts from Manasquan Inlet, New Jersey to the Mexican border. Aids to navigation marking these waters have some portion of them marked with yellow. Otherwise, the coloring and numbering of the aids to navigation follow the same system as that in other U.S. waterways. In order that vessels may readily follow the Intracoastal Waterway route, special markings are employed. These marks consist of a yellow square and yellow triangle and indicate which side the aid to navigation should be passed when following the conventional direction of buoyage. The yellow square indicates that the aid to navigation should be kept on the left side and the yellow triangle indicates that the aid to navigation should be kept on the right side.

NOTE: The conventional direction of buoyage in the Intracoastal Waterway is generally southerly along the Atlantic coast and generally westerly along the Gulf coast.

The Western Rivers System, a variation of the standard U.S. Aids to Navigation System described in the preceding sections, is employed on the Mississippi River and its tributaries above Baton Rouge, LA and on certain other rivers which flow toward the Gulf of Mexico. The Western Rivers System varies from the standard U.S. system as follows:

1) Aids to navigation are not numbered.

2) Numbers on aids to navigation do not have lateral significance, but, rather, indicate mileage from a fixed point (normally the river mouth).

3) Diamond shaped crossing dayboards, red or green as appropriate, are used to indicate where the river channel crosses from one bank to the other.

4) Lights on green aids to navigation show a single-flash characteristic which may be green or white.

5) Lights on red aids to navigation show a group-flash characteristic which may be red or white.

6) Isolated danger marks are not used.

Uniform State Waterway Marking System (USWMS): This system was developed in 1966 to provide an easily understood system for operators of small boats. While designed for use on lakes and other inland waterways that are not portrayed on nautical charts, the USWMS was authorized for use on other waters as well. It supplements the existing federal marking system and is generally compatible with it.

The conventional direction of buoyage is considered upstream or towards the head of navigation.

The USWMS varies from the standard U.S. system as follows:

1) The color black is used instead of green.

2) There are three aids to navigation which reflect cardinal significance:

a. A white buoy with red top represents an obstruction and the buoy should be passed to the south or west.

b. A white buoy with black top represents an obstruction and the buoy should be passed to the north or east.

c. A red and white vertically striped buoy indicates that an obstruction exists between that buoy and the nearest shore.

3) Mooring buoys are white buoys with a horizontal blue band midway between the waterline and the top of the buoy. This buoy may be lighted and will generally show a slow flashing white light.

BRIDGE MARKINGS

Bridges across navigable waters are generally marked with red, green and/or white lights for nighttime navigation. Red lights mark piers and other parts of the bridge. Red lights are also used on drawbridges to show when they are in the closed position.

Green lights are used on drawbridges to show when they are in the open position. The location of these lights will vary according to the bridge structure. Green lights are also used to mark the centerline of navigable channels through fixed bridges. If there are two or more channels through the bridge, the preferred channel is also marked by three white lights in a vertical line above the green light.

Red and green retro-reflective panels may be used to mark bridge piers and may also be used on bridges not required to display lights.

Main channels through bridges may be marked by lateral red and green lights and dayboards. Adjacent piers should be marked with fixed yellow lights when the main channel is marked with lateral aids to navigation.

Centerlines of channels through fixed bridges may be marked with a safe water mark and an occulting white light when lateral marks are used to mark main channels. The centerline of the navigable channel through the draw span of floating bridges may be marked with a special mark. The mark will be a yellow diamond with yellow retro-reflective panels and may exhibit a yellow light that displays a Morse code "B" (– . . .).

Clearance gauges may be installed to enhance navigation safety. The gauges are located on the right channel pier or pier protective structure facing approaching vessels. They indicate the vertical clearance available under the span.

Drawbridges equipped with radiotelephones display a blue and white sign which indicates what VHF radiotelephone channels should be used to request bridge openings.

ELECTRONIC AIDS TO NAVIGATION

Racons

Aids to navigation may be enhanced by the use of radar beacons (racons). Racons, when triggered by pulses from a vessel's radar, will transmit a coded reply to the vessel's radar. This reply serves to identify the racon station by exhibiting a series of dots and dashes which appear on the radar display emanating radially from the racon. This display will represent the approximate range and bearing to the racon. Although racons may be used on both laterally significant and non-laterally significant aids to navigation, the racon signal itself is for identification purposes only, and therefore carries no lateral significance. Racons are also used as bridge marks to mark the point of best passage.

3

All racons operate in the marine radar X-band from 9,300 to 9,500 MHz. Some frequency-agile racons also operate in the 2,900 to 3,000 MHz marine radar S-band.

Racons have a typical output of 100 to 300 milliwatts and are considered a short range aid to navigation. Reception varies from a nominal range of 6 to 8 nautical miles when mounted on a buoy to as much as 17 nautical miles for a racon with a directional antenna mounted at a height of 50 feet on a fixed structure. It must be understood that these are nominal ranges and are dependent upon many factors.

The beginning of the racon presentation occurs about 50 yards beyond the racon position and will persist for a number of revolutions of the radar antenna (depending on its rotation rate).

Distance to the racon can be measured to the point at which the racon flash begins, but the figure obtained will be greater than the ship's distance from the racon. This is due to the slight response delay in the racon apparatus.

Radar operators may notice some broadening or spoking of the racon presentation when their vessel approaches closely to the source of the racon. This effect can be minimized by adjustment of the IF gain or sweep gain control of the radar. If desired, the racon presentation can be virtually eliminated by operation of the FTC (fast time constant) controls of the radar.

Radar Reflectors

Many aids to navigation incorporate special fixtures designed to enhance the reflection of radar energy. These fixtures, called radar retlectors, help radar equipped vessels to detect buoys and beacons which are so equipped. They do not however, positively identity a radar target as an aid to navigation.

For more information on electronic aids to navigation see Chapter 8.

THE CANADIAN AIDS TO NAVIGATION SYSTEM

We offer here a brief discussion of the Canadian system. For more information consult the Canadian coast pilots and small craft guides. The Canadian Coast Guard publishes a book titled The Canadian Aids to Navigation System.

Canada uses the same IALA Region B system used in the United States. A combined lateral and cardinal system is used. The shape, color and light characteristics all indicate the function of the aid to navigation.

In general, the "red right returning" rule applies, as it does in the United States. Additionally, a system of cardinal marks indicates the relative position of an obstruction. The cardinal buoys have double cone topmarks. The diagram on page 67 at the begining of this Chapter illustrates the significance of the various topmarks:

Canada also has special purpose buoys which are usually similar to U.S. buoys designed for the same purpose. Daymarks include red triangles and green squares, somewhat similar to marks used in the U.S. Intracoastal Waterway.

A point to keep in mind, is the universal use of the metric system in Canada. Lighthouse heights are given in meters, rather than feet as currently done in the U.S. Ranges of lights are still listed in terms of nautical miles.

Boating Regulations

4

BOATING SAFETY HOTLINE

To reach the Coast Guard's Boating Safety Hotline call (800) 368-5647. You can obtain information on boating safety recalls, report defects in boats, comment on U.S. boarding procedures, receive answers to boating safety questions and obtain boating safety literature.

This service also offers information on the Recreational Vessel Fee. For information on boating courses in your area call the course line at (800) 336-2628, or 800-245-2628 in Virginia.

STATE REGISTRATION

To obtain information on state boat registrations and rules contact the appropriate office from the following list. Federal Law requires all vessels propelled by machinery (with the exception of racing vessels and tenders under 10 HP) to be registered with the state of principal use, if that state has an approved numbering system, or with the Coast Guard. A certificate of number will be issued upon registering the vessel. Federal Law requires the registration certificate to be on board whenever the boat is in use. When the boat is moved to a new State of principal use, the certificate is valid for 60 days.

NOTE: Some states require state registration in addition to Coast Guard Documentation.

State numbers must be painted or permanently attached to each side of the forward half of the vessel. The validation stickers must be affixed within six inches of the registration number. Check your state's instructions as to the exact position for the validation sticker. With the exception of the Recreational Vessel Fee sticker, no other letters or numbers may be displayed nearby.

The owner of a vessel must notify the agency which issued the certificate of number within 15 days if:

> The vessel is transferred, destroyed, abandoned, lost, stolen or recovered.
>
> The certificate of number is lost, destroyed or the owner's address changes.

If the certificate of number becomes invalid for any reason, it must be surrendered in the manner prescribed to the issuing authority within 15 days.

Some states have registration requirements that differ from or exceed the Coast Guard rules. Check with the state agency for any differences in your area.

ALABAMA
Marine Police Division
64 North Union Street
Montgomery, AL 36130
(205) 242-3679

ALASKA
The Coast Guard registers all boats in Alaska. The motor vehicle office will register boat trailers.
(907) 269-5511

ARIZONA
Arizona Game and Fish Department
2222 West Greenway Road
Phoenix, AZ 85023
(602) 942-3000

CALIFORNIA
Department of Motor Vehicles
P.O. Box 942869
Sacramento, CA 94269
(916) 657-7669

COLORADO
Colorado Division of Parks
P.O. Box 231
Littleton, CO 80160
(303) 791-1920

CONNECTICUT
Department of Motor Vehicles
60 State Street
Wethersfield, CT 06161
(203) 566-3781 Not open Mondays

DELAWARE
Division of Fish and Wildlife
Boat Registration Office
P.O. Box 1401
Dover, DE 19903
(302) 739-3498

DISTRICT OF COLUMBIA
Boat Registration
Metropolitan Police Department
550 Water Street SW
Washington, DC 20024
(202) 727-4582

FLORIDA
Department of Natural Resources
3900 Commonwealth Blvd.
Tallahassee, FL 32399
(904) 488-1195

GEORGIA
Department of Natural Resources
Boat Registration
2189 North Lake Parkway
Building 10, Suite 108
Tucker, GA 30084
(404) 493-5774

HAWAII
DLNR-BOR
79 South Nimitz Highway
Honolulu, HI 96813
(808) 587-1970

IDAHO
Idaho Department of Parks and Recreation
State House Mail
Boise, ID 83720
(208) 327-7444

ILLINOIS
Department of Conservation
Watercraft
P.O. 19226
Springfield, IL 62794
(217) 782-2138

INDIANA
Bureau of Motor Vehicles
100 North Senate Ave.
IGN 440
Indianapolis, IN 46204
(317) 232-2859

IOWA
Iowa Department of Natural Resources
Wallace Building
Des Moines, IO 50319
(515) 281-5267

KANSAS
Wildlife and Parks
Rt. 2, Box 54A
Pratt, KS 67124
(316) 672-5911

KENTUCKY
Division of Water Patrol
Department of Natural Resources
107 Mero Street
Frankfurt, KY 40601
(502) 564-2184

LOUISIANA
Department of Wildlife and Fisheries
P.O. Box 14796
Baton Rouge, LA 70898
(504) 765-2898

MAINE
Licensing Division
Department of Inland Fisheries and Wildlife
284 State Street, Station 41
Augusta, ME 04333
(207) 289-2043

MARYLAND
Department of Natural Resources
P.O. Box 1869
Annapolis, MD 21404
(410) 974-3219

MASSACHUSETTS
Division of Environmental Law Enforcement
100 Nashua Street
Boston, MA 02214
(617) 727-3900

MICHIGAN
Michigan Department of State
Direct Mail Unit
7064 Crowner Drive
Lansing, MI 48918
(517) 322-1473

MINNESOTA
Minnesota Department of Natural Resources
Licensing Bureau
500 Lafayette Road
St. Paul, MN 55155
(612) 296-6157

MISSISSIPPI
Wildlife Fisheries and Parks
Boat Registration Division
2906 North State Street
Jackson, MS 39216
(601) 364-2035

MISSOURI
Motor Vehicle Department
Truman Building
Room 370
301 West High Street
Jefferson City, MO 65105
(314) 751-4509

MONTANA
Title Registration Bureau
Motor Vehicle Division
Department of Justice
Deer Lodge, MT 59722
(406) 846-1423

NEBRASKA
Nebraska State Game and Parks Commission
Boating Division
P.O. Box 30370
Lincoln, NE 68503
(402) 471-5462

NEVADA
Nevada Department of Wildlife
1100 Valley Road
Reno, NV 89520
(702) 688-1511

NEW HAMPSHIRE
Department of Safety
Boat Desk
10 Hazen Drive
Concord, NH 03305
(603) 271-2251

NEW JERSEY
Motor Vehicles Service
1 SM Correspondence
CN 403
Trenton, NJ 08666
(609) 588-2424

NEW MEXICO
Department of Motor Vehicles
P.O. Box 1028
Santa Fe, NM 87504
(505) 827-2245

NEW YORK
Department of Motor Vehicles
P.O. Box 2650-ESP
Albany, NY 12220
(518) 473-5595

NORTH CAROLINA
WRC Boat Registration Section
Archdale Building
512 North Salisbury Street
Raleigh, NC 27604
(919) 662-4373

NORTH DAKOTA
Licensing Department
North Dakota State Game and Fish Department
100 North Bismarck Expressway
Bismarck, ND 58501
(701) 221-6300

OHIO
Division of Watercraft
1952 Belcher Drive C2
Columbus, OH 43224
(614) 265-6480

OKLAHOMA
Motor Vehicle Department
409 NE 28th Street
Oklahoma City, OK 73105
(405) 521-2437

OREGON
State Marine Board
435 Commercial Street NE
Salem, OR 97310
(503) 378-8587

PENNSYLVANIA
Pennsylvania Fish and Boat Commission
P.O. Box 1852
Harrisburg, PA 17105
(717) 657-4551

PUERTO RICO
Commissioner of Navigation
Department of Natural Resources
P.O. Box 5887
Puerto de Tierra Station
San Juan, PR 00906
(809) 724-2340

RHODE ISLAND
Division of Boating Safety
Office of Boating Registration and Licensing
22 Hayes Street
Providence, RI 02908
(401) 277-6647

SOUTH CAROLINA
Boat Titling and Registration
P.O. Box 167
Columbia, SC 29202
(803) 734-3857

SOUTH DAKOTA
Department of Motor Vehicles
118 West Capital Ave.
Pierre, SD 57501
(605) 773-3541

TENNESSEE
Tennessee Wildlife Resources Agency
P.O. Box 40747
Nashville, TN 37204
(615) 781-6522

TEXAS
Parks and Wildlife Department
4200 Smith School Rd.
Austin, TX 78744
(512) 389-4800

UTAH
Motor Vehicle Division
1095 Motor Avenue
Salt Lake City, UT 84116
(801) 538-8300

VERMONT
Vermont Department of Motor Vehicles
120 State Street
Montpelier, VT 05603
(802) 828-2000

VIRGIN ISLANDS
Boat Registration
Department of Planning and Natural Resources
231 Nisky Center
45A Estate Nisky
St. Thomas, VI 00802
(809) 774-3320

VIRGINIA
Department of Game and Inland Fisheries
4010 West Broad Street
Richmond, VA 23230
(804) 367-0939

WASHINGTON
Department of Licensing
Highway Licenses Building PB-01
Olympia, WA 98504
(206) 586-2183

WASHINGTON, DC see DISTRICT OF COLUMBIA
WEST VIRGINIA
Title and Registration Services
West Virginia Division of Motor Vehicles
Building 3, Room 113
1800 Kanawha Blvd. East
Charleston, WV 25317
(800) 642-9066 In State
(304) 558-3900 Out of State

WISCONSIN
Boat Registration
Department of Natural Resources
P.O. Box 7236
Madison, WI 53707
(608) 266-2621

WYOMING
Boat Registration
Game and Fish Department
Cheyenne, WY 82006
(307) 777-4597

DOCUMENTATION

Larger recreational vessels may be documented by the U.S. Coast Guard. A variety of measurements determine the "tonnage" of the vessel for documentation purposes. The vessel must measure a minimum of 5 net tons to be documented. This generally means a minimum length of about 30 feet.

The major advantage of documentation for most owners is the establishment of clear title to your boat. Many banks and lenders will require documentation before the loan will be issued. The document is also an internationally recognized proof of ownership and origin. This can smooth customs clearance in many foreign countries.

To obtain documentation you must make an application to one of the Documentation Offices listed later on. The application must be on Coast Guard forms filled out precisely as instructed. Forms include declaration of citizenship (for the owners), vessel measurements, builders certification, certificate of marking and a special bill of sale. It is highly advisable to fill out an official Coast Guard bill of sale whenever buying or selling a boat. Do this even if you are planning on obtaining state registration. If you later decide to obtain documentation, the official bill of sale will avoid having to recontact previous owners who may be hard to reach.

Your official number will have to be carved into a beam, or otherwise attached permanently to some interior part of your vessel. The number must be at least 3 inches high, in block letters and preceded by the abbreviation No.

The name of the vessel, and its hailing port must be marked together with letters not less than 4 inches high. Commercial vessels have similar requirements.

Bills of sale must be error free and notarized. They must be submitted in duplicate. The Coast Guard is notoriously finicky about perfection on these forms. Many private agencies provide documentation services for those desiring assistance in this exacting process.

Contact the documentation office nearest your homeport to obtain application forms and more information:

Vessel Documentation Office
U.S. Coast Guard
447 Commercial Street
Boston, MA 02109

Vessel Documentation Office
U.S. Coast Guard
Battery Park Building
Governors Island
New York, NY 10004

Vessel Documentation Office
U.S. Coast Guard
1 Washington Avenue
Philadelphia, PA 19147

Vessel Documentation Office
U.S. Coast Guard
Norfolk Federal Building
200 Granby Mall
Norfolk, VA 23510

Vessel Documentation Office
U.S. Coast Guard
Justice Building
155 South Miami Avenue
Miami, FL 33130

Vessel Documentation Office
U.S. Coast Guard
F. Edward Herbert Building
600 South Maestri Place
New Orleans, LA 70130

Vessel Documentation Office
U.S. Coast Guard
Suite 210
8876 Gulf Freeway
Houston, TX 77017

Vessel Documentation Office
U.S. Coast Guard
1240 East Ninth Street
Cleveland, OH 44199

Vessel Documentation Office
U.S. Coast Guard
Building 14
Coast Guard Island
Alameda, CA 94501

Vessel Documentation Office
U.S. Coast Guard
165 North Pico Avenue
Los Angeles, CA 90802

Vessel Documentation Office
U.S. Coast Guard
6767 North Basin Avenue
Portland, OR 97217

Vessel Documentation Office
U.S. Coast Guard
1519 Alaskan Way South
Seattle, WA 98134

Vessel Documentation Office
U.S. Coast Guard
2760 Sherwood Lane
Juneau, AK 99801

U.S. COAST GUARD SAFETY REQUIREMENTS

For complete details of Coast Guard required safety equipment refer to Chapter 13, Safety at Sea. In addition to emergency equipment all vessels must comply with the Navigation Rules with regard to navigation lights and sound signals. Refer to Chapters 1 and 2 for this information on the Rules of the Road. For information on FCC licensing requirements refer to Chapter 9, Communications.

The FCC now requires a Ship Station License for all vessels equipped with marine VHF, EPIRB, Radar, SSB or other transmitting equipment. CB radios alone do not require a Ship Station License. The Coast Guard is now checking for these licenses.

The operators of vessels 12m or more in length are responsible for having on board and maintaining a copy of the Inland Navigation Rules.

Your local Coast Guard Auxiliary is a volunteer organization dedicated to assisting the Coast Guard in promoting boating safety. They offer a free boat inspection called a Courtesy Marine Examination (CME). The CME requirements are at least as stringent as the Coast Guard's guidelines, and in many cases stricter. The examination is to promote safety - not for law enforcement purposes. If your boat passes the test you will receive a special Seal of Safety decal for display on your boat.

VESSEL BRIDGE-TO-BRIDGE RADIOTELEPHONE REGULATIONS

The vessel Bridge-to-Bridge Radiotelephone Act is applicable on navigable waters of the United States inside of the boundary lines established in 46 CFR 7. In all cases, the Act applies on waters subject to the three mile limit, depending on where the boundary lines are located. In no instance does the Act apply beyond the three mile limit.

§ 26·01 Purpose

(a) The purpose of this part is to implement the provisions of the Vessel Bridge-to-Bridge Radiotelephone Act. This part –

(1) Requires the use of the vessel bridge-to-bridge Radiotelephone;

(2) Provides the Coast Guard's interpretation of the meaning of important terms in the Act.

(3) Prescribes the procedures for applying for an exemption from the Act and the regulations issued under the Act and a listing of exemptions.

(b) Nothing in this part relieves any person form the obligation of complying with the rules of the road and the applicable pilot rules.

§ 26·02 Definitions

For the purpose of this part and interpreting the Act –

"Secretary" means the Secretary of the department in which the Coast Guard is operating;

"Act" means the "Vessel Bridge-to-Bridge Radiotelephone Act", 33 U.S.C. sections 1201-1208;

"Length" is measured from end to end over the deck excluding sheer;

"Power-driven vessel" means any vessel propelled by machinery; and

"Towing vessel" means any commercial vessel engaged in towing another vessel astern, alongside, or by pushing ahead.

§ 26·03 Radiotelephone required.

(a) Unless an exemption is granted under §26·09 and except as provided in paragraph (a)(4) of this section, this part applies to :

(1) Every power-driven vessel of 20 meters or over in length while navigating:

(2) Every vessel of 100 gross tons and upward carrying one or more passengers for hire while navigating;

(3) Every towing vessel of 26 feet or over in length while navigating; and

(4) Every dredge and floating plant engaged in or near a channel or fairway in operations likely to restrict or affect navigation of other vessels except for an unmanned or intermittently manned floating plant under the control of a dredge.

(b) Every vessel, dredge or floating plant described in paragraph (a) of this section must have a radiotelephone on board capable of operation from its navigational bridge, or in the case of a dredge, from its main control station, and capable of transmitting and receiving on the frequency or frequencies within the 156-162 Mega-Hertz band using the classes of emissions designated by the Federal Communications Commission for the exchange of navigational information.

(c) The radiotelephone required by paragraph (b) of this section must be carried on board the described vessels, dredges, and floating plants upon the navigable waters of the United States.

(d) The radiotelephone required by paragraph (b) of this section must be capable of transmitting and receiving on VHF FM channel 22A (157·1 MHz).

(e) While transiting any of the following waters, each vessel described in paragraph (a) of this section also must have on board a radiotelephone capable of transmitting and receiving on VHF FM channel 67 (156·375 MHz):

(1) The lower Mississippi River from the territorial sea boundary,and within either the Southwest Pass safety fairway or the South Pass safety fairway specified in 33 CFR 166·200, to mile 242·4 AHP (Above Head of Passes) near Baton Rouge:

(2) The Mississippi River – Gulf Outlet from the territorial sea boundary, and within the Mississippi River – Gulf Outlet safety fairway specified in 33 CFR 166·200, to that channel's junction with the Inner harbor Navigation Canal; and

(3) The full length of the Inner Harbor Navigation Canal from its junction with the Mississippi River to that canal's entry to Lake Pontchartrain at the New Seabrook vehicular bridge.

§ 26·04 Use of the designated frequency

(a) No person may use the frequency designated by the Federal Communications Commission under section 8 of the Act, 33 U.S.C. 1207(a), to transmit any information other than information necessary for the safe navigation of vessels or necessary tests.

(b) Each person who is required to maintain a listening watch under Section 5 of the Act shall, when necessary, transmit and confirm, on the designated frequency, the intentions of his vessel and any other information necessary for the safe navigation of vessels.

(c) Nothing in these regulations may be construed as prohibiting the use of the designated frequency to communicate with shore stations to obtain or furnish information necessary for the safe navigation of vessels.

(d) On navigable waters of the United States, channel 13 (156·65 MHz) is the designated frequency required to be monitored in accordance with §26·05(a) except that in the area prescribed in §26·03(e), channel 67 (156·375 MHz) is the designated frequency.

§ 26·05 Use of radiotelephone.

Section 5 of the Act states –

(a) The radiotelephone required by this Act is for the exclusive use of the master or person in charge to pilot or direct the movement of the vessel, who shall maintain a listening watch on the designated frequency. Nothing contained herin shall be interpreted as precluding the use of portable radiotelephone equipment to satisfy the requirements of this Act.

§ 26·06 Maintenance of radiotelephone; failure of radiotelephone.

Section 6 of the Act states –

(a) Whenever radiotelephone capability is required by this Act, a vessel's radiotelephone equipment shall be maintained in effective operating condition. If the radiotelephone equipment carried aboard a vessel ceases to operate, the master shall exercise due diligence to restore it or cause it to be restored to effective operating condition at the earliest practicable time. The failure of a vessel's radioelephone equipment shall not, in itself, constitute a violation of this Act, nor shall it obligate the master of any vessel to moor or anchor his vessel;however, the loss of radiotelephone capability shall be given consideration in the navigation of the vessel.

§ 26·07 English Language

No person may use the services of, and no person may serve a person required to maintain a listening watch under section 5 of the Act, 33 U.S.C. section 1204 unless he can speak the English language.

§ 26·08 Exemption procedures

(a) Any person may petition for an exemption from any provision of the Act or this part;

(b) Each petion must be submitted in writing to U.S. Coast Guard (G-N), 2100 Second Street, SW., Washington, D.C. 20593, and must state –

(1) The provisions of the Act or this part from which an exemption is requested; and

(2) The reasons why marine navigation will not be adversely affected if the exeption is granted and if the exemption releates to a local communication system how that system would fully comply with the intent of the concept of the Act but would not conform in detail if the exemption is granted.

§ 26·09 List of exemptions.

(a) All vessels navigating on those waters governed by the navigation rules for the Great Lakes and their connecting and tributary waters (33 U.S.C. 241 et seq.) are exempt from the requirements of the Vessel Bridge-to-Bridge Radiotelephone Act and this part until May 6, 1975.

(b) Each vessel navigating on the Great Lakes as defined in the Inland Navigation Rules Act of 1980 (33 U.S.C. 2001 et seq.) and to which the Vessel Bridge-to-Bridge Radiotelephone Act (33 U.S.C. 1201-1208) applies is exempt from the requirements in 33 U.S.C.1203, 1204, and 1205 and the regulations under §26·03, 26·05, 26·06, and 26·07. Eachof these vessels and each person to whom 33 U.S.C. 1208(a) applies must comply with Articles VII, X, XI, XII, XIII, XV, and XVI and Technical Regulations 1-9 of "The Agreement Between the United States of America and Canada for Promotion of Safety on the Great Lakes by Means of Radio, 1973."

§ 26·10 Penalties.

Section 9 of the Act states –

(a) Whoever, being the master or person in charge of a vessel subject to the Act, fails to enforce or comply with the Act or the regulations hereunder; or whoever, being designated by the master or person in charge of a vessel subject to the Act to pilot or direct the movement of a vessel fails to enforce or comply with the Act or the regulations hereunder – is liable to a civil penalty of not more than $500 to be assessed by the Secretary.

(b) Every vessel navigated in violation of the Act or the regulations hereunder is liable to a civil penalty of not more than $500 to be assessed by the Secretary, for which the vessel may be proceeded against in any District Court of the United States having jurisdiction.

(c) any penalty assessed under this section may be remitted or mitigated by the Secretary, upon such terms as he may deem proper.

CANADIAN VESSEL LICENSING

Every vessel principally maintained or operated in Canada must be licensed that has a motor exceeding 7.5 kW (about 10 HP), or a combination of motors exceeding 7.5 kW total. Owners may register any vessel voluntarily, even if it is not required by law to be registered. This would be wise if you are planning any trips outside of Canada with your boat. Foreign customs officials will want to see proof of ownership for the boat.

Pleasure vessels over 20 tons measurement must be measured by a government surveyor of ships. A special formula is used to compute registered tonnage. The tonnage of an open vessel under 5.5m in length shall be deemed not to exceed 5 tons.

A customs officer can provide the boat owner with the proper forms to apply for a license. The vessel will be issued with a license number which much be displayed in block characters not less than 75mm high, and in a color that contrasts with the background. The numbers should be displayed on each side of the bow, or on a board attached to each side of the bow. This number is a permanent number for the vessel and remains with it through any subsequent transfers of ownership.

A transfer form allows the license to be transferred to the new owner. Both parties must notify customs of this change, and a new license will be issued with the same number. All owners must be able to produce this license when requested by a peace officer.

For complete information on Canadian regulations order the publication Small Vessel Regulations (P218) from:

Hydrographic Chart Distribution Office
Department of Fisheries and Oceans
1675 Russell Road
P.O. Box 8080
Ottawa, Ontario, Canada K1G 3H6
(613) 998-4931, 4932, 4933
FAX (613) 998-1217

CANADIAN SAFETY REGULATIONS

Canada has stricter equipment requirements than the United States. For complete information on these regulations order the publication Small Vessel Regulations as mentioned previously. We give here a short description of the basic requirements:

Vessels not over 5.5m in length

1) One approved small vessel lifejacket, or approved flotation device for each person aboard.

2) Two oars and oarlocks, or two paddles.

3) One bailer, or one manual pump.

4) If equipped with an inboard motor, permanent fuel tanks or a stove using liquid or gaseous fuel, one Class BI fire extinguisher.

Vessels over 5.5m, but not over 8m in length

1) One approved small vessel lifejacket, or approved flotation device for each person aboard.

2) Two oars and oarlocks, or two paddles, or one anchor with not less than 15m of cable, rope or chain.

3) One bailer, or one manual pump.

4) If equipped with an inboard motor, permanent fuel tanks or a stove using liquid or gaseous fuel, one Class BI fire extinguisher.

5) One approved throwable device. Either a cushion, a buoyant heaving line, or an approved lifebuoy.

Vessels over 8m, but not over 12m in length

1) One approved small vessel lifejacket for each person aboard.

2) One approved lifebuoy.

3) One approved buoyant heaving line not less than 15m in length.

4) One bailer and one manual or power-driven bilge pump.

5) 12 pyrotechnic distress signals in a waterproof container, not more than 6 may be daytime smoke signals.

6) One anchor with not less than 15m of cable, rope or chain.

7) If equipped with an inboard motor, permanent fuel tanks or a stove using liquid or gaseous fuel, one Class BI fire extinguisher.

8) Proper lights and sound signaling apparatus to comply with the International Rules of the Road (see Chapter 2).

Sailing vessels that have no enclosed cabin with sleeping facilities, and are under 12m in length, may carry an approved personal flotation device in lieu of the lifejackets described in 1 above.

Vessels over 12m, but not over 20m in length

1) One approved standard lifejacket, or one small vessel lifejacket for each person aboard.

2) One approved 762mm lifebuoy, or two 610mm lifebuoys.

3) One approved buoyant heaving line not less than 15m in length.

4) Six pyrotechnic signals of any type, and six signals of type A, B or C.

5) One anchor with not less than 15m of cable, rope or chain.

6) Two fire buckets.

7) Either a manual pumped, or powered fire hose located outside the machinery spaces, or 2 Class B II fire extinguishers. One of the extinguishers must be located near the entrance to the accommodation space, and the other near the entrance to the machinery space.

8) Efficient bilge pumping arrangements.

9) If equipped with an inboard motor, permanent fuel tanks or a stove using liquid or gaseous fuel, one Class BII fire extinguisher.

10) One fire axe.

11) Proper lights and sound signaling apparatus to comply with the International Rules of the Road (see Chapter 2).

Vessels over 20m in length

1) One approved standard lifejacket, or one small vessel lifejacket for each person aboard.

2) Two approved 762mm lifebuoys, one with an automatic light.

3) One buoyant heaving line not less than 27.5m in length.

4) Six pyrotechnic signals of any type, and six signals of type A, B or C.

5) One anchor with not less than 15m of cable, rope or chain.

6) Four fire buckets.

7) Two fire axes.

8) One power driven fire hose located outside the machinery spaces.

9) Efficient bilge pumping arrangements.

10) In each accommodation space one Class A II fire extinguisher (maximum of three need be carried).

11) In the machinery space two Class B II fire extinguishers, with one located near the entrance.

12) Proper lights and sound signaling apparatus to comply with the International Rules of the Road (see Chapter 2).

Racing type vessels have somewhat less stringent requirements when actively engaged in a race.

Other regulations govern construction rules, power and capacity plates for motor vessels and lighting requirements. The regulations contain specifications for pyrotechnic devices and fire extinguishers.

RECREATIONAL VESSEL FEE

The Omnibus Budget Reconciliation Act of 1990 requires owners of recreational boats longer than 16 feet operated on certain navigable U.S. waters to pay an annual fee. Owners of vessels covered by the law are required to display a valid set of decals indicating the annual fee has been paid.

President Bush signed a repeal of this law in the fall of 1992. The fees will be phased out through 1994. As of 1992, boats under 21 feet no longer need a decal. In October 1993 boats 37 feet and under will be exempt. In October 1994 all boats will be exempt.

For 1993 the fees are as follows:

$35.00 for vessels over 21 feet, but less than 27 feet

$50.00 for vessels at least 27 feet, but less than 40 feet

$100.00 for vessels 40 feet or longer

The decals must be securely attached within 6 inches of the vessel's registration number, or where such a number would be located on a documented vessel.

The fee does not apply to the following vessels:

Vessels under 16 feet long.

Public vessels.

Sailboards and seaplanes.

Manually propelled vessels like canoes, kayaks and row boats.

Foreign vessels operated less than 30 days a calendar year in the U.S.

Vessel tenders or life boats (less than 10 HP) for numbered or documented vessels used only for transportation between that vessel and shore, and for no other purpose.

Unpowered barges or houseboats normally moored or at anchor.

Vessels owned by charitable nonprofit organizations specified by regulation.

Rescue vessels owned by fire departments, etc.

Decals are issued annually and are valid until December 31st for the year purchased. To obtain an application, or to purchase a decal using your Visa or MasterCard, call (800) 848-2100. Mail applications may be sent to:

U.S. RVF
P.O. Box 740169
Atlanta, GA 30321

There is a civil penalty for failure to display the proper decals. The Coast Guard has been inspecting RVF stickers during routine boardings and inspections. For further information concerning the vessel fee, call the Boating Safety Hotline (800) 368-5647.

POLLUTION REGULATIONS

The Refuse Act of 1899 prohibits throwing, discharging or depositing any refuse matter of any kind (including trash, garbage, oil and other liquid pollutants) into the waters of the United States.

The Federal Water Pollution Control Act prohibits the discharge of oil or hazardous substances which may be harmful into U.S. navigable waters. Vessels 26 feet in length and over must display a placard at least 5 by 8 inches, made of durable material, fixed in a conspicuous place in the machinery spaces, or at the bilge pump control station, stating the following:

Discharge of Oil Prohibited

The Federal Water Pollution Control Act prohibits the discharge of oil or oily waste into or upon the navigable waters of the United States or the waters of the contiguous zone if such discharge causes a film or sheen upon, or discoloration of, the surface of the water, or causes a sludge or emulsion beneath the surface of the water. Violators are subject to a penalty of $5,000.

You must have the capacity to retain oily wastes on board. No person may intentionally drain these wastes into the bilge.

If you discharge oil or hazardous substances you must immediately notify the Coast Guard at (800) 424-8802 (in Washington, DC at 202-267-2675).

The Act to Prevent Pollution from Ships (MARPOL ANNEX V) places limitations on the discharge of garbage from vessels. It is illegal to dump plastic trash anywhere in the ocean or navigable waters of the United States. It is also illegal to discharge garbage in the navigable waters of the United States, including the Great Lakes. The discharge of other types of garbage is permitted outside of specific distances offshore as determined by the nature of the garbage.

U.S. vessels 26 feet or longer must display in a prominent location, a durable placard at least 4 by 9 inches notifying the crew and passengers of the discharge restrictions.

U.S. vessels of 40 feet or more in length which are engaged in commerce, or are equipped with a galley and berthing must have a written Waste Management Plan describing the procedures for collecting, processing, storing and discharging garbage.

A designated person must be in charge of carrying out the plan.

MARPOL ANNEX V

1) Plastics including synthetic ropes, fishing nets and plastic bags may not be discharged in any area.

2) Floating dunnage, lining and packing materials may not be discharged less than 25 miles from the nearest land.

3) Food waste, paper, rags, glass, metal, bottles, crockery and similar refuse may not be discharged less than 12 miles from the nearest land.

4) Comminuted or ground food waste, paper, rags, glass etc. may not be discharged less than 3 miles from the nearest land.

MARINE SANITATION DEVICES

All recreational boats with installed toilet facilities must have an operable marine sanitation device (MSD) on board. Vessels 65 feet and under may use a Type I, II or III MSD. Vessels over 65 feet must install a Type II or III MSD. All MSDs must be Coast Guard certified.

Type I and II MSDs are flow-through treatment systems that treat the sewage using, chemical, electrical and/or incineration methods before discharging the waste overboard. A Type II MSD treats the sewage more completely than a Type I. If you have this type of treatment system avoid discharging when in shallow water, near shellfish beds, in confined harbors or near bathing areas.

Type III MSDs are holding tanks for storing the sewage aboard the boat. The tank may be discharged outside of the 3 mile U.S. territorial limit. Within the limit, or in no-discharge zones, the tank must be emptied at a shoreside pumpout station. When within the limit, the handle of the discharge valve should be removed or padlocked in the closed position to prevent unauthorized use.

COAST GUARD BOARDINGS

The United States Coast Guard may hail your vessel while underway, and you must heave to, or maneuver in a manner allowing a Coast Guard boarding officer to come aboard. Other Federal, State and local law enforcement authorities can also board and examine your vessel.

Unfortunately, the war on drugs has lead to the increased likelihood of boarding in many places. In addition, the Coast Guard conducts routine inspections as part of its normal operating procedures. They do not need a search warrant, or in fact any reason whatsoever - so be prepared to be boarded!

Usually the Coast Guard vessel will approach your boat close enough to alert you to the fact they want to inspect you. A rotating blue (police type) light indicates a law enforcement craft. If you have not had your radio turned on, you should do so now. Monitor channel 16 for messages from the Coast Guard vessel. They will ask you to switch to a working channel. If you are alone, be careful to set your autopilot or lock your wheel if you must leave the helm to use the radio. Some autopilots act erratically when a radio is used nearby. You should maintain your course and speed until requested to do otherwise by the Coast Guard. Do not slow down, or change course suddenly!

You will usually be asked several questions such as your registration number, your next port of call, the number of passengers aboard and your home address. They will ask if you have any firearms aboard. This may be the end of your encounter, or it may be the beginning of a boarding. Needless to say, a cooperative and polite attitude is helpful.

If you are to be boarded you will be instructed exactly what to do. The Coast Guard will suggest a course of action. If you feel this may endanger your vessel or your passengers, discuss your reservations immediately. The Coast Guard will be very receptive to your suggestions. On the other hand, they have conducted many boardings and are very experienced in the procedure. You will usually be instructed to simply maintain a steady course and speed.

In calm coastal waters the Coast Guard vessel may simply approach your stern so the boarding officers can step across onto your boat. All loose items should be cleared from the decks and the officers alerted to faulty lifelines, weak stanchions or antennas that should not be grabbed. The boarding officers will have on appropriate foot gear and lifejackets. Most of the crew should stay clear of the boarding area, but it is wise to have one strong person ready to assist if needed.

If you must go on deck to assist the boarding, wear a lifejacket and safety harness if available.

In rough seas or offshore waters the boarding will usually be accomplished by using a large inflatable boat, or hard-bottomed inflatable. They may be able to simply pull alongside and step aboard. If your boat has unusually high freeboard, the stern may again be the best boarding place. Do not hold onto the Coast Guard boat! The boats are very heavy and can cause injury or even pull you overboard. The boarding party's boat will not be tied off to your boat.

Once aboard, the formalities proceed swiftly. An officer will ask the captain a series of questions on the vessel's safety equipment, radio licenses and registration or documentation. The appropriate documents and equipment will be examined. A standard form and checklist is used to speed the process. At the end of the procedure you will be given a copy of this form which will detail the time, location and personnel involved. If all goes well, you may get a "Very Cooperative" in the comments area!

LAW ENFORCEMENT

The Coast Guard may impose a civil penalty up to $1,000 for failure to comply with equipment requirements, for failure to report a boating accident, or for failure to comply with other Federal regulations. Failure to comply with the Inland Navigation Rules Act of 1980 can result in a civil penalty of up to $5,000.

Improper use of a radiotelephone is a criminal offense. The use of obscene, indecent or profane language during radio communications is punishable by a $10,000 fine, imprisonment for two years or both. Other penalties exist for misuse of a radio, such as improper use of channel 16 on a VHF radio.

Operating a boat while intoxicated became a Federal offense on January 13, 1988. If the blood alcohol level is .10% (.08% in some States) or higher violators are subject to a civil penalty of up to $1,000, or a criminal penalty of up to $5,000, 1 year of imprisonment, or both.

The Coast Guard may impose a civil penalty for Negligent or Grossly Negligent Operation of a vessel which endangers lives and/or property. Grossly Negligent Operation is a criminal offense with fines up to $5,000, imprisonment for one year, or both. Examples of Grossly Negligent Operation include:

- Operating a boat in a swimming area
- Operating a boat under the influence of alcohol or drugs
- Speeding near other boats or in dangerous waters
- Hazardous water skiing practices
- Bowriding, riding on seatback, riding on gunwale, riding on transom

The Coast Guard can terminate a voyage if they feel a boat is being operated in an unsafe condition, or if an especially hazardous condition exists. You may be directed to port, or told to immediately correct the hazardous situation. Your voyage may be terminated if it is declared a "Manifestly Unsafe Voyage". This is the catch all that can be used whenever the Coast Guard feels you are operating in an unsafe manner.

An operator who refuses to terminate the unsafe use of a vessel can be cited for failure to comply with the directions of a Coast Guard officer. Violators may be fined up to $1,000, imprisoned for one year, or both.

REPORTING ACCIDENTS

A formal report must be filed with the law enforcement authorities in the state where an accident occurred if more than $500.00 of damage is done, or a vessel is lost. You have 10 days to file a report.

In the case of fatal accidents you must notify the authorities immediately. If a person has died or disappeared you must provide officials with the following information:

- Date, time and exact location of the accident
- Name of the person (or persons) involved
- Number and name of the vessel
- Name and address of the owner and operator

In an accident with injuries requiring more than first aid, a formal report must be filed within 48 hours.

RENDERING ASSISTANCE

The master of a vessel is obligated by law to provide assistance to any person in danger at sea. The master is subject to a fine and/or imprisonment for failure to do so. Many boaters refer to this great tradition as "The Law of the Sea".

BASIC NAVIGATION

5

Page

BASIC NAVIGATION

The widespread use of position fixing systems such as Loran and G.P.S. make the work of the navigator very easy. It is tempting to rely entirely on this method but very unwise – instruments are fallible and it is essential for the navigator to understand the basic principles of navigation.

The primary object of this section is to act as a general *aide memoire* for the inexperienced navigator, with the hope that the more experienced one may find it useful at times.

The essence of good navigation in small ships is adequate preparation before the start of the voyage, careful observation and recording, thus enabling the dead reckoning to be kept up to date at regular intervals.

THE NAVIGATOR'S EQUIPMENT

The following list should be regarded as the minimum for navigation.

Charts

The basic essential for navigation – dealt with more fully later.

Current Charts

Available from all good chart agents, various editions for different areas give hour by hour diagrams of current direction and strength. Extremely useful for the small ship navigator.

Sailing Directions and Coast Pilots

Many available, issued by the various hydrographic offices, and many commercially published ones. Highly desirable for reading before a trip into unfamiliar waters and should be available on passage.

Reed's Nautical Almanac

Is essential to provide all the information required relating to tides, lights, buoys, radio aids and navigational tables, etc.

Ship's Log Book

It is important to record all the information relating to the navigation of the ship as well as the D.R. position on the chart. A ship's position about which the navigator is subsequently doubtful can thus be rechecked if the facts and calculations are readily available. It is customary to keep a rough or "deck" log, entering it up in the ship's log at the end of the day or other suitable interval. Reed's Log Book embodies preplanning sheets which enable important information to be readily available.

Dividers and Pencil Compasses

Essential for chart work.

Parallel Ruler or Patent Protractor

The traditional instrument for laying off courses on the chart is the parallel ruler, but for small ship navigation where motion may be violent and space restricted the patent protractor is more convenient with less chance of error. The patent protractor consists of a compass rose on a transparent base with a rotating arm which permits a course to be read or laid off without reference to the chart rose.

Chart Magnifier

An illuminated chart magnifier can be extremely useful for reading fine detail on a chart under difficult conditions.

Clock

A good marine clock is a useful item of equipment as is a stopwatch for timing the frequency of lights.

Barometer

A good marine barometer is necessary to maintain a check on the weather situation. Remember that marine forecasts are invaluable in that they cover a large area – it is useful and it may be vital to know the trend of pressure locally.

Compass

A good compass is an essential piece of equipment in any vessel. A particularly useful type for small vessels with possible inexperienced helmsmen is the grid compass. In this type the compass bowl is surmounted by a plastic plate with an annular ring marked with 0-360°. The course is set by rotating the annular ring on to the desired heading and the helmsman then keeps the N-S line on the compass card parallel to two lines engraved on the plastic grid. This renders the helmsman's task much easier, especially at night and when fatigue sets in.

A small hand bearing compass is invaluable for position fixing from fixed objects and lights.

Patent Log

A towed or hull fitted log will help immeasurably with the dead reckoning calculations.

Pocket Calculators

Useful for rapid calculations. The scientific type, programmed for calculating SIN, COS and TAN are especially useful in navigation provided the navigator understands the fundamentals involved.

Depth Sounder

Apart from the useful ability to predict when the ship is likely to run aground, the electronic depth sounder is a very useful aid to navigation, especially in fog.

Sextant

Not an essential item of equipment for the coastal navigator but useful for measuring horizontal and vertical angles for fixing positions. Dealt with more fully later.

Radio Aids

A radio set for weather forecasts is really essential. R.D.F. sets are of considerable assistance to navigators but should never be relied on to the exclusion of normal navigation methods.

THE CHART

The chart is obviously the key piece of equipment required by the navigator and should be treated as such and kept up to date.

Notices to Mariners are issued weekly and can be obtained from chart agents or directly from the Coast Guard.

This weekly notice contains navigational warnings – amendments to dangerous areas, corrections to Lists of Lights, fog signals, radio signals and any important navigational alterations or additions necessary to safe navigation.

The navigator should always carry a number of charts to cover the area of the projected voyage, together with those necessary to cover any area to which the vessel may be driven by reason of bad weather. In the case of a fairly lengthy trip, one small scale passage chart to cover the whole trip is required together with larger scale charts covering the coastline and port approaches.

TYPES OF CHARTS AND DETAILS

There are basically two different types of navigational chart, the difference being in the method of construction or "projection". These two projections are called the Mercator and the Gnomonic projections, the latter being used for large scale charts covering small areas. From the small ship navigator's point of view, the projection has no practical significance in coastal navigation.

The National Ocean Service produces chart catalogs showing what charts are available for U.S. coasts, islands, and the Great Lakes. These catalogs give the names and addresses of local chart agents.

In addition to navigational charts, charts for special purposes such as Loran charts are also issued. Various other specialised charts such as Tidal Current Charts and Marine Weather Services charts are also available.

Compass Rose

Compass Roses have inner and outer circles covering 0°-360°. The outer ring gives true north, while the inner ring shows magnetic headings. In the center of the rose is printed the local magnetic variation and its annual change.

To obtain Local Notices to Mariners contact the Coast Guard at the following addresses:

Commander, First Coast Guard District
(ME to Toms River,NJ)
Aids to Navigation Office
408 Atlantic Avenue
Boston, MA 02110
(617) 223-8338

Commander, Fifth Coast Guard District
(Toms River, NJ to NC)
Aids to Navigation Office
431 Crawford Street
Portsmouth, VA 23704
(804) 398-6223

Commander, Seventh Coast Guard District
(SC to St. Marks River, FL including PR and VI)
Aids to Navigation Office
909 SE 1st Avenue
Miami, FL 33131
(305) 536-5621

Commander, Eight Coast Guard District
(FL from St. Marks River west to Texas)
Aids to Navigation Office
501 Magazine Street
New Orleans, LA 70130
(504) 589-6234

Commander Second Coast Guard District
(MS River System, portions of the Tombigbee and the Illinois River
Aids to Navigation Office
1222 Spruce Street
St Louis, MO 63103
(314) 539-3714

Commander Ninth Coast Guard District
(The Great Lakes and St. Lawrence River)
Aids to Navigation Office
1240 East Ninth Street
Cleveland, OH 44199
(216) 522-3991

Commander Eleventh Coast Guard District
(California)
Aids to Navigation Office
400 Oceangate Blvd.
Long Beach, CA 90822
(310) 499-5410

Commander Thirteenth Coast Guard District
(OR, WA, ID, MT)
Aids to Navigation Office
915 Second Avenue
Seattle, WA 98174
(206) 553-5864

Commander Fourteenth Coast Guard District
(HI, American Samoa, Marshall, Marianas, Caroline Islands and Subic Bay, Phillipines)
Aids to Navigation Office
300 Ala Moana Blvd.
Honolulu, HI 96850
(808) 541-2316

Commander Seventeenth Coast Guard District
(Alaska)
Aids to Navigation Office
P.O. Box 25517
Juneau, AK 99802
(907) 463-2245

To obtain Notices to Mariners for areas outside the United States contact:

Director Defense Mapping Agency
Combat Support Center
Attn: PMSS
6001 MacArthur Blvd.
Bethersda, MD 20816
(301) 227-2426

To obtain Canadian Notices to Mariners contact:

Director General
Aids and Waterways
Canadian Coast Guard
Transport Canada
Ottawa, Canada K1A 0N7

Depths

All depths are given below Chart Datum and the units are stated under the title. In places where there is no appreciable tide, depths are given below sea level.

On metric charts depths are given in whole meters, shallow depths are given in meters and decimeters – e.g., 5_3 which means 5.3 meters.

Heights

Heights, other than drying heights are given in feet above Chart Datum, except in places where there is no appreciable tide, in such cases heights are referred to sea level.

Drying Heights are given in feet above Chart Datum and underlined, thus $\underline{1}$, $\underline{4}$,etc. Should there be insufficient space for printing the figures in the drying area, such height may be stated alongside the area; e.g., *"Dries 4 feet."*

Depth Contours

Depth contours are drawn in fine firm lines, broken in places where there are figures indicating the depth.

Vertical Clearances

Vertical clearances (under bridges, etc.) are given in feet, the figures are printed between two lines like this $\overline{\underline{20}}$.

Horizontal Clearances

Horizontal clearance between bridge abutments etc, are listed in feet between two vertical lines like this |30|.

Submerged Wrecks

Sounded or swept depths over wrecks are given in feet or fathoms.

Tints and Colours

The land tint is buff and drying areas are green, but vary on other nationality charts. Blue tints are used to show shallow water. White indicates deeper water.

CHART SYMBOLS

For a full understanding of all symbols used in NOAA charts, reference should be made to Chart No. 1 now published in book form. This gives full details of every symbol and abbreviation used and should be included in the equipment of everyone who takes their navigation seriously. Some useful chart symbols and abbreviations are included in this section. Charts of other nationalities may have varying symbols and the appropriate key should always be consulted.

CULTURAL FEATURES

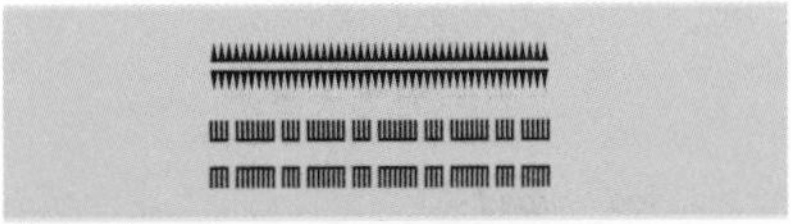

Embankment

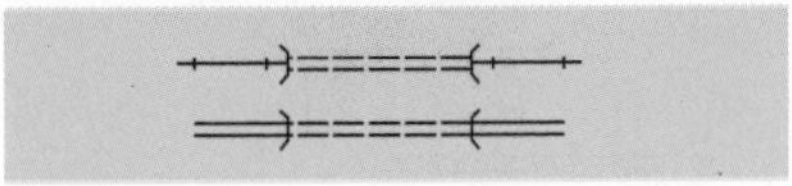

Tunnel

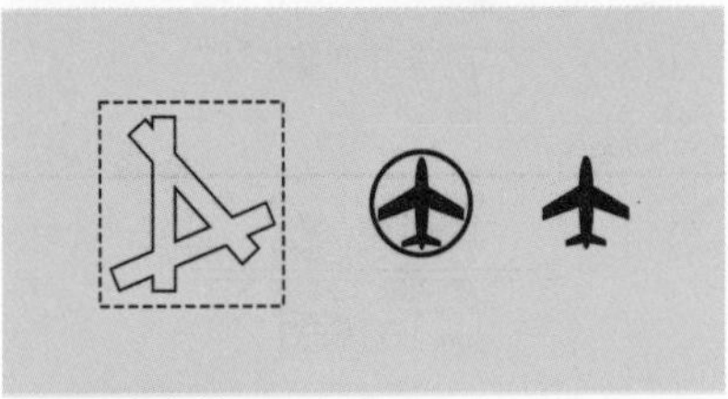

Airport, Airfield

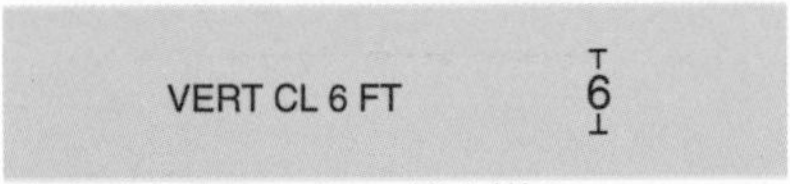

Vertical clearance above High Water

Horizontal clearance

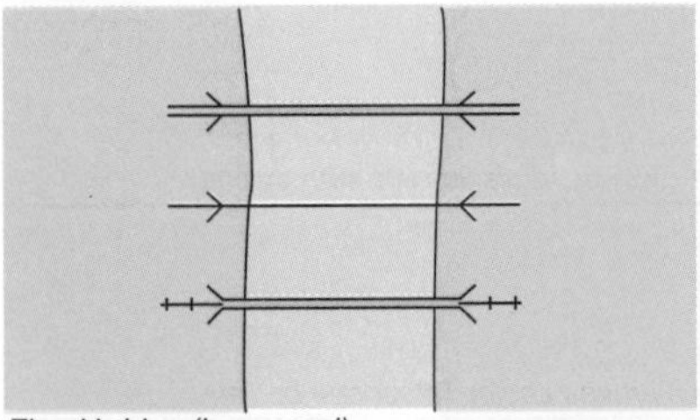

Fixed bridge (in general)

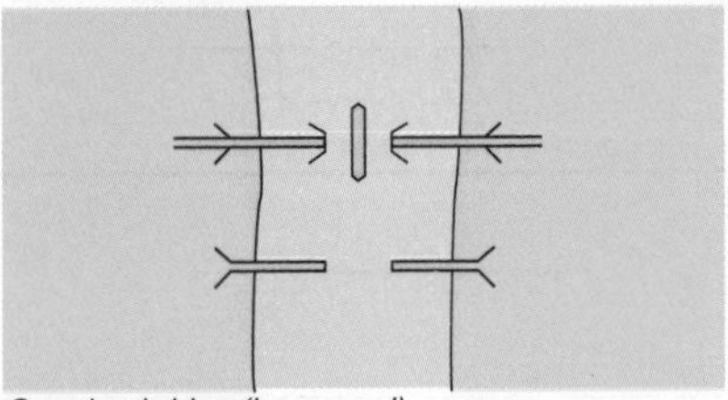

Opening bridge (in general)

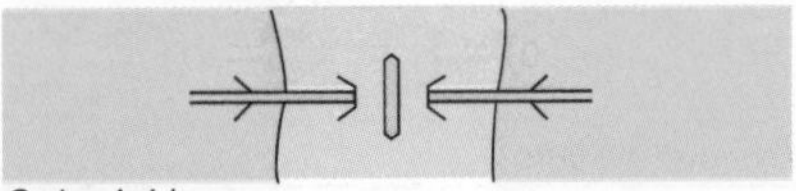

Swing bridge

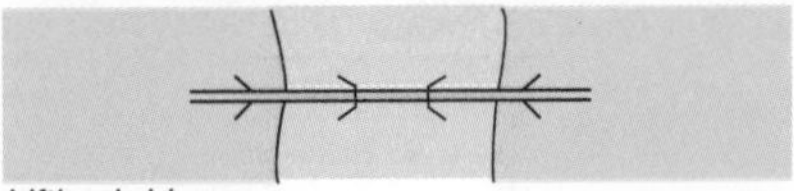

Lifting bridge

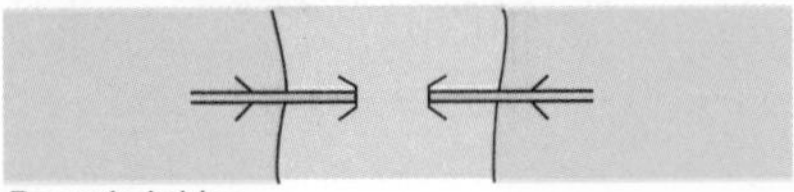

Bascule bridge

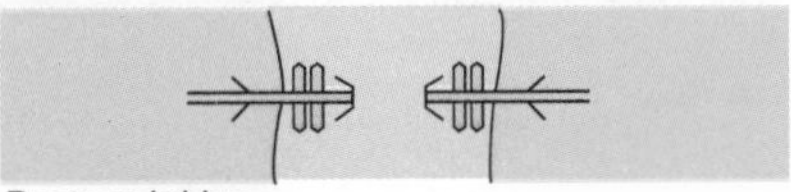

Pontoon bridge

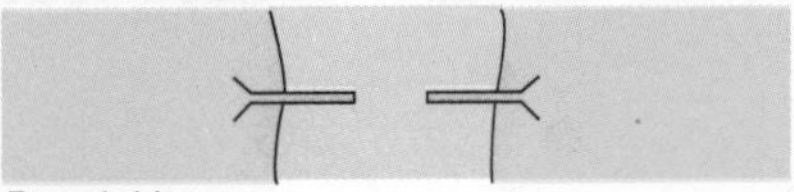

Draw bridge

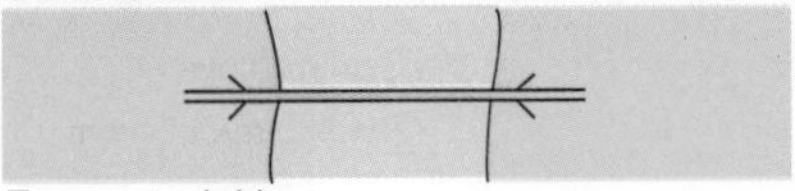

Transporter bridge

CULTURAL FEATURES AND LANDMARKS

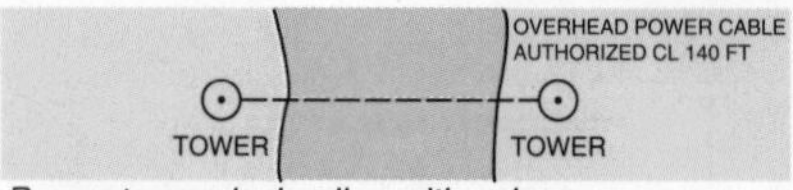

Power transmission line with pylons

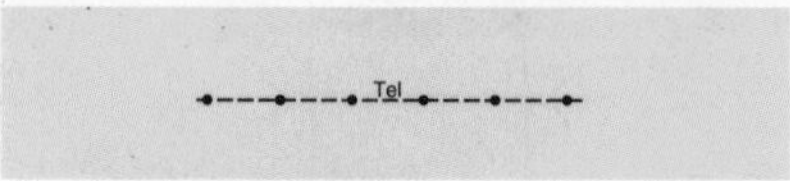

Overhead cable, Telephone or Telegraph line

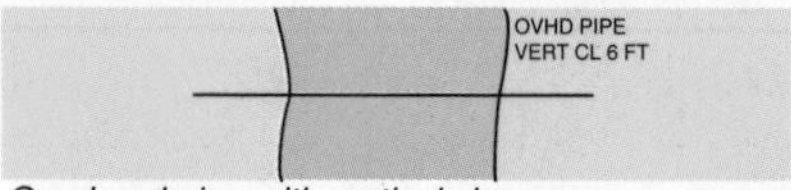

Overhead pipe with vertical clearance

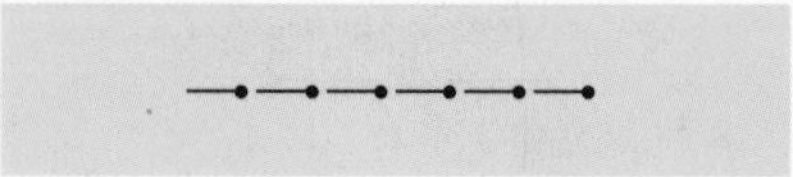

Pipeline on land

Highway markers

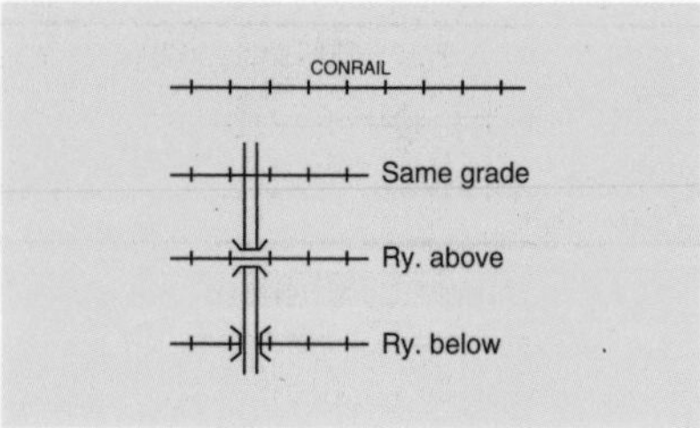

Railway (Ry) (single or double track) Railroad (RR)

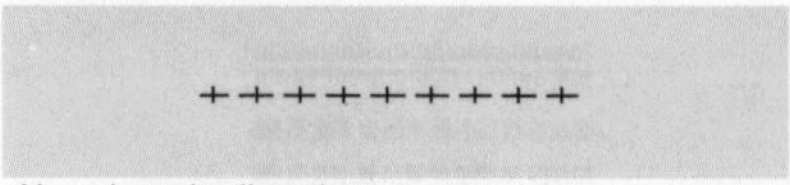

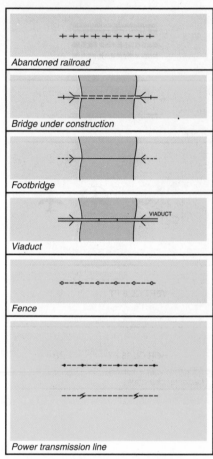

Abandoned railroad

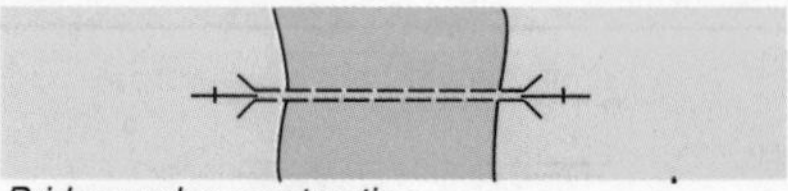

Bridge under construction

Footbridge

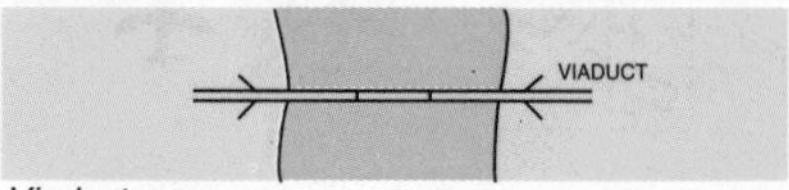

Viaduct

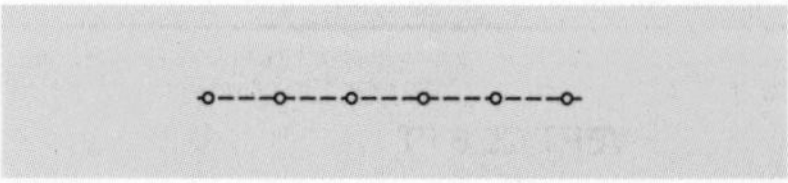

Fence

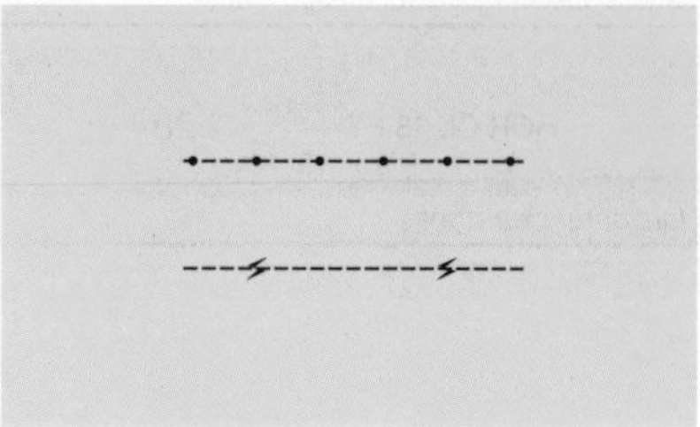

Power transmission line

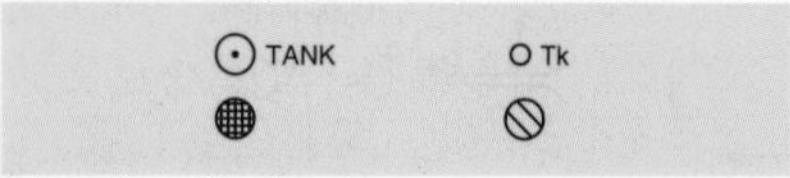

Examples of landmarks

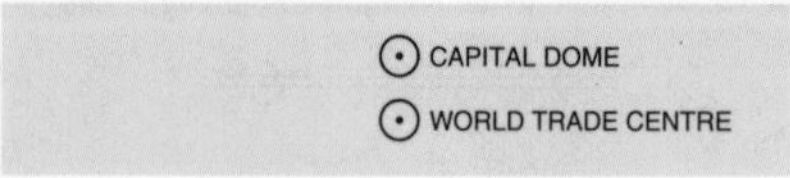

Examples of conspicuous landmarks

Height of structure above ground level

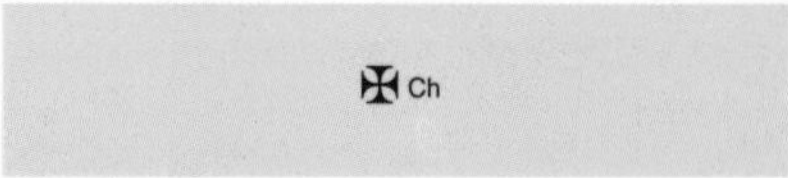

Church

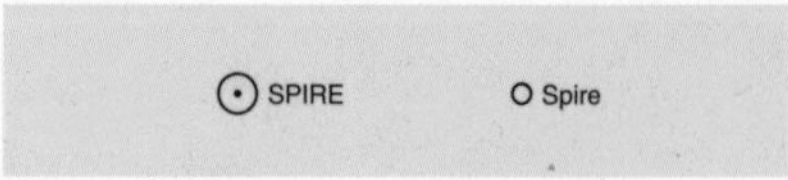

Church Spire

Church Cupola

DEPTHS

ED

Existance doubtful

SD

Sounding doubtful

Rep

Reported, but not surveyed

(3) *Rep (1983)*

Reported with year of report, but not surveyed

(3) *Rep*

Reported but not confirmed sounding or danger

19 8_2 $7\frac{3}{4}$ 8_2 19

Sounding in true position (Upright soundings are used on English unit charts and Sloping soundings are used on Metric charts)

(23) . —1036

Sounding out of position

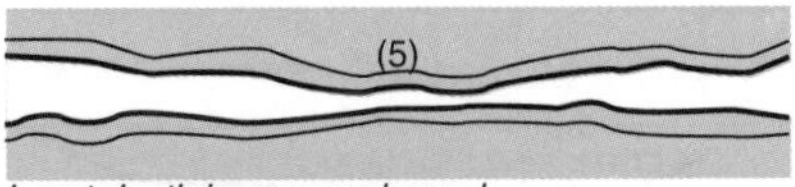

Least depth in narrow channel

$\dot{\overline{65}}$

No bottom found at depth shown

8_2 19 8_2 19

Soundings which are unreliable or taken from a smaller-scale source (Upright soundings are used on English unit charts and Sloping soundings are used on Metric charts)

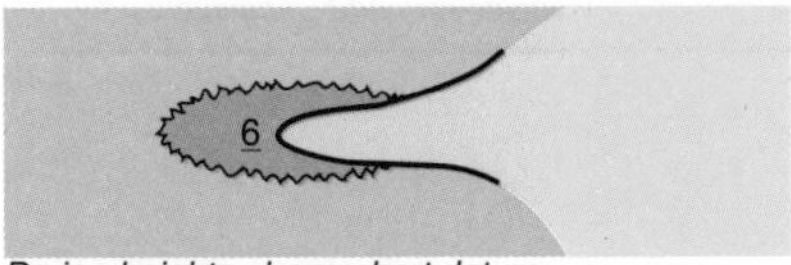

Drying heights above chart datum

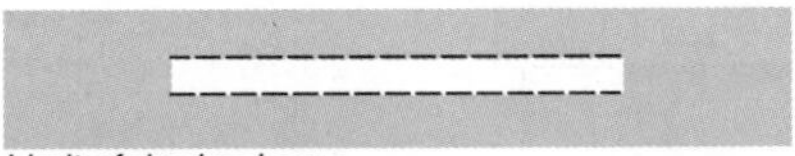

Limit of dredged area

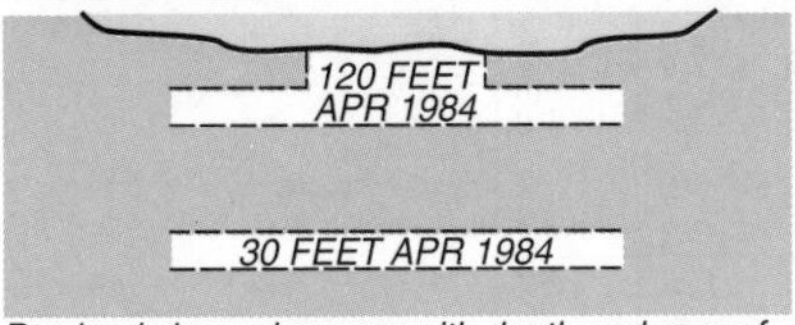

Dredged channel or area with depth and year of the latest control survey

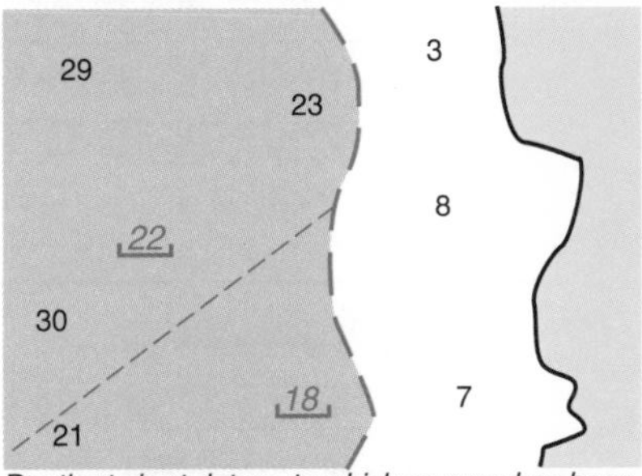

Depth at chart datum, to which an area has been swept by wire drag. The latest date of sweeping may be shown in parentheses

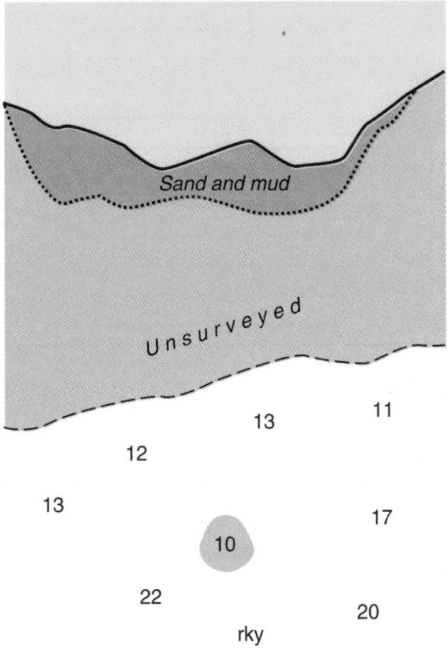

Unsurveyed or inadequately surveyed area; area with inadequate depth information

DEPTHS/NATURE OF SEABED

Feet	Fm/Mtrs
0	0
6	1
12	2
18	3
24	4
30	5
36	6
60	10
120	20
180	30
240	40
300	50
600	100
1,200	200
1,800	300
2,400	400
3,000	500
6,000	1,000

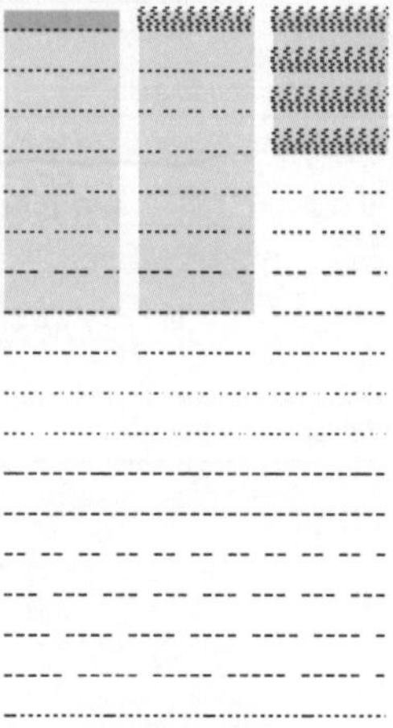

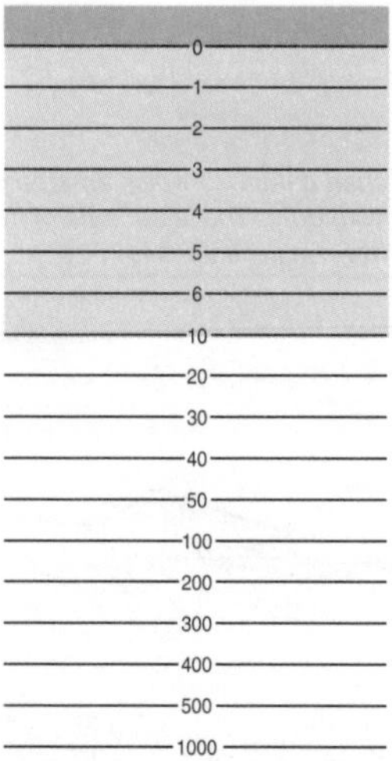

Approximate depth contour

5 *(blue or black)* **100**

Continuous lines, with values

NOTE
The extent of the blue tint varies with the scale and purpose of the chart, or its sources.
On some charts, contours and figures are printed in blue.

S	*Sand*
M	*Mud*
Cy;Cl	*Clay*
Si	*Silt*
St	*Stones*
G	*Gravel*
P	*Pebbles*
Cb	*Cobbles*
Rk; Rky	*Rock; Rocky*
Co	*Coral and Coralline algae*
Sh	*Shells*
S/M	*Two layers, eg. Sand over mud*
Wd	*Weed (including Kelp)*
 *Kelp*	*Kelp, Seaweed*
 *Sandwaves*	*Mobile bottom (sand waves)*
 *Spring*	*Freshwater springs in seabed*

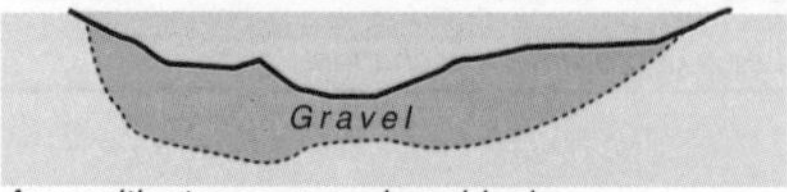

Area with stones, gravel or shingle

Rocky area, which covers and uncovers

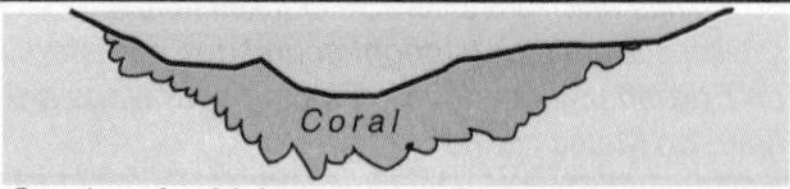

Coral reef, which covers and uncovers

LIGHTS/BUOYS BEACONS

Major light, minor light, light, lighthouse

Lighted offshore platform

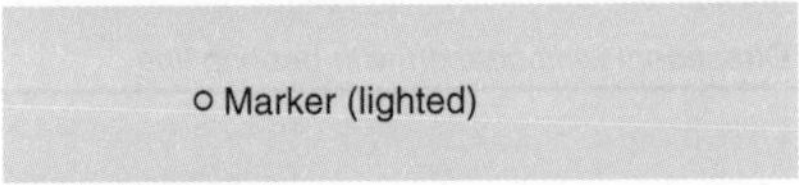

Lighted beacon tower

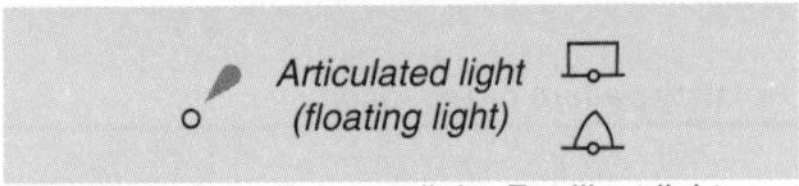

Articulated light, Buoyant light, Resilient light

Light vessel; Lightship; Manned light-vesel

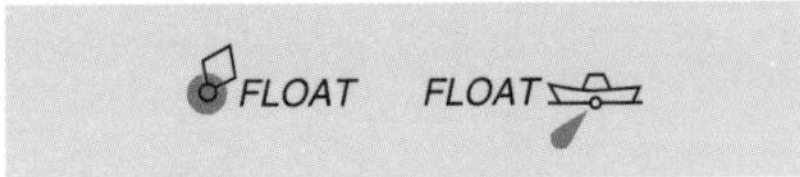

Unmanned light-vessel; light float

LANBY, superbuoy as navigational aid

Conical buoy, nun buoy

Can or cylindrical buoy

Spherical buoy

Pillar buoy

Spar buoy, spindle buoy

Barrel buoy

Super buoy

Light float as part of IALA System

Mooring bouys

Light mooring buoy (Example)

RADAR, RADIO, ELECTRONIC POSITION-FIXING SYSTEMS

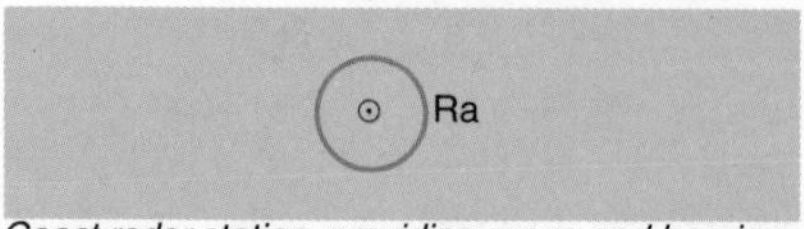

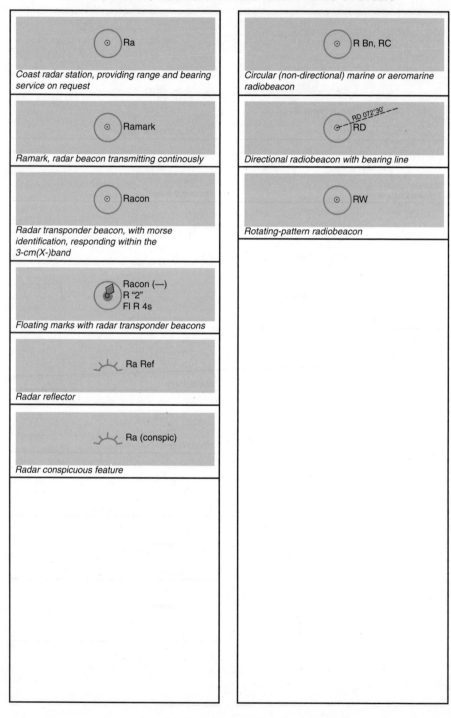

Coast radar station, providing range and bearing service on request

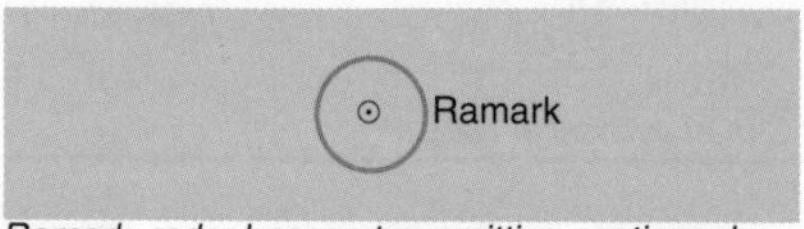

Ramark, radar beacon transmitting continously

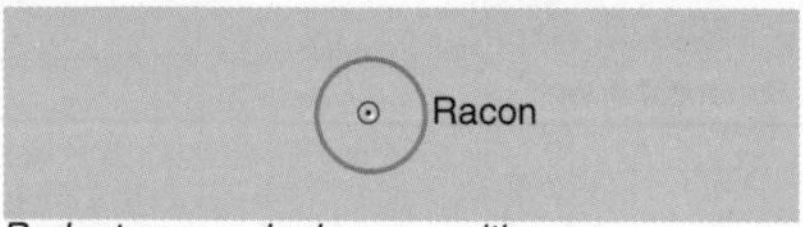

Radar transponder beacon, with morse identification, responding within the 3-cm(X-)band

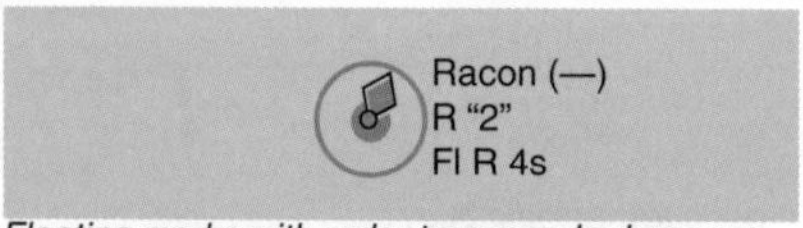

Floating marks with radar transponder beacons

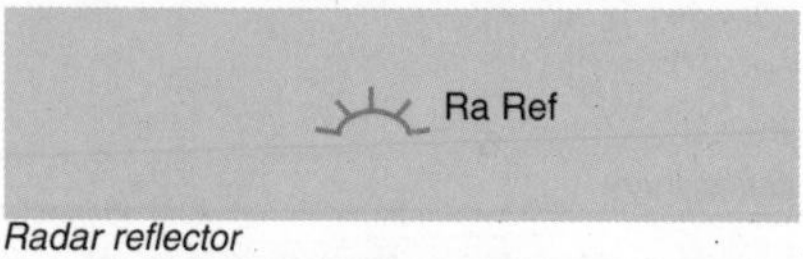

Radar reflector

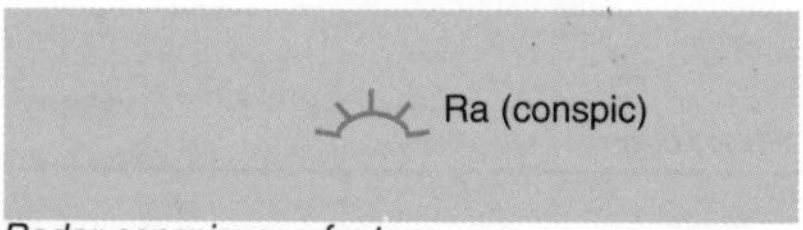

Radar conspicuous feature

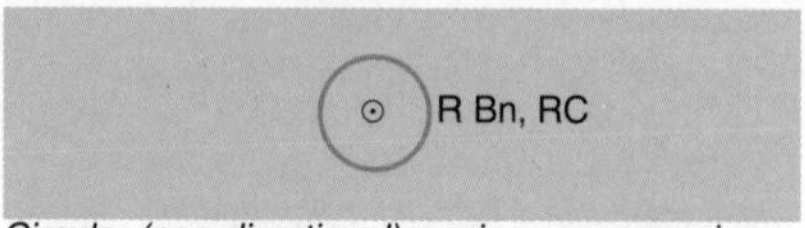

Circular (non-directional) marine or aeromarine radiobeacon

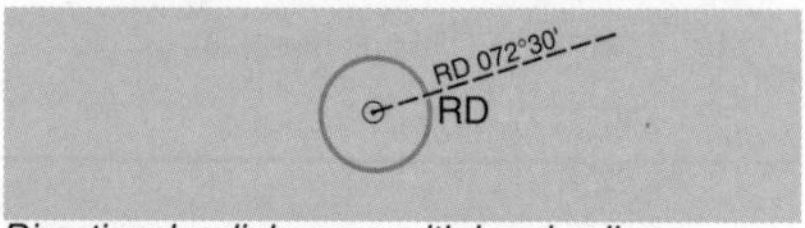

Directional radiobeacon with bearing line

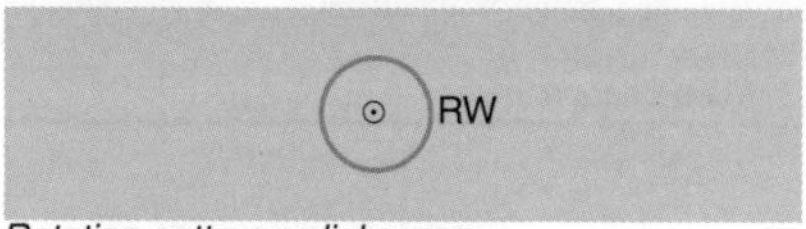

Rotating-pattern radiobeacon

ROCKS, WRECKS AND OBSTRUCTIONS

+ 35 Rk	35 Rk	Non-dangerous rock, depth known
+ Co + 3₁ + Reef Line		Coral reef which covers
Breakers	Br	Breakers
Hk	Hk	Wreck, hull always dry, on large-scale charts
	Hk	Wreck, covers and uncovers, on large-scale charts
	Hk	Submerged wreck, depth unknown, on large-scale charts
	PA	Wreck showing any portion of hull or superstructure at level of chart datum
Masts Mast (10 ft) Funnel		Wreck showing mast or masts above chart datum only
5½ Wk		Wreck, least depth known by sounding only
21 Wk 5 Wk	21 Wk 5½ Wk 5 Wk	Wreck, least depth known, swept by wire drag or diver
+++		Dangerous wreck, depth unknown
+++		Sunken wreck, not dangerous to surface navigation
8 Wk		Wreck, least depth unknown, but considered to have safe clearance to the depth shown

Foul Wks #	Foul Wks Wreckage	Remains of a wreck or other foul area, non-dangerous to navigation but to be avoided by vessels anchoring, trawling etc.
Obstn	Obstn	Obstruction, depth unknown
5½ Obstn	5½ Obstn	Obstruction, least depth known
21 Obstn 5 Obstn	21 Obstn 5 Obstn	Obstruction, least depth known, swept by wire drag or diver
Stakes, Perches	Subm piles Subm piling	Stumps of posts or piles, wholly submerged
Snags Stumps		Submerged pile, stake, snag, well or stump (with exact position)
Fsh stks		Fishing stakes
		Fish trap, fish weirs, tunny nets
		Fish trap area, tunny nets area
Obstruction (Fish haven) (actual shape)		Fish haven (artificial fishing reef)
Obstn Fish haven (auth min 42ft)		Fish haven with minimum depth
Oys		Shellfish cultivation (stakes visible)

TIDES AND CURRENTS

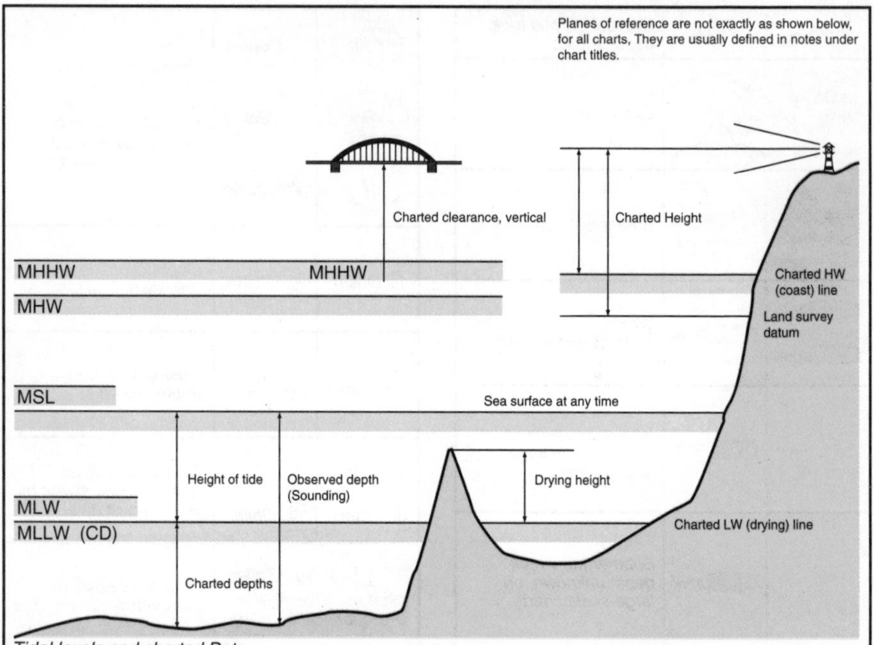

Tidal levels and charted Data

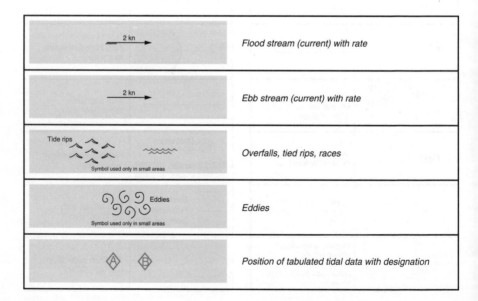

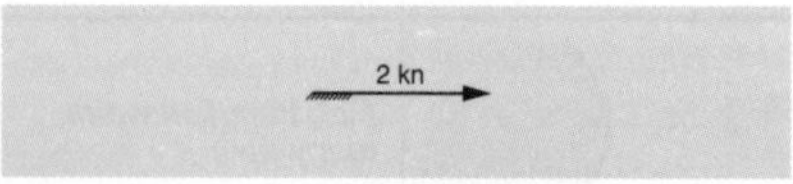2 kn	*Flood stream (current) with rate*
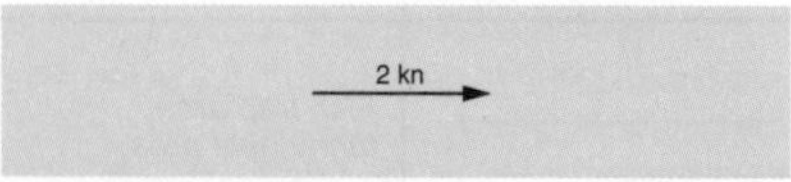2 kn	*Ebb stream (current) with rate*
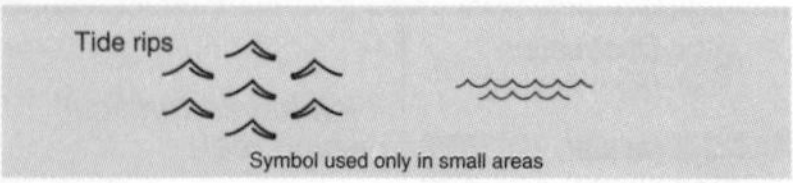Tide rips Symbol used only in small areas	*Overfalls, tied rips, races*
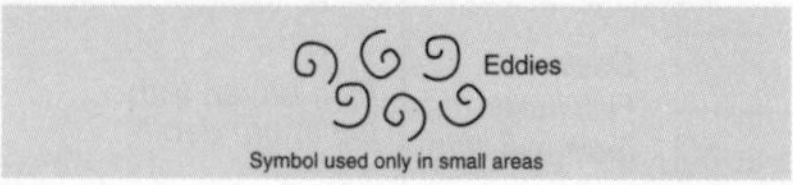Eddies Symbol used only in small areas	*Eddies*
A B	*Position of tabulated tidal data with designation*

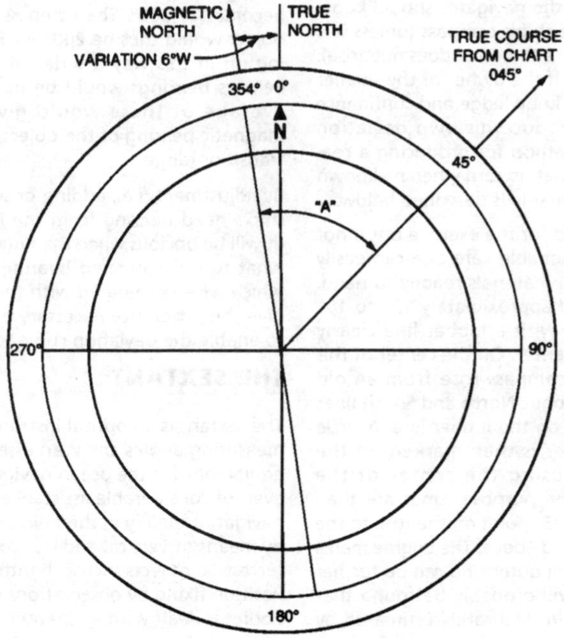

VARIATION AND DEVIATION

Basically variation is the angle between the Magnetic North Pole and the True Pole – which could perhaps be described as the Geometric Pole. This angle varies over the earth's surface.

Deviation is an error induced in a vessel's compass by local conditions, i.e., magnetic material near to the compass. This error varies with the ship's heading and should therefore be known on all points of the compass, for which purpose a deviation card is required. This card can be prepared by a professional compass adjuster or, with care, by the mariner himself. One method of preparing such a card is described later.

METHOD OF APPLYING VARIATION

When the *True* course has been laid on the chart, it is then necessary to convert it to a *Magnetic* course for use on the mariner's compass. Consider the diagram above and assume a course of 045° *True* is required. It will be observed that the *Variation* angle in this example is 6° West, i.e., *Magnetic North* is 6° West of *True North.*

The angle between the *True* course of 45° and the *Magnetic North* is therefore 45° + 6° = 51° (angle A). The course to be steered on the compass is therefore 51° Magnetic. Similarly, if the Variation angle was to be East of *True North* it will be seen that the Variation is subtracted from the True Course, i.e., if the variation was 6° East the above-mentioned course of 45° True would become 45° True – 6° = 39° Magnetic.

To assist in remembering this fact when converting from True to Magnetic courses under difficult conditions the following may help:

"West is best (i.e. greater); East is least (i.e. less)."

Applying Variation and Deviation

The same rule applies to Deviation. For example a True Course of 254° T, Variation 6° W; Magnetic Course will be 254° T + 6° W = 260° M, and from the Deviation Card (page 10) Dev. for this course will be 4° E. ∴ Compass Course will be 254° T + 6° W Var. = 260° – 4° E. Dev. = 256° C.

The two components, Var. and Dev. can be combined, i.e., + 6° W. – 4° E = 2° Compass error for the particular course. 254° T + 2° = 256° C.

It is essential when converting from True to Compass to apply Var. and Dev. in that order.

PREPARING A DEVIATION CARD

It is important that the navigator should know the deviation of the ship's compass (unless it is a gyro compass where this error does not arise). It is also very useful if the owner of the smaller vessel has sufficient knowledge and confidence in his ability to produce his own deviation card. One useful method for producing a reasonably accurate deviation card when no known transit is readily available is described below.

A Pelorus is required for the exercise but if not available, with reasonable care one can easily be constructed with materials readily to hand. A sheet of plywood approximately 12" to 18" square is prepared with a lubber line clearly marked along the center. On the center of this square is glued a compass rose from an old chart with the magnetic North and South lines accurately lined up on the lubber line. A circle of say 12" diameter is then marked on the plywood square using the center of the compass rose for the purpose. Lines are then drawn through each 5° point on the rose to the outer circle mentioned above. The degree marks then obtained on the outer ring can be further subdivided but it will probably be found that readings can be quite accurately estimated by eye. A small wooden pointer about 9" long with the appropriate sighting marks is then mounted in the center of the rose and the Pelorus is complete.

The Pelorus is then mounted in such a position that the lubber line is on the fore and aft line of the vessel and sights can be taken all round. It will be appreciated that the purpose of the Pelorus is to take bearings of an object relative to the ship's head.

A position is then selected where the vessel can be maneuvered through 360° as far as possible in the same position, for example near a buoy, and bearings taken on a distant object, ideally at least 5 miles away. The magnetic bearing of this object is immaterial at this stage. The procedure is as follows:

The ship is swung until her head is on due North (Compass) and the bearing of the object is noted on the Pelorus. This procedure is repeated for each quadrant of the compass so that 8 bearings of the object are obtained relative to the main compass headings. The compass bearings of the object with the ship's head on the different compass headings can then be calculated and the deviation card prepared in the usual way. For example, with the ship's head on compass North, the Pelorus reading will be the actual bearing of the object as it would be read from the ship's compass. Assume that this figure is 250°. The ship's head would then be swung to 45° and the Pelorus bearing would become say 200°. The compass bearing of the object would thus be 200° + 45° = 245°. Carrying on in this way a series of roughly similar Pelorus bearings would be obtained and the average of these would give the correct magnetic bearing of the object, i.e., in effect a transit or range.

By adjustment, i.e., adding or subtracting each ship's head bearing from the Pelorus bearing (it will be obvious when the figures are obtained what to do) corrected bearings are obtained, which when compared with the mean bearing give the difference necessary on each heading to enable the deviation curve to be prepared.

THE SEXTANT

The sextant is an optical instrument used for measuring angles and is an essential item of equipment for the ocean navigator. It is, however, of considerable assistance to the coastal navigator, mainly in the field of position fixing by means of vertical and horizontal angles of terrestrial objects such as lighthouses, etc. Position fixing by observations of celestial bodies is dealt with in Chapter 7. Like most instruments practice is necessary to achieve proficiency in its use – coastal navigation will afford plenty of opportunity. Those wishing to attain a high standard of proficiency should refer to *The Sextant Simplified* by Captain O.M. Watts, published by Reed's.

INDEX ERROR

Any residual error left in the sextant after it has been properly adjusted is called *Index Error* and this value should be applied as a correction to all sextant readings. There are several methods by which Index Error can be found, one simple method is:

To find Index Error by the sea horizon

1. Clamp the index at approximately zero.
2. Hold the sextant vertically and look through the telescope at the sea horizon.
3. Turn the tangent screw until the true and reflected horizons together form an unbroken line.
4. The *reading* on the sextant now indicates the Index Error which should be applied as a subtractive correction if the reading is on the arc, and additive if off the arc.

A clear horizon is essential to ensure accurate results.

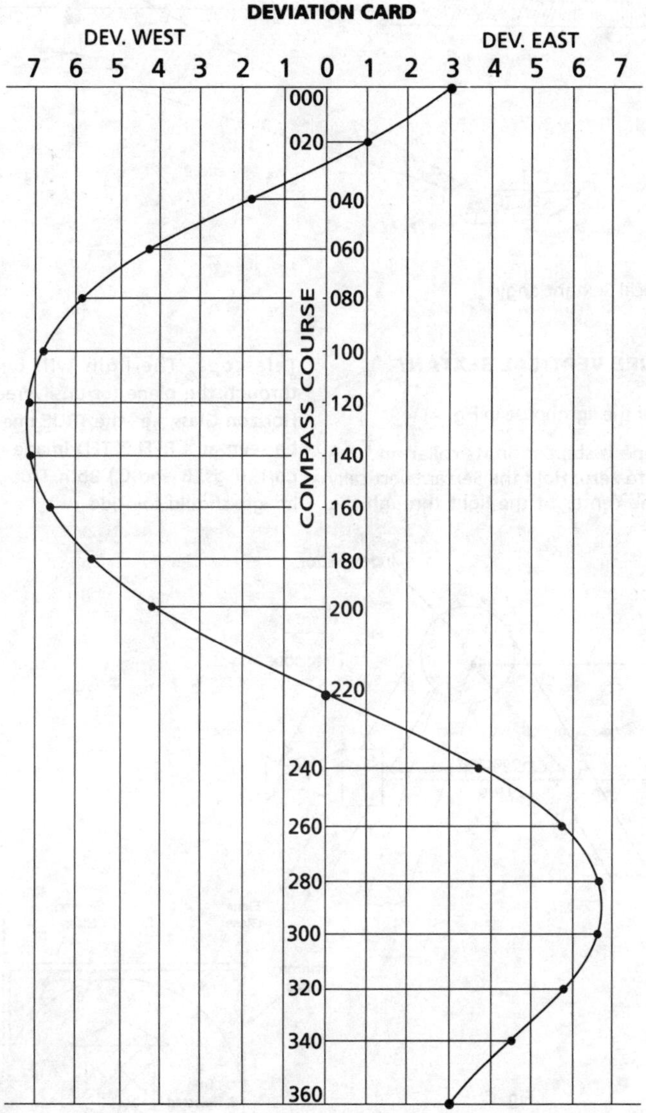

A typical deviation card which shows the method of construction

TAKING HORIZONTAL AND VERTICAL SEXTANT ANGLES

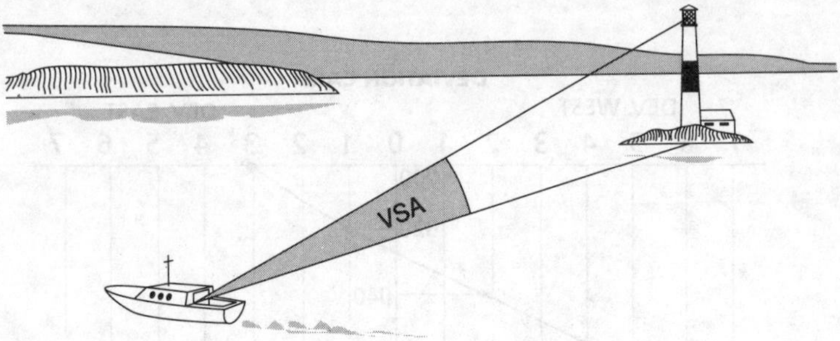

Fig. A. Vertical Sextant angle

TO MEASURE VERTICAL SEXTANT ANGLES

(e.g. those of the lighthouse in Fig. A)

The Telescope is shipped in its collar and the Index is set to zero. Hold the Sextant vertically and view the center of the light through the Telescope. The light will be seen direct through the plane (or unsilvered) part of the Horizon Glass, i.e., the TRUE image. It will also be seen as a REFLECTED image in the silvered part. (Figs. B and C.) Both True and Reflected images should coincide.

Fig. B

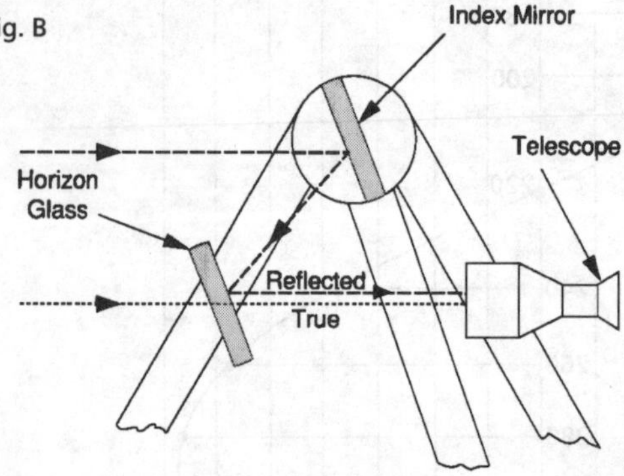

Fig. C

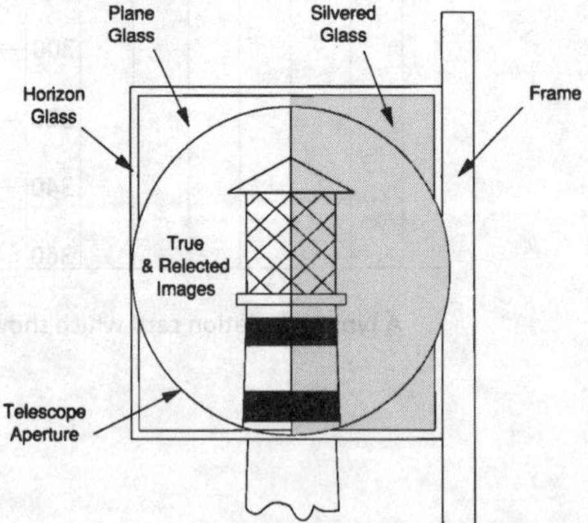

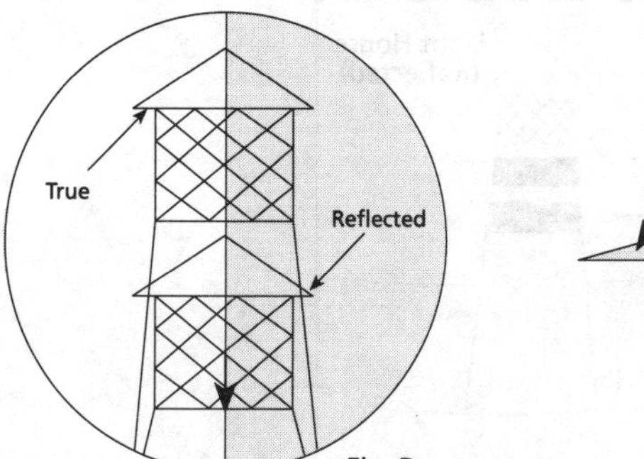

Fig. D

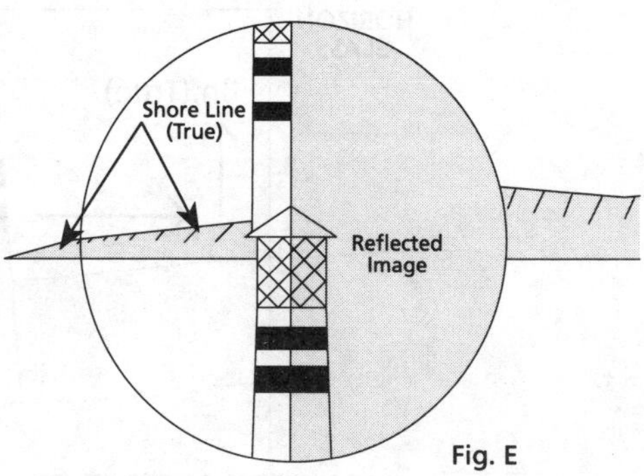

Fig. E

The Micrometer Head is now turned with the left hand so that the Index moves along the Arc, away from the Telescope end. As soon as the Micrometer is turned the True and Reflected images will separate, the Reflected image moving downwards. (Fig. D). As the Reflected image of the light "falls" the Sextant is tilted downwards to follow its movement. When the center of the light reaches the shoreline the reading is noted. (Fig. E.)

Using the sextant should first be practised on dry land and then on a yacht. Try bringing a chimney top down to the base of a wall to begin with.

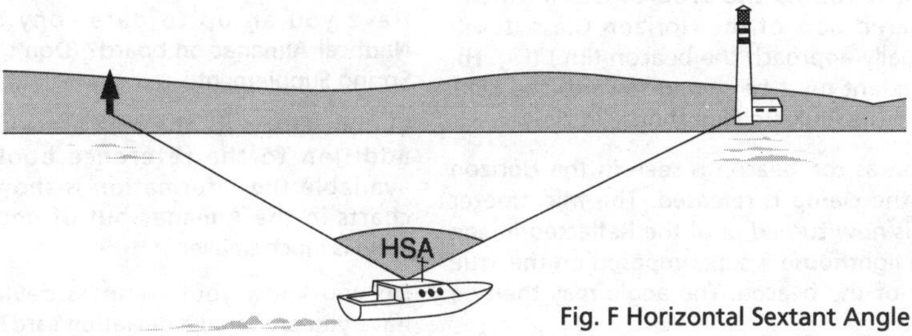

Fig. F Horizontal Sextant Angle

TO MEASURE HORIZONTAL SEXTANT ANGLES

(Fig. F)

The Horizontal Sextant Angle between, say, a lighthouse and a beacon is measured by holding the Sextant horizontally with the Handle downwards. As with the Vertical Sextant Angle the Index is set to zero. The Telescope is now pointed at the right hand object, in Fig. G, the Lighthouse.

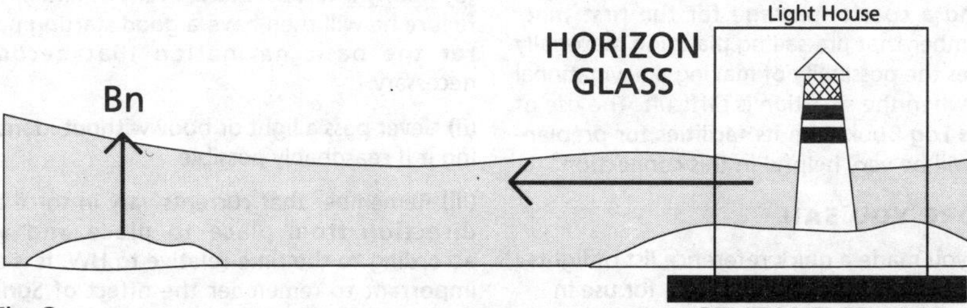

Fig. G

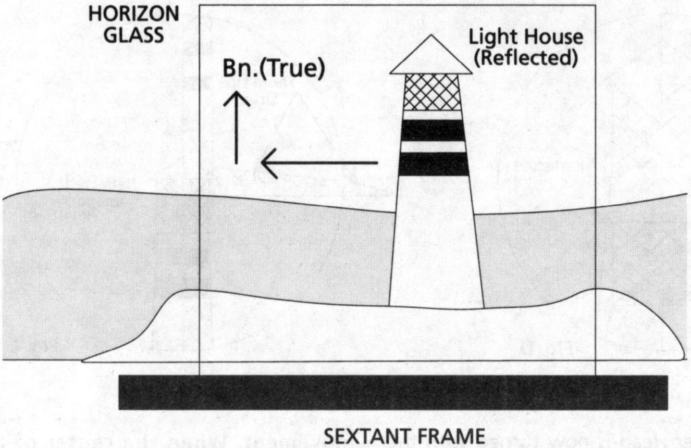

Fig. H

Since the angle to be measured will be relatively large the Index is now moved along the Arc by means of the Quick Release Clamp. Make sure a firm pressure is exerted on the clamp otherwise the gear teeth may be damaged.

The Reflected image of the Lighthouse will appear to move towards the LEFT, so that by letting it follow the True coastline in the unsilvered part of the Horizon Glass it will eventually approach the beacon (Bn.) (Fig. H). The Sextant must be swung towards the LEFT to keep the Reflected lighthouse in view.

As soon as the beacon is seen in the Horizon Glass the clamp is released. The Micrometer Head is now turned until the Reflected image of the lighthouse is superimposed on the True image of the beacon. The angle may then be read.

Some navigators prefer to point the sextant initially at the left hand object and move the index bar forward so that the right hand object eventually comes into view.

NAVIGATOR'S CHECK LIST

The following check list may be helpful to those making a coastal passage for the first time. Remember that pre-sailing planning materially reduces the possibility of making a navigational error when the situation is difficult. The use of Reed's Log Book with its facilities for preplanning will be very helpful in this connection.

BEFORE YOU SAIL

Have you made a quick reference list of lights and buoys with their ranges, etc., for use in the cockpit if necessary?

Check that all charts required are available on board and corrected up to date.

Are the desired course lines marked on the charts to assist navigation at sea?

Have alternative courses been considered in case stress of weather dictates a departure from the planned trip?

Have you an up to date copy of Reed's Nautical Almanac on board? (Don't forget the Spring Supplement.}

Current Charts for the area are a most useful addition to the reference books. If not available the information is shown on the charts in the Almanac but of necessity the scale is much smaller.

Do you know your compass deviation and have you prepared a deviation card?

POINTS TO CONSIDER WHEN ON PASSAGE

(i) In yachts equipped with Loran etc., there is always the temptation to rely on it entirely but the prudent navigator will always maintain an estimated position on the chart at say hourly intervals. In the event of equipment failure he will then have a good starting point for the basic navigation that becomes necessary.

(ii) Never pass a light or buoy without identifying it if reasonably possible.

(iii) Remember that currents vary in force and direction from place to place and also according to the time relative to HW. It is also important to remember the effect of Springs and Neaps on the force of the current.

(iv) Do not forget leeway angle when setting courses and do not overlook the effect of surface drift which may occur due to a hard and prolonged blow.

(v) When navigating in fog if it is not possible to anchor in safety out of shipping lanes try to maintain a constant speed – it makes calculations easier.

(vi) Remember the textbook approach to an unfamiliar but well lighted shore – close the coast before dawn to obtain an accurate fix from lights and then make your entry with daylight.

(vii) Finally – when approaching an unfamiliar destination, if uncertain of your position and there is a possibility of danger as a result – heave to or stand out to sea again until you have clarified the situation.

THE VESSEL'S COURSE

One of the first essentials before commencing a trip is to decide upon the different courses to be made good between the start and the destination. The standard terms used in connection with the vessel's course are given below and it is recommended that these should always be used, particularly in discussions between the navigator and helmsman.

The word "course" by itself can have several quite different meanings. It may refer to a course to steer, a leeway course, a required course, or a course to make good, which is not always the same thing as the required course.

Heading refers only to the vessel's fore-and-aft line. It is the direction in which she is pointing, regardless of her actual track, and is designated as True (T), Magnetic (M) or Compass (C), as appropriate. Whenever the true heading is plotted on the chart, the line should be marked for identification with a single arrow head pointing in the appropriate direction.

Track refers to the direction of the ship's track over the sea bed. It may be designated as True (T) or Magnetic (M), as convenient, and when drawn on the chart should be marked for identification with two arrow heads and clearly labelled, e.g., 286° (T). The Required Track is the direction of the intended track between two points. The line drawn on the chart to indicate the required track is often referred to as the "course line".

Current – when plotted on the chart should be marked with three arrow heads.

Course to Steer is the heading required to make good a specified track.

Course Steered refers to the heading that was steered over a specified time.

Leeway is the angle between the ship's fore-and-aft line and her line of movement through the water.

Leeway Course is the direction of the vessel's line of movement through the water. Thus when she is making leeway the leeway course always lies to leeward of the true heading; and if there is a significant current, too, the track may be different to both the heading and leeway courses.

PLOTTING THE REQUIRED TRACK

Any reader wishing to use a calculator should, after studying the following basic information, refer to the use of the electronic calculator later in this section.

On a coastal passage the configuration of the coastline may necessitate many changes of course and it is a wise practice to plot all the required courses on the chart before the commencement of the passage. The prudent navigator will also plot the courses of any "escape route" that may be necessitated by bad weather.

A close examination of the course lines should then be made to ensure that adequate clearance is given to all possible dangers. The courses can be marked in on the course lines or preferably noted separately. The reason for not writing them on the chart is to ensure that it is as uncluttered as possible before the normal chartwork of recording estimated positions, etc., commences as the passage progresses.

SETTING THE COURSE

With Allowance for Leeway only:

Some sea-going experience and a knowledge of the ship's likely behavior under existing conditions is required when estimating the allowance to be made for leeway. For any one course this allowance must be adjusted from time to time as dictated by change in the force and/or direction of the wind.

The leeway angle is the angle between the fore and aft line of the vessel and her wake and should be measured or estimated for various speeds and sea conditions.

To determine the true course to steer: apply leeway to windward of the required true track.

To determine the true track being made good: apply leeway to leeward of the true course being steered.

Always apply leeway angle before variation and deviation have been applied to the course to steer.

When there is no current or tidal effect, the track and the wake course are the same.

Allowance for Tide or Current and Leeway

The term speed refers always to the ship's speed through the water; her speed over the sea bed is called speed over the ground.

EXAMPLE: It is required to set course to make good a track of 080° (T) when the current is setting 180° at 3 knots, wind northerly and leeway 5°. If the vessel's speed is 9 knots, what course should she steer, and what will be her speed over the ground?

In the diagram AB represents the required track drawn on the chart.

1. Take any convenient point C and lay off the current vector CD representing 3 kts. (using units from any convenient scale) at 180° (T).

2. With center D and radius equal to ship's speed of 9 kts. strike an arc cutting AB at E.

3. DE represents True Course required, i.e., 061° (T).

4. Apply Southerly leeway angle of 5°; course will be 056° (T).

5. Compass course will be 056° + 6° Var. W. –3° Dev. E. = 059° (C).

6. CE measured in the same units as CD gives 8 kts. – the speed over the ground.

When out of sight of land or in low visibility with no navigational fixing aids available, allowance for leeway and tide should be adjusted continually, as required, so as to "make good" the required track over the sea bed. In continued low visibility, soundings taken at regular intervals often provide a useful check on the distance off the coast.

COURSE CORRECTION

Every prudent navigator when setting a course makes allowance for leeway, and the effects of a current.

The following Table has been designed to save the navigator of a small vessel having to work the problem on the chart to find out what course allowance he should make to counteract the effect of a current of an estimated speed and taking into account the speed of his vessel.

It will be realised, of course, that the slower the vessel's speed, the more it will be affected by any current; and the more this current is abeam, the more it will push the vessel sideways from her course, and, therefore, the more allowance that must be made. Should the stream be directly ahead or astern, no course allowance need be made, but the speed will be advanced or retarded according to the speed of the current.

The Table – in addition to giving in the shortest time the allowance to be made to the

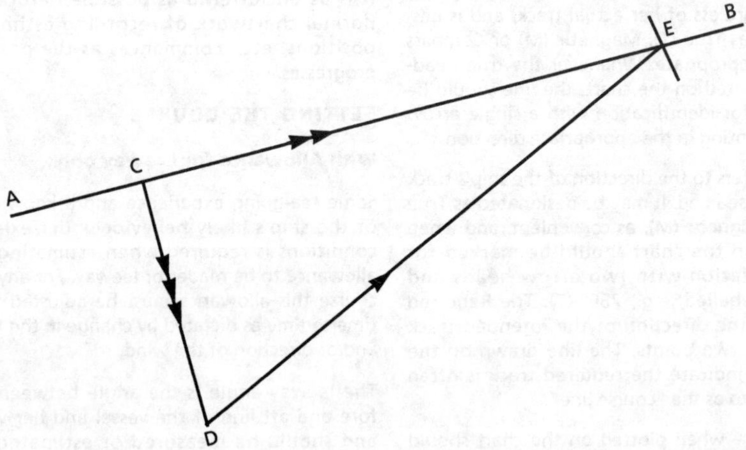

course – gives also the speed made good over the ground. While this latter may sometimes be required, it is more necessary in practical navigation to find the course allowance to be made at frequent intervals.

This Table saves any chart plotting and enables the course allowance for current to be found mentally in the quickest possible manner.

HOW TO FIND THE COURSE TO STEER TO COUNTERACT THE EFFECT OF CURRENT

(1). Find the speed of the current at the top of the page and with the relative angle of the current from the desired track to be made good in the left hand column, C, read value from the Table.

(2) Find at the top of the Table the speed of the vessel (through the water) and look down this column until the value in (1) above is found (or closely approximated). Then read off in the left hand column C, the number of degrees allowance to be made to the course.

(3) Allow this course correction to the same side, port or starboard, as the current; i.e., in order to counteract a current setting towards the vessel on the starboard side, you naturally make the course allowance towards the starboard side.

Example I. Vessel steering 060° (T) at 10 knots estimates a current will set 290° (T) at 3½ knots. What allowance should be made, and what course should be steered?

1) Find speed of current, 3½ knots, in column at top of page, and 50° (relative angle of the current to the vessel's course) on the left hand side of the page giving a value of 2.681.

(2) Find speed of vessel, 10 knots, at the top of the Table and value 2.681 in this column – 2,760 is the nearest. The course allowance in column C on this line is seen to be 16° C.

(3) As the current is on the starboard bow, the 16° must be allowed to starboard to counteract its effect. Therefore, the course to steer is 076° (T).

Example II. Vessel steering 200° (T), speed 8 knots, current estimated to set 230° (T) at 1½ knots (i.e., 30° from dead astern). With 1.5 knots on top and 30° in column C, value is 0.750. With 8 knots on top and value 0.750 in same column, in column C is found 5°.

Current is on port quarter, so allow 5° to port, i.e., the course to steer is 195° (T).

Example III. Vessel steering 337° at 14½ knots, current setting 247° at 2½ knots. What course should the vessel steer to counteract the effect of the current?

With 2½ knots on top and 90° in column C value is 2.500. With 14½ knots on top and value 2.500 in the same column, in column C is found 10°.

Current is abeam to starboard so allow 10° to starboard. Course to steer therefore is 347°.

HOW TO FIND THE SPEED MADE GOOD OVER THE GROUND (EFFECTIVE SPEED)

(1) Enter the Table from the top with speed of the current and from the right hand column S with relative angle of the stream. Read from the Table the factor and name it T.C. (Tidal Contribution to vessel's speed over ground).

(2) Enter Table from the top with ship's speed (through the water) and from the right hand column S with course correction. Read from the Table the factor and name it S.C. (Ship's Contribution to vessel's speed over ground).

(3) If current is on the bow, (i.e., before the beam), the vessel's speed over the ground is the difference between S.C. and T.C.

If current is on the quarter (i.e., abaft the beam), the vessel's speed over the ground is the sum of S.C. and T.C.

5

COURSE CORRECTION TABLE
(Designed by R. C. Fisher)

SPEED OF TIDAL STREAM (OR CURRENT) OVER THE GROUND AND SHIP'S SPEED THROUGH THE WATER

C	Knots 0.5	1.0	1.5	2.0	2.5	Knots 3.0	3.5	4.0	4.5	Knots 5.0	S
0	0	0	0	0	0	0	0	0	0	0	90
1	0.009	0.019	0.026	0.035	0.044	0.052	0.061	0.070	0.079	0.087	89
2	0.017	0.035	0.052	0.070	0.087	0.105	0.122	0.139	0.157	0.174	88
3	0.026	0.052	0.079	0.105	0.131	0.157	0.183	0.209	0.236	0.262	87
4	0.035	0.070	0.105	0.140	0.174	0.209	0.244	0.279	0.314	0.349	86
5	0.044	0.087	0.131	0.174	0.218	0.261	0.305	0.349	0.392	0.436	85
6	0.052	0.105	0.157	0.209	0.261	0.314	0.366	0.418	0.470	0.523	84
8	0.070	0.139	0.209	0.278	0.348	0.418	0.487	0.557	0.626	0.696	82
10	0.087	0.174	0.260	0.347	0.434	0.521	0.608	0.695	0.781	0.868	80
12	0.104	0.208	0.312	0.416	0.520	0.624	0.728	0.832	0.936	1.040	78
14	0.121	0.242	0.363	0.484	0.605	0.726	0.847	0.968	1.089	1.210	76
16	0.138	0.276	0.413	0.551	0.689	0.827	0.965	1.103	1.240	1.378	74
18	0.155	0.309	0.464	0.618	0.773	0.927	1.082	1.236	1.391	1.545	72
21	0.179	0.358	0.538	0.717	0.896	1.075	1.254	1.433	1.613	1.792	69
24	0.203	0.407	0.610	0.813	1.017	1.220	1.424	1.627	1.830	2.034	66
27	0.227	0.454	0.681	0.908	1.135	1.362	1.589	1.816	2.043	2.270	63
30	0.250	0.500	0.750	1.000	1.250	1.500	1.750	2.000	2.250	2.500	60
33	0.272	0.545	0.817	1.089	1.362	1.634	1.906	2.179	2.451	2.723	57
36	0.294	0.588	0.882	1.176	1.469	1.763	2.057	2.351	2.645	2.939	54
39	0.315	0.629	0.944	1.259	1.573	1.888	2.203	2.517	2.832	3.147	51
42	0.335	0.669	1.004	1.338	1.673	2.007	2.342	2.667	3.011	3.346	48
46	0.360	0.719	1.079	1.439	1.798	2.158	2.518	2.877	3.237	3.597	44
50	0.383	0.766	1.149	1.532	1.915	2.298	2.681	3.064	3.447	3.830	40
54	0.405	0.809	1.214	1.618	2.023	2.427	2.832	3.236	3.641	4.045	36
58	0.424	0.848	1.272	1.696	2.120	2.540	2.986	3.392	3.816	4.240	32
62	0.442	0.883	1.324	1.766	2.207	2.649	3.090	3.532	3.973	4.415	28
66	0.457	0.914	1.370	1.827	2.284	2.741	3.197	3.754	4.111	4.568	24
70	0.470	0.940	1.410	1.879	2.349	2.819	3.289	3.759	4.229	4.698	20
75	0.483	0.966	1.449	1.932	2.415	2.898	3.381	3.864	4.347	4.830	15
80	0.492	0.985	1.477	1.970	2.462	2.954	3.447	3.939	4.432	4.924	10
85	0.498	0.996	1.494	1.992	2.490	2.989	3.487	3.985	4.483	4.981	5
90	0.500	1.000	1.500	2.000	2.500	3.000	3.500	4.000	4.500	5.000	0
C	0.5	1.0	1.5	2.0	2.5	3.0 Knots	3.5	4.0	4.5	5.0	S

C	Knots 6	7	8	9	10	Knots 12	14	16	18	Knots 20	S
0	0	0	0	0	0	0	0	0	0	0	90
1	0.105	0.120	0.140	0.160	0.170	0.210	0.240	0.280	0.310	0.350	89
2	0.209	0.240	0.280	0.310	0.350	0.420	0.490	0.560	0.503	0.700	88
3	0.314	0.370	0.420	0.470	0.520	0.630	0.730	0.840	0.940	1.050	87
4	0.419	0.490	0.560	0.630	0.700	0.840	0.980	1.120	1.260	1.400	86
5	0.523	0.610	0.700	0.780	0.870	1.050	1.220	1.390	1.570	1.740	85
6	0.627	0.730	0.840	0.940	1.050	1.250	1.460	1.670	1.880	2.080	84
8	0.835	0.970	1.110	1.250	1.390	1.670	1.950	2.230	2.510	2.780	82
10	1.040	1.220	1.390	1.560	1.740	2.080	2.430	2.780	3.130	3.470	80
12	1.247	1.460	1.660	1.870	2.080	2.490	2.910	3.330	3.740	4.160	78
14	1.452	1.690	1.940	2.180	2.420	2.900	3.390	3.870	4.350	4.840	76
16	1.654	1.930	2.210	2.480	2.760	3.310	3.860	4.410	4.960	5.510	74
18	1.854	2.160	2.470	2.780	3.090	3.710	4.330	4.940	5.560	6.180	72
21	2.150	2.510	2.870	3.230	3.580	4.300	5.020	5.730	6.450	7.170	69
24	2.440	2.850	3.250	3.660	4.070	4.880	5.690	6.510	7.320	8.130	66
27	2.724	3.180	3.630	4.090	4.540	5.450	6.360	7.260	8.170	9.080	63
30	3.000	3.500	4.000	4.500	5.000	6.000	7.000	8.300	9.000	10.00	60
33	3.268	3.810	4.360	4.900	5.450	6.540	7.620	8.710	9.800	10.89	57
36	3.527	4.110	4.700	5.290	5.880	7.050	8.230	9.400	10.58	11.76	54
39	3.776	4.410	5.030	5.660	6.290	7.550	8.810	10.07	11.33	12.59	51
42	4.015	4.680	5.350	6.020	6.690	8.030	9.370	10.71	12.04	13.38	48
46	4.316	5.040	5.750	6.470	7.190	8.630	10.07	11.51	12.95	14.39	44
50	4.596	5.360	6.130	6.890	7.660	9.190	10.72	12.26	13.79	15.32	40
54	4.854	5.660	6.470	7.280	8.090	9.710	11.33	12.94	14.56	16.18	36
58	5.088	5.940	6.780	7.630	8.480	10.18	11.87	13.57	15.26	16.96	32
62	5.298	6.180	7.060	7.950	8.830	10.60	12.36	14.13	15.89	17.66	28
66	5.481	6.390	7.310	8.220	9.140	10.96	12.79	14.62	16.44	18.27	24
70	5.638	6.580	7.520	8.460	9.400	11.28	13.16	15.04	16.91	18.79	20
75	5.796	6.760	7.730	8.690	9.660	11.59	13.52	15.45	17.39	19.32	15
80	5.909	6.890	7.880	8.860	9.850	11.82	13.79	15.76	17.73	19.70	10
85	5.977	6.970	7.970	8.970	9.960	11.95	13.95	15.94	17.93	19.92	5
90	6.000	7.000	8.000	9.000	10.00	12.00	14.00	16.00	18.00	20.00	0
C	6	7	8	9	10 Knots	12	14	16	18	20	S

Example I. Vessel's speed 10 knots, current 3½ knots, 50° on the starboard bow. What is the vessel's speed over the ground?

(1) With 3½ knots at top and 50° on the right in column S, gives (by interpolation) 2.249.

(2) With 10 knots at the top and 16° course correction on the T.C. right in column S gives (by interpolation) S.C. 9.608.

(3) As the current is ahead of the vessel (i.e., 50° on the starboard bow) and pushing her back, the difference between S.C. and T.C. – 9.608 and 2.249 gives 7.359* knots, the vessel's speed over the ground.

Should the current have been on the starboard quarter (i.e., helping the vessel along) the sum of T.C. and S.C. i.e., 11.857 knots, would have been the speed over the ground.

*If interpolation had not been done but the nearest tabulated figures used, i.e., T.C. 2.203 and S.C. 9.660, the result would be 7.457, which is quite accurate enough for ordinary purposes.

Example II. Vessel's speed, 8 knots, current speed 1½ knots, 30° on the quarter. Course allowance 5°. What speed did the vessel make good over the ground?

1. With 1½ knots and 30° T.C. equals 1.300.
2. With 8 knots and 5° S.C. equals 7.970.
3. As stream is behind vessel, the sum 9.27 is the speed over the ground.

Example III. Vessel's speed 14½ knots, current 2½ knots abeam. Course allowance 10°. What was the vessel's speed over the ground?

1. With 2½ knots and 90° T.C. equals 0.
2. With 14½ knots and 10° S.C. equals 14¼.

As current is abeam the sum (or difference) is 14¼, so vessel's speed over the ground is 14¼ knots.

POSITION FIXING

A "Fix" is obtained by the intersection of two or more position lines; more than two should be used whenever possible. If the position lines are obtained all at the same time it is commonly called a Simultaneous Fix. If, however, there is a significant time interval between the observations, so that the first position time has to be transferred up to the time of the last one, it is termed a Running Fix. All other things being equal, a simultaneous fix is more reliable than a running fix.

There are various types of position lines; but those which are normally available to the average yacht are obtained by:

(1) A compass bearing of a fixed object ashore.

(2) A transit bearing i.e., two fixed objects seen in line with one another, e.g., a point of land in line with a conspicuous chimney – very accurate.

(3) A vertical sextant angle of an object of known height coupled with its compass bearing – very accurate.

(4) A horizontal sextant angle between two fixed objects – very accurate.

(5) A dipping range.

(6) A sounding corresponding to a clearly defined fathom line on the chart.

(7) A radio D/F bearing;

(8) An astronomical observation.

A fix can be obtained by any combination of the position lines listed above. A quick and accurate method by day is to combine the distance of an object (e.g., headland or lighthouse) obtained from a vertical sextant angle with the simultaneous bearing of the object.

Compass bearings are obtained with the use of a pelorus on the main compass or, in the case of smaller vessels, by means of a Hand Bearing Compass.

There are many occasions when a single position line may prove useful, for example:

(a) A position line which is parallel or nearly parallel to the required track shows whether or not the vessel is maintaining that track.

(b) A position line which cuts the track at or near 90° will often provide a good check on speed over the ground and ETA at the next point.

(c) Two marks or beacons in transit (a range) may provide a leading line into a harbor, or clear a danger.

(d) A single bearing may be used as a clearing line – danger being avoided by keeping to one side of the bearing line.

When making a passage it is necessary to have an accurate assessment of the vessel's position at all times – especially important in coastal navigation. The ocean navigator may only plot his position at noon each day – the coastal navigator should plot his at least once each hour. The standard terms used in position fixing are:

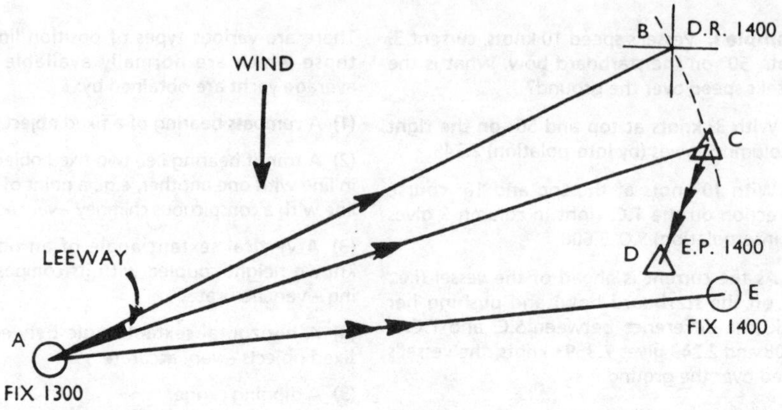

DEAD RECKONING (DR) – a position obtained from the course steered by the vessel and her speed through the water and no other factors. The distance run through the water is laid off along the course line steered and the position so obtained marked with a small cross, the letters DR and the time, thus – + DR 1030.

ESTIMATED POSITION (EP) – a position obtained by adjusting the DR position for the effects of leeway and current. It is marked on the chart by means of a dot in a triangle thus ⚠ EP 1030.

A FIX – provided by reliable observations of terrestrial or celestial bodies and is shown thus ⊙ Fix 1030.

With practice the symbols only should be used – clarity on the chart reduces the chances of error.

The figure above illustrates the different kinds of position as defined above. Assuming point A to be the last reliable fix (obtained at, say, 1300 hours), AB the course steered and the log distance for one hour; then B is the DR position for 1400 hours – i.e., the position the vessel would be in if there was no leeway, no current, the course had been accurately steered and the distance run through the water accurately indicated.

If the ship had been making leeway (angle BAC) due to a northerly wind, but was not affected by current, then C would be the EP at 1400 hours. Note that the distance AB and AC are always the same.

If, however, a current setting (say) 200° (T) at 3 knots was encountered, then the set and drift for one hour (200° (T) – 3 miles) would be laid off on the chart from point C – i.e., CD, and point D is now the EP for 1400 hours. Note that the effect of current is marked by three arrow heads.

Should a reliable fix, E, be obtained at 1400 hours, the current actually experienced during the last hour would be determined by measuring the direction and distance from C to E (not drawn in figure). The track and distance made good, and the effective speed, would be determined by the straight line AE.

THE RUNNING FIX

A Running Fix is primarily for use on those frequent occasions (particularly during night passage) when only one known object is visible, so that simultaneous cross bearings cannot be obtained. Although less reliable than a simultaneous fix, it does have many valuable applications which should never be neglected.

To obtain a Running Fix from bearings of the same object with a time interval between them:

(1) Take the first bearing and note the reading of the log, plot the position line on the chart and mark it with a single arrowhead at one end and also the time at which the observation was made.

(2) When the bearing has altered enough to make a good angle of "cut" with the first position line repeat the procedure.

(3) From any convenient point on the first position line lay off the "run" (the run being the track and the distance made good over the ground during the time interval between the bearings) – AB.

(4) Through the end of the run draw a line parallel to the first position line. This line is the first position line "transferred", and it should be marked by two arrow heads at each end.

(5) The point where the transferred position line cuts the second bearing is the "fix" and should be marked accordingly.

Important Notes:

(a) The accuracy of this method of fixing is dependent, not only on the accuracy of the bearings and their angle of cut, but also on the accuracy with which the "run" between the bearings has been estimated – remember leeway and effect of tide.

(b) The reliability of a running fix can be better assessed when two bearings are transferred up to the time of a third. A small "cocked hat" thus formed can generally be treated with a greater degree of confidence than a running fix from only two bearings.

(c) The principle of the running fix applies whether or not the position lines are obtained from the same point of origin. A bearing of one object may be transferred to cross with a bearing of a different object which was not sighted until after the first one was lost to view.

Example of a Running fix with no tide Fig. 1:

Vessel steering 270° (T) and making no leeway. At 2300 hrs. a lighthouse, P, bore 315° (T), Patent Log read 86.2. At 2330 hrs. the same light bore 040° (T), Patent Log read 90.7. If the tidal effect was estimated to be nil during the interval between the bearings, what was the ship's position at 2330 hours?

(1) Plot the two position lines as described.

(2) From any convenient point A on the first position line lay off the run (AB) 270° 4.5 miles.

(3) Through B draw the transferred position line parallel to PA, and the point where it cuts the second bearing is the fix.

Example of a Running fix in a current Fig. 2:

Vessel steering 270° (T) and making 5° leeway due to a northerly wind. At 2300 hours a Lighthouse, P, bore 315° (T), Patent Log reading 86.2. At 2330 hours the same light bore 040° (T), Patent Log reading 90.7. The current was estimated to be setting 010° at 2 knots. Required: the vessel's position at 2330.

Referring to the figure overleaf:

(1) Plot the two position lines as described above.

(2) From any convenient point A on the first position line lay off AB (4.5 miles along the Wake Course – 265°).

(3) From point B lay off BC the tidal effect for 30 minutes (set 010°, drift 1 mile). The estimated run then is AC.

(4) Through point C draw the transferred position line parallel to PA, and the point where it cuts the second bearing is the fix.

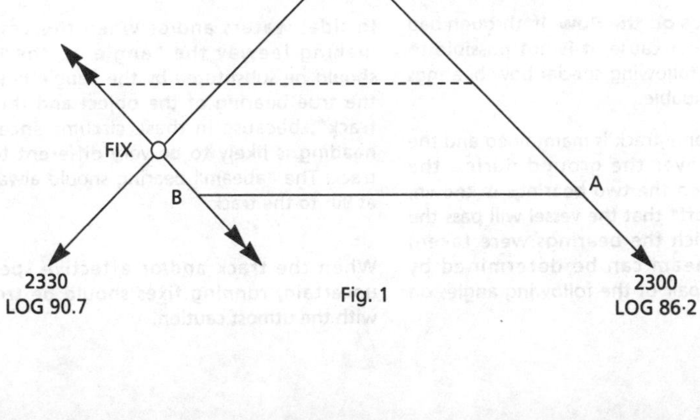

Fig. 1

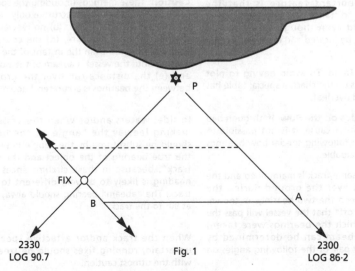

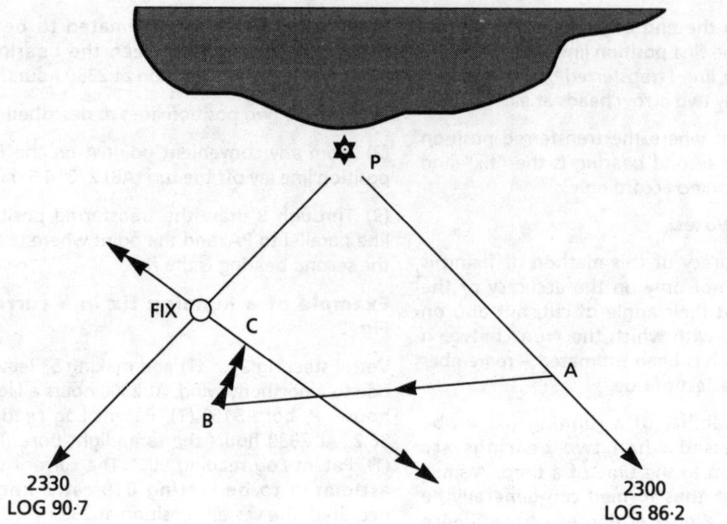

Fig. 2

SOME USEFUL VARIATIONS IN THE RUNNING FIX METHOD

One particular advantage of any of the methods which follow is that the approximate distance off a terrestrial object can be found before it comes abeam and, if necessary, the track can be altered at once to avoid passing too close to a danger.

Another important feature is that the approximate "distance off" any fixed object can be found even though the observed object cannot be located and identified on the chart.

Running Fix Table: To avoid having to plot these bearings on the chart, a special table has been included overleaf.

Bearing-Angles on the Bow. If, through bad weather or other cause, it is not possible to use tables the following special bow bearings may be very valuable.

Provided the same track is maintained and the distance run over the ground during the interval between the two bearings is known, the "distance off" that the vessel will pass the object (of which the bearings were taken) when it is abeam can be determined by observing any pair of the following angles on the bow:

Pairs of angles: (a) 22° and 34° ; (b) 25° and 41°; (c) 26½° and 45°; (d) 32° and 59° ; (e) 35° and 67°; (f) 37° and 72°; (g) 45° and 90°.

The distance off when abeam of the object will be equal to the distance run (over the ground) between the bearings in any one pair.

Caution: These methods (including the special cases described below are accurate only when: (a) there is no tidal effect; (b) no leeway; (c) the bearings are accurate; (d) the course is accurately steered from the instant of the first bearing until the vessel is abeam of the object; and (e) the distance run over the ground between the bearings is accurately known.

In tidal waters and/or when the vessel is making leeway the "angle on the bow" should be substituted by the "angle between the true bearing of the object and the true track", because in these circumstances the heading is likely to be very different to the track. The "abeam" bearing should always be at 90° to the track.

When the track and/or effective speed is uncertain, running fixes should be treated with the utmost caution.

RUNNING FIX TABLE

DISTANCE OFF (at Second Bearing) By TWO BEARINGS AND RUN BETWEEN THEM

EXAMPLE OF USING TABLES. At 0600 steering East (Magnetic) a vessel takes a bearing of a lighthouse 160° (M). Patent Log 56. half an hour later the Patent Log reads 60 and the bearing is found to be 210° (M). Find the distance off at the second bearing. Angle between Course Line and First bearing equals 70°. Angle between First and Second bearing equals 50°. Using Table, with above angles 70° at top and 50° at side, gives 1.2M.

Distance run between bearings (PL 60 – 56) = 4 miles. Therefore, 1.2 × 4 = 4.8 miles.

Vessel's bearing and distance from the lighthouse is therefore 210°, distance 4.8 miles.

Speed must be estimated as accurately as possible if Patent Log is not available.

Angle between 1st and 2nd Bearings	Angle between Course Line (i.e. Ship's Head) and First Bearing															Angle between 1st and 2nd Bearings
	20°	25°	30°	35°	40°	45°	50°	55°	60°	65°	70°	75°	80°	85°	90°	
10°	2·0	2·4	2·9	3·3	3·7	4·1	4·4	4·7	5·0	5·2	5·4	5·5	5·7	5·7	5·8	
15°	1·3	1·6	1·9	2·2	2·5	2·7	3·0	3·2	3·3	3·5	3·7	3·8	4·0	4·0	4·0	
20°	1·0	1·2	1·5	1·7	1·9	2·1	2·2	2·4	2·5	2·6	2·8	2·8	2·9	2·9	2·9	160°
25°	0·8	1·0	1·2	1·4	1·6	1·7	1·8	1·9	2·0	2·1	2·2	2·3	2·3	2·4	2·4	155°
30°	0·7	0·9	1·0	1·1	1·3	1·4	1·5	1·6	1·7	1·8	1·9	1·9	2·0	2·0	2·0	150°
35°	0·6	0·8	0·9	1·0	1·1	1·3	1·4	1·5	1·5	1·6	1·7	1·7	1·7	1·7	1·7	145°
40°	0·5	0·7	0·8	0·9	1·0	1·1	1·2	1·3	1·4	1·4	1·5	1·5	1·5	1·6	1·6	140°
45°	0·5	0·6	0·7	0·8	0·9	1·0	1·1	1·2	1·2	1·3	1·3	1·4	1·4	1·4	1·4	135°
50°	0·4	0·6	0·7	0·8	0·8	0·9	1·0	1·1	1·1	1·2	1·2	1·3	1·3	1·3	1·3	130°
55°	0·4	0·5	0·6	0·7	0·8	0·9	0·9	1·0	1·1	1·1	1·1	1·2	1·2	1·2	1·2	125°
60°	0·4	0·5	0·6	0·7	0·7	0·8	0·9	0·9	1·0	1·1	1·1	1·1	1·1	1·2	1·2	120°
65°	0·4	0·5	0·5	0·6	0·7	0·8	0·9	0·9	0·9	1·0	1·0	1·1	1·1	1·1	1·1	115°
70°	0·4	0·5	0·5	0·6	0·7	0·7	0·8	0·8	0·9	0·9	1·0	1·0	1·1	1·1	1·1	110°
75°	0·3	0·4	0·5	0·6	0·7	0·7	0·8	0·8	0·9	0·9	1·0	1·0	1·0	1·0		105°
80°	0·3	0·4	0·5	0·6	0·7	0·7	0·8	0·8	0·9	0·9	0·9	1·0	1·0			100°
85°	0·3	0·4	0·5	0·6	0·6	0·7	0·8	0·8	0·9	0·9	0·9	1·0				95°
90°	0·3	0·4	0·5	0·6	0·6	0·7	0·8	0·8	0·9	0·9	0·9					90°
	160°	155°	150°	145°	140°	135°	130°	125°	120°	115°	110°	105°	100°	95°	90°	
	Angle between Course Line (i.e. Ship's Head) and First Bearing															

Note: **When the angles exceed 90° use the right vertical column for the difference between bearings and the bottom horizontal row for the angle between Course Line and First Bearing. Interpolate for accuracy.**

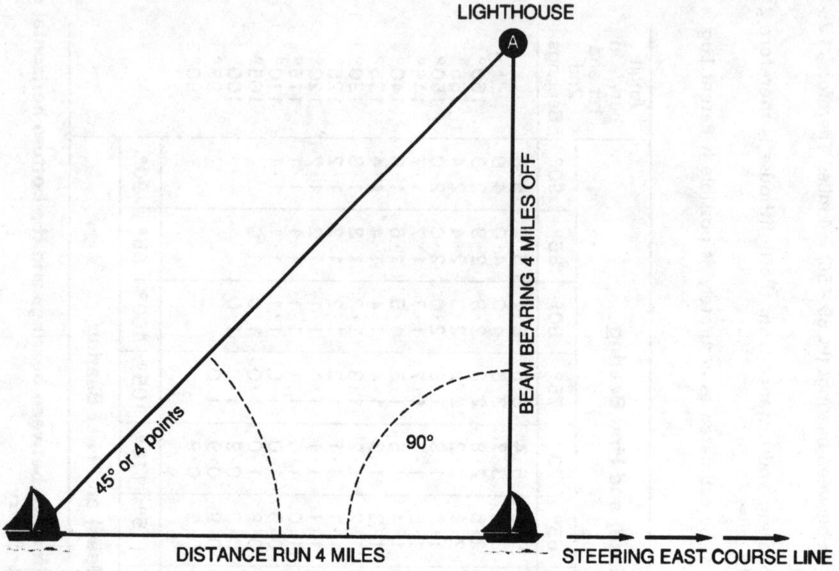

SPECIAL CASES OF RUNNING FIXES

Although tables will give the distance off for any bearing, it requires pencil, paper, nd, of course, the table itself. The following well-known methods of fixing a vessel's position can be used mentally hence their great value in small vessels.

(1) The Four Point Bearing.

(2) Doubling the Angle on the Bow.

The term "4 Points" derives its name from the old sailing ship days. The compass card used to be divided into 32 points, and courses were given in points and quarter points, each point being 11¼°. hence, 45° = 4 points.

1. The Four Point Bearing

It is customary in Coastal Navigation (where no special dangers lie near the Course Line) to fix the position when a point of land or a light is abeam, as it is then the Tack is usually altered.

Method. Take a bearing of an object when it bears 4 points (i.e., 45°) on the bow (assuming there is no leeway or current, otherwise take the bearing when it makes an angle of 45° with the track) and note the time and Log. Again take the time and log when it is abeam (i.e., at 90° to the track). Then - the distance made good over the ground in the interval between the two bearings equals the distance off when abeam.

Example. Steering 022° at 8½ knots, a lighthouse bears 067° at 1638 Log 36. At 1704 it came abeam (Log 39½). What was the distance off when abeam? At 8½ knots in 26 mins. vessel goes 3·7 miles (see Time, Speed and Distance Tables) check by the Log which shows 3½ miles has been run. Therefore the vessel is 3½ miles off.

2. Doubling the Angle on the Bow

The 4 point bearing method gives the distance off when abeam, but by "doubling the angle on the bow" the vessel's position may be found in advance, and therefore how far off a point the vessel will be when it comes abeam.

Method. Take a bearing of an object when more that 2 point (22½°) on the bow and take the time and Log. Note down this angle and watch the compass bearing carefully until it is exactly doubled then note the log and time again. The distance made good over the ground between the bearings is the distance off at the time of taking the second bearing.

Example. Steering 231° at 5 knots a lighthouse bears 259°. One hour 13 minutes later it bears287°. What is the position at the second bearing?

As the first angle on the bow had been doubled, i.e., 28° to 56° the distance run must be the distance off.

In 1hr. 13 min. at 5 knots the vessels steams 6·1 miles therefore the vessel's position is with the lighthouse bearing 287° 6·1 miles off.

POSITION BY VERTICAL

SEXTANT ANGLE

If the height of any object is known, its distance off can be measured by a vertical sextant angle and if a bearing of the object is taken at the same time the result is an accurate fix.

When measuring the angle remember that the height is measured to the center of the light - not to the top of the lighthouse.

In practice no allowance is made for the height of tide or observer's eye unless the object is very low.

TABLE FOR FINDING "DISTANCE OFF" UP TO 7 MILES

The following table gives the "distance off" by inspection of an object whose height is known and of which a sextant angle has been obtained. Where the height of the object is small, the distances cannot be found beyond 6 miles, so for this reason the first page extends only to 6 miles. The columns are for every3m. (10ft.) up to 122m (400ft.) and every 15m. (50ft.) thence to 213m. (700ft.) The distance column is for every cable* up to 3 miles and every 2 cables from 3 to 6 miles.

***Note:** A cable, or cable's length, is 100 fathoms, or 600 feet, or about 0·1 nautical miles.

Example 1. The sextant angle of a lighthouse 40m. above HW was taken and found to be 0°24'. Required, the distance off. First find the column for 40m. Glance down this column until the "angle off" is sighted i.e., 24'. Cast the eye along this line to the left when the 'Distance off" in miles and cables will be seen – in this case 3 miles exactly. The distance off is therefore 3 miles.

Example 2. There vertical angle of a lighthouse 70m. high was 1°26' which gives 1 mile 5 cables. The position of the vessel is therefore on a bearing of 202° from the lighthouse, 1·5 miles off – a reliable fix if the bearing is reasonable accurate.

If it is desired to keep 1 mile off this lighthouse, the necessary sextant angle to do so can be found from the table, 70m. high, 1 mile off is 2°10'.

TABLE FOR FINDING DISTANCE OFF WITH SEXTANT UP TO 6 MILES

Distance in Miles & Cables	HEIGHT OF OBJECT, TOP LINE METERS–LOWER LINE FEET												Distance in Miles & Cables
	12 40	15 50	18 60	21 70	24 80	27 90	30 100	33 110	37 120	40 130	43 140	46 150	
m c	° ′	° ′	° ′	° ′	° ′	° ′	° ′	° ′	° ′	° ′	° ′	° ′	m c
0 1	3 46	4 42	5 38	6 34	7 30	8 25	9 20	10 15	11 10	12 04	12 58	13 52	0 1
0 2	1 53	2 21	2 49	3 18	3 46	4 14	4 42	5 10	5 38	6 06	6 34	7 02	0 2
0 3	1 15	1 34	1 53	2 12	2 31	2 49	3 08	3 27	3 46	4 05	4 23	4 42	0 3
0 4	0 57	1 11	1 25	1 39	1 53	2 07	2 21	2 35	2 49	3 04	3 18	3 32	0 4
0 5	0 45	0 57	1 08	1 19	1 30	1 42	1 53	2 04	2 16	2 27	2 38	2 49	0 5
0 6	0 38	0 47	0 57	1 06	1 15	1 25	1 34	1 44	1 53	2 02	2 12	2 21	0 6
0 7	0 32	0 40	0 48	0 57	1 05	1 13	1 21	1 29	1 37	1 45	1 53	2 01	0 7
0 8	0 28	0 35	0 42	0 49	0 57	1 04	1 11	1 18	1 25	1 32	1 39	1 46	0 8
0 9	0 25	0 31	0 38	0 44	0 50	0 57	1 03	1 09	1 15	1 22	1 28	1 34	0 9
1 0	0 23	0 28	0 34	0 40	0 45	0 51	0 57	1 02	1 08	1 14	1 19	1 25	1 0
1 1	0 21	0 26	0 31	0 36	0 41	0 46	0 51	0 57	1 02	1 07	1 12	1 17	1 1
1 2	0 19	0 24	0 28	0 33	0 38	0 42	0 47	0 52	0 57	1 01	1 06	1 11	1 2
1 3	0 17	0 22	0 26	0 30	0 35	0 39	0 44	0 48	0 52	0 57	1 01	1 05	1 3
1 4	0 16	0 20	0 24	0 28	0 32	0 36	0 40	0 44	0 48	0 53	0 57	1 01	1 4
1 5	0 15	0 19	0 23	0 26	0 30	0 34	0 38	0 41	0 45	0 49	0 53	0 57	1 5
1 6	0 14	0 18	0 21	0 25	0 28	0 32	0 35	0 39	0 42	0 46	0 49	0 53	1 6
1 7	0 13	0 17	0 20	0 23	0 27	0 30	0 33	0 37	0 40	0 43	0 47	0 50	1 7
1 8	0 13	0 16	0 19	0 22	0 25	0 28	0 31	0 35	0 38	0 41	0 44	0 47	1 8
1 9	0 12	0 15	0 18	0 21	0 24	0 27	0 30	0 33	0 36	0 39	0 42	0 45	1 9
2 0	0 11	0 14	0 17	0 20	0 23	0 25	0 28	0 31	0 34	0 37	0 40	0 42	2 0
2 1	0 10	0 14	0 16	0 19	0 22	0 24	0 27	0 30	0 32	0 35	0 38	0 40	2 1
2 2	0 10	0 13	0 15	0 18	0 21	0 23	0 26	0 28	0 31	0 33	0 36	0 39	2 2
2 3	0 10	0 12	0 14	0 17	0 20	0 22	0 25	0 27	0 30	0 32	0 34	0 37	2 3
2 4	0 10	0 12	0 14	0 17	0 19	0 21	0 24	0 26	0 28	0 31	0 33	0 35	2 4
2 5	0 9	0 11	0 13	0 16	0 18	0 20	0 23	0 25	0 27	0 29	0 32	0 34	2 5
2 6	0 9	0 11	0 13	0 15	0 17	0 20	0 22	0 24	0 26	0 28	0 30	0 33	2 6
2 7	0 9	0 10	0 12	0 15	0 17	0 19	0 21	0 23	0 25	0 27	0 29	0 31	2 7
2 8	0 8	0 10	0 12	0 14	0 16	0 18	0 20	0 22	0 24	0 26	0 28	0 30	2 8
2 9	0 8	0 10	0 11	0 14	0 16	0 18	0 20	0 21	0 23	0 25	0 27	0 29	2 9
3 0	0 8	0 9	0 10	0 13	0 15	0 17	0 19	0 21	0 23	0 24	0 26	0 28	3 0
3 2				0 12	0 14	0 16	0 18	0 19	0 21	0 23	0 25	0 27	3 2
3 4				0 12	0 13	0 15	0 17	0 18	0 20	0 22	0 23	0 25	3 4
3 6				0 11	0 13	0 14	0 16	0 17	0 19	0 20	0 22	0 24	3 6
3 8				0 10	0 12	0 13	0 15	0 16	0 18	0 19	0 21	0 22	3 8
4 0				0 10	0 11	0 13	0 14	0 16	0 17	0 18	0 20	0 21	4 0
4 2						0 12	0 14	0 15	0 16	0 17	0 19	0 20	4 2
4 4						0 12	0 13	0 14	0 15	0 17	0 18	0 19	4 4
4 6						0 11	0 13	0 14	0 15	0 16	0 17	0 18	4 6
4 8						0 11	0 12	0 13	0 14	0 15	0 16	0 18	4 8
5 0						0 10	0 11	0 12	0 14	0 15	0 16	0 17	5 0
5 2								0 12	0 13	0 14	0 15	0 16	5 2
5 4								0 12	0 13	0 14	0 15	0 16	5 4
5 6								0 11	0 12	0 13	0 14	0 15	5 6
5 8								0 11	0 12	0 13	0 14	0 15	5 8
6 0								0 10	0 11	0 12	0 13	0 14	6 0

TABLE FOR FINDING DISTANCE OFF WITH SEXTANT UP TO 7 MILES

Distance in Miles & Cables	HEIGHT OF OBJECT, TOP LINE METERS—LOWER LINE FEET												Distance in Miles & Cables
	49 160	52 170	55 180	58 190	61 200	64 210	67 220	70 230	73 240	76 250	79 260	82 270	
m c	° ′	° ′	° ′	° ′	° ′	° ′	° ′	° ′	° ′	° ′	° ′	° ′	m c
0 1	14 45	15 37	16 29	17 21	18 13	19 03	19 54	20 43	21 32	22 21	23 09	23 57	0 1
0 2	7 30	7 58	8 25	8 53	9 20	9 48	10 15	10 43	11 10	11 37	12 04	12 31	0 2
0 3	5 01	5 19	5 38	5 57	6 15	6 34	6 53	7 11	7 30	7 48	8 07	8 25	0 3
0 4	3 46	4 00	4 14	4 28	4 42	4 56	5 10	5 24	5 38	5 52	6 06	6 20	0 4
0 5	3 01	3 12	3 23	3 35	3 46	3 57	4 08	4 20	4 31	4 42	4 53	5 05	0 5
0 6	2 31	2 40	2 49	2 59	3 08	3 18	3 27	3 36	3 46	3 55	4 05	4 14	0 6
0 7	2 09	2 17	2 25	2 33	2 41	2 49	2 58	3 06	3 14	3 22	3 30	3 38	0 7
0 8	1 53	2 00	2 07	2 14	2 21	2 28	2 35	2 42	2 49	2 57	3 04	3 11	0 8
0 9	1 40	1 47	1 53	1 59	2 06	2 12	2 18	2 24	2 31	2 37	2 43	2 49	0 9
1 0	1 30	1 36	1 42	1 47	1 53	1 59	2 04	2 10	2 16	2 21	2 27	2 33	1 0
1 1	1 22	1 27	1 33	1 38	1 43	1 48	1 53	1 58	2 03	2 08	2 14	2 19	1 1
1 2	1 15	1 20	1 25	1 30	1 34	1 39	1 44	1 48	1 53	1 58	2 02	2 07	1 2
1 3	1 10	1 14	1 18	1 23	1 27	1 31	1 36	1 40	1 44	1 49	1 53	1 57	1 3
1 4	1 05	1 09	1 13	1 17	1 21	1 25	1 29	1 33	1 37	1 41	1 45	1 49	1 4
1 5	1 00	1 04	1 8	1 12	1 15	1 19	1 23	1 27	1 30	1 34	1 38	1 42	1 5
1 6	0 57	1 00	1 04	1 07	1 11	1 14	1 18	1 21	1 25	1 28	1 32	1 35	1 6
1 7	0 53	0 57	1 00	1 03	1 07	1 10	1 13	1 16	1 20	1 23	1 26	1 30	1 7
1 8	0 50	0 53	0 57	1 00	1 03	1 06	1 09	1 12	1 15	1 19	1 22	1 25	1 8
1 9	0 48	0 51	0 54	0 57	1 00	1 02	1 05	1 08	1 11	1 14	1 17	1 20	1 9
2 0	0 45	0 48	0 51	0 54	0 57	0 59	1 02	1 05	1 08	1 11	1 14	1 16	2 0
2 1	0 43	0 46	0 48	0 51	0 54	0 57	0 59	1 02	1 05	1 07	1 10	1 13	2 1
2 2	0 41	0 44	0 46	0 49	0 51	0 54	0 57	0 59	1 02	1 04	1 07	1 09	2 2
2 3	0 39	0 42	0 44	0 47	0 49	0 52	0 54	0 57	0 59	1 01	1 04	1 06	2 3
2 4	0 38	0 40	0 42	0 45	0 47	0 49	0 52	0 54	0 57	0 59	1 01	1 04	2 4
2 5	0 36	0 38	0 41	0 43	0 45	0 48	0 50	0 52	0 54	0 57	0 59	1 01	2 5
2 6	0 35	0 37	0 39	0 41	0 44	0 46	0 48	0 50	0 52	0 54	0 57	0 59	2 6
2 7	0 34	0 36	0 38	0 40	0 42	0 44	0 46	0 48	0 50	0 52	0 54	0 57	2 7
2 8	0 32	0 34	0 36	0 38	0 40	0 42	0 44	0 46	0 48	0 50	0 53	0 55	2 8
2 9	0 31	0 33	0 35	0 37	0 39	0 41	0 43	0 45	0 47	0 49	0 51	0 53	2 9
3 0	0 30	0 32	0 34	0 36	0 38	0 40	0 41	0 43	0 45	0 47	0 49	0 51	3 0
3 2	0 28	0 30	0 32	0 34	0 35	0 37	0 39	0 41	0 42	0 44	0 46	0 48	3 2
3 4	0 27	0 28	0 30	0 32	0 33	0 35	0 37	0 38	0 40	0 42	0 43	0 45	3 4
3 6	0 25	0 27	0 28	0 30	0 31	0 33	0 35	0 36	0 38	0 39	0 41	0 42	3 6
3 8	0 24	0 25	0 27	0 28	0 30	0 31	0 33	0 34	0 36	0 37	0 39	0 40	3 8
4 0	0 23	0 24	0 25	0 27	0 28	0 30	0 31	0 33	0 34	0 35	0 37	0 38	4 0
4 2	0 22	0 23	0 24	0 26	0 27	0 28	0 30	0 31	0 32	0 34	0 35	0 36	4 2
4 4	0 21	0 22	0 23	0 24	0 26	0 27	0 28	0 30	0 31	0 32	0 33	0 35	4 4
4 6	0 20	0 21	0 22	0 23	0 25	0 26	0 27	0 28	0 30	0 31	0 32	0 33	4 6
4 8	0 19	0 20	0 21	0 22	0 24	0 25	0 26	0 27	0 28	0 30	0 31	0 32	4 8
5 0	0 18	0 19	0 20	0 21	0 23	0 24	0 25	0 26	0 27	0 28	0 29	0 31	5 0
5 2	0 17	0 18	0 20	0 21	0 22	0 23	0 24	0 25	0 26	0 27	0 28	0 29	5 2
5 4	0 17	0 18	0 19	0 20	0 21	0 22	0 23	0 24	0 25	0 26	0 27	0 28	5 4
5 6	0 16	0 17	0 18	0 19	0 20	0 21	0 22	0 23	0 24	0 25	0 26	0 27	5 6
5 8	0 16	0 17	0 18	0 19	0 19	0 20	0 21	0 22	0 23	0 24	0 25	0 26	5 8
6 0	0 15	0 16	0 17	0 18	0 19	0 20	0 21	0 22	0 23	0 24	0 25	0 25	6 0
6 2					0 18	0 19	0 20	0 21	0 22	0 23	0 24	0 25	6 2
6 4					0 18	0 19	0 20	0 21	0 21	0 22	0 23	0 24	6 4
6 6					0 17	0 18	0 19	0 20	0 21	0 21	0 22	0 23	6 6
6 8					0 17	0 18	0 18	0 19	0 20	0 21	0 22	0 22	6 8
7 0					0 16	0 17	0 18	0 19	0 19	0 20	0 21	0 22	7 0

TABLE FOR FINDING DISTANCE OFF WITH SEXTANT UP TO 7 MILES

Distance in Miles & Cables	HEIGHT OF OBJECT, TOP LINE METERS—LOWER LINE FEET												Distance in Miles & Cables
	85 280	88 290	91 300	94 310	97 320	101 330	104 340	107 350	110 360	113 370	116 380	119 390	
m c	° ′	° ′	° ′	° ′	° ′	° ′	° ′	° ′	° ′	° ′	° ′	° ′	m c
0 1	24 44	25 30	26 16	26 01	27 46	28 29	29 13	29 56	30 38	31 19	32 00	32 41	0 1
0 2	12 58	13 25	13 52	14 08	14 45	15 11	15 37	16 03	16 29	16 55	17 21	17 47	0 2
0 3	8 44	9 02	9 20	9 39	9 57	10 15	10 34	10 52	11 10	11 28	11 46	12 04	0 3
0 4	6 34	6 48	7 02	7 16	7 30	7 44	7 58	8 11	8 25	8 39	8 53	9 07	0 4
0 5	5 16	5 27	5 38	5 49	6 01	6 12	6 23	6 34	6 45	6 56	7 08	7 19	0 5
0 6	4 23	4 33	4 42	4 51	5 01	5 10	5 19	5 29	5 38	5 47	5 47	6 06	0 6
0 7	3 46	3 54	4 02	5 10	4 18	4 26	4 43	4 42	4 50	4 58	5 06	5 14	0 7
0 8	3 18	3 25	3 32	3 39	3 46	3 53	4 00	4 07	4 14	4 21	4 28	4 35	0 8
0 9	2 56	3 02	3 08	3 15	3 21	3 27	3 33	3 40	3 46	3 52	3 58	4 05	0 9
1 0	2 38	2 44	2 49	2 55	3 01	3 06	3 12	3 18	3 23	3 29	3 35	3 40	1 0
1 1	2 24	2 29	2 34	2 39	2 44	2 49	2 55	3 00	3 05	3 10	3 15	3 20	1 1
1 2	2 12	2 17	2 21	2 26	2 31	2 35	2 40	2 45	2 49	2 54	2 59	3 04	1 2
1 3	2 02	2 06	2 10	2 15	2 19	2 23	2 28	2 32	2 36	2 41	2 45	2 49	1 3
1 4	1 53	1 57	2 01	2 05	2 09	2 13	2 17	2 21	2 25	2 29	2 37	2 37	1 4
1 5	1 46	1 49	1 53	1 57	2 01	2 04	2 08	2 12	2 16	2 19	2 23	2 27	1 5
1 6	1 39	1 42	1 46	1 50	1 53	1 57	2 00	2 04	2 07	2 11	2 14	2 18	1 6
1 7	1 33	1 36	1 40	1 43	1 46	1 50	1 53	1 56	2 00	2 03	2 06	2 10	1 7
1 8	1 28	1 31	1 34	1 37	1 40	1 44	1 47	1 50	1 53	1 56	1 59	2 02	1 8
1 9	1 23	1 26	1 29	1 32	1 35	1 38	1 41	1 44	1 47	1 50	1 53	1 56	1 9
2 0	1 19	1 22	1 25	1 28	1 30	1 33	1 36	1 39	1 42	1 45	1 47	1 50	2 0
2 1	1 15	1 18	1 21	1 23	1 26	1 29	1 32	1 34	1 37	1 40	1 42	1 45	2 1
2 2	1 12	1 15	1 17	1 20	1 22	1 25	1 27	1 30	1 33	1 35	1 38	1 40	2 2
2 3	1 09	1 11	1 14	1 16	1 19	1 21	1 24	1 26	1 29	1 31	1 33	1 36	2 3
2 4	1 06	1 08	1 11	1 13	1 15	1 18	1 20	1 22	1 25	1 27	1 30	1 32	2 4
2 5	1 03	1 06	1 08	1 10	1 12	1 15	1 17	1 19	1 21	1 24	1 26	1 28	2 5
2 6	1 01	1 03	1 05	1 07	1 10	1 12	1 14	1 16	1 18	1 20	1 23	1 25	2 6
2 7	0 59	1 01	1 03	1 05	1 07	1 09	1 11	1 13	1 15	1 17	1 20	1 23	2 7
2 8	0 57	0 59	1 01	1 03	1 05	1 07	1 09	1 11	1 13	1 15	1 17	1 19	2 8
2 9	0 55	0 57	0 58	1 00	1 02	1 04	1 06	1 08	1 10	1 12	1 14	1 16	2 9
3 0	0 53	0 55	0 57	0 58	1 00	1 02	1 04	1 06	1 08	1 10	1 12	1 14	3 0
3 2	0 49	0 51	0 53	0 55	0 57	0 58	1 00	1 02	1 04	1 05	1 07	1 09	3 2
3 4	0 47	0 48	0 50	0 52	0 53	0 55	0 57	0 58	1 00	1 02	1 03	1 05	3 4
3 6	0 44	0 46	0 47	0 49	0 50	0 52	0 53	0 55	0 57	0 58	1 00	1 01	3 6
3 8	0 42	0 43	0 45	0 46	0 48	0 49	0 51	0 52	0 54	0 55	0 57	0 58	3 8
4 0	0 40	0 41	0 42	0 44	0 45	0 47	0 48	0 49	0 51	0 52	0 54	0 55	4 0
4 2	0 38	0 39	0 40	0 42	0 43	0 44	0 46	0 47	0 48	0 50	0 51	0 53	4 2
4 4	0 36	0 37	0 39	0 40	0 41	0 42	0 44	0 45	0 46	0 48	0 49	0 50	4 4
4 6	0 34	0 36	0 37	0 38	0 39	0 41	0 42	0 43	0 44	0 45	0 47	0 48	4 6
4 8	0 33	0 34	0 35	0 37	0 38	0 39	0 40	0 41	0 42	0 44	0 45	0 46	4 8
5 0	0 32	0 33	0 34	0 35	0 36	0 37	0 38	0 40	0 41	0 42	0 43	0 44	5 0
5 2	0 30	0 32	0 33	0 34	0 35	0 36	0 37	0 38	0 39	0 40	0 41	0 42	5 2
5 4	0 29	0 30	0 31	0 32	0 34	0 34	0 36	0 37	0 38	0 39	0 40	0 41	5 4
5 6	0 28	0 29	0 30	0 31	0 32	0 33	0 34	0 35	0 36	0 37	0 38	0 39	5 6
5 8	0 27	0 28	0 29	0 30	0 31	0 32	0 33	0 34	0 35	0 36	0 37	0 38	5 8
6 0	0 26	0 27	0 28	0 29	0 30	0 31	0 32	0 33	0 34	0 35	0 36	0 37	6 0
6 2	0 26	0 26	0 27	0 28	0 29	0 30	0 31	0 32	0 33	0 34	0 35	3 06	6 2
6 4	0 25	0 26	0 27	0 27	0 28	0 29	0 30	0 31	0 32	0 33	0 34	0 34	6 4
6 6	0 24	0 25	0 26	0 27	0 27	0 28	0 29	0 30	0 31	0 32	0 33	0 33	6 6
6 8	0 23	0 24	0 25	0 26	0 27	0 27	0 28	0 29	0 30	0 31	0 32	0 32	6 8
7 0	0 23	0 23	0 24	0 25	0 26	0 27	0 37	0 38	0 29	0 30	0 31	0 31	7 0

TABLE FOR FINDING DISTANCE OFF WITH SEXTANT UP TO 7 MILES

Distance in Miles & Cables	HEIGHT OF OBJECT, TOP LINE METERS—LOWER LINE FEET												Distance in Miles & Cables
	122 400	137 450	152 500	168 550	183 600	198 650	213 700	244 800	274 900	305 1000	457 1500	610 2000	
m c	° ′	° ′	° ′	° ′	° ′	° ′	° ′	° ′	° ′	° ′	°	° ′	m c
0 1	33 20	36 30	39 26	42 08	44 37								0 1
0 2	18 13	20 18	22 21	24 20	26 16	28 08	29 56	33 20	36 30	39 26			0 2
0 3	12 22	13 52	15 20	16 47	18 13	19 37	21 00	23 41	26 16	28 44			0 3
0 4	9 20	10 29	11 37	12 45	13 52	14 58	16 03	18 13	20 18	22 21			0 4
0 5	7 30	8 25	9 20	10 15	11 10	12 04	12 58	14 45	16 30	18 13	26 15		0 5
0 6	6 15	7 02	7 48	8 34	9 20	10 06	10 52	12 22	13 52	15 20	22 20	28 44	0 6
0 7	5 22	6 02	6 42	7 22	8 01	8 41	9 20	10 39	11 56	13 13	19 25	25 10	0 7
0 8	4 42	5 17	5 52	6 27	7 02	7 37	8 11	9 20	10 29	11 37	17 08	22 21	0 8
0 9	4 11	4 42	5 13	5 44	6 15	6 46	7 17	8 19	9 20	10 21	15 19	20 05	0 9
1 0	3 46	4 14	4 42	5 10	5 38	6 06	6 34	7 30	8 25	9 20	13 51	18 13	1 0
1 1	3 25	3 51	4 17	4 42	5 08	5 33	5 59	6 49	7 40	8 30	12 38	16 39	1 1
1 2	3 08	3 32	3 55	4 19	4 42	5 05	5 29	6 15	7 02	7 48	11 37	15 20	1 2
1 3	2 54	3 16	3 37	3 59	4 20	4 42	5 04	5 47	6 30	7 13	10 45	14 12	1 3
1 4	2 41	3 02	3 22	3 42	4 02	4 22	4 42	5 22	6 02	6 42	10 00	13 13	1 4
1 5	2 31	2 49	3 08	3 27	3 46	4 05	4 23	5 01	5 38	6 15	9 20	12 22	1 5
1 6	2 21	2 39	2 57	3 14	3 32	3 49	4 07	4 42	5 17	5 52	8 46	11 37	1 6
1 7	2 13	2 30	2 46	3 03	3 19	3 36	3 52	4 26	4 59	5 32	8 15	10 57	1 7
1 8	2 06	2 21	2 37	2 53	3 08	3 24	3 40	4 11	4 42	5 13	7 48	10 21	1 8
1 9	1 59	2 14	2 29	2 44	2 58	3 13	3 28	3 58	4 27	4 57	7 25	9 50	1 9
2 0	1 53	2 07	2 21	2 35	2 49	3 04	3 18	3 46	4 14	4 42	7 02	9 20	2 0
2 1	1 48	2 01	2 15	2 28	2 41	2 55	3 08	3 35	4 02	4 29	6 41	8 53	2 1
2 2	1 43	1 56	2 08	2 21	2 34	2 47	3 00	3 25	3 51	4 17	6 23	8 30	2 2
2 3	1 38	1 51	2 03	2 15	2 27	2 40	2 52	3 16	3 41	4 05	6 07	8 09	2 3
2 4	1 34	1 46	1 58	2 10	2 21	2 33	2 45	3 08	3 32	3 55	5 52	7 48	2 4
2 5	1 30	1 42	1 53	2 04	2 16	2 27	2 38	3 01	3 23	3 46	5 38	7 30	2 5
2 6	1 27	1 38	1 49	2 00	2 10	2 21	2 32	2 54	3 16	3 37	5 25	7 13	2 6
2 7	1 24	1 34	1 45	1 55	2 06	2 16	2 27	2 47	3 08	3 29	5 13	6 57	2 7
2 8	1 21	1 31	1 41	1 51	2 01	2 11	2 21	2 41	3 02	3 22	5 02	6 42	2 8
2 9	1 18	1 28	1 37	1 47	1 57	2 07	2 16	2 36	2 55	3 15	4 52	6 28	2 9
3 0	1 15	1 25	1 34	1 44	1 53	2 02	2 12	2 31	2 49	3 08	4 42	6 15	3 0
3 2	1 11	1 20	1 28	1 37	1 46	1 55	2 04	2 21	2 39	2 57	4 24	5 52	3 2
3 4	1 07	1 15	1 23	1 31	1 40	1 48	1 56	2 13	2 30	2 46	4 09	5 32	3 4
3 6	1 03	1 11	1 19	1 26	1 34	1 42	1 50	2 06	2 21	2 37	3 55	5 13	3 6
3 8	1 00	1 07	1 14	1 22	1 29	1 37	1 44	1 59	2 14	2 29	3 43	4 57	3 8
4 0	0 57	1 04	1 11	1 18	1 25	1 32	1 39	1 53	2 07	2 21	3 31	4 42	4 0
4 2	0 54	1 01	1 07	1 14	1 21	1 28	1 34	1 48	2 01	2 15	3 21	4 29	4 2
4 4	0 51	0 58	1 04	1 11	1 17	1 24	1 30	1 43	1 56	2 08	3 12	4 17	4 4
4 6	0 49	0 55	1 01	1 08	1 14	1 20	1 26	1 38	1 51	2 03	3 04	4 05	4 6
4 8	0 47	0 53	0 59	1 05	1 11	1 17	1 22	1 34	1 46	1 58	2 57	3 55	4 8
5 0	0 45	0 51	0 57	1 02	1 08	1 14	1 19	1 30	1 42	1 53	2 50	3 46	5 0
5 2	0 43	0 49	0 54	1 00	1 05	1 11	1 16	1 27	1 38	1 49	2 44	3 38	5 2
5 4	0 42	0 47	0 52	0 58	1 03	1 08	1 13	1 24	1 34	1 45	2 28	3 30	5 4
5 6	0 40	0 45	0 50	0 56	1 01	1 06	1 11	1 21	1 31	1 41	2 32	3 22	5 6
5 8	0 39	0 44	0 49	0 54	0 58	1 03	1 08	1 18	1 28	1 37	2 26	3 15	5 8
6 0	0 38	0 42	0 47	0 52	0 57	1 01	1 06	1 15	1 25	1 34	2 21	3 09	6 0
6 2	0 36	0 41	0 46	1 50	1 55	0 59	1 04	1 13	1 22	1 31	2 16	3 02	6 2
6 4	0 35	0 40	0 44	0 49	0 53	0 57	1 02	1 11	1 20	1 28	2 12	2 57	6 4
6 6	0 34	0 38	0 43	0 47	0 51	0 56	1 00	1 09	1 17	1 26	2 08	2 51	6 6
6 8	0 33	0 37	0 42	0 46	0 50	0 54	0 58	1 07	1 15	1 23	2 04	2 46	6 8
7 0	0 32	0 36	0 40	0 44	0 48	0 53	0 57	1 05	1 13	1 21	2 01	2 42	7 0

HORIZONTAL SEXTANT ANGLE FIX

An accurate fix can be obtained by measuring the angles between three objects marked on the chart and using the tables overleaf to fix the vessel's position. The best results are obtained when the objects are roughly in a straight line and the angles separating them are at least 30°.

Explanation and examples of how to use the Tables.

The diagram illustrates a vessel (S) whose navigator, when coasting, has taken simultaneous (or nearly so) horizontal sextant angles. The first angle taken was between the center object a Church (✝) and the right hand object – a high Rock (R); and the second angle was taken immediately between the same center object, a Church (✝) and the left hand object, a Lighthouse (L), all marked conspicuously on the chart and clearly visible to the navigator.

Angle between Rock (R) and Church (C) (right hand angle) = 30°. Distance between R and C = 3.2 miles. Angle between Lighthouse (L) and Church (C) (left hand angle) = 45°, and Distance between L and C = 7.1 miles.

Instructions

With the angle RSC (30°), subtended by the right hand and center objects enter the table on page 30 from the side and find the Radius of one of the Position Circles in the column headed by the Distance between the objects. In this case with 30° at the side and 3.2 miles at the top the Radius (by simple interpolation) is 3.2. Therefore with 3.2 miles in the compasses as Radius strike short arcs from both R and C and mark P – their point of intersection. With the same radius describe round P the circle RCS.

Proceeding in a similar way, describe arcs LQ and CQ and draw circle LCS.

The intersection of the two circles (S in the figure) gives the desired Fix and the Ship's position.

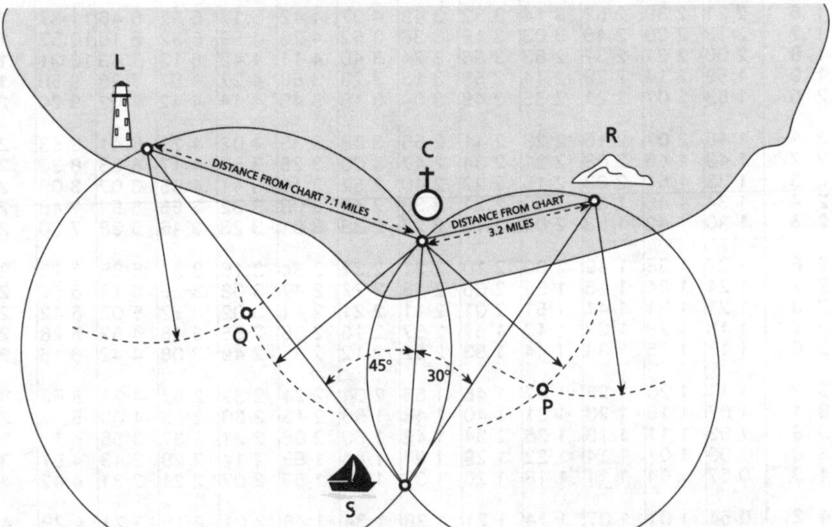

Note: The distances, tabulated at the top of the table are for full miles. For tenfolds and decimals of full miles use ten times or tenths respectively, of the tabulated radii and add, thus:

Subtended Angle 50°
Distance between objects 23.7 miles.

For 20 miles (ten times two) 10 x 1.31	13.1 miles
For 3 miles (from table)	1.96 miles
For 0.7 miles (column 7 divided by 10)	0.46 miles
Radius	15.5 miles

In general no interpolation between the tabulated angles will be necessary and in any case most Navigators would prefer to interpolate at sight.

HORIZONTAL SEXTANT ANGLE FIX

Angle Subtended by Objects °	'	Distance between Objects 1	2	3	4	5	6	7	8	9	Angle Subtended by Objects °	'
30		1.00	2.00	3.00	4.00	5.00	6.00	7.00	8.00	9.00	150	
	10	1.00	1.99	2.99	3.98	4.98	5.97	6.97	7.96	8.96		50
	20	0.99	1.98	2.97	3.96	4.95	5.94	6.93	7.92	8.91		40
	30	0.99	1.97	2.96	3.94	4.93	5.91	6.90	7.88	8.87		30
	40	0.98	1.96	2.94	3.92	4.90	5.88	6.86	7.84	8.83		20
	50	0.98	1.95	2.93	3.90	4.88	5.85	6.83	7.80	8.78		10
31		0.97	1.94	2.91	3.88	4.86	5.83	6.80	7.77	8.74	149	
	10	0.97	1.93	2.90	3.86	4.83	5.80	6.76	7.73	8.70		50
	20	0.96	1.92	2.89	3.85	4.81	5.77	6.73	7.70	8.65		40
	30	0.96	1.91	2.87	3.83	4.79	5.74	6.70	7.66	8.61		30
	40	0.95	1.91	2.86	3.81	4.76	5.72	6.67	7.62	8.57		20
	50	0.95	1.90	2.84	3.79	4.74	5.69	6.64	7.58	8.53		10
32		0.94	1.89	2.83	3.77	4.72	5.66	6.61	7.55	8.49	148	
	10	0.94	1.88	2.82	3.76	4.70	5.63	6.57	7.51	8.45		50
	20	0.94	1.87	2.81	3.74	4.68	5.61	6.55	7.48	8.42		40
	30	0.93	1.86	2.79	3.72	4.65	5.58	6.51	7.44	8.38		30
	40	0.93	1.85	2.78	3.71	4.63	5.56	6.49	7.41	8.34		20
	50	0.92	1.84	2.77	3.69	4.61	5.53	6.45	7.38	8.30		10
33		0.92	1.84	2.75	3.67	4.59	5.51	6.43	7.34	8.26	147	
	10	0.92	1.83	2.75	3.66	4.58	5.49	6.41	7.32	8.24		50
	20	0.91	1.82	2.73	3.64	4.55	5.46	6.37	7.28	8.19		40
	30	0.91	1.81	2.72	3.62	4.53	5.44	6.34	7.25	8.15		30
	40	0.90	1.80	2.71	3.61	4.51	5.41	6.31	7.22	8.12		20
	50	0.90	1.80	2.69	3.59	4.49	5.39	6.29	7.18	8.08		10
34		0.89	1.79	2.68	3.58	4.47	5.36	6.26	7.15	8.05	146	
	10	0.89	1.78	2.67	3.56	4.45	5.34	6.23	7.12	8.02		50
	20	0.89	1.77	2.66	3.55	4.43	5.32	6.21	7.09	7.98		40
	30	0.88	1.77	2.65	3.53	4.42	5.30	6.18	7.06	7.95		30
	40	0.88	1.76	2.64	3.52	4.40	5.27	6.15	7.03	7.91		20
	50	0.88	1.75	2.63	3.50	4.38	5.25	6.13	7.00	7.88		10
35		0.87	1.74	2.62	3.49	4.36	5.23	6.10	6.97	7.84	145	
	12	0.87	1.74	2.60	3.47	4.34	5.21	6.07	6.94	7.81		48
	24	0.86	1.73	2.59	3.45	4.32	5.18	6.04	6.90	7.77		36
	36	0.86	1.72	2.58	3.44	4.30	5.15	6.01	6.87	7.73		24
	48	0.86	1.71	2.57	3.42	4.28	5.13	5.99	6.84	7.70		12
36		0.85	1.70	2.55	3.40	4.25	5.10	5.95	6.80	7.66	144	
	12	0.85	1.69	2.54	3.39	4.23	5.08	5.93	6.77	7.62		48
	24	0.84	1.69	2.53	3.37	4.21	5.06	5.90	6.74	7.58		36
	36	0.84	1.68	2.52	3.35	4.19	5.03	5.87	6.71	7.55		24
	48	0.83	1.67	2.50	3.34	4.17	5.01	5.84	6.68	7.51		12
37		0.83	1.66	2.49	3.32	4.16	4.99	5.82	6.65	7.48	143	
	12	0.83	1.65	2.48	3.31	4.14	4.96	5.79	6.62	7.44		48
	24	0.82	1.65	2.47	3.29	4.12	4.94	5.76	6.58	7.41		36
	36	0.82	1.64	2.46	3.28	4.10	4.92	5.74	6.56	7.38		24
	48	0.82	1.63	2.45	3.26	4.08	4.90	5.71	6.53	7.34		12
38		0.81	1.62	2.44	3.25	4.06	4.87	5.68	6.50	7.31	142	
	12	0.81	1.62	2.43	3.23	4.04	4.85	5.66	6.47	7.28		48
	24	0.81	1.61	2.42	3.22	4.03	4.83	5.64	6.44	7.25		36
	36	0.80	1.60	2.41	3.21	4.01	4.81	5.61	6.41	7.21		24
	48	0.80	1.60	2.39	3.19	3.99	4.79	5.59	6.38	7.18		12
39		0.79	1.59	2.38	3.18	3.97	4.77	5.56	6.36	7.15	141	
	12	0.79	1.58	2.37	3.16	3.96	4.75	5.54	6.33	7.12		48
	24	0.79	1.58	2.36	3.15	3.94	4.73	5.52	6.30	7.09		36
	36	0.79	1.57	2.35	3.14	3.92	4.71	5.49	6.28	7.06		24
	48	0.78	1.56	2.34	3.12	3.91	4.69	5.47	6.25	7.03		12
40		0.78	1.56	2.33	3.11	3.89	4.67	5.45	6.22	7.00	140	
	20	0.77	1.55	2.32	3.09	3.86	4.64	5.41	6.18	6.95		40
	40	0.77	1.54	2.30	3.07	3.84	4.61	5.37	6.14	6.91		20
41		0.76	1.52	2.29	3.05	3.81	4.57	5.33	6.10	6.86	139	
	20	0.76	1.51	2.27	3.03	3.79	4.54	5.30	6.06	6.81		40
	40	0.75	1.50	2.26	3.01	3.76	4.51	5.26	6.02	6.77		20
42		0.75	1.50	2.24	2.99	3.74	4.49	5.23	5.98	6.73	138	
	20	0.74	1.49	2.23	2.97	3.71	4.46	5.20	5.94	6.68		40
	40	0.74	1.48	2.21	2.95	3.69	4.43	5.17	5.90	6.64		20
43		0.73	1.47	2.20	2.93	3.67	4.40	5.13	5.86	6.60	137	
°	'										°	'

HORIZONTAL SEXTANT ANGLE FIX

Angle Subtended by Objects		Distance between Objects									Angle Subtended by Objects	
		1	2	3	4	5	6	7	8	9		
°	′										°	′
43		0.73	1.47	2.20	2.93	3.67	4.40	5.13	5.86	6.60	137	
	20	0.73	1.46	2.19	2.91	3.64	4.37	5.10	5.83	6.56		40
	40	0.72	1.45	2.17	2.90	3.62	4.34	5.07	5.79	6.52		20
44		0.72	1.44	2.16	2.88	3.60	4.32	5.04	5.76	6.48	136	
	20	0.72	1.43	2.15	2.86	3.58	4.29	5.01	5.72	6.44		40
	40	0.71	1.42	2.14	2.85	3.56	4.27	4.98	5.69	6.40		20
45		0.71	1.41	2.12	2.83	3.54	4.24	4.95	5.66	6.36	135	
	20	0.70	1.41	2.11	2.81	3.52	4.22	4.92	5.62	6.33		40
	40	0.70	1.40	2.10	2.80	3.50	4.19	4.89	5.59	6.29		20
46		0.70	1.39	2.09	2.78	3.48	4.17	4.87	5.56	6.26	134	
	20	0.69	1.38	2.07	2.76	3.46	4.15	4.84	5.53	6.22		40
	40	0.69	1.38	2.06	2.75	3.44	4.13	4.81	5.50	6.19		20
47		0.68	1.37	2.05	2.73	3.42	4.10	4.79	5.47	6.15	133	
	20	0.68	1.36	2.04	2.72	3.40	4.08	4.76	5.44	6.12		40
	40	0.68	1.35	2.03	2.71	3.38	4.06	4.74	5.41	6.09		20
48		0.67	1.35	2.02	2.69	3.37	4.04	4.71	5.38	6.06	132	
	20	0.67	1.34	2.01	2.68	3.35	4.02	4.69	5.36	6.03		40
	40	0.67	1.33	2.00	2.66	3.33	4.00	4.66	5.33	5.99		20
49		0.66	1.33	2.00	2.65	3.31	3.98	4.64	5.30	5.96	131	
	20	0.66	1.32	1.98	2.64	3.30	3.95	4.61	5.27	5.93		40
	40	0.66	1.31	1.97	2.62	3.28	3.94	4.59	5.25	5.90		20
50		0.65	1.31	1.96	2.61	3.26	3.92	4.57	5.22	5.87	130	
	30	0.65	1.30	1.94	2.59	3.24	3.89	4.54	5.18	5.83		30
51		0.64	1.29	1.93	2.57	3.22	3.86	4.51	5.15	5.79	129	
	30	0.64	1.28	1.92	2.56	3.20	3.83	4.47	5.11	5.75		30
52		0.63	1.27	1.90	2.54	3.17	3.81	4.44	5.08	5.71	128	
	30	0.63	1.26	1.89	2.52	3.15	3.78	4.41	5.04	5.68		30
53		0.63	1.25	1.88	2.50	3.13	3.76	4.38	5.01	5.63	127	
	30	0.62	1.24	1.87	2.49	3.11	3.73	4.35	4.98	5.60		30
54		0.62	1.24	1.85	2.47	3.09	3.71	4.33	4.94	5.56	126	
	30	0.61	1.23	1.84	2.46	3.07	3.68	4.30	4.91	5.53		30
55		0.61	1.22	1.83	2.44	3.05	3.66	4.27	4.88	5.50	125	
	30	0.61	1.21	1.82	2.43	3.03	3.64	4.25	4.85	5.46		30
56		0.60	1.21	1.81	2.41	3.02	3.62	4.22	4.82	5.43	124	
	30	0.60	1.20	1.80	2.40	3.00	3.60	4.20	4.80	5.40		30
57		0.60	1.19	1.79	2.38	2.98	3.58	4.17	4.77	5.36	123	
	30	0.59	1.19	1.78	2.37	2.97	3.56	4.15	4.74	5.34		30
58		0.59	1.18	1.77	2.36	2.95	3.54	4.13	4.72	5.31	122	
	30	0.59	1.17	1.76	2.35	2.93	3.52	4.11	4.69	5.28		30
59		0.58	1.17	1.75	2.33	2.92	3.50	4.09	4.67	5.25	121	
	30	0.58	1.16	1.74	3.32	2.90	3.48	4.06	4.64	5.23		30
60		0.58	1.16	1.73	2.31	2.89	3.47	4.04	4.62	5.20	120	
61		0.57	1.14	1.72	2.29	2.86	3.43	4.00	4.57	5.14	119	
62		0.57	1.13	1.70	2.27	2.83	3.40	3.97	4.53	5.10	118	
63		0.56	1.12	1.68	2.24	2.81	3.37	3.93	4.49	5.05	117	
64		0.56	1.11	1.67	2.23	2.78	3.34	3.90	4.45	5.01	116	
65		0.55	1.10	1.66	2.21	2.76	3.31	3.86	4.41	4.96	115	
66		0.55	1.10	1.64	2.19	2.74	3.29	3.83	4.38	4.93	114	
67		0.54	1.09	1.63	2.17	2.72	3.26	3.80	4.34	4.89	113	
68		0.54	1.08	1.62	2.16	2.70	3.24	3.78	4.32	4.86	112	
69		0.54	1.07	1.61	2.14	2.68	3.21	3.75	4.28	4.82	111	
70		0.53	1.06	1.60	2.13	2.66	3.19	3.72	4.26	4.79	110	
71		0.53	1.06	1.59	2.12	2.65	3.17	3.70	4.23	4.76	109	
72		0.53	1.05	1.58	2.10	2.63	3.16	3.68	4.21	4.73	108	
73		0.52	1.05	1.57	2.09	2.62	3.14	3.66	4.18	4.71	107	
74		0.52	1.04	1.56	2.08	2.60	3.12	3.64	4.16	4.68	106	
76		0.52	1.03	1.55	2.06	2.58	3.09	3.61	4.12	4.64	104	
78		0.51	1.02	1.53	2.04	2.56	3.07	3.58	4.09	4.60	102	
80		0.51	1.02	1.52	2.03	2.54	3.05	3.55	4.06	4.57	100	
82		0.51	1.01	1.52	2.02	2.53	3.03	3.54	4.04	4.55	98	
84		0.50	1.01	1.51	2.01	2.52	3.02	3.52	4.02	4.53	96	
86		0.50	1.00	1.50	2.00	2.51	3.01	3.51	4.01	4.51	94	
90		0.50	1.00	1.50	2.00	2.50	3.00	3.50	4.00	4.50	90	
°	′										°	′

FINDING THE DISTANCE OF OBJECTS AT SEA

Owing to the Earth's curvature, the distance to the sea horizon is governed by the height of the observer's eye. The figure below illustrates this and also that, in conditions of clear visibility, the distance at which the top of an object first shows itself on the horizon depends upon its height as well as the height of eye.

In this example the distance of the horizon from the observer using the tables overleaf is 3.25 miles and the distance of the light from the horizon is 13.1 miles. The light will appear to the observer when it is 16.35 miles distant.

Range of lights

Luminous range is the maximum distance at which a light can be seen as determined by the intensity of the light and the meteorological visibility prevailing at the time; it takes no account of elevation, observer's height of eye or the curvature of the earth.

Nominal range is the luminous range when the meteorological visibility is unlimited.

Geographical range is the maximum distance at which light from a light can theoretically reach an observer, as limited only by the curvature of the earth and the refraction of the atmosphere, and by the elevation of the light and the height of the observer. Geographical ranges are based on a height of eye of 15 ft (5 meters).

The range shown on modern charts for U.S. waters is the nominal range.

All heights of lights are given above High Water. Allowance for the state of the tides should be made with lights of small elevation.

Tables I and II allow for the effect of normal atmospheric refraction but would be of no use when conditions are abnormal.

Glare from background lighting will reduce considerably the range at which lights are sighted. A light of 100,000 candle power has a nominal range of about 20 miles; with minor background lighting as from a populated coastline this range will be reduced to about 14 miles, and with major background lighting as from a city or from harbor installations to about 9 miles.

Yachtsmen with a near horizon and utilising the powerful lights around the U.S. coastline will probably be more concerned with the Geographical range of lights.

From the yachtsman's point of view it is useful to know when a charted light will become visible. For example a light with a charted range of 20 miles is 46 m high and the observer's eye is 2.1 m above sea level.

From Table 1 the light to horizon distance is 14.1 miles and observer to horizon is 3.04 miles, the light will therefore become visible when it is 17 miles distant.

To check whether or not a newly sighted light is actually on the horizon, if practicable, lower the eye immediately to find out if the light dips below the horizon again. In clear visibility and a heavy swell the light should alternately rise above and dip below the horizon with the ship's movement. The distance off from the light at this moment is often referred to as the "dipping range" or "dipping distance".

Table II will be found very useful for finding the dipping range of a light immediately by inspection.

Fix by dipping range and bearing: The light "X" has just appeared on the horizon in clear visibility and bearing 068°. If the height of eye is 3 m what is the ship's position?

The Visual Aids to Navigation Section gives the height of Light "X" as 40 m and the charted visibility as 17 miles. With height of eye 3 m at the top and 40 m at the side, Table II gives 16¾ miles.

The ship's position is, therefore, 16¾ miles 248° from Light "X".

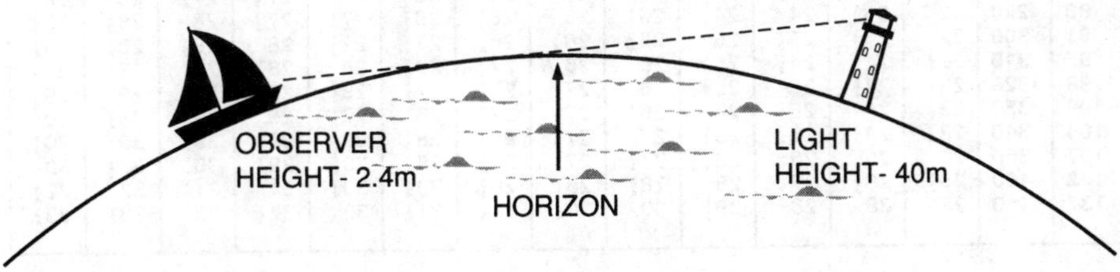

TABLE I DISTANCE OF SEA HORIZON IN NAUTICAL MILES

Height in Meters	Height in Feet	Distance in Miles	Height in Meters	Height in Feet	Distance in Miles	Height in Meters	Height in Feet	Distance in Miles	Height in Meters	Height in Feet	Distance in Miles
0.3	1	1.15	4.3	14	4.30	12.2	40	7.27	55	180	15.4
0.6	2	1.62	4.9	16	4.60	12.8	42	7.44	61	200	16.2
0.9	3	1.99	5.5	18	4.87	13.4	44	7.62	73	240	17.8
1.2	4	2.30	6.1	20	5.14	14.0	46	7.79	85	280	19.2
1.5	5	2.57	6.7	22	5.39	14.6	48	7.96	98	320	20.5
1.8	6	2.81	7.3	24	5.62	15.2	50	8.1	110	360	21.8
2.1	7	3.04	7.9	26	5.86	18	60	8.9	122	400	23.0
2.4	8	3.25	8.5	28	6.08	20	70	9.6	137	450	24.3
2.7	9	3.45	9.1	30	6.30	24	80	10.3	152	500	25.7
3.0	10	3.63	9.8	32	6.50	27	90	10.9	183	600	28.1
3.4	11	3.81	10.4	34	6.70	30	100	11.5	213	700	30.4
3.7	12	3.98	11.0	36	6.90	40	130	13.1	244	800	32.5
4.0	13	4.14	11.6	38	7.09	46	150	14.1			

TABLE II DISTANCE OF LIGHTS RISING OR DIPPING

Height of Light		HEIGHT OF EYE												
		Meters												
		1.5	3	4.6	6.1	7.6	9.1	10.7	12.2	13.7	15.2	16.8	18.3	19.8
		Feet												
m	ft	5	10	15	20	25	30	35	40	45	50	55	60	65
12	40	9¾	11	11¾	12½	13	13½	14	14½	15	15½	15¾	16¼	16½
15	50	10¾	11¾	12½	13¼	14	14½	15	15½	15¾	16¼	16¾	17	17½
18	60	11½	12½	13½	14	14¾	15¼	15¾	16¼	16½	17	17½	17¾	18¼
21	70	12¼	13¼	14	14¾	15½	16	16½	17	17¼	17¾	18	18½	19
24	80	13	14	14¾	15½	16	16½	17	17½	18	18½	18¾	19¼	19½
27	90	13½	14½	15½	16	16¾	17¼	17¾	18¼	18½	19	19½	19¾	20¼
30	100	14	15	16	16½	17¼	17¾	18¼	18¾	19¼	19½	20	20½	20¾
34	110	14½	15¾	16½	17¼	17¾	18¼	19	19¼	19¾	20¼	20½	21	21¼
37	120	15¼	16¼	17	17¾	18¼	19	19½	20	20¼	20¾	21	21½	22
40	130	15¾	16¾	17½	18¼	19	19½	20	20½	20¾	21¼	21½	22	22½
43	140	16¼	17¼	18	18¾	19½	20	20½	21	21¼	21¾	22	22½	23
46	150	16¾	17¾	18½	19¼	19¾	20½	21	21¼	21¾	22¼	22½	23	23¼
49	160	17	18¼	19	19¾	20¼	20¾	21½	21¾	22¼	22¾	23	23½	23¾
52	170	17½	18½	19½	20	20¾	21¼	21¾	22¼	22¾	23	23½	24	24¼
55	180	18	19	20	20½	21¼	21¾	22¼	22¾	23	23½	24	24¼	24¾
58	190	18½	19½	20¼	21	21½	22	22¾	23	23½	24	24½	24¾	25
61	200	18¾	20	20¾	21½	22	22½	23	23½	24	24½	24¾	25¼	25½
64	210	19¼	20¼	21	21¾	22½	23	23½	24	24½	24¾	25¼	25½	26
67	220	19½	20¾	21½	22¼	22¾	23¼	24	24¼	24¾	25¼	25½	26	26¼
70	230	20	21	22	22½	23¼	23¾	24¼	24¾	25	25½	26	26¼	26¾
73	240	20½	21½	22¼	23	23½	24	24½	25	25½	26	26¼	26¾	27
76	250	20¾	21¾	22½	23¼	24	24½	25	25½	26	26¼	26¾	27	27½
79	260	21	22¼	23	23¾	24¼	24¾	25¼	25¾	26¼	26¾	27	27½	27¾
82	270	21½	22½	23¼	24	24½	25¼	25¾	26¼	26½	27	27½	27¾	28¼
85	280	21¾	23	23¾	24½	25	25½	26	26½	27	27½	27¾	28	28½
88	290	22	23¼	24	24¾	25¼	26	26½	26¾	27¼	27¾	28	28½	28¾
91	300	22½	23½	24½	25	25¾	26¼	26¾	27¼	27½	28	28½	28¾	29¼
95	310	22¾	24	24¾	25½	26	26½	27	27½	28	28½	28¾	29	29½
98	320	23	24¼	25	25¾	26¼	27	27½	27¾	28¼	28¾	29	29½	29¾
100	330	23½	24½	25¼	26	26½	27¼	27¾	28	28½	29	29½	29¾	30
104	340	23¾	24¾	25¾	26¼	27	27½	28	28½	29	29¼	29¾	30	30½
107	350	24	25	26	26¾	27¼	27¾	28¼	28¾	29¼	29½	30	30½	30¾
122	400	25½	26½	27½	28	28¾	29¼	29¾	30¼	30¾	31	31½	32	32¼
137	450	27	28	28¾	29½	30	30¾	31¼	31¾	32	32½	33	33¼	33¾

MEASURING SPEED

At a number of places on the coast marks have been erected which indicate specific measured distances (usually 1 mile) which can be used for checking the accuracy of speed indicating instruments.

The method is to travel at a constant speed between the two transits, ideally at slack water, noting the exact time elapsed. With only a single run allowance must be made for any current; in practice several runs should be made.

The downstream speed is found by dividing the distance by the downstream time and the upstream similarly and the vessel's speed through the water will be half the total sum.

Example. Using a measured mile and the time and knot table ascertain the time taken on the measured mile in minutes and seconds and look up the table (minutes at the top and seconds at the side) to find the vessel's speed in knots.

Having covered the measured mile in 6 minutes 18 seconds, what is the speed? This will be found to be 9.524 knots.

For speeds lower than 5 knots simply halve the time taken and then halve the speed found, e.g., if the time taken on the mile is 17 minutes then look out under 8 min. 30 sec. The speed given is 7.059 which divided by 2 gives the speed of 3.529 knots (i.e., 3½ knots).

If the speed through the water determined by the Patent Log is required; record accurately the time taken to travel one mile; then read off the speed in knots from the table.

MEASURED MILE (TIME AND KNOT) TABLE

The above figures indicate the speed in knots according to a particular time in minutes and

Secs.	2 min.	3 min.	4 min.	5 min.	6 min.	7 min.	8 min.	9 min.	10 min.	11 min.
0	30.000	20.000	15.000	12.000	**10.000**	8.571	7.500	6.667	6.000	5.455
1	29.752	19.890	14.938	11.960	**9.972**	8.551	7.484	6.654	5.990	5.446
2	29.508	19.780	14.876	11.921	**9.945**	8.531	7.469	6.642	5.980	5.438
3	29.268	19.672	14.815	11.881	**9.917**	8.511	7.453	6.630	5.970	5.430
4	29.032	19.565	14.754	11.842	**9.890**	8.491	7.438	6.618	5.960	5.422
5	28.800	19.459	14.694	11.803	**9.863**	8.471	7.423	6.606	5.950	5.414
6	28.571	19.355	14.634	11.765	**9.836**	8.451	7.407	6.593	5.941	5.405
7	28.346	19.251	14.575	11.726	**9.809**	8.431	7.392	6.581	5.931	5.397
8	28.125	19.149	14.516	11.688	**9.783**	8.411	7.377	6.569	5.921	5.389
9	27.907	19.048	14.458	11.650	**9.756**	8.392	7.362	6.557	5.911	5.381
10	27.692	18.947	14.400	11.613	**9.730**	8.372	7.347	6.545	5.902	5.373
11	27.481	18.848	14.343	11.576	**9.704**	8.353	7.332	6.534	5.892	5.365
12	27.273	18.750	14.286	11.538	**9.677**	8.333	7.317	6.522	5.882	5.357
13	27.068	18.653	14.229	11.502	**9.651**	8.314	7.302	6.510	5.873	5.349
14	26.866	18.557	14.173	11.465	**9.626**	8.295	7.287	6.498	5.863	5.341
15	26.667	18.461	14.118	11.429	**9.600**	8.276	7.273	6.486	5.854	5.333
16	26.471	18.367	14.062	11.392	**9.574**	8.257	7.258	6.475	5.844	5.325
17	26.277	18.274	14.008	11.356	**9.549**	8.238	7.243	6.463	5.835	5.318
18	26.087	18.182	13.953	11.321	**9.524**	8.219	7.229	6.452	5.825	5.310
19	25.899	18.090	13.900	11.285	**9.499**	8.200	7.214	6.440	5.816	5.302
20	25.714	18.000	13.846	11.250	**9.474**	8.182	7.200	6.429	5.806	5.294
21	25.532	17.910	13.793	11.215	**9.449**	8.163	7.186	6.417	5.797	5.286
22	25.352	17.822	13.740	11.180	**9.424**	8.145	7.171	6.406	5.788	5.279
23	25.175	17.734	13.688	11.146	**9.399**	8.126	7.157	6.394	5.778	5.271
24	25.000	17.647	13.636	11.111	**9.375**	8.108	7.143	6.383	5.769	5.263
25	24.828	17.561	13.585	11.077	**9.351**	8.090	7.129	6.372	5.760	5.255
26	24.658	17.476	13.534	11.043	**9.326**	8.072	7.115	6.360	5.751	5.248
27	24.490	17.391	13.483	11.009	**9.302**	8.054	7.101	6.349	5.742	5.240
28	24.324	17.308	13.433	10.976	**9.278**	8.036	7.087	6.338	5.732	5.233
29	24.161	17.225	13.383	10.942	**9.254**	8.018	7.073	6.327	5.723	5.225
30	24.000	17.143	13.333	10.909	**9.231**	8.000	7.059	6.316	5.714	5.217
31	23.841	17.062	13.284	10.876	**9.207**	7.982	7.045	6.305	5.705	5.210
32	23.684	16.981	13.235	10.843	**9.184**	7.965	7.031	6.294	5.696	5.202
33	23.529	16.901	13.187	10.811	**9.160**	7.947	7.018	6.283	5.687	5.195
34	23.377	16.822	13.139	10.778	**9.137**	7.930	7.004	6.272	5.678	5.187
35	23.226	16.744	13.091	10.746	**9.114**	7.912	6.990	6.261	5.669	5.180
36	23.077	16.667	13.043	10.714	**9.091**	7.895	6.977	6.250	5.660	5.172
37	22.930	16.590	12.996	10.682	**9.068**	7.877	6.963	6.239	5.651	5.165
38	22.785	16.514	12.950	10.651	**9.045**	7.860	6.950	6.228	5.643	5.158
39	22.642	16.438	12.903	10.619	**9.023**	7.843	6.936	6.218	5.634	5.150
40	22.500	16.364	12.857	10.588	**9.000**	7.826	6.923	6.207	5.625	5.143
41	22.360	16.290	12.811	10.557	**8.978**	7.809	6.910	6.196	5.616	5.136
42	22.222	16.216	12.766	10.526	**8.955**	7.792	6.897	6.186	5.607	5.128
43	22.086	16.143	12.721	10.496	**8.933**	7.775	6.883	6.175	5.599	5.121
44	21.951	16.071	12.676	10.465	**8.911**	7.759	6.870	6.164	5.590	5.114
45	21.818	16.000	12.632	10.435	**8.889**	7.742	6.857	6.154	5.581	5.106
46	21.687	15.929	12.587	10.405	**8.867**	7.725	6.844	6.143	5.573	5.099
47	21.557	15.859	12.544	10.375	**8.845**	7.709	6.831	6.133	5.564	5.092
48	21.429	15.789	12.500	10.345	**8.824**	7.692	6.818	6.122	5.556	5.085
49	21.302	15.721	12.457	10.315	**8.802**	7.676	6.805	6.112	5.547	5.078
50	21.176	15.652	12.414	10.286	**8.780**	7.660	6.792	6.102	5.538	5.070
51	21.053	15.584	12.371	10.256	**8.759**	7.643	6.780	6.091	5.530	5.063
52	20.930	15.517	12.329	10.227	**8.738**	7.627	6.767	6.081	5.521	5.056
53	20.809	15.451	12.287	10.198	**8.717**	7.611	6.754	6.071	5.513	5.049
54	20.690	15.385	12.245	10.169	**8.696**	7.595	6.742	6.061	5.505	5.042
55	20.571	15.319	12.203	10.141	**8.675**	7.579	6.729	6.050	5.496	5.035
56	20.455	15.254	12.162	10.112	**8.654**	7.563	6.716	6.040	5.488	5.028
57	20.339	15.190	12.121	10.084	**8.633**	7.547	6.704	6.030	5.479	5.021
58	20.225	15.126	12.081	10.056	**8.612**	7.531	6.691	6.020	5.471	5.014
59	20.112	15.063	12.040	10.028	**8.592**	7.516	6.679	6.010	5.463	5.007
Secs.	2 min.	3 min.	4 min.	5 min.	6 min.	7 min.	8 min.	9 min.	10 min.	11 min.

The above figures indicate the speed in knots according to a particular time in minutes and seconds

TIME, SPEED and DISTANCE TABLE
for finding distance run in a given time at various Speeds, 2½ to 22 knots

	KNOTS													
Min	**2½**	**3**	**3½**	**4**	**4½**	**5**	**5½**	**6**	**6½**	**7**	**7½**	**8**	**8½**	**Min**
1	0.1	0.1	0.1	0.1	0.1	0.1	0.1	0.1	0.1	0.1	0.1	0.1	0.2	**1**
2	0.1	0.1	0.1	0.2	0.2	0.2	0.2	0.2	0.2	0.2	0.3	0.3	0.3	**2**
3	0.1	0.2	0.2	0.2	0.3	0.3	0.3	0.3	0.3	0.3	0.4	0.4	0.4	**3**
4	0.1	0.2	0.3	0.3	0.3	0.3	0.4	0.4	0.4	0.5	0.5	0.5	0.6	**4**
5	0.2	0.3	0.3	0.4	0.4	0.4	0.5	0.5	0.6	0.6	0.6	0.7	0.7	**5**
6	0.3	0.3	0.4	0.4	0.5	0.5	0.6	0.6	0.7	0.7	0.8	0.8	0.9	**6**
7	0.3	0.4	0.4	0.5	0.6	0.6	0.6	0.7	0.8	0.8	0.9	0.9	1.0	**7**
8	0.4	0.4	0.5	0.6	0.6	0.7	0.7	0.8	0.9	0.9	1.0	1.0	1.1	**8**
9	0.4	0.5	0.6	0.6	0.7	0.8	0.8	0.9	1.0	1.1	1.1	1.2	1.3	**9**
10	0.4	0.5	0.6	0.7	0.8	0.8	0.9	1.0	1.1	1.2	1.3	1.3	1.4	**10**
11	0.5	0.6	0.7	0.8	0.9	0.9	1.0	1.1	1.2	1.3	1.4	1.5	1.6	**11**
12	0.5	0.6	0.7	0.8	0.9	1.0	1.1	1.2	1.3	1.4	1.5	1.6	1.7	**12**
13	0.6	0.7	0.8	0.9	1.0	1.1	1.2	1.3	1.4	1.5	1.6	1.7	1.8	**13**
14	0.6	0.7	0.8	1.0	1.1	1.2	1.3	1.4	1.5	1.6	1.8	1.9	2.0	**14**
15	0.7	0.8	0.9	1.0	1.2	1.3	1.4	1.5	1.6	1.8	1.9	2.0	2.1	**15**
16	0.7	0.8	1.0	1.1	1.2	1.3	1.5	1.6	1.7	1.9	2.0	2.1	2.3	**16**
17	0.7	0.9	1.0	1.2	1.3	1.4	1.6	1.7	1.8	2.0	2.1	2.3	2.4	**17**
18	0.8	0.9	1.1	1.2	1.4	1.5	1.7	1.8	2.0	2.1	2.3	2.4	2.6	**18**
19	0.8	1.0	1.1	1.3	1.5	1.6	1.7	1.9	2.1	2.2	2.4	2.5	2.7	**19**
20	0.9	1.0	1.2	1.4	1.5	1.7	1.8	2.0	2.2	2.3	2.5	2.7	2.8	**20**
21	0.9	1.1	1.3	1.4	1.6	1.8	1.9	2.1	2.3	2.5	2.6	2.8	3.0	**21**
22	0.9	1.1	1.3	1.5	1.7	1.8	2.0	2.2	2.4	2.6	2.8	2.9	3.1	**22**
23	1.0	1.2	1.4	1.6	1.8	1.9	2.1	2.3	2.5	2.7	2.9	3.0	3.3	**23**
24	1.0	1.2	1.4	1.6	1.8	2.0	2.2	2.4	2.6	2.8	3.0	3.2	3.4	**24**
25	1.1	1.3	1.5	1.7	1.9	2.1	2.3	2.5	2.7	2.9	3.1	3.3	3.5	**25**
26	1.1	1.3	1.5	1.8	2.0	2.2	2.4	2.6	2.8	3.0	3.3	3.5	3.7	**26**
27	1.2	1.4	1.6	1.8	2.1	2.3	2.5	2.7	2.9	3.2	3.4	3.6	3.9	**27**
28	1.2	1.4	1.7	1.9	2.1	2.3	2.6	2.8	3.0	3.3	3.5	3.7	4.0	**28**
29	1.2	1.5	1.7	2.0	2.2	2.4	2.7	2.9	3.1	3.4	3.6	3.9	4.1	**29**
30	1.3	1.5	1.8	2.0	2.3	2.5	2.8	3.0	3.3	3.5	3.8	4.0	4.3	**30**
31	1.3	1.6	1.8	2.1	2.4	2.6	2.8	3.1	3.4	3.6	3.9	4.1	4.4	**31**
32	1.4	1.6	1.9	2.2	2.4	2.7	2.9	3.2	3.5	3.7	4.0	4.3	4.5	**32**
33	1.4	1.7	2.0	2.3	2.5	2.8	3.0	3.3	3.6	3.9	4.1	4.4	4.7	**33**
34	1.4	1.7	2.0	2.3	2.6	2.9	3.1	3.4	3.7	4.0	4.3	4.5	4.8	**34**
35	1.5	1.8	2.1	2.4	2.7	2.9	3.2	3.5	3.8	4.1	4.4	4.7	5.0	**35**
36	1.5	1.8	2.1	2.4	2.7	3.0	3.3	3.6	3.9	4.2	4.5	4.8	5.1	**36**
37	1.6	1.9	2.2	2.5	2.8	3.1	3.4	3.7	4.0	4.3	4.6	4.9	5.2	**37**
38	1.6	1.9	2.2	2.6	2.9	3.2	3.5	3.8	4.1	4.4	4.8	5.0	5.4	**38**
39	1.7	2.0	2.3	2.6	2.9	3.3	3.6	3.9	4.2	4.6	4.9	5.2	5.5	**39**
40	1.7	2.0	2.4	2.7	3.0	3.3	3.7	4.0	4.3	4.7	5.0	5.3	5.7	**40**
41	1.7	2.1	2.4	2.8	3.1	3.4	3.8	4.1	4.4	4.8	5.1	5.5	5.8	**41**
42	1.8	2.1	2.5	2.8	3.2	3.5	3.9	4.2	4.6	4.9	5.3	5.6	6.0	**42**
43	1.8	2.2	2.5	2.9	3.3	3.6	3.9	4.3	4.7	5.0	5.4	5.7	6.1	**43**
44	1.9	2.2	2.6	3.0	3.3	3.7	4.0	4.4	4.8	5.1	5.5	5.9	6.2	**44**
45	1.9	2.3	2.7	3.0	3.4	3.8	4.1	4.5	4.9	5.3	5.6	6.0	6.4	**45**
46	1.9	2.3	2.7	3.1	3.5	3.8	4.2	4.6	5.0	5.4	5.8	6.1	6.5	**46**
47	2.0	2.4	2.8	3.2	3.6	3.9	4.3	4.7	5.1	5.5	5.9	6.3	6.7	**47**
48	2.0	2.4	2.8	3.2	3.6	4.0	4.4	4.8	5.2	5.6	6.0	6.4	6.8	**48**
49	2.1	2.5	2.9	3.3	3.7	4.1	4.5	4.9	5.3	5.7	6.1	6.5	6.9	**49**
50	2.1	2.5	2.9	3.4	3.8	4.2	4.6	5.0	5.4	5.8	6.3	6.7	7.1	**50**
51	2.2	2.6	3.0	3.4	3.9	4.3	4.7	5.1	5.5	6.0	6.4	6.8	7.2	**51**
52	2.2	2.6	3.1	3.5	3.9	4.3	4.8	5.2	5.6	6.1	6.5	6.9	7.4	**52**
53	2.2	2.7	3.1	3.6	4.0	4.4	4.9	5.3	5.7	6.2	6.6	7.0	7.5	**53**
54	2.3	2.7	3.2	3.6	4.1	4.5	5.0	5.4	5.9	6.3	6.8	7.1	7.6	**54**
55	2.3	2.8	3.2	3.7	4.2	4.6	5.0	5.5	6.0	6.4	6.9	7.3	7.8	**55**
56	2.4	2.8	3.3	3.8	4.2	4.7	5.1	5.6	6.1	6.5	7.0	7.5	7.9	**56**
57	2.4	2.9	3.4	3.8	4.3	4.8	5.2	5.7	6.2	6.7	7.1	7.6	8.1	**57**
58	2.4	2.9	3.4	3.9	4.4	4.8	5.3	5.8	6.3	6.8	7.3	7.7	8.2	**58**
59	2.5	3.0	3.5	3.9	4.5	4.9	5.4	5.9	6.4	6.9	7.4	7.9	8.4	**59**
60	2.5	3.0	3.5	4.0	4.5	5.0	5.5	6.0	6.5	7.0	7.5	8.0	8.5	**60**
Min	**2½**	**3**	**3½**	**4**	**4½**	**5**	**5½**	**6**	**6½**	**7**	**7½**	**8**	**8½**	**Min**

Example 1. if steaming 7½ knots, what distance has been covered in 41 minutes? Answer = 5·1 miles

TIME, SPEED and DISTANCE TABLE

	KNOTS													
Min	**9**	**9½**	**10**	**10½**	**11**	**11½**	**12**	**12½**	**13**	**13½**	**14**	**14½**	**15**	**Min**
1	0.2	0.2	0.2	0.2	0.2	0.2	0.2	0.2	0.2	0.2	0.2	0.2	0.3	**1**
2	0.3	0.3	0.3	0.4	0.4	0.4	0.4	0.4	0.5	0.5	0.5	0.5	0.5	**2**
3	0.5	0.5	0.5	0.5	0.6	0.6	0.6	0.6	0.7	0.7	0.7	0.7	0.8	**3**
4	0.6	0.6	0.7	0.7	0.7	0.8	0.8	0.8	0.9	0.9	0.9	1.0	1.0	**4**
5	0.8	0.8	0.8	0.9	0.9	1.0	1.0	1.1	1.1	1.2	1.2	1.2	1.3	**5**
6	0.9	1.0	1.0	1.1	1.1	1.2	1.2	1.3	1.3	1.4	1.4	1.5	1.5	**6**
7	1.1	1.1	1.2	1.2	1.3	1.3	1.4	1.5	1.5	1.6	1.6	1.7	1.8	**7**
8	1.2	1.3	1.3	1.4	1.5	1.5	1.6	1.7	1.7	1.8	1.9	1.9	2.0	**8**
9	1.4	1.4	1.5	1.6	1.7	1.7	1.8	1.9	2.0	2.0	2.1	2.2	2.3	**9**
10	1.5	1.6	1.7	1.8	1.8	1.9	2.0	2.1	2.2	2.3	2.3	2.4	2.5	**10**
11	1.7	1.7	1.8	1.9	2.0	2.1	2.2	2.3	2.4	2.5	2.6	2.7	2.8	**11**
12	1.8	1.9	2.0	2.1	2.2	2.3	2.4	2.5	2.6	2.7	2.8	2.9	3.0	**12**
13	2.0	2.1	2.2	2.3	2.4	2.5	2.6	2.7	2.8	2.9	3.0	3.1	3.2	**13**
14	2.1	2.2	2.3	2.5	2.6	2.7	2.8	2.9	3.0	3.2	3.3	3.4	3.5	**14**
15	2.3	2.4	2.5	2.6	2.8	2.9	3.0	3.1	3.3	3.4	3.5	3.6	3.8	**15**
16	2.4	2.5	2.7	2.8	2.9	3.1	3.2	3.3	3.5	3.6	3.7	3.9	4.0	**16**
17	2.6	2.7	2.8	3.0	3.1	3.3	3.4	3.5	3.7	3.8	4.0	4.1	4.3	**17**
18	2.7	2.9	3.0	3.2	3.3	3.5	3.6	3.8	3.9	4.1	4.2	4.4	4.5	**18**
19	2.9	3.1	3.2	3.3	3.5	3.6	3.8	4.0	4.2	4.3	4.4	4.6	4.8	**19**
20	3.0	3.2	3.3	3.5	3.7	3.8	4.0	4.2	4.4	4.5	4.7	4.8	5.0	**20**
21	3.2	3.3	3.5	3.7	3.9	4.0	4.2	4.4	4.6	4.7	4.9	5.1	5.3	**21**
22	3.3	3.5	3.7	3.9	4.0	4.2	4.4	4.6	4.8	5.0	5.1	5.3	5.5	**22**
23	3.5	3.6	3.8	4.0	4.2	4.4	4.6	4.8	5.0	5.2	5.4	5.6	5.7	**23**
24	3.6	3.8	4.0	4.2	4.4	4.6	4.8	5.0	5.2	5.4	5.6	5.8	6.0	**24**
25	3.8	4.0	4.2	4.4	4.6	4.8	5.0	5.2	5.4	5.6	5.8	6.1	6.3	**25**
26	3.9	4.1	4.3	4.6	4.8	5.0	5.2	5.4	5.6	5.9	6.1	6.3	6.5	**26**
27	4.1	4.3	4.5	4.7	5.0	5.2	5.4	5.6	5.9	6.1	6.3	6.5	6.8	**27**
28	4.2	4.4	4.7	4.9	5.1	5.4	5.6	5.8	6.1	6.3	6.5	6.8	7.0	**28**
29	4.4	4.6	4.8	5.1	5.3	5.6	5.8	6.0	6.3	6.5	6.8	7.0	7.3	**29**
30	4.5	4.8	5.0	5.3	5.5	5.8	6.0	6.3	6.5	6.8	7.0	7.3	7.5	**30**
31	4.7	4.9	5.2	5.4	5.7	5.9	6.2	6.5	6.7	7.0	7.2	7.5	7.8	**31**
32	4.8	5.0	5.3	5.6	5.9	6.1	6.4	6.7	6.9	7.2	7.5	7.7	8.0	**32**
33	5.0	5.2	5.5	5.8	6.1	6.3	6.6	6.9	7.2	7.4	7.7	8.0	8.3	**33**
34	5.1	5.4	5.7	6.0	6.2	6.5	6.8	7.1	7.4	7.7	8.0	8.2	8.5	**34**
35	5.3	5.5	5.8	6.1	6.4	6.7	7.0	7.3	7.6	7.9	8.2	8.5	8.8	**35**
36	5.4	5.7	6.0	6.3	6.6	6.9	7.2	7.5	7.8	8.1	8.4	8.7	9.0	**36**
37	5.6	5.9	6.2	6.5	6.8	7.1	7.4	7.7	8.0	8.3	8.6	8.9	9.3	**37**
38	5.7	6.0	6.3	6.7	7.0	7.3	7.6	7.9	8.2	8.6	8.9	9.2	9.5	**38**
39	5.9	6.2	6.5	6.8	7.1	7.5	7.8	8.1	8.5	8.8	9.1	9.4	9.8	**39**
40	6.0	6.3	6.7	7.0	7.3	7.7	8.0	8.3	8.7	9.0	9.3	9.7	10.0	**40**
41	6.2	6.5	6.8	7.3	7.5	7.9	8.2	8.5	8.9	9.2	9.6	9.9	10.3	**41**
42	6.3	6.7	7.0	7.4	7.7	8.1	8.4	8.8	9.1	9.5	9.8	10.2	10.5	**42**
43	6.5	6.8	7.2	7.5	7.9	8.2	8.6	9.0	9.3	9.7	10.0	10.4	10.8	**43**
44	6.6	7.0	7.3	7.7	8.0	8.4	8.8	9.2	9.5	9.9	10.3	10.6	11.0	**44**
45	6.8	7.1	7.5	7.9	8.2	8.6	9.0	9.4	9.8	10.1	10.5	10.9	11.3	**45**
46	6.9	7.3	7.7	8.1	8.4	8.8	9.2	9.6	10.0	10.4	10.7	11.1	11.5	**46**
47	7.1	7.4	7.8	8.2	8.6	9.0	9.4	9.8	10.2	10.6	11.0	11.4	11.8	**47**
48	7.2	7.6	8.0	8.4	8.8	9.2	9.6	10.0	10.4	10.8	11.2	11.6	12.0	**48**
49	7.4	7.8	8.2	8.6	9.0	9.4	9.8	10.2	10.6	11.0	11.4	11.8	12.3	**49**
50	7.5	7.9	8.3	8.7	9.1	9.6	10.0	10.4	10.8	11.3	11.7	12.1	12.5	**50**
51	7.7	8.1	8.5	8.9	9.4	9.8	10.2	10.6	11.1	11.5	11.9	12.3	12.8	**51**
52	7.8	8.2	8.7	9.1	9.5	10.0	10.4	10.8	11.3	11.7	12.1	12.6	13.0	**52**
53	8.0	8.4	8.8	9.3	9.7	10.2	10.6	11.0	11.5	11.9	12.4	12.8	13.3	**53**
54	8.1	8.6	9.0	9.5	9.9	10.4	10.8	11.3	11.7	12.2	12.6	13.1	13.5	**54**
55	8.3	8.7	9.2	9.6	10.0	10.5	11.0	11.5	11.9	12.4	12.8	13.3	13.8	**55**
56	8.4	8.9	9.3	9.8	10.2	10.7	11.2	11.7	12.1	12.6	13.1	13.5	14.0	**56**
57	8.6	9.0	9.5	10.0	10.5	10.9	11.4	11.9	12.4	12.8	13.3	13.8	14.3	**57**
58	8.7	9.2	9.7	10.2	10.6	11.1	11.6	12.1	12.6	13.1	13.5	14.0	14.5	**58**
59	8.9	9.3	9.8	10.3	10.8	11.3	11.8	12.3	12.8	13.3	13.8	14.3	14.8	**59**
60	9.0	9.5	10.0	10.5	11.0	11.5	12.0	12.5	13.0	13.5	14.0	14.5	15.0	**60**
Min	**9**	**9½**	**10**	**10½**	**11**	**11½**	**12**	**12½**	**13**	**13½**	**14**	**14½**	**15**	**Min**

Example 2. How long will it take to steam 6·8 miles (when the course is to be altered)? Vessel's speed. 10½ knots. Answer = 39 minutes.

TIME, SPEED and DISTANCE TABLE

	KNOTS														
Min	**15½**	**16**	**16½**	**17**	**17½**	**18**	**18½**	**19**	**19½**	**20**	**20½**	**21**	**21½**	**22**	**Min**
1	0.3	0.3	0.3	0.3	0.3	0.3	0.3	0.3	0.3	0.3	0.3	0.4	0.4	0.4	**1**
2	0.5	0.5	0.5	0.6	0.6	0.6	0.6	0.6	0.6	0.7	0.7	0.7	0.7	0.7	**2**
3	0.8	0.8	0.8	0.9	0.9	0.9	0.9	1.0	1.0	1.0	1.0	1.1	1.1	1.1	**3**
4	1.0	1.1	1.1	1.1	1.1	1.2	1.2	1.3	1.3	1.3	1.3	1.4	1.4	1.5	**4**
5	1.3	1.3	1.3	1.4	1.4	1.5	1.5	1.6	1.6	1.7	1.7	1.8	1.8	1.8	**5**
6	1.5	1.6	1.6	1.7	1.7	1.8	1.8	1.9	1.9	2.0	2.0	2.1	2.1	2.2	**6**
7	1.8	1.9	1.9	2.0	2.0	2.1	2.1	2.2	2.2	2.3	2.4	2.5	2.5	2.6	**7**
8	2.0	2.1	2.2	2.3	2.3	2.4	2.4	2.5	2.6	2.7	2.7	2.8	2.8	2.9	**8**
9	2.3	2.4	2.5	2.6	2.6	2.7	2.8	2.9	2.9	3.0	3.1	3.2	3.2	3.3	**9**
10	2.6	2.7	2.7	2.8	2.9	3.0	3.1	3.2	3.2	3.3	3.4	3.5	3.6	3.7	**10**
11	2.8	2.9	3.0	3.1	3.2	3.3	3.4	3.5	3.6	3.7	3.8	3.9	3.9	4.0	**11**
12	3.1	3.2	3.3	3.4	3.5	3.6	3.7	3.8	3.9	4.0	4.1	4.2	4.3	4.4	**12**
13	3.4	3.5	3.6	3.7	3.8	3.9	4.0	4.1	4.2	4.3	4.4	4.6	4.7	4.8	**13**
14	3.6	3.7	3.8	4.0	4.1	4.2	4.3	4.4	4.5	4.7	4.8	4.9	5.0	5.1	**14**
15	3.9	4.0	4.1	4.3	4.4	4.5	4.6	4.8	4.9	5.0	5.1	5.3	5.4	5.5	**15**
16	4.2	4.3	4.4	4.5	4.6	4.8	4.9	5.1	5.2	5.3	5.4	5.6	5.7	5.9	**16**
17	4.4	4.5	4.6	4.8	4.9	5.1	5.2	5.4	5.5	5.7	5.8	6.0	6.1	6.2	**17**
18	4.7	4.8	4.9	5.1	5.2	5.4	5.5	5.7	5.8	6.0	6.1	6.3	6.4	6.6	**18**
19	4.9	5.1	5.2	5.4	5.5	5.7	5.8	6.0	6.1	6.3	6.5	6.7	6.8	7.0	**19**
20	5.1	5.3	5.5	5.7	5.8	6.0	6.1	6.3	6.5	6.7	6.8	7.0	7.1	7.3	**20**
21	5.4	5.6	5.8	6.0	6.1	6.3	6.5	6.7	6.8	7.0	7.2	7.4	7.5	7.7	**21**
22	5.7	5.9	6.0	6.2	6.4	6.6	6.8	7.0	7.1	7.3	7.5	7.7	7.9	8.1	**22**
23	5.9	6.1	6.3	6.5	6.7	6.9	7.1	7.3	7.5	7.7	7.9	8.1	8.2	8.4	**23**
24	6.2	6.4	6.6	6.8	7.0	7.2	7.4	7.6	7.8	8.0	8.2	8.4	8.6	8.8	**24**
25	6.5	6.7	6.9	7.1	7.3	7.5	7.7	7.9	8.1	8.3	8.5	8.8	9.0	9.2	**25**
26	6.7	6.9	7.1	7.4	7.6	7.8	8.0	8.2	8.4	8.7	8.9	9.1	9.3	9.5	**26**
27	7.0	7.2	7.4	7.7	7.9	8.1	8.3	8.6	8.8	9.0	9.2	9.5	9.7	9.9	**27**
28	7.2	7.5	7.7	7.9	8.1	8.4	8.6	8.9	9.1	9.3	9.5	9.8	10.0	10.3	**28**
29	7.5	7.7	7.9	8.2	8.4	8.7	8.9	9.2	9.4	9.7	9.9	10.2	10.4	10.6	**29**
30	7.8	8.0	8.2	8.5	8.7	9.0	9.2	9.5	9.7	10.0	10.2	10.5	10.7	11.0	**30**
31	8.0	8.3	8.5	8.8	9.0	9.3	9.5	9.8	10.0	10.3	10.6	10.9	11.1	11.4	**31**
32	8.2	8.5	8.8	9.1	9.3	9.6	9.9	10.2	10.4	10.7	10.9	11.2	11.4	11.7	**32**
33	8.5	8.8	9.1	9.4	9.6	9.9	10.2	10.5	10.7	11.0	11.3	11.6	11.8	12.1	**33**
34	8.8	9.1	9.3	9.6	9.9	10.2	10.5	10.8	11.0	11.3	11.6	11.9	12.2	12.5	**34**
35	9.0	9.3	9.6	9.9	10.2	10.5	10.8	11.1	11.4	11.7	12.0	12.3	12.5	12.8	**35**
36	9.3	9.6	9.9	10.2	10.5	10.8	11.1	11.4	11.7	12.0	12.3	12.6	12.9	13.2	**36**
37	9.6	9.9	10.2	10.5	10.8	11.1	11.4	11.7	12.0	12.3	12.6	13.0	13.3	13.6	**37**
38	9.8	10.1	10.4	10.8	11.1	11.4	11.7	12.0	12.3	12.7	13.0	13.3	13.6	13.9	**38**
39	10.1	10.4	10.7	11.1	11.4	11.7	12.0	12.4	12.7	13.0	13.3	13.7	14.0	14.3	**39**
40	10.4	10.7	11.0	11.3	11.7	12.0	12.3	12.7	13.0	13.3	13.6	14.0	14.3	14.7	**40**
41	10.6	10.9	11.2	11.6	12.0	12.3	12.6	13.0	13.3	13.7	14.0	14.4	14.7	15.0	**41**
42	10.8	11.2	11.5	11.9	12.3	12.6	12.9	13.3	13.6	14.0	14.3	14.7	15.0	15.4	**42**
43	11.1	11.5	11.8	12.2	12.5	12.9	13.2	13.6	13.9	14.3	14.7	15.1	15.4	15.8	**43**
44	11.3	11.7	12.1	12.5	12.8	13.2	13.5	13.9	14.3	14.7	15.0	15.4	15.7	16.1	**44**
45	11.6	12.0	12.4	12.8	13.1	13.5	13.8	14.3	14.6	15.0	15.4	15.8	16.1	16.5	**45**
46	11.9	12.3	12.6	13.0	13.4	13.8	14.2	14.6	14.9	15.3	15.7	16.1	16.5	16.9	**46**
47	12.2	12.5	12.9	13.3	13.7	14.1	14.5	14.9	15.3	15.7	16.1	16.5	16.8	17.2	**47**
48	12.4	12.8	13.2	13.6	14.0	14.4	14.8	15.2	15.6	16.0	16.4	16.8	17.2	17.6	**48**
49	12.7	13.1	13.5	13.9	14.3	14.7	15.1	15.5	15.9	16.3	16.7	17.2	17.6	18.0	**49**
50	12.9	13.3	13.7	14.2	14.6	15.0	15.4	15.8	16.2	16.7	17.1	17.5	17.9	18.3	**50**
51	13.2	13.6	14.0	14.5	14.9	15.3	15.7	16.2	16.6	17.0	17.5	17.9	18.3	18.7	**51**
52	13.5	13.9	14.3	14.7	15.1	15.6	16.0	16.5	16.9	17.3	17.8	18.2	18.6	19.1	**52**
53	13.7	14.1	14.5	15.0	15.4	15.9	16.3	16.8	17.2	17.7	18.1	18.6	19.0	19.4	**53**
54	14.0	14.4	14.8	15.3	15.7	16.2	16.6	17.1	17.5	18.0	18.4	18.9	19.3	19.8	**54**
55	14.2	14.7	15.1	15.6	16.0	16.5	16.9	17.4	17.8	18.3	18.8	19.3	19.7	20.2	**55**
56	14.4	14.9	15.4	15.9	16.3	16.8	17.2	17.7	18.2	18.7	19.1	19.6	20.0	20.5	**56**
57	14.7	15.2	15.7	16.2	16.6	17.1	17.6	18.1	18.5	19.0	19.5	20.0	20.4	20.9	**57**
58	15.0	15.5	16.0	16.4	16.9	17.4	17.9	18.4	18.8	19.3	19.8	20.3	20.8	21.3	**58**
59	15.2	15.7	16.2	16.7	17.2	17.7	18.2	18.7	19.2	19.7	20.2	20.7	21.1	21.6	**59**
60	15.5	16.0	16.5	17.0	17.5	18.0	18.5	19.0	19.5	20.0	20.5	21.0	21.5	22.0	**60**
Min	**15½**	**16**	**16½**	**17**	**17½**	**18**	**18½**	**19**	**19½**	**20**	**20½**	**21**	**21½**	**22**	**Min**

Example 3. How far will a vessel steam at 17·5 knots in 25 minutes? Answer 7·3 miles

THE ELECTRONIC CALCULATOR IN COASTAL NAVIGATION

Coastal Navigation can be an almost continuous process and aids which can be utilised for rapid calculation should be seriously considered. It must always be understood, however, that the calculator is an aid – it is a piece of electronic equipment which is fallible, but useful for supplementing the basic skills of the navigator by enabling rapid checks to be carried out to calculations already made, and as confidence grows, of carrying out initial calculations. It would be most unwise to use a calculator without fully understanding the fundamental principles involved and being able to work out the problem in longhand. Trigonometrical tables should therefore always be carried on board.

Calculators can be divided into three main groups – the inexpensive arithmetical type with a decimal base, the scientific or slide rule calculator with algebraic, trigonometrical and logarithmic functions and a number of memories, and the most expensive calculators which can be programmed for repetition work either manually or by the insertion of magnetic cards and sometimes having printout facilities.

The middle range of scientific calculators with trigonometrical and logarithmic functions, square root, exponents and reciprocals, with two to three memories, would fulfil the needs of the average coastal navigator. The better the calculator the fewer the key sequences required. Key sequences and functions vary with different calculators and the maker's handbook should always first be studied.

The examples in this section have all been worked using sin, cos, tan and inverse (sometimes shown as ARC) keys together with the normal arithmetical functions, all of which are included on most scientific calculators.

BASIC TRIGONOMETRICAL FUNCTIONS

Before using these functions consider the method by which they are derived as this will assist in the solution of triangular problems. Given any right angle triangle ABC (Fig. 1) trigonometrical functions are:

$$\text{sin angle ABC} = \frac{\text{opposite}}{\text{hypotenuse}} = \frac{AC}{AB}$$

$$\text{cos angle ABC} = \frac{\text{adjacent}}{\text{hypotenuse}} = \frac{BC}{AB}$$

$$\text{tan angle} = \frac{\text{opposite}}{\text{adjacent}} = \frac{AC}{BC}$$

For example:

$$\text{sin angle BAC} = \frac{\text{opposite}}{\text{hypotenuse}} = \frac{BC}{AB}$$

These functions are the same for angle BAC except that adjacent and opposite sides are different.

Thus it will be seen that triangular problems can easily be solved if they can be reduced to right angle triangles.

SIMPLE NAVIGATIONAL PROBLEMS

Consider now the solution of one of the simplest navigational problems, finding the distance "off" from a fixed point. If using the "four points" rule or "doubling the angle" on the bow one has to wait for specific bearings to appear, i.e., 45° or 30° and 60°.

Using trigonometrical functions, however, the navigator can take the initial bearing at any suitable time. Consider the example in Fig. 2 where the vessel is on a course of 105° T and requires to know the distance off the headland when abeam.

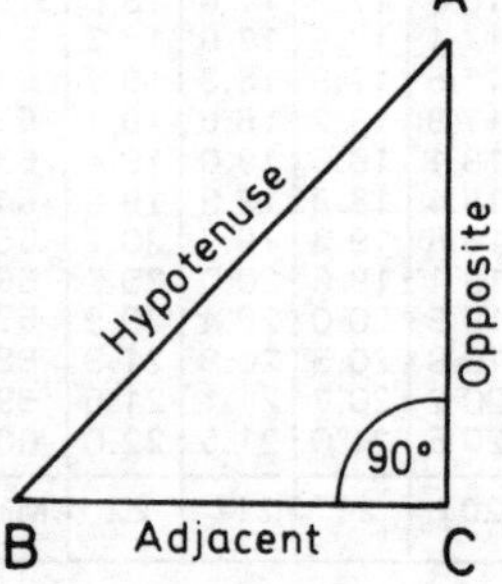

Fig. 1

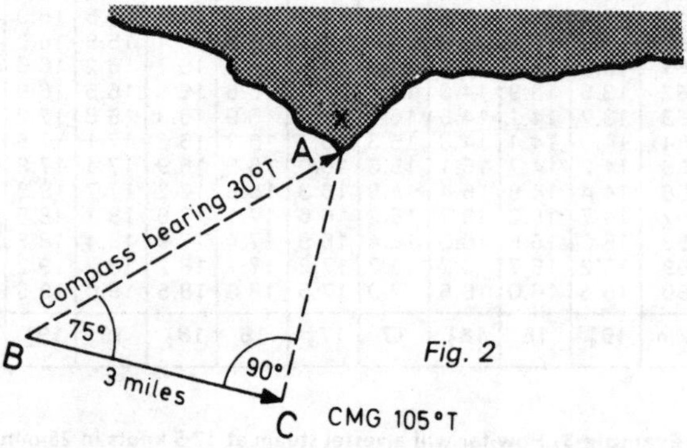

Fig. 2

In this example tidal set and leeway angle are ignored for the sake of simplicity.

Vessel's course = 105° T.

Compass bearing of A = 030° T.

∴ Relative Bearing (RB) = 75° (Angle ABC).

When the vessel is abeam of the fixed point A the relative bearing will be 90° and the log reads 3 miles.

From Fig. 1 it will be seen that:

$$\frac{AC}{BC} = \tan \text{angle } ABC$$

$$\therefore AC = BC \times \tan 75$$

$$AC = 3 \times 3.732$$

$$= \underline{11.19 \text{ miles}}$$

Using the calculator to solve the problem the following steps are necessary:

Quantity	**Entry**	**Reading**
Clear calculator	C	0
Enter Relative Bearing (RB)	75	75
	tan	3.732
	×	3.732
Distance Run	3	3
Answer	=	11.19

Distance off = 11.19 miles

It will be appreciated that the distance run must be the distance over the ground and the log reading must therefore be adjusted for tidal set and leeway angle (read on for method of calculating this).

In many cases the navigator will wish to know his "distance off" before reaching the abeam position if for example there are outlying dangers as in the following example (Fig. 3).

The vessel is somewhere in vicinity of A on a course of 080° T and wishes to know if this will clear outlying danger.

At A first compass bearing is 050° T.
∴ first RB = 30°

Second compass bearing after 3 miles run is 035° T.
∴ second RB = 45°

Now consider the solution to obtain both a "fix" and a probable distance off using trigonometrical functions. (This working will be used to derive a formula which will considerably simplify later calculations.)

In Fig. 4 opposite the triangle ABD is completed by drawing BD at right angles to AX.

To find XC it is first necessary to evaluate BD and then BX

(1) To find DB referring again to Fig. 1 it will be seen that:

$$\sin 30° = \frac{DB}{AB} = \frac{DB}{3}$$

Since sin 30° = ½, DB= 1.5 m

(2) To find XB angle DXB is first required. This is (45-30) = 15°

$$\sin 15° = \frac{DB}{XB} = 0.258$$

$$\therefore XB = \frac{DB}{0.258} = \frac{1.5}{0.258} = 5.8 \text{ m.}$$

(3) To find XC

$$\sin 45° = \frac{XC}{5.8}$$

$$\therefore XC = \sin 45° \times 5.8 = 4.1 \text{ m.}$$

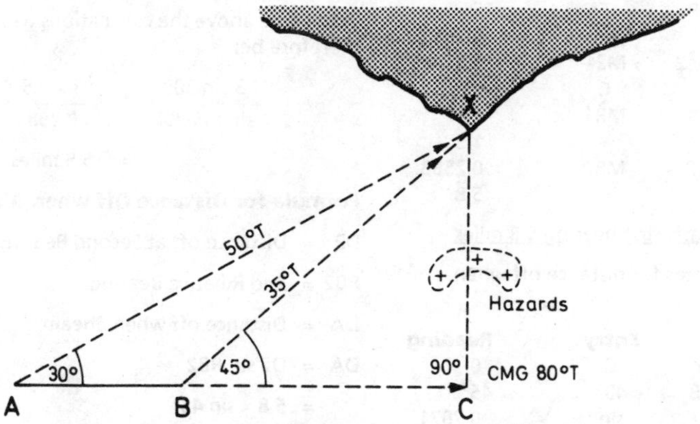

Fig. 3

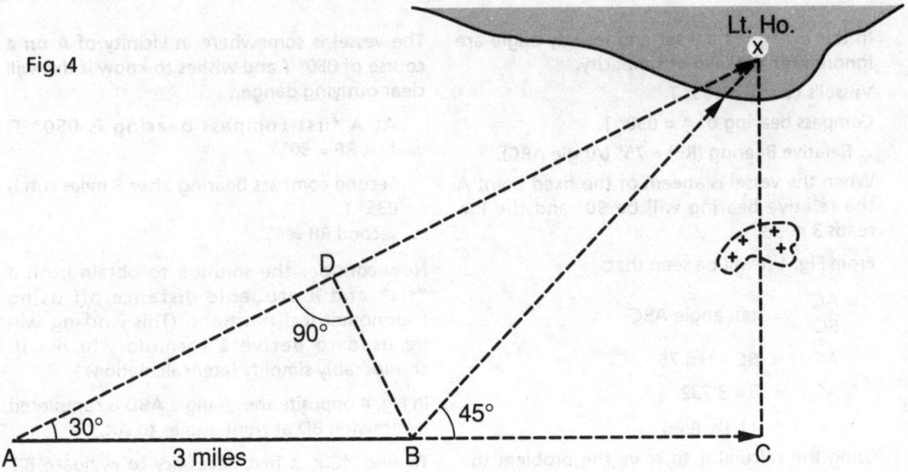

Referring to Fig. 4 the position at B can be established by describing a circle of radius 5.8 miles with center at X and then drawing XB, the True bearing (*not* the relative bearing) and the point of intersection is the fix. Similarly with XC, giving the probable position when abeam.

Consider now the key sequences necessary on the calculator, first using the somewhat lengthy calculation shown earlier.

Quantity	**Entry**	**Reading**
Clear calculator	C	0
Enter first RB	30°	30°
	sin	0.5
	×	0.5
Enter Distance Run	3	3
	=	1.5
Store – Memory 1	M1+	1.5
Clear display	C	0
Enter angle DXB	15°	15°
	sin	0.2588
Store – Memory 2	M2+	0.2588
Clear display	C	0
Recall Memory 1	MR1	1.5
	÷	1.5
Recall Memory 2	MR2	0.2588
Answer	=	5.8

Distance off first bearing 5.8 miles

The key sequences for distance off when abeam will be:

Quantity	**Entry**	**Reading**
Clear calculator	C	0
Enter second RB	45°	45°
	sin	0.7071
	×	0.7071
Enter distance off at second RB	5.8	5.8
	=	4.1

Distance off when abeam = 4 miles

These somewhat lengthy calculations can be reduced and simplified to the following two formulae, thus obviating the necessity for any chartwork until the final fix is obtained.

Formula for Distance Off at 2nd Bearing

D2 = Distance off at 2nd Bearing.

R = Distance between 1st and 2nd Bearings.

RB1 = First Relative Bearing

RB2 = Second Relative Bearing

$$D2 = \frac{R \sin RB1}{\sin (RB2 - RB1)}$$

In the case above the calculations will therefore be:

$$\frac{3 \sin 30°}{\sin (45-30)} = \frac{3 \times 0.5}{0.258}$$

$$= 5.8 \text{ miles}$$

Formula for Distance Off when Abeam

D2 = Distance off at Second Bearing

RB2 = 2nd Relative Bearing

DA = Distance off when abeam

$$DA = D2 \sin RB2$$

$$= 5.8 \times \sin 45°$$

$$= \underline{4.1 \text{ miles.}}$$

From the calculations above it will be seen that the formula derived from the original rather lengthy calculations reduces the work to a short key sequence which is rapidly performed and requires no plotting until the navigator wishes to plot his position on the chart.

Fig. 5

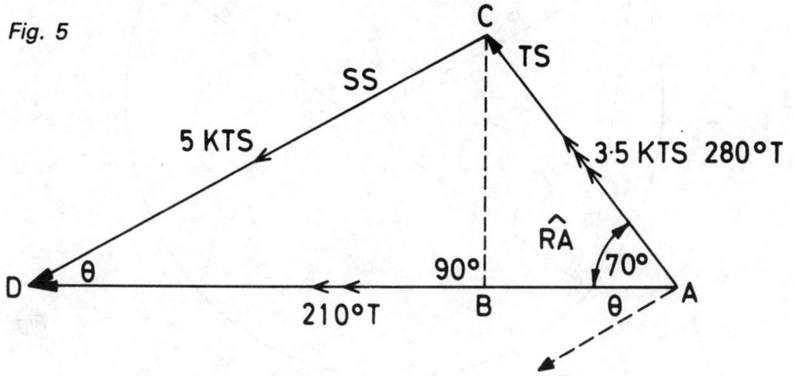

Tide Correction Angle and Speed Made Good (Fig. 5)

Similarly a formula can be derived for calculating the tidal correction angle. Omitting the step by step calculation this formula is:

$$\text{Sin}\ \theta = \frac{\text{TS} \times \sin \text{RA}}{\text{SS}}$$

where θ = Tidal Correction Angle

TS = Tide Speed

RA = Relative angle between tide and course to be made good

SS = Ship's Speed

Example:

current 3.5 kts. 280° T
Ship's Speed 5 kts.
Course to be made good 210° T
∴ RA = 70°

$$\text{CB} = \text{CA} \times \sin 70°$$

$$\therefore \sin\theta = \frac{\text{CA} \times \sin 70°}{\text{CD}}$$

$$= \frac{3.5 \sin 70°}{5} = \frac{3.5 \times 0.94}{5} = 0.658$$

$$\theta = 41°$$

NOTE: To convert 0.658 use invert and sine keys. Method may vary with different types of calculator.

Speed made good = AD

= CD cos θ + AC cos 70°

in standard terms

= (Ship's speed × cos θ) + (Tide speed × cos RA)

= (5 × 0.754) + (3.5 × 0.342)

= 4.97 kts.

When $\hat{RA}$ is greater than 90° the complementary angle is used (e.g., $\hat{RA}$ = 150°, complementary angle = 180 – 150 = 30°) in both correction angle and speed calculations. The latter formula becomes SS cos θ – TS cos $\hat{RA}$ where $\hat{RA}$ is the complementary angle.

HORIZONTAL ANGLE FIX

A quick method of calculating the radius of the circle required in the horizontal angle fix omitting the step by step calculation is:

$$\text{Radius} = \frac{\frac{1}{2}\text{AB}}{\text{SIN}\ \theta}$$

Where AB is the horizontal distance between the two points and θ is the angle subtended at the vessel.

In the example opposite, if the distance AB = 7 miles and angle θ is 55°

$$\text{Radius} = \frac{\text{AB}}{2\ \text{SIN}\ \theta} = \frac{7}{2 \times .819} = 4.27\ \text{m}$$

It will be appreciated that a position line cutting the circle will give a fix.

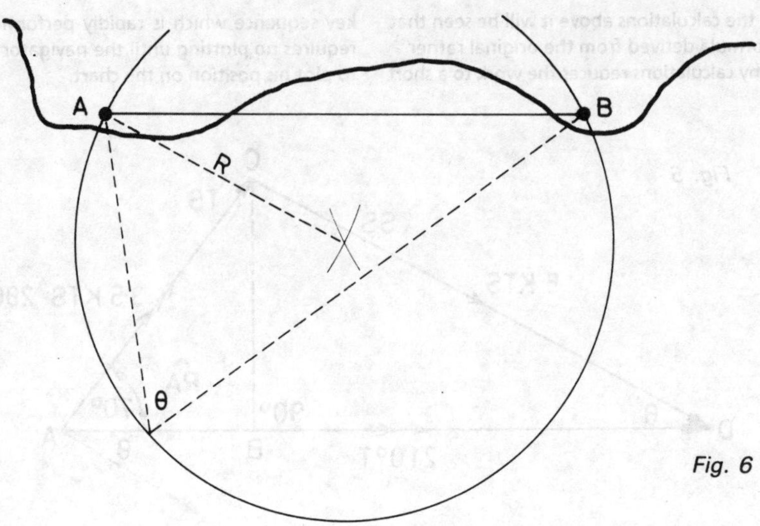

Fig. 6

Fast Boat Navigation

6

Page

FAST BOAT NAVIGATION

The modern planing-hulled motorboat will often make short work of passagemaking. Cruising speeds of 20 knots or more bring flexibility over the choice of course and departure time, the relative effect of tidal currents will be much less, and the risk of being caught by bad weather certainly reduced.

However, that is not to say that the fast boat navigator can completely turn his back on basic principles, or be encouraged to do less preparation before leaving the slip. In fact, the opposite is true, even if the methods of staying on a safe course are considerably different from the traditional divider and parallel rule approach.

UNDERSTANDING THE FAST BOAT AT SEA

To see why fast boat navigation techniques are essentially different from standard chart plotting, consider briefly the simplified case of two boats making an identical passage at the same time, one a fast planing-hulled design cruising at 24 knots, the other, a slow displacement craft running at 6 knots. Assuming the weather and other factors remain constant throughout, both boats will encounter the same number of waves, but the faster one will hit them four times faster. In doing so, it will accentuate the uneven pattern of the waves, something not noticed as much in a boat which stays in the water, rather than skims across it. Good hull design will cushion the ride, but the motion will nevertheless be lively in all but the calmest waters.

Other factors apply. Not every fast boat has the room, or the right layout, for a practical chart area, so the navigator has often to use a difficult working space made lively by the fast motion. In addition, on sportscruisers (open cockpit designs), this area will be relatively exposed, sheltered only from the 20 knot plus wind of the boat's high speed progress by a windscreen and possibly, a bimini.

Staying with our example, the fast boat moves towards navigation marks, conspicuous objects and potential hazards four times faster than its slower partner. At 24 knots, if the navigator dips his head for just one minute to check the details of the next buoy, as yet unseen, the boat will have covered nearly half-a-mile by the time he once again turns to search the sea. If the course-keeping is incorrect and the boat is approaching a sandbank which runs from deep water to 2 feet depth in ¼ mile, the helmsman will only have 38 seconds to detect the problem before running aground.

Fortunately, the answers to safe navigation at speed are quite simple — full preparation before departure and disciplined observation while at sea.

PREPARATION

There is a satisfying skill in putting together a good course and passage plan for a fast boat.

All of the basic chartwork skills described elsewhere in this companion are still required, but the aim in this instance is to plot a full course before leaving which anticipates as much as possible what will be encountered on the passage. A major advantage is the speed capability of the boat, which brings greater flexibility to planning, if used wisely.

TIDE AND WIND

The fast boat navigator should look at tides with a different eye. While the effect of cross-currents must still be kept in mind, the importance of 'catching' a tide to speed progress along a coast is less important than choosing the tide which is most favorable when considered with the wind direction. In this respect, advice in pilot books on suitable departure times for given passages, written with an eye to helping the sailing boat navigator, will often have to be ignored. A higher speed cruise into an adverse current with wind and tide together is often a far more efficient way of making progress than punching through choppy wind against tide waters riding a favorable current.

Wind direction is also important in other ways. Planing-hulled boats have differing capabilities, and courses should wherever possible be planned to encounter seas which are favorable for the craft concerned. At high speed, diversions from the most direct route are often not significant regarding the extra distance they entail and a good idea if calmer seas or a more favorable wave direction results. In some cases, given prevailing conditions, the decision may be taken to head for a harbor in an entirely different direction from that originally planned.

With a crosswind, some allowance should be made for leeway, especially on motor yachts with high superstructures.

PILOTAGE

A less direct course may also be appropriate to maximise the number of navigation marks encountered along the way.

Straightforward pilotage between buoys is a sensible approach to fast boat navigation, allowing quick and easy confirmation of current position, provided that positive identification is made. At high cruising speeds, navigation marks may not be seen until shortly before they are due to appear, although the higher vantage point of a flybridge helm position on a motor yacht is helpful in this respect.

RANGE AND DURATION

Fast motorboats use a lot of fuel and a 20% safety margin is the minimum when calculating range. This not only allows for unforeseen diversions, but avoids the bad practice of draining the bottom of the tank, where water and other contaminants might be lurking.

Head seas will tend to increase consumption. Also, for twin-engined boats with separate tanks and no switchover system, the range on one engine draining from one tank with the boat just off the plane may be less than with both motors working, and must be taken into account in case of breakdown.

Fuel gauges should not be trusted; logging the consumption over a number of passages is a more accurate way of assessing maximum working range. Not every harbor has suitable fueling facilities and a telephone call to check availability is often sensible.

A fast passage is exhilarating, but also tiring. The quick motion and often high noise levels promote fatigue, especially for inexperienced crew. Extended cruising should be planned accordingly.

HARBORS

Just about all fast motorboats with inboard engines, and even a good number with outdrives, are not built to sit aground and non-drying harbors are essential. Access may be restricted by tides, and departure time planned accordingly. This should not only reflect the anticipated passage time, but incorporate a generous margin for slow speed maneuvers at both ends and for a delay, or the need to set a slower cruising speed, en-route.

As with any navigation plan, suitable alternative harbors along the route should be considered if these are available, but for the faster boat, again the course can be shaped to make these quickly accessible as a safeguard against bad weather or breakdown.

CHARTWORK

With a broad idea of a plan, it is time to transfer to the chart. The first consideration before pencil hits paper is where will the chart be used?

Limited space and/or an exposed area should be considered. If paper charts are being used outside, these can be covered in transparent plastic, slipped inside proper covers manufactured for the purpose, or even encapsulated. If the working area is not satisfactory, or the chart is in danger of blowing away, it can be securely mounted to a suitable piece of board.

For the actual passage, it is easier to use a small scale chart. For planning, a larger scale is better, and any important features not shown on the passage chart can be transferred over.

Wind, tide, pilotage and harbor considerations will already have given the gist of a basic course, but this can be further tailored. A defensive approach is sensible, with generous allowance for anticipated cross tides and winds. Places where overfalls form are best avoided, as are areas where experience tells that fishing gear — lobster pot markers, drift nets etc — might be found. A course through shallower water could present the hazard of running aground, but will be clear of main shipping routes.

Ideally, courses should always be chosen which are easy to steer i.e. either ending in 0 or 5. Given a steady hand on the helm and an accurate compass, it is possible to achieve very good results at high speed under dead reckoning alone.

The chosen course, along with alternatives, should be marked very clearly, and major features ringed or highlighted. The navigator's concentration is constantly tested by the motion and noise of a fast boat, so any technique which makes the chart easier to read is sensible.

PASSAGE PLANNING

With a course to work from, a passage plan can be drawn up. This is another familiar part of any style of navigation, but on the fast boat, the priority is on producing a precise account of what the navigator expects to see, when he expects to see it and what courses to steer — in effect, a navigation checklist. The more detail, the better.

Estimated time of arrival at each point can be shown either as real time, if the departure hour is assured, or as elapsed time from departure. The stopwatch facility fitted to a number of electronic logs is useful on motorboats for the latter.

This vital piece of paper needs to be protected and secured so that it is readily available to those who will use it.

OUT AT SEA

The major deviation from conventional navigation on a fast boat is that accurate plotting on a paper chart is rarely possible — the reason for completing all of the paperwork before departure. Certain chart instruments, are easier to use on a lively chart table, but even with such devices, just a small jolt could throw a pencil position more than a mile or more out.

Instead, the chart is often only used for reference and a log account takes on greater importance. Because of the distances covered in a relatively short period, regular entries every half hour, or even 20 minutes, are common, rather than the customary hourly interval. If the boat's formal log book is not practical to use for this purpose, a rough version can be kept and written up later. Once again, this needs to be protected and secured.

A good grasp of basic navigation principles pays dividends at high speed. The fast boat navigator needs an ability to register all the information available to him — from the log, compass, depth sounder and what can be seen all around — and visualize that as a position on the chart. Cultivating an ability to accurately estimate distances off, and understanding the optical illusions that the coastline can present to the observer, are equally important.

In cases where doubt overcomes confidence — where a navigation mark fails to appear on schedule for instance — the navigator still has the ultimate safeguard; to request a slower speed, or even to stop, until the boat's position has been re-established.

ELECTRONIC NAVIGATION ON FAST BOATS

So far, we have concentrated on the ways in which traditional navigation techniques can be modified to suit high speed boating, But the appearance of a whole new generation of electronic instruments will bring about further changes as we move through the 1990s.

ELECTRONIC NAVIGATORS

Electronic navigators lie at the core of any modern set-up. The various land-based and satellite systems work on the same basic principal of an onboard receiver which provides a regularly-updated readout of position in latitude and longitude and at the next level, of assisting the navigator in steering between 'waypoints'. Waypoints are simply those turning points on a passage plan which we have already described above – navigation marks or other places where a course change is required to follow the desired track on the chart.

Electronic navigators vary greatly in complexity. The simplest types just give a lat/long position, the ability to store a single waypoint and enough steering information to find it. The most complex units can take 100 waypoints or more into a memory (which is retained after power is switched off). plus several routes (a string of waypoints or in effect, an electronic navigator's passage plan). The display can be changed to show the distance and direction of the next waypoint, cross track error (the distance from one side or the other of the straight track between the waypoint which has been passed and the one which lies ahead), speed over ground, satellite availability or strength of land-based transmitter signals, estimated accuracy and a host of other facts.

Three things are required for successful operation. The first is a basic understanding of traditional navigation techniques so that this plethora of information can be read, understood, appreciated and correctly interpreted. The second is to ensure good installation according to manufacturers' recommendations. Last but not least is a long evening or two spent making the acquaintance of any unfamiliar electronic navigator. Manuals vary widely in their ability to educate the potential user and delving through them is much easier if the unit itself is available.

With an electronic navigator fitted, it is common to express all waypoints on the passage plan in latitude and longitude form, along with an identification number or name. Before departure, these figures have to be accurately entered into the unit's memory and checked.

Once at sea, there are any number of ways in which the electronic navigator can be used by a fast boat navigator.

At its most basic level, it is possible to take a lat/long reading and check this against the chart. Another technique using the position information is to observe this in a defensive way. By noting that safe water lies above or below a certain latitude or to one side of a specified longitude (expressed in degrees and minutes only and allowing a good margin for error), it is possible to make a quick at-a-glance check that all is as it should be.

However, the waypoint facilities give far more accurate ways of using an electronic navigator to its best. Cross track error gives an instant indication of how far the boat is off course and what correction needs to be made, also showing the influence of cross tides and any leeway. This facility too can be used defensively; if it is known that a hazard lies to one side or the other in the track, the helmsman can bias his steering accordingly.

THE CHANGING FACE OF FAST BOAT NAVIGATION.

The electronic navigator, used even in its most passive role, confirms the position of the boat in relation to what is calculated from conventional techniques. But advances in technology are making it possible for those roles to become reversed.

The helmsman may choose to steer using cross track error, rather than following the gyrations of an inadequately damped compass. A correctly-located electronic navigator display – either the unit itself, or a repeater by the helm – can actually be easier to interpret, and provided allowances are made for potential errors in the system, bring about a far higher level of accuracy than conventional techniques could provide in similar circumstances.

AUTOPILOTS

Taking things one stage further, by interfacing (a compatible electronic connection) the electronic navigator to a compatible autopilot, course-keeping becomes an automatic function, leaving more time to monitor the equipment itself, other navigational factors and keep a better watch.

Modern autopilots designed for fast boats are simple to operate, with automatic trim controls and easy-to-understand helm functions. Whether or not used in conjunction with an electronic navigator, they are a real aid to safe navigation if used wisely.

PLOTTERS AND ELECTRONIC CHARTS

More equipment can be added. By interfacing a compatible plotter (which shows the track only according to other interfaced instruments) or more usefully, an electronic chart (which shows the same track but on an electronic representation of a chart), the navigator has a second reference source and a real time plot of perceived position.

Electronic chart units have undergone much refinement in the last five years. Most are based around bulky cathode ray displays and are of a similar size to a radar display unit, although flat LED screens are under development. But the main consideration when choosing a unit is the cartography available.

Software to produce the actual chart images on screen is usually supplied in the form of plug-in cartridges which contain microchips with the digitized information burnt into memory. Two companies, C-Map and Navionics have established themselves as major suppliers of these cartridges, plus the necessary operating software and hardware. One or the other system is employed by most mainstream electronic chart manufacturers in their units, but they are not compatible with each other.

OTHER ELECTRONICS

It is possible to extend the principal of interfacing boat instruments far beyond the trio of electronic navigator, autopilot and chart or plotter.

Basic instruments such as an electronic log, compass and depth sounder are now available as integrated systems, or even single display units. These can be connected, for instance, to easily provide repeat information around the boat and a dead reckoned track (or estimated position if manually-entered tidal information can be entered) on the electronic chart display if no positional data is available from an electronic navigator.

Radar, if used correctly, will provide another independent source of information for the hard-pressed navigator. Additionally, an interfaced radar will be able to display repeat information from other instruments on screen.

Some units have a 'north-up' facility which, if connected with a compatible electronic compass, allows the display to show true north in the 12 o'clock position, rather than the boat's heading. Latest developments will allow the screen to alternate between the radar image and an electronic chart, or even to super-impose the two.

INTERFACING AND RELIABILITY

To make each individual instrument 'speak' to each other, it is important that they can send and receive data as a common electronic signal.

The industry standard has emerged around a set of 'languages' formulated by the National Marine Electronic Association (NMEA) in the United States. NMEA 0180 and NMEA 0183 are the most common standards, using a simple two wire interconnection.

In addition, especially for integrated instrument systems, individual manufacturers have developed their own languages and cabling systems. Mostly, these are incompatible with one another, although they additionally offer facilities for sending and receiving NMEA messages, but even within the NMEA protocol, there are some differences from company to company.

When planning any interfaced electronic system, from the simplest autopilot to electronic navigator arrangement, to the most complex array, it is important to seek the advice of manufacturers and dealers before proceeding.

The same is true of installation and maintenance work.

Much of the argument against greater reliance on electronics for navigation at sea has to do with reliability, which is perceived as poor. Errors which are due to aberrations in satellite or land-based transmitter signals are well documented and can be allowed for. The biggest reason for breakdowns, or misinformation, is faulty installation and subsequently, failure to routinely check that all is in order.

It also makes good sense to plan any system so that there is a degree of redundancy – if the power supply to the radar fails, for instance, the rest of the instruments can still operate.

7

Ocean Navigation

OCEAN NAVIGATION

THE MODERN SCENE

Top venture on an ocean passage is the ambition or dream of nearly every yachtsman. Only a few years ago he was able to call upon very little in the way of navigational aids to enable him to fix his position. Nowadays there is no such lack; and the advent of reasonably priced GPS receivers means that nearly all yachts heading for blue waters will carry equipment which will give a constant readout of position anywhere in the world - with an accuracy of 100 yards. A description of the various radio navigational aids which are available to yachtsmen can be found in Section 10.

It is helpful if the modern yachtsman understands the principles behind his electronic gear, and obviously he must master the "procedures" which will enable him to get the best out of his particular set. Will this equipment and this knowledge therefore allow him to embark on his passage with complete confidence that he will always be able to answer the question, "Where am I?" The answer must be no.

PITFALLS

There are three ways in which electronic navigational aids may be disabled: firstly, the set itself is as vulnerable to breakdown as other items of electrical equipment on board; secondly, it may be deprived of the electrical power necessary to run it; thirdly, lightning strike will cause serious damage. The chances of these mishaps occurring may be small, but they must be recognised by the prudent mariner.

SEXTANT NAVIGATION

We advocate therefore that the ocean navigator should carry a sextant, should practise how to use it effectively and should have at his fingertips a method of doing the associated arithmetic, i.e. sight reduction. There is the added stimulus that the art of celestial-navigation gives a great deal of pleasure and satisfaction, and that is surely why the yachtsman goes to sea.

REED'S POLICY

We, at Reed's, have made the deliberate decision that we will continue to provide the oceangoing yachtsman with the data necessary for him to perform all the necessary celestial-navigation tasks so that the partnership of the yachtsman, his sextant and his almanac will keep him out of trouble when the going gets tough. To this end we have retained, with some small revision, the descriptions, explanations, examples and tables which have appeared in Reed's for many years. Moreover, we have not been tempted to "update" the elegant prose style of much of the original material, which came from the pen of Captain O. M. Watts himself.

SIGHT REDUCTION

Getting good sextant altitudes is the most difficult part of celestial-navigation, and this can only be achieved by practice. The business of manipulating figures in order to perform the sight reduction is merely a matter of arithmetic. Not so long ago this was an onerous task, bedevilled by potential error. Nowadays it can be done relatively easily by a number of different methods, using tables, calculators or computers. Essentially, these are all ways of solving the spherical triangle by trigonometry, using long established formulae.

Some calculators and computers carry all or part of the ephemeris in their memories, thus appearing to make redundant the same data that we print. While not decrying this obvious use of computer power, it is our view that no sensible navigator would go to sea without carrying his ephemeris in (indestructible) book form. If this is accepted, the need for also carrying the data in an electronic memory is debatable.

One further point; those navigators who use tabular methods of sight reduction usually require the ephemeris to be presented in degrees and minutes of arc; those who use calculators or computers may prefer the presentation in degrees and decimal parts of a degree. We have decided to continue with the former, traditional, method. Our reason is that users of calculators almost always have a quick and simple means of making the conversion, whereas the same is not true for users of tabular methods.

REED'S METHODS

Reed's offers well tried and inexpensive methods of doing the arithmetic. *Firstly,* we provide the data and the guidance for doing the work, without going outside the almanac, using the versine method and ABC tables. This method is still used by many navigators all over the world, and we regard it as an essential "fall-back" feature of the almanac. *Secondly,* we show in the text, how to do the job using a simple scientific calculator.

THE ALMANAC - NEW FORMAT

Reed's is now divided into two parts, all the data which is unchanging (or changes seldom) in the Companion, and the material which changes annually in a separate edition. However, there is an important exception to this general rule; we have arranged things so that the sight reduction process, whichever method the navigator uses, can be accomplished by using the annual volume alone. This is because we believed it would be inefficient for him to switch from book to book during his work. In order to ensure coherence, there is some data which is carried in both books.

AN INVITATION

We hope these new arrangements will be approved by ocean navigators, and also by those who are engaged in teaching the art. As ever, we are open to any suggestions aimed at improving our content or presentation.

THE ART OF NAVIGATION

The Art of Navigation is the means by which vessels of any size are sailed from one safe place to another. The art is the same essentially, whether the vessel is large or small or under sail or power. Larger vessels carry more responsibilities; but smaller vessels, where conditions are much more difficult - owing to space and motion - call for the same art of navigation; but it is carried out in a different manner.

The knowledge required may conveniently be split up into two parts - the practice of navigation in sight of (or close to) the land, generally termed Coastal navigation; while the practice of navigation out of sight of land over the boundless ocean is termed Celestial, Ocean, Deep Sea or Astronomical navigation, or frequently and perhaps more correctly, just navigation.

Pilotage is generally defined as the art of navigating a vessel in enclosed waters or in harbors and estuaries.

As it is obvious that Coastal navigation cannot be carried out without a knowledge of pilotage - one must enter harbor sometimes - it is equally clear that Ocean navigation cannot be carried out without a knowledge of Coastal navigation - as one must leave and arrive from some coastline.

Where countries or islands are adjacent, or separated by short distances, then the two types of navigation mentioned overlap somewhat and short voyages can be carried out without the instruments required for longer voyages. Conversely the instruments or knowledge required essentially for long voyages can be employed usefully on the coast.

It is essential also that anyone who wishes to navigate anywhere must acquire the art of seamanship. Each art is really dependent on the other. One may be able to navigate successfully in all weathers; but if for example the navigator cannot handle his ship - then there probably will not be any ship left to navigate.

CELESTIAL NAVIGATION

Celestial navigation has two main functions:

1) To determine the azimuth (bearing) of the sun (star, planet, moon) and thereby establish the compass error and

2) To determine a position line when coastal methods of fixing are not available.

(**Note:** two or more position lines are necessary to fix the observer's position.)

Celestial navigation has the advantage that it is cheap - all you need is Reed's Almanac, a sextant and a watch accurate to the nearest second or so, and you have a system that can be used anywhere at any time, provided the cloud is not too dense.

Beginners to celestial navigation must not let the theory or the threat of massive calculations deter them. The theory can be largely ignored if simple routines are adopted and the calculations considerably reduced by a variety of ways, many of which are indicated on the following pages.

The beginner should start by finding the latitude from the sun and pole star.

PRINCIPLES OF CELESTIAL POSITION LINE NAVIGATION

To obtain a position line from a celestial body the following principles are involved.

The actual distance of the heavenly bodies from the earth is disregarded (as only angular measurements from the earth's center are involved), and all bodies are assumed to be on

THE NAVIGATIONAL TRIANGLE

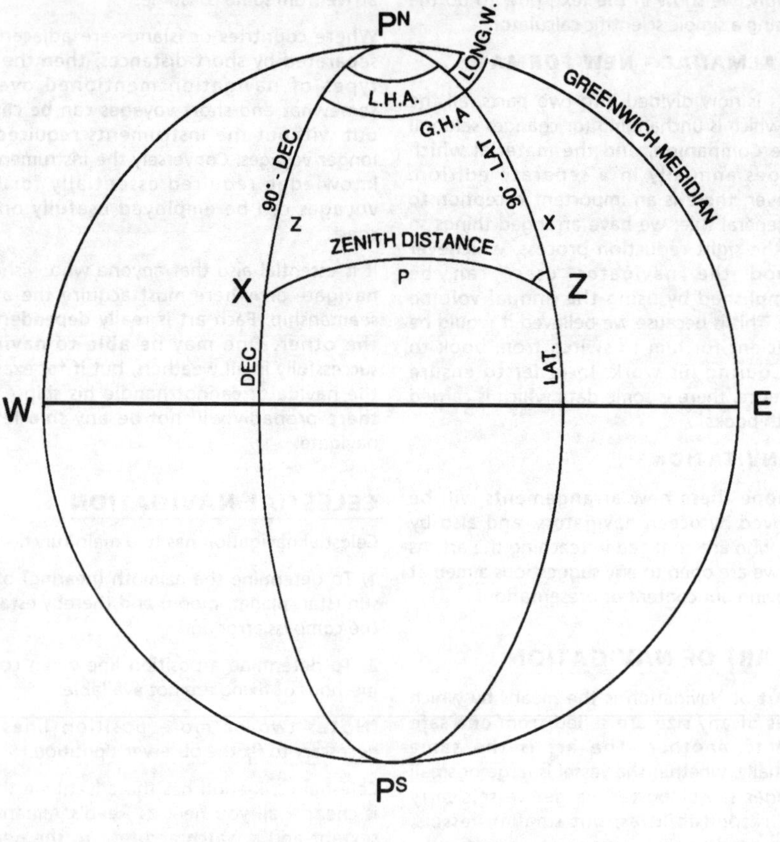

A Glossary of terms used in celestial navigation is given later in this section.

the surface of an imaginary sphere, "the Celestial Sphere", with the center of the earth at the center. Angular measurements on the celestial sphere correspond to those on the earth, i.e., the celestial equator is on the same plane as the terrestrial equator and north or south latitude (called (Declination on the Celestial Sphere) correspond. Longitude on the celestial sphere, or hour angle, is the angle at the pole measured from the meridian of Greenwich westward from 0° to 360°.

The Navigational Triangle

Thus, as shown in the diagram above, it can be seen that obtaining a "Position Line" from a celestial observation requires resolving a spherical triangle PZX, the "Navigational Triangle". All calculations for celestial observations are related to this PZX triangle as will be readily appreciated throughout the following examples.

In the triangle, the angle ZPX is the angle at the nearest Pole (N or S) between the observer's meridian (longitude) and the meridian of the body at the time of observation. It is therefore the Local Hour Angle (LHA) of the body and is found (as shown in the annual volume) for the sun.

Z is the position of the observer, the Observer's Zenith; X is the position of the observed body.

PZ is the arc of the observer's meridian betweenthe Pole and the Observer's Zenith and is therefore the Observer's Latitude subtracted from 90°. (Co-latitude.)

PX is the arc of the body's meridian between the Pole and the observed body and is therefore the body's Declination subtracted from 90° (Polar Distance).

ZX is the Zenith Distance, or the arc of a great circle contained between the Observer's Zenith and the observed body. It is therefore the altitude of the body subtracted from 90°.

The angle PZX is the Azimuth or True Bearing of the observed body.

THE CELESTIAL POSITION LINE

The corrected sextant altitude subtracted from 90 does therefore give you the distance in nautical miles (as 1' of arc = 1 nautical mile) from the point on the earth's surface directly beneath the body observed (i.e., the geographical position).

In practice this zenith distance is too large to plot so the observer compares his actual distance (True Zenith Distance) with the distance he has calculated from some assumed position (Calculated Zenith Distance). This comparison tells the observer that he is so many miles nearer or further away from the body than he had assumed.

i.e. True Zenith Distance = 40 10
Calc " " = 40 5
Intercept 5 miles away

that is the observer is five miles further away from the G.P. than he had assumed.

As the radius of the position circle is so large, the small section the observer is concerned with can be drawn as a straight line at right angles to the Azimuth

Note. The easiest position line to obtain is when the body lies due north or south. In this case the calculation is minimal and the position line obtained can be assumed to be the latitude.

See annual volume.

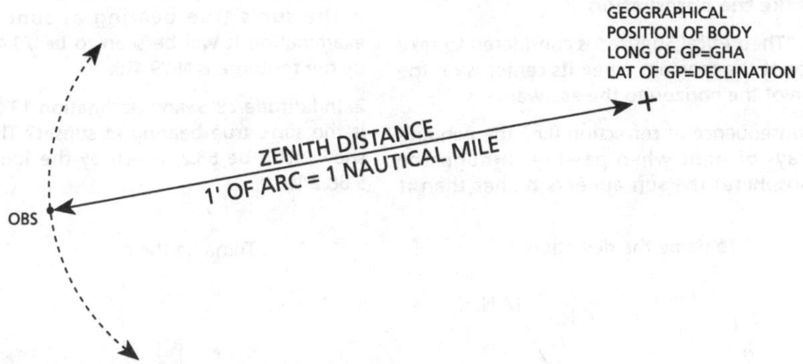

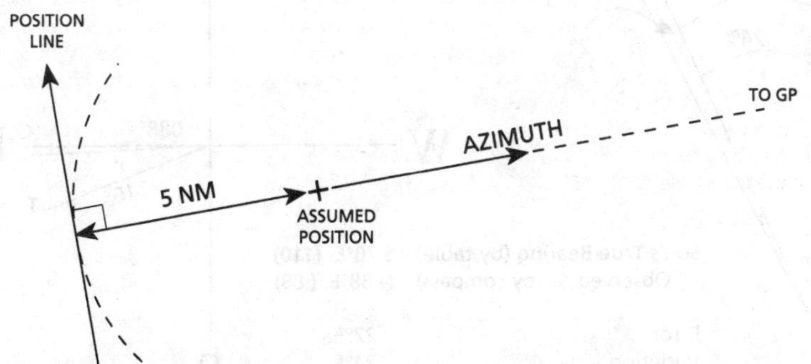

AMPLITUDES AND AZIMUTHS

The bearing of the sun when rising or setting is known as its Amplitude.

It is the quickest and easiest method of obtaining the compass error as "Time" does not enter into the problem at all. Also the Amplitude is the only astronomical sight that can be made accurately without the aid of any instrument (other than the compass), Nature's own instrument the horizon being used.

All that is required is to know the approximate latitude from the chart, and the approximate declination from this Almanac, see annual volume.

With these quantities a simple inspection of the table on following pages will give the True Bearing of the Sun at Sunrise or Sunset in any part of the world up to Latitude 66°; which, when compared with the compass bearing at sunrise or sunset will give the error of the compass. The Deviation can then be found immediately.

To take the observation

The "Theoretical Sunrise" is considered to take place at the moment when its center is on the edge of the horizon to the eastward.

In consequence of refraction (i.e., the bending of rays of light when passing through the atmosphere) the sun appears higher than it actually is and it must therefore be remembered that it apparently rises before it is actually above the horizon, and it is actually set when you can still see a small portion of the limb.

Amplitudes should therefore be taken, both at rising and setting, when the sun's lower limb is about half the sun's diameter above the horizon, as it is then that the center of the sun may be taken as being on the horizon.

This table can also be used for true bearing at rising and setting of any celestial body other than the moon, within these declinations.

Example - On November 18th, in latitude 18°N. declination 19°S. the sun rose bearing by compass N88°E (or 088°). The Variation from the chart was 24°E. Find the deviation.

Draw diagrams as shown at foot of page to help in naming the error (D) and deviation (C).

Further Examples of the Use of the Table on following pages

1. In latitude 20°N. and declination 10°N. what is the sun's true bearing at sunrise? On examination it will be seen to be 79.4, which by the footnote is N 79.4°E.

2. In latitude 29°S. and declination 19°S., what is the sun's true bearing at sunset? The table shows it to be 68.2, which by the footnote is S 68.2°W.

To name the deviation

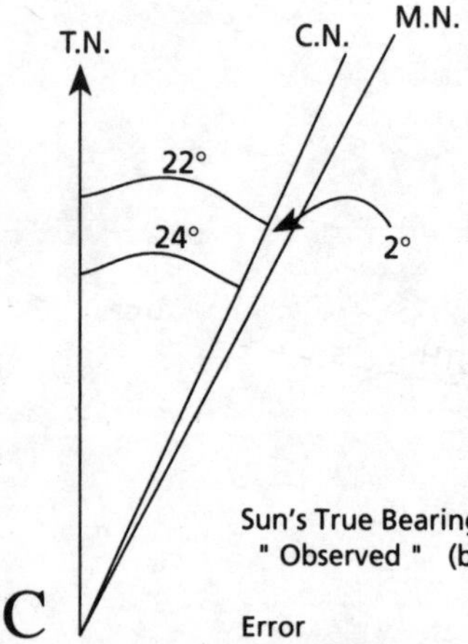

To name the error

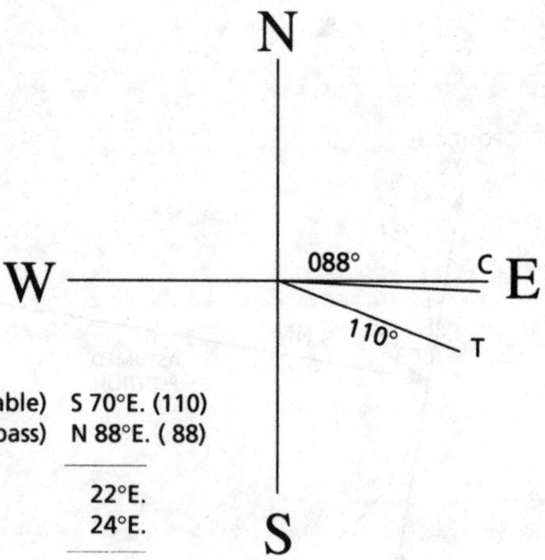

Sun's True Bearing (by table)	S 70°E. (110)
" Observed " (by compass)	N 88°E. (88)
Error	22°E.
Variation	24°E.
Deviation	2°W.

SUN'S TRUE BEARING AT SUNRISE AND SUNSET

LATITUDES 0° to 66° DECLINATIONS 0° to 11°

	DECLINATION											
LAT	0°	1°	2°	3°	4°	5°	6°	7°	8°	9°	10°	11°
	°	°	°	°	°	°	°	°	°	°	°	°
0° to 5°	90	89	88	87	86	85	84	83	82	81	80	79
6°	90	89	88	87	86	85	84	83	82	81	79.9	78.9
7°	90	89	88	87	86	85	84	83	81.9	80.9	79.9	78.9
8°	90	89	88	87	86	85	84	82.9	81.9	80.9	79.9	78.9
9°	90	89	88	87	86	85	83.9	82.9	81.9	80.9	79.8	78.9
10°	90	89	88	87	86	84.9	83.9	82.9	81.9	80.9	79.8	78.8
11°	90	89	88	87	86	84.9	83.9	82.9	81.9	80.8	79.8	78.8
12°	90	89	88	87	85.9	84.9	83.9	82.9	81.8	80.8	79.8	78.8
13°	90	89	88	86.9	85.9	84.9	83.8	82.8	81.8	80.8	79.7	78.7
14°	90	89	88	86.9	85.9	84.8	83.8	82.8	81.8	80.7	79.7	78.7
15°	90	89	88	86.9	85.9	84.8	83.8	82.8	81.7	80.7	79.6	78.6
16°	90	89	87.9	86.9	85.8	84.8	83.8	82.7	81.7	80.6	79.6	78.6
17°	90	89	87.9	86.9	85.8	84.8	83.7	82.7	81.6	80.6	79.5	78.5
18°	90	89	87.9	86.9	85.8	84.8	83.7	82.6	81.6	80.5	79.5	78.4
19°	90	89	87.9	86.8	85.8	84.7	83.7	82.6	81.5	80.5	79.4	78.4
20°	90	88.9	87.9	86.8	85.8	84.7	83.6	82.6	81.5	80.4	79.4	78.3
21°	90	88.9	87.9	86.8	85.7	84.7	83.6	82.5	81.4	80.4	79.3	78.2
22°	90	88.9	87.9	86.8	85.7	84.6	83.5	82.5	81.4	80.3	79.2	78.1
23°	90	88.9	87.9	86.7	85.7	84.6	83.5	82.4	81.3	80.2	79.1	78.0
24°	90	88.9	87.8	86.7	85.6	84.5	83.4	82.3	81.2	80.1	79.0	78.0
25°	90	88.9	87.8	86.7	85.6	84.5	83.4	82.3	81.2	80.1	79.0	77.9
26°	90	88.9	87.8	86.7	85.6	84.4	83.3	82.2	81.1	80.0	78.9	77.8
27°	90	88.9	87.8	86.6	85.5	84.4	83.3	82.1	81.0	79.9	78.8	77.6
28°	90	88.9	87.8	86.6	85.5	84.4	83.2	82.1	80.9	79.8	78.7	77.5
29°	90	88.9	87.8	86.6	85.5	84.3	83.1	82.0	80.9	79.7	78.6	77.4
30°	90	88.9	87.7	86.5	85.4	84.2	83.1	81.9	80.8	79.6	78.5	77.3
31°	90	88.9	87.7	86.5	85.4	84.2	83.0	81.8	80.7	79.5	78.3	77.1
32°	90	88.9	87.7	86.5	85.3	84.1	82.9	81.7	80.6	79.4	78.2	77.0
33°	90	88.8	87.7	86.4	85.3	84.0	82.8	81.7	80.5	79.3	78.0	76.9
34°	90	88.8	87.6	86.4	85.2	84.0	82.7	81.5	80.3	79.1	77.9	76.7
35°	90	88.8	87.5	86.3	85.1	83.9	82.7	81.4	80.2	79.0	77.8	76.5
36°	90	88.8	87.5	86.3	85.0	83.8	82.6	81.3	80.1	78.8	77.6	76.3
37°	90	88.7	87.5	86.2	85.0	83.7	82.5	81.2	80.0	78.7	77.4	76.2
38°	90	88.7	87.5	86.2	84.9	83.6	82.4	81.1	79.8	78.5	77.3	76.0
39°	90	88.7	87.4	86.1	84.8	83.6	82.3	81.0	79.7	78.4	77.1	75.8
40°	90	88.7	87.4	86.1	84.8	83.5	82.1	80.8	79.5	78.2	76.9	75.6
41°	90	88.7	87.3	86.0	84.7	83.4	82.0	80.7	79.4	78.0	76.7	75.3
42°	90	88.6	87.3	86.0	84.6	83.3	81.9	80.6	79.2	77.8	76.5	75.1
43°	90	88.6	87.3	85.9	84.5	83.1	81.8	80.4	79.0	77.6	76.4	74.9
44°	90	88.6	87.2	85.8	84.4	83.0	81.6	80.2	78.8	77.4	76.0	74.6
45°	90	88.6	87.2	85.7	84.3	82.9	81.5	80.1	78.6	77.2	75.8	74.3
46°	90	88.6	87.1	85.7	84.2	82.8	81.3	79.9	78.4	77.0	75.5	74.0
47°	90	88.5	87.1	85.6	84.1	82.6	81.2	79.7	78.2	76.7	75.2	73.7
48°	90	88.5	87.0	85.5	84.0	82.5	81.0	79.5	78.0	76.5	75.0	73.4
49°	90	88.5	86.9	85.4	83.9	82.4	80.8	79.3	77.7	76.2	74.6	73.1
50°	90	88.4	86.9	85.3	83.8	82.2	80.7	79.1	77.5	75.9	74.3	72.7
51°	90	88.4	86.8	85.2	83.6	82.0	80.4	78.8	77.2	75.6	74.0	72.3
52°	90	88.4	86.7	85.1	83.5	81.9	80.2	78.6	76.9	75.3	73.6	71.9
53°	90	88.3	86.7	85.0	83.3	81.7	80.0	78.3	76.6	74.9	73.2	71.5
54°	90	88.3	86.6	84.9	83.2	81.5	79.7	78.0	76.3	74.6	72.8	71.0
55°	90	88.2	86.5	84.8	83.0	81.3	79.5	77.7	75.9	74.2	72.4	70.6
56°	90	88.2	86.4	84.6	82.8	81.0	79.2	77.4	75.6	73.7	71.9	70.0
57°	90	88.2	86.3	84.5	82.6	80.8	78.9	77.1	75.2	73.3	71.4	69.5
58°	90	88.1	86.2	84.3	82.4	80.5	78.6	76.7	74.8	72.8	70.9	68.9
59°	90	88.0	86.1	84.2	82.2	80.2	78.3	76.3	74.3	72.3	70.3	68.2
60°	90	88.0	86.0	84.0	82.0	80.0	77.9	75.9	73.8	71.8	69.7	67.6
61°	90	87.9	85.9	83.8	81.7	79.6	77.5	75.4	73.3	71.2	69.0	66.8
62°	90	87.9	85.7	83.6	81.4	79.3	77.1	74.9	72.7	70.5	68.3	66.0
63°	90	87.8	85.6	83.4	81.2	78.9	76.7	74.4	72.1	69.8	67.5	65.1
64°	90	87.7	85.4	83.1	80.8	78.5	76.2	73.9	71.5	69.1	66.7	64.2
65°	90	87.6	85.3	82.9	80.5	78.1	75.7	73.2	70.8	68.3	65.7	63.2
66°	90	87.5	85.1	82.6	80.1	77.6	75.1	72.6	70.0	67.4	64.7	62.0

Name the Bearing the same as the Declination NORTH or SOUTH and EAST if rising, WEST if setting. For example of use of this Table see previous page.

SUN'S TRUE BEARING AT SUNRISE AND SUNSET

LATITUDES 0° to 66° DECLINATIONS 12° to 23°

	DECLINATION											
LAT.	12°	13°	14°	15°	16°	17°	18°	19°	20°	21°	22°	23°
	°	°	°	°	°	°	°	°	°	°	°	°
0° to 5°	77.9	76.9	75.9	74.9	73.9	72.9	71.9	70.9	69.9	68.8	67.9	66.9
6°	77.9	76.9	75.9	74.9	73.9	72.9	71.9	70.9	69.9	68.8	67.9	66.9
7°	77.9	76.9	75.9	74.9	73.9	72.9	71.9	70.8	69.8	68.8	67.8	66.8
8°	77.9	76.9	75.9	74.8	73.8	72.8	71.8	70.8	69.8	68.8	67.8	66.8
9°	77.8	76.8	75.8	74.8	73.8	72.8	71.8	70.7	69.7	68.7	67.7	66.7
10°	77.8	76.8	75.8	74.8	73.7	72.7	71.7	70.7	69.7	68.7	67.6	66.6
11°	77.8	76.8	75.7	74.7	73.7	72.7	71.6	70.6	69.6	68.6	67.6	66.5
12°	77.7	76.7	75.7	74.6	73.6	72.6	71.6	70.6	69.5	68.5	67.5	66.4
13°	77.7	76.6	75.6	74.6	73.6	72.5	71.5	70.5	69.4	68.4	67.4	66.4
14°	77.6	76.6	75.6	74.5	73.5	72.5	71.4	70.4	69.4	68.3	67.3	66.2
15°	77.6	76.5	75.5	74.4	73.4	72.4	71.3	70.3	69.3	68.2	67.2	66.1
16°	77.5	76.5	75.4	74.4	73.3	72.3	71.2	70.2	69.1	68.1	67.1	66.0
17°	77.4	76.4	75.3	74.3	73.3	72.2	71.1	70.1	69.0	68.0	66.9	65.9
18°	77.4	76.3	75.3	74.2	73.2	72.1	71.0	70.0	68.9	67.9	66.8	65.7
19°	77.4	76.2	75.2	74.1	73.0	72.0	70.9	69.9	68.8	67.7	66.7	65.6
20°	77.2	76.1	75.1	74.0	72.9	71.9	70.8	69.7	68.6	67.6	66.5	65.4
21°	77.1	76.0	75.0	73.9	72.8	71.7	70.7	69.6	68.5	67.4	66.3	65.2
22°	77.0	76.0	74.9	73.8	72.7	71.6	70.5	69.4	68.3	67.3	66.2	65.1
23°	76.9	75.9	74.8	73.7	72.6	71.5	70.4	69.3	68.2	67.1	66.0	64.9
24°	76.8	75.7	74.6	73.5	72.5	71.3	70.2	69.1	68.0	66.9	65.8	64.7
25°	76.7	75.6	74.5	73.4	72.3	71.2	70.1	68.9	67.8	66.7	65.6	64.5
26°	76.6	75.5	74.4	73.3	72.1	71.0	69.9	68.8	67.6	66.5	65.4	64.2
27°	76.5	75.4	74.3	73.1	72.0	70.8	69.7	68.6	67.4	66.3	65.1	64.0
28°	76.4	75.2	74.1	73.0	71.8	70.7	69.5	68.4	67.2	66.1	64.9	63.8
29°	76.2	75.1	73.9	72.8	71.6	70.5	69.3	68.2	67.0	65.8	64.6	63.5
30°	76.1	75.0	73.8	72.6	71.4	70.3	69.1	67.9	66.7	65.5	64.4	63.2
31°	76.0	74.8	73.6	72.4	71.2	70.0	68.9	67.6	66.5	65.3	64.1	62.9
32°	75.8	74.6	73.4	72.2	71.0	69.8	68.6	67.4	66.2	65.0	63.8	62.6
33°	75.7	74.4	73.2	72.0	70.8	69.6	68.4	67.1	65.9	64.7	63.5	62.2
34°	75.5	74.2	73.0	71.8	70.6	69.3	68.1	66.9	65.6	64.4	63.1	61.9
35°	75.3	74.1	72.8	71.6	70.3	69.1	67.8	66.6	65.3	64.0	62.8	61.5
36°	75.1	73.8	72.6	71.3	70.1	68.8	67.5	66.3	65.0	63.7	62.4	61.1
37°	74.9	73.6	72.4	71.1	69.8	68.5	67.2	65.9	64.6	63.3	62.0	60.7
38°	74.7	73.4	72.1	70.8	69.5	68.2	66.9	65.6	64.3	62.9	61.6	60.3
39°	74.5	73.2	71.9	70.5	69.2	67.9	66.6	65.2	63.9	62.5	61.2	59.8
40°	74.2	72.9	71.6	70.2	68.9	67.6	66.2	64.8	63.5	62.1	60.7	59.3
41°	74.0	72.7	71.3	70.0	68.6	67.2	65.8	64.4	63.0	61.6	60.2	58.8
42°	73.7	72.4	71.0	69.6	68.2	66.8	65.4	64.0	62.6	61.2	59.7	58.3
43°	73.5	72.1	70.7	69.3	67.9	66.4	65.0	63.6	62.1	60.7	59.2	57.7
44°	73.2	71.8	70.3	68.9	67.5	66.0	64.6	63.1	61.6	60.1	58.6	57.1
45°	72.9	71.4	70.0	68.5	67.0	65.6	64.1	62.6	61.1	59.5	58.0	56.4
46°	72.6	71.1	69.6	68.1	66.6	65.1	63.6	62.1	60.5	58.9	57.4	55.8
47°	72.2	70.7	69.2	67.7	66.2	64.6	63.0	61.5	59.9	58.3	56.7	55.0
48°	71.9	70.3	68.8	67.2	65.7	64.1	62.5	60.9	59.3	57.6	55.9	54.3
49°	71.5	69.9	68.4	66.8	65.1	63.5	61.9	60.2	58.6	56.9	55.2	53.4
50°	71.1	69.5	67.9	66.2	64.6	63.0	61.3	59.6	57.8	56.1	54.3	52.6
51°	70.7	69.0	67.4	65.7	64.0	62.3	60.6	58.8	57.1	55.3	53.5	51.6
52°	70.3	68.6	66.9	65.1	63.4	61.6	59.9	58.1	56.2	54.4	52.5	50.6
53°	69.8	68.0	66.3	64.5	62.7	60.9	59.1	57.2	55.4	53.4	51.5	49.5
54°	69.3	67.5	65.7	63.9	62.0	60.2	58.3	56.4	54.4	52.4	50.4	48.3
55°	68.7	67.9	65.0	63.2	61.3	59.3	57.4	55.4	53.4	51.3	49.2	47.1
56°	68.2	66.3	64.4	62.4	60.5	58.5	56.4	54.4	52.3	50.1	47.9	45.7
57°	67.6	65.6	63.6	61.6	59.6	57.5	55.4	53.3	51.1	48.8	46.5	44.2
58°	66.9	64.9	62.8	60.8	58.6	56.5	54.3	52.1	49.8	47.4	45.0	42.5
59°	66.2	64.1	62.0	59.8	57.6	55.4	53.1	50.8	48.4	45.9	43.3	40.6
60°	65.4	63.3	61.1	58.8	56.5	54.2	51.8	49.4	46.8	44.2	41.5	38.6
61°	64.6	62.3	60.1	57.7	55.3	52.9	50.4	47.8	45.1	42.3	39.4	36.3
62°	63.7	61.4	59.0	56.5	54.0	51.5	48.8	46.1	43.2	40.2	37.1	33.7
63°	62.7	60.3	57.8	55.2	52.6	49.9	47.1	44.2	41.1	37.9	34.4	30.6
64°	61.7	59.1	56.5	53.8	51.0	48.2	45.2	42.0	38.7	35.2	31.3	27.0
65°	60.5	57.8	55.1	52.2	49.3	46.2	43.0	39.6	36.0	32.0	27.6	22.4
66°	59.2	56.4	53.5	50.5	47.3	44.0	40.5	36.8	32.8	28.2	22.9	16.1

Name the Bearing the same as the Declination NORTH or SOUTH and EAST if rising. WEST if setting.

CELESTIAL SIGNS AND ABBREVIATIONS

SIGNS OF THE PLANETS

☉ The Sun.	⊕ The Earth.	♄ Saturn.
☾ The Moon.	♂ Mars.	♅ Uranus.
☿ Mercury.	♃ Jupiter.	♆ Nepturn.
♀ Venice.		

SIGNS OF THE ZODIAC

The Zodiac is the belt or zone extending 8° on either side of the Ecliptic, which contains the apparent paths of the Sun, Moon and the principal planets. It is divided into twelve angular portions of 30° (equalling the circle of 360°), each portion containing one constellation or sign, termed collectively The Signs of the Zodiac.

The seasons associated with these signs are given below, however, owing to the precession of the equinoxes the vernal equinox now actuallv occurs during Pisces instead of marking the First Point of Aries.

Northern Signs

Spring Signs	1. ♈ Aries	0°
	2. ♉ Taurus	30°
	3. ♊ Gemini	60°
Summer Signs	4. ♋ Cancer	90°
	5. ♌ Leo	120°
	6. ♍ Virgo	150°

Southern signs

Autumn Signs	1. ♎ Libra	180°
	2. ♏ Scorpio	210°
	3. ♐ Sagittarius	240°
Winter Signs	4. ♑ Capricornus	270°
	5. ♒ Aquarius	300°
	6. ♓ Pices	330°

ASPECTS

☌	Conjunction, or having the same Longitude or Right Ascension.
□	Quadrature, or differing ±90° in Longitude or Right Ascension.
☍	Opposition, or differing 180° in Longitude or Right Ascension.

ABBREVIATIONS

☊	Ascending Node
☋	Descending Node
N	North
S	South
E	East
W	West
°	Degrees
′	Minutes or Arc
″	Seconds of Arc
h	Hours
m	Minutes of Time
s	Seconds of Time

GREEK ALPHABET

Letter	Name	Letter	Name	Letter	Name
α	Alpha	ι	Iota	ρ	Rho
β	Beta	κ	Kappa	σ	Sigma
γ	Gamma	λ	Lambda	τ	Tau
δ	Delta	μ	Mu	υ	Upsilon
ε	Epsilon	ν	Nu	φ	Phi
ζ	Zeta	ξ	Xi	χ	Chi
η	Eta	ο	Omicron	ψ	Psi
θ	Theta	π	Pi	ω	Omega

GLOSSARY OF TERMS USED IN NAUTICAL ASTRONOMY AND CELESTIAL NAVIGATION

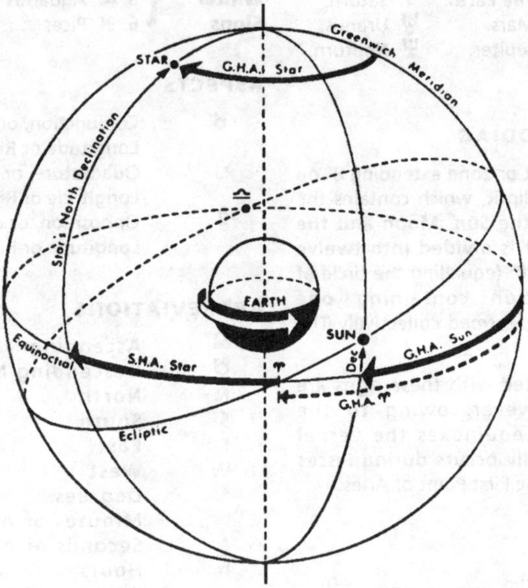

The Celestial Sphere (also termed the Celestial Concave—or the Heavens) illustrated above, is really the "Space" around the Earth into which we gaze at the Stars. Although it has no defined outline, being so far away it is assumed for practical purposes to be a hollow Sphere, of very large radius, having the Earth at its center, and all heavenly bodies located on its surface.

Owing to the Earth's radius being so small in comparison, the observer's eye may be assumed to be at the center of the Earth. Positions on the Earth's surface may be projected from the center outwards on to the celestial sphere, also Parallels of Latitude and Meridians of Longitude.

Altitude. The Observed Altitude is the angular height of an object above the visible horizon, measured on a Vertical Circle (which is a great Circle perpendicular to the horizon) by a Sextant. After correcting this Observed Altitude for Dip, Refraction, Semi-Diameter and Parallax (all embodied in a Total Correction Table in this Almanac) the True Altitude is obtained.

Amplitude. The bearing of a heavenly body when rising or setting measured from the east or west points of the observer's horizon.

Apogee. The position in the orbit of the Moon which is farthest from the Earth. Opposite to Perigee.

Aphelion. When the Earth or other Planet is at the farthest point (in its orbit) from the Sun, opposite to Perihelion.

Apparent Time. Time measured by the Apparent Sun.

Apparent Sun, The, is the "True" and actually visible Sun of which observations can be taken.

An Apparent Solar Day is the interval between two consecutive transits of the Apparent Sun over an observer's meridian.

Apparent Noon at a place is the time when the Apparent Sun is on the Meridian of that place.

Ship Apparent Time (S.A.T.) **or Local Apparent Time** at any instant is the L.H.A. of the True (or actual) Sun ± 12h., S.A.T. is reckoned Westwards (Oh. to 24h.) from the antimeridian of the place.

The measurement of Apparent Solar Time at any place is simply the measurement of the Apparent Sun's angular distance from the antimeridian of that place. As the Apparent Sun does not move uniformly, it is of no use as a standard time-keeper so another unit is adopted, called Mean Time (q.v.)

Arc. A part of the circumference of any circle.

Aries. One of the constellations of the Zodiac (see First Point of Aries).

Ascension (Right). See Right Ascension.

Astronomical Day, The. is composed of 24 mean solar hours, and begins at midnight on the civil day. It is reckoned from Oh. to 24h.

Autumnal Equinox. The time of the year – September 23rd – when the Sun crosses the Equator from North to South declinations.

Azimuth of a body is the arc of the horizon contained between the observer's meridian and a vertical circle through the center of the body. It is simply the bearing of a Heavenly Body measured from the North or South points of the horizon.

Azimuth Tables. A set of Tables to determine the true bearing of a Heavenly Body for any Latitude and time.

Calendar Month. The ordinary month having 30, 31 or 28 (and in a leap year 29) days in general use.

Celestial Poles, The. are the N. and S. poles of the Earth projected from the Earth's center on to the Celestial Sphere.

Circumpolar Stars. Stars which never set below the horizon at the place of observation, and to get this phenomenon the Latitude of the place must be more than the Polar distance of such Stars. Hence, there are no circumpolar stars at the Terrestrial Equator; but at the Terrestrial Poles all the Stars visible are circumpolar.

Civil Time is composed of 24 mean solar hours divided into two equal portions, the first marked A.M., from midnight to noon, the second marked P.M., from noon to midnight.

The civil year is 365 days (366 every 4 years – Leap Year).

Conjunction. When two Celestial bodies are in the same direction from the Earth they are said to be in conjunction.

Constellations. The groups into which the stars are divided for identification purposes; the ancients gave these groups names of a fish, bird or figure which they were thought to resemble.

Culmination. The time of a Heavenly body reaching its highest altitude in the Heavens, when it crosses the observer's meridian or "culminates".

Cycle. The period of time between some celestial phenomenon and its repetition.

Day. See Apparent Time, Mean Day and Sidereal Day.

Declination. The Declination (Dec.) of a body is its angular distance North (N) or South (S) of the Celestial Equator. Declination on the Celestial Sphere corresponds to Latitude on the Earth. North is sometimes written as + (plus) and South as - (minus), but this form of notation is not in general use.

Eclipse. The period when one Celestial body passes through the shadow of another.

The Ecliptic is the Great circle on the Celestial Sphere in which the Sun appears to move during its annual movement round the Earth. Its plane is inclined 23° 27′ (which is the Sun's maximum Declination) to the plane of the Celestial Equator, which angle is called the Obliquity of the Ecliptic.

Elevated Pole. The Celestial Pole which is above the observer's horizon.

Ephemeris (Ephemerides). The special calendar showing the predicted timetable of the moving Celestial Bodies.

Ephemeris Time (E.T.). A conception of time for presentation of Ephemerides of the Sun, Moon and Planets.

Equation of Time (Eq.T.). The excess of Mean Solar Time over Apparent Solar Time. When Apparent Time is greater than Mean Time the equation of time is a negative quantity and is prefixed with a minus sign.

Equinoctial (or Celestial Equator). The Equinoctial is a Great Circle dividing the Celestial Sphere into two equal parts. It is in the same plane as the Earth's Equator.

Equinox. See Autumnal Equinox, also Vernal Equinox.

First Point of Libra. The Autumnal Equinoctial Point; the point where the Sun's center crosses the Equinoctial as it moves along the Ecliptic and changes its Declination from North to South on the 23rd of September each year. It is diametrically opposite to the First point of Aries.

First Point of Aries. The starting point for measuring right ascensions. The point where the Sun's center crosses the Celestial Equator (Equinoctial) when moving along the Ecliptic and changing from South to North Declination on March 21st. It is called the Vernal (or Spring) Equinox.

At this time the lengths of the day and night are equal throughout the world. See also Transit of Aries.

Full Moon. When the Moon is in "opposition" to the Sun, or on the Sun's antimeridian; i.e., when it is on the Meridian about midnight – 12 hours different from the Sun.

Geographical Position. The. of a Heavenly body is the point on the Earth's surface directly underneath that object (i.e., the object is in this position's Zenith). Its actual position is found by its Declination (i.e., Latitude) and its G.H.A. (i.e., Longitude).

G.H.A. in the Heavens corresponds to the Longitude (measured 0° to 360° westwards from the Prime Meridian) of the Geographical Position of the body.

Gibbous Moon. The phases of the Moon when the Moon's disc is more than half illuminated; i.e., between First Quarter and Full Moon and also between Full Moon and Last Quarter.

Greenwich Mean Time (G.M.T.) is the Time at Greenwich by the Mean Sun and is the standard to which all observations can be referred.

Greenwich Hour Angle, The. is the angle at the pole between the Meridian at Greenwich and the Meridian or hour circle through the body. As can be seen clearly from the figure p.10: it may also be measured Westward from 0° to 360° along the Celestial Equator from the Celestial Meridian of Greenwich.

Greenwich Sidereal Time (G.S.T.) is the same as G.H.A. Aries.

Harvest Moon. The Full Moon nearest the Autumnal Equinox (Sept. 23rd).

Hemisphere. Half of the Sphere. A plane (Equator) passing through the center of a Sphere (the Earth) divides it into two equal parts (the Northern and Southern Hemispheres).

Horizontal Parallax (H.P.). Any Heavenly body on an observer's horizon would have no altitude, but if observed from the Earth's center there would be an altitude as it would be above the horizon from the different viewpoint. The angle between these two positions is termed the Horizontal Parallax.

Hour Angle (of the Heavenly Bodies). The Hour Angle of a heavenly body is the angle at the Pole between the observer's meridian and the meridian through the Body. It is purely a system of measurement, but because it often expresses "time" it is termed the Hour Angle, and when it is measured Westward from the Meridian (0° to 360° in arc or 0 to 24 hours in time) it is called "Local Hour Angle" (L.H.A.); but if measured Eastwards from the Meridian it is called "Easterly Hour Anglen and labelled E.H.A.

As the earth is rotating slowly unceasingly, the hour angle of any body that is fixed in the celestial concave will increase constantly during the 24 hours. When the body is on the observer's meridian the Hour Angle is 0 hours; and it is 24 hours later when it again returns to the observer's meridian.

The Local Hour Angle (L.H.A.) of the True (or actual) Sun is denoted by L.H.A.T.S. and that of the Mean Sun by L.H.A.M.S. (See also under Greenwich Hour Angle above.).

The L.H.A. of a Heavenly Body is also the sum of the L.H.A. of the First Point of Aries (i.e., the local Sidereal time) and the Sidereal Hour Angle (S.H.A.) of the body.

Hunter's Moon. The Full Moon nearest October 21st; but it is not so pronounced as the phenomenon of the Harvest Moon.

Inferior Planet. A Planet whose orbit round the Sun is between the Earth and the Sun. Only Mercury and Venus are Inferior Planets.

Latitude. (Terrestrial). The angular distance of a place on the Earth's surface North or South of the Equator.

Latitude. (Celestial). The angular distance of a Celestial Body North or South of the Ecliptic.

Leap Year. The year really consists of 365¼ days; but as the Civil year consists of 365 days, the extra 6 hours (¼ day) is added at the end of the fourth year as an extra day in February to give Leap Year.

Limb. The edge (Upper or Lower) of the Sun, Moon or Planet's disc..

Line, The. The Seaman's name for the Equator. When a vessel moves from South to North Latitude or vice versa she is said to "Cross the Linen".

Local Hour Angle (L.H.A.) (or the Hour Angle at the ship), is the difference between the Longitude of the Geographical Position of the body and the Longitude of the Observer. It is measured WESTWARDS (0° to 360°) from the Observer's Meridian.

The modern Navigator who determines his position by celestial observation and "position lines" is first and foremost concerned with obtaining his Local Hour Angle (L.H.A.).

Local Mean Time. The mean time at any place on the Earth's surface (see Ship Mean Time).

Local Sidereal Time (or Sidereal time of a place at any instant) is the L.H.A. of the First Point of Aries at that instant reckoned (0-24 hours) Westward from the meridian of the place. It is also the angular distance of the meridian Eastward from the First Point of Aries of the Right Ascension of the meridian (R.A.M.).

Longitude. The angular distance between the Greenwich Meridian and the meridian passing through any place, measured along the Equator, and named E or W of 6reenwich from 0° to 1 80°.

Longitude of Time is the difference between S.M.T. and G.M.T. and the difference of longitude between two places is the difference between the local mean times of the places. From which statements we get the rhyme – Longitude East, Greenwich Time Least, Longitude West, 6reenwich Time best – which gives the rule for turning Ship Time into Greenwich Time (and vice-versa). As the Mean Sun moves westwards through 360° of longitude in 24 hours, the difference in time between the two places 15° of longitude apart is 1h. and so on in proportion. In other words time can be converted into arc at the rate of 15° to 1h., 1° to 4min., or 1′ to 4 sec. (See annual volume.) As the earth rotates from West to East, Easterly meridians will pass under the Mean Sun before that of Greenwich; hence the time for a place East of Greenwich is in advance of Greenwich time, i.e., S.M.T. is for any instant greater than G.M.T. for the same instant.

Lunar Distance. The angular distance of the Moon from other Heavenly Bodies.

Lunar – of the Moon. (A Lunar Day is the time between two successive transits of the Moon over the same meridian.)

Magnitude. Relative brightness of a Star or Planet.

Mean Time. The Mean Solar Day, which is the average of all the Apparent solar days throughout a large number of years, may also be defined as the interval of time between two consecutive transits of the Mean Sun over an observer's meridian. This Mean Sun is an imaginary celestial body supposed to move along the celestial equator with a uniform speed equal to the average speed of the true Sun in the ecliptic.

Meridian. An imaginary great circle extending from North to South Pole. Any heavenly body reaching the highest point of its arc is said to be "on the Meridian" of any observer.

Meridian Altitude. The highest altitude above the horizon of a heavenly body when "on the Meridian".

Meridian, Prime. The Meridian of Greenwich (England) – Longitude 0°.

Moon's Age. The Moon's Age is the number of days that have passed since the previous New Moon.

Nadir. The point opposite to the Zenith, i.e., the point of the heavens directly below the observer.

New Moon. When the Sun and Moon are on the same celestial longitude, i.e., are in conjunction, it is called "New Moon". Is often incorrectly applied to the time when the Moon is first visible as a crescent in the West after Sunset.

Noon (Apparent). When the center of the actual Sun is on the observer's meridian.

Obliquity of the Ecliptic. See Ecliptic.

Occultation. When one heavenly body eclipses another.

Opposition. When a heavenly body is 180° of Longitude from another. At Full Moon the Moon is in opposition to the Sun.

Orbit. The elliptical path of one heavenly body round another body.

Parallax. The apparent movement of an object when viewed from two different positions.

7

Perigee. The position in the Moon's orbit nearest to the Earth, opposite to Apogee.

Perihelion. The point in the orbit of the Earth or other Planet when it is nearest to the Sun, opposite to Aphelion.

Phase. The particular aspects of a heavenly body as Phases of the Moon, etc.

Polar Distance. the angular distance of a heavenly body from the nearer celestial Pole.

Prime Meridian. See Meridian, Prime.

Prime Vertical. Vertical Circle of the celestial sphere passing through East and West points of the horizon. a heavenly body is on the "Prime Vertical" when it bears East or West (true).

Quadrature. When the positions of the heavenly bodies differ by 90° of longitude. At First Quarter and Last Quarter the Moon is in Quadrature.

Quarter, First and Last. At "Half Moon", when the Sun and Moon are 90° apart – the Phases of the Moon when the body is half illuminated.

Right Ascension. The Right Ascension (R.A.) of a heavenly body is the angular distance Eastward from the First Point of Aries, to the point where the Great Circle through the Pole and the body cuts the Equator, always expressed in hours 0-24.

Rising. The appearance of a heavenly body above the horizon of the observer. Owing to refraction, the object appears above the horizon when it is really still below it.

Seasons. The variation in the length of day and night is due to the inclining of the Earth's axis to the plane of its orbit.

Semi-Diameter (S.D.). Half the angular diameter of a heavenly body. The S.D. of the Sun and Moon is roughly 16′.

Sun's Semi-Diameter. The Sun has a perceptible disc and so its center cannot be observed. The part of the circumference actually observed is called the Limb. If the lower limb be observed in an altitude, the semi-diameter must be added to get the altitude of the center; but from an altitude of the upper limb, the semi-diameter must be subtracted.

Ship Mean Time (S.M.T.) or Local Mean Time at any instant is the H.A. of the Mean Sun ± 12h. S.M.T. is reckoned Westward (Oh. to 24h.) from the antimeridian of the ship.

Sidereal. In relation to the Stars. Time is an element of the highest importance in all observations of heavenly bodies. One unit of time is provided by the rotation of the earth on its axis from West to East.

A Sidereal Day is the time occupied in one complete rotation of the Earth upon its axis, or more particularly it is the interval between two successive transits of the First Point of Aries over an observer's meridian. (See First Point of Aries.) Sidereal Time is used by astronomers.

Sidereal Hour Angle (The) S.H.A. of a star, is the angle at the pole measured (from 0° to 360°) from the meridian of Aries to the meridian of the Star in a WESTERLY direction.

Signs of the Zodiac. The twelve constellations through which the Ecliptic runs.

Solstices. When the Sun is farthest from the Celestial Equator (i.e., Declination 23.5° North or South) June 21st, December 22nd, the "longest" and "shortest" days, respectively, in northern latitudes.

Superior Planets. Those Planets whose orbits are outside that of the Earth, and farthest from the Sun. That is all Planets except Mercury and Venus.

Time. See Apparent, Mean, Sidereal.

Transit. The passage of a heavenly body across the observer's Meridian.

Transit of Aries. The Transit of the First Point of Aries and of the fixed Stars occurs approximately 4 minutes earlier on each successive day; so that every month the Transit occurs 2 hours (approx.) earlier and thus 24 hours per year in completing the cycle.

Twilight. The periods of the day when, although the Sun is below the visible horizon, the observer does not experience complete darkness because indirect light is received from the Sun through reflection and scattering by the upper atmosphere. Complete darkness occurs when the Sun's center is18° below the horizon. Civil Twilight begins or ends when the Sun is 6° below the horizon, at which time the sea horizon is clear and the brightest stars are visible – the most favorable time for stellar observations.

Universal Time (U.T.). Another name for G.M.T. (Greenwich Mean Time).

Vernal Equinox. Also called the Spring Equinox, when the Sun crosses the Equinoctial from South to North (about March 21st). See First Point of Aries.

Waxing and waning. The Moon is said to be waxing between New Moon and Full Moon when its light increases and waning when its light decreases between Full Moon and New Moon.

Zenith, Zenith Distance is the angular distance of an object from the observer's Zenith (the point vertically overhead in the celestial sphere). It is the complement of the Altitude, i.e., 90° minus the Altitude. Zenith is opposite to Nadir.

Zodiac. An imaginary belt of sky along the Ecliptic, in which the Sun, Moon and larger Planets perform their revolutions.

THE FIXED STARS

These are called "fixed" as their position in relation to one another changes but a fraction. All stars appear to move across the sky from East to West, and across the meridian about four minutes earlier each day. They do not move about the heavens at random as the Moon and the Planets appear to do. The Stars are at an immense distance from the Earth and, unlike the Moon and Planets, which shine with the reflected light of the Sun, shine with their own light.

At first sight there appears to be an immense number of Stars in the heavens; but on due examination it will be seen that there are relatively few bright Stars and only some hundreds of smaller ones, which latter, of course, are of no use for Navigational purposes.

STELLAR MAGNITUDES

The stars are classified according to the amount of light which is received from them on Earth. The magnitude of a star is a measure of its relative brilliance; the actual grading being based on the definition that na star of magnitude 1 is one from which the Earth receives 100 times as much light as it receives from a star of magnitude 6". Thus a star of magnitude 2 is 1OO times brighter than a star of magnitude 7; a star of magnitude 3 is 100 times brighter than a star of magnitude 8. It follows therefore that a star of magnitude 0 is 100 times brighter than a star of magnitude 5, and a star which is 100 times brighter than a star of magnitude 4 must have a magnitude of -1. Sirius, the brightest star in the heavens, has a magnitude of -1.6.

In practice, the terms "stars of the first magnitude" (of which there are 12 only) refers to all those whose magnitude is less than 1.0.

Note: A sixth-magnitude star is only just visible to the naked eye.

The Planets Venus and Jupiter have variable minus magnitudes in the nature of -3.5 and -2.0, respectively. An interesting comparison also is that of the Sun and the Full Moon which have magnitudes of -26.7 and -12.5 respectively.

CONSTELLATIONS

From ancient times Stars have been divided into groups called Constellations; and as it would be impossible to name each Star with a proper name the Stars were named according to their Constellation. The brightest Star in a constellation is prefixed with the Greek Letter α (alpha), the second brightest Star is prefixed β (Beta); and so on in order of their brightness as, for example, α Andromedae and β Andromedae. Proper Names have also been given to the brightest of the Fixed Stars – especially in the Northern Hemisphere – as, for example, Alpheratz (α Andromedae); Mirach (β Andromedae); Vega (Alpha Lyrae); Altair (Alpha Aquiliae); Canopus (Alpha * Carinae); and Denebola (Beta Leionis), etc.

It is frequently of advantage to be able to judge the angular distance between heavenly bodies, and this can be done by comparing the distance with the known angular distance between specified stars or arcs.

The following examples of varying sized angles may be useful to serve as a guide to the estimation of apparent distances in the sky when using Star Charts.

360°	All round the horizon.
180°	East to West along the horizon or through Zenith.
90°	Horizon to Zenith.
60°	Dubhe (Great Bear) to Caph (,B Cassiopeiae).
30°	Polaris to Caph (~ Cassiopeiae).
23°	Vega to Deneb.
20°	Betelguese to Rigel (Orion).
5°	Merak to Dubhe (Pointers to the Plough).
4°	Castorto Pollux.

* Formerly Argus

HOW TO FIND THE PRINCIPAL FIXED STARS LISTED IN REED'S NAUTICAL ALMANAC

The Navigator will usually find a Star Map or Atlas of great benefit, especially if he is not able to take Star Sights often; but as many Star Maps are still graduated in Right Ascension, for the purposes of identification, we give the R.A. of each Star as well as its S.H.A.

Generally, of course, the brighter Planets and Stars are used to take observations and Azimuths, so the annual edition of Reed's Almanac has tabulated each month the position, i.e., Declination and G.H.A., etc. of 60 Principal Stars. Each of these Stars is numbered as follows, and to assist the beginner especially, we give the following notes on how to find every one of these navigational Stars in the same numerical order as in the Almanac.

Pronunciations are also given for some of the Stars. Always accent the syllable marked.

(1) Alpheratz. A line from the Pole Star through β Cassiopeiae (Caph) and produced the same distance beyond leads to Alpheratz (α Andromedae), which together with the Stars Markab, Algenib and Scheat form the Square of Pegasus with Markab at the south-west corner. These are all bright Stars, and make almost an exact square which is easily found.

(2) Ankaa. (α Phoenicis). A second magnitude Star situated just east of a line from Achernar to Fomalhaut.

(3) Schedar. The brightest Star in Cassiopeiae. This constellation is on the opposite side of the Pole to the Dipper and about the same distance away. It is in the shape of a "W" and is known as Cassiopeiae's Chair.

When the Great Bear (or Big Dipper) is on the meridian above the Pole, Cassiopeiae is on the meridian below the Pole, and the two constellations appear to revolve round the Pole Star at equi-distances. A line drawn from Aldebaran through Algol will intersect Schedar.

(4) Diphda. A Star of second magnitude which lies by itself about half way between the Square of Pegasus and Achernar.

(5) Achernar. (Ak'-er-nar). The brightest Star in the constellation Eridanus in the Southern Hemisphere. Lies about 70° west of Canopus just off a line between Canopus and Fomalhaut.

(6) POLARIS (or POLE STAR). See diagram of the Great Bear and description on page 20.

(7) Hamal. The brightest Star in the constellation Aries. A line from Betelgeuse through Aldebaran leads to Hamal which lies midway between Aldebaran and the Great Square of Pegasus.

(8) Acamar. A third magnitude Star situated about 20° N.E. of Achernar.

(9) Menkar. A second magnitude Star which lies S.W. of Aldebaran and forms the apex of a triangle (upside down) with Aldebaran and Hamal. A line from Sirius through Rigel about the same distance beyond points to Menkar (a Ceti).

(10) Mirfak. Lies North of Algol and on a line from Capella to Cassiopeiae.

(11) Aldebaran (Al-deb'-ar-an). See the diagram of the constellation of Orion on p. 20. This very bright red Star lies to the North of Orion just a little off the line of the Belt. It lies at the top of one of the arms of a V-shaped cluster of small Stars – the Hyades. The Pleiades, a well defined cluster of Stars (The Seven Sisters) lie close to the Hyades, and form a valuable skymark.

(12) Rigel (Ri'-jel). See diagram of the constellation of Orion on p. 20.

(13) Capella (Ca-pel'-la). A line drawn from the Pole Star away from the Great Bear but perpendicular to the Pointers leads to Capella. It will readily be recognised as a bright yellow Star.

A line from Polaris to Rigel nearly intersects Capella, which is 45° from the Pole Star and 55° from Rigel. It may be recognised also from being in a line from Menkar through the Pleiades about 30° N.E. of that cluster of Stars.

(14) Bellatrix (Bel'-la-trix). See the diagram of the constellation of Orion on p. 20.

(15) Elnath (Nath). The second brightest Star to Aldebaran in the constellation Taurus, and lies about halfway along a line between Orion's Belt and Capella.

(16) Alnilam. The middle Star of the three bright Stars in the center of Orion forming the Belt.

(17) Betelgeuse (Bet'-eljoox). See the diagram of the constellation of Orion. Betelgeuse has a reddish appearance rather like Aldebaran.

(18) Canopus (Can-o'-pus). a Carinae (formerly Argus). The second brightest Star in the sky, but situated in 52° South declination. A line drawn from Bellatrix through the northern star in Orion's Belt passes to Canopus. It is almost due South from Sirius and a pale blue colour.

(19) Sirius (Sir'-e-us). The Dog Star – is magnificent – in that he is the brightest Star in the sky (surpassing in brilliance the Planets, Mars and Saturn), and has a gorgeous pale blue colour. The three Stars in the Belt of Orion lead directly away from Aldebaran to Sirius which lies S.E. of Orion.

A fine heavenly curve is formed by Capella, Castor, Pollux, Procyon and Sirius. See diagram of the constellation of Orion.

(20) Adhara. This is a first magnitude star which lies about 10° South of Sirius.

(21) Castor and Pollux (Kas'-ter and Pol'-lux). Known as the Twins – these two Stars lie nearly halfway between the Dipper and Orion. A line from Rigel through the center Star in Orion's Belt points to Castor. Pollux (the brighter Star of the two) will be found 4.5° to the southward.

(22) Procyon (Pro'-se-on). A line drawn from Castor and Pollux to Sirius passes almost through Procyon, the little Dog Star.

(23) Pollux. (See No. 21.)

(24) Avior. This first magnitude Star lies far South (60° declination) about 30° S.E. of Canopus and a little to the East of a line joining Canopus to Miaplacidus.

(25) Suhail (ν Velorum). A second magnitude Star South of Alphard and E.N.E. of Canopus.

(26) Miaplacidus (β Carinae formerly Argus). A far southerly first magnitude Star, situated about halfway between Canopus and Acrux, but about 10° S.W. of a line joining them.

(27) Alphard. This second magnitude Star lies on a line drawn from the Great Bear Star Alioth through Regulus and about 20° beyond to the S.S.W. Its name means "the solitary one" because there is no other bright star near it.

(28) Regulus (Reg'-u-lus). A line from the Pole Star through the Pointers of the Dipper, and continued about 4S° leads close to Regulus. This Star may be found easily, as it is situated at the end of the "handle" of the "Sickle" (which shape the constellation Leo takes), and is the brightest Star in the group.

(29) Dubhe. The northern and brightest of the two Pointers of the Great Bear.

(30) Denebola (De-neb'-o-la). The second brightest Star in the constellation of Leo. Lies about halfway along a line from Arcturus to Regulus.

(31) Gienah (γ Corvi). A second magnitude Star situated S.W. of Spica.

(32) Acrux. The brightest and most southerly Star in the Southern Cross or Crux. Together with the bright Stars, a and ,13 Centauri, the Southern Cross, or Crux, forms the most remarkable constellation in the Southern Hemisphere. It is unfortunately not visible far North, and only shows up over the horizon when sailing South and the Latitude 20's are reached.

(33) Gacrux (γ Crucis) is nearly as bright as Mimosa (β Crux) and is situated at the top (North) of the Cross.

(34) Mimosa (γ Crucis). Is the second brightest Star in the Crux and lies at the eastern arm of the Cross.

(35) Alioth. One of the Stars in the Tail of the Great Bear.

(36) Spica (Spi'-ka). When the curve of three Stars in the Tail of the Great Bear is continued through Arcturus, and about 30° beyond it passes through Spica, a first magnitude Star. Just South-West of Spica are four Stars which look exactly like a Spanker sail, and are known as Spica's Spanker, the gaff of which always points to Spica.

(37) Alkaid (Benetnasch). A first magnitude Star situated at the extreme Tail of the Great Bear.

(38) Hadar (β Centauri). The two Stars β and α Centauri lie close Eastward of the Southern Cross, and are called the Southern Cross Pointers. β Centauri is the nearer of the two to Crux.

(39) Menkent (θ Centauri). A second magnitude Star situated about halfway between Spica and β Centauri and slightly east of a direct line.

(40) Arcturus (Ark-tu-rus). If the Great Bear is followed southwards away from the Pole Star for the same distance as the length of the Dipper itself, it will lead to Arcturus (a yellow Star). There are three small Stars just to the Westward of Arcturus which form a small triangle. Arcturus is the second brightest Star in the Northern heavens.

(41) Rigil Kent (α Centauri). See No. 38 above. a Centauri is the nearest fixed Star to the Earth.

(42) Zuben'ubi (α Librae). A second magnitude Star situated on a line about halfway between Spica and Antares.

(43) Kochab. A second magnitude Star in Ursa Minor.

(44) Alphecca. A second magnitude Star in the constellation Corona Borealis but the brightest in the heavenly jewel, the Northern Crown. A line drawn from Megrez through Alkaid (the last Star in the tail of the Great Bear) leads to Alphecca in the Northern Crown – an almost perfect semi-circular group of small Stars. It lies a third of the distance from Arcturus to Vega about 20° E.N.E. of Arcturus.

(45) Antares (An'-ta-rez). A line from Regulus through Spica the same distance beyond leads to Antares – a bright red Star. It lies about 45 S.W. of Altair.

(46) Atria (α Trianguli Australis). A first magnitude Star and the brightest of the three Stars lying at the S.E. apex of the Southern Triangle, which lies S.E. of Centaurus and about 45° due 5outh of Antares.

(47) Sabik (π Ophuchi). A second magnitude Star situated N.E. of Antares about a quarter of the way towards Altair.

(48) Shaula. A first magnitude Star lying 15° S.E. of Antares about a quarter of the way on a line drawn from Antares to Peacock (α Pavonis).

(49) Rasalhague. A second magnitude Star lying about 25° W,N.W. of Altair. It lies also on a line between Vega and Antares. It forms a triangle with Altair and Vega.

(50) Eltanin. A second magnitude Star lying about 10° N.N.W. of Vega on a line from Altair through Vega.

(51) Kaus Australis. A second magnitude Star lying with the many Stars of the constellation of Sagittarius. It is difficult to identify and lies about 25° E.S.E. of Antares, but East of a line from Antares to Peacock (No. 55).

(52) Vega (Ve'-ga). A line curving through Dubhe, Megrez, Alioth and Mizar (see diagram of the Great Bear) and following to the west for about thirty five degrees leads close to Vega – the brightest and most beautiful Star in the Northern heavens, and of a fine pale blue colour. Vega may also be found by a line from Arcturus through the Northern Crown Star (Alphecca) and extending about 40° beyond.

(53) Nunki. A second magnitude Star lying among many others of the constellation Sagittarius about 35° due East of Antares.

(54) Altair (Al-tair'). Is easily recognised as a bright Star lying between two smaller Stars which are close in line and point in the direction of Vega. A line from the Pole Star between Vega and Deneb and extended the same distance beyond leads to Altair.

(55) Peacock. This second magnitude Star lies alone in 57° South declination about halfway between Achernar and Centauri on the same parallel of latitude (West from Achernar). It lies S.E. of Antares and S.W. of Fomalhaut and about 65° due South of Altair.

(56) Deneb (Den'-eb). This first magnitude Star lies E.N.E. of Vega and is the brightest Star in the constellation of Cygnus (the Swan). A line drawn from Castor and Pollux through the Pole Star and extended the same distance beyond passes through Deneb, which is readily found as it is at the top of a "Cross" of Stars (very similar to the Southern Cross). The constellation is usually known as the "Kite" – it is exactly this shape. It lies about 25° Eastward of Vega.

(57) Enif (ε Pegasi). A second magnitude Star situated about halfway between Altair and Markab (Square of Pegasus).

(58) Al Na'ir (α Gruis). This second magnitude Star lies West of β Gruis and is situated on a line about halfway between Fomalhaut and Peacock.

(59) Fomalhaut (Fom'-al-haut). A line drawn from Scheat through Markab (which Stars form one side of the Great Square of Pegasus) passes through Fomalhaut, which may be found readily as it has a small square of Stars near it. Situated about 45° South of Markab.

(60) Markab. Is in the S.W. Corner of the Square of Pegasus. A line from Altair N.E. through the Dolphin 50° from Altair will lead to Scheat. It lies about 45° to the east of Altair and about 45° North of Fomalhaut.

ALPHABETICAL INDEX OF PRINCIPAL STARS

PROPER NAME	Constellation Name	Mag.	R.A.	Dec.	S.H.A.	No.
			h. m.	°	°	
Acamar	θ **Eridani**	**3.1**	2 58	S 40	315	**8**
Achernar	α **Eridani**	**0.6**	1 37	S 57	336	**5**
Acrux	α **Crucis**	**1.1**	12 26	S 63	173	**32**
Adhara	ϵ **Canis Majoris**	**1.6**	6 58	S 29	255	**20**
Aldebaran	α **Tauri**	**1.1**	4 36	N 16	291	**11**
Alioth	ϵ **Ursae Majoris**	**1.7**	12 54	N 56	167	**35**
Alkaid	η **Ursae Majoris**	**1.9**	13 47	N 49	153	**37**
Al Na'ir	α **Gruis**	**2.2**	22 08	S 47	28	**58**
Alnilam	ϵ **Orionis**	**1.8**	5 36	S 1	276	**16**
Alphard	α **Hydrae**	**2.2**	9 27	S 9	218	**27**
Alphecca	α **Coronae Bor**	**2.3**	15 34	N 27	126	**44**
Alpheratz	α **Andromedae**	**2.2**	0 08	N 29	358	**1**
Altair	α **Aquilae**	**0.9**	19 51	N 9	62	**54**
Ankaa	α **Phoenicis**	**2.4**	0 26	S 42	354	**2**
Antares	α **Scorpii**	**1.2**	16 29	S 26	113	**45**
Arcturus	α **Bootis**	**0.2**	14 15	N 19	146	**40**
Atria	α **Triang Aust**	**1.9**	16 48	S 69	108	**46**
Avior	ϵ **Carinae**	**1.7**	8 22	S 59	234	**24**
Bellatrix	γ **Orionis**	**1.7**	5 25	N 6	279	**14**
Betelgeuse	α **Orionis**	**0.1-1.2**	5 55	N 7	271	**17**
Canopus	α **Carinae**	**-0.9**	6 24	S 53	264	**18**
Capella	α **Aurgae**	**0.2**	5 16	N 46	281	**13**
Castor	α **Geminorum**	**1.6**	7 34	N 32	246	**21**
Deneb	α **Cygni**	**1.3**	20 41	N 45	50	**56**
Denebola	β **Leonis**	**2.2**	11 49	N 15	183	**30**
Diphda	β **Ceti**	**2.2**	0 43	S 18	349	**4**
Dubhe	α **Ursae Majoris**	**2.0**	11 03	N 62	194	**29**
Elnath	β **Tauri**	**1.8**	5 26	N 29	279	**15**
Eltanin	γ **Draconis**	**2.4**	17 56	N 51	91	**50**
Enif	ϵ **Pegasi**	**2.5**	21 44	N 10	34	**57**
Fomalhaut	α **Piscis Aust.**	**1.3**	22 57	S 30	16	**59**
Gacrux	γ **Crucis**	**1.6**	12 31	S 57	172	**33**
Gienah	λ **Corvi**	**2.8**	12 15	S 18	176	**31**
Hadar	β **Centauri**	**0.9**	14 03	S 60	149	**38**
Hamal	α **Arietis**	**2.2**	2 07	N 23	328	**7**
Kaus Aust.	ϵ **Sagittarii**	**2.0**	18 24	S 34	84	**51**
Kochab	β **Ursae Minoris**	**2.2**	14 51	N 74	137	**43**
Markab	α **Pegasi**	**2.6**	23 04	N 15	14	**60**
Menkar	α **Ceti**	**2.8**	3 02	N 4	315	**9**
Menkent	θ **Centauri**	**2.3**	14 06	S 36	148	**39**
Miaplacidus	β **Carinae**	**1.8**	9 13	S 70	222	**26**
Mimosa	β **Crucis**	**1.5**	12 47	S 60	168	**34**
Mirfak	α **Persei**	**1.9**	3 24	N 50	309	**10**
Nunki	σ **Sagittarii**	**2.1**	18 55	S 26	76	**53**
Peacock	α **Pavonis**	**2.1**	20 25	S 57	54	**55**
POLARIS	α **Ursae Minoris**	**2.1**	2 25	N 89	324	**6**
Pollux	β **Geminorum**	**1.2**	7 45	N 28	244	**23**
Procyon	α **Canis Minoris**	**0.5**	7 39	N 5	245	**22**
Rasalhague	α **Ophiuchi**	**2.1**	17 35	N 13	96	**49**
Regulus	α **Leonis**	**1.3**	10 08	N 12	208	**28**
Rigel	β **Orionis**	**0.3**	5 14	S 8	281	**12**
Rigil Kent	α **Centauri**	**0.1**	14 39	S 61	140	**41**
Sabik	η **Ophiuchi**	**2.6**	17 10	S 16	102	**47**
Schedar	α **Cassiopaiae**	**2.5**	0 40	N 56	350	**3**
Shaula	λ **Scorpii**	**1.7**	17 33	S 37	97	**48**
Sirius	α **Canis Majoris**	**-1.6**	6 45	S 17	259	**19**
Spica	α **Virginis**	**1.2**	13 25	S 11	159	**36**
Suhail	λ **Velorum**	**2.2**	9 08	S 43	223	**25**
Vega	α **Lyrae**	**0.1**	18 37	N 39	81	**52**
Zuben'ubi	α **Librae**	**2.9**	14 51	S 16	137	**42**

The last column refers to the number given to the Star in the annual volume of this Almanac. The Star's exact position may be found according to this number on the monthly pages.

AUXILIARY STAR CHARTS

POLE-DIPPER-DUBHE-BENETNASCH-KOCHAB

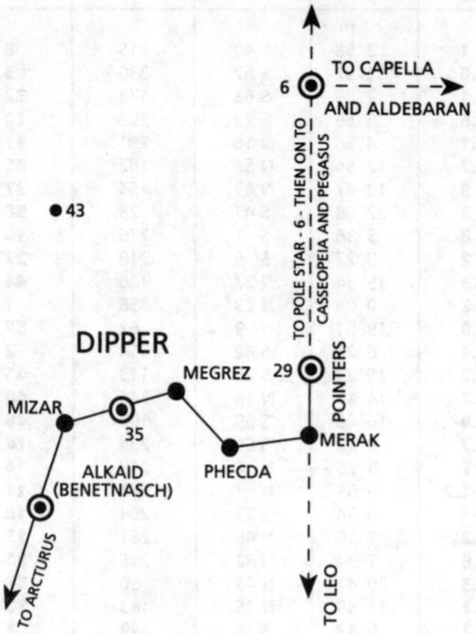

No. 6. POLARIS
No. 29. DUBHE.
No. 35. ALIOTH.
No. 43. KOCHAB.
No. 11. ALDERBARAN.
No. 13. CAPELLA.

Polaris – the Pole Star – familiar in the Northern Hemishpere is always seen in the same part of the heavens, over the Pole of the Earth. It is the brightest star in the Little Bear (Ursa Minor). The position of Polaris in the Little Bear corresponds to the position of Alkaid (Benetnasch) 37, in the Great Bear. The Dipper or Great Bear (Ursa Major) is the easiest recognisable constellation in the northern heavens, a straight line through Merak and Dubhe – the Pointers – leads to the Pole Star.

CAPELLA-POLLUX-SIRIUS-ORION-ALDEBARAN

No. 11. ALDEBARAN.
No. 12. RIGEL.
No. 13. CAPELLA.
No. 14. BELLATRIX.
No. 17. BETELGEUSE.
No. 19. SIRIUS.
No. 21. CASTOR.
No. 22. PROCYON.
No. 23. POLLUX.

Orion is the finest constellation visible in the Northern Hemisphere, is easily recognised, and the many fine stars around it make it invaluable. The three bright stars in line form Orion's belt with Alnilam at the center and the sword hanging down below the belt. Four bright stars surround Orion – Betelgeuse, Bellatrix, Rigel and Saiph. Orion is near the meridian at midnight late in the year, and therefore is only visible in northern latitudes in winter and early spring.

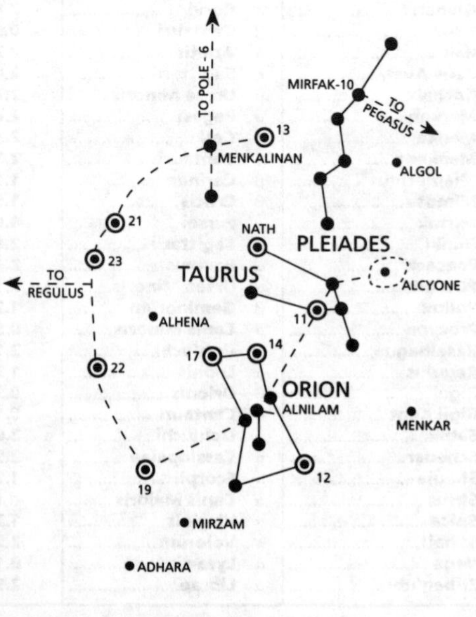

Further instructions will be found in the Star Index.

STAR CHART OF NORTHERN HEMISPHERE

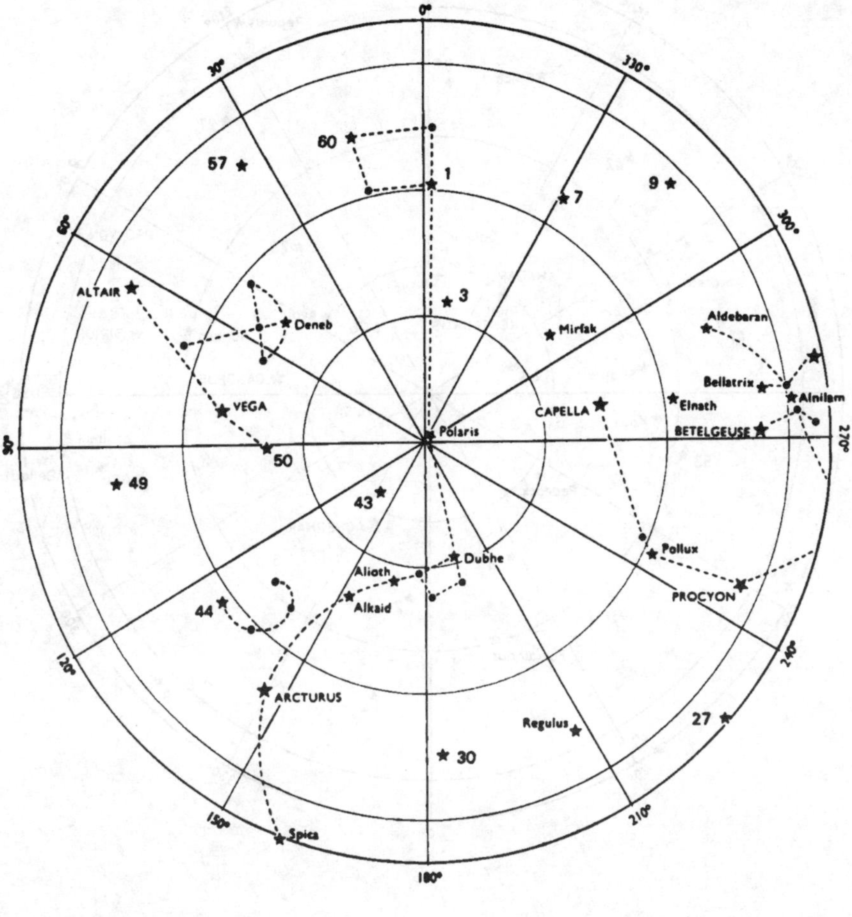

* **Stars of the first magnitude**

(capital letters)

● **Stars of magnitude 2.0 to 1.0**

(small letters)

Key to numbered stars

1. Alpheratz	27. Alphard	49. Rasalhague
3. Schedar	30. Denebola	50. Eltanin
7. Hamal	43. Kochlab	57. Enif
9. Menkar	44. Alphecca	60. Markab

START CHART OF SOUTHERN HEMISPHERE

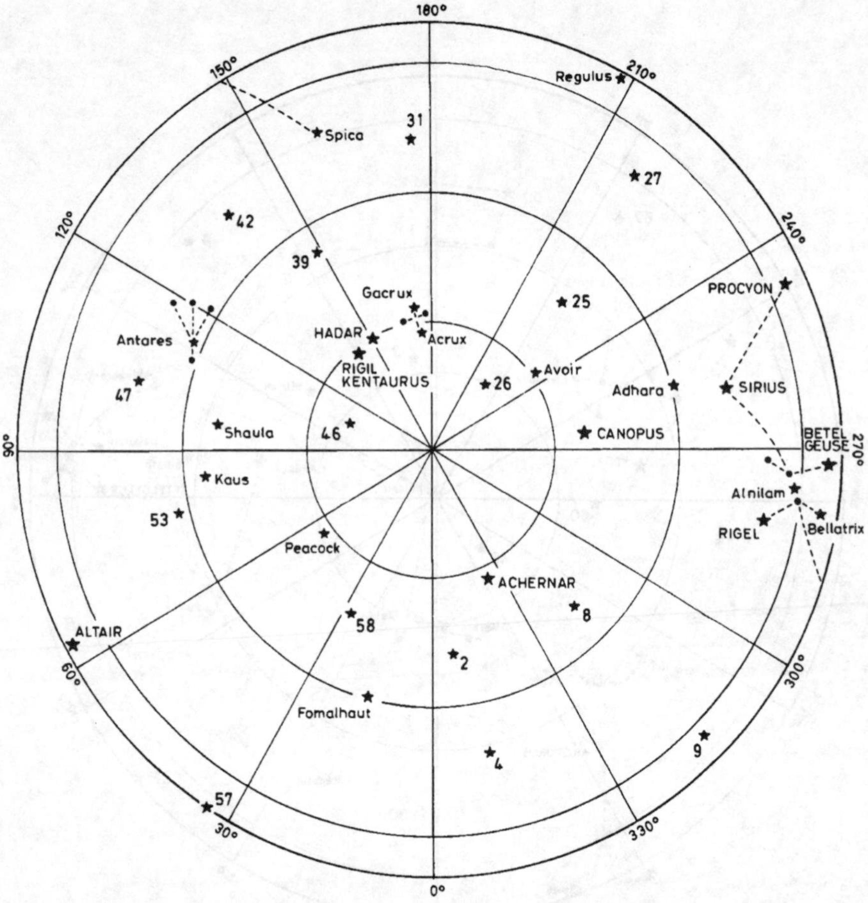

*** Stars which are less bright than mag. 2.0 but are listed and numbered as Selected Stars**

● Stars of lesser magnitude, included to help identification of some constellations.

Key to numbered stars

2. Ankaa	26. Miaplacidus	46. Atria
4. Diphda	27. Alphard	47. Sabik
8. Acamar	31. Gienah	53. Nunki
9. Menkar	39. Menkent	57. Enif
25. Suhail	42. Zuben'ubi	58. Al Na'ir

HOW TO RECOGNISE THE PLANETS

The principal planets are Mercury, Venus, the Earth, Mars, Jupiter, Saturn, Uranus and Neptune. (see page 155 for symbols)

Planets are heavenly bodies of which our Earth is an example – which revolve round the Sun in their own particular orbits (or paths). These planets are situated at varying distances from the Sun and thus have entirely different periods of revolution.They are all, however, situated in a belt of the celestial sphere about 8° on either side of the Ecliptic called the Zodiac.

The planets, like the Earth's satellite – the Moon – (and the Comets when visible), all receive their light from the reflected rays of the Sun. Those between the Earth and the Sun are Mercury and Venus and are called Inferior planets; the others are outside the Earth's Orbit and are called Superior planets.

On account of their position varying so much in comparison with the fixed stars, the planets are often termed "wandering stars".

None of the visible planets ever twinkle like the Stars so they may readily be recognised in consequence.

Mercury is very close to the Sun and being seldom seen is of little use to the Navigator. Uranus on the other hand, is not visible, except perhaps with a telescope, so is of no service either. The remainder of the planets are never visible to the naked eye, except Venus, Jupiter, Mars and Saturn, which are all four of great importance and assistance to the practical Navigator.

Venus is only visible for a short time after sunset and before sunrise, because its orbit is between the Earth and the Sun, and it appears to cross and recross the Sun continually. In practice, the time of the meridian passage of Venus is constantly changing from about 9 a.m. to 3 p.m. As Venus is so bright, she can, at all times, during clear weather and when not too near the Sun, be observed during the daytime, even though not visible to the naked eye. Many Navigators get a splendid position during the day by taking Venus on the meridian crossed with a Sun position line.

Venus has a bluish light and with the exception of the Sun and Moon, is by far the brightest object in the heavens. She is outstanding for easy navigation and may readily be observed during twilight.

Jupiter, while not so bright as Venus, is nevertheless brighter than any fixed star and may be used for a daytime fix with a powerful sextant telescope.

Mars' distance from the Earth varies and in consequence is sometimes very bright and at others very faint. Mars has a reddish color.

Saturn is the least bright of the four planets and shines at the equivalent of a first magnitude star. Saturn has a yellowish color.

The diameter of Jupiter is quite appreciable and is about three times that of Saturn. As their semi-diameters vary, it is customary to observe the center of the planet to avoid any correction for semi-diameter.

The notes on monthly Planet pages in the annual volume show whether the Planet is a Morning or Evening Planet and whether it is too close to the Sun for observation and give an indication of its position in the heavens.

When the meridian passage (given daily) occurs at midnight the body is in Opposition to the Sun and is visible all night so may be observed in both morning and evening twilights; it bears to the east of the meridian before meridian passage.

THE MOON'S PHASES

The time required for the Moon to make one orbit using the Sun as a reference point, i.e., the interval between two successive New Moons, is approximately 29.5 days and is called a Synodical Month or a Lunation.

A Sidereal Month is the time taken for one complete orbit with reference to a fixed star. It is the time interval from Perigee to Perigee or Apogee to Apogee, and is approximately 27 days.

A Lunar Day is the time interval between two successive transits of the Moon over the same meridian. It averages about 24 hours and 50 minutes. The minutes in excess of 24 hours vary from 38 to 66 minutes due to the irregular speed of the Moon along its orbit.

Because the Moon crosses the meridian later each day, there is always a day in each synodical month in which there is no meridian passage, another in which there is no moonrise and another with no moonset. For example, if Moonrise occurs at, say, 2330 on a Monday, the following Moonrise may not occur until 0020 on Wednesday.

AN EXPLANATION OF THE MOON'S PHASES

The Moon's Phases are changes in the appearance of the Moon's disc due to variations in its position with reference to the Earth and Sun. Some knowledge of this is of good practical use to the seaman because, at a single glance at the Moon he will know without reference to books or tables, its phase, rough time of meridian passage and the state of the tides in regard to Springs and Neaps.

The Sun is so far away from us that, for all practical purposes, its light is considered to reach the whole of the Earth-Moon system in parallel rays.

Figure 1 - looking down onto the North pole of the Earth – shows 8 successive positions of the Moon as it orbits the Earth in an counter-clockwise direction. It also shows how at all times one hemisphere of the Moon is illuminated by the Sun's rays whilst the opposite hemisphere is in total darkness. The 8 positions are numbered consecutively commencing at the New Moon, Position 1.

Figure 2 illustrates the appearance of the Moon's disc corresponding to each of the positions, numbered 1 to 8, in Figure 1. This shows how the Moon looks to an observer in any latitude from which the Moon bears South at its meridian passage.

When comparing Figures 1 and 2, remember that an observer looks from the Earth towards the Moon. Thus if Figure 1 is turned upside down to look at the Moon in Position 7, its corresponding appearance in Figure 2 (not upside down) is obvious.

Figure 2, when turned upside down, shows the appearance of the Moon at each phase (keeping the same numbers as before) when seen from latitudes in which it passes North of the observer at meridian passage.

PHASES OF THE MOON

Referring again to Figures 1 and 2:

Position No.	Moon's Phase	Age	Time of Mer. Pass (Approx)	Remarks
		Days	**Hrs.**	
1.	**New Moon**	0	1200	Sun and Moon "in conjunction". Moon not visible because only the dark hemisphere faces the Earth.
2	**Between New Moon and First Quarter**	3-4	1500	Visible as a crescent with its bow towards the West. Waxing.
3	**First Quarter**	7	1800	Moon 90° East of Sun (in East Quadrature). Visible as a half-disc with its bow towards the West. Waxing.
4	**Between First Quarter**	11-12	2100	Three quarters of the disc visible (called a Gibbous Moon), the more rounded side towards the West. Waxing.
5	**Full Moon**	15	2400	Moon on Sun's antimeridian, i.e., "in opposition'. The whole of the illuminated hemishpere is visible.
6	**Between Full Moon and Last Quarter**	18-19	0300	Three quarters of the disc visible (called a Gibbous Moon), the more rounded side towards the East. Waning.
7	**Last Quarter**	22	0600	Moon 90° West of the Sun (in West Quadrature). Visible as a half-disc with its bow towards the East. Waning.
8	**Between Last Quarter and New Moon**	25-26	0900	Visible as a crescent with its bow towards the East. Waning.

In low latitudes, Moonrise and Moonset occur a few minutes more than 6 hours before and after mer. pass., respectively. In high latitudes the times vary with changes in the Moon's Declination.

THE MOON'S PHASES

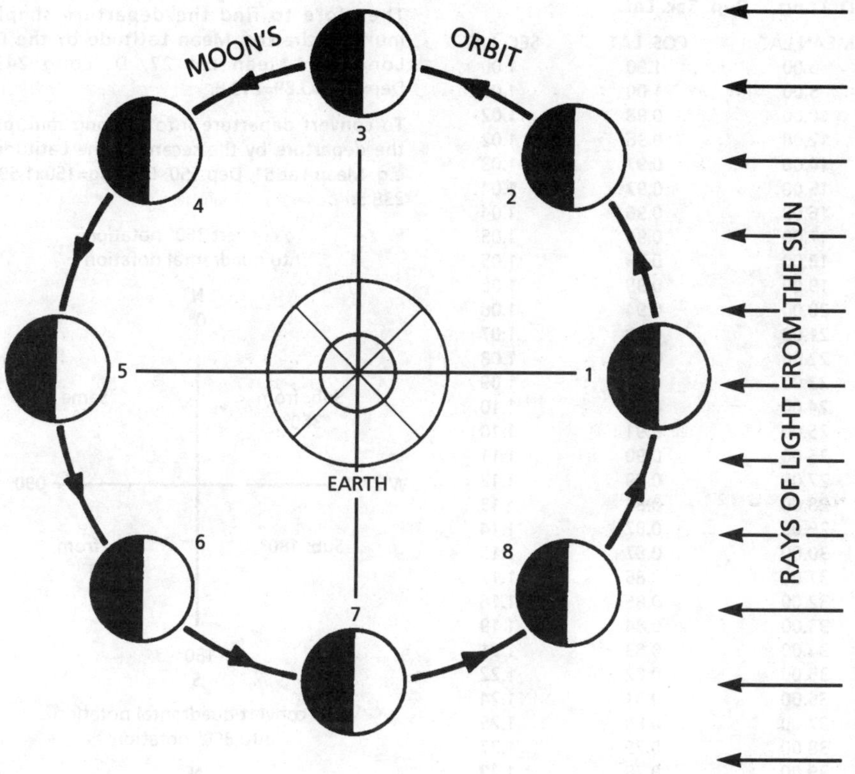

Figure 1

Successive positions (1 to 8) of the Moon along its orbit round the Earth.

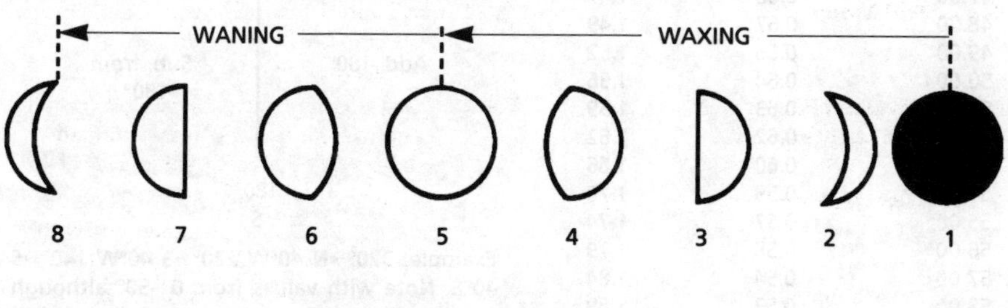

Figure 2

Phases of the Moon as viewed from the Earth's surface.

DEPARTURE* INTO D. LONG AND VICE VERSA

Dep = D.. Long Cos. Mean Lat.
D. Long. = Dep. Sec. Lat.

MEAN LAT	COS. LAT	SEC. LAT
0.00	1.00	1.00
5.00	1.00	1.00
10.00	0.98	1.02
12.00	0.98	1.02
14.00	0.97	1.03
15.00	0.97	1.04
16.00	0.96	1.04
17.00	0.96	1.05
18.00	0.95	1.05
19.00	0.95	1.06
20.00	0.94	1.06
21.00	0.93	1.07
22.00	0.93	1.08
23.00	0.92	1.09
24.00	0.91	1.10
25.00	0.91	1.10
26.00	0.90	1.11
27.00	0.89	1.12
28.00	0.88	1.13
29.00	0.87	1.14
30.00	0.87	1.15
31.00	0.86	1.17
32.00	0.85	1.18
33.00	0.84	1.19
34.00	0.83	1.21
35.00	0.82	1.22
36.00	0.81	1.24
37.00	0.80	1.25
38.00	0.79	1.27
39.00	0.78	1.29
40.00	0.77	1.31
41.00	0.75	1.33
42.00	0.74	1.35
43.00	0.73	1.37
44.00	0.72	1.39
45.00	0.71	1.41
46.00	0.69	1.44
47.00	0.68	1.47
48.00	0.67	1.49
49.00	0.66	1.52
50.00	0.64	1.56
51.00	0.63	1.59
52.00	0.62	1.62
53.00	0.60	1.66
54.00	0.59	1.70
55.00	0.57	1.74
56.00	0.56	1.79
57.00	0.54	1.84
58.00	0.53	1.89
59.00	0.52	1.94
60.00	0.50	2.00
61.00	0.48	2.06
62.00	0.47	2.13
63.00	0.45	2.20
64.00	0.44	2.28
65.00	0.42	2.37

Therefore to find the departure simply multiply the cos. Mean Latitude by the D. Long e.g. Mean Lat 27, D. Long 247, Dep=247xO.89=219.8.

To convert departure into D. Long multiply the departure by the secant of the Latitude, e.g. Mean Lat 51, Dep 150, D. Long=150x1.59= 238.5.

To convert 360° notation into quadrantal notation

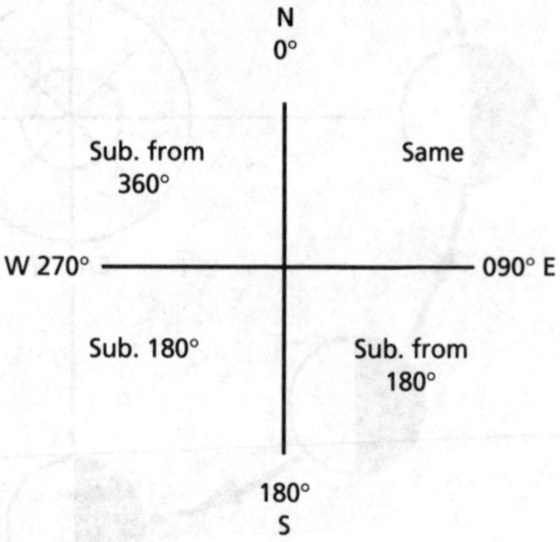

To convert quadrantal notation into 360° notation

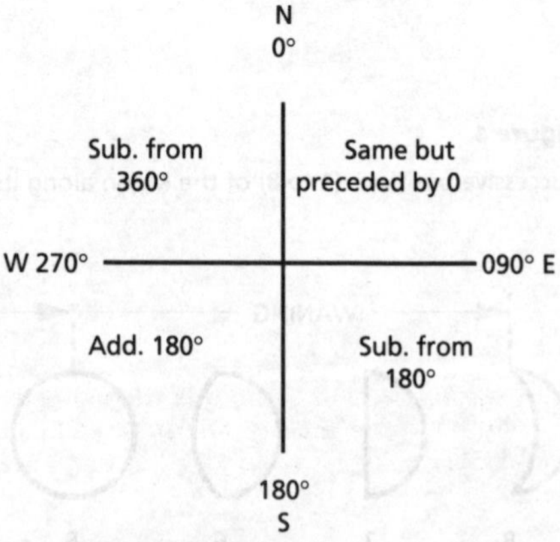

Example: 320°→N 40°W 220°→S 40°W 140°→S 40°E. Note with values from 0°–90° although numerically the same they are written as N 40 E or 0400.

* See opposite.

TRAVERSE TABLES

For those with scientific calculators see the calculator section later on.

These Tables have many uses but briefly it may be said that if the values for any two of the four things, viz. the Course, Distance, Difference of Latitude and the Departure be given, and these two be found together in the Tables, the values for the two remaining parts will be found in their respective places on the same page.

As the Tables are abbreviated, when any of the given parts (excepting the Course, which should never be multiplied or divided) exceed the table limits, any aliquot part, as a half, third, fourth or tenth, may be taken and the corresponding figures found are to be doubled, trebled, etc., that is multiplied by the same figure that the given number is divided by.

The Tables will be found useful for the run between sights where a large scale chart is not available – also to find the vessel's D.R. position at any time, or to find the Course to steer and distance to run over Short Navigation Distances of a few hundred miles or less.

The Tables are entered by using the Mean Latitude between any two positions, the Difference of Latitude (D. Lat.) in minutes of arc; and the Departure (Dep.) in nautical miles. Departure is the Distance made good in an east/west direction in nautical miles.

Departure may be changed into difference of longitude by using the table opposite.

Example (A). To find vessel's D.R. Position

A vessel in Lat. 17°20′N., Long. 38°41′W. steers 320°. Distance 54 miles. What position has she arrived at? From example on previous page we see that 320°=N 40°W.

So we require the D. Lat. and Dep. for 40° and 54 miles; It is easier to divide the distance by 2 (and multiply the figures found by 2) so on page 30 we find:

Under 40°and 27′ D. Lat. =20.7x2=41.4and Dep. 17.4x2=34.8.

Now Lat. from= 17°20′N	*Mean Lat. is therefore 18° by*	Now. Long. from= 38°41′ W
D. Lat.. 41′.4N	*the table on page 26 against*	D. Long.. 36′.5W
	Lat. 18 the Secant = 1.05	
Lat. in.. 18°01′.4N	*D. Long=34.8 x1.05=36.5*	Long. in.. 39°17′.5W

Hence the vessel's position is Lat. 18°01′.4N., Long. 39°17′.5W. (approx.)

Example (B). To find the Course and Distance

What is the True Course and Distance to steer from Lat. 49°57′N., Long. 6°00′W to Lat. 43°04′N., Long. 9°38′W.? Mean Lat. is about 46°.

Lat. from	49°57′N	Long . from	6°00′W
Lat. to	43°04′N	Long. to	9°38′W
D. Lat =	6°53′S. x 60 = 413′S.	D. Long. =	3°38′W x 60 = 218′W

Using Mean Lat. 46° we find that cos 46 is 0.69. Therefore the Dep. = 218 x 0.69 = 150. So we search the Traverse Table to find D. Lat. 4.13 and Dep. 1.5 (both divided by 100). We find them adjacent on the next page on the line of Course 20° and half way between Distance columns 4′ and 5′, i.e., 4.4 x 100 = 440.

So the Course is S20°W. and the Distance 440 miles.

Practice with interpolation will give greater accuracy, but the table – abbreviated as it is – will give quite close results with care.

TRAVERSE TABLES

COURSE	DISTANCE																						
	1′		2′		3′		4′		5′		6′		7′		8′		9′		10′		11′		
	D. Lat	Dep	D. Lat	Dep	D. Lat	Dep	D. Lat	Dep	D. Lat	Dep	D. Lat	Dep	D. Lat	Dep	D. Lat	Dep	D. Lat	Dep	D. Lat	Dep	D. Lat	Dep	
°	′	′	′	′	′	′	′	′	′	′	′	′	′	′	′	′	′	′	′	′	′	′	°
0	1.0	0.0	2.0	0.0	3.0	0.0	4.0	0.0	5.0	0.0	6.0	0.0	7.0	0.0	8.0	0.0	9.0	0.0	10.0	0.0	11.0	0.0	90
1	1.0	0.0	2.0	0.0	3.0	0.1	4.0	0.1	5.0	0.1	6.0	0.1	7.0	0.1	8.0	0.1	9.0	0.2	10.0	0.2	11.0	0.2	89
2	1.0	0.0	2.0	0.1	3.0	0.1	4.0	0.1	5.0	0.2	6.0	0.2	7.0	0.2	8.0	0.3	9.0	0.3	10.0	0.3	11.0	0.4	88
3	1.0	0.1	2.0	0.1	3.0	0.2	4.0	0.2	5.0	0.3	6.0	0.3	7.0	0.4	8.0	0.4	9.0	0.5	10.0	0.5	11.0	0.6	87
4	1.0	0.1	2.0	0.1	3.0	0.2	4.0	0.3	5.0	0.3	6.0	0.4	7.0	0.5	8.0	0.6	9.0	0.6	10.0	0.7	11.0	0.8	86
5	1.0	0.1	2.0	0.2	3.0	0.3	4.0	0.3	5.0	0.4	6.0	0.5	7.0	0.6	8.0	0.7	9.0	0.8	10.0	0.9	11.0	1.0	85
6	1.0	0.1	2.0	0.2	3.0	0.3	4.0	0.4	5.0	0.5	6.0	0.6	7.0	0.7	8.0	0.8	9.0	0.9	9.9	1.0	10.9	1.1	84
7	1.0	0.1	2.0	0.2	3.0	0.4	4.0	0.5	5.0	0.6	6.0	0.7	6.9	0.9	7.9	1.0	8.9	1.1	9.9	1.2	10.9	1.3	83
8	1.0	0.1	2.0	0.3	3.0	0.4	4.0	0.6	5.0	0.7	5.9	0.8	6.9	1.0	7.9	1.1	8.9	1.3	9.9	1.4	10.9	1.5	82
9	1.0	0.2	2.0	0.3	3.0	0.5	4.0	0.6	4.9	0.8	5.9	0.9	6.9	1.1	7.9	1.3	8.9	1.4	9.9	1.6	10.9	1.7	81
10	1.0	0.2	2.0	0.3	3.0	0.5	3.9	0.7	4.9	0.9	5.9	1.0	6.9	1.2	7.9	1.4	8.9	1.6	9.8	1.7	10.8	1.9	80
11	1.0	0.2	2.0	0.4	2.9	0.6	3.9	0.8	4.9	1.0	5.9	1.1	6.9	1.3	7.9	1.5	8.8	1.7	9.8	1.9	10.8	2.1	79
12	1.0	0.2	2.0	0.4	2.9	0.6	3.9	0.8	4.9	1.0	5.9	1.2	6.8	1.5	7.8	1.7	8.8	1.9	9.8	2.1	10.8	2.3	78
13	1.0	0.2	1.9	0.4	2.9	0.7	3.9	0.9	4.9	1.1	5.8	1.3	6.8	1.6	7.8	1.8	8.8	2.0	9.7	2.2	10.7	2.5	77
14	1.0	0.2	1.9	0.5	2.9	0.7	3.9	1.0	4.9	1.2	5.8	1.5	6.8	1.7	7.8	1.9	8.7	2.2	9.7	2.4	10.7	2.7	76
15	1.0	0.3	1.9	0.5	2.9	0.8	3.9	1.0	4.8	1.3	5.8	1.6	6.8	1.8	7.7	2.1	8.7	2.3	9.7	2.6	10.6	2.8	75
16	1.0	0.3	1.9	0.6	2.9	0.8	3.8	1.1	4.8	1.4	5.8	1.7	6.7	1.9	7.7	2.2	8.7	2.5	9.6	2.8	10.6	3.0	74
17	1.0	0.3	1.9	0.6	2.9	0.9	3.8	1.2	4.8	1.5	5.7	1.8	6.7	2.0	7.7	2.3	8.6	2.6	9.6	2.9	10.5	3.2	73
18	1.0	0.3	1.9	0.6	2.9	0.9	3.8	1.2	4.8	1.5	5.7	1.9	6.7	2.2	7.6	2.5	8.6	2.8	9.5	3.1	10.5	3.4	72
19	0.9	0.3	1.9	0.7	2.8	1.0	3.8	1.3	4.7	1.6	5.7	2.0	6.6	2.3	7.6	2.6	8.5	2.9	9.5	3.3	10.4	3.6	71
20	0.9	0.3	1.9	0.7	2.8	1.0	3.8	1.4	4.7	1.7	5.6	2.1	6.6	2.4	7.5	2.7	8.5	3.1	9.4	3.4	10.3	3.8	70
21	0.9	0.4	1.9	0.7	2.8	1.1	3.7	1.4	4.7	1.8	5.6	2.2	6.5	2.5	7.5	2.9	8.4	3.2	9.3	3.6	10.3	3.9	69
22	0.9	0.4	1.9	0.7	2.8	1.1	3.7	1.5	4.6	1.9	5.6	2.2	6.5	2.6	7.4	3.0	8.3	3.4	9.3	3.7	10.2	4.1	68
23	0.9	0.4	1.8	0.8	2.8	1.2	3.7	1.6	4.6	2.0	5.5	2.3	6.4	2.7	7.4	3.1	8.3	3.5	9.2	3.9	10.1	4.3	67
24	0.9	0.4	1.8	0.8	2.7	1.2	3.7	1.6	4.6	2.0	5.5	2.4	6.4	2.8	7.3	3.3	8.2	3.7	9.1	4.1	10.0	4.5	66
25	0.9	0.4	1.8	0.8	2.7	1.3	3.6	1.7	4.5	2.1	5.4	2.5	6.3	3.0	7.3	3.4	8.2	3.8	9.1	4.2	10.0	4.6	65
26	0.9	0.4	1.8	0.9	2.7	1.3	3.6	1.8	4.5	2.2	5.4	2.6	6.3	3.1	7.2	3.5	8.1	3.9	9.0	4.4	9.9	4.8	64
27	0.9	0.5	1.8	0.9	2.7	1.4	3.6	1.8	4.5	2.3	5.3	2.7	6.2	3.2	7.1	3.6	8.0	4.1	8.9	4.5	9.8	5.0	63
28	0.9	0.5	1.8	0.9	2.6	1.4	3.5	1.9	4.4	2.3	5.3	2.8	6.2	3.3	7.1	3.8	7.9	4.2	8.8	4.7	9.7	5.2	62
29	0.9	0.5	1.7	1.0	2.6	1.5	3.5	1.9	4.4	2.4	5.2	2.9	6.1	3.4	7.0	3.9	7.9	4.4	8.7	4.8	9.6	5.3	61
30	0.9	0.5	1.7	1.0	2.6	1.5	3.5	2.0	4.3	2.5	5.2	3.0	6.1	3.5	6.9	4.0	7.8	4.5	8.7	5.0	9.5	5.5	60
31	0.9	0.5	1.7	1.0	2.6	1.5	3.4	2.1	4.3	2.6	5.1	3.1	6.0	3.6	6.9	4.1	7.7	4.6	8.6	5.2	9.4	5.7	59
32	0.8	0.5	1.7	1.1	2.5	1.6	3.4	2.1	4.2	2.6	5.1	3.2	5.9	3.7	6.8	4.2	7.6	4.8	8.5	5.3	9.3	5.8	58
33	0.8	0.5	1.7	1.1	2.5	1.6	3.4	2.2	4.2	2.7	5.0	3.3	5.9	3.8	6.7	4.4	7.5	4.9	8.4	5.4	9.2	6.0	57
34	0.8	0.6	1.7	1.1	2.5	1.7	3.3	2.2	4.1	2.8	5.0	3.4	5.8	3.9	6.6	4.5	7.5	5.0	8.3	5.6	9.1	6.2	56
35	0.8	0.6	1.6	1.1	2.5	1.7	3.3	2.3	4.1	2.9	4.9	3.4	5.7	4.0	6.6	4.6	7.4	5.2	8.2	5.7	9.0	6.3	55
36	0.8	0.6	1.6	1.2	2.4	1.8	3.2	2.4	4.0	2.9	4.9	3.5	5.7	4.1	6.5	4.7	7.3	5.3	8.1	5.9	8.9	6.5	54
37	0.8	0.6	1.6	1.2	2.4	1.8	3.2	2.4	4.0	3.0	4.8	3.6	5.6	4.2	6.4	4.8	7.2	5.4	8.0	6.0	8.8	6.6	53
38	0.8	0.6	1.6	1.2	2.4	1.8	3.2	2.5	3.9	3.1	4.7	3.7	5.5	4.3	6.3	4.9	7.1	5.5	7.9	6.2	8.7	6.8	52
39	0.8	0.6	1.6	1.3	2.3	1.9	3.1	2.5	3.9	3.1	4.7	3.8	5.4	4.4	6.2	5.0	7.0	5.7	7.8	6.3	8.5	6.9	51
40	0.8	0.6	1.5	1.3	2.3	1.9	3.1	2.6	3.8	3.2	4.6	3.9	5.4	4.5	6.1	5.1	6.9	5.8	7.7	6.4	8.4	7.1	50
41	0.8	0.7	1.5	1.3	2.3	2.0	3.0	2.6	3.8	3.3	4.5	3.9	5.3	4.6	6.0	5.2	6.8	5.9	7.5	6.6	8.3	7.2	49
42	0.7	0.7	1.5	1.3	2.2	2.0	3.0	2.7	3.7	3.3	4.5	4.0	5.2	4.7	5.9	5.4	6.7	6.0	7.4	6.7	8.2	7.4	48
43	0.7	0.7	1.5	1.4	2.2	2.0	2.9	2.7	3.7	3.4	4.4	4.1	5.1	4.8	5.9	5.5	6.6	6.1	7.3	6.8	8.0	7.5	47
44	0.7	0.7	1.4	1.4	2.2	2.1	2.9	2.8	3.6	3.5	4.3	4.2	5.0	4.9	5.8	5.6	6.5	6.3	7.2	6.9	7.9	7.6	46
45	0.7	0.7	1.4	1.4	2.1	2.1	2.8	2.8	3.5	3.5	4.2	4.2	4.9	4.9	5.7	5.7	6.4	6.4	7.1	7.1	7.8	7.8	45
	Dep	D. Lat	Dep	D. Lat	Dep	D. Lat	Dep	D. Lat	Dep	D. Lat	Dep	D. Lat	Dep	D. Lat	Dep	D. Lat	Dep	D. Lat	Dep	D. Lat	Dep	D. Lat	COURSE
	1′		2′		3′		4′		5′		6′		7′		8′		9′		10′		11′		
	DISTANCE																						

Read the columns downwards for Courses 0° – 45° and upwards from 45° – 90°

TRAVERSE TABLES

COURSE	DISTANCE																		
	12′		13′		14′		15′		16′		17′		18′		19′		20′		
	D. Lat.	Dep.	D. Lat.	Dep.	D. Lat.	Dep.	D. Lat.	Dep.	D. Lat.	Dep.	D. Lat.	Dep.	D. Lat.	Dep.	D. Lat.	Dep.	D. Lat.	Dep.	
°	′	′	′	′	′	′	′	′	′	′	′	′	′	′	′	′	′	′	°
0	12.0	0.0	13.0	0.0	14.0	0.0	15.0	0.0	16.0	0.0	17.0	0.0	18.0	0.0	19.0	0.0	20.0	0.0	90
1	12.0	0.2	13.0	0.2	14.0	0.2	15.0	0.3	16.0	0.3	17.0	0.3	18.0	0.3	19.0	0.3	20.0	0.3	89
2	12.0	0.4	13.0	0.5	14.0	0.5	15.0	0.5	16.0	0.6	17.0	0.6	18.0	0.6	19.0	0.7	20.0	0.7	88
3	12.0	0.6	13.0	0.7	14.0	0.7	15.0	0.8	16.0	0.8	17.0	0.9	18.0	0.9	19.0	1.0	20.0	1.0	87
4	12.0	0.8	13.0	0.9	14.0	1.0	15.0	1.0	16.0	1.1	17.0	1.2	18.0	1.3	19.0	1.3	20.0	1.4	86
5	12.0	1.0	13.0	1.1	13.9	1.2	14.9	1.3	15.9	1.4	16.9	1.5	17.9	1.6	18.9	1.7	19.9	1.7	85
6	11.9	1.3	12.9	1.4	13.9	1.5	14.9	1.6	15.9	1.7	16.9	1.8	17.9	1.9	18.9	2.0	19.9	2.1	84
7	11.9	1.5	12.9	1.6	13.9	1.7	14.9	1.8	15.9	1.9	16.9	2.1	17.9	2.2	18.9	2.3	19.9	2.4	83
8	11.9	1.7	12.8	1.8	13.9	1.9	14.9	2.1	15.8	2.2	16.8	2.4	17.8	2.5	18.8	2.6	19.8	2.8	82
9	11.9	1.9	12.8	2.0	13.8	2.2	14.8	2.3	15.8	2.5	16.8	2.7	17.8	2.8	18.8	3.0	19.8	3.1	81
10	11.8	2.1	12.8	2.3	13.8	2.4	14.8	2.6	15.8	2.8	16.7	3.0	17.7	3.1	18.7	3.3	19.7	3.5	80
11	11.8	2.3	12.8	2.5	13.7	2.7	14.7	2.9	15.7	3.1	16.7	3.2	17.7	3.4	18.7	3.6	19.6	3.8	79
12	11.7	2.5	12.7	2.7	13.7	2.9	14.7	3.1	15.7	3.3	16.6	3.5	17.6	3.7	18.6	4.0	19.6	4.2	78
13	11.7	2.7	12.7	2.9	13.6	3.1	14.6	3.4	15.6	3.6	16.6	3.8	17.5	4.0	18.5	4.3	19.5	4.5	77
14	11.6	2.9	12.6	3.1	13.6	3.4	14.6	3.6	15.5	3.9	16.5	4.1	17.5	4.4	18.4	4.6	19.4	4.8	76
15	11.6	3.1	12.6	3.4	13.5	3.6	14.5	3.9	15.5	4.1	16.4	4.4	17.4	4.7	18.4	4.9	19.3	5.2	75
16	11.5	3.3	12.5	3.6	13.5	3.9	14.4	4.1	15.4	4.4	16.3	4.7	17.3	5.0	18.3	15.2	19.2	5.5	74
17	11.5	3.5	12.4	3.8	13.4	4.1	14.3	4.4	15.3	4.7	16.3	5.0	17.2	5.3	18.2	5.6	19.1	5.8	73
18	11.4	3.7	12.4	4.0	13.3	4.3	14.3	4.6	15.2	4.9	16.2	5.3	17.1	5.6	18.1	5.9	19.0	6.2	72
19	11.3	3.9	12.3	4.2	13.2	4.6	14.2	4.9	15.1	5.2	16.1	5.5	17.0	5.9	18.0	6.2	18.9	6.5	71
20	11.3	4.1	12.2	4.4	13.2	4.8	14.1	5.1	15.0	5.5	16.0	5.8	16.9	6.2	17.9	6.5	18.8	6.8	70
21	11.2	4.3	12.1	4.7	13.1	5.0	14.0	5.4	14.9	5.7	15.9	6.1	16.8	6.5	17.7	6.8	18.7	7.2	69
22	11.1	4.5	12.1	4.9	13.0	5.2	13.9	5.6	14.8	6.0	15.8	6.4	16.7	6.7	17.6	7.1	18.5	7.5	68
23	11.0	4.7	12.0	5.1	12.9	5.5	13.8	5.9	14.4	6.3	15.6	6.6	16.6	7.0	17.5	7.4	18.4	7.8	67
24	11.0	4.9	11.9	5.3	12.8	5.7	13.7	6.1	14.6	6.5	15.5	6.9	16.4	7.3	17.4	7.7	18.3	8.1	66
25	10.9	5.1	11.8	5.5	12.7	5.9	13.6	6.3	14.5	6.8	15.4	7.2	16.3	7.6	17.2	8.0	18.1	8.5	65
26	10.8	5.3	11.7	5.7	12.6	6.1	13.5	6.6	14.4	7.0	15.3	7.5	16.2	7.9	17.1	8.3	18.0	8.8	64
27	10.7	5.4	11.6	5.9	12.5	6.4	13.4	6.8	14.3	7.3	15.1	7.7	16.0	8.2	16.9	8.6	17.8	9.1	63
28	10.6	5.6	11.5	6.1	12.4	6.6	13.2	7.0	14.1	7.5	15.0	8.0	15.9	8.5	16.8	8.9	17.7	9.4	62
29	10.5	5.8	11.4	6.3	12.2	6.8	13.1	7.3	14.0	7.8	14.9	8.2	15.7	8.7	16.6	9.2	17.5	9.7	61
30	10.4	6.0	11.3	6.5	12.1	7.0	13.0	7.5	13.9	8.0	14.7	8.5	15.6	9.0	16.5	9.5	17.3	10.0	60
31	10.3	6.2	11.1	6.7	12.0	7.2	12.9	7.7	13.7	8.2	14.6	8.8	15.4	9.3	16.3	9.8	17.1	10.3	59
32	10.2	6.4	11.0	6.9	11.9	7.4	12.7	7.9	13.6	8.5	14.4	9.0	15.3	9.5	16.1	10.1	17.0	10.6	58
33	10.1	6.5	10.9	7.1	11.7	7.6	12.6	8.2	13.4	8.7	14.3	9.3	15.1	9.8	15.9	10.3	16.8	10.9	57
34	9.9	6.7	10.8	7.3	11.6	7.8	12.4	8.4	13.3	8.9	14.1	9.5	14.9	10.1	15.8	10.6	16.6	11.2	56
35	9.8	6.9	10.6	7.5	11.5	8.0	12.3	8.6	13.1	9.2	13.9	9.8	14.7	10.3	15.6	10.9	16.4	11.5	55
36	9.7	7.1	10.5	7.6	11.3	8.2	12.1	8.8	12.9	9.4	13.8	10.0	14.6	10.6	15.4	11.2	16.2	11.8	54
37	9.6	7.2	10.4	7.8	11.2	8.4	12.0	9.0	12.8	9.6	13.6	10.2	14.4	10.8	15.2	11.4	16.0	12.0	53
38	9.5	7.4	10.2	8.0	11.0	8.6	11.8	9.2	12.6	9.9	13.4	10.5	14.2	11.1	15.0	11.7	15.8	12.3	52
39	9.3	7.6	10.1	8.2	10.9	8.8	11.7	9.4	12.4	10.1	13.2	10.7	14.0	11.3	14.8	12.0	15.5	12.6	51
40	9.2	7.7	10.0	8.4	10.7	9.0	11.5	9.6	12.3	10.3	13.0	10.9	13.8	11.6	14.6	12.2	15.3	12.9	50
41	9.1	7.9	9.8	8.5	10.6	9.2	11.3	9.8	12.1	10.5	12.8	11.2	13.6	11.8	14.3	12.5	15.1	13.1	49
42	8.9	8.0	9.7	8.7	10.4	9.4	11.1	10.0	11.9	10.7	12.6	11.4	13.4	12.0	14.1	12.7	14.9	13.4	48
43	8.8	8.2	9.5	8.9	10.2	9.5	11.0	10.2	11.7	10.9	12.4	11.6	13.2	12.3	13.9	13.0	14.6	13.6	47
44	8.6	8.3	9.4	9.0	10.1	9.7	10.8	10.4	11.5	11.1	12.2	11.8	12.9	12.5	13.7	13.2	14.4	13.9	46
45	8.5	8.5	9.2	9.2	9.9	9.9	10.6	10.6	11.3	11.3	12.0	12.0	12.7	12.7	13.4	13.4	14.1	14.1	45
	Dep.	D. Lat.	Dep.	D. Lat.	Dep.	D. Lat.	Dep.	D. Lat.	Dep.	D. Lat.	Dep.	D. Lat.	Dep.	D. Lat.	Dep.	D. Lat.	Dep.	D. Lat.	COURSE
	12′		13′		14′		15′		16′		17′		18′		19′		20′		
	DISTANCE																		

Read the columns downwards for Courses 0° – 45° and upwards from 45° – 90°

TRAVERSE TABLES

COURSE	DISTANCE 21′		22′		23′		24′		25′		26′		27′		28′		29′		
	D. Lat.	Dep.	D. Lat.	Dep.	D. Lat.	Dep.	D. Lat.	Dep.	D. Lat.	Dep.	D. Lat.	Dep.	D. Lat.	Dep.	D. Lat.	Dep.	D. Lat.	Dep.	
°	′	′	′	′	′	′	′	′	′	′	′	′	′	′	′	′	′	′	°
0	21.0	0.0	22.0	0.0	23.0	0.0	24.0	0.0	25.0	0.0	26.0	0.0	27.0	0.0	28.0	0.0	29.0	0.0	90
1	21.0	0.4	22.0	0.4	23.0	0.4	24.0	0.4	25.0	0.4	26.0	0.5	27.0	0.5	28.0	0.5	29.0	0.5	89
2	21.0	0.7	22.0	0.8	23.0	0.8	24.0	0.8	25.0	0.9	26.0	0.9	27.0	0.9	28.0	1.0	29.0	1.0	88
3	21.0	1.1	22.0	1.2	23.0	1.2	24.0	1.3	25.0	1.3	26.0	1.4	27.0	1.4	28.0	1.5	29.0	1.5	87
4	20.9	1.5	21.9	1.5	22.9	1.6	23.9	1.7	24.9	1.7	25.9	1.8	26.9	1.9	27.9	2.0	28.9	2.0	86
5	20.9	1.8	21.9	1.9	22.9	2.0	23.9	2.1	24.9	2.2	25.9	2.3	26.9	2.4	27.9	2.4	28.9	2.5	85
6	20.9	2.2	21.9	2.3	22.9	2.4	23.9	2.5	24.9	2.6	25.9	2.7	26.9	2.8	27.8	2.9	28.8	3.0	84
7	20.8	2.6	21.8	2.7	22.8	2.8	23.8	2.9	24.8	3.0	25.8	3.2	26.8	3.3	27.8	3.4	28.8	3.5	83
8	20.8	2.9	21.8	3.1	22.8	3.2	23.8	3.3	24.8	3.5	25.7	3.6	26.7	3.8	27.7	3.9	28.7	4.0	82
9	20.7	3.3	21.7	3.4	22.7	3.6	23.7	3.8	24.7	3.9	25.7	4.1	26.7	4.2	27.7	4.4	28.6	4.5	81
10	20.7	3.6	21.7	3.8	22.7	4.0	23.6	4.2	24.6	4.3	25.6	4.5	26.6	4.7	27.6	4.9	28.6	5.0	80
11	20.6	4.0	21.6	4.2	22.6	4.4	23.6	4.6	24.5	4.8	25.5	5.0	26.5	5.2	27.5	5.3	28.5	5.5	79
12	20.5	4.4	21.5	4.6	22.5	4.8	23.5	5.0	24.5	5.2	25.4	5.4	26.4	5.6	27.4	5.8	28.4	6.0	78
13	20.5	4.7	21.4	4.9	22.4	5.2	23.4	5.4	24.4	5.6	25.3	5.8	26.3	6.1	27.3	6.3	28.3	6.5	77
14	20.4	5.1	21.3	5.3	22.3	5.6	23.3	5.8	24.3	6.0	25.2	6.3	26.2	6.5	27.2	6.8	28.1	7.0	76
15	20.3	5.4	21.3	5.7	22.2	6.0	23.2	6.2	24.1	6.5	25.1	6.7	26.1	7.0	27.0	7.2	28.0	7.5	75
16	20.2	5.8	21.1	6.1	22.1	6.3	23.1	6.6	24.0	6.9	25.0	7.2	26.0	7.4	26.9	7.7	27.9	8.0	74
17	20.1	6.1	21.0	6.4	22.0	6.7	23.0	7.0	23.9	7.3	24.9	7.6	25.8	7.9	26.8	8.2	27.7	8.5	73
18	20.0	6.5	20.9	6.8	21.9	7.1	22.8	7.4	23.8	7.7	24.7	8.0	25.7	8.3	26.6	8.7	27.6	9.0	72
19	19.9	6.8	20.8	7.2	21.7	7.5	22.7	7.8	23.6	8.1	24.6	8.5	25.5	8.8	26.5	9.1	27.4	9.4	71
20	19.7	7.2	20.7	7.5	21.6	7.9	22.6	8.2	23.5	8.6	24.4	8.9	25.4	9.2	26.3	9.6	27.3	9.9	70
21	19.6	7.5	20.5	7.9	21.5	8.2	22.4	8.6	23.3	9.0	24.3	9.3	25.2	9.7	26.1	10.0	27.1	10.4	69
22	19.5	7.9	20.4	8.2	21.3	8.6	22.3	9.0	23.2	9.4	24.1	9.7	25.0	10.1	26.0	10.5	26.9	10.9	68
23	19.3	8.2	20.3	8.6	21.2	9.0	22.1	9.4	23.0	9.8	23.9	10.2	24.9	10.5	25.8	10.9	26.7	11.3	67
24	19.2	8.5	20.1	8.9	21.0	9.4	21.9	9.8	22.8	10.2	23.8	10.6	24.7	11.0	25.6	11.4	26.5	11.8	66
25	19.0	8.9	19.9	9.3	20.8	9.7	21.8	10.1	22.7	10.6	23.6	11.0	24.5	11.4	25.4	11.8	26.3	12.3	65
26	18.9	9.2	19.8	9.6	20.7	10.1	21.6	10.5	22.5	11.0	23.4	11.4	24.3	11.8	25.2	12.3	26.1	12.7	64
27	18.7	9.5	19.6	10.0	20.5	10.4	21.4	10.9	22.3	11.3	23.2	11.8	24.1	12.3	24.9	12.7	25.8	13.2	63
28	18.5	9.9	19.4	10.3	20.3	10.8	21.2	11.3	22.1	11.7	23.0	12.2	23.8	12.7	24.7	13.1	25.6	13.6	62
29	18.4	10.2	19.2	10.7	20.1	11.2	21.0	11.6	21.9	12.1	22.7	12.6	23.6	13.1	24.5	13.6	25.4	14.1	61
30	18.2	10.5	19.1	11.0	19.9	11.5	20.8	12.0	21.7	12.5	22.5	13.0	23.4	13.5	24.2	14.0	25.1	14.5	60
31	18.0	10.8	18.9	11.3	19.7	11.8	20.6	12.4	21.4	12.9	22.3	13.4	23.1	13.9	24.0	14.4	24.9	14.9	59
32	17.8	11.1	18.7	11.7	19.5	12.2	20.4	12.7	21.2	13.2	22.0	13.8	22.9	14.3	23.7	14.8	24.6	15.4	58
33	17.6	11.4	18.5	12.0	19.3	12.5	20.1	13.1	21.0	13.6	21.8	14.2	22.6	14.7	23.5	15.2	24.3	15.8	57
34	17.4	11.7	18.2	12.3	19.1	12.9	19.9	13.4	20.7	14.0	21.6	14.5	22.4	15.1	23.2	15.7	24.0	16.2	56
35	17.2	12.0	18.0	12.6	18.8	13.2	19.7	13.8	20.5	14.3	21.3	14.9	22.1	15.5	22.9	16.1	23.8	16.6	55
36	17.0	12.3	17.8	12.9	18.6	13.5	19.4	14.1	20.2	14.7	21.0	15.3	21.8	15.9	22.7	16.5	23.5	17.0	54
37	16.8	12.6	17.6	13.2	18.4	13.8	19.2	14.4	20.0	15.0	20.8	15.6	21.6	16.2	22.4	16.9	23.2	17.5	53
38	16.5	12.9	17.3	13.5	18.1	14.2	18.9	14.8	19.7	15.4	20.5	16.0	21.3	16.6	22.1	17.2	22.8	17.9	52
39	16.3	13.2	17.1	13.8	17.9	14.5	18.7	15.1	19.4	15.7	20.2	16.4	21.0	17.0	21.8	17.6	22.5	18.3	51
40	16.1	13.5	16.9	14.1	17.6	14.8	18.4	15.4	19.2	16.1	19.9	16.7	20.7	17.4	21.4	18.0	22.2	18.6	50
41	15.8	13.8	16.6	14.4	17.4	15.1	18.1	15.7	18.9	16.4	19.6	17.1	20.4	17.7	21.1	18.4	21.9	19.0	49
42	15.6	14.1	16.3	14.7	17.1	15.4	17.8	16.1	18.6	16.7	19.3	17.4	20.1	18.1	20.8	18.7	21.6	19.4	48
43	15.4	14.3	16.1	15.0	16.8	15.7	17.6	16.4	18.3	17.0	19.0	17.7	19.7	18.4	20.5	19.1	21.2	19.8	47
44	15.1	14.6	15.8	15.3	16.5	16.0	17.3	16.7	18.0	17.4	18.7	18.1	19.4	18.8	20.1	19.5	20.9	20.1	46
45	14.8	14.8	15.6	15.6	16.3	16.3	17.0	17.0	17.7	17.7	18.4	18.4	19.1	19.1	19.8	19.8	20.5	20.5	45
	Dep.	D. Lat.	Dep.	D. Lat.	Dep.	D. Lat.	Dep.	D. Lat.	Dep.	D. Lat.	Dep.	D. Lat.	Dep.	D. Lat.	Dep.	D. Lat.	Dep.	D. Lat.	COURSE
	21′		22′		23′		24′		25′		26′		27′		28′		29′		
	DISTANCE																		

Read the columns downwards for Courses 0° – 45° and upwards from 45° – 90°

TRAVERSE TABLES

COURSE	DISTANCE																		
	30′		40′		50′		60′		70′		80′		90′		100′		200′		
	D. Lat.	Dep.	D. Lat.	Dep.	D. Lat.	Dep.	D. Lat.	Dep.	D. Lat.	Dep.	D. Lat.	Dep.	D. Lat.	Dep.	D. Lat.	Dep.	D. Lat.	Dep.	
°	′	′	′	′	′	′	′	′	′	′	′	′	′	′	′	′	′	′	°
0	30.0	0.0	40.0	0.0	50.0	0.0	60.0	0.0	70.0	0.0	80.0	0.0	90.0	0.0	100.0	0.0	200.0	0.0	90
1	30.0	0.5	40.0	0.7	50.0	0.9	60.0	1.0	70.0	1.2	80.0	1.4	90.0	1.6	100.0	1.7	200.0	3.5	89
2	30.0	1.0	40.0	1.4	50.0	1.7	60.0	2.1	70.0	2.4	80.0	2.8	89.9	3.1	99.9	3.5	199.9	7.0	88
3	30.0	1.6	39.9	2.1	49.9	2.6	59.9	3.1	69.9	3.7	79.9	4.2	89.9	4.7	99.9	5.2	199.7	10.5	87
4	29.9	2.1	39.9	2.8	49.9	3.5	59.9	4.2	69.8	4.9	79.8	5.6	89.8	6.3	99.8	7.0	199.5	14.0	86
5	29.9	2.6	39.8	3.5	49.8	4.4	59.8	5.2	69.7	6.1	79.7	7.0	89.7	7.8	99.6	8.7	199.2	17.4	85
6	29.8	3.1	39.8	4.2	49.7	5.2	59.7	6.3	69.6	7.3	79.6	8.4	89.5	9.4	99.5	10.5	198.9	20.9	84
7	29.8	3.7	39.7	4.9	49.6	6.1	59.6	7.3	69.5	8.5	79.4	9.7	89.3	11.0	99.3	12.2	198.5	24.4	83
8	29.7	4.2	39.6	5.6	49.5	7.0	59.4	8.4	69.3	9.7	79.2	11.1	89.1	12.5	99.0	13.9	198.1	27.8	82
9	29.6	4.7	39.5	6.3	49.4	7.8	59.3	9.4	69.1	11.0	79.0	12.5	88.9	14.1	98.8	15.6	197.5	31.3	81
10	29.5	5.2	39.4	6.9	49.2	8.7	59.1	10.4	68.9	12.2	78.8	13.9	88.6	15.6	98.5	17.4	197.0	34.7	80
11	29.4	5.7	39.3	7.6	49.1	9.5	58.9	11.4	68.7	13.4	78.5	15.3	88.3	17.2	98.2	19.1	196.3	38.2	79
12	29.3	6.2	39.1	8.3	48.9	10.4	58.7	12.5	68.5	14.6	78.3	16.6	88.0	18.7	97.8	20.8	195.6	41.6	78
13	29.2	6.7	39.0	9.0	48.7	11.2	58.5	13.5	68.2	15.7	77.9	18.0	87.7	20.2	97.4	22.5	194.9	45.0	77
14	29.1	7.3	38.8	9.7	48.5	12.1	58.2	14.5	67.9	16.9	77.6	19.4	87.3	21.8	97.0	24.2	194.1	48.4	76
15	29.0	7.8	38.6	10.4	48.3	12.9	58.0	15.5	67.6	18.1	77.3	20.7	86.9	23.3	96.6	25.9	193.2	51.8	75
16	28.8	8.3	38.5	11.0	48.1	13.8	57.7	16.5	67.3	19.3	76.9	22.1	86.5	24.8	96.1	27.6	192.3	55.1	74
17	28.7	8.8	38.3	11.7	47.8	14.6	57.4	17.5	66.9	20.5	76.5	23.4	86.1	26.3	95.6	29.2	191.3	58.5	73
18	28.5	9.3	38.0	12.4	47.6	15.5	57.1	18.5	66.6	21.6	76.1	24.7	85.6	27.8	95.1	30.9	190.2	61.8	72
19	28.4	9.8	37.8	13.0	47.3	16.3	56.7	19.5	66.2	22.8	75.6	26.0	85.1	29.3	94.6	32.6	189.1	65.1	71
20	28.2	10.3	37.6	13.7	47.0	17.1	56.4	20.5	65.8	23.9	75.2	27.4	84.6	30.8	94.0	34.2	187.9	68.4	70
21	28.0	10.8	37.3	14.3	46.7	17.9	56.0	21.5	65.4	25.1	74.7	28.7	84.0	32.3	93.4	35.8	186.7	71.7	69
22	27.8	11.2	37.1	15.0	46.4	18.7	55.6	22.5	64.9	26.2	74.2	30.0	83.4	33.7	92.7	37.5	185.4	74.9	68
23	27.6	11.7	36.8	15.6	46.0	19.5	55.2	23.4	64.4	27.4	73.6	31.3	82.8	35.2	92.1	39.1	184.1	78.1	67
24	27.4	12.2	36.5	16.3	45.7	20.3	54.8	24.4	63.9	28.5	73.1	32.5	82.2	36.6	91.4	40.7	182.7	81.3	66
25	27.2	12.7	36.3	16.9	45.3	21.1	54.4	25.4	63.4	29.6	72.5	33.8	81.6	38.0	90.6	42.3	181.3	84.5	65
26	27.0	13.2	36.0	17.5	44.9	21.9	53.9	26.3	62.9	30.7	71.9	35.1	80.9	39.5	89.9	43.8	179.8	87.7	64
27	26.7	13.6	35.6	18.2	44.6	22.7	53.5	27.2	62.4	31.8	71.3	36.3	80.2	40.9	89.1	45.4	178.2	90.8	63
28	26.5	14.1	35.3	18.8	44.1	23.5	53.0	28.2	61.8	32.9	70.6	37.6	79.5	42.3	88.3	46.9	176.6	93.9	62
29	26.2	14.5	35.0	19.4	43.7	24.2	52.5	29.1	61.2	33.9	70.0	38.8	78.7	43.6	87.5	48.5	174.9	97.0	61
30	26.0	15.0	34.6	20.0	43.3	25.0	52.0	30.0	60.6	35.0	69.3	40.0	77.9	45.0	86.6	50.0	173.2	100.0	60
31	25.7	15.5	34.3	20.6	42.9	25.8	51.4	30.9	60.0	36.1	68.6	41.2	77.1	46.4	85.7	51.5	171.4	103.0	59
32	25.4	15.9	33.9	21.2	42.4	26.5	50.9	31.8	59.4	37.1	67.8	42.4	76.3	47.7	84.8	53.0	169.6	106.0	58
33	25.2	16.3	33.5	21.8	41.9	27.2	50.3	32.7	58.7	38.1	67.1	43.6	75.5	49.0	83.9	54.5	167.7	108.9	57
34	24.9	16.8	33.2	22.4	41.5	28.0	49.7	33.6	58.0	39.1	66.3	44.7	74.6	50.3	82.9	55.9	165.8	111.8	56
35	24.6	17.2	32.8	22.9	41.0	28.7	49.1	34.4	57.3	40.2	65.5	45.9	73.7	51.6	81.9	57.4	163.8	114.7	55
36	24.3	17.6	32.4	23.5	40.5	29.4	48.5	35.3	56.6	41.1	64.7	47.0	72.8	52.9	80.9	58.8	161.8	117.6	54
37	24.0	18.1	31.9	24.1	39.9	30.1	47.9	36.1	55.9	42.1	63.9	48.1	71.9	54.2	79.9	60.2	159.7	120.4	53
38	23.6	18.5	31.5	24.6	39.4	30.8	47.3	36.9	55.2	43.1	63.0	49.3	70.9	55.4	78.8	61.6	157.6	123.1	52
39	23.3	18.9	31.1	25.2	38.9	31.5	46.6	37.8	54.4	44.1	62.2	50.3	69.9	56.6	77.7	62.9	155.4	125.9	51
40	23.0	19.3	30.6	25.7	38.3	32.1	46.0	38.6	53.6	45.0	61.3	51.4	68.9	57.9	76.6	64.3	153.2	128.6	50
41	22.6	19.7	30.2	26.2	37.7	32.8	45.3	39.4	52.8	45.9	60.4	52.5	67.9	59.0	75.5	65.6	150.9	131.2	49
42	22.3	20.1	29.7	26.8	37.2	33.5	44.6	40.1	52.0	46.8	59.5	53.5	66.9	60.2	74.3	66.9	148.6	133.8	48
43	21.9	20.5	29.3	27.3	36.6	34.1	43.9	40.9	51.2	47.7	58.5	54.6	65.8	61.4	73.1	68.2	146.3	136.4	47
44	21.6	20.8	28.8	27.8	36.0	34.7	43.2	41.7	50.4	48.6	57.5	55.6	64.7	62.5	71.9	69.5	143.9	138.9	46
45	21.2	21.2	28.3	28.3	35.4	35.4	42.4	42.4	49.5	49.5	56.6	56.6	63.6	63.6	70.7	70.7	141.4	141.4	45
	Dep.	D. Lat.	Dep.	D. Lat.	Dep.	D. Lat.	Dep.	D. Lat.	Dep.	D. Lat.	Dep.	D. Lat.	Dep.	D. Lat.	Dep.	D. Lat.	Dep.	D. Lat.	COURSE
	30′		40′		50′		60′		70′		80′		90′		100′		200′		
	DISTANCE																		

Read the columns downwards for Courses 0° – 45° and upwards from 45° – 90°

7

TO FIND THE D.R. POSITION AND COURSE AND DISTANCE BY CALCULATOR

The same results as obtained by the Traverse Tables can be achieved very simply by the use of a scientific calculator.

The same examples as given previously are repeated below. The working as shown may look somewhat lengthy but with practice the calculation can be done very quickly and accurately.

Example (A) To find vessel's D.R. Position

A vessel in Lat. 17°20′N., Long. 38°41′W. steers 320° (N.40°W.) for 54 miles. What position has she arrived at?

To find D. Lat. D. Lat. = Distance x cos Co.

Quantity		**Entry**	**Reading**
Course	→	40	40
		cos	0.76604
		STO 1	0.76604
Dist.	→	54	54
		x	54
		RCL 1	0.76604
D. Lat.	←	=	41.4

To find D. Lat. Dep = Distance x sin Co.

Quantity		**Entry**	**Reading**
Course	→	40	40
		sin	0.64279
		STO 1	0.64279
Dist.	→	54	54
		x	54
		RCL 1	0.64279
D. Lat.	←	=	37.7

To find D. Long. $\text{D. Long.} = \frac{\text{Dep.}}{\text{cos Mean Lat.}}$

Mean Lat. = Initial Lat. + 2 D. Lat. = 17°20′N. + 20′.5 - 17°40′.5N. (N.B. a mental approximation for Mean Lat. will do.)

Quantity		**Entry**	**Reading**
Mean Lat.	→	17.68	17.68
		cos	0.95277
		STO 1	0.95277
Dep.	→	34.7	34.7
		+	34.7
		RCL 1	0.95277
D. Long.	←	=	36.4

Lat. from	17°20′N.	Long. from	38°41′W.
D. Lat.	41′.4N.	D. Long.	36′.4W
D.R. Position	18°01′.4N.		39°17′.4W.

Example (B) To find the Course and Distance

What is the True Course and Distance to steer from Lat. 49°57′N., Long. 6°00′W. to Lat. 43°04′N., Long. 9°38′W.

Lat. from	49°57′N.	Long. from	6°00′W.
Lat. to	43°04′N.	Long to.	9°38′W.
D. Lat.	6°53′.5. = 312′S	D. Long.	3°38′W. = 218′W.

Mean Lat. = 43°04′ + 3°26′.5 = 46°30′.5N. (N.B. a mental approximation for Mean Lat. will do.)

To find D. Lat. Departure = D. Long. x cos. mean Lat.

Quantity		**Entry**	**Reading**
Mean Lat.	→	46.5	46.5
		cos	0.68835
		STO 1	0.68835
D. Long.	→	218	218
		x	218
		RCL 1	0.68835
Dep	←	=	150

To find the Course. $\tan Co. = \frac{Dep.}{D.\ Lat.}$

Quantity		**Entry**	**Reading**
Dep	→	150	150
		÷	150
D. Lat.	→	413	413
		=	0.3632
		arc	0.3632
Course	←	tan	20

Therefore the Course is S.20°W.

To find the Distance. $Distance = \frac{D.\ Lat.}{\cos Co.}$

Quantity		**Entry**	**Reading**
Course	→	20	20
		cos	0.93969
		STO 1	0.93969
D. Lat.	→	413	413
		÷	413
		RCL 1	0.93969
Distance	←	=	439.5

So the course is S.20°W. and the Distance 439.5 miles.

Note: These formulae assume that the earth is flat which is why this routine is often referred to as Plane Sailing. This assumption is reasonable for distances up to 500 or 600 miles. Therefore do not use for distances greater than this.

MIDDLE LATITUDE SAILING

For distances greater than 500-600 miles the same procedures can be followed except that a correction has to be applied to the mean latitude.

This corrected MEAN latitude is called the MIDDLE latitute.

Correction to apply to MEAN LAT. to obtain MIDDLE LAT.

MEAN LAT.	DIFFERENCE OF LATITUDE																MEAN LAT.
	2°	**4°**	**6°**	**8°**	**10°**	**11°**	**12°**	**13°**	**14°**	**15°**	**16°**	**17°**	**18°**	**19°**	**20°**	**21°**	
°																	°
11	-129	-125	-118	-110	-100	-93	-87	-80	-72	-64	-57	-48	-38	-29	-18	-8	**11**
12	-114	-111	-105	-98	-89	-83	-77	-71	-64	-57	-49	-42	-33	-23	-15	-5	**12**
13	-102	-100	-95	-88	-79	-75	-69	-63	-57	-51	-43	-36	-27	-20	-12	-3	**13**
14	-93	-90	-86	-80	-72	-67	-62	-57	-51	-45	-38	-31	-24	-16	-9	0	**14**
15	-85	-83	-79	-73	-65	-61	-56	-51	-46	-40	-34	-27	-21	-13	-6	+1	**15**
16	-79	-76	-72	-66	-60	-56	-51	-46	-41	-36	-30	-24	-17	-10	-4	+4	**16**
17	-72	-70	-66	-61	-55	-51	-47	-42	-37	-32	-27	-21	-15	-8	-2	+6	**17**
18	-67	-65	-61	-56	-50	-46	-43	-38	-34	-29	-24	-18	-12	-6	+1	+8	**18**
19	-62	-60	-57	-52	-46	-43	-39	-35	-30	-25	-21	-15	-9	-3	+3	+10	**19**
20	-58	-56	-53	-48	-42	-39	-35	-31	-27	-22	-18	-13	-7	-1	+5	+13	**20**
22	-50	-48	-45	-41	-36	-33	-29	-25	-22	-17	-13	-8	-3	+3	+9	+15	**22**
24	-44	-42	-40	-36	-31	-28	-24	-21	-17	-13	-8	-4	+1	+6	+12	+17	**24**
26	-39	-37	-35	-31	-26	-23	-20	-16	-13	-9	-5	0	+5	+10	+15	+21	**26**
28	-34	-32	-30	-26	-22	-19	-16	-12	-9	-5	-1	+3	+8	+13	+18	+23	**28**
30	-30	-29	-26	-22	-18	-15	-12	-9	-6	-2	+2	+6	+11	+16	+21	+26	**30**
35	-22	-21	-18	-15	-10	-7	-5	-1	+2	+6	+10	+14	+18	+23	+28	+33	**35**
40	-16	-14	-12	-8	-4	-1	+2	+5	+8	+12	+16	+20	+25	+29	+34	+40	**40**
45	-11	-10	-7	-3	+1	+4	+7	+11	+14	+18	+22	+27	+31	+36	+41	+47	**45**
50	-8	-6	-3	+1	+6	+9	+12	+16	+20	+24	+28	+33	+38	+44	+49	+55	**50**
55	-5	-3	0	+5	+10	+14	+17	+21	+25	+30	+35	+40	+46	+52	+58	65	**55**
60	-3	-1	+3	+8	+14	+18	+22	+27	+32	+37	+43	+49	+55	+62	+69	+77	**60**

Examples:

To find course and distance from 42°03'N 70°04'W to 36°59'N 25°10'W.

Departure position	42°03'N	70°04'W
Destination position	36°59'N	25°10'W
	D. Lat. 5°04'S	D. Long 44°54'E
	" = 304	" = 2694
	Mean Lat. = 39°31'N	
	(from table) corr. = - 13'	
	Middle Lat. 39°18'	

To find Departure
Dep = d.long Cos middle Lat.

Quantity		**Entry**	**Reading**
Middle Lat.	→	39.3	39.3
		cos	0.77384
		STO 1	0.77384
D. Long.	→	2694	2694
		x	2694
		RCL 1	0.77384
Departure	←	=	2084.73

To find the Course. $\tan Co. = \dfrac{\text{Departure}}{\text{D. Lat.}}$

Quantity		Entry	Reading
Dep	→	2084.73	2084.73
		÷	2084.73
D. Lat.	→	304	304
		=	6.85765
		avc Tan	81.7035

Course = S 81°42′.17E

To find the Distance. $\text{Distance} = \dfrac{\text{D. Lat.}}{\text{cos course.}}$

Quantity		Entry	Reading
Course		81.7035	81.7035
		cos	0.14430
		STO 1	0.14430
D. Lat.	→	304	304
		÷	304
		RCL 1	0.14430
Distance	←	=	2106.77

Distance = 2106.8

Conversely suppose the vessel starts form a position 42°03′N 70°04′W and steers S81°42′E for a distance of 2106.8 miles. What would be her D.R.

To find D. Lat. D. Lat. = distance x cox Co.

Quantity		Entry	Reading
Course	→	81.7	81.7
		cos	0.14436
		STO 1	0.14436
Distance	→	2106.8	2106.8
		x	
		RCL 1	0.14436
D. Lat.	←	=	304.13

Latitude departure	= 42°03′N	Mean Lat.	= 39°31′
D. Lat. (304)	= 5°04′S	Corr.	= - 13′
Arrival D.R. Lat.	= 36°59′N	Middle Lat.	= 39°18′

To find Departure Dep. = Dist x Sin Co

Quantity		Entry	Reading
Course	→	81.7	81.7
		sin	0.98953
		STO 1	0.98953
Distance	→	2106.8	2106.8
		x	2106.8
		RCL 1	0.98953
Departure	←	=	2084.73

To find D. Long $\text{D. Long.} = \dfrac{\text{Dep.}}{\text{cos mid. lat.}}$

Quantity		Entry	Reading
Mid. Lat.	→	39.3	39.3
		cos	0.77384
		STO 1	0.77384
Departure	→	2084.5	2084.73
		÷	2084.73
		RCL 1	0.77384
D. Long.	←	=	2694

Longitude departure	= 70°04′W
D. Long. 2694	= 44°54′E
Arrival D.R. Long.	= 25°10′W

OCEAN PASSAGE PLANNING

It may be practical, though hardly desirable, to embark upon a short coastal passage with a minimum of planning; but this is not true of an ocean passage. Thousands of small craft each year complete happy and successful ocean passages. These vessels are of many different types and sizes; one thing they have in common is that the skipper or the navigator has taken a great deal of care in planning the passage.

The planning of objectives are simple: to stay out of trouble, and to take maximum advantage of the elements. The planning itself is also relatively straightforward given all the data which is readily available.

Staying out of trouble means; first, avoiding the risk of encountering tropical revolving storms (hurricanes); second, making sure that passages are not unduly slowed by constant headwinds or unfavorable currents, or made dangerous by poor visibility.

The elements are harnessed by planning a route which takes advantage of favorable currents and also gives a good chance of being able to sail free and lay your objective.

TROPICAL REVOLVING STORMS

This is the technical name given to violent storms which have their beginnings in some equatorial ocean, and in which winds exceeding one hundred knots are not unknown. Normally, the TRS is known locally by another name. Broad indications about months where these may be expected are as shown in the Table at foot of page.

Tropical revolving storms do not occur in the South Atlantic, nor in the eastern South Pacific.

It is an important responsibility of the ocean passage planner to limit to a minimum the risk of encountering a TRS. Indeed, it is unlikely thatinsurance coverage can be obtained unless this is done. Note that the data shown at foot of page are merely indications, and navigators should use the best possible recorded data.

PILOT CHARTS

The main planning tool is the pilot charts; these are published by the DMA.

The charts are based on observations made over many years and show practically all the information you need in order to plan your route: winds, frequency of strong winds (force seven and above), currents, ice limits, fog and low visibility frequency, air temperatures, sea temperatures, tracks of tropical revolving storms or a t note that none has been observed in that month, shipping routes.

Much of the data can be relied upon without serious reservation; but winds do not come into that category because they are dependant upon a, perhaps temporary, weather system. The method of depicting winds enables you to say, for example, "In that position, in January, there is an 80% chance of wind from North through East." One in five navigators will be disappointed and therefore may look disapprovingly at the pilot chart; but this does not negate its value!

PLANNING THE ROUTE

The best route to choose depends mainly on the avoidance of ice, TRS and other adverse weather, and the harnessing of favorable winds and currents. The windward ability of the vessel and the requirement of the crew should also be considered.

A good example is the traditional route from Europe to the Caribbean. A direct route would lead the boat through unfavorable winds and probably unpleasant weather. The route which nearly all navigators choose takes in the Canary Islands, then leads further south, nearing the Cape Verde Islands, where the

Area	*Months*	*Local Name*
Western North Atlantic	June to November	Hurricane
Southern Indian Ocean	November to May	Cyclone
Australasia	December to April	Willy-willy
Western North Pacific	Any; but most likely June to November	Typhoon
Eastern North Pacific	June to November	Hurricane
Bay of Bengal and Arabian Sea	Mainly April to December	Cyclone

north-east trade winds and the north equatorial current can be picked up, culminating in a "downhill" passage on the great circle to the south and west.

A great circle track may save scores or hundreds of miles compared with a rhumb line. Big ships plan the great circle course before the passage starts, and usually keep to it, making slight alterations a few times each day. This practice is not useful for sailing boats because it is rare to be able to follow with absolute precision a pre-planned track. A method used in small boats is to calculate a new great circle course daily, after a good position has been obtained.

CHARTS

Charts are expensive, and stowage space may be limited. A policy which many navigators have used with success is to hold what may be called "port approach" charts of areas which may be visited (scale about 1:150,000), and to rely on sailing directions (pilot books), for entry and anchorage details. You will also need small scale charts of ocean areas. Graph paper is useful for many jobs, including the plotting of sights.

SAILING DIRECTIONS

Published by the DMA, and covering the world, these volumes are often known as "pilots". They contain essential pilotage information for specific areas. Many other pilot books are also published commercially; and the navigator should give himself plenty of time to consider the options and make his choice.

OTHER PUBLICATIONS

You will, of course, need your almanac. Do not be tempted to go to sea with your ephemerides in a computer! Problems can arise when your passage takes you past the end of a calendar year. Reed's contains guidance for you to use last year's almanac for this year's sights; but it is better to remember to buy ahead. Reed's is published each September for the following year. A further volume for the serious passage maker is "Reed's Ocean Navigator"; this goes into great detail for everything from celestial navigation to traffic separation schemes.

The DMA publishes volumes entitled "List of Lights and Fog Signals". It also produces books entitled Radio Navigational Aids; the latter cover communications, navigational aids and weather information. You will need the volumes which relate to your planned areas and activities.

Two books written by Jimmy Cornell and published by Adlard Coles have received favorable attention by ocean navigators. These are "World Cruising Routes" – the title is self-explanatory – and "World Cruising Handbook", which is a tourist guide cum pilot book.

Finally, there is the famous "Ocean Passages For The World", published by the British Admiralty. This has an excellent section on passage planning, supported by many charts and illustrations, as well as detailed advice on practically every conceivable ocean route.

Happy landfalls!

Electronic Navigation Aids

8

ELECTRONIC NAVIGATION AIDS

Over the past few decades, electronic aids for yachtsmen have advanced dramatically in sophistication and ease of operation.

For years the most advanced aid for the navigation of small vessels was the RDF set, by means of which radio bearings were taken of fixed DF stations. This system is still in use but the advent of more accurate and advanced systems has led to declining importance from the yachtsman's point of view. Full information on its use, is still included for the benefit of those navigators who use the method.

Automatic position-fixing has been in use commercially for many years, using groups of shore stations. The advent of the microchip and miniaturisation generally, allowed the development to take place of very small, highly sophisticated units, which could easily be accommodated in small vessels. Thus GPS and Loran became practical possibilities for small craft. Omega, although having worldwide coverage, is of little interest to yachtsmen.

RADIO DIRECTION FINDING (RDF)

RDF bearings consist of two types:

(a) Bearings taken by the navigator of fixed stations.

(b) Bearings taken by a fixed station of a vessel which are then radioed to the vessel concerned, giving its position.

Range

The range of radiobeacons, where known, is shown in nautical miles, in some cases, however, only the output (in kilowatts) is known. Where this is the case the following table will act as an approximate guide for converting to nautical miles.

Output	*Range*	*Output*	*Range*
0.025	45	1.0	240
0.05	80	1.5	280
0.1	100	2.0	300
0.2	130	3.0	330
0.3	155	5.0	400
0.4	170	10.0	500
0.5	180		

In areas where radiobeacons are numerous, the power output at night is reduced. In these cases both day and night ranges are given, eg. 200/70.

MARINE RADIOBEACONS

The automatic DF sets used by the majority of merchant ships require an uninterrupted carrier wave from the beacon to enable the set to 'lock on' when using automatic control rather than the interruption which occurs when the carrier is switched. Continuous carrier wave emission was introduced primarily for this purpose, but it also has considerable advantages for the small hand-held DF set. Before the introduction of this type of emission the modulated carrier wave was switched so that nothing was radiated during the intervals between the Morse Code letters. With the A2A system the carrier wave is emitted continuously and the modulation is also switched on during the DF period. However, with aerobeacons the modulation is switched off during the DF period.

The following is a summary of radiobeacon emissions used by Marine and Aeronautical stations:

A1A	Unmodulated carrier frequency during DF period; on-off keying of unmodulated carrier frequency during identification.
A2A	Carrier frequency with modulating audio frequency during DF period; on-off keying of modulating audio frequency. Carrier frequency either continuous or keyed with audio frequency.
NON A2A	Unmodulated carrier frequency during DF period; continuous carrier frequency with on-off keying of modulating audio frequency during identification.

The majority of marine radiobeacons use the A2A emission system, including all beacons administered by the U.S. Coast Guard.

In 1987 the Coast Guard Began a program of modernizing the Marine Radiobeacon system. Groups of radiobeacons in the United States were formerly sequenced in operation. This meant several beacons on the same frequency would broadcast alternately in a specific order. This practice has been discontinued by the U.S. Coast Guard. Many of these beacons have had recent frequency changes, and they are all now continuous in operation. It had been found most boaters were using the system for homing on individual beacons. These changes will allow continued use of the homing function, and should increase reliability.

Certain marine radiobeacons emit an additional signal for the transmission of GPS differential corrections. See Section on GPS.

AERO BEACONS

A glimpse at the list of aero beacons in the annual volume will show that these are few in number compared to Marine radiobeacons, bearing in mind that only those of use to surface vessels are included. These beacons, however, have the advantage that in general they are more powerful than the coastal marine beacons. The normal transmission consists of a long dash interrupted at approximately 15 second intervals with the call sign, although some may repeat the call sign continuously. The facility of being able to pick up a transmission at any moment without reference to a time sequence is often extremely useful, particularly when used in conjunction with a marine beacon.

The receiver should be used exactly as for marine beacons. However, in this case if the operator should forget to select DF/BFO position when he is taking his bearing, all he will hear is background noise. This once again illustrates the importance of developing an automatic procedure with respect to the operating controls of the particular set in use.

ERRORS AND CALIBRATION OF DF SETS

Quadrantal Error

The accuracy of an RDF set should not be relied upon until it has been checked for errors. The main error due to the vessel itself is quadrantal error which is caused by the re-radiation of radio waves from metal structures or rigging of the vessel. This re-radiated signal is picked up by the DF aerial and the set then indicates the resultant direction of the two waves. In the case of a sailing yacht the effect can be minimised by 'breaking' the closed loops of the rigging by inserting insulation but it is debatable whether this is really worth doing in most cases. It is much easier and more worthwhile to break the loops formed by steel life lines by using a rope seizing at one end of each line instead of a shackle. To calibrate for quadrantal error it is necessary to be within sight of a radiobeacon or in a known position so that the magnetic bearing of the beacon can be accurately determined. The visual (magnetic) and the DF bearings are compared at regular intervals, say 10°, while the vessel is rotated through 360°. A curve can then be plotted of the quadrantal error for each 10° of a relative bearing. Before plotting the curve it is important to remember to correct the compass bearings for deviation if any.

Night Effect

During the hours of darkness or more correctly between one hour before sunset to one hour after sunrise the radiobeacon signals are reflected back from the ionosphere and are picked up by the DF set slightly out of phase with the direct ground waves, resulting in a blurring of the null. The effect increases with distance from the beacon but close to the beacon, say within 15 miles, the effect is less noticeable. It is advisable to assume that MF beacons in general are not to be relied on at ranges of more than 70 miles in the presence of 'Night Effect', particularly around sunset and sunrise.

Coastal Refraction

Radio waves crossing a coastline at 90° are unaffected directionally but as the angle decreases refraction occurs, that is, the radio wave is bent in towards the land. The error, however, is really only significant when the angle is small and will always give a fix closer to the coastline than the actual position. Similarly, aerobeacons situated well inland may have the path of their ground waves seriously 'bent' due to the presence of high ground.

Remember

1. A beacon selected should not be beyond its official range and not more than 25 miles at night whatever its range othèrwise bearings may be unreliable.

2. Try to ensure that the ship's head is kept on a steady bearing during the operation. This is essential with the loop type aerial as the ship's heading will be needed at the instant the beacon bearing is taken.

8

3. The DF set bearing is corrected for deviation and quadrantal error if appropriate.

4. When choosing the beacon make sure that the bearing does not make a small angle with the coastline, that high ground does not intervene between the beacon and the vessel and that bearings should be as widely divergent as possible. As with visual bearings, considerable reliance can be placed on three well spaced bearings producing a small cocked hat.

5. Other aerial circuits near a loop aerial should be disconnected from their sets.

6. Radiobeacons may be suspended from operation without notice due to defects, maintenance.

SUPPRESSION OF ELECTRICAL APPARATUS

When any radio equipment is to be used on board it is important to ensure that any rotating electrical plant in the form of dynamos, alternators etc. is effectively suppressed. Normally, installations of this type are properly suppressed by the manufacturer, but if this has not been done or it has become defective it should be remedied if the best results are to be obtained from the radio equipment. It is incidentally worth bearing in mind that a very obtrusive static discharge can occur when the auxiliary of a sailing yacht is not in use but the propeller is allowed to rotate. A shaft brake should be fitted, alternatively a contact brush fitted on the shaft near the stern gland and suitably grounded will alleviate the trouble. All equipment should be grounded down to the engine bed plate and cathodic protection system.

RADIO BEARING CORRECTION TABLE

Radio bearings of a ship (Q.T.G.s) which have been taken by a distant radio station are great circle bearings and they are represented on a Mercator chart by curved lines, except when they coincide with a meridian or the equator. As meridians are shown as parallel lines on a Mercator chart, these great circle curves will cut each meridian at a different angle.

Convergency is the difference in the angles formed by the intersection of a great circle with two meridians. Its value between any two points on the Earth can be found from the approximate formula:

Convergency = difference of longitude x sin. mean latitude.

If two places on the chart are joined, first by a great circle and then by a straight line, the latter makes an angle with the great circle at each end. Each of these two angles may, for all practical purposes, be regarded as being equal to the **Half Convergency.**

It is important to remember that the straight line bearing on the Mercator chart always lies on the equatorial side of the great circle bearing.

D/F bearings are all great circle bearings and must, therefore, be corrected for Half Convergency before they can be plotted on a Mercator chart.

Rule for applying Half Convergency

It is usual for the ship to take a Radio D/F bearing of the shore station but in any case the following rule holds good even if the shore station has taken the bearings.

Always apply the Half Convergency TOWARDS THE EQUATOR.

A Half Convergency Correction table appears opposite.

OMEGA

Omega is a long range hyperbolic fixing system operating in the very low frequency (VLF) band. Eight transmitting stations are sufficient to provide world-wide coverage.

Radio Frequency: The basic frequency is 10.2 kHz but signals of 11.33 kHz and 13.6 kHz are also transmitted. Each station transmits the same frequencies in turn, according to a schedule which repeats at 10 second intervals. The signals from individual stations are identified by the duration and sequence of the transmissions.

Principle: The phase of signals of pairs of stations from pairs of stations are compared (as in the Decca system) and a number of possible hyperbolic position lines are defined by an observed phase difference.

Accuracy: Observations of phase difference must be corrected for the phase variations which may be predicted according to the time of the day, season of the year and geographical location. When these corrections are applied, fixing accuracy may be expected to be of the order of ±1 nm by day and ± 2 nm by night (95 per cent probability).

HALF CONVERGENCY CORRECTION TABLE

Mean Lat	Longitude Difference between Radio Station and Ship												
	2°	**4°**	**6°**	**8°**	**10°**	**12°**	**14°**	**16°**	**18°**	**20°**	**22°**	**24°**	**26°**
	0.1	0.1	0.2	0.2	0.3	0.3	0.4	0.4	0.5	0.5	0.6	0.6	0.7
3	0.1	0.2	0.3	0.4	0.5	0.6	0.7	0.8	0.9	1.0	1.1	1.2	1.3
6	0.2	0.3	0.5	0.6	0.9	0.9	1.1	1.2	1.4	1.5	1.7	1.8	2.0
9	0.2	0.4	0.6	0.8	1.1	1.2	1.5	1.6	1.9	2.0	2.3	2.5	2.7
12	0.3	0.5	0.8	1.0	1.3	1.6	1.9	2.0	2.3	2.5	2.8	3.1	3.3
15	0.3	0.6	1.0	1.2	1.6	1.9	2.2	2.4	2.8	3.0	3.4	3.7	4.0
18	0.3	0.7	1.1	1.4	1.9	2.2	2.5	2.8	3.2	3.5	3.9	4.3	4.6
21	0.4	0.8	1.2	1.6	2.1	2.5	2.9	3.2	3.6	4.0	4.4	4.8	5.2
24	0.4	0.9	1.3	1.8	2.3	2.8	3.2	3.6	4.0	4.5	5.0	5.4	5.9
27	0.5	1.0	1.4	2.0	2.5	3.0	3.5	4.0	4.5	5.0	5.5	6.0	6.5
30	0.5	1.1	1.5	2.2	2.7	3.3	3.8	4.4	4.9	5.4	6.0	6.5	7.1
33	0.6	1.2	1.7	2.4	2.9	3.5	4.1	4.7	5.3	5.9	6.5	7.0	7.6
36	0.6	1.3	1.8	2.6	3.1	3.8	4.4	5.0	5.6	6.3	7.0	7.5	8.1
39	0.7	1.4	1.9	2.8	3.3	4.0	4.7	5.3	6.0	6.7	7.5	8.0	8.7
42	0.7	1.5	2.0	2.9	3.5	4.2	5.0	5.6	6.3	7.1	7.9	8.5	9.2
45	0.7	1.5	2.1	3.0	3.7	4.5	5.3	5.9	6.7	7.4	8.2	8.9	9.6
48	0.8	1.6	2.3	3.2	3.9	4.7	5.5	6.2	7.0	7.8	8.5	9.3	10.0
51	0.8	1.6	2.4	3.4	4.1	4.9	5.7	6.5	7.3	8.1	8.9	9.7	10.5
54	0.8	1.7	2.5	3.5	4.3	5.1	5.9	6.8	7.6	8.4	9.2	10.0	10.9
57	0.9	1.8	2.6	3.6	4.4	5.2	6.1	7.0	7.9	8.7	9.5	10.3	11.2

Example: A vessel in Lat. 15°20'N,. Long. 50°20'W. obtains a Radio D/F bearing from a Station in Lat. 53°40'N., Long 5°10'W. True bearing signalled as 070°.

Enter the above table with the mean latitude (53°40' + 50°20' = 104°00' ÷ 2) = 52°00', and the Diff. Long. (15°20'– 5°10') = 10°10'W., and by inspection the approximate correction is found to be 4°. By the rule above this must be applied towards the Equator so 070° + 4° = 074°, which is the correct mercatorial bearing to plot.

OMEGA STATIONS

Ident Letter	Location	Lat.	Long.
A	Norway	66°25'N	13°09'E
B	Liberia	6°18'N	10°40'W
C	Hawaii	21°24'N	157°50'W
D	N. Dakota	46°22'N	98°20'W
E	La Réunion	20°58'S	55°17'E
F	Argentina	43°03'S	65°11'W
G	Australia	38°29'S	146°56'E
H	Japan	34°37'N	129°27E

LORAN C

Loran C is a development from the less successful Loran A. The radio Frequency is 100 kHz which is low enough to give a ground wave range of 800-1200 nm. Also sky waves may be used at longer ranges.

Principle: A Loran C chain consists of a master transmitting station and two to four slaves designated W,X,Y, and Z. The time interval between reception of signals from master and slave pairs is measured coarsely by comparing pulse envelopes and then finely by comparing the phase of the radio frequency cycles within the envelopes. The measured time difference defines the observer's position as on a hyperbola which can be identified on the appropriate Loran C lattice chart. Two master-slave pairs are needed to obtain a fix. Each chain is identified by a unique group repetition interval (GRI) at which the complete pattern of signals is repeated.

Range: The ground wave coverage of 800-1200 nm is increased to over 2000 nm by the use of sky waves but with reduced accuracy.

Accuracy: Within ground wave coverage the fixing accuracy is usually better than ± 500 metres (95 per cent probability).

LORAN-C RATE TABLES

Pair	Location (Master station listed first)	
GULF OF ALASKA, U.S.A.		
7960-X	Tok Junction, AK	Narrow Cape, AK
7960-Y	Tok Junction, AK	Shoal Cove, AK
7960-Z	Tok Junction, AK	Pt. Clarence, AK
WEST COAST, CANADA		
5990-X	Williams Lake, BC	Shoal Cove, Revillagigedo I., AK
5990-Y	Williams Lake, BC	George, WA
5990-Z	Williams Lake, BC	Port Hardy, Vancouver I., Canada
CENTRAL PACIFIC	**THIS CHAIN HAS BEEN DISCONTINUED IN 1992**	
WEST COAST U.S.A.		
9940-W	Fallon, NV	George, WA
9940-X	Fallon, NV	Middletown, CA
9940-Y	Fallon, NV	Searchlight, NV
EAST COAST, CANADA		
5930-X	Caribou, ME	Nantucket, MA
5930-Y	Caribou, ME	Cape Race, Newfoundland
5930-Z	Caribou, ME	Fox Harbor, Newfoundland
NORTHEAST, U.S.A.		
9960-W	Seneca, NY	Caribou, ME
9960-X	Seneca, NY	Nantucket, MA
9960-Y	Seneca, NY	Carolina Beach, NC
9960-Z	Seneca, NY	Dana, IN
SOUTHEAST, U.S.A.		
7980-W	Malone, FL	Grangeville, LA
7980-X	Malone, FL	Raymondville, TX
7980-Y	Malone, FL	Jupiter, FL
7980-Z	Malone, FL	Carolina Beach, NC
GREAT LAKES, U.S.A.		
8970-W	Dana, IN	Malone,FL
8970-X	Dana, IN	Seneca, NY
8970-Y	Dana, IN	Baudette, MN

TRANSIT SATELLITE SYSTEM

Originally developed for the U.S. Navy, the system consists of five satellites orbiting the earth at a height of 1000 km and transmitting data on frequencies of 400MHz and 150MHz.

The transmission frequency received by an observer decreases as the satellite passes overhead due to the Doppler effect. The rotation of the earth brings the receiver under each satellite orbit in turn, and as the receiver 'sights' the satellite, it computes its position from the data transmitted.

The time between suitable satellite 'passes' varies between 90 minutes in the low latitudes and 30 minutes in the high latitudes. The actual time of the satellite pass overhead varies between 10 and 15 minutes, during which time the receiver calculates the navigator's position.

SatNav does not provide continuous position-fixing like Decca and Loran C, and it is therefore necessary to maintain a D.R. Position on the chart between fixes. The accuracy of the system is basically good—of the order of ± 100m—but correct input of the vessel's speed is necessary for this accuracy. The speed of the vessel will affect the Doppler effect and therefore the calculated position. This error can be of the order of ± 400m for every knot of velocity error. In some sets speed and compass course can be keyed in manually and in the more sophisticated sets it can be done automatically by interfacing with automatic log and compass units.

Satellite fixes are based on the World Geodetic System (WGS72) Datum and for the best accuracy the receiver coordinates should be amended by the local 'shift' where mentioned on a particular chart.

GLOBAL POSITIONING SYSTEM (GPS)

GPS has been developed in the USA for military purposes by the Department of Defense, and by arrangement with the Department of Transportation a degraded version is utilized for civilian use. The system will eventually consist of 21 satellites with 3 spares in orbit at an altitude of 20,000km, each satellite rotating round the earth at 12-hour intervals. There are at least 4 satellites visible to a receiver at sea level at any one time, thus providing continuous position fixing.

The method of operation, basically is that each satellite broadcasts its exact position at an exact time, the receiver then notes the time taken for the transmission to reach it and converts that time into the distance from the satellite. This operation is carried out on 4 satellites and the receiver obtains 4 'position lines' or circles, the point of intersection being the navigator's position. The timing is of extreme importance and this is achieved by equipping the satellites with atomic clocks with an error of ± 1 second in 300,000 years.

Each satellite transmits data on two frequencies, the first designed for military purposes and not available for civilian use, giving extremely accurate position-fixing, probably of the order of 6 to 8 metres error. The transmission available to civilian users is deliberately degraded and the error will be of the order of ± 100m.

It should be noted that the position obtained by GPS should be amended for chart datum in exactly the same way as SatNav positions are amended.

Differential Transmissions (GPS)

The accuracy of satellite navigation systems (e.g GPS) can be improved considerably by the transmission of differential corrections obtained from suitably located stations. These stations can be radiobeacons operating on the maritime radiobeacon frequencies.

The differential corrections are transmitted on an additional signal (within 0·5 kHz of the radiobeacon frequency), with Minimum Shift Keying (MSK) and G1D class of emission. This additional signal should not affect the radiobeacon.

Radiobeacon stations may also be used to transmit supplementary navigational information using narrow-band techniques, provided that the prime function of the beacon is not significantly affected.

GPS Information

For more information on GPS contact the Coast Guard's Global Positioning Information Center (GPSIC). A 24 hour-a-day recording may be heard by calling 703-866-3826. You can access the 24 hour computer bulletin board at 703-866-3890 (up to 2400 baud). For up to 9600 baud call 703-866-3894.

To get your GPS questions answered call 703-866-3806 of FAX 703-866-3825. A GPSIC watchstander will help you. Watchstanders are on duty from 0600 to 2200, Monday through Sunday.

The Coast Guard broadcasts warnings and information on GPS in their regular Marine Information Broadcasts. These may be heard by listening on VHF channel 16 (switching 22A) and on medium frequency 2182 (switching 2670). Messages are also broadcast on NAVTEX. Those with a modem link to NAVINFONET can access GPS information.

Radio station WWV also broadcasts GPS status reports at 14 and 15 minutes past the hour on 2.5, 5, 10, 15 and 20MHz. WWVH broadcasts these reports at 43 and 44 minutes past the hour on 2.5, 5, 10 and 15MHZ. For more information on WWV and WWVH broadcasts see the Communications and Weather Services chapter of the Almanac.

GPS and Omega publications are available from:

Commanding Officer
Omega NAVSYSCEN/GPSIC
7323 Telegraph Road
Alexandria, VA 22310-3998

RADAR

Radar is probably the most useful of all the electronic navigation aids when coasting. It not only gives position but also indicates the dangers of collision or stranding.

Radar consists of four basic units: transmitter, aerial (scanner), receiver and display.

A very short pulse of powerful electromagnetic energy is transmitted from the aerial in a narrow, horizontal beam at the speed of light (300 million meters/sec.) at the same time a stream of electrons (the trace) is deflected from the centre of the cathode ray tube out towards the circumference of the tube face at a controlled rate, variable with the range scale in use. Only the outward trace is used.

Any object on the bearing of the transmitted pulse will re-radiate the energy in many directions and only a very small portion will return to the aerial.

REFLECTION

This signal once detected needs to be greatly amplified and changed to + D.C. voltage. The D.C. pulse allows an increase in the flow of electrons to make a bright mark on the screen

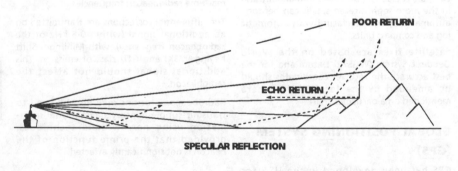

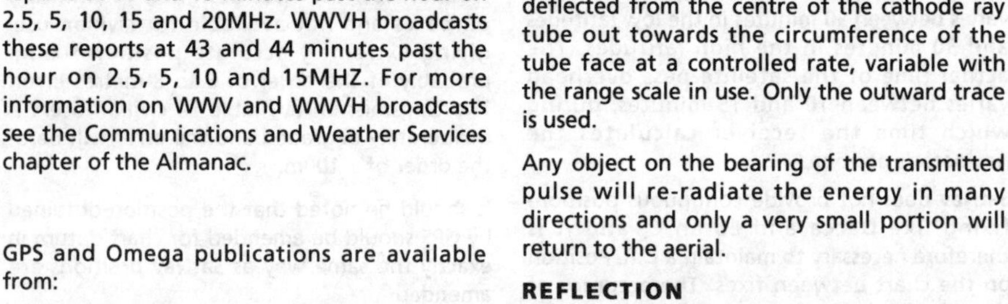

SPECULAR REFLECTION

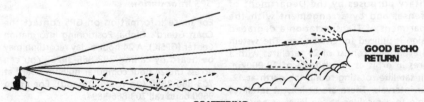

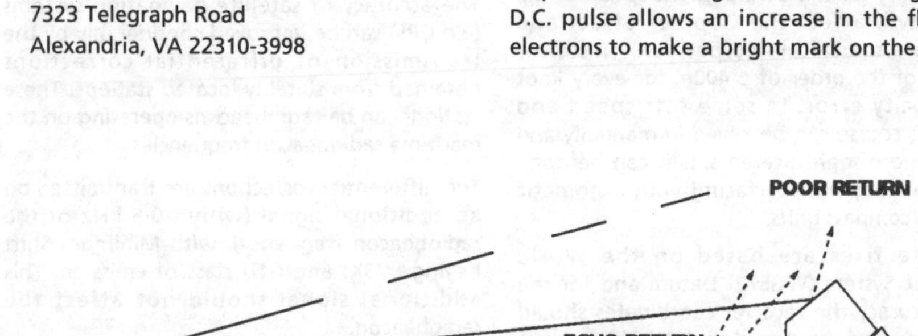

SCATTERING

Small objects, buoy (A) boat (B) small fishing vessel (C) in an area of rough sea.

to record the 'echo'. This sequence takes place many times each second (Pulse Repetition Frequency), the space between is to allow a returned echo to be detected and displayed before the next transmission. PRFs vary with range and/or make of set. Between 500-2000 per second. The aerial is set to rotate at about 20 revs. per minute and the trace rotation is synchronised with the direction of the rotating aerial (scanner) so the direction of every echo from the observer is shown on the display.

Even the smallest object will return several echoes before the beam moves on. This provides a storage effect of the returned energy to help display the weaker echoes.

A most important point of reference is the Heading Marker. To enable the radar to give direction, a switch device is placed at the aerial unit. When the aerial is pointing ahead a pulse is sent from the aerial to the radar display which causes a line to show on the screen which represents the ship's head so that any echo displayed on the screen can be referred to the ship's head and the bearing of the echo obtained. If the Heading Marker switch is not pointing exactly ahead, relative bearings will be in error. A quick check is to head towards a small prominent visible object and see if the echo is under the Heading Marker, noting any difference.

The narrow horizontal beam is determined by the size of the aerial. The larger the scanner the smaller is the horizontal beam. The 6m. shore scanners have 0.5° beams. Merchant ships must have less than 2°. These large scanners are not practicable on small craft and the usual yacht scanner of about 0.5m. has a 6° beam.

To allow for the motion at sea the vertical beam is about 20°. The transmitted pulse has to contain sufficient energy to travel many miles and produce a detectable echo return. If a peak power of 1.5 kW. is transmitted for 0.5 millionths of a second (½ microsecond) this produces a pulse 150 m. long. The pulse is shorter on lower ranges (0.1 sec. = 30 m.)

This combined effect of pulse length and horizontal beam width will determine the picture resolution and ability to discriminate between objects close to each other. The beam distortion of echoes can be seen by apparently large echoes at the longer ranges, getting smaller as they near the centre. Small river or harbor entrances may not be detected, buoyed channels may close. Any objects within the beam at the same range will show on the radar at that bearing as a single echo.

The pulse length gives apparent length to an echo. Any two objects within the pulse appear as one. This is why the shortest pulse possible for detection is used on lower ranges.

8

The detection of objects is also determined by their shape, size aspect and material. Metal is a perfect reflector, while glass fibre is almost transparent to radar. This is why a metal reflector is a must for small glass fibre vessels (the metal reflectors may be set inside a fiberous material). Sea water is a very good re-radiator, most of the energy reflecting away but the scattered return from waves may give stronger echoes than objects within the waves. Sea clutter normally is more noticeable to windward, the backs of the lee waves giving less return to the aerial.

To remove this clutter around the center of the display a special variable suppression is provided which works outward from the center decreasing to nil at about 3 miles. This control, 'Sea Clutter', is regarded as the most dangerous control on the set, as 'wanted' real echoes may be removed without the observer realising the extent of the 'hole' in the picture. This is worse for small craft which may not be detected from a larger ship's radar display. 2(a) & 2(b)

Navigating Using Radar

Bearing in mind all the above limitations, radar is a most useful navigational aid. The presentation is a plan view of the locality which will relate to the chart in use. However, the picture will not be quite the same as the chart. Small insignificant objects may be enhanced while small prominent objects may not give a detectable return. Lower parts of the coast may be below the radar horizon and the coast on the radar will be inland from the charted coast.

Bearings are quite difficult to take on a small craft radar. The heading must be read at the instant the bearing is read and converted to a true bearing and unless the object is identified the bearing may be laid off from the wrong place. Lighthouses are not usually at the exact point of land. The ends of land will be displaced by half beam width. The best position is obtained by taking a visual bearing of an isolated object and the best radar only position is by taking three or more radar ranges from the land. This will produce a 'cocked hat'. Take the closest to danger to be your position. In fog always 'stand off' to seaward of your intended track.

Racons

To aid radar navigation, important objects such as lightships or fairway buoys are fitted with responder beacons, 'Racons', which produce a 'flash' away from the racon, usually about two miles long. The racon searches the whole marine radar X band and may only strike your frequency once or twice each 100 or so seconds.

Radar presentations not yet widely available to small craft radars are North up, where a

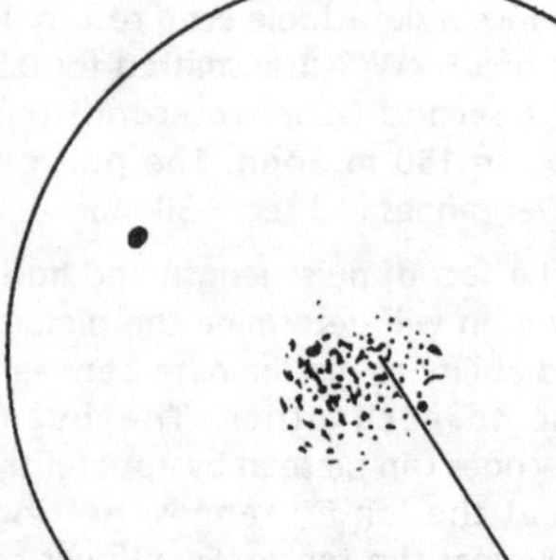

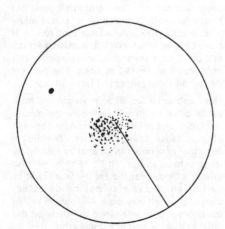

2(a)Sea Clutter masking echoes from A. B.and C.

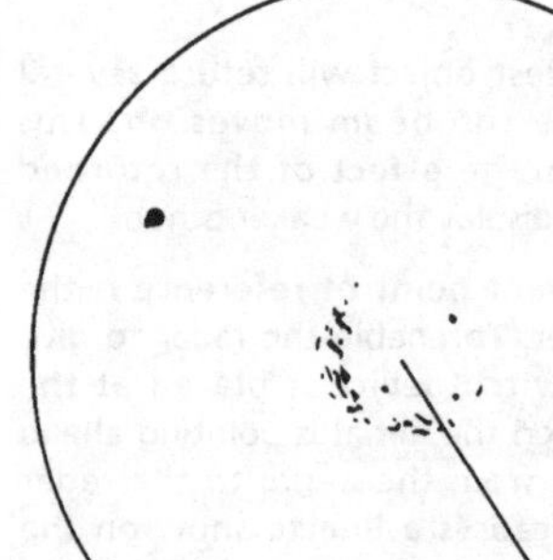

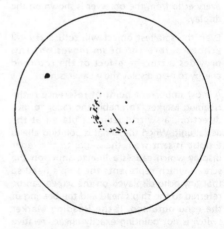

2(b) Sea Clutter Suppression applied echoes A, B. – not detected and C – just visible.

RADAR (HEAD UP)

6 MILE RANGE

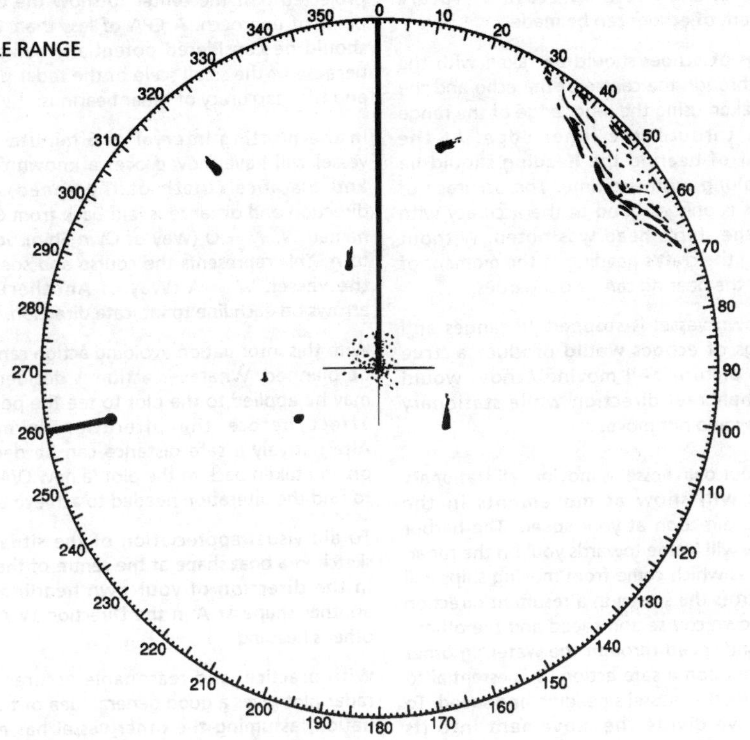

Course 240°T, Speed 8 knots. Land to starboard.
Racon 'Flash' marks structure to port.
5 echoes detected. Echoes at 340° and 130° visible beacons.
Echo at 240° vessel same course/speed.
Echo at 015° crossing clear.
Echo at 320° to be plotted.

compass heading is introduced. As the vessel yaws the Heading Marker moves while the picture is stable. Also true motion, where the center spot is set to move across the screen at own vessel's course and speed.

Plenty of clear weather practice is essential to build confidence in your own ability, or attend a radar course where all these points will be amplified.

THE RADAR PLOT

In order to comply with the International Collision Regulations 'correct assessment' of a situation using radar can only be ascertained by carefully plotting the movement of an approaching vessel. Clear weather practice is essential before attempting radar navigation in fog.

The Relative Plot

The majority of small craft radars are only capable of a 'ship's head up' display. This is where the heading marker is always at zero and any movement of the craft will show as lateral rotating movement of the radar picture. When plotting in this mode it is better to convert the relative bearings into compass bearings for plotting — (no need to apply variation or deviation) — the vessel's course steered is drawn on the plotting diagram. Continuity of the plot after course alterations by your own vessel will be preserved as the only thing to be altered is the heading line. If the plot were to be made 'head up' all echoes will have to be transferred each time the course is changed. This is a frequent cause of mistakes.

The relative plot is a reproduction of the radar picture and on it a forecast of future movement of echoes can be made.

Bearings of echoes should be taken with the cursor through the centre of the echo and the range taken using the inner edge of the range marker through the inner edge. At the moment of bearing the heading should be noted along with the time. The accuracy of the plot is only as good as the accuracy with which the ship's head was noted. Without knowing the craft's heading at the moment of reading the bearing can be dangerous.

If our own vessel is stopped all ranges and bearings of echoes would produce a 'true motion picture'. All moving echoes would show their real direction while stationary objects would not move.

When your own vessel is moving, all stationary objects will show as movements in the opposite direction at your speed. The harbor entrance will 'come towards you' on the radar. All echoes which come from moving ships will move across the screen in a resultant direction of your own course and speed and the other's course and speed through the water. In order to decide upon a safe action, it is essential to know the other vessel's heading and speed. To do this we divide the movement into its known components to produce a triangle. By looking at the radar screen the afterglow from echo movements produces dim 'tails' behind the echo. This is only an indication of resultant movement, but useful in deciding which echoes may be closing.

To allow time to plot and assess which action to take the plot should start when the echo is some distance from the center.

The triangle of motions is named in a standard form W.O. and A.A. series of three ranges and bearings are taken in a time interval of six minutes (1/10th hour)

The first position is named O and the time noted. On 3 minutes a check position is taken. After the six minutes the range and bearing is taken and marked A. If the O → A line is reasonably straight it may be assumed the other vessel has probably not altered course during the plotting interval. This O → A line is projected past the center to show the closest point of approach. A CPA of less than 1 mile should be considered potentially dangerous because of the small scale of the radar picture and the inaccuracy of radar bearings.

In the plotting interval of 6 minutes own vessel will have moved over a known course and distance (1/10th of the speed). This direction and distance is laid back from O and named W. W → O (Way of Own Ship). Join W to A. This represents the course and speed of the vessel. W → A (Way of Another). Use arrows on each line to indicate direction.

With this information avoiding action can now be planned. Whatever action is decided this may be applied to the plot to see the possible effect before the alteration is made. Alternatively a safe distance can be decided on and taken back to the plot (a new O/A line) to find the alteration needed to achieve this.

To aid visual appreciation of the situation, sketch in a boat shape at the centre of the plot in the direction of your own heading and another shape at A in the Direction W A, the other's heading.

With practice, and reasonable accuracy the radar plot gives a good general idea of the situation, assuming the other vessel has maintained course and speed. It is important to continue plotting an approaching echo until it is past and clear, especially after you have made an alteration, to see what effect has been made to the CPA.

The need for radar plotting became apparent soon after radar was introduced for use at sea in the 1940s. Many collisions in the early days were caused by misunderstanding of what was 'seen' on the screen. Since then technology and regulations have come a long way to improve the situation.

Very few of the modern developments extend to the small ship's radar and most are only able to present the original 'ships head up' display. The information may be filtered to the 'Rasterscan' type (television) display. Guard rings are available but the plotting and forecasting of subsequent movements are left to the observer.

RADAR PLOTTING SHEET

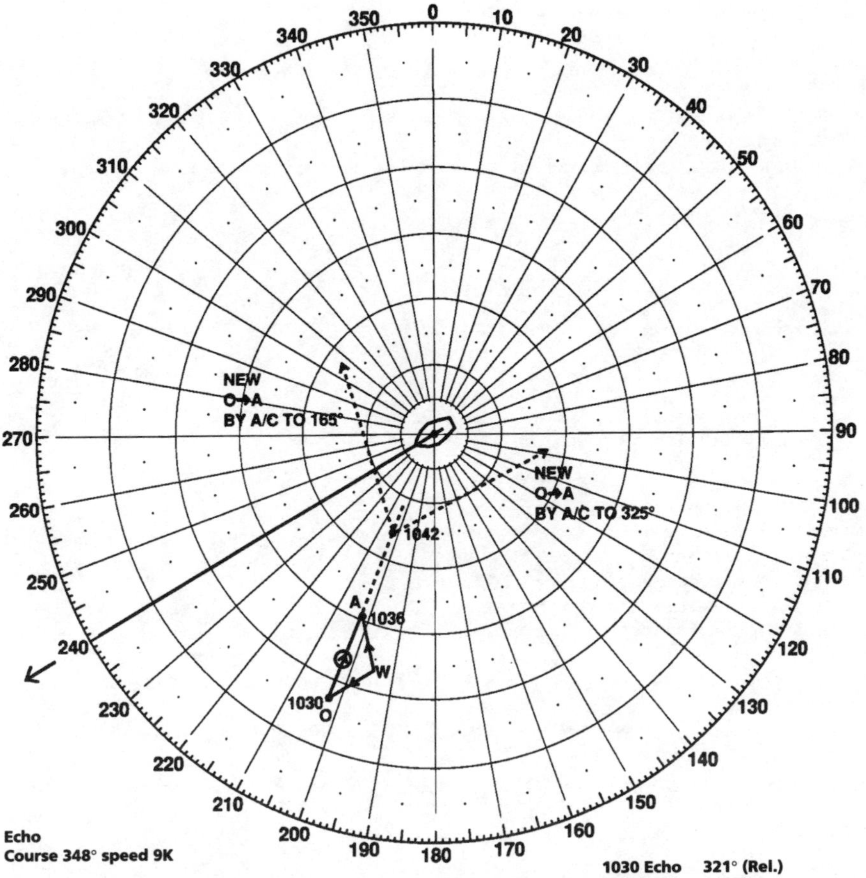

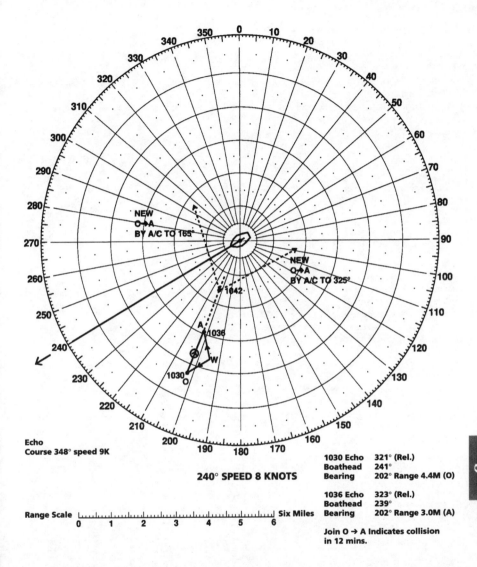

Echo
Course 348° speed 9K

240° SPEED 8 KNOTS

Range Scale 0 1 2 3 4 5 6 **Six Miles**

1030 Echo	**321° (Rel.)**
Boathead	**241°**
Bearing	**202° Range 4.4M (O)**
1036 Echo	**323° (Rel.)**
Boathead	**239°**
Bearing	**202° Range 3.0M (A)**

Join O → A Indicates collision in 12 mins.

Assuming no significant changes in O → A, Plot the forecast position say in 6 min. at 1042. From this position lay off tangents to the chosen pass distance (1 mile ring). Take this line back to A on the plot. Rotate W – O about W to touch this new O – A line at O_1. W → O_1 is the new course. Repeat with the other O_1 – A line.

Note: From the plot an alteration to starboard will mean running on a near parallel course for a long time. An alteration to port is not recommended as the other vessel may be altering to starboard as we alter to port — most dangerous. In this situation stopping own vessel before 1042 will allow the other to pass well ahead. Remember the craft on your port quarter will now overtake you.

9

COMMUNICATIONS

RADIO TELEPHONE ALPHABET

When sending any communication at sea in plain language, the following phonetic alphabet is used Internationally:

Letter	*Word*	*Pronunciation*
A	Alfa	AL FAH
B	Bravo	BRAH VOH
C	Charlie	CHAR LEE or SHAR LEE
D	Delta	DELL TAH
E	Echo	ECK OH
F	Foxtrot	FOKS TROT
G	Golf	GOLF
H	Hotel	HOH TELL
I	India	IN DEE AH
J	Juliett	JEW LEE ETT
K	Kilo	KEY LOH
L	Lima	LEE MAH
M	Mike	MIKE
N	November	NO VEM BER
O	Oscar	OSS CAH
P	Papa	PAH PAH
Q	Quebec	KEH BECK
R	Romeo	ROW ME OH
S	Sierra	SEE AIR RAH
T	Tango	TANG GO
U	Uniform	YOU NEE FORM or OO NEE FORM
V	Victor	VIK TAH
W	Whiskey	WISS KEY
X	X-ray	ECKS RAY
Y	Yankee	YANG KEY
Z	Zulu	ZOO LOO

The syllables to be emphasized underlined.

RADIO LICENSING

All vessels using marine VHF, marine Single Sideband (SSB), Radar and Emergency Position Indicating Radiobeacons (EPIRBS) must obtain a Ship Radio Station License from the Federal Communications Commission (FCC). The application must be made on FCC form 506 accompanied by a $35.00 application fee. You may obtain a form from the following office:

Federal Communications Commission
Forms Distribution Center
2803 52nd Avenue
Hyattsville, MD 20781
202-632-3676

Information required includes your name and address, the registration or documentation number of your boat, your boat's type and size and the type of radio equipment you are requesting a license for. The fee of $35.00 must accompany the application in the form of a check or money order. Do not send cash. Questions may be directed to the FCC's Private Radio Bureau Consumer Assistance Branch at 717-337-1212. Completed applications should be sent to:

Federal Communications Commission
Marine Ship Service
P.O. Box 358275
Pittsburgh, PA 15251-5275

A temporary permit to operate your radio station is included with your application. The permit is valid for 90 days, or until you receive your Ship Station License. The term of a license is normally five years. All changes to vessel status, address and radio equipment must be reported to the FCC. The U.S. Coast Guard is now checking Ship Station Licenses routinely during vessel inspections, and the FCC can fine those not in compliance.

A Digital Selective Calling Ship Station Identity (SSI) may be obtained by using Form 506. After you obtain your SSI you will need to enter it into your radio. This number may be used by others to call you using the Digital Selective calling system.

Restricted Radiotelephone Operator Permit

This license must be obtained by those intending to make foreign voyages or intending to use SSB radiotelephone transmitters. This permit is not required for VHF operation within the U.S. An application is made on FCC form 753 and is free. No test is required. This is a permanent permit issued for the lifetime of the licensee.

A Marine Radio Operator Permit is required for vessels carrying more than six passengers for hire, or for vessels over 65 feet operating on the Great Lakes. The application is made on FCC form 756 and requires a test. Contact the FCC for more information. For general information contact:

Private Radio Bureau Licensing Division
Gettysburg, PA 17325-7245
717-337-1212

VHF-FM

VHF Channel 16 (156.8 MHz) is the distress, safety and calling frequency that is mandatory in all VHF marine installations. Its use is for inter-ship and for ship-to-shore as a distress and calling channel. It is monitored by all Coast Guard stations and commercial vessels and all vessels should monitor Channel 16 whenever the radio is in operation and the vessel is underway. Vessels should also have available Channel 22A (157.1 MHz) to contact the Coast Guard in the event of heavy traffic on Channel 16. All transmissions on Channel 16 should be kept to an absolute minimum.

REMINDER: YOU ARE PROHIBITED FROM MAKING ROUTINE RADIO CHECKS ON THE VHF EMERGENCY CHANNEL.

Channel 6 (156.3 MHz) is the inter-ship safety frequency and is used for ship-to-ship traffic. It is also mandatory on all VHF marine installations.

Channel 13 is the Bridge to Bridge Navigational channel used by commercial vessels in meeting and passing situations. It should be monitored in certain restricted areas such as The Chesapeake and Delaware Canal and Norfolk Harbor. This channel is also used for talking to bridges and locks. In many areas bridge tenders prefer to be called on channel 13, to reduce congestion on channel 16.

Channel 09 has been designated as a secondary calling channel for New England, eastern New York and New Jersey north of Toms River. This area includes Lake Champlain. VHF channel 09 should be used as the general purpose calling channel in these areas. Vessels using channel 09 in this manner may monitor channel 09 instead of channel 16. When underway all vessels should monitor channel 09.

The Coast Guard will not monitor channel 09, but it will make emergency broadcasts and announce marine information broadcasts on the channel. The Coast Guard will continue to monitor channel 16, which is reserved for distress and safety communications only.

SHIP-SHIP COMMUNICATION

Channel 22A (157.1 MHz) is assigned to the US Coast Guard, and can be used by the public for communication with the Coast Guard. Channel 22A is not monitored continuously but regularly scheduled Marine Information Broadcasts are made on this channel.

CHANGES IN THE VESSEL BRIDGE-TO-BRIDGE RADIOTELEPHONE REGULATIONS

On August 19, 1992, several changes to the Vessel Bridge-To-Bridge Radiotelephone Regulations will become effective. These changes were published in the Federal Register on April 21, 1992 (57 FR 14483), and will be published as a change to *Navigation Rules: International – Inland* in August. The following is a summary of the substantive changes:

For power driven vessels, the minimum size requirements for application of the regulations will change from 300 gross tons to 20 metres (65·5 feet) in length. This means that all power driven vessels 20 metres in length or greater, passenger vessels of 100 gross tons or greater, towing vessels 26 feet in length or greater, and most dredges will be required to abide by these regulations.

All vessels subject to the regulations must be capable of transmitting and receiving on VHF-FM channel 22A (157·1 MHz) (Coast Guard Marine Information Broadcast and Communications Channel). Note: most VHF-FM Marine radios commercially available in the United States are already capable of transmitting and receiving on this channel.

Vessels subject to these regulations, operating in a designated area on the lower Mississippi River and its approaches, must have equipment capable of transmitting and receiving on channel 67 VHF-FM (156·375 MHz) and are required to monitor this channel instead of channel 13.

RECREATIONAL, MILITARY AND OTHER UNINSPECTED VESSELS 20 METRES IN LENGTH OR GREATER ARE REQUIRED TO COMPLY WITH THE BRIDGE-TO-BRIDGE RADIOTELEPHONE REGULATIONS.

Important: Provisions of the Vessel Bridge-To-Bridge Radiotelephone Regulations:

The operator, or whomever it designated to pilot the vessel, must maintain a listening watch on the designated frequency while underway on the navigable waters of the United States. The designated frequency is VHF-FM Channel 13 (156·65MHz), exept on portions of the lower Mississippi River, where VHF-FM channel 67 (156·375 MHz) is the designated frequency.

The Bridge-To-Bridge VHF-FM maritime channel shall only be used to exchange navigational information or necessary tests. The person maintaining the listening watch must be able to communicate in English.

Each vessel must have on board a radio operator who holds a restricted radio-telephone operator permit or higher class license, as well as a FCC ship station license.

Note: All vessels operating on the Great Lakes are exempt from these regulataions (33 CFR 26), but must comply with the provisions of "The agreement between the United States of America and Canada for Promotion of Safety on the Great Lakes by Means of Radio, 1973 (47 CFR 80·951-80·971).

In order to maintain an effective and continuous watch on the designated Bridge-To-Bridge channel (channel 13 or 67), a second VHF-FM radio must be available to meet watch requirements on channel 16 (156·8 MHz – Distress, Safety and Calling channel) or separately assigned Vessel Traffic Service (VTS) channel, and to communicate on other required channels (e.g., port operations channel, or designated working channel). Any of the following combinations of equipment are acceptable to meet these requirements:

Two multi-channel VHF-FM radios capable of transmitting and receiving on the Bridge-to-Bridge channel (channel 13 or 67), channel 16, channel 22A and such other channels as required for the vessel's service.

One single channel VHF-FM radio capable of transmitting and receiving on channel 13 or 67, and a second multi-channel VHF-FM radio capable of transmitting and receiving on channels 16, 22A and such other channels as required for the vessel's service.

One multi-channel VHF-FM channel 13 or 67 through one receiver, and channel 16, or a separately assigned VTS channel through the other receiver. Note: A single VHF-FM radio capable of scanning, or sequential monitoring (often referred to as "dual watch" capability), will not satisfy this requirement.

NOTE: A portable (hand held) radio may be used to meet the bridge-to-bridge requirements. However, this radio must be permanently associated with the vessel, and it must have a connection for an external antenna (FCC regulations 47 CFR 80·1017). Foreign vessels entering into U.S. waters may use portable equipment, not permanently associated with the vessel, that is brought abroad by the pilot. However, foreign vessels transiting U.S. waters without a pilot on board must still meet the provisions above.

For more information on VHF-FM marine radiotelephone requirements call 202-267-0352, or write to:

Commandant (G-NSR-3), U.S. Coast Guard, 2100 2nd Street SW, Washington DC 20593-0001.

REQUIRED FREQUENCIES AND EQUIPMENT CHANNELIZATION

All ship radiotelephone stations in the 156 to 162 MHz band MUST be equipped to operate on:

1. Ch. 16 (156.8 MHz) International Distress, Safety and Calling frequency for VHF

2. Ch. 6 (156.3 MHz) Intership Safety Channel.

3. At least one working frequency.

The following table lists the marine band VHF frequencies available and explains the use of the various channels.

If your set is equipped with a synthesizer, you will normally be able to tune to any of the channels in the maritime mobile band. If your set is not equipped with a synthesizer, you will only be able to tune to such channels as have been previously set up in your equipment. For non- synthesized equipment, the number of channels installed in your set will depend largely on how the set will be used, where the vessel will be operated, and what coast stations are operating in your area. While fewer than twelve channels may be satisfactory for some vessels, installation of a radiotelephone with less than twelve channel capability is not recommended.

The more channels you are able to use, the better your communication capability will be. Caution must be exercised, however, in selecting and using channels in accordance with their authorized purpose.

AVAILABLE MARINE CHANNELS AND THEIR USES

Frequencies(MHz)		Channel Usage	
Channel Number	**Ship Transmit**	**Ship Receive**	**Intended Use**
1A	156.050	156.050	PORT OPERATIONS AND COMMERCIAL and (Intership and Ship-to-Coast)
63A	156.175	156.175	Available for use within the U.S.C.G designated Vessel Traffic Services (VTS) area of New Orleans, and the Lower Mississippi River.
5A	156.250	156.250	PORT OPERATIONS (Intership and Ship-to Coast). Available for use within the U.S.C.G Vessel Traffic Service radio protection areas of Seattle.
6	156.300	156.300	INTERSHIP SAFETY. Required or all VHF-FM equipped vessels. For intership safety purposes and search and rescue (SAR) communications with ships and aircraft of the U.S. Coast Guard. Must not be used for non-safety communications.
7	156.350	160.950	INTERNATIONAL USE.
7A	156.350	156.350	COMMERCIAL (INTERSHIP AND SHIP-TO COAST). A working channel for commercial vessels to fulfil a wide scope of business and operational needs
8	156.400	156.400	COMMERCIAL (INTERSHIP). Same as channel 7A except limited to intership communications.
9	156.450	156.450	COMMERCIAL LAND NON-COMMERCIAL (INTERSHIP AND SHIP-TO-COAST). Some examples of use are communications with commercial marinas and public docks to obtain supplies or schedule repairs and contacting commercial vessels about matters of common concern.
10	156.500	156.500	COMMERCIAL (INTERSHIP AND SHIP- TO-COAST). Same as channel 7A.
12			restricted to the operational handling, movement and safety of ships and, in emergency, to the safety of persons. It should be noted, however, in certain ports 11, 12 and 14 are used selectively for the U.S.C.G. Vessel Traffic Service or the Great Lakes ship movement service.
13	156.650	156.650	NAVIGATIONAL – (SHIP'S) BRIDGE TO (SHIP'S) BRIDGE. This channel is available to all vessels and is required on large passenger and commercial vessels (including many tugs). Use is limited to navigational communications such as in meeting and passing situations. Abbreviated operating procedures (call signs omitted) and 1 watt maximum power (except in certain special instances) are used on this channel for both calling and working. For recreational vessels, this channel should be used for listening to determine the intentions of large vessels. This is also the primary channel used at locks and bridges.
14	156.700	156.700	PORT OPERATIONS (INTERSHIP AND SHIP- TO-COAST). Same as channel 12.

AVAILABLE MARINE CHANNELS AND THEIR USES

Frequencies(MHz)			Channel Usage
Channel Number	**Ship Transmit**	**Ship Receive**	**Intended Use**
15		156.750	ENVIRONMENTAL (RECEIVE ONLY). A receive only channel used to broadcast environmental information to ships such as weather, sea conditions, time signals for navigation, notices to mariners, etc. Most of this information is also broadcast on the weather (WX) channels. Class C EPIRBs also operate on this channel.
16	156.800	156.800	DISTRESS, SAFETY AND CALLING (INTERSHIP AND SHIP-TO-COAST), ALSO EPIRB's. Required channel for all VHF-FM equipped vessels. Must be monitored at all times station is in operation (except when actually communicating on another channel). This channel is monitored, also, by the Coast Guard, public coast stations and many other limited coast stations. Calls to other vessels are normally initiated on this channel. Then, except in an emergency, you must switch to a working channel.
17	156.850	156.850	STATE CONTROL. Available to all vessels to communicate with ships and coast stations operated by state or local governments. Messages are restricted to regulation and control, or rendering assistance. Use of low power (1 watt) setting is required by international treaty.
18	156.900	161.500	INTERNATIONAL USE.
18A	156.900	156.900	COMMERCIAL (INTERSHIP AND SHIP-TO- COAST). Same as channel 7A.
19	156.950	161.550	INTERNATIONAL USE.
19A	156.950	156.950	COMMERCIAL (INTERSHIP AND SHIP-TO- COAST). Same as channel 7A.
20	157.000	161.600	PORT OPERATIONS (INTERSHIP AND SHIP- TO-COAST). Available to all vessels. This is a traffic advisory channel for use by agencies directing the movement of vessels in or near ports, locks, or waterways. Messages are restricted to the operational handling, movement and safety of ships and, in emergency, to the safety of persons.
21	157.050	156.050	INTERNATIONAL USE. (or 161.650)
21A	157.050	157.050	U.S. GOVERNMENT ONLY.
22	157.100	161.700	INTERNATIONAL USE.
22A	157.100	157.100	COAST GUARD LIASON AND MARITIME SAFETY INFORMATION BROADCASTS. This channel is used for communications with U.S. Coast Guard ship, coast and aircraft stations after first establishing communications on channel 16. Navigational warnings and, where not available on WX channels, Marine Weather forecasts are made on this frequency. It is strongly recommended that every VHF radiotelephone include this channel.
23	157.150	161.750	INTERNATIONAL USE.

AVAILABLE MARINE CHANNELS AND THEIR USES

Frequencies(MHz)			Channel Usage
Channel Number	**Ship Transmit**	**Ship Receive**	**Intended Use**
23A	157.150	157.150	U.S. GOVERNMENT ONLY.
24	157.200	161.800	PUBLIC CORRESPONDENCE (SHIP-TO- COAST). Available to all vessels to communicate with public coast stations. Channels 26 and 28 are the primary public correspondence channels and therefore become the first choice for the cruising vessel having limited channel capacity.
25	157.250	161.850	PUBLIC CORRESPONDENCE (SHIP-TO COAST). Same as channel 24.
26	157.300	161.900	PUBLIC CORRESPONDENCE (SHIP-TO- COAST). Same as channel 24.
27	157.350	161.950	PUBLIC CORRESPONDENCE (SHIP-TO COAST). Same as channel 24.
28	157.400	162.000	PUBLIC CORRESPONDENCE (SHIP-TO COAST). Same as channel 24.
65	156.275	160.875	INTERNATIONAL USE.
65A	156.275	156.275	PORT OPERATIONS (INTERSHIP AND SHIP- TO-COAST). Same as channel 12.
66	156.325	160.925	INTERNATIONAL USE.
66A	156.325	156.325	PORT OPERATIONS (INTERSHIP AND SHIP- TO-COAST). Same as channel 12.
67	156.375	156.375	COMMERCIAL (INTERSHIP). Same as channel 7A except limited to intership communications. In the New Orleans U.S.C.G. Vessel Traffic Service protection area, use is limited to navigational bridge- to-bridge intership purposes.
68	156.425	156.425	NON-COMMERCIAL (INTERSHIP AND SHIP- TO-COAST). A working channel for non- commercial vessels. May be used for obtaining supplies, scheduling repairs, berthing and accommodations, etc. from yacht clubs or marinas, and intership operational communications such as piloting or arranging for rendezvous with other vessels. It should be noted that channel 68 (and channel 70 for intership only) is the most popular non-commercial channel and therefore is the first choice for vessels having limited channel capacity.
69	156.475	156.475	NON-COMMERCIAL (INTERSHIP AND SHIP- TO-COAST). Same as channel 68.
70	156.525	156.525	DIGITAL SELECTIVE CALLING.
71	156.575	156.575	NON-COMMERCIAL (INTERSHIP AND SHIP- TO-COAST). Same as channel 68.
72	156.625	156.625	NON-COMMERCIAL (INTERSHIP). Same as channel 68, except limited to intership communications.
73	156.675	156.675	PORT OPERATIONS (INTERSHIP AND SHIP- TO-COAST). Same as channel 12.

6

AVAILABLE MARINE CHANNELS AND THEIR USES

Frequencies(MHz)		Channel Usage	
Channel Number	**Ship Transmit**	**Ship Receive**	**Intended Use**
74	156.725	156.725	PORT OPERATIONS (INTERSHIP AND SHIP- TO-COAST). Same as channel 12.
77	156.875	156.875	PORT OPERATIONS (INTERSHIP). Limited to intership communications to and from pilots concerning the docking of ships.
78	156.925	161.525	INTERNATIONAL USE.
78A	156.925	156.925	NON-COMMERCIAL (INTERSHIP AND SHIP- TO COAST). Same as channel 68.
79	156.975	161.575	INTERNATIONAL USE.
79A	156.975	156.975	COMMERCIAL (INTERSHIP AND SHIP-TO- COAST). Same as channel 7A.*
80	157.025	161.625	INTERNATIONAL USE.
80A	157.025	157.025	COMMERCIAL (INTERSHIP AND SHIP-TO COAST). Same as channel 7A*.
81	157.075	161.675	INTERNATIONAL USE.
81A	157.075	157.075	U.S. GOVERNMENT ONLY.
82	157.125	161.725	INTERNATIONAL USE.
82A	157.125	157.125	U.S. GOVERNMENT ONLY.
83	157.175	156.175	INTERNATIONAL USE. (or 161.775)
83A	157.175	157.175	U.S. GOVERNMENT ONLY.
84	157.225	161.825	PUBLIC CORRESPONDENCE (SHIP-TO- COAST). Same as channel 24.
85	157.275	161.875	PUBLIC CORRESPONDENCE (SHIP-TO- COAST). Same as channel 24.
86	157.325	161.925	PUBLIC CORRESPONDENCE (SHIP-TO- COAST). Same as channel 24.
87	157.375	161.975	PUBLIC CORRESPONDENCE (SHIP-TO COAST). Same as channel 24.
88	157.425	162.025	In the areas of the Puget Sound and of the Great Lakes except Lake Michigan and along the St. Lawrence Seaway available for use by ship stations for public correspondence Same as channel 24.
		*	Sharing by non-commercial permitted on the Great Lakes. Other regions may be authorized in the future.
88A	157.425	157.425	COMMERCIAL (INTERSHIP). Except in Lakes Erie, Huron, Ontario, and Superior and along the St Lawrence Seaway. Same as channel 7A except limited to Intership communications and between commercial fishing vessels and associated aircraft while engaged in commercial fishing.

NOTE: The addition of the letter "A" to the channel number indicates that operations on this channel in the United States are different than international operations on this channel. In the United States, stations transmit and receive on the same frequency. Internationally, stations transmit on one frequency and receive on another (different) frequency. The table above lists international use of affected frequencies. When in the service area of a foreign coast station where channels are used in the duplex mode (different transmit and receive frequencies), these international channels should be used. Some VHF transceivers are equipped with a switch for this purpose, i.e. "International - U.S.".

The Coast Guard broadcasts maritime safety information on VHF Channel 22A (157.1 MHz), the ship station transmit frequency portion of international Channel 22 (Appendix 18 of the International Telecommunications Union (ITU) Radio Regulations). Urgent broadcasts are first announced on Channel 16 (156.8 MHz). This simplex use of channel 22A (157.1 MHz) is not compatible with the international duplex arrangement of the channel (coast transmit 161.7 MHz, ship transmit 157.1 MHz). As a result, approximately half of foreign vessels in U.S. waters are unable to receive these safety broadcasts. Operators of vessels who plan to operate in U.S. waters and who do not have VHF radios tunable to USA Channel 22A are encouraged to obtain the necessary equipment.

SINGLE SIDEBAND MARINE RADIO (SSB)

Contacting the U.S. Coastguard

2182 kHz is the international hailing and distress frequency in the medium frequency band. It is monitored by all Coast Guard stations and all commercial vessels when underway.

Emergency Medical Advice may be obtained by contacting the Coast Guard on 2182 kHz or via one of the high frequency channels listed below. The stations listed in the section on High Seas Radiotelephone Service (in the *Almanac*) will immediately transfer emergency calls to the nearest Coast Guard station. No charge is made for such calls when the ship states it is an emergency involving the safety of life or property at sea.

2670 kHz is the Coast Guard working frequency in the MF band. It is used for marine safety, Notice to Mariners and weather broadcasts.

4125 kHz, 6215 kHz, 8291 kHz, 12290 kHz and 16420 kHz are primary high frequency distress and safety calling frequencies. Distress traffic is given precedence over all other traffic. When such traffic is received the U.S. Coast Guard will be notified immediately.

In addition the Coast Guard monitors the following frequencies as part of the CALL (Contact and Long Range Liason) system. These frequencies are also used for voice weather broadcasts, navigation warnings and medical communications. Allow at least one minute for a response before switching channels. The Coast Guard is monitoring many channels at once and may not be able to respond immediately.

Channel	Transmit	Receive
424	4134 kHz	4426 kHz
601	6200 kHz	6501 kHz
816	8240 kHz	8764 kHz
1205	12242 kHz	13089 kHz
1625	16432 kHz	17314 kHz

MARINE RADIOTELEPHONE SERVICES

Three types of marine radio service, described on the following pages, provide full communications coverage for a wide range of needs.

I. HIGH SEAS RADIOTELEPHONE SERVICE (HF)
II. COASTAL HARBOR SERVICE (MF)
III. VHF RADIOTELEPHONE SERVICE

A network of marine radio stations along the nation's coastal waters and major inland waterways is maintained by common carriers. The Marine or High Seas operators at these stations are available to establish your calls at any time of the day or night. The radiotelephone equipment on board your vessel should be capable of radiating adequate power and should be equipped with appropriate radio channels for the radiotelephone service desired. Your radiotelephone equipment dealer can recommend a specific radiotelephone unit to meet your particular needs.

If you plan regular use of Public Marine Radio Telephone Service it is important that you make arrangements with that service. These arrangements can be made at no charge and can expedite calling by saving the air time it would take to otherwise process your call. Users of Coastal Harbor and VHF are assigned Marine Identification Numbers (MINS). These can be obtained by contacting your local telephone company.

1. HIGH SEAS RADIOTELEPHONE SERVICE (HIGH FREQUENCY)

The High Seas Service uses high frequencies to provide long-range radiotelephone communications with similarly equipped vessels throughout the world. Service is provided via coast stations licensed in the United States. These stations operate on various radio channels in the 4 through 23 MHz bands and are equipped for single side band operation.

Single sideband propagation on the radio channels assigned to this service differs with the time of day, season and vessel location. A good rule of thumb is to use the frequency on which you best hear the coast station. Vessel operators contemplating use of this service may obtain information concerning choice of channels for given location, time and season by placing a call or writing to the station operations manager. The addresses, telephone numbers and operating frequencies for WOO, WOM, WAH and WLO are listed in the *Almanac*.

Radio equipment for High Seas operation should be capable of employing various channels in 4 to 23 MHz bands. The following modes of transmission may be used:

A3A – Single Sideband, Reduced Carrier.

A3J – Single Sideband, Suppressed Carrier.

Normally the higher radio frequency channels propagate greater distances so the most important factors are those bands selected. For example, at noon 4 MHz will only operate 100 miles or a little more. When the sun nears the horizon, the range increases. At night 4 MHz is excellent for over 800 miles. The 8 MHz band, on the other hand, has a noon time range of about 600 miles, while at night the signal will travel several thousand miles. Higher frequency bands will generally cover distances up to 10,000 miles.

See the Frequency Selection Guide for more information.

PLACING HIGH SEAS CALLS

Ship-to-Shore

First select the channel for the coast station you wish to contact. Then LISTEN. Don't call until transmissions in progress have been completed. Before completing your call, the High Seas Traffic Operator will ask for your name, the name and telephone number of the party you wish to reach, and the method of billing – paid, collect, marine credit card or third number. Should you need time and charges, advise the operator of this before your call is connected. After your call is completed, stand by until the Technical Operator releases the channel.

RECEIVING HIGH SEAS CALLS

You can receive an incoming call only when your receiver is TURNED ON and TUNED to the frequency of the coast station through which the call is being channelled.

When your vessel is called, answer the Coast Station on a working channel stating your vessel's name, call sign, and location. After contact has been established the Coast Station operator will make any necessary adjustments to provide you with the best possible circuit for your telephone call.

Shore-to-ship

Dial your local operator from any private or pay telephone and ask for the High Seas Operator. Give the vessel's name, call letters (if known) and approximate location, and then follow the operator's instructions. More special information about the vessel is often useful, such as the channel generally monitored for receiving calls and the coast station through which calls can generally be received.

Remember that the ship station generally operates using push-to-talk techniques so that it is impossible for you to break in while the ship station is being received.

High Seas Coast Stations' Facts

Ships, aircraft and coast stations must transmit and receive on their assigned paired channels. "Crossband" operation is strictly forbidden.

All High Seas stations continuously monitor the vessel's transmitting channels.

Do not wait for a traffic list broadcast before making a call. Demand Calling is encouraged.

No calls are accepted on a channel just before it is scheduled to carry a traffic list or weather broadcast. However, when a call is in progress, the broadcast is omitted on the busy channel.

II. COASTAL HARBOR SERVICE (MF)

Public Class II-B Coast Stations

The operating range of this service is normally to distances up to 300 miles. Channels operating in the 2 MHz range are used along the East and West Coast. Vessels may be registered for VHF and Coastal Harbor (MF) Radiotelephone Service by contacting the Telephone company office serving the area in which your account is to be billed – normally a home or business location.

Placing MF or VHF Calls – Ship-to-shore Calls

Monitor the desired coast station channel to determine that it is idle. If known, give the name of the coast station you are calling. When the Marine Operator answers announce: "This is (ship's call sign), and my Marine Identification Number or MIN is (give number)." If you don't have one, give the ship's name and call sign and full billing information. Give the city and telephone number you wish to call. Proceed as directed. At the end of the conversation, repeat your ship's name and call sign and say "out".

Shore-to-ship Calls (MF or VHF) – To Contact a Vessel

Contact the local telephone operator from any private or pay phone and ask for the Marine Operator. Give the Marine Operator the name of the ship you are calling, its call sign, and location if known. If the ship has a Selective Signalling Number, give this to the Marine Operator. Then follow the Marine Operator's instructions.

To Receive a Call From Shore

A vessel's equipment must be operating and tuned to the appropriate channel before receiving public coast station calls. Coast stations routinely make contact through VHF Channel 16 (156.8 MHz) unless the vessel is equipped with selective signalling which permits direct dialling on the coast station transmitting channel.

Vessels are normally contacted directly on the working channel of the (MF) Coastal Harbor coast station. However, if requested by the calling party, initial contact can be made on the distress and call channel (2182 kHz). After initial contact on 156.8 MHz or 2182 kHz, the operator will designate the working channel to which you should shift to complete your call.

If the boatowner expects a call on Coastal Harbor (MF) frequencies, he should notify the prospective caller whether he will be monitoring a working frequency.

Since it is mandatory on commercial vessels that a watch be maintained on the Distress and Calling channels 16 or 2182 kHz, an additional receiver may be used on board to monitor for calls on the working channel of the local coast station. This receiver may also be equipped with a selective calling device.

When your vessel is called, announce: "This is (name your vessel and call sign), over." Then proceed as instructed.

Ship-to-ship Calls (MF or VHF) – Via Marine Operator

Your Marine Operator can connect you with vessels which may be beyond your normal vessel-to-vessel transmitting range. To do so, contact the Marine Operator in the regular ship-to-shore fashion, and give the name, call sign, location and Selective Signalling Number (if known) of the vessel you are calling.

On completion of the call, sign off by announcing your vessel's name and call sign.

Direct Calls

Direct contact with another vessel requires that compatible equipment operating on the same channel be used on each vessel.

Most direct ship-to-ship calls are initiated on the distress safety and calling frequency – VHF Channel 16 (156.8 MHz), or on Coastal Harbor (MF) 2182 kHz.

When the channel is clear, give the name of the vessel being called, and give your own call sign and ship's name. When the called vessel answers, an intership frequency should be chosen on which to continue the conversation. Limit calls to three minutes except for emergencies. On completion of the call, sign off with the name of your vessel and its call sign. Except for distress and safety traffic no repeat calls to the same party can be made for at least 10 minutes.

Technical Data

VHF licensed equipment must be provided prior to installing SSB equipment.

III. VHF RADIO TELEPHONE SERVICE

This system provides reliable operation and good transmission quality over distances of 20 to 50 miles, via FM and channels in the 156-162 MHz range. Since VHF provides essentially line-of-sight communications, antenna height and equipment quality aboard your vessel are basic to the distance of transmission. This service performs better than systems operating on the lower frequencies because there is less atmospheric noise at the higher VHF frequencies and there is virtually no ionispheric "skip" which could bring in interfering signals from hundreds or thousands of miles away.

FREQUENCY SELECTION GUIDE

This chart is greatly simplified. The winter/ summer cycle and sunspot activity will alter propagation. In general, if you can hear traffic clearly you will be able to transmit successfully on the same channel or band. Always listen for other traffic before transmitting on a particular channel. After transmitting wait several minutes for a response before trying again.

Listen to traffic lists and weather reports at various times. Use your radio log to record the best times and frequencies for communicating with these stations.

	Distance in Nautical Miles		
Local Time	*200-750 NM*	*750-1500 NM*	*More Than 1500 NM*
0000	3-5 MHz	6-9 MHz	6-11 MHz
0400	3-5 MHz	4-7 MHz	6-9 MHz
0800	3-7 MHz	6-11 MHz	11-22MHz
1200	4-7 MHz	8-13 MHz	13-22 MHz
1600	4-7 MHz	8-13 MHz	13-22 MHz
2000	3-7 MHz	6-11 MHz	11-22 MHz

Except for the hand held variety, all VHF sets are rated at 25 watts with the capability of reducing to one watt as required by law. There are two general categories: those covering all the U.S. frequencies and those covering U.S. plus international frequencies.

Under current FCC rules, VHF must be aboard ship before MF equipment can be licensed. In addition, VHF must be used in preference to MF when the vessel is within range of VHF shore station. For information on placing or receiving calls on VHF, see the Coastal Harbor Service section.

INMARSAT SYSTEMS

The idyllic remoteness of the high seas is one of the attractions of sailing, but as any ocean-going yachtsman knows, this isolation can have serious disadvantages.

The high seas can be an unpredictable and dangerous environment where reliable communications for information and assistance are indispensable and for some in the business world, the possibility of being cut off for even a few hours from their offices might prevent them from going to sea at all. Access to a reliable, easy to use communications link can make any voyage better, more enjoyable and safer. Today, a growing number of yachts of 80 ft. and beyond, are being fitted with mobile satcoms equipment that enables world-wide direct-dial telephone, fax and data communications.

Known as Inmarsat-A, this global communications system is available around the clock for ocean-going yachts wherever they may be sailing. Fig. 1 shows a yacht fitted with an Inmarsat-A terminal, the white radome antenna visible at the top. Each satellite terminal has a unique number, and making a call either to or from is as simple as using the telephone in the office or at home. The facsimile, telex and data communications facilities are just as easy to use. Inmarsat-A also connects easily into the world's electronic mail networks, using a built-in personal computer.

A range of specialized services is also offered, e.g. using modern data compression techniques it is possible to send and receive high quality photographs to and from an on-board terminal. These techniques can also enable the system to be used for transmitting still and moving video images. A video signal coming from a camera can be manipulated by a computer as an ordinary graphic. This graphic can in turn be enlarged or decreased in size or rotated; colors and contrasts can be changed and then the graphic is saved as a file, compressed and transmitted via Inmarsat-A to an office onshore where, for instance, it can be imported into desk-top publishing software. Ships at sea can receive instant advice on the repair of engines and other critical parts by faxing a photograph of the faulty section to an on-shore agent who can then pinpoint the defect and suggest methods of repair immediately.

The ability to transmit text, graphics and photographs via the system has enabled news networks on shore to reach a ship on the high seas and many yacht owners have up-to-date electronic 'newspapers' and weather charts delivered to them.

Even with all of these advanced capabilities, Inmarsat-A is extremely easy to operate and does not require the skills of a radio officer. Thirteen terminal models are available. Essentially, these consist of an above-the-deck parabolic antenna encased in a weatherproof radome. Below decks is the electronics and peripheral equipment such as a telephone, facsimile and computer. Terminals are available with up to four channels. Some large yachts are fitted with two separate terminals for different applications.

SATCOMS FOR SMALL YACHTS

The size and cost of Inmarsat-A equipment means that smaller yachts may not find it suitable to their requirements. Many yachtsmen with craft as small as 30 ft. and those for whom voice communications are not critical, need an affordable communications system that can fit on to even the smallest yacht. Until recently, no such communication link existed for those small boat owners and operators who ventured into high seas.

The alternative for the small boat owner is Inmarsat-C, a store-and-forward data messaging system, which is able to send messages in any language or character set. These messages can be originated or delivered in many forms such as telex, electronic mail, switched data, or a message forwarded as a fax from your yacht to a shore destination. Fig. 2 shows a sailing yacht fitted with this equipment.

Inmarsat-C antennas are small enough to be fitted to a vessel of any size or even to be carried in one hand. They are also light, omnidirectional and the terminals have low power requirements. Below-decks equipment is neat, compact and simple to install on any boat. Fig. 3 shows a typical below-decks installation.

The system's simplicity extends to its operation. Anyone who has used a personal computer, word processor or a telex machine can use Inmarsat-C and touchscreen computers can be connected to send handwritten messages.

Every terminal in the system is allocated a discrete identity number and only messages addressed to that number are received. This, along with its digital transmission mode, automatically provides a high level of security for users.

While Inmarsat-C is a store-and-forward communications system, it can deliver messages in a very short time to anybody in the world, possible because of its connectibility into international data networks. It also makes possible a range of services such as data reporting, position reporting and polling.

Yacht captains can program their terminals to transmit regular data reports of the condition of vessels and other operational information to shore-based offices. Alternatively, shore-based managers and yacht owners can 'poll' or interrogate ships, automatically or manually, for receiving the same information.

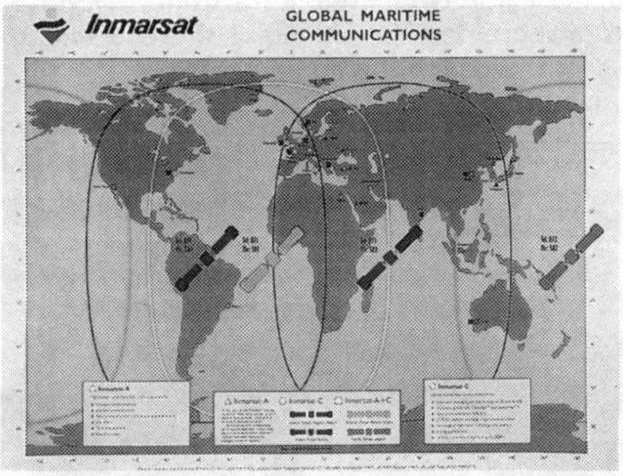

Inmarsat-C can also be connected to positioning devices like GPS receivers to enable ships at sea to send periodic position reports to shore. The terminals can be programmed to do this automatically at regular intervals or they can transmit position reports manually. Besides GPS, Inmarsat-C can also use inputs from other positioning systems such as Glonass, Decca and Loran.

While Inmarsat-C is used primarily for two-way messaging communications between mobile terminals and fixed communications points on shore, its flexibility is such that it can support many value-added services. Shore based service providers offer regularly updated weather reports, stock market information. news and electronic mail services.

Terminals fitted with an optional Enhanced Group Call capability, are able to receive two categories of messages known As SafetyNET™ and FleetNET™. SafetyNET™ is specifically designed for the distribution of safety information provided by hydrographic, meteorological, coastguard and search and rescue coordination authorities. Messages can be targeted to boats in or approaching specific geographic regions, such as the area around a hazard or a ship in distress.

FleetNET™ can be used to transmit trade information, such as company news or market prices, simultaneously to selected groups of ships. Using FleetNET™, subscription services can provide ships with up-to-the-minute news and stock prices.

Fig.4 depicts the global satellite coverage operated by Inmarsat, a London-based international enterprise with 64 member countries. The satellites are in orbit over the equator, providing communications to all of the earth's surface except the extreme polar regions.

Users can also choose to route their calls through any of a growing number of Coast Earth Stations around the world which act as gateways, delivering messages into public telephone and data networks on shore, and also channelling calls from shore onward to mobile terminals.

Significantly, fitting Inmarsat-C and/or Inmarsat-A terminals on yachts is also an efficient way for boats operating outside of coastal radio coverage, to meet the long range communications requirement of the Global Maritime Distress and Safety Systems (GMDSS). See Chapter 15. The Inmarsat-C Safety NET™ service meets GMDSS requirements for shore-to-ship distress alerting.

A further system. Inmarsat-M will provide satellite telephone services through lightweight, low-cost terminals, offering all-digital telephony and facsimile services. Inmarsat-M specifications will allow the customer terminals to be smaller than Inmarsat-A, have lower power requirements, and low terminal and operating costs.

For those who require it, combinations of Inmarsat-C with Inmarsat-M/A will allow for substantial flexibility of Satcoms to suit individual needs. Satellite communications will be available to more boats than ever before and the idyll of the high seas will never be ominous again.

Tides and Tidal Currents

10

TIDE PREDICTIONS

Reed's Nautical Almanac contains the predicted times and heights of the high and low waters for each day of the year at a number of places which are designated as *reference stations.* By using tidal differences one can calculate the approximate times and heights of the tide at many other places which are called *subordinate stations.*

High water is the maximum height reached by each rising tide, and low water is the minimum height reached by each falling tide. High and low waters can be selected from the predictions by the comparison of consecutive heights. Because of diurnal inequality at certain places, however, there may be a difference of only a few tenths of a foot between one high water and low water of a day, but a marked difference in heights between the other high water and low water. It is essential, therefore, in using the tide tables to note carefully the heights as well as the times of the tides.

Time: The kind of time used for the predictions at each reference station is indicated by the time meridian on each page. Daylight saving time is used in Reed's.

Datum: The datum from which the predicted heights are recorded is the same as that used for the charts of the locality. The datum for the Atlantic coast of the United States is mean lower low water (MLLW). The datum for the Pacific coast of the United States (including Hawaii and Alaska) is the mean of the lower of the two low waters of each day. For foreign coasts a datum approximating to mean low water springs, Indian spring low water, or the lowest possible low water is generally used. The depression of the datum below mean sea level (MSL) for each of the reference stations in Reed's is given in table 1.

Depth of water: The nautical charts published by the United States and other maritime nations show the depth of the water as referred to a low water datum corresponding to that from which the

TIDAL DEFINITIONS

A DIAGRAM OF SPECIFIC TIDAL HEIGHTS (USA)

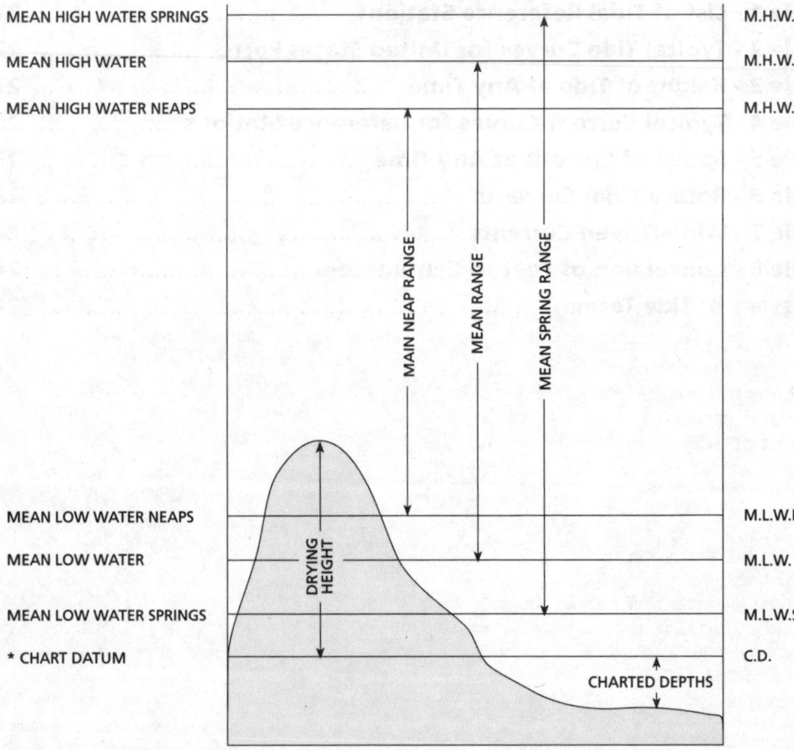

predicted tidal heights are recorded. To find the actual depth of water at any time the height of the tide should be added to the charted depth. If the height of the tide is negative – that is, if there is a minus sign (–) before the tabular height – the height should be subtracted from the charted depth. For any time between high and low water, the height of the tide may be estimated from the heights of the preceding and the following tides, or table 3 may be used.

Variation in sea level: Changes in winds and barometric conditions cause variations in sea level from day to day. In general, with onshore winds or a low barometer the heights of both the high and low waters will be higher than predicted while with offshore winds or a high barometer they will be lower. There are also seasonal variations in sea level, but these variations have been included in the predictions for each station. At ocean stations the seasonal variation in sea level is usually less than half a foot.

At stations on tidal rivers the average seasonal variation in river level due to freshets and droughts may be considerably more than a foot. The predictions for these stations include an allowance for this seasonal variation representing average freshet and drought conditions. Unusual freshets or droughts, however, will cause the tides to be higher or lower, respectively, than predicted.

Number of tides: There are usually two high and two low waters in a day. Tides follow the moon more closely than they do the sun, and the lunar or tidal day is about 50 minutes longer than the solar day. This causes the tide to occur later each day, and a tide that has occurred near the end of one calendar day will be followed by a corresponding tide that may skip the next day and occur in the early morning of the third day. Thus on certain days of each month only a single high or a single low water occurs. At some stations, during portions of each months, the tide becomes diurnal – that is, only one high and one low water will occur during the period of a lunar day.

Relation of tide to current: In using tables of tide predictions it must be borne in mind that they give the times and heights of high and low waters and not the times of turning of the current or slack water. For stations on the outer coast there is usually but little difference between the time of high or low on tidal rivers, the time of slack water may differ by several hours from the time of high or low water stand. The relation of the times of high and low water to the turning of the current depends upon a number of factors, so no simple or general rule can be given. For the predicted time of slack water, and other current data, reference should be made to the tidal current tables.

Typical tide curves: The variations in the tide from day to day and from place to place are illustrated in Table 2 by the tide curves for representative ports along the Atlantic and Pacific coasts of the United States. It will be noted that the range of tide for stations along the Atlantic coast varies from place to place but that the type is uniformly semidiurnal with the principal variations following the changes in the Moon's distance and phase. In the Gulf of Mexico, however, the range of tide is uniformly small but the type of tide differs considerably. At certain ports such as Pensacola there is usually but one high and one low water a day while at other ports such as Galveston the inequality is such that the tide is semidiurnal around the times the moon is on the Equator but becomes diurnal around the times of maximum north or such declination of the moon. In the Gulf of Mexico, consequently, the principal variations in the tide are due to the changing declination of the moon. Key West, at the entrance to the Gulf of Mexico, has a type of tide which is a mixture of semidaily and daily types. Here the tide is semidiurnal but there is considerable inequality in the heights of high and low waters. By reference to the curves it will be seen that where the inequality is large there are times when there is but a few tenths of a foot difference between high water and low water.

Table 2 also shows tide curves for representative parts along the Pacific coast. It will be noted that one of the chief characteristics of the tide in this region is diurnal inequality, i.e., the difference in heights in successive high waters or low waters. The largest inequality is in the low waters although at Seattle there is also considerable difference between the two high waters on certain days. The importance of this inequality at Seattle is brought out by the curve which shows that at times the two high waters of a day differ by over 4 feet and the two low waters differ by more than 8 feet. At Ketchikan and Anchorage the inequality is less pronounced because of the large range of tide. In these localities the principal variations in the tide follow the changes in the Moon's phase and distance. The tide at Anchorage is one of the largest in the world. At Unalaska and Dutch Harbor the type of tide is such that it is semidiurnal around the times the moon is on the Equator, but becomes diurnal around the times of maximum north or south declination of the moon.

TIDAL DIFFERENCES

The publication of full daily predictions in Reed's Nautical Almanac is necessarily limited to a comparatively small number of stations. Tide predictions for many other places, however, can be obtained by applying certain differences to the predictions for the reference stations. These differences or ratios are to be applied to the predictions for the proper reference station which is listed above the differences for the subordinate station. The stations are arranged in geographical order. The index at the end of Reed's Nautical Almanac will assist in locating a particular station.

Caution: The time and height differences listed are average differences derived from comparisons of simultaneous tide observations at the subordinate location and its reference station. Because these figures are constant, they may not always provide for the daily variations of the actual tide, especially if the subordinate station is some distance from the reference station. Therefore, it must be realized that although the application of the time and height differences will generally provide reasonably accurate approximations, they cannot result in as accurate predictions as those for the reference stations which are based upon much larger periods of analyses and which do provide for daily variations.

Time differences: To determine the time of high water or low water at any station there is given in the columns headed "Time Differences" the hours and minutes to be added to or subtracted from the time of high or low water at some reference station. A plus (+) sign indicated that the tide at the subordinate station is later than at the reference station and the difference should be added, a minus (–) sign that it is earlier and should be subtracted.

To obtain the tide at a subordinate station on any date apply the difference to the tide at the reference station for that same date. In some cases, however, to obtain an a.m. tide it may be necessary to use the preceding day's p.m. tide at the reference station, or to obtain a p.m. tide it may be necessary to use the following day's a.m. tide. For example, if a high water occurs at a reference station at 2200 on July 2, and the tide at the subordinate station occurs 3 hours later, then high water will occur at 0100 on July 3 at the subordinate station. For the second case, if a high water at a reference station occurs at 0200 on July 17, and the tide at the subordinate station occurs 5 hours earlier, the high water at the subordinate station will occur at 2100 on July 16.

Differences in time meridians between a subordinate station and its reference station have been accounted for and no further adjustment by the reader is necessary. Daylight Saving Time is used in Reed's.

Height differences: The height of the tide, referred to the datum of charts, is obtained by means of the height differences or ratios. A plus (+) sign indicates that the difference should be added to the height at the reference station and a minus (–) sign that it should be subtracted. All height differences, ranges, and levels are in feet but may be converted to centimeters by the use of table 8.

Ratio: For some stations height differences would give unsatisfactory predictions. In such cases they have been omitted and one or two ratios are given. Where two ratios are given, one in the "height of high water" column and one in the "height of low water" column, the high waters and low waters at the reference station should be multiplied by these respective ratios. Where only one is given, the omitted ratio is either unreliable or unkown.

(1)		(2)	(3)	(4)		
Time H.m.	Height Ft.	Time Corrections	Height Corrections	Time H.m.	Height Ft	Height Centimeters
0313	3.8	+0 46	X0.48 + 2.8	0359	4.6	140
0921	15.2	+0 34	X0.48 + 2.8	0955	10.1	308
1601	-0.4	+0 46	X0.48 + 2.8	1647	2.6	79
2230	14.1	+0 34	X0 48 + 2.8	2304	9.6	293

For some subordinate stations there is given in parentheses a ratio as well as a correction in feet. In those instances, each predicted high and low water at the reference station should first be multiplied by the ratio and then the correction in feet is to be added to or subtracted from each product as indicated.

As an example, at Treadwell Bay the values in the time and height difference columns are given as +0 34, +0 46, and (*0.48 + 2.8) as referred to the reference station at Ketchikan, Alaska. If we assume that the tide predictions in column (1) below are those of Ketchikan on a particular day, application of the time and height corrections in columns (2) and (3) would result in the tide predictions for Treadwell Bay in column (4).

Datum: The datum of the predictions obtained through the height differences or ratios is also the datum of the largest scale chart for the locality. To obtain the depths at the time of high or low water, the predicted heights should be added to the depth on the chart unless such height is negative (–), when it should be subtracted. To find the height at times between high and low water see Table 3. On some charts the depths are given in meters or centimeters and in such cases the heights of the tide can be reduced to other units by the use of Table 8. Chart datums for the portion of the world covered by these tables are approximately as follows: *Mean lower low water* for the Pacific coast of the United States, Alaska and the Hawaiin Islands; *mean low water springs* for Central America and Mexico. For the rest of the area covered by these tables the datums generally used are approximately *mean low water springs, Indian spring low water,* or the *lowest possible low water.*

CURRENT PREDICTIONS

Current tables give the predicted times of slack water and the predicted times and speeds of maximum current-flood and ebb-for each day of the year. The times are given in hours and minutes and the speeds in knots.

Time: The kind of time used for the predictions at each reference station is indicated by the time meridian on each page.

Slack water and maximum current: The columns headed "Slack time" contain the predicted times at which there is no current; or, in other words, the times at which the current has stopped setting in a given direction and is about to begin to set in the opposite direction. Offshore, where the current is rotary, slack water denotes the time of minimum current. Beginning with the slack water before flood the current increases in speed until the strength or maximum speed of the flood current is reached; it then decreases until the following slack water or slack before ebb. The ebb current now begins, increases to a maximum speed, and then decreases to the next slack. The predicted times and speeds of maximum current are given in the columns headed "Max Time".

Direction of set: As the terms flood and ebb do not in all cases clearly indicate the direction of the current, the approximate direction toward which the currents flow are given at the top of each page to distinguish the two streams.

Number of slacks and strengths: There are usually four slacks and four maximums each day. When a vacancy occurs in any day, the slack or maximum that seems to be missing will be found to occur soon after midnight as the first slack or maximum of the following day. At some stations where the diurnal inequality is large, there may be on certain days a continous flood or ebb current with varying speed throughout half the day giving only two slacks and two maximums on that particular day.

Current and tide: It is important to notice that the predicted slacks and strengths given in these tables refer to the horizontal motion of the water and not to the vertical rise and fall of the tide. The relation of current to tide is not constant, but varies from place to place, and the time of slack water does not generally coincide with the time of high or low water, nor does the time of maximum speed of the current usually coincide with the time of most rapid change in the vertical height of the tide. At stations located on a tidal river or bay the time of slack water may differ from 1 to 3 hours from the time of high or low water.

Variations from predictions: In using this table it should be borne in mind that actual times of slack or maximum occasionally differ from the predicted times by as much as half an hour and in rare instances the difference may be as much as an hour. Comparisons of predicted with observed times of slack water indicate that more than 90 percent of the slack waters occurred within half an hour of the predicted times. To make sure, therefore, of getting the full advantage of a favorable current or slack water, the navigator should reach the entrance or strait at least half an hour before the predicted time of the desired condition of current. Currents are frequently disturbed by wind or variations in river discharge. On days when the current is affected by such disturbing influences the times and speeds will differ from those given in the table, but local knowledge will enable one to make proper allowance for these effects.

Typical current curves: The variations in the tidal current from day to day and from place to place are illustrated in Table 4 by the current curves for representative ports along the Atlantic and Pacific coast of the United States. Flood current is represented by the solid line curve above the zero speed (slack water) line and the ebb current by the broken line curve below the slack water line. The curves show clearly that the currents along the Atlantic coast are semi-daily (two floods and two ebbs in a day) in character with their principal variations following changes in the moon's distance and phase. In the Gulf of Mexico, however, the currents are daily in character. As the dominant factor is the change in the moon's declination the currents in the Gulf tend to become semi-daily when the moon is near the Equator. By reference to the curves it will be noted that with this daily type of current there are times when the current may be erratic (marked with an asterisk), or one flood or ebb current of the day may be quite weak. Therefore in using the predictions of the current it is essential to carefully note the speeds as well as the times.

The tables also have current curves for representative ports, along the Pacific Coast.

The outstanding feature of the currents in this region is the diurnal inequality, i.e., the difference in speed of two consecutive flood or two consecutive ebb maximums. This inequality varies directly with the moon's declination; consequently it tends to disappear when the moon is near the Equator. By reference to the curves it will be noted that at certain places the inequality is chiefly in the flood currents. At Seymour Narrows the two floods of a day sometimes differ by 5 knots. At other places the inequality is chiefly in the ebb currents, while at still other places there is a marked inequality in both flood and ebb currents. The effect of the inequality at some places is such that there are times when the current may be erratic (marked by an asterisk) or one flood or ebb current of the day may be quite weak. Therefore in using the predictions of the current it is essential to carefully note the speeds as well as the times.

CURRENT DIFFERENCES

Reed's Nautical Almanac reference stations are those for which daily predictions are listed. The principal purpose of Current Differences is to present data that will enable one to determine the approximate times of minimum currents (slack waters) and the times and speeds of maximum currents at numerous subordinate stations. By applying the specific corrections given to the predicted times and speeds of the current at the appropriate reference station, reasonable approximations of the current at the subordinate station may be compiled.

Locations and Depths: Because the latitude and longitude are listed according to the exactness recorded in the original survey records, the locations of the subordinate stations are presented in varying degrees of accuracy. Since a minute of latitude is nearly equivalent to a mile, a location given to the nearest minute may not indicate the exact position of the station. This should be remembered, especially in the case of a narrow stream, where the nearest minute of latitude or longtidue may locate a station inland. In such cases, unless the descrption locates the station elsewhere, reference is made to the current in the center of the channel. In some instances, the charts may not present a convenient name for locating a station. In those cases, the position may be described by a bearing from some prominent place on the chart.

Although current measurements may have been recorded at various depths in the past, the data listed here for most of the subordinate stations are mean values determined to have been representative of the current at each location. For that reason, no specific current meter depths for those stations are given. Beginning with the Boston Harbor tidal current survey in 1971, data for individual meter depths were published and subsequent new data may be presented in a similar manner.

Since most of the current data came from meters suspended from survey vessels or anchored buoys, the listed depths are those measured downward from the surface. Some later data have come from meters anchored at fixed depths from the bottom. Those meter positions were defined as depths below chart datum. Such depths in Reed's will be accompanied by the small letter "d".

Minimum Currents: The reader may note that at many locations the current may not diminish to a true slack water or zero speed stage. For that reason, the phrases, "minimum before flood" and "minimum before ebb' are used rather than "slack water" although either or both minimums may actually reach a zero speed value at some locations.

Maximum Currents: Near the coast and in inland tidal waters, the current increases from minimum current (slack water) for a period of about 3 hours until the maximum speed or the strength of the current is reached. The speed then decreases for another period of about 3 hours when minimum current is again reached and the current begins a similar cycle in the opposite direction. The current that flows toward the coast or up a stream is known as the flood current; the opposite flow is known as the ebb current.

Differences and Speed Ratios: Current Difference tables contain mean time differences by which the reader can compile approximate times for the minimum and maximum current phases at the subordinate stations. It will be seen upon inspection that some subordinate stations exhibit either a double flood or a double ebb stage, or both. Explanations of these stages can be found in the glossary located elsewhere in this publication. In those cases, a separate time difference is listed for each of the three flood (or ebb) phases and these should be applied only to the daily maximum flood (or ebb) phase at the reference station. The results obtained by the application of the time differences will be based upon the time meridian shown above the name of the subordinate station. Differences of time meridians between a subordinate station and its reference station have been accounted for and no further adjustment by the reader is needed. Daylight Saving Time is used in Reed's.

The speed ratios are used to compile approximations of the daily current speeds at the subordinate stations and refer only to the maximum floods and ebbs. No attempt is made to predict the speeds of the minimum currents. Normally, these ratios should be applied to the corresponding maximum current phases at the reference station. As mentioned above, however, some subordinate stations may exhibit either a double flood or a double ebb or both. As with the time differences, separate ratios are listed for each of the three flood (or ebb phases) and should be applied only to the daily maximum flood (or ebb) speed at the reference station. It should be noted that although the speed of a given current phase at a subordinate station is obtained by reference to the corresponding phase at the reference station, the directions of the current at the two places may differ considerably.

WIND-DRIVEN CURRENTS

A wind continuing for some time will produce a current the speed of which depends on the speed of the wind, and unless the current is deflected by some other cause, the deflective force of the Earth's rotation will cause it to set to the right of the direction of the wind in the northern hemisphere and to the left in the southern hemishpere.

The current produced at off-shore locations by local winds of various strengths and directions has been investigated from observations made at lightships (some of which have since been moved). The averages obtained are given below and may prove helpful in estimating the probable current that may result from various winds at the several locations.

Caution: There were of course many departures from these averages of speed and direction, for the wind-driven current often depends not only on the length of time the wind blows but also on factors other than the local wind at the time and place of the current. The mariner must not, therefore, assume that the given wind will always produce the indicated current.

It should be remembered, too, that the current which a vessel experiences at any time is the resultant of the combined actions of the tidal current, the wind-driven current, and any other currents such as the Gulf Stream or currents due to river discharge.

Speed: The following table shows the average speed of the current due to winds of various strengths.

Direction: The position of the shoreline with respect to the station influences considerably the direction of the currents due to certain winds. Table 7 shows for each station the average number of degrees by which the wind-driven current is deflected to the right or

Wind speed (miles per hour)	10	20	30	40	50
Average current speed (knots) due to wind at following lightship stations					
Boston and Barnegat	0·1	0·1	0·2	0·3	0·3
Diamond Shoal and Cape Lookout Shoals	0·5	0·6	0·7	0·8	1.0
All other locations on the Atlantic Coast	0·2	0·3	0·4	0·5	0·6
Wind speed (miles per hour)	10	20	30	40	50
Average current speed (knots) due to wind at following lightship stations:*					
San Francisco	0·3	0·3	0·5	0·6	0·7
Blunts Reef	0·2	0·3	0·4	0·7	0·8
Columbia River	0·4	0·5	0·6	0·8	0·8
Umatilla Reef	0·2	0·6	0·9	1·0	0·9
Swiftsure Bank	0·5	0·5	0·5	0·7	0·8

*** All of these lightships have since been removed.**

left of the wind. Thus at the former location of the San Francisco Lightship the table indicates that with a north wind the wind-driven current flows on the average 061° west of south, and with an east wind if flows 023° north of west.

THE COMBINATION OF CURRENTS

In determining from the current tables the speed and direction of the current at any time, it is frequently necessary to combine the tidal current with the wind-driven current. The following methods indicate how the resultant of two or more currents may be easily determined.

Currents in the same direction: When two or more currents set in the same direction it is a simple matter to combine them. The resultant current will have a speed which is equal to the sum of all the currents and it will set in the same direction.

For example, a vessel is near the Nantucket Shoals station at a time when the tidal current is setting 120° with a speed of 0.6 knot, and at the same time a wind of 40 miles per hour is blowing from the west; what current will the vessel be subject to at that time? Since a wind of 40 miles per hour from the west will give rise to a current setting 120° with a speed of 0.5 knot, the combined tidal and wind-driven currents will set in the same direction (120°) with a speed of 0.6 +0.5 = 1.1 knots.

Currents in opposite directions: The combination of currents setting in opposite directions is likewise a simple matter. The speed of the resultant current is the difference between the opposite setting currents, and the direction of the resultant current is the same as that of the greater current.

As an example, let it be required to determine the speed of the current at the Nantucket Shoals station when the tidal current is setting 205° with a speed of 0.8 knot, and when a wind of 40 miles per hour is blowing from the south. The current produced by a wind of 40 miles per hour from the south would set 025° with a speed of 0.5 knot. The tidal and wind-driven currents therefore set in opposite directions, the tidal current being the stronger. Hence the resultant current will set in the direction of the tidal current (205°) with a speed of 0.8 – 0.5 = 0.3 knot.

Currents in different directions: The combination of two or more currents setting neither in the same nor in opposite direction, while not as simple as in the previous cases, is nevertheless not difficult, the best method being a graphic method. Taking the combination of two currents as the simplest case, we draw from a given point as origin, a line the direction of which is the direction of one of the currents to be combined and whose length represents the speed of that current to some suitable scale; from the end of this line we draw another line the direction and length of which, to the same scale, represents the other of the currents to be combined; then a line joining the origin with the end of our second line gives the direction and speed of the resultant current.

As an example, let us take Nantucket Shoals station at a time when the tidal current is 0.7 knot setting 355° and a wind of 50 miles per hour is blowing from the west-southwest; the wind-driven current according to the preceding chapter would therefore be about 0.6 knot setting 085°.

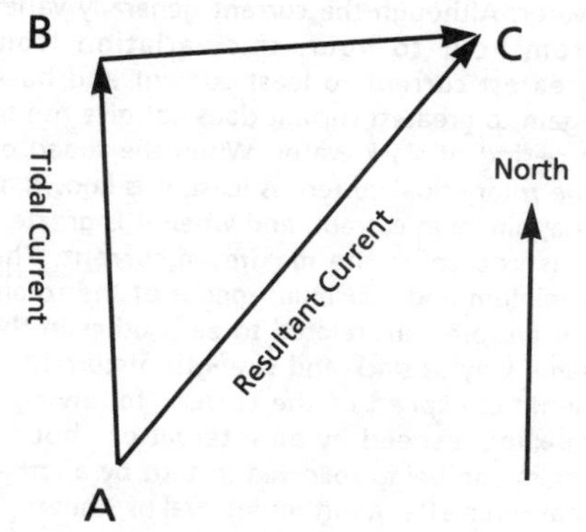

Combination of tidal current and wind-driven current

Using a scale of 2 inches to the knot we draw from point A in the diagram above, the line AB 1.4 inches in length directed 355° to represent the tidal current. From B we then draw the line BC 1.2 inches in length directed 085° to represent the wind current. The line AC represents the resultant current and on being measured is found to be about 1.8 inches in length directed 035° with a speed of 0.9 knot.

The combination of three or more currents is made in the same way as above, the third current to be combined being drawn from point C, the resultant current being given by joining the origin A with the end of the last line. For drawing the lines, a parallel rule and compass rose will be found convenient, or a protractor or polar coordinate paper may be used.

ROTARY TIDAL CURRENTS

Offshore and in some of the wider indentations of the coast, the tidal current is quite different from that found in the more protected bays and rivers. In these inside waters the tidal current is of the reversing type. It sets in one direction for a period of about 6 hours after which it ceases to flow momentarily and then sets in the opposite direction during the following 6 hours. Offshore the current, not being confined to a definite channel, changes its direction continually and never comes to a slack, so that in a tidal cycle of about 12.5 hours it will have set in all directions of the compass. This type of current is therefore called a rotary current.

A characteristic feature of the rotary current is the absence of slack water. Although the current generally varies from hour to hour, this variation from greatest current to least current and back again to greatest does not give rise to a period of slack water. When the speed of the rotary tidal current is least, it is known as the minimum current, and when it is greatest it is known as the maximum current. The minimum and maximum speeds of the rotary current are thus related to each other in the same way as slack and strength of current, a minimum speed of the current following a maximum speed by an interval of about 3 hours and being followed in turn by another maximum after a further interval of 3 hours.

In Table 6 there are given for a number of offshore stations the direction and average speed of the rotary tidal current for each hour of the tidal cycle referred to predictions for a station in Reed's Nautical Almanac.

The speeds given in the table are average. The Moon at new, full, or perigee tends to increase the speeds 15 to 20 percent above average. When perigee occurs at or near the time of new or full Moon the speeds will be 30 to 40 percent above average. Quadrature and apogee tend to decrease the speeds below average by 15 to 20 percent. When apogee occurs at or near quadrature they will be 30 to 40 percent below average. The speeds will be about average when apogee occurs at or near the time of new or full Moon and also when perigee occurs at or near quadrature.

The direction of the current is given in degrees, true, reading clockwise from 0° at north, and is the direction toward which the water is flowing.

The speeds and directions are for the tidal current only and do not include the effect of winds. When a wind is blowing, a wind-driven current will be set up which will be in addition to the tidal current, and the actual current encountered will be a combination of the wind-driven current and tidal current. See the section on "Wind-Driven Currents" and "The Combination of Currents".

As an example, in the following table the current at Nantucket Shoals is given for each hour after maximum flood at Pollock Rip Channel. Suppose it is desired to find the direction and speed of the current at Nantucket Shoals at 3:15 p.m. (15:15) eastern standard time on a day when maximum flood at Pollock Rip Channel is predicted to occur at 13:20 eastern standard time. The desired time is therefore about 2 hours after maximum flood at Pollock Rip Channel, and from the following table the tidal current at Nantucket Shoals at this time is setting 15° true with an average speed of 0.8 knot. If this day is near the time of new Moon and about halfway between apogee and perigee, then the distance effect of the Moon will be nil and the phase effect alone will operate to increase the speed by about 15 percent, to 0.9 knot. If a wind has been blowing, determine the direction and speed of the wind-driven current from the section on "Wind-Driven Currents" and combine it with the above tidal current as explained in the section on "The Combination of Currents."

Caution: Speeds from 1.5 to 3 knots have been observed at most of the stations in this table. Near Diamond Shoal Light a speed of 4 knots has been recorded.

At some offshore stations, such as near the entrance to Chesapeake Bay, the tidal current is directed alternately toward and away from the bay entrance with intervening periods of slack water, so that it is essentially a reversing current. For such places, differences for predicting are given after the applicable reference station in Reed's Nautical Almanac.

PACIFIC COASTAL TIDAL CURRENTS

The term coastal tidal current is used here to designate the tidal current found offshore from 5 to 20 miles from the coast. The data were based upon observations made through the cooperation of the U.S. Coast Guard at a number of lightship stations along the Pacific coast from San Francisco to Swiftsure Bank, off the coast of Washington.

Rotary current: Offshore, away from the immediate influences of the coast, the tidal current is quite different from the current found in inland tidal waters. Instead of setting in one direction for a period of 6 hours and in the opposite direction during the following period of 6 hours, the tidal current offshore changes its direction continually, so that in a period of about 12.5 hours it will have set in all directions of the compass. This type of current is therefore called a rotary current.

Minimum current: A characteristic feature of the rotary current is the absence of slack water. Although the current generally varies from hour to hour, this variation from greatest current to least current and back again to greatest current does not give rise to a period of slack water. When the speed of the rotary tidal current is least, it is known as the minimum current, and when it is greatest it is known as the maximum current. The minimum and maximum speeds of the rotary current are thus related to each other in the same way as slack and strength of current, a minimum speed of the current following a maximum speed by an interval of about 3 hours and being followed in turn by another maximum after a further interval of 3 hours.

Changes in tidal current: The speeds of the tidal current given here are average speeds. Near the times when the Moon is full or new the speeds of the tidal current will be about 20 percent, or one-fifth greater than the average, and near the times of the Moon's first and third quarters the speeds will be smaller than the average by one-fifth.

Effect of wind: It is to be carefully noted that, when a wind is blowing, the current a vessel will encounter is the resultant of the tidal and wind currents. Only the tidal currents together with the greatest observed speed of the current at each light vessel are given here, and the mariner is cautioned to combine with the tidal current the current brought about by any wind that may be blowing. Wind currents are given under the heading, "Wind-driven Currents".

Direction and Speed of current: The direction of the current is true, not magnetic, and is the direction toward which the current is setting, while the wind when given is in the direction from which it is blowing. The speed of the current is given in knots or nautical miles per hour.

Reference to tides: The tidal currents on the Pacific coast, like the tides, exhibit the feature known as diurnal inequality; that is, the two floods of a day are unequal and likewise the two ebbs. In the case of the tides the higher of the two high waters of a day is known as higher high water, while the lower of the two is known as lower high water. For the two low water of a day there are likewise distinctive names, the lower one being known as lower low water while the higher one is known as higher low water. In certain instances it is convenient to refer the currents to the tides, and where this is done the following symbols are used to designate the different tides: HH

Time	Speed	Direction	Time	Speed	Direction
Tide Hrs	Knot	True	Tide Hrs	Knot	True
HH–3	0·1	060°	LL–3	0·2	170°
HH–2	0·1	070°	LL–2	0·3	180°
HH–1	0·1	085°	LL–1	0·3	210°
HH	0·1	100°	LL	0·3	240°
HH+1	0·1	120°	LL+1	0·3	275°
HH+2	0·1	145°	LL+2	0·4	300°
HH+3	0·2	160°	LL+3	0·4	325°
LH–2	0·3	000°	HL–2	0·2	110°
LH–1	0·3	015°	HL–1	0·2	125°
LH	0·2	030°	HL	0·2	140°
LH+1	0·2	050°	HL+1	0·2	150°
LH+2	0·2	080°	HL+2	0·1	130°

for higher high water, LH for lower high water, LL for lower low water, and HL for higher low water.

Point Lobos, 8.7 miles WSW. of (former location of San Francisco Lightship), Calif: The tidal current here is rotary, turning clockwise, as shown in figure 1, in which the average currents have been referred to each hour of the tides at San Francisco (Golden Gate). The diurnal inequality here is so great that the current is very largely diurnal; that is, during the greater part of the month the current changes direction at the rate of about 15° per hour, giving but one strength of flood and one strength of ebb in a day.

The speed of the tidal current here is generally small, as shown in the above table, which represents the average conditions of figure 1.

In the column headed "Time," in the table above, the minus (—) sign before the hours indicates that the time referred to is before the particular tide, while the plus (+) sign indicates that the time is after the tide. Thus, HH–3 in figure 1 and in the table means 3 hours before higher high water, and LL+1 means 1 hour after lower low water.

The current observations at this location indicated a permanent current in a northwesterly direction of about 0.1 knot. This was especially noticeable during the winter months. This permanent current, therefore, increases the speed of the tidal currents that set in the northwesterly direction and decreases the speed of the tidal currents setting in the southeasterly direction.

When there is considerable runoff from San Francisco Bay, the combined tidal and nontidal current at the former lightship location generally attains a speed of 1.5 knots in a northwesterly direction. The greatest observed speed was 2.9 knots.

Cape Mendocino Light, 4.6 miles west of (former location of Blunts Reef Lightship), Calif: The tidal current here is rotary, but quite weak, being on the average less than 0.1 knot. At strength of flood the current sets north, and at strength of ebb it sets south. Since the tidal current is weak, it is generally masked by wind currents or other nontidal currents. The observations indicated the existence of a nontidal current setting southwesterly with an average speed of 0.2 knot from March to November and northwesterly with a like average speed from November to March. The greatest observed speed was 3 knots.

Columbia River Approach Lighted Horn Buoy R"C" (former location of the Columbia River Lightship), coast of Oregon: The tidal current here is rotary, turning clockwise, but rather weak. The speed of the current at strength being about 0.3 knots setting 020° on the flood and 200° on the ebb.

The current from the Columbia River completely masks the flood current; observations showing that there is a nontidal current at the buoy location with an average speed of 0.4 knots setting 235° from February to October; and 295° from October to February. When there is considerable runoff from the river, the combined tidal and nontidal current at the buoy frequently attains a speed of 2 knots or more in a southwesterly direction: The greatest observed speed here is 3.5 knots.

Cape Alava, 4.4 miles west of (former location of Umatilla Reef Lightship), Wash: The tidal current here is only slightly rotary. Strength of flood comes about one-fourth hour after the

Figure 1

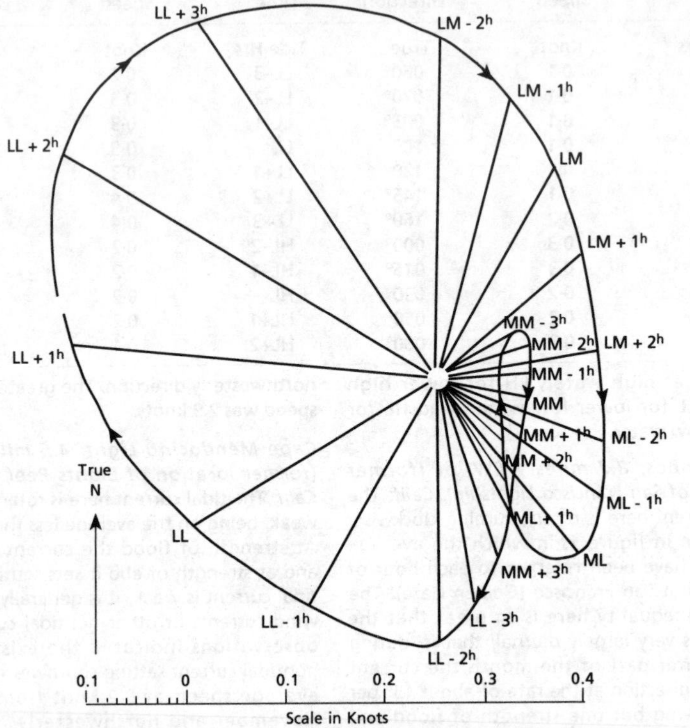

Tidal Current Curve, former location of San Francisco Lightship Referred to predicted time of the tide at San Francisco (Golden Gate), Calif.

strength of flood in the entrance to the Strait of Juan be Fuca; setting 345° with a speed of 0.3 knot. Strength of ebb comes about one-fourth hour after the strength of ebb in the strait and sets 165° with a speed of 0.3 knot.

The tidal current here is generally masked by nontidal currents brought about by winds or other causes. Observations indicated the existence of a nontidal current, setting about 350° with a speed of 0.7 knot from November to April, with the greatest speed during the month of December, when it averaged about 1 knot. From April to November the nontidal current was variable, averaging 0.4 knot, generally in a southeasterly direction. With strong southeasterly winds the combined tidal and nontidal current attains a speed of 2 to 3 knots in a northerly direction. The greatest observed speed was 3.3 knots.

Swiftsure Bank (Latitude 48°32'N.; Longitude 125°00'W.): The tidal current is distinctly rotary, turning clockwise twice each day, as shown in figure 2, in which the average currents have been referred to every hour of the tides at Astoria, Oreg. As there is considerable difference between the speeds of the two revolutions which the tidal currents make each day, there are two distinct values for the flood and for the ebb currents, corresponding to the diurnal inequality of the tides.

The speed of the tidal currents here is generally small, being less than 1 knot, as shown in the following table, which represents the average conditions of Figure 2.

In the first column of the following table the letters under "Tide" refer to the different tides of the day, HH standing for higher high water, LH for lower high water, LL for lower low water, and HL for higher low water. The corresponding letters on Figure 2 have a similar meaning. The minus (—) sign before the hours indicates that the time referred to is earlier than the particular tide, while the plus (+) sign indicates that the time is after the tide. Thus, HH—3 means 3 hours before higher high water, and LL+1 means 1 hour after lower low water at Astoria, Oreg.

Time	Speed	Direction	Time	Speed	Direction
Tide Hrs	Knot	True	Tide Hrs	Knot	True
HH–3	0·5	325°	LL–3	0·4	230°
HH–2	0·4	000°	LL–2	0·6	260°
HH–1	0·3	045°	LL–1	0·7	280°
HH	0·4	080°	LL	0·8	295°
HH+1	0·5	110°	LL+1	0·8	310°
HH+2	0·4	135°	LL+2	0·6	335°
HH+3	0·4	170°	LL+3	0·4	020°
LH–2	0·5	060°	HL–2	0·5	175°
LH–1	0·7	085°	HL–1	0·4	225°
LH	0·8	100°	HL	0·5	265°
LH+1	0·9	115°	HL+1	0·6	290°
LH+2	0·8	130°	HL+2	0·6	305°

It is to be noted that the speeds and directions of the current given in the table refer only to the tidal current. Observations indicate the existence of a permanent current setting 315° with an average speed of 0.5 knot. This makes the northwesterly currents considerably stronger than the southeasterly. A southeasterly current of as much as 1.5 knots does not occur except with strong westerly or northwesterly winds, while northwesterly currents of 2 knots or more occur frequently.

The greatest observed speed at Swiftsure Bank is 3 knots.

Maui Island, Hawaii (Latitude 20° 46′ N.; Longitude 155° 58′ W.). Observations indicate the existence of a permanent current setting north with an average speed of 0.7 knot. Combined with the tidal current, the northward current may have an average speed varying from slack to 1.4 knots. The greatest observed speed off Maui island was 2.7 knots.

Figure 1

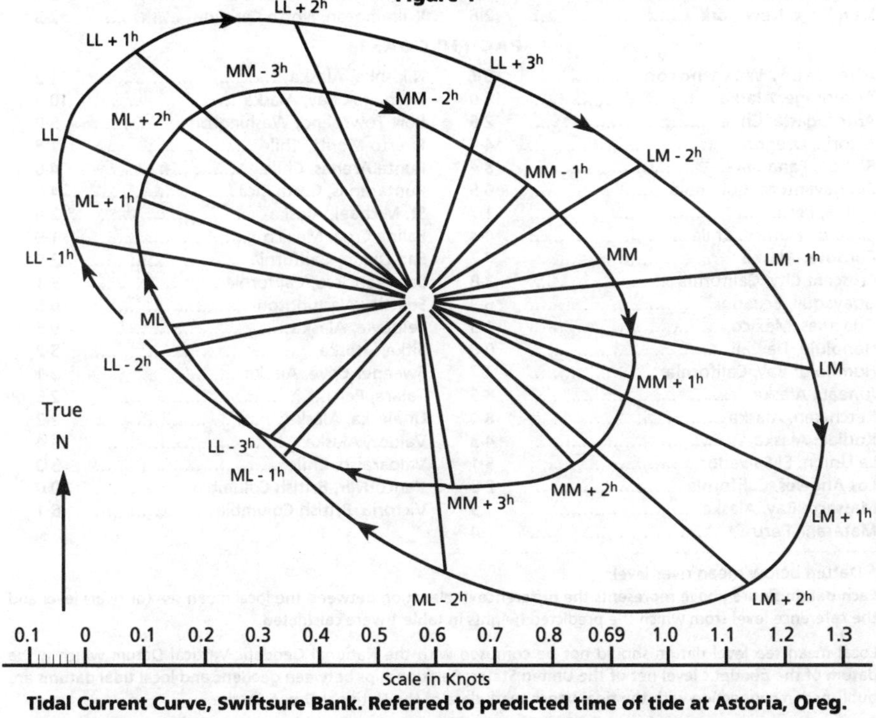

Tidal Current Curve, Swiftsure Bank. Referred to predicted time of tide at Astoria, Oreg.

TABLE 1 – LIST OF TIDAL REFERENCE STATIONS

ATLANTIC COAST

Name of station	*Datum below mean sea-level*	*Name of station*	*Datum below mean sea-level*
Albany, New York	*2·5	Pensacola, Florida	0·6
Amuay, Venezuela	0·6	Philadelphia, Pennsylvania	*3·5
Argentia, Newfoundland	4·3	Pictou, Nova Scotia	3·9
Baltimore, Maryland	0·8	Portland, Maine	4·9
Boston, Massachusetts	5·2	Puerto Ingeniero White, Argentina	8·5
Breakwater Harbor, Delaware	2·3	Punta Gorda, Venezuela	3·3
Bridgeport, Connecticut	3·6	Punta Loyola, Argentina	20·3
Buenos Aires, Argentina	2·6	Quebec, Quebec	*8·5
Charleston, South Carolina	3·0	Recife, Brazil	3·7
Comodoro Rivadavia, Argentina	10·3	Reedy Point, Delaware	3·0
Cristobal, Panama	0·5	Rio de Janeiro, Brazil	2·3
Easport, Maine	9·7	St. John, New Brunswick	14·5
Galveston, Texas	0·8	St. Marks River Entrance, Florida	1·9
Halifax, Nova Scotia	4·3	St. Petersburg, Florida	1·2
Hampton Roads, Virginia	1·4	Sandy Hook, New Jersey	2·6
Harrington Harbour, Quebec	3·5	San Juan, Puerto Rico	0·8
Isla Zapara, Venezuela	2.7	Santos, Brazil	2·5
Key West, Floriday	0·9	Savannah, Georgia	4·4
Mayport, Florida	2·5	Savannah River Entrance, Georgia	3·8
Miami Harbor Entrance, Florida	1·4	Suriname River, Surinam	4·3
Mobile, Alabama	0·8	Tampico Harbor, Mexico	0·8
New London, Connecticut	1·6	Washington, D.C.	*1·6
Newport, Rhode Island	1·8	Willets Point, New York	3·9
New York, New York	2·6	Wilmington, North Carolina	*2·3

PACIFIC COAST

Name of station	*Datum below mean sea-level*	*Name of station*	*Datum below mean sea-level*
Aberdeen, Washington	5·6	Nikishka, Alaska	11·2
Anchorage, Alaska	16·0	Nushagak Bay, Alaska	10·3
Antofagasta, Chile	2·6	Port Townsend, Washington	5·0
Astoria, Oregon	*4·4	Puerto Montt, Chile	11·8
Balboa, Panama	8·4	Punta Arenas, Chile	4·0
Buenaventura, Columbia	6·5	Puntarenas, Costa Rica	4·6
Calloa, Peru	1·7	St. Michael, Alaska	2·0
Cabo de Hornos, Chile	4·4	Salina Cruz, Mexico	1·9
Cordova, Alaska	6·7	San Diego, California	2·9
Crescent City, California	3·8	San Francisco, California	3·1
Guayaquil, Ecuador	*6·3	Seattle, Washington	6·6
Guaymas, Mexico	1·5	Seldovia, Alaska	9·5
Honolulu, Hawaii	0·8	Sitka, Ataska	5·2
Humboldt Bay, California	3·7	Sweeper Cove, Alaska	2·1
Juneau, Alaska	8·5	Talara, Peru	2·6
Ketchikan, Alaska	8·0	Unalaska, Alaska	2·2
Kodiak, Alaska	4·3	Valdez, Alaska	6·4
La Union, El Salvador	5·1	Valparaiso, Chile	3·0
Los Angeles, California	2·8	Vancouver, British Columbia	10·0
Massacre Bay, Alaska	1·9	Victoria, British Columbia	6·1
Matarani, Peru	1·4		

* Datum below mean river level.

Each datum figure above represents the difference in elevation between the local mean sea (or river) level and the reference level from which the predicted heights in table 1 were calculated.

Local mean sea level datum should not be confused with the National Geodetic Vertical Datum which is the datum of the geodetic level net of the United States. Relationships between geodetic and local tidal datums are published in connection with the tidal bench mark data of the National Ocean Service.

TABLE 2 – TYPICAL TIDE CURVES FOR UNITED STATES PORTS

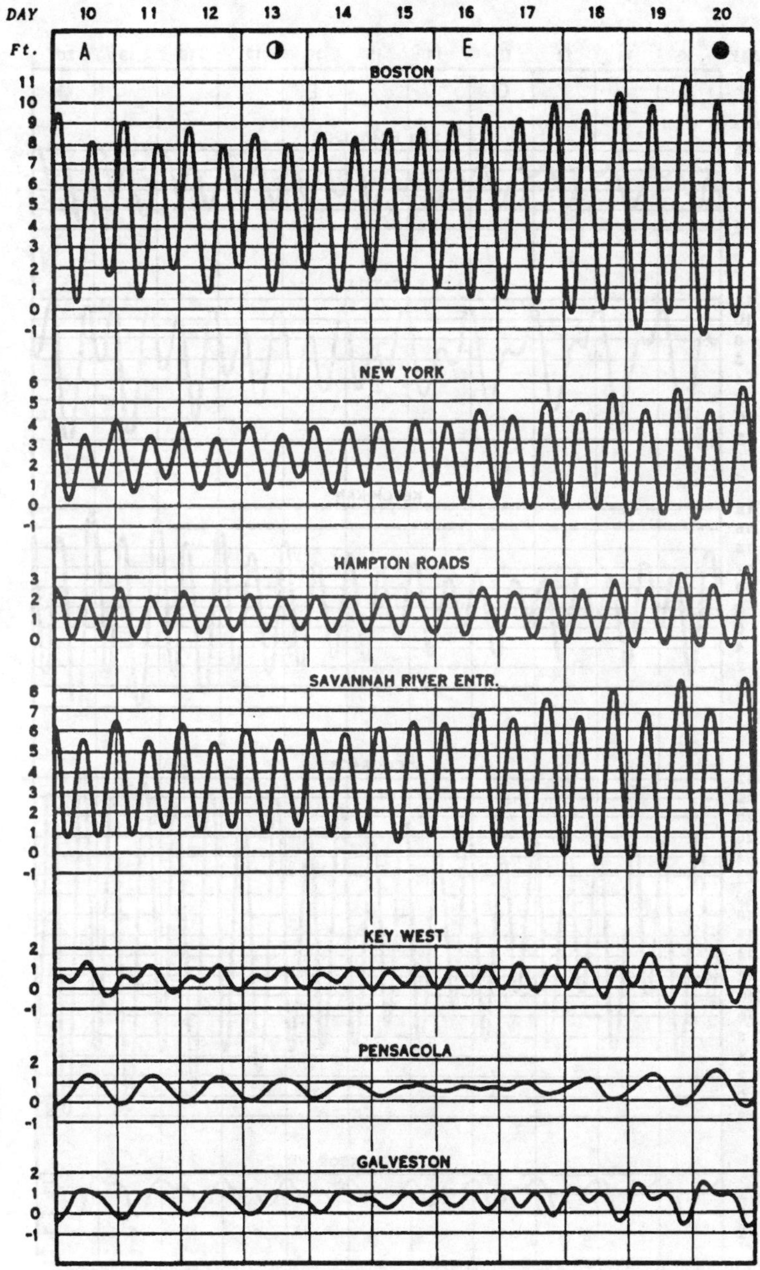

Lunar data: A – Moon in apogee
◑ – last quarter
E – Moon on Equator
● – new Moon

TABLE 2 – TYPICAL TIDE CURVES FOR UNITED STATES PORTS

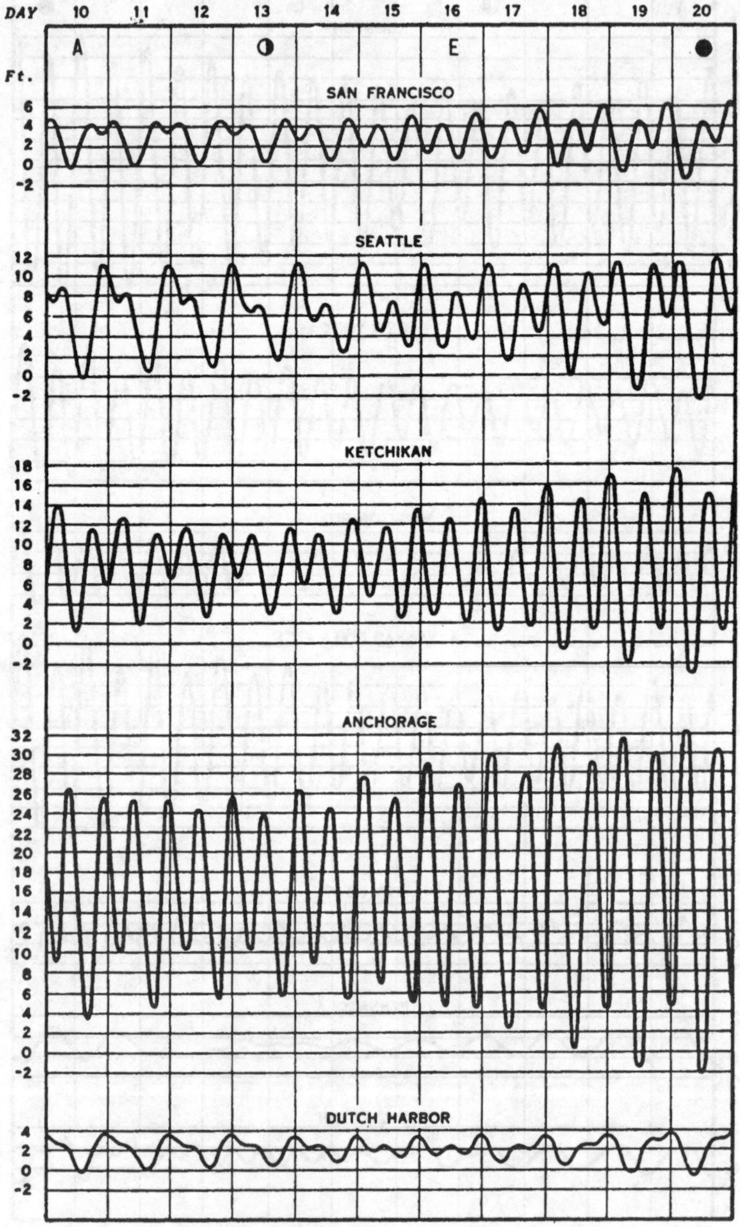

Lunar data: A – Moon in apogee
◑ – last quarter
E – Moon on Equator
● – new Moon

TABLE 3 – HEIGHT OF TIDE AT ANY TIME

EXPLANATION OF TABLE

Although the footnote of Table 3 may be sufficient explanation, two examples are given here to illustrate its use.

Example 1: Find the height of the tide at 0755 at New York (The Battery), N.Y., on a day when the predicted tide are given as:

Low Water		*High Water*	
Time h.m.	*Height ft*	*Time h.m.*	*Height ft*
0522	0·1	1114	4·2
1741	0·6	2310	4·1

An inspection of the above example shows that the desired time falls between the two morning tides.

The duration of rise is 11^h 14^m – 5^m 22^m = 5^h 52^m.

The time after low water for which the height is required is 7^h 55^m – 5^h 22^m = 33^m.

The range of tide is 4·2 – 0·1 - 4·1 feet.

The duration of rise or fall in table 3 is given in heavy-faced type for each 20 minutes from 4^h 00m to 10^h 40^m. The nearest taburlar value to 5^h 52^m, the above duration of rise, is 6^h 00^m; and on the horizontal line of 6^h 00^m the nearest tabular time to 2^h 33^m after low water for which the height is required is 2^h 36^m. Following down the column in which this 2^h 36^m is found to its intersection with the line of the range 4.0 feet (the nearest tabular value to the above range of 4.1 feet), the correction is found to be 1.6 feet, which being reckoned from low water, must be added, making 0·1 + 1·6 = 1·7 feet or 52 centimeters which is the required height above mean lower low water, the datum for New York.

Example 2: Find the height of the tide at 0300 at Somewhere, U.S.A. on a day when the predicted tides are given as:

High Water		*Low Water*	
Time h.m.	*Height ft*	*Time h.m.*	*Height ft*
0012	11·3	0638	-2·0
1251	11·0	1853	-0·8

The duration of fall is 6^h 38^m – 6^h 26^m = 5^h 52^m.

The time after high water for which the height is required is 3^h 00^m – 00^h 12^m = 48^m.

The range of tide is 11·3 – (-2·0) = 13·3 feet.

Entering Table 3 at the duration of fall of 6^h 20^m, which is the nearest value of 6^h 26^m, the nearest value on the horizontal line to 2^h 48^m is 2^h 45^m after high water. Follow down this column to its intersection with a range of 13·5 feet which is the nearest tabular value to 13·3 feet, one obtains 5·3 which, being calculated from high water, must be subtracted from it. The approximate height at 03^h 00^m is therefore, 11·3 – 5·3 = 6·0 feet or 183 centimeters.

When the duration of rise or fall is greater than 10^h 40^m, enter the table with one-half the given duration and with one-half the time from the nearest high or low water; but if the duration of rise or fall is less than 4 hours, enter the table with double the given duration and with double the time from the nearest high or low water.

Similarly, when the range of tide is greater than 20 feet, enter the table with one-half the given range. The tabular correction should then be doubled before applying it to the given high or low water height. if the range of tide is greater than 40 feet, take one-third of the range and multiply the tabular correction by 3.

GRAPHIC METHOD

If the height of the tide is required for a number of times on a certain day the full tide curve for the day may be obtained by the *one-quarter, one-tenth rule.* The procedure is as follows:

1. On cross-section paper plot the high and low water points in the order of their occurence for the day, measuring time horizontally and height vertically. These are the basic points for the curve.
2. Draw light straight lines connecting the points representing successive high and low waters.
3. Divide each of these straight lines into four equal parts. The halfway point of each line gives another point for the curve.
4. At the quarter point adjacent to high water draw a vertical line above the point and at the quarter point adjacent to low water draw a vertical line below the point, making the length of these lines equal to one-tenth of the range between the high

and low waters used. The points marking the ends of these vertical lines give two additional intermediate points for the curve.

5. Draw a smooth curve through the points of high and low waters and the intermediate points, making the curve well rounded near high and low waters. This curve will approximate the actual tide curve and heights for any time of the day may be readily scaled from it.

Caution: Both methods presented are based on the assumption that the rise and fall conform to simple cosine curves. Therefore the heights obtained will be approximate. The roughness of approximation will vary as the tide curve differs from a cosine curve.

An example of the use of the graphical method is illustrated below. Using the same predicted tides as in example 2, the approximate height at $3^h\ 00^m$ could be determined as shown below.

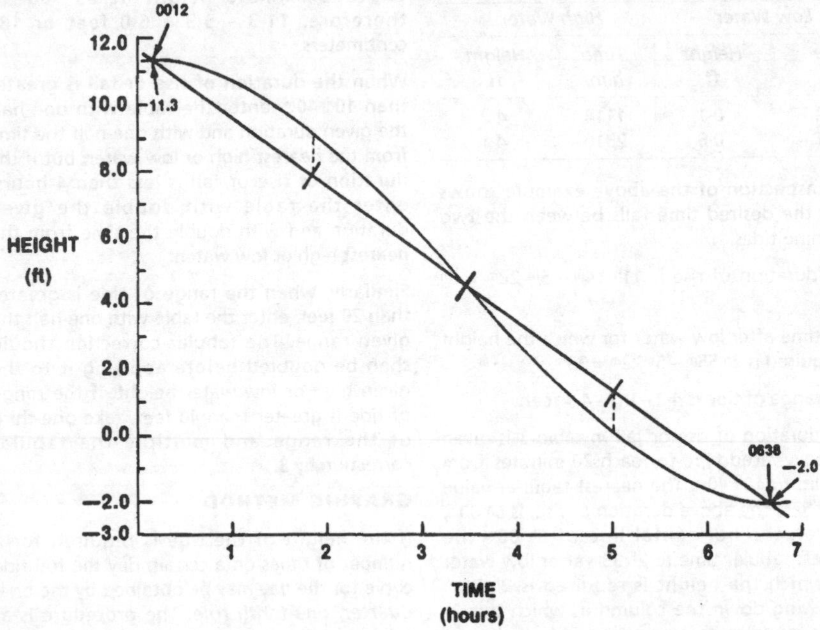

TABLE 3 – HEIGHT OF TIDE AT ANY TIME															
Duration of rise or fall, see footnote	***Time from the nearest high water or low water***														
h.m.	*h.m.*	*h.m.*	*h.m.*	*h.m.*	*h.m.*	*h.m.*	*h.m.*	*h.m.*	*h.m.*	*h.m.*	*h.m.*	*h.m.*	*h.m.*	*h.m.*	*h.m.*
4 00	0 08	0 16	0 24	0 32	0 40	0 48	0 56	1 04	1 12	1 20	1 28	1 36	1 44	1 52	2 00
4 20	0 09	0 17	0 26	0 35	0 43	0 52	1 01	1 09	1 18	1 27	1 35	1 44	1 53	2 01	2 10
4 40	0 09	0 19	0 28	0 37	0 47	0 56	1 05	1 15	1 24	1 33	1 43	1 52	2 01	2 11	2 20
5 00	0 10	0 20	0 30	0 40	050	1 00	1 10	1 20	1 30	1 40	1 50	2 00	2 10	2 20	2 30
5 20	0 11	0 21	0 32	0 43	0 53	1 04	1 15	1 25	1 36	1 47	1 57	2 08	2 19	2 29	2 40
5 40	0 11	0 23	0 34	0 45	0 57	1 08	1 19	1 31	1 42	1 53	2 05	2 16	2 27	2 39	2 50
6 00	0 12	0 24	0 36	0 48	1 00	1 12	1 24	1 36	1 48	2 00	2 12	2 24	2 36	2 48	3 00
6 20	0 13	0 25	0 38	0 51	1 03	1 16	1 29	1 41	1 54	2 07	2 19	2 32	2 45	2 57	3 10
6 40	0 13	0 27	0 40	0 53	1 07	1 20	1 33	1 47	2 00	2 13	2 27	2 40	2 53	3 07	3 20
7 00	0 14	0 28	0 42	0 56	1 10	1 24	1 38	1 52	2 06	2 20	2 34	2 48	3 02	3 16	3 30
7 20	0 15	0 29	0 44	0 59	1 13	1 28	1 43	1 57	2 12	2 27	2 41	2 56	3 11	3 25	3 40
7 40	0 15	0 31	0 46	1 01	1 17	1 32	1 47	2 03	2 18	2 33	2 49	3 04	3 19	3 35	3 50
8 00	0 16	0 32	0 48	1 04	1 20	1 36	1 52	2 08	2 24	2 40	2 56	3 12	3 28	3 44	4 00
8 20	0 17	0 33	0 50	1 07	1 23	1 40	1 57	2 13	2 30	2 47	3 03	3 20	3 37	3 53	4 10
8 40	0 17	0 35	0 52	1 09	1 27	1 44	2 01	2 19	2 36	2 53	3 11	3 28	3 45	4 03	4 20
9 00	0 18	0 36	0 54	1 12	1 30	1 48	2 06	2 24	2 42	3 00	3 18	3 36	3 54	4 12	4 30
9 20	0 19	0 37	0 56	1 15	1 33	1 52	2 11	2 29	2 48	3 07	3 25	3 44	4 03	4 21	4 40
9 40	0 19	0 39	0 58	1 17	1 37	1 56	2 15	2 35	2 54	3 13	3 33	3 52	4 11	4 31	4 50
10 00	0 20	0 40	1 00	1 20	1 40	2 00	2 20	2 40	3 00	3 20	3 40	4 00	4 20	4 40	5 00
10 20	0 21	0 41	1 02	1 23	1 43	2 04	2 25	2 245	3 06	3 27	3 47	4 08	4 29	4 49	5 10
10 40	0 21	0 43	1 04	1 25	1 47	2 08	2 29	2 51	3 12	3 33	3 55	4 16	4 37	4 59	5 20
Range of tide, see footnote	***Correction to height***														
Ft.	*Ft.*	*Ft.*	*Ft.*	*Ft.*	*Ft.*	*Ft.*	*Ft.*	*Ft.*	*Ft.*	*Ft.*	*Ft.*	*Ft.*	*Ft.*	*Ft.*	*Ft.*
0.5	0.0	0.0	0.0	0.0	0.0	0.0	0.1	0.1	0.1	0.1	0.1	0.2	0.2	0.2	0.2
1.0	0.0	0.0	0.0	0.0	0.1	0.1	0.1	0.2	0.2	0.2	0.3	0.3	0.4	0.4	0.5
1.5	0.0	0.0	0.0	0.1	0.1	0.1	0.2	0.2	0.3	0.4	0.4	0.5	0.6	0.7	0.8
2.0	0.0	0.0	0.0	0.1	0.1	0.2	0.3	0.3	0.4	0.5	0.6	0.7	0.8	0.9	1.0
2.5	0.0	0.0	0.1	0.1	0.2	0.2	0.3	0.4	0.5	0.6	0.7	0.9	1.0	1.1	1.2
3.0	0.0	0.0	0.1	0.1	0.2	0.3	0.4	0.5	0.6	0.8	0.9	1.0	1.2	1.3	1.5
3.5	0.0	0.0	0.1	0.2	0.2	0.3	0.4	0.6	0.7	0.9	1.0	1.2	1.4	1.6	1.8
4.0	0.0	0.0	0.1	0.2	0.3	0.4	0.5	0.7	0.8	1.0	1.2	1.4	1.6	1.8	2.0
4.5	0.0	0.0	0.1	0.2	0.3	0.4	0.6	0.7	0.9	1.1	1.3	1.6	1.8	2.0	2.2
5.0	0.0	0.1	0.1	0.2	0.3	0.5	0.6	0.8	1.0	1.2	1.5	1.7	2.0	2.2	2.5
5.5	0.0	0.1	0.1	0.2	0.4	0.5	0.7	0.9	1.1	1.4	1.6	1.9	2.2	2.5	2.8
6.0	0.0	0.1	0.1	0.3	0.4	0.6	0.8	1.0	1.2	1.5	1.8	2.1	2.4	2.7	3.0
6.5	0.0	0.1	0.2	0.3	0.4	0.6	0.8	1.1	1.3	1.6	1.9	2.2	2.6	2.9	3.2
7.0	0.0	0.1	0.2	0.3	0.5	0.7	0.9	1.2	1.4	1.8	2.1	2.4	2.8	3.1	3.5
7.5	0.0	0.1	0.2	0.3	0.5	0.7	1.0	1.2	1.5	1.9	2.2	2.6	3.0	3.4	3.8
8.0	0.0	0.1	0.2	0.3	0.5	0.8	1.0	1.3	1.6	2.0	2.4	2.8	3.2	3.6	4.0
8.5	0.0	0.1	0.2	0.4	0.6	0.8	1.1	1.4	1.8	2.1	2.5	2.9	3.4	3.8	4.2
9.0	0.0	0.1	0.2	0.4	0.6	0.9	1.2	1.5	1.9	2.2	2.7	3.1	3.6	4.0	4.5
9.5	0.0	0.1	0.2	0.4	0.6	0.9	1.2	1.6	2.0	2.4	2.8	3.3	3.8	4.3	4.8
10.0	0.0	0.1	0.2	0.4	0.7	1.0	1.3	1.7	2.1	2.5	3.0	3.5	4.0	4.5	5.0
10.5	0.0	0.1	0.3	0.5	0.7	1.0	1.3	1.7	2.2	2.6	3.1	3.6	4.2	4.7	5.2
11.0	0.0	0.1	0.3	0.5	0.7	1.1	1.4	1.8	2.3	2.8	3.3	3.8	4.4	4.9	5.5
11.5	0.0	0.1	0.3	0.5	0.8	1.1	1.5	1.9	2.4	2.9	3.4	4.0	4.6	5.1	5.8
12.0	0.0	0.1	0.3	0.5	0.8	1.1	1.5	2.0	2.5	3.0	3.6	4.1	4.8	5.4	6.0
12.5	0.0	0.1	0.3	0.5	0.8	1.2	1.6	2.1	2.6	3.1	3.7	4.3	5.0	5.6	6.2
13.0	0.0	0.1	0.3	0.6	0.9	1.2	1.7	2.2	2.7	3.2	3.9	4.5	5.1	5.8	6.5
13.5	0.0	0.1	0.3	0.6	0.9	1.3	1.7	2.2	2.8	3.4	4.0	4.7	5.3	6.0	6.8
14.0	0.0	0.2	0.3	0.6	0.9	1.3	1.8	2.3	2.9	3.5	4.2	4.8	5.5	6.3	7.0
14.5	0.0	0.2	0.4	0.6	1.0	1.4	1.9	2.4	3.0	3.6	4.3	5.0	5.7	6.5	7.2
15.0	0.0	0.2	0.4	0.6	1.0	1.4	1.9	2.5	3.1	3.8	4.4	5.2	5.9	6.7	7.5
15.5	0.0	0.2	0.4	0.7	1.0	1.5	2.0	2.6	3.2	3.9	4.6	5.4	6.1	6.9	7.8
16.0	0.0	0.2	0.4	0.7	1.1	1.5	2.1	2.6	3.3	4.0	4.7	5.5	6.3	7.2	8.0
16.5	0.0	0.2	0.4	0.7	1.1	1.6	2.1	2.7	3.4	4.1	4.9	5.7	6.5	7.4	8.2
17.0	0.0	0.2	0.4	0.7	1.1	1.6	2.2	2.8	3.5	4.2	5.0	5.9	6.7	7.6	8.5
17.5	0.0	0.2	0.4	0.8	1.2	1.7	2.2	2.9	3.6	4.4	5.2	6.0	6.9	7.8	8.8
18.0	0.0	0.2	0.4	0.8	1.2	1.7	2.3	3.0	3.7	4.5	5.3	6.2	7.1	8.1	9.0
18.5	0.1	0.2	0.5	0.8	1.2	1.8	2.4	3.1	3.8	4.6	5.5	6.4	7.3	8.3	9.2
19.0	0.1	0.2	0.5	0.8	1.3	1.8	2.4	3.1	3.9	4.8	5.6	6.6	7.5	8.5	9.5
19.5	0.1	0.2	0.5	0.8	1.3	1.9	2.5	3.2	4.0	4.9	5.8	6.7	7.7	8.7	9.8
20.0	0.1	0.2	0.5	0.9	1.3	1.9	2.6	3.3	4.1	5.0	5.9	6.9	7.9	9.0	10.0

Obtained from the predictions the high water and low water, one of which is before and the other after the time for which the height is required. The difference between the times of occurence of these tides is the duration of rise or fall, and the difference between their heights is the range of tide for the above table. Find the difference between the nearest high or low water and the time for which the height is required. Enter the table with the duration of rise or fall, printed in heavy-faced type, which most nearly agrees with the actual value, and on that horizontal line find the time from the nearest high or low water which agrees most nearly with the corresponding actual difference. The correction sought is in the column directly below, on the line with the range of tide. When the nearest tide is high water, subtract the correction. When the nearest tide is low water, add the correction.

TABLE 4 – TYPICAL CURRENT CURVES FOR REFERENCE STATIONS

(Flood: Solid line, Ebb: Broken Line)

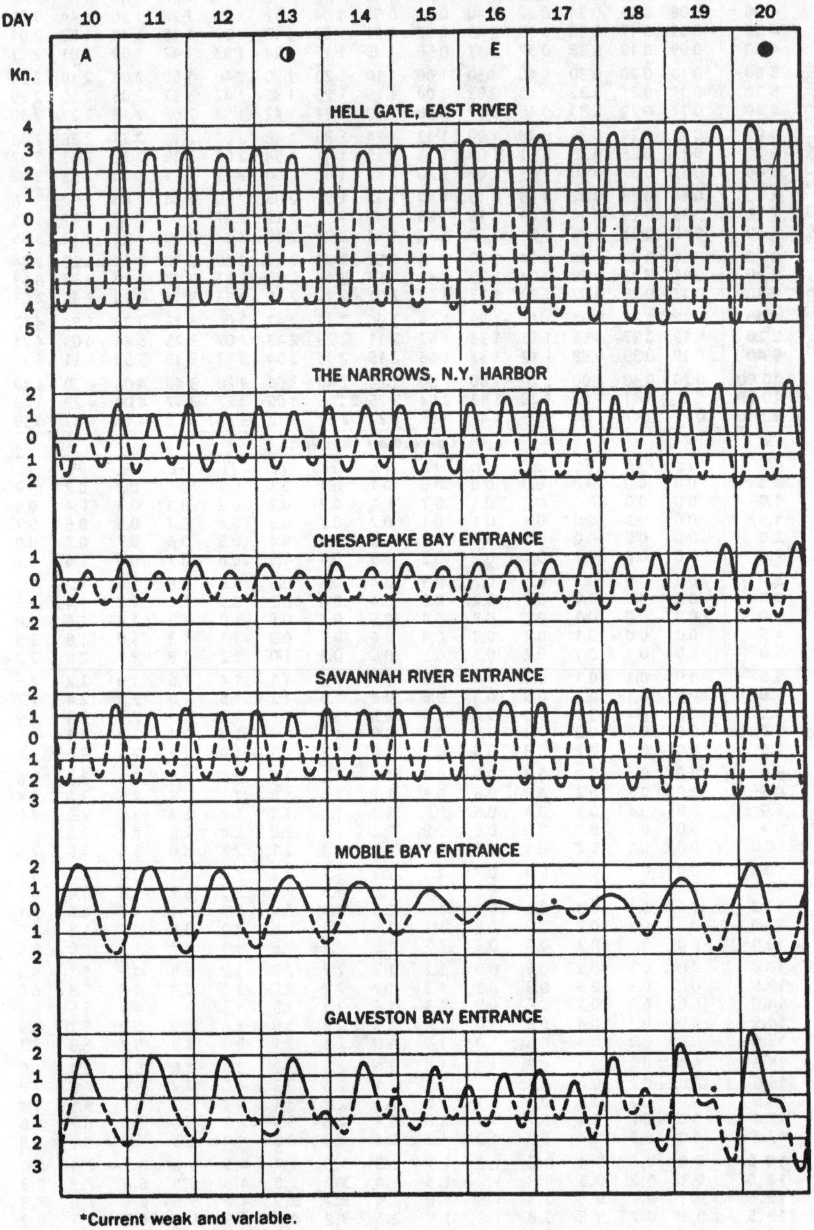

*Current weak and variable.

Lunar data: A—moon in apogee
◑—last quarter
E—moon on equator
●—new moon

TABLE 4 – TYPICAL CURRENT CURVES FOR REFERENCE STATIONS

(Flood: Solid line, Ebb: Broken Line)

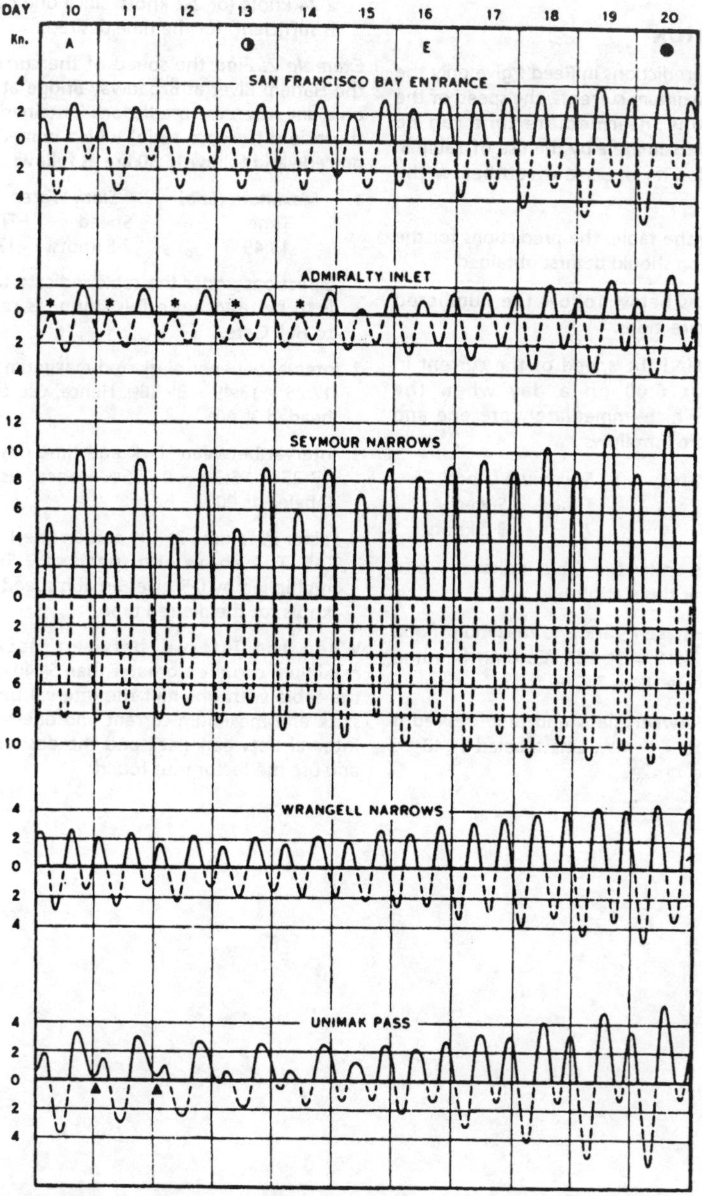

*Current weak and variable.
▲Minimum flood.

Lunar data: A – Moon in apogee
◐ – last quarter
E – Moon on Equator
● – new Moon

TABLE 5 – SPEED OF CURRENT AT ANY TIME

EXPLANATION

Though the predictions in Reed's give only the slacks and maximum currents, the speed of the current at any intermediate time can be obtained approximately by the use of Table 5. Directions for its use are given below the table.

Before using the table, the predictions for the day in question should be first obtained.

The examples below follow the numbered steps in the directions.

Example 1: Find the speed of the current in The Race at 6:00 on a day when the predictions which immediately precede and follow 6:00 are as follows:

1.

Slack Water	*Maximum (Flood)*	
Time	Time	Speed
4:18	7:36	3·2 knots

Directions under the table indicate A is to be used for this station.

2. Interval between slack and maximum flood is 7:36 – 4:18 = 3h 18m. Column heading nearest to 3h 18m is 3h 20m.
3. Interval between slack and time desired is 6:00 – 4:18 = 1h 42m. Line labeled 1h 40m is nearest to 1h 42m.
4. Factor in column 3h 20m and on line 1h 40m is 0·7. The above flood speed is 3·2 knots multiplied by 0·7 gives a flood speed of 2·24 knots (or 2·2 knots, since one decimal is sufficient) for the time desired.

Example 2: Find the speed of the current in the Harlem River at Broadway Bridge at 16:30 on a day when the predictions (obtained using the tide difference ratio) which immediately precede and follow 16:30 are as follows:

1.

Maximum (Ebb)		*Slack Water*
Time	Speed	Time
13:49	2·5 knots	17:25

Directions under the table indicate table B is to be used, since this station is referred to Hell Gate.

2. Interval between slack and maximum ebb is 17:25 – 13:49 = 3h 36m. Hence, use column headed 3h 40m.
3. Interval between slack and time desired is 17:25 – 16:30 = 0h 55m. Hence, use line labeled 1h 00m.
4. Factor in column 3h 40m and on line 1h 00m is 0·5. The above ebb speed of 2·5 knots multiplied by 0·5 gives an ebb speed of 1·2 knots for the desired time.

When the interval between slack and maximum current is greater than 5h 40m, enter the table with one-half the interval between slack and maximum current and one-half the interval between slack and the desired time and use the factor thus found.

TABLE 5 – SPEED OF CURRENT AT ANY TIME

TABLE A

Interval between slack and desired time	*Interval between slack and maximum current*													
	h.m. 1 20	*h.m.* 1 40	*h.m.* 2 00	*h.m.* 2 20	*h.m.* 2 40	*h.m.* 3 00	*h.m.* 3 20	*h.m.* 3 40	*h.m.* 4 00	*h.m.* 4 20	*h.m.* 4 40	*h.m.* 5 00	*h.m.* 5 20	*h.m.* 5 40
h. m.	f.	f.	f.	f.	f.	f.	f.	f.	f.	f.	f.	f.	f.	f.
0 20	0.4	0.3	0.3	0.2	0.2	0.2	0.2	0.1	0.1	0.1	0.1	0.1	0.1	0.1
0 40	0.7	0.6	0.5	0.4	0.4	0.3	0.3	0.3	0.3	0.2	0.2	0.2	0.2	0.2
1 00	0.9	0.8	0.7	0.6	0.6	0.5	0.5	0.4	0.4	0.4	0.3	0.3	0.3	0.3
1 20	1.0	1.0	0.9	0.8	0.7	0.6	0.6	0.5	0.5	0.5	0.4	0.4	0.4	0.4
1 40	---	1.0	1.0	0.9	0.8	0.8	0.7	0.7	0.6	0.6	0.5	0.5	0.5	0.4
2 00	---	---	1.0	1.0	0.9	0.9	0.8	0.8	0.7	0.7	0.6	0.6	0.6	0.5
2 20	---	---	---	1.0	1.0	0.9	0.9	0.8	0.8	0.7	0.7	0.7	0.6	0.6
2 40	---	---	---	---	1.0	1.0	1.0	0.9	0.9	0.8	0.8	0.7	0.7	0.7
3 00	---	---	---	---	---	1.0	1.0	1.0	0.9	0.9	0.8	0.8	0.8	0.7
3 20	---	---	---	---	---	---	1.0	1.0	1.0	0.9	0.9	0.9	0.8	0.8
3 40	---	---	---	---	---	---	---	1.0	1.0	1.0	0.9	0.9	0.9	0.9
4 00	---	---	---	---	---	---	---	---	1.0	1.0	1.0	1.0	0.9	0.9
4 20	---	---	---	---	---	---	---	---	---	1.0	1.0	1.0	1.0	0.9
4 40	---	---	---	---	---	---	---	---	---	---	1.0	1.0	1.0	1.0
5 00	---	---	---	---	---	---	---	---	---	---	---	1.0	1.0	1.0
5 20	---	---	---	---	---	---	---	---	---	---	---	---	1.0	1.0
5 40	---	---	---	---	---	---	---	---	---	---	---	---	---	1.0

TABLE B

Interval between slack and desired time	*Interval between slack and maximum current*													
	h.m. 1 20	*h.m.* 1 40	*h.m.* 2 00	*h.m.* 2 20	*h.m.* 2 40	*h.m.* 3 00	*h.m.* 3 20	*h.m.* 3 40	*h.m.* 4 00	*h.m.* 4 20	*h.m.* 4 40	*h.m.* 5 00	*h.m.* 5 20	*h.m.* 5 40
h. m.	f.	f.	f.	f.	f.	f.	f.	f.	f.	f.	f.	f.	f.	f.
0 20	0.5	0.4	0.4	0.3	0.3	0.3	0.3	0.3	0.2	0.2	0.2	0.2	0.2	0.2
0 40	0.8	0.7	0.6	0.5	0.5	0.5	0.4	0.4	0.4	0.4	0.3	0.3	0.3	0.3
1 00	0.9	0.8	0.8	0.7	0.7	0.6	0.6	0.5	0.5	0.5	0.4	0.4	0.4	0.4
1 20	1.0	1.0	0.9	0.8	0.8	.07	0.7	0.6	0.6	0.6	0.5	0.5	0.5	0.5
1 40	---	1.0	1.0	0.9	0.9	0.8	0.8	0.7	0.7	0.7	0.6	0.6	0.6	0.6
2 00	---	---	1.0	1.0	0.9	0.9	0.9	0.8	0.8	0.7	0.7	0.7	0.7	0.6
2 20	---	---	---	1.0	1.0	1.0	0.9	0.9	0.8	0.8	0.8	0.7	0.7	0.7
2 40	---	---	---	---	1.0	1.0	1.0	0.9	0.9	0.9	0.8	0.8	0.8	0.7
3 00	---	---	---	---	---	1.0	1.0	1.0	0.9	0.9	0.9	0.8	0.8	0.8
3 20	---	---	---	---	---	---	1.0	1.0	1.0	1.0	0.9	0.9	0.9	0.9
3 40	---	---	---	---	---	---	---	1.0	1.0	1.0	1.0	0.9	0.9	0.9
4 00	---	---	---	---	---	---	---	---	1.0	1.0	1.0	1.0	0.9	0.9
4 20	---	---	---	---	---	---	---	---	---	1.0	1.0	1.0	1.0	0.9
4 40	---	---	---	---	---	---	---	---	---	---	1.0	1.0	1.0	1.0
5 00	---	---	---	---	---	---	---	---	---	---	---	1.0	1.0	1.0
5 20	---	---	---	---	---	---	---	---	---	---	---	---	1.0	1.0
5 40	---	---	---	---	---	---	---	---	---	---	---	---	---	1.0

Use Table A for all places except those listed below for Table B.

Use Table B for Cape Cod Canal, hell Gate, C and D Canal, Deception Pass, Seymour Narrows, Isanotski Strait and all stations referenced to these tables.

1. From predictions find the time of slack water and the time and speed of maximum current (flood or ebb), one of which is immediately before and the other after the time for which the speed is desired.
2. Find the interval of time between the above slack and maximum current, and enter the top of Table A or B with the interval which most nearly agrees with this value.
3. Find the interval of time between the above slack and the time desired, and enter the side of Table A or B with the intervbal which most nearly agrees with this value.
4. Find, in the table, the factor corresponding to the above two intervals, and multiply the maximum speed by this factor. The result will be the approximate speed at the time desired.

TABLE 6 – ROTARY TIDAL CURRENTS

Georges Bank
Lat. 41°50′N, Long. 66°37′W

Time	Direction (true) Degrees	Velocity Knots
0	285	0.9
1	304	1.1
2	324	1.2
3	341	1.1
4	10	1.0
5	43	0.9
6	89	1.0
7	127	1.3
8	147	1.6
9	172	1.4
10	197	0.9
11	232	0.8

Georges Bank
Lat. 41°54′N, Long. 67°08′W

Time	Direction (true) Degrees	Velocity Knots
0	298	1.1
1	325	1.4
2	344	1.5
3	0	1.2
4	33	0.7
5	82	0.8
6	118	1.1
7	138	1.5
8	153	1.2
9	178	1.1
10	208	0.9
11	236	0.8

Georges Bank
Lat. 41°48′N, Long. 67°34′W

Time	Direction (true) Degrees	Velocity Knots
0	325	1.5
1	332	2.1
2	342	2.0
3	358	1.3
4	35	0.7
5	99	0.8
6	126	1.3
7	150	2.0
8	159	1.9
9	169	1.7
10	197	1.2
11	275	0.9

Georges Bank
Lat. 41°42′N, Long. 67°37′W

Time	Direction (true) Degrees	Velocity Knots
0	316	1.1
1	341	1.3
2	356	1.0
3	16	0.8
4	43	0.6
5	92	0.8
6	122	1.0
7	146	1.1
8	170	1.1
9	195	1.0
10	215	1.0
11	272	0.9

Georges Bank
Lat. 41°41′N, Long. 67°49′W

Time	Direction (true) Degrees	Velocity Knots
0	318	1.6
1	320	1.8
2	325	1.4
3	330	0.8
4	67	0.3
5	111	0.9
6	117	1.5
7	126	1.7
8	144	1.7
9	160	1.1
10	242	0.8
11	292	1.2

Georges Bank
Lat. 41°30′N, Long. 68°07′W

Time	Direction (true) Degrees	Velocity Knots
0	312	1.5
1	338	1.7
2	346	1.5
3	14	1.1
4	59	0.9
5	99	0.9
6	123	1.3
7	144	1.7
8	160	1.6
9	187	1.3
10	244	1.0
11	274	1.1

Georges Bank
Lat. 41°29′N, Long. 67°04′W

Time	Direction (true) Degrees	Velocity Knots
0	277	1.0
1	302	1.2
2	329	1.4
3	348	1.3
4	15	1.2
5	48	1.1
6	85	1.2
7	122	1.4
8	145	1.5
9	166	1.3
10	194	1.2
11	223	1.1

Georges Bank
Lat. 41°14′N, Long. 67°38′W

Time	Direction (true) Degrees	Velocity Knots
0	305	1.4
1	332	1.6
2	355	1.6
3	15	1.4
4	38	1.1
5	77	0.9
6	112	1.2
7	141	1.6
8	162	1.6
9	187	1.5
10	214	1.4
11	252	1.2

Georges Bank
Lat. 41°13′N, Long. 68°20′W

Time	Direction (true) Degrees	Velocity Knots
0	319	1.5
1	332	2.0
2	345	1.4
3	9	0.8
4	42	0.6
5	80	0.7
6	118	1.0
7	138	1.3
8	154	1.4
9	169	1.5
10	188	1.3
11	236	0.9

Georges Bank
Lat. 40°48′N, Long. 67°40′W

Time	Direction (true) Degrees	Velocity Knots
0	304	0.9
1	340	0.9
2	353	0.8
3	29	0.6
4	56	0.6
5	83	0.6
6	107	0.9
7	140	1.0
8	156	1.0
9	175	0.9
10	202	0.8
11	245	0.8

Georges Bank
Lat. 40°49′N, Long. 68°34′W

Time	Direction (true) Degrees	Velocity Knots
0	301	1.2
1	326	1.5
2	345	1.4
3	8	1.1
4	36	0.8
5	69	0.8
6	106	1.0
7	139	1.4
8	153	1.5
9	175	1.4
10	201	1.1
11	237	0.9

Great South Channel, Georges Bank
Lat. 40°31′N, Long. 68°47′W

Time	Direction (true) Degrees	Velocity Knots
0	320	0.7
1	331	0.9
2	342	1.1
3	3	1.0
4	23	0.8
5	63	0.4
6	129	0.7
7	140	0.9
8	164	1.0
9	179	1.0
10	190	0.8
11	221	0.6

Hours after maximum flood at Pollock Rip Channel

TABLE 6 – ROTARY TIDAL CURRENTS

Nantucket Shoals
Lat. 40°37′N, Long. 69°37′W

Time	Direction (true) Degrees	Velocity Knots
0	323	0.6
1	355	0.7
2	15	0.8
3	38	0.8
4	55	0.8
5	85	0.7
6	125	0.6
7	162	0.7
8	192	0.8
9	212	0.8
10	232	0.8
11	257	0.7

Great South Channel, Georges Bank
Lat. 41°10′N, Long. 68°56′W

Time	Direction (true) Degrees	Velocity Knots
0	318	0.5
1	349	0.7
2	352	1.1
3	356	1.0
4	359	0.7
5	18	0.4
6	106	0.4
7	157	0.7
8	165	1.0
9	173	1.0
10	180	0.8
11	204	0.6

Davis Bank, Nantucket Shoals 15 miles SE of Nantucket I.
Lat. 41°07′N, Long. 69°41′W

Time	Direction (true) Degrees	Velocity Knots
0	15	1.5
1	28	2.1
2	33	2.4
3	35	2.1
4	37	1.1
5	128	0.4
6	197	1.2
7	204	1.9
8	205	2.2
9	206	2.2
10	213	1.6
11	307	0.7

Davis Bank, Nantucket Shoals (west) 15 miles SE of Nantucket I.
Lat. 41°03′N, Long. 69°47′W

Time	Direction (true) Degrees	Velocity Knots
0	346	0.9
1	28	1.2
2	47	1.3
3	73	1.1
4	103	0.8
5	132	0.9
6	182	0.8
7	215	1.2
8	240	1.1
9	251	0.9
10	267	0.7
11	302	0.7

Davis Bank, Nantucket Shoals (mid) 17.5 miles SE of Nantucket I.
Lat. 41°02′N, Long. 69°43′W

Time	Direction (true) Degrees	Velocity Knots
0	23	0.8
1	27	1.5
2	28	1.9
3	29	1.8
4	46	1.1
5	115	0.4
6	191	1.2
7	202	1.9
8	215	1.7
9	225	1.5
10	233	0.9
11	270	0.2

Davis Bank, Nantucket Shoals (east) 18.5 miles SE of Nantucket I.
Lat. 41°02′N, Long. 69°41′W

Time	Direction (true) Degrees	Velocity Knots
0	30	0.6
1	36	1.3
2	38	1.5
3	50	1.4
4	80	1.1
5	105	0.8
6	178	0.6
7	230	1.3
8	235	1.7
9	238	1.4
10	241	1.0
11	265	0.3

Nantucket Island, 28 miles east of
Lat. 41°20′N, Long. 69°21′W

Time	Direction (true) Degrees	Velocity Knots
0	19	0.9
1	7	1.3
2	359	1.4
3	351	1.1
4	334	0.5
5	221	0.3
6	198	0.8
7	185	1.1
8	184	1.1
9	184	0.9
10	183	0.7
11	60	0.1

Monomoy Point, 23 miles east of
Lat. 41°35′N, Long. 69°30′W

Time	Direction (true) Degrees	Velocity Knots
0	320	0.7
1	324	1.0
2	326	0.9
3	330	0.7
4	334	0.3
5	144	0.1
6	145	0.5
7	146	0.8
8	147	0.9
9	148	0.8
10	150	0.4
11	230	0.1

Nauset Beach Light, 5 miles NE of
Lat. 41°56′N, Long. 69°54′W

Time	Direction (true) Degrees	Velocity Knots
0	315	0.5
1	327	0.6
2	340	0.5
3	357	0.2
4	16	0.1
5	124	0.2
6	132	0.4
7	135	0.6
8	139	0.6
9	145	0.4
10	269	0.2
11	297	0.2

Great Round Shoal Channel ent, Nantucket Sound ent
Lat. 41°26′N, Long. 69°44′W

Time	Direction (true) Degrees	Velocity Knots
0	32	1.6
1	45	1.4
2	68	1.3
3	95	1.1
4	140	0.8
5	192	1.2
6	210	1.5
7	220	1.5
8	235	1.2
9	264	0.9
10	303	0.8
11	350	1.2

Great Round Shoal Channel Buoy 9, 0.3 ,miles NE of
Lat. 41°24′N, Long. 69°55′W

Time	Direction (true) Degrees	Velocity Knots
0	47	1.0
1	60	1.3
2	70	1.3
3	91	0.8
4	153	0.5
5	211	0.7
6	234	0.9
7	247	1.3
8	252	1.1
9	260	0.9
10	305	0.3
11	35	0.4

Great Round Shoal Channel, 4 miles NE of Great Pt., Nantucket Sound
Lat. 41°26′N, Long. 69°59′W

Time	Direction (true) Degrees	Velocity Knots
0	80	0.8
1	88	1.1
2	96	1.3
3	104	1.0
4	129	0.5
5	213	0.5
6	267	1.1
7	275	1.4
8	280	1.2
9	284	0.7
10	328	0.2
11	42	0.4

Hours after maximum flood at Pollock Rip Channel

TABLE 6 – ROTARY TIDAL CURRENTS

Cuttyhunk I., 3.25 miles SW of
Lat. 41°23′N, Long. 71°00′W

Hours after maximum flood at Pollock Rip Channel

Time	Direction (true) Degrees	Velocity Knots
0	356	0.4
1	15	0.3
2	80	0.2
3	123	0.3
4	146	0.5
5	158	0.5
6	173	0.4
7	208	0.3
8	267	0.2
9	306	0.3
10	322	0.3
11	335	0.4

Gooseberry Neck, 2 miles SSE of Buzzards Bay entrance
Lat. 41°27′N, Long. 71°01′W

Hours after maximum flood at Pollock Rip Channel

Time	Direction (true) Degrees	Velocity Knots
0	52	0.6
1	65	0.4
2	108	0.2
3	168	0.3
4	210	0.4
5	223	0.5
6	232	0.5
7	249	0.3
8	274	0.2
9	321	0.2
10	16	0.3
11	38	0.5

Browns Ledge, Massachusetts
Lat. 41°20′N, Long. 71°06′W

Hours after maximum flood at Pollock Rip Channel

Time	Direction (true) Degrees	Velocity Knots
0	330	0.3
1	12	0.3
2	28	0.3
3	104	0.4
4	118	0.4
5	123	0.4
6	168	0.3
7	205	0.2
8	201	0.3
9	270	0.3
10	282	0.4
11	318	0.5

Point Judith, Harbor of Refuge, Block Island Sound (west entrance)
Lat. 41°22′N, Long. 71°31′W

Hours after maximum flood at The Race

Time	Direction (true) Degrees	Velocity Knots
0	197	0.2
1	160	0.2
2	151	0.4
3	159	0.5
4	146	0.5
5	124	0.5
6	109	0.4
7	104	0.2
8	90	0.1
9	30	0.1
10	336	0.1
11	209	0.1

Point Judith, 4.5 miles SW of Block Island Sound
Lat. 41°18′N, Long. 71°33′W

Hours after maximum flood at The Race

Time	Direction (true) Degrees	Velocity Knots
0	264	0.6
1	270	0.6
2	270	0.5
3	280	0.2
4	62	0.2
5	70	0.6
6	78	0.7
7	95	0.5
8	105	0.3
9	120	0.1
10	286	0.1
11	277	0.3

Grace Point, 2 miles NW of Block Island Sound
Lat. 41°12′N, Long. 71°38′W

Hours after maximum flood at The Race

Time	Direction (true) Degrees	Velocity Knots
0	304	0.2
1	2	0.2
2	28	0.4
3	28	0.6
4	37	0.7
5	71	0.6
6	86	0.6
7	126	0.4
8	137	0.2
9	213	0.1
10	256	0.1
11	267	0.1

Little Gull I., 3.7 miles ESE of Block island Sound
Lat. 41°11′N, Long. 72°02′W

Hours after maximum flood at The Race

Time	Direction (true) Degrees	Velocity Knots
0	271	0.8
1	284	0.5
2	320	0.2
3	68	0.2
4	77	0.7
5	95	1.1
6	118	1.6
7	128	1.2
8	150	0.6
9	171	0.2
10	221	0.4
11	228	0.7

Sandy Hook Approach Lighted Horn Buoy 2A, 0.2 mile W of
Lat. 40°27′N, Long. 73°55′W

Hours after maximum flood at The Narrows, N.Y. Harbor

Time	Direction (true) Degrees	Velocity Knots
0	313	0.4
1	325	0.3
2	356	0.2
3	55	0.2
4	94	0.3
5	118	0.4
6	136	0.6
7	147	0.5
8	177	0.2
9	256	0.2
10	290	0.3
11	298	0.4

Fenwick Shoal Lighted Whistle Buoy 2, off Delaware coast
Lat. 38°25′N, Long. 74°46′W

Hours after maximum flood at Delaware Bay Entrance

Time	Direction (true) Degrees	Velocity Knots
0	342	0.2
1	349	0.2
2	357	0.1
3	43	0.1
4	110	0.1
5	135	0.2
6	150	0.3
7	165	0.3
8	185	0.2
9	226	0.1
10	282	0.1
11	318	0.2

***Frying Pan Shoals, off Cape Fear**
Lat. 33°34′N, Long. 77°49′W

Hours after maximum flood at Charleston

Time	Direction (true) Degrees	Velocity Knots
0	335	0.3
1	10	0.2
2	50	0.2
3	90	0.3
4	110	0.3
5	128	0.3
6	150	0.3
7	188	0.2
8	235	0.2
9	268	0.3
10	290	0.3
11	305	0.3

Cape Romain, 5 miles SE of
Lat. 32°57′N, Long. 79°17′W

Hours after maximum flood at Charleston

Time	Direction (true) Degrees	Velocity Knots
0	6	0.2
1	38	0.2
2	55	0.3
3	67	0.3
4	93	0.3
5	114	0.3
6	167	0.2
7	212	0.2
8	242	0.3
9	244	0.4
10	262	0.3
11	292	0.3

Cape Romain, 6.9 miles SW of
Lat. 32°54′N, Long. 79°26′W

Hours after maximum flood at Charleston

Time	Direction (true) Degrees	Velocity Knots
0	317	0.3
1	350	0.2
2	19	0.2
3	71	0.3
4	115	0.3
5	111	0.3
6	132	0.2
7	160	0.2
8	216	0.2
9	251	0.2
10	266	0.3
11	303	0.3

Current during June-August usually sets eastward, average velocity ½ knots.

TABLE 6 – ROTARY TIDAL CURRENTS

Capers Inlet, 1.9 miles east of Lat. 32°50′N, Long. 79°40′W

Time	*Direction (true) Degrees*	*Velocity Knots*
0	12	0.1
1	58	0.1
2	52	0.2
3	53	0.2
4	67	0.1
5	98	0.1
6	129	0.1
7	214	0.1
8	222	0.2
9	254	0.2
10	246	0.1
11	247	0.1

Capers Inlet, 3.6 miles SE of Lat. 32°49′N, Long. 79°38′W

Time	*Direction (true) Degrees*	*Velocity Knots*
0	302	0.2
1	357	0.1
2	34	0.1
3	17	0.2
4	89	0.2
5	94	0.2
6	112	0.2
7	116	0.2
8	189	0.1
9	249	0.2
10	268	0.2
11	282	0.2

Charleston Entrance, 37 miles east of Lat. 32°42′N, Long. 79°06′W

Time	*Direction (true) Degrees*	*Velocity Knots*
0	328	0.3
1	350	0.3
2	20	0.2
3	65	0.2
4	95	0.3
5	118	0.3
6	140	0.3
7	163	0.3
8	195	0.2
9	235	0.2
10	268	0.2
11	295	0.3

Charleston Lighted Whistle Buoy 2C off Charleston Harbor entrance Lat. 32°41′N, Long. 79°43′W

Time	*Direction (true) Degrees*	*Velocity Knots*
0	300	0.2
1	332	0.2
2	17	0.1
3	55	0.2
4	77	0.3
5	93	0.3
6	117	0.3
7	153	0.2
8	207	0.2
9	242	0.2
10	260	0.3
11	275	0.3

Folly Island, 2 miles east of Lat. 32°39′N, Long. 79°52′W

Time	*Direction (true) Degrees*	*Velocity Knots*
0	346	0.1
1	24	0.2
2	58	0.3
3	76	0.3
4	102	0.3
5	121	0.2
6	164	0.1
7	222	0.2
8	256	0.2
9	256	0.3
10	271	0.3
11	290	0.2

Folly Island, 3.5 miles east of Lat. 32°38′N, Long. 79°50′W

Time	*Direction (true) Degrees*	*Velocity Knots*
0	322	0.1
1	47	0.2
2	69	0.2
3	86	0.2
4	96	0.2
5	115	0.2
6	148	0.1
7	215	0.1
8	256	0.2
9	260	0.2
10	265	0.2
11	285	0.1

Martins Industry, 5 miles east of, off Port Royal Sound Lat. 32°06′N, Long. 80°28′W

Time	*Direction (true) Degrees*	*Velocity Knots*
0	282	0.4
1	293	0.3
2	330	0.1
3	30	0.1
4	75	0.3
5	92	0.4
6	102	0.5
7	110	0.4
8	140	0.2
9	200	0.2
10	250	0.3
11	271	0.4

Savannah Light, 1.2 miles SE of Lat. 31°57′N, Long. 80°40′W

Time	*Direction (true) Degrees*	*Velocity Knots*
0	296	0.3
1	308	0.2
2	326	0.1
3	45	0.1
4	90	0.2
5	107	0.3
6	114	0.3
7	123	0.3
8	145	0.2
9	213	0.1
10	267	0.2
11	283	0.3

Hours after maximum flood atSavannah River Entrance

Hours after maximum flood at Charleston

Fire Island Inlet, N. Y., 22 mile south of:
Tidal current is weak, averaging about 0·1 knot at strength.

Fire Island Lighted Whistle Buoy 2 Fl:
Tidal current is weak, averaging about 0.2 knot at strength.

Ambrose Light, New York Harbor entrance:
Tidal current is weak, averaging about 0·2 knot at strength.

Cape May, N.J., 72 miles east of:
Tidal current is weak, averaging about 0·1 knot at strength.

Five-Fathom Bank Northeast Lighted Whistle Buoy 2FB:
Tidal current is weak, averaging about 0·2 knot at strength.

Winter-Quarter Shoal Lighted Whistle Buoy 6WQS, 9·2 miles SE of, off Assateague I:
Tidal current is weak, averaging less than 0·1 knot.

Cape Charles, 70 miles east of:
Tidal current is weak, averaging about 0·2 knot at strength.

Chesapeake Light, 4.4 miles NE of, off Chesapeake Bay entrance, Va:
Tidal current is weak and variable.

Cape Lookout Shoals Lighted Whistle Buoy 14:
Tidal current is weak, averaging about 0·2 knot at strength.
Current during June-August usually sets eastward, averaging speed 0·5 knot.

Ocracoke Inlet, 3.5 miles SSE of:
Tidal current is weak, averaging about 0·1 knot at strength.

Diamond Shoal Light, 3·9 miles SSW of:
Tidal current is weak, averaging less than 0·1 knot at strength.
Current during June-August usually sets northeastward, average speed 0·75 knot.

Frying Pan Shoals Light, 14·3 miles NW of:
Tidal current is weak, averaging about 0·2 knot at strength.
Current during June-August usually sets eastward, average speed 0·5 knot.

St. Johns Point, 5 miles east of, Fla:
Tidal current is weak and averaging about 0.2 knot at strength.

Fowey Rocks Light, 1.5 miles SW of:
Tidal current is weak and variable.

TABLE 7 – WIND-DRIVEN CURRENTS

AVERAGE DEVIATION OF CURRENT TO RIGHT OR LEFT OF WIND DIRECTION

Pacific Coast

Light Station*	San Francisco		Blunts Reef		Columbia River		Umatilla Reef		Swiftsure Bank	
	Left	Right	Left	Right	Left	Right	Left	Right	Left	Right
Wind from:	*	*	*	*	*	*	*	*	*	*
N	---	061	---	020	---	035	---	044	---	100
NNE...........	---	027	---	006	---	027	---	018	---	054
NE	---	030	---	010	---	009	---	034	---	048
ENE	---	031	---	032	---	029	---	048	---	033
E	---	023	---	028	---	017	---	052	---	027
ESE	---	029	---	007	---	002	---	038	---	018
SE	---	021	011	---	008	---	---	025	---	009
SSE	---	005	---	013	007	---	---	006	---	001
S	020	---	---	001	019	---	006	---	015	---
SSW...........	030	---	011	---	044	---	013	---	021	---
SW	049	---	018	---	074	---	032	---	068	--
WSW	040	---	028	---	121	---	052	---	088	---
W.............	051	---	060	000	000	145	077	---	090	---
WNW	---	033	---	002	---	105	006	---	---	082
NW	---	016	---	031	---	078	---	037	---	130
NNW	---	017	---	043	---	053	---	025	---	111

* All of these lightships have since been removed.

TABLE 7 – WIND-DRIVEN CURRENTS ATLANTIC COAST

Average deviation of current to right of wind direction

[A minus sign (–) indicates that the current sets to the left of the wind]

Wind from			N	NNE	NE	ENE	E	ESE	SE	SSE	S	SSW	SW	WSW	W	WNW	NW	NNW
Old Lightship Stations	Lat.	Long.																
	° ′	° ′	°	°	°	°	°	°	°	°	°	°	°	°	°	°	°	°
Portland	43 32	70 06	24	14	9	8	-2	-14	0	26	15	18	18	24	15	34	13	18
Boston	42 20	70 45	---	-1	---	21	---	32	---	29	---	20	---	2	---	19	---	15
Pollock Rip Slue	41 37	69 54	6	5	48	-38	30	-53	-24	-75	-25	167	70	59	36	53	20	19
Nantucket Shoals	40 37	69 37	44	46	28	24	9	16	12	3	25	0	6	18	30	39	41	48
Hen and Chickens	41 27	71 01	16	14	-7	-1	-14	3	-39	-36	25	55	35	30	20	16	16	8
Brenton Reef	41 26	71 23	34	25	22	19	25	1	-7	8	27	48	23	41	41	31	21	24
Fire Island	40 29	73 11	35	23	15	8	2	-17	31	55	40	41	31	14	-2	0	25	37
Ambrose Channel	40 27	73 49	36	40	21	11	18	72	27	112	82	70	63	46	37	22	23	21
Scotland	40 27	73 55	16	-12	-26	-36	-61	-36	-92	-150	90	33	77	44	15	30	27	13
Barnegat	39 46	73 56	6	5	-13	-9	-16	-7	33	54	55	30	14	8	0	-5	21	29
Northeast End	38 58	74 30	30	14	-3	-11	-20	-31	-42	-28	37	44	25	18	7	16	25	18
Overfalls	38 48	75 01	28	-6	-1	2	-40	-56	-78	-22	68	28	55	54	32	31	32	45
Winter-Quarter Shoal	37 55	74 56	18	-1	-5	-21	-27	-35	-19	31	23	20	4	14	9	8	28	27
Chesapeake	36 59	75 42	18	-2	-4	5	-6	23	73	71	57	38	27	26	22	18	15	22
Diamond Shoal	35 05	75 20	11	3	-3	36	65	88	74	52	40	22	7	-10	-13	-17	-25	-4
Cape Lookout Shoals	34 18	76 24	30	24	2	2	-29	---	21	80	54	31	32	21	2	18	5	-5
Frying Pan Shoals	33 34	77 49	34	34	18	6	2	9	48	55	48	38	26	14	-7	-12	-27	-6
Savannah	31 57	80 40	12	12	-9	-18	-23	-46	17	50	43	17	7	-8	-10	7	15	33
Brunswick	31 00	81 10	17	-2	-10	-28	-18	-21	37	29	23	2	6	-21	-21	-26	16	18
St. Johns	30 23	81 18	3	-12	-27	-47	-84	30	35	26	26	27	1	16	-8	-17	6	8

TABLE 8 – CONVERSION OF FEET TO CENTIMETERS

Feet	TENTHS OF A FOOT 0.0	0.1	0.2	0.3	0.4	0.5	0.6	0.7	0.8	0.9	Feet
0	0	3	6	9	12	15	18	21	24	27	**0**
1	30	34	37	40	43	46	49	52	55	58	**1**
2	61	64	67	70	73	76	79	82	85	88	**2**
3	91	94	98	101	104	107	110	113	116	119	**3**
4	122	125	128	131	134	137	140	143	146	149	**4**
5	152	155	158	162	165	168	171	174	177	180	**5**
6	183	186	189	192	195	198	201	204	207	210	**6**
7	213	216	219	223	226	229	232	235	238	241	**7**
8	244	247	250	253	256	259	262	265	268	271	**8**
9	274	277	280	283	287	290	293	296	299	302	**9**
10	305	308	311	314	317	320	323	326	329	332	**10**
11	335	338	341	344	347	351	354	357	360	363	**11**
12	366	369	372	375	378	381	384	387	390	393	**12**
13	396	399	402	405	408	411	415	418	421	424	**13**
14	427	430	433	436	439	442	445	448	451	454	**14**
15	457	460	463	466	469	472	475	479	482	485	**15**
16	488	491	494	497	500	503	506	509	512	515	**16**
17	518	521	524	527	530	533	536	539	543	546	**17**
18	549	552	555	558	561	564	567	570	573	576	**18**
19	579	582	585	588	591	594	597	600	604	607	**19**
20	610	613	616	619	622	625	628	631	634	637	**20**
21	640	643	646	649	652	655	658	661	664	668	**21**
22	671	674	677	680	683	686	689	692	695	698	**22**
23	701	704	707	710	713	716	719	722	725	728	**23**
24	732	735	738	741	744	747	750	753	756	759	**24**
25	762	765	768	771	774	777	780	783	786	789	**25**
26	792	796	799	802	805	808	811	814	817	820	**26**
27	823	826	829	832	835	838	841	844	847	850	**27**
28	853	856	860	863	866	869	872	875	878	881	**28**
29	884	887	890	893	896	899	902	905	908	911	**29**
30	914	917	920	924	927	930	933	936	939	942	**30**
31	945	948	951	954	957	960	963	966	969	972	**31**
32	975	978	981	985	988	991	994	997	1000	1003	**32**
33	1006	1009	1012	1015	1018	1021	1024	1027	1030	1033	**33**
34	1036	1039	1042	1045	1049	1052	1055	1058	1061	1064	**34**
35	1067	1070	1073	1076	1079	1082	1085	1088	1091	1094	**35**
36	1097	1100	1103	1106	1109	1113	1116	1119	1122	1125	**36**
37	1128	1131	1134	1137	1140	1143	1146	1149	1152	1155	**37**
38	1158	1161	1164	1167	1170	1173	1177	1180	1183	1186	**38**
39	1189	1192	1195	1198	1201	1204	1207	1210	1213	1216	**39**
40	1219	1222	1225	1228	1231	1234	1237	1241	1244	1247	**40**
41	1250	1253	1256	1259	1262	1265	1268	1271	1274	1277	**41**
42	1283	1283	1286	1289	1292	1295	1298	1301	1305	1308	**42**
43	1311	1314	1317	1320	1323	1326	1329	1332	1335	1338	**43**
44	1341	1344	1347	1350	1353	1356	1359	1362	1366	1369	**44**
45	1372	1375	1378	1381	1384	1387	1390	1393	1396	1399	**45**
46	1402	1405	1408	1411	1414	1417	1420	1423	1426	1430	**46**
47	1433	1436	1439	1442	1445	1448	1451	1454	1457	1460	**47**
48	1463	1466	1469	1472	1475	1478	1481	1484	1487	1490	**48**
49	1494	1497	1500	1503	1506	1509	1512	1515	1518	1521	**49**
50	1524	1527	1530	1533	1536	1539	1542	1545	1548	1551	**50**

Feet to Meters = Centimeters divided by 100 (from above table).
Example: 09.40 feet = (287 centimeters) / (100) = 02.87 meters.

1 Meter = 100 centimeters
1 Meter = 3.2808399 feet

1 Foot = 0.30480061 meters
1 Foot = 30.480061 centimeters

GLOSSARY OF TIDE TERMS

Annual Inequality: Seasonal variation in the water level or current, more or less periodic, due chiefly to meteorological causes.

Apogean Tides or Tidal Currents: Tides of decreased range or currents of decreased speed occurring monthly as the result of the moon being in apogee (farthest from the Earth).

Automatic Tide Gage: An instrument that automatically registers the rise and fall of the tide. In some instruments, the registration is accomplished by recording the heights at regular intervals in digital format, in others by a continuous graph in which the height, versus corresponding time of the tide, is recorded.

Bench Mark (BM): A fixed physical object or marks used as reference for a vertical datum. A tidal bench mark is one near a tide station to which the tide staff and tidal datums are referred. A *Geodetic bench mark* identifies a surveyed point in the National Geodetic Vertical Network.

Chart Datum: The tidal datum to which soundings on a chart are referred. It is usually taken to correspond to low water elevation of the tide, and its depression below mean sea level is represented by the symbol Zo.

Current: Generally, a horizontal movement of water. Currents may be classified as *tidal and nontidal*. Tidal currents are caused by gravitational interactions between the sun, moon, and earth and are a part of the same general movement of the sea that is manifested in the vertical rise and fall, called *tide*. Nontidal currents include the permanent currents in the general circulatory systems of the sea as well as temporary currents arising from more pronounced meteorological variability.

Current Difference: Difference between the time of slack water (or minimum current) or strength of current in any locality and the time of the corresponding phase of the tidal current at a reference station, for which predictions are given in the *Tidal Current Tables*.

Current Ellipse: A graphic representation of a rotary current in which the velocity of the current at different hours of the tidal cycle is represented by radius vectors and vectorial angles. A line joining the extremities of the radius vectors will form a curve roughly approximating an ellipse. The cycle is completed in one-half tidal day or in a whole tidal day according to whether the tidal current is of the semidiurnal or the diurnal type. A current of the mixed type will give a curve of two unequal loops each tidal day.

Current Meter: An instrument for measuring the speed and direction or just the speed of a current. The measurements are usually Eulerian since the meter is most often fixed or moored at a specific location.

Datum (vertical): For marine applications, a base elevation used as a reference from which to reckon heights or depths. It is called a *tidal datum* when defined by a certain phase of the tide. Tidal datums are local datums and should not be extended into areas which have differing topographic features without substantiating measurements. In order that they may be recovered when needed, such datums are referenced to fixed points known as *bench marks*.

Daylight Saving Time: A time used during the summer in some localities in which clocks are advanced 1 hour from the usual standard time.

Diurnal: Having a period or cycle of approximately 1 tidal day. Thus, the tide is said to be diurnal when only one high water and one low water occur during a tidal day, and the tidal current is said to be diurnal when there is a single flood and single ebb period in the tidal day. A rotary current is diurnal if it changes its directions through all points of the compass once each tidal day.

Diurnal Inequality: The difference in height of the two high waters or of the two low waters of each day; also the difference in speed between the two flood tidal currents or the two ebb tidal currents of each day. The difference changes with the declination of the moon and to a lesser extent with the declination of the sun. In general, the inequality tends to increase with an increasing declination, either north or south, and to diminish as the moon approaches the Equator. *Mean diurnal high water inequality* (DHQ) is one-half the average difference between the two high waters of each day observed over a specific 19-year Metonic cycle (the National Tidal Datum Epoch). It is obtained by subtracting the mean of all high waters from the mean of the higher high waters. Mean diurnal low water inequality (DLQ) is one-half the average difference between the two low waters of each day observed over a specific 19-year Metonic cycle (the National Tidal Datum Epoch). It is obtained by subtracting the mean of the lower low waters from the mean of all low waters. Tropic high water inequality

(HWQ) is the average difference between the two high waters of the day at the times of the tropic tides. Tropic low water inequality (LWQ) is the average difference between the two low waters of the day at the times of the tropic tides. Mean and tropic inequalities as defined above are applicable only when the type of tide is either semidiurnal or mixed. Diurnal inequality is sometimes called declinational inequality.

Double Ebb: An ebb tidal current where, after ebb begins, the speed increases to a maximum called first ebb; it then decreases, reaching a minimum ebb near the middle of the ebb period (and at some places it may actually run in a flood direction for a short period); it then again ebbs to a maximum speed called second ebb after which it decreases to slack water.

Double Flood: A flood tidal current where, after flood begins, the speed increases to a maximum called first flood; it then decreases, reaching a minimum flood near the middle of the flood period (and at some places it may actually run in an ebb direction for a short period); it then again floods to a maximum speed called second flood after which it decreases to slack water.

Double Tide: A double-headed tide, that is, a high water consisting of two maxima of nearly the same height separated by a relatively small depression, or a low water consisting of two minima separated by a relatively small elevation. Sometimes, it is called an agger.

Duration of Flood and Duration of Ebb: Duration of flood is the interval of time in which a tidal current is flooding, and the duration of ebb is the interval in which it is ebbing. Together they cover, on an average, a period of 12.42 hours for a semidiurnal tidal current or a period of 24.84 hours for a diurnal current. In a normal semidiurnal tidal current, the duration of flood and duration of ebb will each be approximately equal to 6.21 hours, but the times may be modified greatly by the presence of a nontidal flow. In a river the duration of ebb is usually longer than the duration of flood because of the freshwater discharge, especially during the-spring when snow and ice melt are the predominant influences.

Duration of Rise and Duration of Fall: Duration of rise is the interval from low water to high water, and duration of fall is the interval from high water to low water. Together they cover, on an average, a period of 12.42 hours for a semidiurnal tide or a period of 24.84 hours for a diurnal tide. in a normal semidiurnal tide, the duration of rise and duration of fall will each be approximately equal to 6.21 hours, but in shallow waters and in rivers there is a tendency for a decrease in the duration of rise and a corresponding increase in the duration of fall.

Ebb Current: The movement of a tidal current away from shore or down a tidal river or estuary. In the mixed type of reversing tidal current, the terms greater ebb and lesser ebb are applied respectively to the ebb tidal currents of greater and lesser speed of each day. The terms maximum ebb and minimum ebb are applied to the maximum and minimum speeds of a current running continuously ebb, the speed alternately increasing and decreasing without coming to a slack or reversing. The expression maximum ebb is also applicable to any ebb current at the time of greatest speed.

Equatorial Tidal Currents: Tidal currents occurring semimonthly as a result of the moon being over the Equator. At these times the tendency of the Moon to produce a diurnal inequality in the tidal current is at a minimum.

Equatorial Tides: Tides occurring semi monthly as the result of the Moon being over the Equator. At these times the tendency of the Moon to produce a diurnal inequality in the tide is at a minimum.

Flood Current: The movement of a tidal current toward the shore or up a tidal river or estuary. In the mixed type of reversing current, the terms greater flood and lesser flood are applied respectively to the flood currents of greater and lesser speed of each day. The terms maximum flood and minimum flood are applied to the maximum and minimum speeds of a flood current, the speed of which alternately increases and decreases without coming to a slack or reversing. The expression maximum flood is also applicable to any flood current at the time of greatest speed.

Great Diurnal Range (Gt): The difference in height between mean higher high water and mean lower low water. The expression may also be used in its contracted form, diurnal range.

Gulf Coast Low Water Datum: A chart datum. Specifically, the tidal datum formerly designated for the coastal waters of the Gulf

Coast of the United States. It was defined as mean lower low water when the type of tide was mixed and mean low water when the type of tide was diurnal.

Half-Tide Level: See mean tide level.

Harmonic Analysis: The mathematical process by which the observed tide or tidal current at any place is separated into basic harmonic constituents.

Harmonic Constants: The amplitudes and epochs of the harmonic constituents of the tide or tidal current at any place.

Harmonic Constituent: One of the harmonic elements in a mathematical expression for the tide-producing force and in corresponding formulas for the tide or tidal current. Each constituent represents a periodic change or variation in the relative positions of the earth, moon, and sun. A single constituent is usually written in the form $y=A\cos(at+\alpha)$, in which y is a function of time as expressed by the symbol t and is reckoned from a specific origin. The coefficient A is called the amplitude of the constituent and is a measure of its relative importance. The angle $(at+\alpha)$ changes uniformly and its value at any time is called the phase of the constituent. The speed of the constituent is the rate of change in its phase and is represented by the symbol a in the formula. The quantity α is the phase of the constituent at the initial instant from which the time is reckoned. The period of the constituent is the time required for the phase to change through 360° and is the cycle of the astronomical condition represented by the constituent.

High Water (HW): The maximum height reached by a rising tide. The height may be due solely to the periodic tidal forces or it may have superimposed upon it the effects of prevailing meteorological conditions. Use of the synonymous term, high tide, is discouraged.

Higher High Water (HHW): The higher of the two high waters of any tidal day.

Higher Low Water (HLW): The higher of the two low waters of any tidal day.

HYDRAULIC CURRENT: A current in a channel caused-by a difference in the surface level at the two ends. Such a current may be expected in a strait connecting two bodies of water in which the tides differ in time or range. The current in the East River, N.Y., connecting Long Island Sound and New York Harbor, is an example.

Knot: A speed unit of 1 international nautical mile (1,852.0 meters or 6,076.11549 international feet) per hour.

Low Water (LW): The minimum height reached by a falling tide. The height may be due solely to the periodic tidal forces or it may have superimposed upon it the effects of meteorological conditions. Use of the synonymous term, low tide, is discouraged.

Lower High Water (LHW): The lower of the two high waters of any tidal day.

Lower Low Water (LLW): The lower of the two low waters of any tidal day.

Lunar Day: The time of the rotation of the earth with respect to the moon, or the interval between two successive upper transits of the Moon over the meridian of a place. The mean lunar day is approximately 24.84 solar hours long, or 1.035 times as long as the mean solar day.

Lunar Interval: The difference in time between the transit of the Moon over the meridian of Greenwich and over a local meridian. The average value of this interval expressed in hours is 0.069 L, in which L is the local longitude in degrees, positive for west longitude and negative for east longitude. The lunar interval equals the difference between the local and Greenwich interval of a tide or current phase.

Lunicurrent Interval: The interval between the Moon's transit (upper or lower) over the local or Greenwich meridian and a specified phase of the tidal current following the transit.

Examples: strength of flood interval and strength of ebb interval, which may be abbreviated to flood interval and ebb interval, respectively.The interval is described as local or Greenwich according to whether the reference is to the moon's transit over the local or Greenwich meridian. When not otherwise specified, the reference is assumed to be local.

Lunitidal Interval: The interval between the moon's transit (upper or lower) over the local or Greenwich meridian and the following high or low water. The average of all high water intervals for all phases of the Moon is known as mean high water lunitidal interval and is abbreviated to high water interval (HWI). Similarly the mean low water lunitidal interval is abbreviated to low water interval (LWI). The interval is described as local or Greenwich according to whether the reference is to the transit over the local or Greenwich meridian. When not otherwise specified, the reference is assumed to be local.

Mean High Water (MHW): A tidal datum. The arithmetic mean of the high water heights observed over a specific l9-year Metonic cycle (the National Tidal Datum Epoch). For stations with shorter series, simultaneous observational comparisons are made with a primary control tide station in order to derive the equivalent of a l9-year value.

Mean Higher High Water (MHHW): A tidal datum. The arithmetic mean of the higher high water heights of a mixed tide observed over a specific 19-year Metonic cycle (the National Tidal Datum Epoch). Only the higher high water of each pair of high waters, or the only high water of a tidal day is included in the mean.

Mean Higher High Water Line (MHHWL): The intersection of the land with the water surface at the elevation of mean higher high water.

Mean Low Water (MLW): A tidal datum. The arithmetic mean of the low water heights observed over a specific l9-year Metonic cycle (the National Tidal Datum Epoch). For stations with shorter series, simultaneous observational comparisons are made with a primary control tide station in order to derive the equivalent of a 19-year value.

Mean Low Water Springs (MLWS): A tidal datum. Frequently abbreviated spring low water. The arithmetic mean of the low water heights occurring at the time of the spring tides observed over a specific l9-year Metonic cycle (the National Tidal Datum Epoch).

Mean Lower Low Water (MLLW): A tidal datum. The arithmetic mean of the lower low water heights of a mixed tide observed over a specific 19-year Metonic cycle (the National Tidal Datum Epoch). Only the lower low water of each pair of low waters, or the only low water of a tidal day is included in the mean.

Mean Range of Tide (Mn): The difference in height between mean high water and mean low water.

Mean River Level: A tidal datum. The average height of the surface of a tidal river at any point for all stages of the tide observed over a 19-year Metonic cycle (the National Tidal Datum Epoch), usually determined from hourly height readings. In rivers subject to occasional freshets the river level may undergo wide variations, and for practical purposes certain months of the year may be excluded in the determination of tidal datums. For charting purposes, tidal datums for rivers are usually based on observations during selected periods when the river is at or near low water stage.

Mean Sea Level (MSL): A tidal datum. The arithmetic mean of hourly water elevations observed over a specific l9-year Metonic cycle (the National Tidal Datum Epoch). Shorter series are specified in the name; e.g., monthly mean sea level and yearly mean sea level.

Mean Tide Level (MTL): Also called half-tide level. A tidal datum midway between mean high water and mean low water.

Mixed Tide: Type of tide with a large inequality in the high and/or low water heights, with two high waters and two low waters usually occurring each tidal day. In strictness, all tides are mixed but the name is usually applied to the tides intermediate to those predominantly semidiurnal and those predominantly diurnal.

Neap Tides or Tidal Currents: Tides of decreased range or tidal currents of decreased speed occurring semimonthly as the result of the Moon being in quadrature. The neap range (Np) of the tide is the average semidiurnal range occurring at the time of neap tides and is most conveniently computed from the harmonic constants. It is smaller than the mean range where the type of tide is either semidiurnal or mixed and is of no practical significance where the type of tide is diurnal. The average height of the high waters of the neap tides is called neap high water or high water neaps (MHWN) and the average height of the corresponding low waters is called neap low water or low water neaps (MLWN).

Perigean Tides or Tidal Currents: Tides of increased range or tidal currents of increased speed occurring monthly as the result of the Moon being in perigee or nearest the Earth. The perigean range (Pn) of tide is the average semi-diurnal range occurring at the time of perigean tides and is most conveniently computed from the harmonic constants. It is larger than the mean range where the type of tide is either semidiurnal or mixed, and is of no practical significance where the type of tide is diurnal.

Range of Tide: The difference in height between consecutive high and low waters, the mean range is the difference in height between mean high water and mean low water. Where the type of tide is diurnal the mean range is the same as the diurnal range. For other ranges, see great diurnal, spring, neap, perigean, apogean, and tropic tides.

Reference Station: A tide or current station for which independent daily predictions are given in the Tide Tables and Tidal Current Tables, and from which corresponding predictions are obtained for subordinate stations by means of differences and ratios.

Reversing Current: A tidal current which flows alternately in approximately opposite directions with a slack water at each reversal of direction. Currents of this type usually occur in rivers and straits where the direction of flow is more or less restricted to certain channels. When the movement is towards the shore or up a stream, the current is said to be flooding, and when in the opposite direction it is said to be ebbing. The combined flood and ebb movement including the slack water covers, on an average, 12.42 hours for the semidiurnal current. If unaffected by a nontidal flow, the flood and ebb movements will each last about 6 hours, but when combined with such a flow, the durations of flood and ebb may be quite unequal. During the flow in each direction the speed of the current will vary from zero at the time of slack water to a maximum about midway between the slacks.

Rotary Current: A tidal current that flows continually with the direction of flow changing through all points of the compass during the tidal period. Rotary currents are usually found offshore where the direction of flow is not restricted by any barriers. The tendency for the rotation in direction has its origin in the coriolis force and, unless modified by local conditions, the change is clockwise in the Northern Hemisphere and counter clockwise in the Southern. The speed of the current usually varies throughout the tidal cycle, passing through the two maxima in approximately opposite directions and the two minima with the direction at time of maximum speed.

Semidiurnal: Having a period or cycle of approximately one-half of a tidal day. The predominating type of tide throughout the world is semi-diurnal, with two high waters and two low waters each tidal day. The tidal current is said to be semidiurnal when there are two flood and two ebb periods each day.

Set (of current): The direction towards which the current flows.

Slack Water: The state of a tidal current when its speed is near zero, especially the moment when a reversing current changes direction and its speed is zero. The term is also applied to the entire period of low speed near the time of turning of the current when it is too weak to be of any practical importance in navigation. The relation of the time of slack water to the tidal phases varies in different localities. For standing tidal waves, slack water occurs near the times of high and low water, while for progressive tidal waves, slack water occurs midway between high and low water.

Spring Tides or Tidal Currents: Tides of increased range or tidal currents of increased speed occurring semi-monthly as the result of the Moon being new or full. The spring range (Sg) of tide is the average semidiurnal range occurring at the time of spring tides and is most conveniently computed from the harmonic constants. It is larger than the mean range where the type of tide is either semidiurnal or mixed, and is of no practical significance where the type of tide is diurnal. The mean of the high waters of the spring tide is called spring high water or mean high water springs (MHWS), and the average height of the corresponding low waters is called spring low water or mean low water springs (MLWS).

Stand of Tide: Sometimes called a platform tide. An interval at high or low water when there is no sensible change in the height of the tide. The water level is stationary at high and low water for only an instant, but the change in level near these times is so slow that it is not usually perceptible. In general, the duration of the apparent stand will depend upon the range of tide, being longer for a small range than for a large range, but where there is a tendency for a double tide the stand may last for several hours even with a large range of tide.

Standard Time: A kind of time based upon the transit of the Sun over a certain specified meridian, called the time meridian, and adopted for use over a considerable area. With a few exceptions, standard time is based upon some meridian which differs by a multiple of 15° from the meridian of Greenwich.

Strength of Current: Phase of tidal current in which the speed is a maximum; also the speed at this time. Beginning with slack before flood in the period of a reversing tidal current (or minimum before flood in a rotary current), the speed gradually increases to flood strength and then diminishes to slack before ebb (or minimum before ebb in a rotary current), after which the current turns in direction, the speed increases to ebb strength and then diminishes to slack before flood completing the cycle. If it is assumed that the speed throughout the cycle varies as the ordinates of a cosine curve, it can be shown that the average speed for an entire flood or ebb period is equal to $2/\pi$ or 0.6366 of the speed of the corresponding strength of current.

Subordinate Current Station: (1) A current station from which a relatively short series of observations is reduced by comparison with simultaneous observations from a control current station. (2) A station listed in the Tidal Current Tables for which predictions are to be obtained by means of differences and ratios applied to the full predictions at a reference station.

Subordinate Tide Station: (1) A tide station from which a relatively short series of observations is reduced by comparison with simultaneous observations from a tide station with a relatively long series of observations. (2) A station listed in the Tide Tables for which predictions are to be obtained by means of differences and ratios applied to the full predictions at a reference station.

Tidal Current Tables: Tables which give daily predictions of the times and speeds of the tidal currents. These predictions are usually supplemented by current differences and constants through which additional predictions can be obtained for numerous other places.

Tidal Difference: Difference in time or height of a high or low water at a subordinate station and at a reference station for which predictions are given in the Tide Tables. The difference, when applied according to sign to the prediction at the reference station, gives the corresponding time or height for the subordinate station.

Tide: The periodic rise and fall of the water resulting from gravitational interactions between the Sun, Moon, and Earth. The vertical component of the particulate motion of a tidal wave. Although the accompanying horizontal movement of the water is part of the same phenomenon, it is preferable to designate the motion as tidal current.

Tide Tables: Tables which give daily predictions of the times and heights of high and low waters. These predictions are usually supplemented by tidal differences and constants through which additional predictions can be obtained for numerous other places.

Time Meridian: A meridian used as a reference for time.

Tropic Currents: Tidal currents occurring semimonthly when the effect of the Moon's maximum declination is greatest. At these times the tendency of the Moon to produce a diurnal inequality in the current is at a maximum.

Tropic Ranges: The great tropic range (Gc), or tropic range, is the difference in height between tropic higher high water and tropic lower low water. The small tropic range (Sc) is the difference in height between tropic lower high water and tropic higher low water. The mean tropic range (Mc) is the mean between the great tropic range and the small tropic range. The small tropic range and the mean tropic range are applicable only when the type of tide is semi-diurnal or mixed. Tropic ranges are most conveniently computed from the harmonic constants.

Tropic Tides: Tides occurring semi-monthly when the effect of the Moon's maximum declination is greatest. At these times there is a tendency for an increase in the diurnal range. The tidal datums pertaining to the tropic tides are designated as tropic higher high water (TcHHW), tropic lower high water (TcLHW), tropic higher low water (TcHLW), and tropic lower low water (TcLLW) .

Type of Tide: A classification based on characteristic forms of a tide curve. Qualitatively, when the two high waters and two low waters of each tidal day are approximately equal in height, the tide is said to be semidiurnal; when there is a relatively large diurnal inequality in the high or low waters or both, it is said to be mixed; and when there is only one high water and one low water in each tidal day, it is said to be dirunal.

Vanishing Tide: In a mixed tide with very large diurnal inequality, the lower high water (or higher low water) frequently becomes indistinct (or vanishes) at time of extreme declinations. During these periods the diurnal tide has such overriding dominance that the semidiurnal tide, although still present, cannot be readily seen on the tide curve.

11

WEATHER

Page

MARINE METEOROLOGY

Meteorology is the science of the atmosphere, embracing both weather and climate.

Marine meteorology deals with the cause and effect of changes in atmospheric conditions over the oceans.

It is important that the Navigator of a small craft should have some idea of what weather he may expect on a certain passage. On this will depend first, whether it is prudent to undertake such a voyage and, second, what course to take, although this course may have to be amended during the voyage, on a further forecast of the weather being obtained.

Generally speaking, it is imprudent to be badly "caught out" at sea when coasting – but if it is unavoidable, then a proper realization of the likely weather will enable the vessel to be snugged down in plenty of time and a proper offing obtained from any lee shore.

If it is decided to seek shelter in a harbor or some good anchorage, then an early recognition of the probable weather will enable this decision to be carried out in safety and before a shift of wind makes it an impossibility.

Weather is a most fascinating study , and happy is the sailor who makes wise use of the official forecast. To lie in a snug anchorage and hear the wind blowing, after having made a decision to seek shelter because of your information, is to have a feeling of mastery over the elements, and members of the crew – whether amateur or professional – will have renewed confidence in the Owner or Master, without which confidence there can never be a "happy ship".

It therefore behooves any Navigator who is unable to pick up the forecasts to do his best to anticipate the probable weather. He should keep a watch on the movement of the barometer, note any tendency to significant variations in the direction and force of the wind, and, perhaps most important of all, keep a very wary eye open for changes in the appearance of the sky. Should he be able to take dry and wet bulb temperature readings, so much the better, as the information gained about the humidity of the air might be a useful guide to any impending change in visibility. The hints given in the following pages, used in conjunction with the observations made, should give some indication as to the kind of weather to expect in the next few hours; but it is unlikely that the mariner, with only these means at his disposal, will become a "forecaster"; this is a highly specialized job. Listen when possible to the official forecasts and be guided by them.

SINGLE OBSERVER FORECASTING

The observer in temperate latitudes who is unable to obtain an official forecast should not expect much success with his own forecasts for periods longer than six hours. It is generally quite impossible from observations at a single place to say today what the weather will be like tomorrow.

Barometer and Barograph. The onset of a gale is often heralded by a fall of the barometer and by a backing of the wind, but sometimes it is associated with a rapidly rising barometer and veering wind. Both the barometer and the wind usually give significant indications of the change to come an appreciable time before the actual gale begins, but the time interval may vary widely. The rate at which the barometer falls depends to some extent on the locality.

A rapid rise or fall does not always bring a gale; in fact the wind will probably not actually reach gale force more than once out of every three occasions of rapid rise or fall. It is, however, not safe to conclude that because a gale has not come with a rapidly falling barometer, it will not come at all. Some of the worst gales come after the barometer has ceased falling or even when it has started rising. Another point worth remembering is that gales with a rapidly rising barometer are generally more squally than gales with a falling barometer. As the barograph may not give a long warning of an approaching gale, it should be looked at frequently.

As regards the direction from which a gale will come, the barograph gives only a rough general indication, *viz.*, S'ly gales are most likely with a falling barometer and NW'ly gales with a rising barometer. If the wind has been W'ly with alternations of good and bad weather, and signs of an approaching gale are observed with a falling barometer, it is very probable that the gale will be from S or SW at first, veering to W or NW suddenly, with the worst squalls as the cold front passes.

Charts of average pressure over the Atlantic show two semi-permanent features which largely control the region's weather: these are the "Icelandic Low" and the "Azores High". The Icelandic Low is the region of lowest average pressure in the N Atlantic and, in most months of the year, is centered near Iceland. It is most fully developed in winter, when the center lies to the SW of Iceland and when the circulation is large enough to embrace all the coasts of NW Europe.

In summer the Icelandic Low is weaker and the Azores High becomes more dominant. Although the center of this pressure system remains to the S or SW of the Azores throughout the year, and the central pressure is slightly higher in July (1025 mb) than in January (1023 mb), pressure on its N flank rises considerably in summer as the Icelandic Low fills.

Apart from the large pressure changes due to travelling or developing systems, there is also a small regular diurnal variation of pressure with maxima at 1000 and 2200 and minima at 0400 and 1600. The variation is 0.5 mb. from minimum to maximum.This small variation should be borne in mind when interpreting barometer readings, although it is normally masked by the much bigger changes due to movement and development of pressure systems.

During April and May in most years, a ridge of high pressure extends NE from the "Azores High" and the"Icelandic Low" is then less dominant. This process causes a gradual veer of the prevailing SW wind to become mainly W. During June to August the pressure distribution is more regular, but in late September and October it becomes changeable and the weather then more disturbed.

The North Pacific High is the dominant feature on the west coast of North America. In the summer it is centered north and east of Hawaii, with its position being an important factor in the choice of routes to and from the islands. Its mean central pressure reaches a maximum of about 1026 mb in July. In the fall the High moves southeast and shrinks in size, while the Aleutian Low reappears over the Gulf of Alaska and the Bering Sea. The High promotes a general clockwise weather rotation in the North Pacific, causing northwest winds all along the coast from Puget Sound to Mexico.

The position of the centers of high and low pressure and the resulting flow of the airstream is more relevant to the weather pattern than the barometer reading at a particular location.

In addition to its usefulness in giving warning of approaching bad weather, the barograph is also of use in foretelling whether a quiet interval will last. If the pressure is above 1020 mb. (30.12 in.) and steady or rising, quiet weather is likely to last for at least 24 hours. Strong winds may occur with a high barometer, but as they come gradually, this increase acts as its own warning. In unsettled weather a rapid rise of barometer is often quickly followed by a fall, but if the rise reaches a comparatively high level, an improvement in the general conditions may be expected. The single observer has no means of foretelling whether the strongest winds will occur before or after the passage of a front. Generally the wind is strongest in the warm sector and decreases on passage of the cold front. Occasionally, however, the wind rises to a maximum shortly before or actually as the cold front passes and continues for several hours to blow harder than it did in the warm sector.

The speed of the wind tends to increase near headlands and straits, and the direction of the wind under these circumstances tends to follow the run of the coast.

Cloud. The single observer forecaster will probably derive more assistance from studying the trend of cloud development than he will from any other single element on its own. Of all the cloud types, cirrus (Ci) and cirrostratus (Cs) are especially to be watched, as these often afford the first indications of the presence – possibly 500-600 miles away – of an advancing warm front or occlusion, with which bad weather is commonly associated. If fine cirrus is approaching, increasing and thickening into a sheet and showing a halo, then it is fairly certain that bad weather will follow before long, especially if the barometer continues to fall and the wind backs and freshens. With these signs to guide him, the prudent mariner will take any necessary precautions to safeguard his craft.

The speed of the forerunning cirrus is not a good guide to the speed of approach of a depression, although slow, moving cirrus is not usually found before a rapidly advancing depression. Upper clouds moving rapidly are not infrequently a sign of unsettled conditions.

Small or medium, sized cumulus (Cu) is a fair weather cloud forming over the land soon after sunrise and disappearing about sunset. Towering cumulus show that there is a large lapse-rate; so showers and squalls should be expected. Any clouds of Cu type observed over land at dawn are more likely to be stratocumulus (Sc) than true cumulus. At sea, as opposed to over the land, large active cumulus may be found by night as well as by day, there being no appreciable diurnal range of temperature at the sea surface.

The increasing and thickening of high and medium cloud does not invariably indicate the approach of frontal weather, as it is not uncommon for the upper cloud associated with cumulonimbus (Cb) to spread over in advance of the main cloud mass. At times the undersurface of this type of cloud presents a rippled or mammillated appearance. Neither the barometer, which is often unsteady, nor the wind can provide any useful indication of future trends in these conditions, but it is well to be prepared for showers and squalls and possibly thunder. The squalls may be quite severe and come from a direction quite different from that of the wind previously experienced.

In the summer, the appearance in the sky of ragged looking altocumulus or Ac of the castellated variety is an almost certain indication that thunderstorms, more widespread than local, will follow before many hours have passed. If the sky clears after the passage of a cold front and the wind veers to NW, an interval of 6 - 12 hours of fair weather should follow. A close watch should however be kept on the barometer and wind. If the former begins to fall and the wind backs towards SW, with increasing upper cloud, renewed bad weather may be expected within a few hours.

The sun setting behind a bank of clouds may well mean the cloud of an advancing front. On the other hand, a "low" sunset shows that there is no frontal cloud within many hours, run. A "high" dawn may be due to the end of frontal cloud, but a "low" dawn has no special significance.

A heavy dew or frost shows that the sky was clear during the night, but this, on its own, is not necessarily an indication of continued good weather throughout the day. A lot of haze in the lower layers shows the presence of an inversion at no great height, probably caused by subsidence in an anticyclone, and so is a sign of good weather. Unfortunately this prognostic is only valid in dry summer weather when it is already obviously fine. Clouds becoming lower indicate the approach of bad weather.

The popular prognostics of red sunrises and sunsets probably refer to the color of clouds when the horizon is clear. Minute dust particles in the atmosphere, not amounting to haze, are responsible for the red color. The tendency seems to be for a red sunrise to precede bad weather and a red sunset good weather, but the type of clouds should be studied in conjunction with the color. If the redness in the morning is caused by high or medium clouds spreading from the west, but not quite extending to the eastern horizon, the warning is emphasized. The season of the year is important, as a sunset in winter reddening the south-western sky may be misleading, since the bad weather, if it comes, may come from the north; or stray clouds in the north-west may be tinged with red at a summer sunset, while the southern horizon is clouding over, due to a depression moving up from south. Cirrus dissolving indicates fine weather.

Temperature and Humidity of the Air. The temperature and humidity of the surface air over the land are not of great assistance to the single observer forecaster as they are so subject to local effects; but if full consideration is given to all existing circumstances, the variation of temperature and humidity from the normal, at the place of observation, for the season and time of day, may provide a clue to forthcoming changes in the weather. When the wind sets in from some cold or warm region, the temperature does not generally reach its minimum or maximum respectively for a day or two.

Temperature of the Sea. Since it is only the surface of the sea which is in contact with the air, the temperature of the surface is of particular importance in meteorology. A comparison of sea and air temperatures is a useful guide in recognizing the type of air stream; air colder than sea meaning polar air and air warmer than sea, tropical air. In a flat calm the actual surface of the sea may be several degrees warmer than the water at a depth of a couple of feet. This is particularly the case when the temperature is rising. Care therefore should be taken to collect water from as near the surface as possible when taking the sea temperature. At times the temperature is uniform from the surface downwards to a variable depth. This is particularly the case when there is interior mixing caused by waves or by tidal currents or when the temperature is falling, as at the end of the day or the end of the summer; cooling occurs by conduction to the air or radiation to the sky, and the surface water becomes denser and sinks .

The water used for taking the sea surface temperature should be drawn in a canvas or special rubber bucket from over the ship's side. The temperature of this water is taken by an ordinary thermometer. Some sea water thermometers have a small reservoir round the bulb so that if it is necessary to remove the thermometer from the bucket to read it, the bulb will remain immersed in water. The temperature should be read as soon as possible after the water has been drawn; many thermometers need to be in the water, provided that it is well stirred, for only about 30 seconds to read correctly.

Cold water from the depths, brought to the surface by shoals, may cause a deterioration of visibility.

A long line of foam is often caused by the meeting of two currents, one of which sinks below the other. There is generally a difference in the temperature of the water on the two sides of the line.

The Gulf Stream presents a good opportunity to use your thermometer. The west side of the stream, known as the "cold wall", shows a marked temperature change. This change is most noticeable north of Cape Hatteras, but can be observed from the Straits of Florida to the Grand Banks.

Fog. Fog is forecast at sea whenever the temperature of the sea is equal to or below the dew-point of the air. If the air is full of salt particles, fog may form before the air is cooled to its dew-point.

A change in tidal stream or an ocean current often brings colder water to the surface and this may cool the air sufficiently to form fog.

An alteration in wind direction or speed may cause the fog to thin or thicken.

If the sky above a fog is free from cloud during the day, a clearance is more likely than if the sky is cloudy.

The clearance of a shallow fog has sometimes been successfully forecast when the top of the fog is observed to start breaking up into wisps. The periodical appearance of the masthead of a nearby ship can be a useful guide in these circumstances.

When sea fog clears, especially at night, it is often difficult to say whether the ship has run out of it or the fog has dispersed or blown away.

In general, fog in the open sea will not finally clear until the arrival of a cold front, though any increase in the sea temperature has a tendency to lift the fog.

Sea and Swell. Swell is often followed by strong winds or a gale from the direction of the swell, but it is far from being an infallible sign, as the depression causing the strong winds which are the cause of the swell may alter course or slow down and fill up. The most profitable use of swell is in showing the existence and rough position of a tropical revolving storm.

A heavy swell may be caused by strong winds at some distance or by moderate winds closer at hand, but a wave-period of ten seconds or a wave-length of 500 feet in the open sea shows that the wind producing the swell must at least have been of gale force.

TABLE OF SEA STATES

1) Swell Waves – Length		*feet*
Short		0-325
Average		325-650
Long		over 650
(2) Swell Waves – Height		*feet*
Low		0-6.5
Moderate		6.5-13
Heavy		over 13
(3) Sea Waves – Height		*feet*
Code		
0	Calm – glassy	0
1	Calm – rippled	0-0.3
2	Smooth wavelets	0.3-1.5
3	Slight	1.5-4.0
4	Moderate	4.0-8.0
5	Rough	8.0-13.0
6	Very Rough	13.0-20.0
7	High	20.0-30.0
8	Very High	30.0-45.0
9	Phenomenal	over 45.0

Note: In each case the exact boundary of length or height is included in the lower category, e.g., a sea of 13 feet is described as "Rough".

* Average wave height.

Change in Wave Height in Opposing or Following Currents.

Following current with a velocity of ¼ that of waves – wave height reduced by 25%.
Opposing current with a velocity of ⅒ that of waves – wave height increased by 21%.
Opposing current with a velocity of ¼ that of waves – wave height increased by 300%.

11

WEATHER FORECASTS FROM DAILY OBSERVATIONS

Sunrise. A low dawn (day breaking on or near the horizon) means FAIR WEATHER.

A high dawn (day breaking above a cloud bank) means WIND.

A purple sky at dawn means BAD WEATHER (much wind or rain – stormy).

A red sunrise, with clouds towering later, means RAIN.

Sunset. A rosy sky at sunset (whether cloudy or clear) means FAIR WEATHER.

A greenish–gray (or pale yellow) sky means RAIN.

A dark red or purple sky means RAIN.

A bright yellow (or copper colored) sky means WIND.

A sickly, looking gray or greenish orange (or copper sky) means WIND and RAIN.

Moon. A Full Moon, rising clear foretells FAIR WEATHER

A Full Moon rising pale yellow brings RAIN.

In the wane of the Moon, a cloudy morning brings a FAIR afternoon.

A large ring around the Moon and high clouds foretells RAIN in several days.

A red Moon means WIND.

Halo (a large circle). A Halo round the Sun or Moon – the larger the Halo the sooner the RAIN. The open side of the Halo tells the quarter from which the rain will come.

A Halo round the Sun or Moon after fine weather means STORMY WEATHER (wind or rain).

Corona (a small circle). A Corona round the Sun or Moon and growing larger indicates FAIR WEATHER.

A Corona round the Sun or Moon and growing smaller means RAIN.

Rainbow. A Rainbow in the evening means FAIR WEATHER. A secondary bow – with colors reversed – may be seen frequently about 10° outside the main Rainbow.

WELL PROVED INDICATION FOR FORECASTING THE WEATHER

Fair weather. Barometer steady (or RISING at a steady rate. Mare's Tail Clouds at great height or Cumulus clouds.

Rain. Barometer falling slowly (about 0.14 mb. or 0.004 inches per hour). Strange hues of clouds with hard, defined ou' lines. White distant watery-looking clouds which increase and are followed by an overcast murky vapor that becomes cloudy –this is a certain sign of rain.

Wind. Barometer falling gradually (0.37 mb. or 0.011 inches per hour).

Hard edges on oily-looking clouds.

High upper clouds crossing a different direction from that of the lower clouds or surface wind. This, when visible, is a useful sign and foretells change of wind towards their direction. Generally the harder the clouds look, the stronger the wind will be.

Wind and Rain together Barometer falling moderately (say 0.51 mb. or 0.015 inches per hour).

Strong-colored clouds at low heights.

Stormy Weather; Strong Winds (perhaps rain). Barometer falling or rising rapidly (say 1.35 mb. or 0.04 inches per hour).

If oily-looking clouds overcast there will be Wind, but if watery-looking clouds overcast there will be rain.

Unusual hues of cloud with hard outlines. Green and black clouds foretell lightning and storm.

SEAMEN'S RHYMES

These rhymes, which are familiar to all seamen, summarize rather neatly, and in a form which is easily remembered, a number of rules for the amateur weather forecaster. Experience has shown there to be a considerable degree of truth in them and on that account they are included here. It should be borne in mind, however, that the rhymes are neither infallible nor always true, and they should be accepted with caution.

The Barometer

Long foretold, long last,
Short notice, soon past,
Quick rise after low,
Sure sign of stronger blow.

When the glass falls low,
Prepare for a blow;
When it slowly rises high,
Lofty canvas you may fly.

At sea with low and falling glass
Soundly sleeps a careless ass,
Only when it's high and rising
Truly rests a careful wise one.

Wind and Weather

A red sky at night is a sailor's delight,
A red sky in the morning is a sailorman's warning.

The evening red and morning gray
Are sure signs of a fine day,
But the evening gray and the morning red,
Makes the sailor shake his head.

Mackerel sky and mares' tails,
Make lofty ships carry low sails.

When the wind shifts against the sun,
Trust it not, for back it will run.

When rain comes before the wind,
Halyards, sheets and braces mind,
But when wind comes before rain
Soon you may make sail again.

If clouds are gathering thick and fast,
Keep sharp look out for sail and mast,
But if they slowly onward crawl,
Shoot your lines, nets and trawl.

FORECASTING INSTRUMENTS

The BAROMETER and – to a much lesser extent – the THERMOMETER are the two most used instruments for forecasting the weather. In any vessel large enough to house it, a BAROGRAPH – which is simply a recording barometer – is of the utmost value, as the movements of the record – whether up or down on the scale – can be seen over any period of several days at a glance without any written recordings being necessary.

Many large vessels and all meteorological voluntary recording vessels carry a Mercurial Barometer which houses a column of mercury, and very accurate readings may be made by this standard barometer from which all other barometers may be set for comparison.

In any small vessel (and of course this is also used in larger vessels too) the Aneroid type barometer is always used. The word "ANEROID" means "no fluid" and relies for its movement on the pressure of the atmosphere and is, therefore, quite unlike the Mercurial Barometer. The Aneroid Barometer should occasionally be compared at sea level with the mercurial type; if the Aneroid requires adjusting, this is done very simply by carefully turning the screw at the back of the instrument (using a thin ended screwdriver), thus turning the indicators on the face of the Aneroid to a higher or lower reading as required.

FORECASTING FACTORS

The essential factors in forecasting the weather at sea are the following in their relationship one to the other:

(a) The direction and force of the wind.

(b) The pressure of the atmosphere (i.e. barometer readings) and its heat (i.e. thermometer readings).

(c) The formation and movement of cloud.

Expected weather cannot be forecast simply by reading the barometer and thermometer at any given time or place. It is very necessary that a record should be kept of their movements, and in practice this means that the barometer and thermometer readings, direction and force of the wind, and cloud appearance should be entered continually in the Log Book so that a more or less constant record may be available.

On a passage in a vessel of any size, watches must be kept, and the watch on deck can find from the Log Book these observations made by previous watch keepers without rousing them from their sleep to ask them questions.

The Mercury Barometer. For purposes of comparison of different barometric readings, any variation from standard gravity has to be corrected by using a formula giving the gravity at the station in terms of the latitude and the height above sea level. Corrections must also be applied for any difference between the temperature of the instrument, and the standard temperature, for the height above m.s.l.* (as it affects the height of atmosphere above the instrument) and for the instrumental errors given on the certificate which accompanies the barometer. When the three corrections for gravity, temperature and height of instrument above sea level have been made, the resultant value can be directly compared with that of any other barometer similarly corrected. These corrections may be

* m.s.l. = mean sea level. Allowances for change of barometric pressure due to height of tide are negligible, as the atmospheric pressure near the surface decreases approximately one millibar for every 28 feet ascent.

simply and rapidly applied by the use of the Gold slide. When reading a barometer, the eye should be exactly on a level with the top of the mercury column, thus eliminating parallax.

The Aneroid Barometer. Also registers atmospheric pressure and consists fundamentally of a shallow box, made of thin corrugated metal, from which almost all the air has been removed. The pressure exerted by the atmosphere on the outside of the box is very great, while that inside is very small, and were it not for the presence of a spring placed between the faces of the box, the latter would be crushed. However, the spring allows a certain degree of controlled "collapse" to occur, and the small relative movements of the faces due to the changes of pressure acting on the outside are magnified by a series of levers and made to actuate a pointer on a dial. For increased sensitivity, a number of boxes are linked together. The aneroid needs no correction for temperature or for gravity – only for height above m.s.l.

To guard against any loss of accuracy of reading, it should be checked fairly often against the corrected readings of a mercury barometer.

Barometer Readings. Seldom does a single reading have important indications; it is the rate of change that counts. As soon as we have two or more readings, separated by time or distance, or both, the observer is in a somewhat better position to deduce probable changes in weather conditions. How accurate these deductions will be depends on the correct interpretation of other factors and the intelligent application of known meteorological facts.

THE HYGROMETER

Water Vapor. The atmosphere at all times has a certain amount of water vapor in it. When it holds the maximum quantity possible at any given temperature, the air is said to be saturated, and any fall in temperature will then cause the excess vapor to be condensed. As it is important to know what this water vapor content actually is, a hygrometer is used to measure it. This usually consists of two thermometers. One, known as the dry-bulb thermometer, indicates the temperature of the air. The other has its bulb wrapped in muslin and is kept moist by being connected by a cotton wick to a small container of distilled water and is known as the wet-bulb thermometer. When evaporation takes place from the surface of the wet-bulb, heat is abstracted from the bulb of the thermometer and its reading is less than that of the dry-bulb thermometer by an amount which indicates the humidity, or dampness of the air. When the air becomes saturated, this so-called depression of the wet-bulb decreases to nothing because no evaporation is occurring at the wet-bulb. Hygrometer observations are important, as by means of a Dewpoint Table it is possible to find what fall in temperature will cause the formation of mist or fog in the local area. The lowest temperature to which air can be cooled without condensation is called the dew point.

The two common types of instruments for measuring humidity are: (a) Mason's hygrometer, consisting of the wet and dry bulb thermometer side by side in a louvered screen – exposed on the weather side of the ship (b) The "aspirated" psychrometer, in which a steady current of air is drawn past the two thermo-meters by means of a small electric, clockwork or hand operated fan.

CLOUDS

Clouds are aggregates of minute water drops or ice crystals or both held in suspension in the atmosphere. Cloud Atlases are available illustrating the many varieties of cloud forms. For practical purposes a classification into ten main types is adopted. This classification is as follows:

(1) *High Clouds*
- Cirrus (Ci)
- Cirrocumulus (Cc)
- Cirrostratus (Cs)

(2) *Middle Clouds*
- Altocumulus (Ac)
- Altostratus (As)
- Nimbostratus (Ns)

(3) *Low Clouds*
- Stratocumulus (Sc)
- Stratus (St)

(4) *Low Clouds of marked vertical extent*
- Cumulonimbus (Cb)
- Cumulus (Cu)

Brief descriptions of the different cloud types are given below.

Cirrus (Ci). Detached clouds composed of ice crystals, of delicate and fibrous appearance, without shading, generally white in color, often of silky appearance. Tufted cirrus clouds are popularly known as "Mares" Tails."

Cirrocumulus (Cc). A cirriform layer or patch composed of small white flakes or of very small globular masses, without shadows, arranged in groups or lines, or more often in ripples resembling those of sand on the sea shore.

Cirrostratus (Cs). A transparent whitish veil of fibrous or smooth appearance, composed of ice crystals, which totally or partially covers the sky and usually produces halo phenomena.

Altocumulus (Ac). A layer, or patches, composed of laminae or rather flattened globular masses, the smallest elements of the regularly arranged layer being fairly small and thin, with or without shading.

Altostratus (As). A striated or fibrous veil, more or less gray or bluish in color. It does not give rise to halo phenomena.

Stratocumulus (Sc). A layer, or patches, composed of globular masses or rolls; the smallest of the regularly arranged elements are fairly large; they are soft and gray with darker parts.

Stratus (St). A uniform layer of cloud, like fog, but not resting on the ground.

Nimbostratus (Ns). A low, amorphous, and rainy layer, of a dark-gray color and nearly uniform.

Cumulus (Cu). Thick clouds with vertical development; the upper surface is dome shaped and exhibits protuberances, while the base is nearly horizontal.

Cumulonimbus (Cb). Heavy masses of cloud with great vertical development, whose cumuliform summits rise in the form of mountains or towers, the upper parts having fibrous texture and often spreading out in the shape of an anvil.

The degree of cloudiness is normally expressed on a scale from 0 to 8, in which 0 represents a sky quite free from cloud and 8 an entirely overcast sky in which no patches of blue are visible. The estimation is one of "eighths of sky covered" (oktas).

The height of base cloud is a factor of great importance to aviation. During the daytime it may be measured by timing the ascent of a small balloon rising at a fixed rate. At night a

HIGH CLOUD

Photo by R. K. Pilsbury

(1) CIRRUS (Ci) (Mares's Tails). Cirrus increasing and thickening is a sign of unsettled weather.

HIGH CLOUD

Photo by R. K. Pilsbury

(2) CIRROCUMULUS (Cc) (Mackerel Sky). When the above clouds move rapidly and become Cirrostratus, unsettled weather is approaching.

HIGH CLOUD

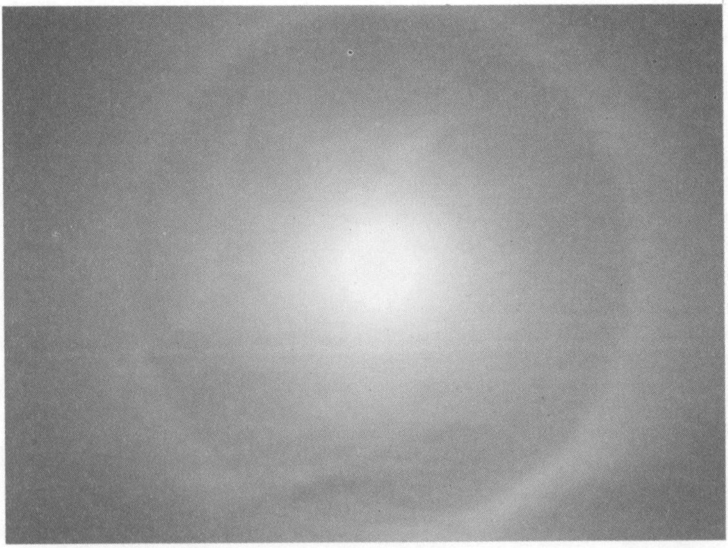

Photo by R. K. Pilsbury

(3) CIRROSTRATUS (Cs). A covering of this cloud with a Halo, as shown, is a sure sign of deteriorating weather approaching.

MIDDLE CLOUD

Photo by R. K. Pilsbury

(4) ALTOCUMULUS (Ac). Similar to a Mackerel Sky but with larger globulues of cloud, often packed in tight lines. If these tend to join and become Altostratus, rain is on the way. Altocumulus in lines with castellated tops, like the battlements on a castle wall, indicate thundery conditions.

MIDDLE CLOUD

Photo by R. K. Pilsbury

(5) ALTOSTRATUS (As). A continuous layer of gray cloud from which rain will soon fall. It is then known as Nimbostratus (Ns) and its base may fall to only a few hundred feet above MSL.

LOW CLOUD

Photo by R. K. Pilsbury

(6) CUMULONIMBUS (Cb). The Thunderstorm Cloud, often accompanied by sudden squalls and rapidly changing winds.

LOW CLOUD

Photo by R. K. Pilsbury

(7) CUMULUS (Cu). Small Cumulus not increasing means fine weather, however, if growing upwards like a cauliflower, showers are likely.

LOW CLOUD

Photo by R. K. Pilsbury

(8) STRATOCUMULUS (SC). More frequent in the colder months, especially near windward coasts. STRATUS (St) (not illustrated). A gray featureless low cloud often shrouding cliff and hill tops on windward coasts. When broken by turbulence, it is call FRACTOSTRATUS (FrSt).

ceiling light projector (cloud searchlight) may be used on large ships. As the use of balloons and searchlights is impracticable in most ships, cloud height is normally estimated at sea.

Approximate Heights of Cloud Bases
High clouds above 18,000 ft.; Middle clouds 8,000 to 18,000 ft.; Low clouds below 8,000 ft..

These limits tend to be higher in low latitudes, and lower, especially for high clouds, in high latitudes.

STATE OF SEA PHOTOGRAPHS FOR ESTIMATING WIND SPEEDS

The following photographs illustrate the appearance of the sea corresponding to the Beaufort wind scale. Their purpose is to assist observers in estimating the wind speed when making weather reports. The description of the sea is according to the SEA CRITERION laid down by the World Meteorological Organization.

The appearance of the sea may be affected also by fetch (the distance which the wind has travelled over a water surface in nearly the same direction), depth of water, swell, heavy rain, tidal streams and the lag affect between the wind getting up and the sea increasing.

Probable wave heights and probable maximum wave heights have been added only as a rough guide to show what may be expected in sea areas remote from land. In enclosed waters, or when near land with an off-shore wind, wave heights will be smaller and the waves steeper.

Aboard a moving vessel it is essential to know the time, wind force and direction and the Beaufort scale provides the best method of making this important observation. The line of sight at right angles to the wave's line of advance indicates the true direction of the wind.

It is difficult at night to estimate wind force by the sea criterion.

Photo by R. R. Baxter (Crown Copyright).

FORCE 0 (CALM) Wind speed less than one knot

(Sea like a mirror)

Photo by R. R. Baxter (Crown Copyright).

FORCE 1 (LIGHT AIR) Wind speed 1-3 knots; mean, 2 knots

(Ripples with the appearance of scales are formed, but without foam crests). Probable wave height, ¼ foot.

Photo by R. R. Baxter (Crown Copyright).

FORCE 2 (LIGHT BREEZE) Wind speed 4-6 knots; mean, 5 knots

(Small wavelets, still short but more pronounced – Crests have a glassy appearance and do not break.) Probable wave height ½ foot - 1 foot maximum.

Photo by R. R. Baxter (Crown Copyright).

FORCE 3 (GENTLE BREEZE) Wind speed 7-10 knots; mean ,9 knots

(Large wavelets. Crests begin to break. Foam of glassy appearance . Perhaps scattered white horses.) Probable wave height 2 feet – maximum, 3 ft.

Photo by R. R. Baxter (Crown Copyright).

FORCE 4 (MODERATE BREEZE) Wind speed 11-16 knots; mean, 13 knots

(Small waves, becoming longer; fairly frequent white horses.) Probable wave height 3½ feet – maximum, 5 feet.

Photo by R. R. Baxter (Crown Copyright).

FORCE 5 (FRESH BREEZE) Wind speed 17-21 knots; mean 19 knots

(Moderate waves, taking a more pronounced long form; many white horses are formed. Chance of some spray.) Probable wave height 6 feet – maximum, 8½ feet.

Photo by R. R. Baxter (Crown Copyright).

FORCE 6 (STRONG BREEZE) Wind speed 22-27 knots; mean, 24 knots

(Large waves begin to form; the white foam crests are more extensive everywhere. Probably some spray.) Probable wave height 9½ feet – maximum, 13 feet.

Photo by R. R. Baxter (Crown Copyright).

FORCE 7 (NEAR GALE) Wind speed 28-33 knots; mean, 30 knots

(Sea heaps up and white foam from breaking waves begins to be blown in streaks along the direction of the wind.) Probable wave height 13½ feet – maximum, 19 feet.

Photo by R. R. Baxter (Crown Copyright).

FORCE 8 (GALE) Wind speed 34-40 knots; mean, 37 knots

(Moderately high waves of greater length; edges of crests begin to break into spindrift. The foam is blown in well-marked streaks along the direction of the wind.) Probable wave height 18 feet – maximum, 25 feet.

Photo by O. R. Bates.

FORCE 9 (STRONG GALE) Wind speed 41-47 knots; mean, 44 knots

(High waves. Dense streaks of foam along the direction of the wind. Crests of waves begin to topple, tumble and roll over. Spray may affect visibility.) Probable wave height 23 feet – maximum, 32 feet.

FORCE 10 (STORM) Wind speed 48-55 knots; mean, 52 knots

Viewed at right angles to the trough. (Very high waves with long overhanging crests. The resulting foam, in great patches, is blown in dense white streaks along the direction of the wind. On the whole, the surface of the sea takes a white appearance. The tumbling of the sea becomes heavy and shock-like. Visibility affected.) Probable wave height 29 feet – maximum, 41 feet.

Photo by J. Hodkinson.

FORCE 11 (VIOLENT STORM) Wind speed 56-63 knots; mean, 60 knots

(Exceptionally high waves. Small and medium-sized ships might be for a time lost to view behind the waves. The sea is completely covered with long white patches of foam lying along the direction of the wind. Everywhere the edges of the wave crests are blown into froth. Visibility affected.) Probable wave height 37 feet – maximum, 52 feet.

Photo by (Crown Copyright).

Photo by (Crown Copyright).

FORCE 12 (HURRICANE) Wind speed 56-63 knots

(The air is filled with foam and spray. Sea completely white with driving spray; visibility very seriously affected.(Probable wave height 45 feet. The Beaufort Scale actually extends to force 17 (up to 118 knots), but Force 12 is the highest which can be identified from the appearance of the sea.

WIND

Wind is the movement of air across the surface of the earth, and basically it is caused by differences of temperature between one large area and another. This in turn gives rise to the pressure differences which are the direct cause of the air movements. The pressure difference over a unit distance is known as the pressure gradient, and the steeper the gradient, the stronger is the wind. (Air also moves upwards and downwards in the atmosphere, and these movements are very largely responsible for the formation or dispersal of cloud and the occurrence of precipitation, thunderstorms, etc.)

Buys Ballot's Law. A useful rule for the observer in the northern hemisphere to remember is that when he faces the wind, the region of lowest barometric pressure will lie towards his right side and the highest, towards his left. The reverse holds good in the southern hemisphere.

Permanent winds which blow in approximately the same direction throughout the year over large parts of the ocean are called "trade winds." Regular winds whose directions depend greatly on the sun's declination are termed "seasonal winds." To this group belong the well-known monsoons of the Indian Ocean and China Sea. Similar periodic winds occur in many other localities, and in nearly all areas on the earth, the "prevailing wind" depends more or less on the season and consequent pressure distribution.

Rotational Effect of the Earth. When considering the motion of air over the earth's surface, it is necessary to take into account the effect of the earth's rotation, which deflects moving air to the right in the Northern Hemisphere and to the left in the Southern Hemisphere. Near the surface of the earth the effect of friction is important, and the air does not move exactly along the isobar but is inclined to it at an angle, inwards towards the low pressure.

Wind Direction and Speed. The direction of a wind is the true bearing of the point from which it blows. Wind force is estimated in the Beaufort Scale. For use in synoptic weather messages, Beaufort force is converted into knots or miles per hour and is generally estimated by the experienced observer with

BEAUFORT WIND SCALE

Beaufort Number	Mean Velocity Knots	Descriptive Term	Deep Sea Criterion	Probable Height of Waves in feet
0	Less than 1	Calm	Sea like a mirror.	
1	1-3	Light	Ripples with the appearance of scales are formed but without foam crests.	.25
2	4-6	Light breeze	Small wavelets, still short but more pronounced Crests have a glassy appearance.	.5-1
3	7-10	Gentle breeze	Large wavelets. Crests begin to break. Foam of glassy appearance. Perhaps scattered white horses	2-3
4	11-16	Mod. breeze	Small waves, becoming longer; fairly frequent horses.	3.5-5
5	17-21	Fresh breeze	Moderate waves, taking a more pronounced long form; many white horses are formed. (Chance of some spray.)	6-8.5
6	22-27	Strong breeze	Large waves begin to form; the white foam crests are more extensive everywhere. (Probably some spray.)	9.5-13
7	28-33	Near gale	Sea heaps up and white foam from breaking waves begins to be blown in streaks along the direction of the wind.	13.5-19
8	34-40	Gale	Moderately high waves of greater length; edges of crests begin to break into spindrift. The foam is blown in well-marked streaks along the direction of the wind.	18-25
9	41-47	Strong gale	High waves. Dense streaks of foam along the direction of the wind. Crests of waves begin to topple, tumble and roll over. Spray may affect visibility.	23-32
10	48-55	Storm	Very high waves with long overhanging crests The resulting foam in great patches is blown in dense white streaks along the direction of the wind. On the whole, the surface of the sea takes a white appearance. The tumbling of the sea becomes heavy and shocklike. Visibility affected.	29-41
11	56-63	Violent storm	Exceptionally high waves. (Small and medium-sized) ships might be for a time lost to view behind the waves.) The sea is completely covered with long white patches of foam lying along the direction of the wind. Everywhere the edges of the waves crests are blown into froth. Visibility affected.	37-52
12	63+	Hurricane	The air is filled with foam and spray. Sea completely white with driving spray; visibility very seriously affected.	45+

Notes:

1. It must be realized that it will be difficult at night to estimate wind force by the sea criterion.
2. The log effect between increase of wind and increase of sea should be borne in mind.
3. Fetch, depth, swell, heavy rain and tide effects should be considered when estimating the wind force from the appearance of the sea.

* This table is intended only as a guide to show roughly what may be expected in the open sea, remote from land. In enclosed waters, or when near land with an off-shore wind, wave heights will be smaller, and the waves steeper. **WARNING:** FOR A GIVEN WIND FORECE, SEA CONDITIONS CAN BE MORE DANGEROUS NEAR LAND THAN IN THE OPEN SEA, IN MANY TIDAL WATERS, WAVE HEIGHTS ARE LIABLE TO INCREASE CONSIDERABLY IN A MATTER OF MINUTES.

THE WEATHER MAP

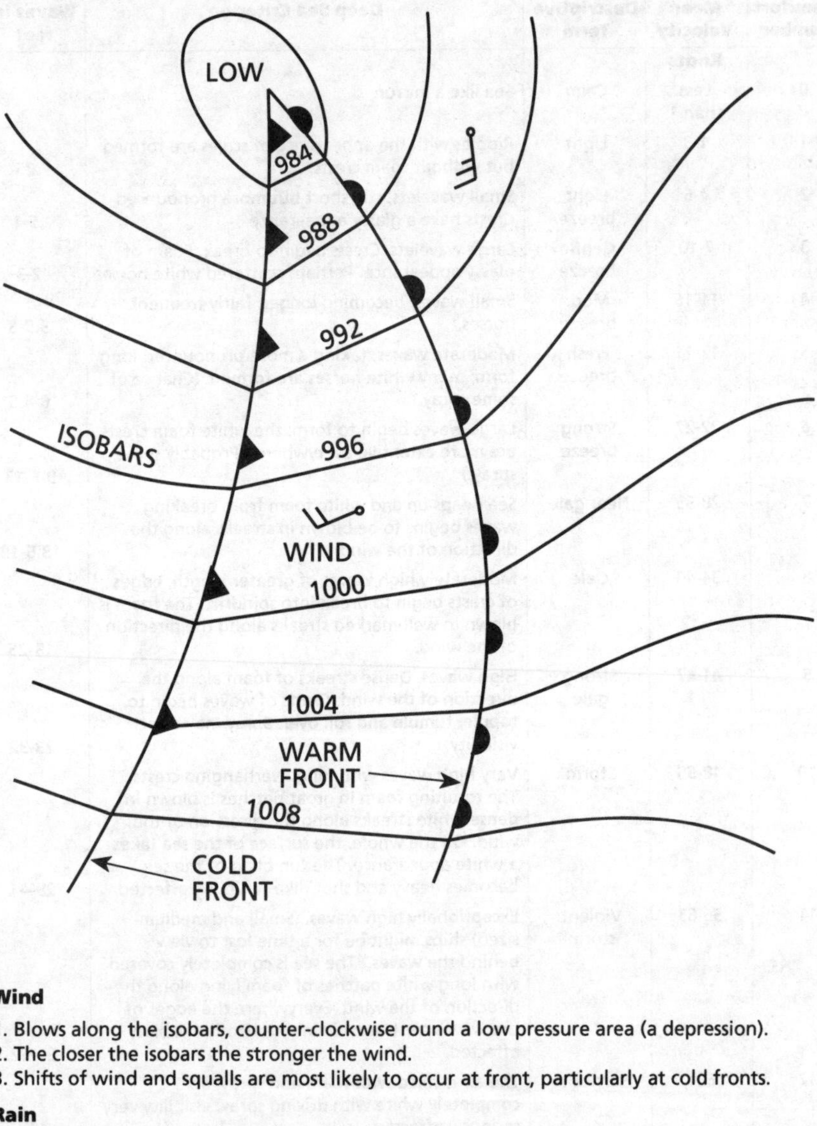

Wind

1. Blows along the isobars, counter-clockwise round a low pressure area (a depression).
2. The closer the isobars the stronger the wind.
3. Shifts of wind and squalls are most likely to occur at front, particularly at cold fronts.

Rain

MOST likely to occur at fronts:

a. Prolonged rain at warm fronts – defined by rounded modules.
b. Showers at cold fronts – defined by triangular modules.

Temperature and Humidity. Air is warm and moist at Warm Fronts. Air is distinctly colder after the passage of a cold Front. Dry air usually follows.

Future Movement of Low. The "Low" will probably move in the direction of the isobars in the warm sector, i.e., the isobars between the warm and cold fronts.

reasonable accuracy, but only practice and careful observation can lead to proficiency in this. It is likely for an inexperienced observer to overestimate slightly the force of light winds and to underestimate the strong ones.

When determining wind direction, care should always be taken to eliminate the effect of the ship's speed and direction from the force and direction of the wind as observed. Tables are available for this purpose.

The effect of wind is always manifested on the surface of the sea. The probable appearance of waves in the open sea remote from land which will be raised by different wind strengths is given in the table of Beaufort Wind Scale.

WHEN INTERPRETING WEATHER FORECASTS and deciding whether it is more prudent to remain (or seek shelter) in harbor until conditions moderate, be sure to consult the Beaufort Wind Scale and give careful consideration to the notes and WARNING at the bottom of the Table.

VISIBILITY SCALE

The numbers 90 - 99 shown below are those used for reporting visibility observations in coded radio weather messages.

*90 – Visibility less than 55 yards.
*91 – Visibility 55-220 yards.
*92 – Visibility 220-550 yards.
*93 – Visibility 550-1,100 yards.
94 – Visibility 1,100-2,200 yards.
95 – Visibility 2,200-2.2 nautical miles.
96 – Visibility 2.2-5.4 nautical miles.
97 – Visibility 5.4-10.8 nautical miles.
98 – Visibility 10.8-27 nautical miles.
99 – Visibility 27 nautical miles or more.
(*Fog.)

Note: In a large vessel, the occasions on which the lowest numbers in the visibility scale 90 and 91 are appropriate, can be determined by noting the distance at which objects on board become invisible in the fog.

If there is any obscurity or abnormal refraction the visible horizon may be very misleading as a means of judging distance, particularly when the height of the eye is great as in the case of an observer on the bridge of a large liner.

Visibility of less than 1,100 yards, however caused, is classed as fog (code figures 90-93 used). As a rough guide, poor visibility, but over 1,100 yards is called mist if the humidity is 95% or higher, and haze if the humidity is less than 95%, i.e. the difference between mist and haze is simply one of damp air.

In the Beaufort notation describing weather, fog is represented by f, mist by m and haze by z. At night it is difficult to judge the density of fog with accuracy and the practice is to use the diffracted blur around the masthead light as a criterion.

Letters to indicate the state of the weather (Beaufort Notation)

"Beaufort Notation," a system of notation devised by Admiral Beaufort, consisting as a rule of the initial letter of the phenomenon to be indicated, has been in use for many years. It affords a simple and concise means of indicating by a group of letters either the actual state of the weather at the hour of observation, "present weather"; or a general summary of the conditions over the interval since the last observation was made, "past weather"

b	=	blue sky (0 - 2/8 clouded).
bc	=	sky partly clouded (3 - 5/8 clouded).
c	=	cloudy (6 --8/8 clouded).
d	=	drizzle.
e	=	wet air (without precipitation).
f	=	fog.
g	=	gale.
h	=	hail.
jp	=	precipitation in sight of ship or station.
kq	=	line squall.
ks	=	storm of drifting snow.
kz	=	sandstorm or dust storm.
l	=	lightning.
m	=	mist.
o	=	overcast sky (the sky completely covered with a uniform layer of thick or heavy cloud.)
q	=	squally weather.
r	=	rain.
rs	=	sleet (rain and snow together).
s	=	snow.
t	=	thunder.
tlr	=	thunderstorm with rain.
tls	=	thunderstorm with snow.
u	=	ugly, threatening sky.
v	=	unusual visibility.
w	=	dew.
x	=	hoar frost.
y	=	dry air.
z	=	haze.

fairly **p,** formerly used as a Beaufort letter, to denote "passing showers", is now only to be used as a prefix, denoting "passing showers of e.g., ph, passing showers of hail; phr passing showers of mixed hail and rain.

The times of commencement and ending of heavy showers should be noted.

Capital letters indicate "intense";l the suffix$_o$ indicates "slight"; repetition of letters denotes continuity. The prefix i indicates "intermittent." Thus R, indicates heavy rain; r_o slight rain; rr, continuous rain; ir_o intermittent slight rain.

g is used to indicate that a wind of at least Beaufort force 8 has persisted for not less than 10 minutes. If the wind in 10 minutes has not fallen below force 10, the capital letter G is used.

d, drizzle, is to be used for precipitation in which the drops are very small. If the drops are of appreciable size, although the rain is small in amount, r_o is used.

DEPRESSIONS

The cyclonic systems of temperate latitudes are now usually referred to as depressions or "lows" to distinguish them from the tropical revolving storms which are often called cyclones or tropical hurricanes.

The depression is a normal feature of temperate latitudes and is an integral part of the general circulation of the atmosphere, forming an essential link in the interchange of air between polar and equatorial regions.

Depressions in general move in both hemispheres in a more or less easterly direction, though considerable variations occur, including sometimes a reversal of direction for a time. More or less stationary and permanent areas of high pressure are to be found in the oceans between latitudes 20° and 40° N and S. In the North Atlantic, North and South Pacific and South Indian Oceans the tropical revolving storms progress round the equatorial sides of these areas and up their western sides in a poleward direction. Occasionally a tropical revolving storm will continue into temperate latitudes, gradually changing its character and becoming a depression.

The concept of the "frontal surface" is vital to the theory of the formation and development of depressions. Warm air masses of tropical origin meet the colder masses of polar origin along a sloping surface of discontinuity, the colder and therefore heavier air lying beneath the warmer lighter air in the form of a wedge of small angle. The sloping surface of discontinuity is called a "frontal surface." The depression is then envisaged as an unstable wave on the surface of discontinuity. Pictured in terms of development at the surface the cold air replaces the warm tropical air along the "cold front," while the warm air replaces the cold air at the "warm front." The movement of the depression as a whole is in the direction of the isobars in its warm sector. The cold front moves faster than the warm front and the warm sector becomes progressively more narrow. Eventually the cold front overtakes the warm front, at first near the center of the depression but progressively further and further away from the center, the warm air being lifted from the surface. This lifting of the warmer air is known as "occlusion." The depression is said to be "occluding", the line at the surface which now takes the place of the warm and cold fronts known as an "occlusion." Much of the bad weather in the temperate zones is associated with the fronts of depression. It is this fact which gives the "frontal theory" of depressions its great value as a forecasting tool.

HURRICANES

Severe tropical cyclones of the North Atlantic Ocean are usually called West Indian Hurricanes, but actually many of these storms form, move and die far out from the mainland and hundreds of miles from the West Indies. The storm field advances in a straight or curved track, sometimes with considerable speed, at other times at a much slower rate. The areas of the individual storms vary from less than 100 to more than 500 miles in width, with a comparatively calm center. Centers ranging from 4 to 22 miles across have been observed. This center is a region of lowest atmospheric pressure around which winds blow in a more or less circular course, spiraling inward in a counterclockwise direction. The wind at the outer edge of the storm area is light to moderate and gusty, and it often increases toward the center to speeds too high for instrument recording. Although the air movement inside the center or eye of the hurricane is usually light and fitful, the seas in this area are in most cases very heavy and confused, rendered so by the shifting violent winds which surround it. Furthermore, after the center has passed a vessel, she may expect a sharp renewal of the gales, but blowing now from a different and more or less opposite direction. The fully developed tropical cyclone, encompassing many tens of thousands of square miles, is perhaps the most destructive of all storms.

Tropical cyclones occur over all the tropical oceans except the South Atlantic. They form in or near the region of doldrums, or light to calm wind movements near the Equator. In the North Atlantic, hurricanes form over a wide range of ocean between the Cape Verde Islands and the Windward Islands, over the western part of the Caribbean Sea, and over the Gulf of Mexico. While some may move northward in the beginning, especially those that form southeast of Bermuda, the majority take a westerly to northwesterly course. Of these, some curve gradually northward, either east of or above the larger islands of the West Indies, then turn northeastward or eastward near to or at some distance from the Atlantic Coast of the United States. Others pass over or to the south of the greater islands and enters the Gulf of Mexico, then curve northward or northeastward and strike some part of the east Gulf Coast, or else continue westward and strike the west Gulf Coast. The most common path is curved, the young storms moving generally in a westward direction at first, turning later to the northwestward and then to the northeastward. A considerable number of hurricanes, however, remain in low latitudes and do not turn appreciably to the northward. Freak movements are not uncommon, and there have been storms describing loops, hairpin-curved paths, and other irregular patterns. Movement toward the southeast is rare in the West Indian region, and when it does occur it is of short duration. The entire Caribbean area, the Gulf of Mexico, the coastal regions bordering these bodies of water, and the Atlantic Coast are in danger of disturbances during the hurricane season.

The hurricane season generally begins in June and closes with November. The months of greatest frequency are August, September, and October. Hurricanes are most likely to be severe during August, September and October. During all the months of the season, however, the chance of encountering an intense storm is great enough to warrant a careful watch of the weather elements in these waters. The June hurricanes which form in the West Indian region usually move in a direction between west and north while they are south of 25° North Latitude.

In late September, October, and November, hurricanes of this region are more likely to move in a direction between north and east, passing through the Yucatan Channel, or over Cuba, Florida, or the Bahamas. Of the hurricanes that come from the Atlantic into the West Indies, the majority occur in August and September, and move on a west-northwesterly course in low latitudes, reaching the coast before curving toward the north and northesast. Late in the season, October or November, the movement of hurricanes that form east of the West Indies is often toward the north in the open Atlantic.

The average speed of movement of West Indian hurricanes is about 10 to 13 knots. This speed, however, varies considerably according to the location of the storm, its development and surrounding meteorological conditions. The highest rates of progression usually occur when the storm is moving northward or northeastward in the middle or higher latitudes.

Signs of approach. One of the earliest signs of a hurricane is the appearance of high cirrus clouds which converge toward a point on the horizon that indicates the direction of the center of the storm. The snow-white fibrous mares' tails appear when the center is about 300 or 400 miles distant. Another usual early indication is a long, heavy swell propagated to a considerable distance, sometimes 2 or 3 days in advance, when there is no intervening land to interrupt it. This swell comes from the general direction in which the storm is approaching. There is usually a slight rise of the barometer at the outset, followed by a continuous fall. In front of the storm, if it is advancing in some westerly direction toward the observer, the winds blow from a northerly point (northeast, north, northwest); if moving in some northerly direction toward the observer, they will blow from an easterly point (southeast, east, or northeast). A further indication is a rough, increasing sea. If one or more of these signs be wanting, there is little cause for anticipating a hurricane.

As the storm center approaches, the barometer continues to fall. The wind increases in speed and blows in heavy squalls and the changes in its direction become more rapid. The wind, in general, will back to the left during this time if the center is moving toward the observer's left, or veer to the right

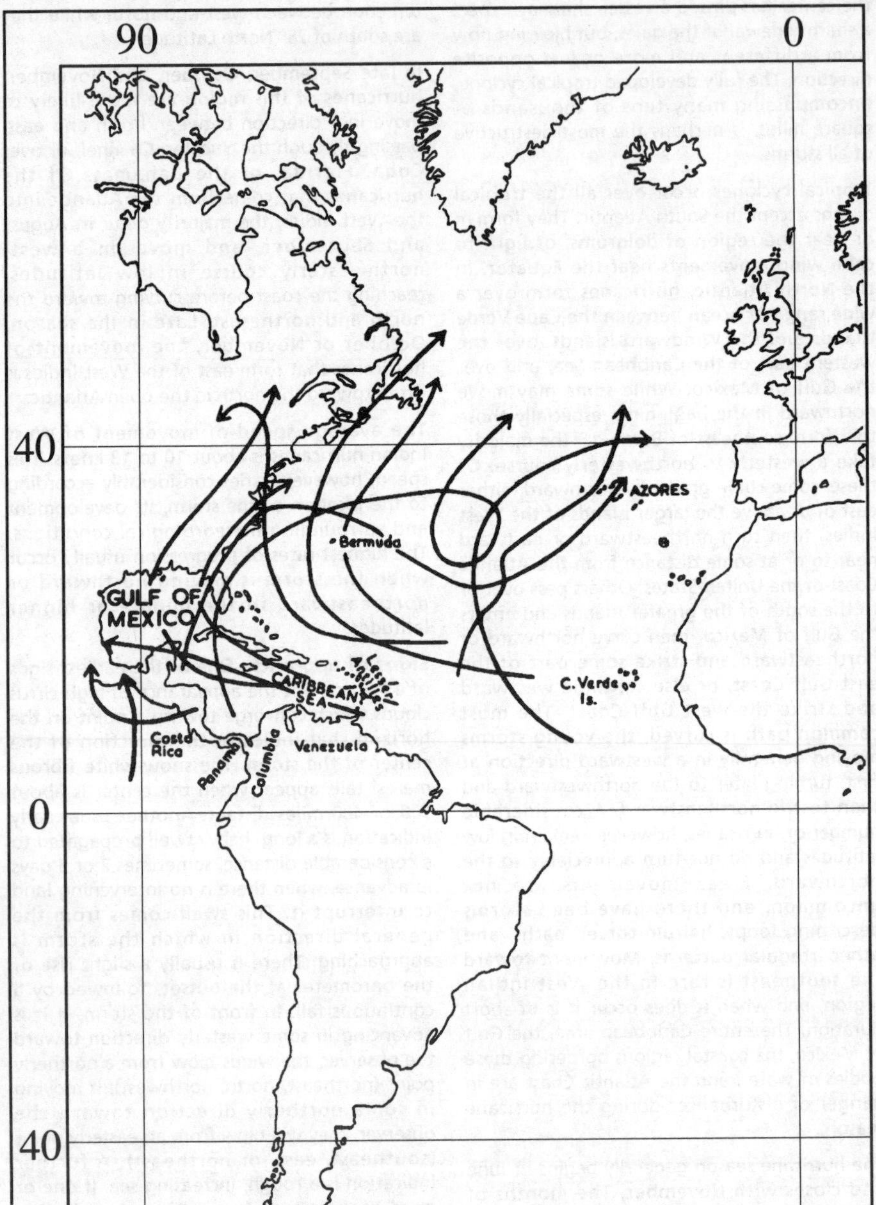

Some tracks followed by hurricanes.

if toward his right as he faces into the wind. Rain in showers accompanies the squalls, and when the center comes closer the rain is usually continuous and is attended by furious gusts of wind. The air is thick with rain and spume drift. Objects at a short distance are often hardly visible. If a vessel is on the line of the hurricane's advance, the wind will remain from the same direction, or nearly so, until the center is close to the vessel, or upon her.

Distance of hurricane center. The distance from the center of a hurricane can be estimated from a consideration of the height of the barometer and the rapidity of its fall, and the velocity of the wind and the rapidity of its changes in direction. If the barometer falls slowly and the wind increases gradually, it may reasonably be supposed that the center is distant. With a rapidly falling barometer and increasing winds, it may reasonably be supposed that the center is approaching dangerously near, the more so if the winds blow closely from the direction of the increasing swell.

Bearing of center. Facing the wind, the storm center will be 8 to 12 points to the right; when the storm is distant it will be from 10 to 12 points, and when the barometer has fallen 5 or 6 tenths of an inch it will be about 8 points.

A line drawn through the center of a hurricane in the direction in which it is moving is called the storm track, or axis of progression. The semicircle on either side of the axis is called, respectively, the right-hand or dangerous semicircle and the left-hand or navigable semicircle.

If the wind shifts to the right, the vessel will be in the right-hand or dangerous semicircle with regard to the direction in which the storm is traveling. In such case the vessel should be kept on the starboard tack and increase her distance from the center.

If the wind shifts to the left, the vessel will be in the left or navigable semicircle. The helm should be put up and the vessel run with the wind on the starboard quarter, preserving the compass course, if possible, until the barometer rises, when the vessel may be hove to on the port tack. If there is not sea room to run, the vessel can be put on the port tack at once.

Should the wind remain steady and the barometer continue to fall, the vessel is in the path of the storm and should run with the wind on the starboard quarter into the navigable semicircle.

In all cases act so as to increase as soon as possible the distance from the center, bearing in mind that the whole storm field is advancing. In receding from the center of a hurricane the barometer will rise and the wind and sea will subside.

Practical rules. When there are indications of a hurricane, vessels should remain in port or seek one if possible. Changes of barometer and wind should be carefully observed and recorded, and every precaution should be taken to avert damage by striking light spars, strengthening moorings, and preparing the engine to assist the moorings. In the ports of the southern States hurricanes are generally accompanied by very high tides, and vessels may be endangered by overriding the wharf where moored if the position is at all exposed.

Vessels in the Straits of Florida may not have sea room to maneuver so as to avoid the storm track, and should try to make a harbor, or to stand out of the straits to obtain sea room. Vessels unable to reach a port and having sea room to maneuver usually observe the following rules:

When there are indications of the near approach of a hurricane, sailing vessels may heave to on the starboard tack. The safety of the vessel often depends on heaving to in time. Steamers may remain stationary. Both should carefully observe and record changes in wind, barometer and swell so as to find the bearing of the center, and to ascertain by the shift of the wind in which semicircle the vessel is situated.

CURRENTS OF THE WORLD

On the following pages are several simplified charts illustrating the basic patterns of ocean currents throughout the world. The average rate of drift is also listed in the first two tables. For more complete information consult the appropriate Pilot Charts from the Defense Mapping Agency, and Ocean Passages For The World (Pub. 136, British Admiralty).

No.	Name	Average Drift miles per day	Remarks
1	N. Equartorial	10-40	Neutral temperature
2	Bahama	10-50	Neutral temperature
3	Caribbean counter current		Neutral temperature
4	Gulf Stream	10-70	Warm at northern limit
5	N. Atlantic drift	10-25	Warm-considerable modifying effect on climate of Western Europe and the U.K.
6	Norwegian		Warm
7	Irminger	9 (average)	Neutral
8	E. and W. Greenland	6-12	Neutral – source of N. Atlantic icebergs
9	Labrador	5-20	Cold – source of fog and icebergs on the Grand Banks.
10	Canary	10-35	Cold – associated with upwelling
11	Azores	11 (average)	Neutral
12	Portuguese	10 (average)	Cold to neutral
13	Counter Equatorial	10-30	Neutral
14	S. Equatorial	10-45	Neutral
15	Guinea	10-60	Neutral
16	Brazil	10-35	Warm
17	Falkland	10-40	Cold
18	Brazil Inshore	15 (average)	Cold. An extension of the Falkland current, may reach as far north as Rio de Janeiro in May to July
19	Southern Ocean Drift	0-30	Neutral – carries S. Atlantic icebergs, common to S. Atlantic, S. Pacific and S. Indian Ocean
20	Benguela	10-50	Cold. Associated with upwelling
21	Western Australian	14 (average)	Inshore current sets south from March to August
22	Equatorial		Similar to Atlantic
23	Counter Equatorial		Similar to Atlantic
24	Mozambique	0-30	Neutral
25	East African coast		Neutral. Average daily drift: November to January 16 miles; February to March 48 miles; May to September 48 miles. From July to September the daily drift may reach 170 miles to the south of Socotra
26	Agulhas	10-40	Warm. A counter current is found close inshore.

Note the change in direction with the change of the monsoon in the Red Sea, Arabian Sea, Bay of Bengal and the China Sea. (See inset on chart for N.E. monsoon.)

CURRENTS OF THE PACIFIC OCEAN

No.	Name	Average Drift miles per day	Remarks
27	N. Equatorial	0-40	Similar to the Atlantic
28	Counter Equatorial	0-40	Similar to the Atlantic
29	S. Equatorial	0-40	Similar to the Atlantic
30	Kuro Shio	10-50	Warm. The "Gulf Stream" of the Pacific
31	Oya Shio	15-30	Cold
32	Tsushima		Warm
33	Liman		Cold
34	Kamchatka	5-10	Neutral
35	N. Pacific drift	10-20	Warm
36	Aleutian	3-7	Neutral
37	Alaskan	6 (average)	Neutral
38	Californian	10-30	Upwelling occurs off the coast of California. Between November and December and Davidson current sets northward close inshore.
39	East Australian	0-25	Warm
40	Peru	0-30	Cold. Upwelling along the coast.
41	Holy Child	Variable	Warm. Flows from January to March but is rather irregular

CURRENTS OF THE WORLD

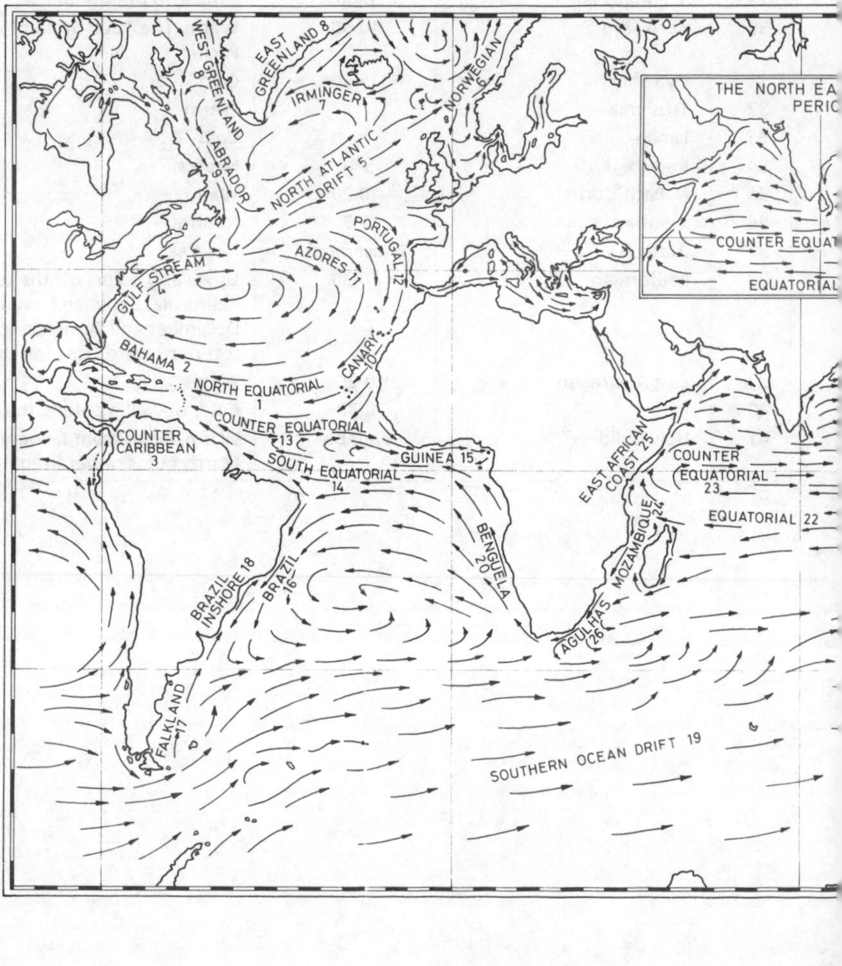

CURRENTS OF THE WORLD

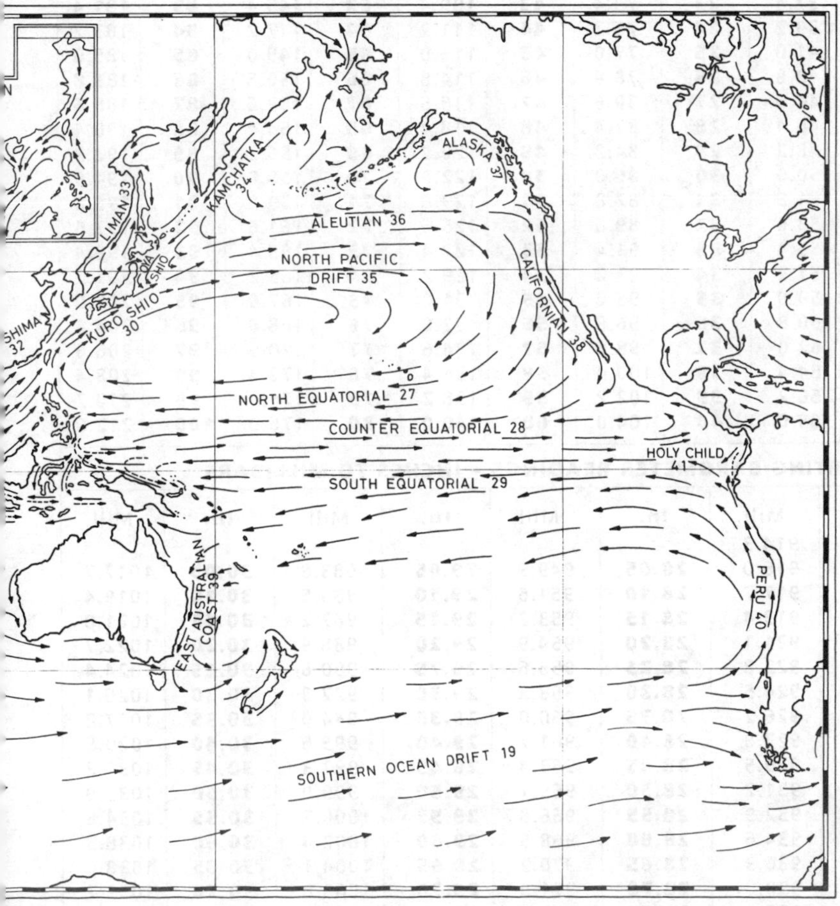

TEMPERATURE CONVERSIONS

C°	F°	C°	F°	C°	F°	C°	F°	C°	F°
00	32.0								
01	33.8	**21**	69.8	**41**	105.8	**61**	141.8	**81**	177.8
02	35.6	**22**	71.6	**42**	107.6	**62**	143.6	**82**	179.6
03	37.4	**23**	73.4	**43**	109.4	**63**	145.4	**83**	181.4
04	39.2	**24**	75.2	**44**	111.2	**64**	147.2	**84**	183.2
05	41.0	**25**	77.0	**45**	113.0	**65**	149.0	**85**	185.0
06	42.8	**26**	78.8	**46**	114.8	**66**	150.8	**86**	186.8
07	44.6	**27**	80.6	**47**	116.6	**67**	152.6	**87**	188.6
08	46.4	**28**	82.4	**48**	118.4	**68**	154.4	**88**	190.4
09	48.2	**29**	84.2	**49**	120.2	**69**	156.2	**89**	192.2
10	50.0	**30**	86.0	**50**	122.0	**70**	158.0	**90**	194.0
11	51.8	**31**	87.8	**51**	123.8	**71**	159.8	**91**	195.8
12	53.6	**32**	89.6	**52**	125.6	**72**	161.6	**92**	197.6
13	55.4	**33**	91.4	**53**	127.4	**73**	163.4	**93**	199.4
14	57.2	**34**	93.2	**54**	129.2	**74**	165.2	**94**	201.2
15	59.0	**35**	95.0	**55**	131.0	**75**	167.0	**95**	203.0
16	60.8	**36**	96.8	**56**	132.8	**76**	168.8	**96**	204.8
17	62.6	**37**	98.6	**57**	134.6	**77**	170.6	**97**	206.6
18	64.4	**38**	100.4	**58**	136.4	**78**	172.4	**98**	208.4
19	66.2	**39**	102.2	**59**	138.2	**79**	174.0	**99**	210.2
20	68.0	**40**	104.0	**60**	140.0	**80**	176.0	**100**	212.0

CONVERTING BAROMETER READINGS – INCHES TO MILLIBARS

In.	Mill.	In.	Mill.	In.	Mill.	In.	Mill.
27.00	914.3						
27.05	916.0	**28.05**	949.9	**29.05**	983.8	**30.05**	1017.7
27.10	917.7	**28.10**	951.6	**29.10**	985.5	**30.10**	1019.4
27.15	919.4	**28.15**	953.2	**29.15**	987.2	**30.15**	1021.0
27.20	921.1	**28.20**	954.9	**29.20**	988.9	**30.20**	1022.7
27.25	922.8	**28.25**	956.6	**29.25**	990.6	**30.25**	1024.4
27.30	924.5	**28.30**	958.3	**29.30**	922.3	**30.30**	1026.1
27.35	926.2	**28.35**	960.0	**29.35**	944.0	**30.35**	1027.8
27.40	927.8	**28.40**	961.7	**29.40**	995.6	**30.40**	1029.5
27.45	929.5	**28.45**	963.4	**29.45**	997.3	**30.45**	1031.2
27.5	931.2	**28.50**	965.1	**29.50**	999.0	**30.50**	1032.9
27.55	932.9	**28.55**	966.8	**29.55**	1000.7	**30.55**	1034.6
27.60	934.6	**28.60**	968.5	**29.60**	1002.4	**30.60**	1036.3
27.65	936.3	**28.65**	970.2	**29.65**	1004.1	**30.65**	1038.0
27.70	938.0	**28.70**	971.9	**29.70**	1005.8	**30.70**	1039.7
27.75	939.7	**28.75**	973.6	**29.75**	1007.5	**30.75**	1041.4
27.80	941.4	**28.80**	975.3	**29.80**	1009.2	**30.80**	1043.1
27.85	943.1	**28.85**	977.0	**29.85**	1010.9	**30.85**	1044.8
27.90	944.8	**28.90**	978.6	**29.90**	1012.6	**30.90**	1046.4
27.95	946.5	**28.95**	980.3	**29.95**	1014.3	**30.95**	1048.1
28.00	948.2	**29.00**	982.1	**30.00**	1016.0	**31.00**	1049.8

BAROMETER INDICATIONS

Certain fundamental principles may be helpful to remember concerning weather, generally:

a **Low Pressure** shows unstable and changin conditions.
b **High Pressure** shows stable and continuing good conditions.
c **Steady Rise** shows good weather approaching.
d **Steady Fall** shows bad weather approaching.
e **Rapid Rise** shows better weather may not last.
f **Rapid Fall** shows stormy weather approaching rapidly.

DEWPOINT (°C) TABLE

Dry Bulb	Depression of Wet Bulb																		Dry Bulb
°C	0°	0.2°	0.4°	0.6°	0.8°	1.0°	2.0°	2.5°	3.0°	3.5°	4.0°	4.5°	5.0°	5.5°	6.0°	6.5°	7.0°	7.5°	°C
40	40	40	40	39	39	39	38	37	36	36	35	34	34	33	32	32	31	30	40
39	39	39	39	38	38	38	37	36	35	35	34	33	33	32	31	31	30	29	39
38	38	38	38	37	37	37	35	35	34	34	33	32	32	31	30	29	29	28	28
37	37	37	37	36	36	36	34	34	33	32	32	31	30	30	29	28	28	27	37
36	36	36	35	35	35	35	33	33	32	31	31	30	29	29	28	27	26	26	36
35	35	35	34	34	34	34	32	32	31	30	30	29	28	28	27	26	25	24	35
34	34	34	33	33	33	33	31	31	30	29	29	28	27	26	26	25	24	23	34
33	33	33	32	32	32	32	30	30	29	28	28	27	26	25	25	24	23	22	33
32	32	32	31	31	31	31	29	29	28	27	26	26	25	24	23	23	22	21	32
31	31	31	30	30	30	30	28	28	27	26	25	25	24	23	22	21	21	20	31
30	30	30	29	29	29	29	27	27	26	25	24	24	23	22	21	20	19	18	30
29	29	29	28	28	28	28	26	25	25	24	23	22	22	21	20	19	18	17	29
28	28	28	27	27	27	27	25	24	24	23	22	21	20	20	19	18	17	16	28
27	27	27	26	26	26	26	24	23	23	22	21	20	19	18	18	17	16	15	26
26	26	26	25	25	25	25	23	22	22	21	20	19	18	17	16	15	14	13	25
25	25	25	24	24	24	24	22	21	20	20	19	18	17	16	15	14	13	12	25
24	24	24	23	23	23	23	21	20	19	19	18	17	16	15	14	13	12	11	24
23	23	23	22	22	22	21	20	19	18	17	17	16	15	14	13	12	10	9	23
22	22	22	21	21	21	20	19	18	17	16	15	14	13	12	11	10	9	8	22
21	21	21	20	20	20	19	18	17	16	15	14	13	12	11	10	9	8	6	21
20	20	20	19	19	19	18	17	16	15	14	13	12	11	10	9	7	6	5	20
19	19	19	18	18	18	17	16	15	14	13	12	11	10	9	7	6	4	3	19
18	18	18	17	17	17	16	15	14	13	12	11	10	8	7	6	4	3	1	18
17	17	17	16	16	16	15	14	13	12	11	9	8	7	6	4	3	1	-0	17
16	16	16	15	15	15	14	12	11	10	9	8	7	6	4	3	1	0	-2	16
15	15	15	14	14	14	13	11	10	9	8	7	6	4	3	1	0	-2	-5	15
14	14	14	13	13	13	12	10	9	8	7	6	4	3	1	0	-2	-4	-7	14
13	13	13	12	12	11	11	9	8	7	6	4	3	1	0	-2	-4	-7	-9	13
12	12	12	11	11	10	10	8	7	6	4	3	1	0	-2	-4	-6	-9	-12	12
11	11	11	10	10	9	9	7	6	4	3	1	0	2	-4	-6	-9	-12	-15	11
10	10	10	9	9	8	8	6	4	3	2	0	-2	-3	-6	-8	-11	-15	-19	10
9	9	9	8	8	7	7	4	3	2	0	-1	-3	-5	-8	-10	-14	-18		9
8	8	8	7	7	6	6	3	2	0	-1	-3	-5	-7	-10	-13	-17			8
7	7	7	6	6	5	5	2	1	-1	-3	-4	-7	-9	-12	-16				7
6	6	6	5	5	4	4	1	-0	-2	-4	-6	-9	-11	-15					6
5	5	5	4	4	3	2	0	-2	-4	-6	-8	-10	-14	-15					5
4	4	4	3	2	2	1	-1	-3	-5	-7	-10	-11	-14	-18					4
3	3	3	2	1	1	0	-3	-5	-7	-8	-11	-14	-17						3
2	2	2	1	0	0	-1	-4	-5	-8	-10	-13	-16							2
1	1	1	0	-1	-1	-2	-5	-7	-9	-12	-15	-10							1
0	0	-1	-1	-2	-2	-3	-7	-9	-11	-14	-18								0

In the table lines are are ruled to draw attention to the fact that above the line evaporation is going on from a water surface, while below the line it is going on from ice surface. Owing to this, interpolation must not be made between figures on different sides of the lines.

11

VISUAL STORM WARNING SIGNALS

These were formerly displayed by the Coast Guard at many locations. They are no longer maintained by the Coast Guard, but may be seen at yacht clubs, marinas or flown by the coast Guard Auxiliary.

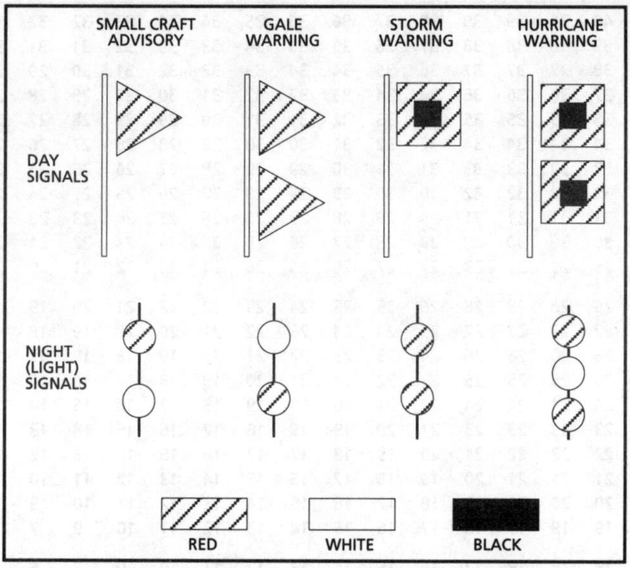

WIND VELOCITY CONVERSION TABLE

Knots	Miles per hour	Knots	Miles per hour	Knots	Miles per hour	Knots	Miles per hour
1	1.15	26	29.92	51	58.69	76	87.46
2	2.30	27	31.07	52	59.84	77	88.61
3	3.45	28	32.22	53	60.99	78	89.76
4	4.60	29	33.37	54	62.14	79	90.91
5	5.75	30	34.52	55	63.29	80	92.06
6	6.90	31	35.67	56	64.44	81	93.21
7	8.05	32	36.82	57	65.59	82	94.36
8	9.21	33	37.98	58	66.74	83	95.51
9	10.36	34	39.13	59	67.89	84	96.67
10	11.51	35	40.28	60	69.05	85	97.82
11	12.66	36	41.43	61	70.20	86	98.97
12	13.81	37	42.58	62	71.35	87	100.12
13	14.96	38	43.73	63	72.50	88	101.27
14	16.11	39	44.88	64	73.65	89	102.42
15	17.26	40	46.03	65	74.80	90	103.57
16	18.41	41	47.18	66	75.95	91	104.72
17	19.56	42	48.33	67	77.10	92	105.87
18	20.71	43	49.48	68	78.25	93	107.02
19	21.86	44	50.63	69	79.40	94	108.17
20	23.02	45	51.78	70	80.55	95	109.32
21	24.17	46	52.94	71	81.70	96	110.47
22	25.32	47	54.09	72	82.86	97	111.62
23	26.47	48	55.24	73	84.01	98	112.78
24	27.62	49	56.39	74	85.16	99	113.93
25	28.77	50	57.54	75	86.31	100	115.08

GLOSSARY OF TERMS USED IN MARINE METEOROLOGY

Air Mass. A mass of air which is largely homogeneous in a horizontal direction. Its physical properties are determined by the nature of the surface over which it forms and may be subsequently modified when the air mass moves over a different type of surface. Air masses are often separated from each other by frontal surfaces, which form discontinuities.

Anemometer. An instrument for measuring the speed of the wind.

Angle of Indraft. The angle between an isobar and the direction of the wind, near the earth's surface.

Anticyclone. A region characterised in the barometric pressure field by a system of closed isobars, with the highest pressure on the inside.

Aurora. Bright streamers of light, ascending from the horizon towards the zenith, or luminous arcs, which are manifestations of electrical energy in the upper atmosphere. The aurora is seen in both hemispheres, in high and sometimes in medium or low latitudes. In the northern hemisphere it is known as Aurora Borealis, the southern as Aurora Australis.

Backing. A change in the direction of the wind, in an counterclockwise direction.

Blizzard. A high wind accompanied by great cold and drifting or falling snow.

Col. The saddle-backed region occurring between two anticyclones and two depressions, arranged alternately.

Cold Front. The boundary line between the advancing cold air at the rear of a depression and the warm sector. Line squalls may occur at the passage of this front, which was formerly called the squall line.

Cold Sector. The part of a depression associated with relatively cold air on the earth's surface.

Convection. In convection, heat is carried from one place to another by the bodily transfer of the matter containing it. In particular, this is the method by which heat raises the temperature of a fluid mass. The part in close contact with the heat rises, and the surrounding fluid moves in to take its place. This action in the atmosphere gives rise to convectional currents, which may produce cumulus or cumulonimbus cloud.

Convergence. Consider an area on the earth's surface. On the sides which face the wind, air will flow into the area, while on the other sides air will flow out. If, however, the wind is not uniform, more air may flow in than flows out, and the amount of air in the area will tend to increase. The air cannot, however, go on accumulating, and the excess will have to flow out over the top, thus leading to a rising air current, and perhaps to clouds and rain. The contrary case, when more air flows out of the area than flows into it is called **Divergence.** In this case there is a deficit of air, which is balanced by a descent of the upper air layers above the area. This descent is called **Subsidence.** The subsiding air warms up, its relative humidity falls, and fine weather is the usual accompaniment of subsidence, though fog may occur under certain conditions.

Corona(ae). A series of colored rings round the sun or moon caused by diffraction of its light by water-drops, chiefly in alto-clouds.

Corposants. Luminous brush discharges of electricity, sometimes observed at the mastheads, and on projecting parts of ships during electrical storms. Also known as **St. Elmo's Fire.** Due to atmospheric electricity.

Cyclone. A name given to the tropical revolving storms of the Bay of Bengal and the Arabian Sea. Sometimes used as a general term for tropical revolving storms of all oceans, or in the form "Tropical Cyclone."

Cyclonic. Refers to wind circulating counter-clockwise round a low pressure area surrounded by an area of higher pressure in North latitudes – clockwise in South latitudes.

Dangerous Quadrant. The forward quadrant of the dangerous semi-circle of a cyclone, which before recurvature is nearer the pole (in both hemispheres).

Depression. A region characterised in the barometric pressure field by a system of closed isobars, having lowest pressure on the inside.

Dew. Water drops deposited by condensation of water vapor from the air, mainly on the hor-izontal surfaces cooled by nocturnal radiation.

Dew Point. The lowest temperature to which air can be cooled without causing condensation.

Diurnal Variation. This term is used to indicate the changes in the course of an average day, in the magnitude of a meteorological element. The most striking example of this is the diurnal variation of barometric pressure in the tropics, the chief component of which has a 12-hourly period. The maxima of this variation are about 10 a.m. and 10 p.m., the minima about 4 a.m. and 4 p.m. local time.

Doldrums. The equatorial oceanic regions of calms and light variable winds, accompanied by heavy rains, thunderstorms and squalls. These belts are variable in position and extent, and as a whole move north and south with the annual changes of the sun's declination.

Eye of Storm. The calm central area of a tropical cyclone. The most noticeable feature of this area is the sudden drop in wind from hurricane force to light unsteady breezes or even to a complete calm, with more or less cloudless sky and absence of rain. The sea in this area is, however, often very high and confused.

Front. The line of separation at or above the earth's surface between cold and warm air masses.

Frontogenesis. The development or marked intensification of a front.

Frontolysis. The disappearance or marked weakening of a front. Subsidence is the most important factor in causing frontolysis.

Gust. A comparatively rapid fluctuation in the strength of the wind, characteristic of winds near the surface of the earth. Gusts are mainly due to the turbulence or eddy motion arising from the friction offered by the ground to the flow of the current of air. (See **Squall**).

Hail. Hard pellets of ice, of various shapes and sizes, and more or less transparent, which fall from cumulonimbus clouds and are often associated with thunderstorms.

Halo. Halo phenomena constitute a large group of phenomena produced by the refraction or reflection of the light of the sun or moon by the ice crystals composing cirrus or cirrostratus cloud.

Hurricane. A name given to the tropical revolving storm of the West Indian region. Also applied to force 12 in the Beaufort Scale, whatever its cause.

Inversion. An abbreviation for "inversion of temperature gradient." The temperature or the air generally decreases with increasing height, but occasionally the reverse is the case; when the temperature thus increases with height there is said to be an inversion. When an inversion exists at the surface, fog often occurs.

Isallobars. Isallobars are lines drawn upon a chart through places at which equal changes of pressure have occurred in some places at the same period of time. Lines of equal change, or isallobars, are drawn to enclose regions of rising or of falling pressure.

Isobars. Lines drawn through positions having the same barometric pressure, when reduced to sea level.

Isotherms. Lines drawn through positions having the same temperatures.

Katabatic Wind. A wind that flows down slopes, usually at night. The air at the top of the slope is cooled to a greater amount by radiation than the air lower down, becomes heavier, and flows down the slope under the influence of gravity. The opposite of katabatic is **anabatic,** applied to a wind blowing up a slope, if it is caused by the convection of heated air.

Land and Sea Breezes. These are caused by the unequal heating and cooling of land and water under the influence of solar radiation by day and radiation to the sky at night, which produce a gradient of pressure near the coast. During the daytime the land is warmer than the sea and a breeze, the sea breeze, blows onshore; at night and in the early morning the land is cooler than the sea and the land breeze blows offshore. Land breeze is usually less developed than sea breeze.

Line Squall. A more or less violent squall, accompanying the passage of the cold front of a depression, distinguished by a sudden or rapid rise of wind strength, a change of wind direction, a rapid rise of the barometer and a fall of temperature. There is usually heavy rain or hail, sometimes a thunderstorm, or snow. The accompanying low black cloud forms a line or arch.

Local Winds. Winds prevalent in particular areas at particular times with special features, eg, the **Bora, Pampero, Mistral, Levanter, Sumatra.**

Mirage. The appearance of one or more images of a terrestrial object in the sky; also all forms of distortion of objects, due to abnormal refraction.

Occlusion, Occluded Depression. When the whole of the warm sector of a depression has been "pushed up" from the earth's surface by the advance of the cold front behind it, this is known as occlusion, and the depression in which it occurs is called an occluded depression.

Orographic Rain. Rain caused by the interference of rising land in the path of moisture laden air. A horizontal air current striking a mountain slope is deflected upwards, and the consequent dynamical cooling associated with the expansion of the air produces cloud and rain, if the air contains sufficient aqueous vapor.

Polar Front. The line of discontinuity, which is developed in suitable conditions between air originating in polar regions and air from low latitudes, and on which the majority of the depressions of temperate latitudes develop. It can sometimes be traced as a continuous wavy line thousands of miles in length, but it is interrupted when polar air breaks through to feed the trade winds, and is often replaced by a very complex series of fronts, or by a more gradual change of temperature.

Precipitation. Any aqueous deposit, in liquid or solid form, derived from the atmosphere. The precipitation at a given station during a given period includes not only the rainfall but also dew and the water equivalent of any solid deposits (snow, hail, or hoar frost) received in the rain gauge.

Recurvature of Storm. This expression refers to the recurvature of the track of a tropical cyclone. In the northern hemisphere a tropical cyclone, after proceeding in a more or less westerly direction, recurves and normally takes a north -easterly direction; in the southern hemisphere the final direction is normally south-easterly.

Ridge. An extension of an anticyclone or high pressure area shown on a pressure chart, corresponding to a ridge running out from the side of a mountain.

Roaring Forties. A nautical expression for the region of westerly winds in south temperate latitudes, which reach their greatest development south of 40°S. A general term for the prevailing westerly winds in the temperate latitudes of both hemispheres is Brave West Winds.

Scud. A word used by sailors to describe ragged fragments of cloud drifting rapidly in a strong wind, often underneath rain clouds. The meteorological term is fractostratus.

Secondary Depression or "Secondary." The isobars around a depression are frequently not quite symmetrical, they sometimes show bulges or distortions, which are accompanied by marked deflections in the general circulation of the wind in the depression; such distortions are called secondaries; they may appear merely as sinuosities in the isobars, but at other times they enclose separate centers of low pressure and show separate wind circulations from that of the parent depression.

Shower. In describing present or past weather, the following distinction is made between the use of the terms "showers" and "occasional precipitation." In general, showers are of short duration, and the fair periods between them are usually characterised by definite clearance of the sky. The clouds which give the showers are, therefore, isolated. The precipitation does not usually last more than fifteen minutes, though it may occasionally last for half an hour or more. Occasional precipitation, on the other hand, usually lasts for a longer time than the showers, and the sky in the periods between the precipitation is usually cloudy or overcast.

Sleet. Precipitation of snow and rain together, or of melting snow and rain.

Snow. Precipitation of ice crystals of feathery or needlelike structure.

Squall. A strong wind that increases suddenly, lasts for some minutes, and decreases again comparatively rapidly. It is frequently, but not necessarily, associated with a temporary change of direction. (See **Gust**)

Stratosphere. The region of the atmosphere immediately above the troposphere (q.v.). In the lower stratosphere temperature may continue to decrease with increase of height (but more slowly than in the troposphere) or may remain practically constant, or may increase with height. The transition from troposphere to stratosphere, judged by change of temperature with height is not always abrupt.

There are other regions, at greater heights, with special characteristics,e.g.:

(a) The ozonosphere, where the concentration of ozone gas is greatest, centered at a height of about 20 miles.

(b) The ionosphere, the highly electrically conducting region of ionised gases, extending upwards from the height of 50 or 60 miles. This region plays an important part in radio propagation. The main subdivisions of this region in order of increasing height are usually referred to as the D,E (or Kennelly-Heaviside), F (or Appleton) regions or layers.

Synoptic. An adjective derived from the noun "synopsis," a brief or condensed statement presenting a combined or general view of something. Thus a synoptic chart shows the weather conditions over a large area at a given instant of time.

Tendency of the Barometer. The amount of change in barometric pressure in the 3 hours preceding the time of observation. The characteristic of the tendency is the type of change during the same period, e.g. "rising," "falling at first then rising," "steady".

Thunder. The noise made by an electric discharge (lightning) from charged raindrops in a cloud to another cloud (or another part of the same cloud) or to the earth, or to the air surrounding the charged cloud. Sound travels 1 mile in about 5 seconds, while the lightning flash is seen as soon as it occurs, hence the interval of time between the two will give the distance from the observer.

Tornado. A violent and destructive whirl accompanying a thunderstorm.

Trade Winds. The name given to the winds which blow from the tropical high pressure belts towards the equatorial region of low pressure, from the N.E in the northern hemisphere and from the S.E. in the southern hemisphere.

Troposphere. The lower region of the atmosphere, throughout which temperature in general decreases as height increases, and within which occur practically all clouds and the various other phenomena normally styled "weather." The upper boundary of the region is known as the tropopause. The height of the tropopause varies with latitude from an average of about 5½ miles in our polar regions to about 11 miles at the equator, but the height also varies from summer to winter and with the general meteorological situation. (See **Stratosphere**).

Trough. The trough line of a circular depression is the line, through the center, perpendicular to the line of advance of the center. During the passage of a depression over any given place the pressure at first falls and later rises; the trough line passes over the place during the period of transition from the falling to the rising barometer. The word trough is also used in a more general sense for any "valley" of low pressure, and is thus the opposite of a "ridge" of high pressure.

Typhoon. A name given to the tropical revolving storms of the China Sea and the west of the North Pacific Ocean.

Veering. A change in the direction of the wind, in a clockwise direction.

Vertex. The westernmost point in the track of a tropical revolving storm.

Vortex. Center of tropical revolving storm, where barometric pressure is least.

Warm Sector, Warm Front. Most depressions in their earlier stages have an area of warm air on the side nearest the equator, known as the warm sector. The warm front is the boundary between the front of the warm sector, as the depression advances, and the colder air in front of it.

Waterspout. An air whirl, normally with a funnel shaped cloud projecting downwards from a cumulonimbus cloud, accompanied by an agitation of the sea surface beneath it, and the formation of a cloud of sprays. The waterspout is formed when the funnel shaped cloud has descended to join up with the cloud of spray; the spout then assumes the appearance of a column of water.

Wedge. An area of high pressure bounded by wedge shaped isobars. It is the converse of a V-shaped depression.

SEAMANSHIP

12

Page

ROPE—ITS USE AND CARE

TYPES OF CONSTRUCTION

There are two main methods of rope construction: laid or twisted ropes (cable laid), the traditional form of manufacture used when natural fiber ropes were in general use, and braided ropes. Braided ropes, usually 4, 8 or 16 plait, have the great advantage of being far less liable to kink than a traditional laid rope and are thus useful for anchor and mooring ropes, where long lengths may require to be rapidly stowed in fairly small places, as they will flake down with no tendency to kink. Braided ropes have very little tendency to kink and are smooth running. This type of construction does of course require special splicing techniques.

Types of Material

There are three main types of man-made fiber: nylon, polyester and polypropylene. Nylon is the strongest of the three followed by polyester and then polypropylene. Nylon, as well as being very strong, is also elastic and is thus most suitable for dealing with shock loads, for example with anchors, but is unsuitable for halyards where minimum stretch is essential.

Polyester has the useful combination of strength with a low stretch characteristic which thus makes it suitable for most purposes on board—it is also available as pre-stretched which is ideal for halyards, in both plaited or three–strand construction. (Dacron is a trademark of polyester rope)

The main advantage of polypropylene is that it floats and is thus the most useful rope to use for dinghy painters and mooring lines where a submerged rope could offer hazards to propellers.

A fourth material, polythene, is relatively cheap and has a "waxy" feel, very popular for fishing net construction but of no great interest to yachtsmen, other than for mooring lines. (Unsuitable where it is necessary to tie knots due to slippery finish.) The latest additions to the man–made fiber groups are 'Spectra' (brand name of Allied Chemicals) and 'Kevlar' (brand name of Du Pont). Both are very light with immensely strong filaments.

In their present form, both ropes are mainly of interest to the racing yachtsman, where great strength and lightness are highly desirable and cost and working life of lesser importance than they are to the cruising sailor. Reference should be made to the manufacturers' publications when it is proposed to use any of such new generation products in view of the varying characteristics and requirements. For example Kevlar is very susceptible to damage by chafe and bending and must be protected from sunlight, whereas with Spectra, variants with adequate resistance to long term creep must be selected .

Generally speaking, man–made fiber ropes used in yachts are larger than is necessary from a strength point of view in order to facilitate ease of handling; for example the modern equivalent strengthwise of the old 1½ inch circumference manila ropes would be far too small to handle comfortably if used for sheets. The surface of the rope also has considerable bearing on its handling properties: ropes formed with a continuous filament (never possible with natural fibers) are immensely strong and very shiny in appearance, while rope formed of the staple or shorter filament has slightly lower strength than the continuous filament rope but has a matt finish, which is obviously more desirable where the rope is frequently handled, as in the case of sheets. With self tailers or stoppers the shiny braid should be used to facilitate long life.

Handling and Care of Ropes

The majority of man–made fibers as well as being much stronger than natural fibers are very tolerant of those factors which reduced the working life of the latter, for example the former can be stored away damp and will not rot although mildew-may appear. Physical damage must be guarded against as with natural fibers, particularly bearing in mind that rope under tension is easily damaged by chafe. Ropes under tension but static (e.g. mooring lines) should be protected at any angular point or rough service by plastic tubing over the rope or parcelling with canvas, etc.

The effects of chafe from normal friction surfaces such as sheaves, fairleads and cleats is considerably reduced if the bearing surfaces are large. In the case of sheaves, the diameter should be not less than five times the diameter of the rope and preferably more. The groove of a sheave should have such a radius that it supports one third of the rope's circumference. Whenever possible sharp "nips" in a rope should be avoided, but if a rope has to be led through a sharp angle the bearing surface of the lead should be at least that required of a sheave and smooth. Rope can be severely damaged if led through a thin shackle or eye bolt, particularly if the angle is sharp.

When coiling a rope always begin at the end which is made fast so that any twists or kinks can be chased along and run out at the far end. It is particularly important to ensure that load is never applied to rope when there is a kink in it as this will almost inevitably damage and weaken it. Rope which has been badly overloaded in any way may indicate this by being unusually hard in parts. This hardness is caused by the heat produced by the overload friction fusing some of the filaments together.

Always avoid heavy shock loads if possible, for example when passing a tow rope between a stationary vessel and a moving one, never make both ends fast at once. The resulting jerk imposes a tremendous strain on the rope which if it does not damage it, may rip a cleat or bollard out. When one end has been made fast the correct procedure at the other end is to make a figure of eight turn round the bitts, or a round turn on a bollard, and allow the rope to render smoothly as the load comes on, then check steadily and make fast as the vessel gathers way.

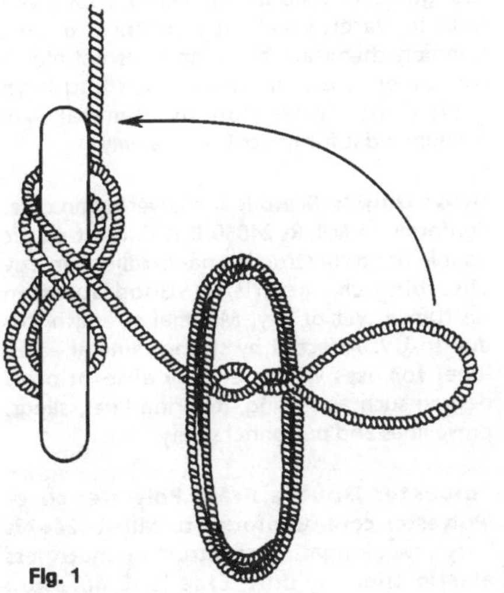

Fig. 1

Unless ropes are properly coiled, kinks will occur with subsequent snags when the rope is run out. Nearly all laid ropes are right handed and should be coiled clockwise to ensure smooth running out.

In practice it is seldom that cleats on yachts are large enough to allow the fall of the halyard to be looped over the horn of the cleat without slipping off and becoming a confused tangle. When the halyard has been made up on the cleat and coiled, hold it close to the cleat, pull a short length through the coil, twist and then loop it over the horn of the cleat (Sketch 1). Alternatively a buntline hitch can be used. After coiling and looping, the last loop can be pushed through the center of the coil, capsized over the top and drawn tight (Sketch 2). A very useful hitch to use when hanging spare lines up in a cockpit locker.

A point to remember in connection with mooring ropes is that the eye of the rope should not be dropped over any lines already on the bollard. The eye should be passed up through the eyes of lines already there and then dropped over the bollard. This will facilitate the removal of any line without disturbing the others.

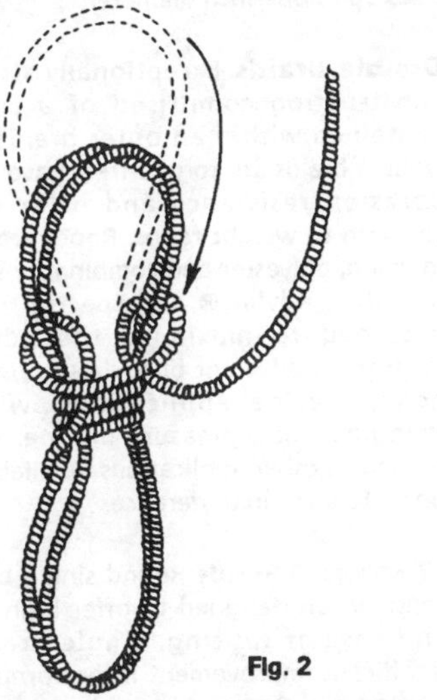

Fig. 2

It is desirable to ensure uniformity of wear in ropes whenever possible by changing end for end occasionally.

Cleaning

The life of a rope can be extended considerably by washing in fresh water to get rid of salt crystal, grit and dirt. This should be done at the end of the season when laying up and will ensure that not only will the rope look clean but will remain soft and pliable. Detergents should not be used, soap powder only should be employed to clean the rope.

(From information supplied by Marlow Ropes)

ROPE SPECIFICATIONS

This section on types of marine rope, breaking strains and size selection has been kindly provided by New England Ropes of New Bedford, Massachusetts. Special rope designs utilizing proprietary fibers and construction will be available only from New England Ropes. Other manufacturers may, or may not, have similar designs. In any case, this information is representative of the types of high-tech line available to today's boater.

ROPE CONSTRUCTIONS

3-Strand Traditional rope construction consisting of three equally sized strands twisted together to produce a very fine, durable rope. Standard designs are available in nylon, polyester, polypropylene and specialized blends. Uses include hand and block lines, anchor and dock lines, safety lines and numerous other applications. Available in sizes up to one-inch diameter.

Double Braids Exceptionally strong rope construction comprised of a core braid contained within an outer braided jacket. Double braids are torque-free, have very good abrasion resistance and offer excellent strength to weight ratios. Ropes are available in nylon, polyester and combinations of fibers, including Kevlar ® and Spectra ® that are designed to maximize the advantages inherent in different fiber classes. Uses include heavy marine applications, winch and stringing lines, pleasure marine ropes and numerous other applications. Available in sizes up to 10-inch circumference.

12-Strand S-Braids Round single braid rope construction designed to offer high strengths and ease of splicing. Single braids offer significant improvement in performance over twisted and 8-strand plaited ropes. Available in nylon, polyester and a polyester/polypropylene blend. Uses include mooring and head lines, hand and block lines and other general purpose applications. Available in sizes up to 6-inch circumference.

Parallel Core Rope Specialized construction consisting of a parallel fiber core wrapped with a double layer of polyester tape and covered with a braided jacket. Unlike other parallel core ropes, this product is easily spliced using a technique similar to that used for double braids. The parallel core rope provides very high strength and exceptionally low elongation and is designed for applications such as stringing lines where low stretch is a primary consideration. Available in sizes up to 1-1/8 inch diameter.

Multiline II A combination rope design in which each strand consists of a polypropylene core securely wrapped with 100% polyester cover yarns made of blended staple and filament fibers. Lighter and lower in strength then Dacron, but with similar stretch characteristics. Excellent UV resistance. Renders well around sheaves and winches.

Nylon Highest strength and elongation. Ideal for uses requiring high energy absorption. Good UV resistance. Not affected by common alkalies or acids. Should not be exposed to strong mineral acids.

Dacron Dupont's trade name for their superior polyester fiber. Much less elastic then nylon with slightly lower strength. Not affected by common alkalies or acids. Excellent UV resistance. Very good wet or dry abrasion resistance. Renders well around capstans or winches.

Polypropylene The lightest and lowest strength fiber used in commercial ropes; will float in water. Excellent resistance to most common chemicals, but highly susceptible to UV. Given a low melting point and high coefficient of friction over metal, we recommend it for noncritical use only.

Nylon Double Braid Nylon cover/Nylon core. Conforms to MIL-R- 24050 B & C. Most elastic double braid construction has excellent energy absorbing characteristics. Good abrasion resistance wet or dry. Minimal strength loss due to UV. Affected by strong mineral acids. Ideal for uses where energy absorption is desired such as towing, mooring lines, slings, purse lines and personnel safety lines.

Polyester Double Braid Polyester cover /Polyester core. Conforms to MIL-R- 24677. Very low elongating construction-much less elastic than nylon . Excellent abrasion resistance wet or dry. Superior resistance to UV degradation.

Excellent chemical resistance except to concentrated sulphuric acid and strong alkalies at elevated temperatures. Ideal for use where controlled elongation is required such as head lines, sailboat halyards and sheets, bull ropes, winch lines, stringing lines and car spotting lines.

Polyester/Nylon Double Braid Polyester cover/Nylon core.Conforms to MIL-R- 44123. Unique combination of fibers designed to provide a balanced rope construction of extremely high strength. Stronger than either nylon or polyester double braid, but offering elasticity similar to that of an all nylon rope. The polyester cover braid offers the same excellent abrasion and chemical resistance as found in the all-polyester rope. Ideal for uses requiring good energy absorption and very high strength such as mooring lines, winch lines, and commercial fishing lines.

Spect-Set Double Braid Polyester cover /Spectra core. The strength member core design utilizes the exceptional performance properties of Spectra. High tensile strength, very low stretch and light weight. The tough durable jacket provides excellent abrasion and chemical resistance. The core is provided with a special coating to reduce slipping between the cover and core. Ideal for winch lines, stringing lines, and replacement for steel cable.

Nylon "S" Braid 100% Nylon 12-strand single braid. Superior in strength and performance characteristics to 3-strand and plaited rope constructions. The single braid design will not rotate under load or hockle when load is released. Stays firm and round under load. Easy to splice. Strips and renders well on winches and capstans. Designed to be used in place of 3-strand and plaited ropes in all applications where improved performance is necessary such as mooring lines, tow surge pennants, head lines and other applications requiring high energy, absorption.

Polyester "S" Braid 100% Polyester single braid. Highest strength S-Braid available. Provides all the advantages associated with polyester in a torque-free, flexible construction that is ideally suited for use in both marine and industrial applications. Uses include mooring lines, pilot lines, head and block lines, slings, bull ropes and commercial fishing lines.

Da-Pro "S" Braid Single braid design in which each strand consists of a polypropylene core sheathed in polyester fiber. Unique unitized strand design produces a high strength, low weight rope with excellent handling properties and superior abrasion resistance. Ideally suited for use in applications such as hand and block lines, slings, bull ropes, pilot lines and underground pulling lines.

Spectwelve 100% Spectra single braid. The strongest, lightest, lowest stretch, torque resistant rope available. Exceptional durability and resistance to chemical contamination. A special coating is applied to identify the rope and provide superior snag and improved abrasion resistance. For winch lines, pilot lines, Underground Pulling Lines, and as a replacement for steel wire.

Nerex 100% Polyester single braid. Unique construction provides the lowest elongation of any braided polyester rope with correspondingly higher strengths. Rope is torque-free and remains firm and round under load. Specially formulated urethane coating provides excellent abrasion resistance and/or color coding. Construction is very easy to splice. Nerex is designed to be used in applications such as distribution and transmission stringing lines, underground pulling lines, winch and pilot lines, slings and other uses requiring a very high strength, low stretch rope.

PC R Patented rope construction consisting of a parallel core of polyester wrapped with a special polyester tape and surrounded by a urethane coated braid of polyester. The parallel core produces very high strengths and the lowest elongation of any polyester rope. Unlike other parallel core ropes, PCR is extremely flexible and very easy to splice. Also works well with mechanical end terminations such as Kellems grips. The urethane coating provides excellent abrasion protection and/or color coding. Uses include transmission and distribution lines, winch lines, lifting lines and other very low stretch applications.

Kevlar # 100 100% braided Kevlar ® core and blended spun/filament polyester cover braid. This design is intended to derive maximum benefit from the ultra high strength, low stretch properties of Kevlar. Due to the susceptibility of Kevlar to abrade in bending situations, this construction is intended for use in situations such as standing rigging where the rope is not subjected to excessive bending loads.

Sta-Set K-900 Core braid consisting of a combination of Kevlar ® and Spectra ® fibers and afilament polyester cover. This design combines the best properties of the two strongest, lowest stretch fibers commercially available. Problems associated with the exclusive use of either of these fibers, such as the poor abrasion resistance of Kevlar or the creep and excessive slipperiness of Spectra are virtually eliminated through the special blending of these two fibers in the core braid. As a result, this product is ideally suited for both standing and running rigging applications, or any application requiring very high strength and low elongation.

® Kevlar is a registered trademark of Dupont ® Spectra is a registered trademark of Allied Corp.

YACHTING APPLICATION GUIDE

New England Ropes ®

Pope's Island New Bedford, MA 02740-7288 USA
(508) 999-2351 Fax # 1-508-999-5972

		3-STRAND NYLON	3-STRAND DACRON	3-STRAND SPUN DACRON	DOUBLE BRAID NYLON	REGATTA BRAID	STA SET	STA SET X	STA SET X LITE	KEVLAR 65	STA SET K-900	SPECT SET	DACRON CORD
CHARACTERISTICS	DURABILITY/WEAR	Very Good	Excellent	Good	Very Good	Good	Excellent	Very Good	Fair	Good	Very Good	Excellent	Excellent
	HANDLING	Good	Very Good	Excellent	Excellent	Excellent	Excellent	Very Good	Fair	Very Good	Excellent	Excellent	Very Good
	SPLICEABILITY	Excellent	Excellent	Excellent	Good	Excellent	Very Good	Very Good	Fair	Very Good	Very Good	Very Good	
	U.V. RESISTANCE	Good	Very Good	Very Good	Good	Excellent	Excellent	Excellent	Fair	Excellent	Excellent	Excellent	Very Good
	STRETCH	VH	ML	ML	H	L	L	VL	VL	VVL	VVL	VVL	L
	STRENGTH	H	H	M	H	H	H	H	H	H	VH	VH	M
APPLICATIONS	ANCHOR LINE	Excellent			Good								
	DOCK LINE	Excellent			Good								
	TOW LINE	Very Good			Excellent								
	HALYARDS		Good	Fair		Fair	Very Good	Excellent	Good	Excellent	Excellent	Good	
	SHEETS		Good	Good		Excellent	Excellent	Very Good	Good	Excellent	Excellent	Excellent	
	GUYS					Fair	Good	Excellent	Good	Excellent	Excellent	Good	
	RUNNING BACKSTAYS							Fair		Excellent	Excellent	Good	
	CONTROL LINES		Fair	Fair		Very Good	Excellent		Good	Excellent	Excellent	Excellent	
	TOPPING LIFT		Good	Fair		Fair	Excellent	Excellent					
	REEF LINES		Good	Good		Excellent	Excellent			Excellent	Excellent	Excellent	
	FURLING SYS.		Fair	Fair		Excellent	Excellent						
	FLAG HALYARD												Excellent
	LIFE PRESERVER LANYARDS								Fair				

KEY

H=HIGH M=MEDIUM
L=LOW V=VERY

EXCELLENT VERY GOOD
GOOD FAIR

3-Strand Ropes

NOMINAL SIZE Dia	NYLON Weight Lbs./100 ft.	NYLON Average Tensile Strength	DACRON Weight Lbs./100 ft.	DACRON Average Tensile Strength	MULTILINE II Weight Lbs./100 ft.	MULTILINE II Average Tensile Strength	POLYPROPELENE Weight Lbs./100 ft.	POLYPROPELENE Average Tensile Strength
3/16*	1.0	1,200	1.2	1,200	...	...	0.7	856
1/4*	1.5	2,000	1.7	2,000	...	...	1.2	1,350
5/16*	2.5	3,000	3.1	3,000	2.5	2,200	1.8	2,050
3/8*	3.5	4,400	4.5	4,400	3.6	3,200	2.8	2,900
7/16*	5.0	5,900	6.2	5,900	5.0	4,100	3.8	3,800
1/2*	6.5	7,500	8.0	6,500	6.5	5,800	4.7	4,700
9/16*	8.2	9,400	10.2	8,900	...	...	6.1	5,450
5/8*	10.5	12,200	13.0	11,700	9.5	8,200	7.5	7,000
3/4*	14.5	16,700	17.5	14,700	12.5	10,800	10.7	9,400
7/8*	20.0	23,500	25.0	21,200	18.0	15,500	15.0	13,000
1*	26.4	29,400	30.4	25,800	21.8	18,700	18.0	15,700

*Average tensile strengths listed in pounds

DOCK & ANCHOR LINE CHART

Boat Length	Dock Lines	Anchorline*	Mooring Pendent**
Up to 20'	3/8	3/8	1/2
21-30	1/2	1/2	5/8
30-35	1/2	1/2	3/4
35-40	5/8	5/8	7/8
40-45	5/8	5/8	1

*Your anchor line should be at least 8 x water depth.
** We recommend twisted 3-strand nylon for mooring pendents.

WIRE HALYARD REPLACEMENT CHART

7 x 19 Wire Size	1/8	5/32	3/16	7/32	1/4
STA SET "X" Replacement Size	5/16	3/8	7/16	1/2	9/16

SUGGESTED LINE SIZES

"T" in feet	20'	25'	30'	35'	40'	45'	50'	55'	60'	65'
MAIN HALYARD	5/16	5/16	3/8	3/8	7/16	7/16	1/2	1/2	1/2	9/16
JIB HALYARD	3/8	3/8	7/16	7/16	1/2	1/2	9/16	9/16	9/16	5/8
SPINNAKER HALYARD	7/16	7/16	1/2	1/2	9/16	9/16	5/8	5/8	5/8	3/4
TOPPING LIFT	5/16	5/16	3/8	3/8	7/16	7/16	1/2	1/2	1/2	9/16
JIB SHEET	1/4	5/16	5/16	3/8	7/16	1/2	9/16	5/8	5/8	3/4
SPIN SHEET	1/4	1/4	5/16	5/16	3/8	7/16	1/2	9/16	9/16	5/8
SPIN GUY	1/4	5/16	5/16	3/8	7/16	1/2	9/16	5/8	5/8	3/4

"T" =Height of foretriangle from the deck. Line recommendations are based on STA-SET strengths.

All line strengths and sizing recommendations are based on new, unused rope. Tensile tests are done to Cordage Institute specifications for testing new, unused rope. Depending on the nature of your rope application use a safety factor of between 5 and 10. Sizing lines for ultra-light displacement boats or multihulls with these tables may not be appropriate.

Double Braid Ropes

12 Strand S-Braids

NOMINAL SIZE (inches)		POLYESTER BRAID		NYLON BRAID		POLYESTER/NYLON		SPECT-SET		POLYESTER S-BRAID		NYLON S-BRAID		DA-PRO S-BRAID	
Dia.	Circ.	Weight Lbs./ 100 ft.	Average Tensile Strength	Weight Lbs./ 100 ft.	Average Tensile Strength	Weight Lbs./ 100 ft.	Average Tensile Strength	Weight Lbs./ 100 ft.	Average Tensile Strength	Weight Lbs./ 100 ft.	Average Tensile Strength	Weight Lbs./ 100 ft.	Average Tensile Strength	Weight Lbs./ 100 ft.	Average Tensile Strength
3/16	9/16	1.1	1.2	0.9	1.2	......	......	......	......	......	......	......	......	......	......
1/4	3/4	2.	2.3	1.6	.2.2	1.9	2.5	2.	4.6	......	......	......	......	......	......
5/16	1	3.1	3.	2.5	3.4	3.	3.9	3.2	7.4	......	......	......	......	......	......
3/8	1-1/8	4.4	4.4	3.4	4.7	4.3	5.6	4.	9.5	4.2	5.3	3.7	5.2	3.2	4.
7/16	1-1/4	6.1	6.6	4.9	6.6	5.8	7.5	5.2	12.5	5.7	7.1	5.1	7.1	4.3	5.4
1/2	1-1/2	8.	8.5	6.3	8.5	7.6	10.5	7.5	16.9	7.4	9.3	6.6	9.2	5.6	7.
9/16	1-3/4	10.1	11.	8.	11.7	9.6	12.5	9.	21.	9.3	11.6	8.4	11.8	7.2	9.
5/8	2	12.6	14.	11.7	13.5	11.9	15.5	11.1	27.	11.5	14.4	10.4	14.6	9.3	11.6
3/4	2-1/4	17.5	22.	14.3	19.4	17.1	23.2	15.7	37.	16.6	20.8	15.	17.	12.6	15.
7/8	2-3/4	23.7	29.9	19.4	26.3	32.3	30.3	19.9	51.5	22.6	24.3	19.3	23.2	17.5	19.
1	3	33.	38.	25.4	34.	30.4	40.	26.	63.5	30.	32.	23.	28.	24.5	26.
1-1/8	3-1/2	42.	46.	35.	46.	38.	50.	35.3	77.	38.	41.	31.	37.	33.9	34.5
1-1/4	3-3/4	49.8	55.	40.	52.	45.	58.	40.6	85.	44.	47.	36.	43.	38.9	39.2
1-5/16	4	57.	61.	45.	58.	57.	73.	46.3	98.	50.	54.	41.	49.	44.3	44.3
1-1/2	4-1/2	68.	72.	58.	74.	68.	87.	58.5	115.	63.	63.	52.	62.	56.	55.4
1-5/8	5	85.	89.	71.	90.	80.	101.	72.3	145.	78.	77.	64.	77.	69.1	67.9
1-3/4	5-1/2	101.	104.	89.	110.	97.	121.	87.4	168.	94.	92.	77.	92.	......	......
2	6	123.	124.	102.	126.	115.	143.	104.	192.	......	......	......	......	......	......
2-1/8	6-1/2	144.	145.	119.	145.	134.	168.	122.1	222.	......	......	......	......	......	......
2-1/4	7	168.	166.	138.	166.	157.	194.	141.6	258.	......	......	......	......	......	......
2-1/2	7-1/2	196.	190.	159.	189.	180.	222.	162.5	285.	......	......	......	......	......	......
2-5/8	8	216.	212.	181.	213.	203.	248.	184.9	318.	......	......	......	......	......	......
2-3/4	8-1/2	246.	234.	204.	237.	......	......	......	......	......	......	......	......	......	......
3	9	293.	278.	228.	261.	......	......	......	......	......	......	......	......	......	......
3-1/4	10	344.	326.	282.	319.	......	......	......	......	......	......	......	......	......	......

Average tensile strength listed in thousands of pounds (1.5 = 1500)

Specialty Braided Ropes

NOMINAL SIZE	NEREX		PCR		SPECTWELVE		KEVLAR 100		STA-SET K900	
(inches) Dia.	Weight Lbs./ 100 ft.	Average Tensile Strength	Weight Lbs./ 100 ft.	Average Tensile Strength	Weight Lbs./ 100 ft.	Average Tensile Strength	Weight Lbs./ 100 ft.	Average Tensile Strength	Weight Lbs./ 100 ft.	Average Tensile Strength
3/16	......	......	......	......	......	......	1.4	2,300	1.3	2,200
1/4	......	......	......	......	1.4	6,200	2.2	3,600	1.9	3,600
5/16	......	......	3.4	4,400	2.2	9,900	3.1	5,000	2.8	5,800
3/8	4.7	6,300	4.4	5,500	3.2	14,400	4.7	8,300	4.2	8,700
7/16	6.4	9,000	5.9	7,400	4.3	18,500	6.5	11,000	5.3	12,200
1/2	8.9	11,900	7.9	9,600	5.8	26,500	8.7	15,500	7.2	15,800
9/16	10.5	15,100	......	......	7.1	32,000	10.9	19,600	9.5	20,100
5/8	13.	17,900	12.3	15,000	8.8	40,000	13.6	22,000	12.0	24,500
3/4	18.	23,500	17.7	21,600	12.7	52,000	......	......	17.0	35,000
7/8	25.5	33,100	24.1	30,700	17.2	69,500	......	......	22.5	48,000
1	33.3	43,300	32.0	38,400	23.3	88,000	......	......	31.0	60,000
1-1/8	......	......	39.5	49,000	29.5	108,000	......	......	......	......

Average tensile strength listed in pounds

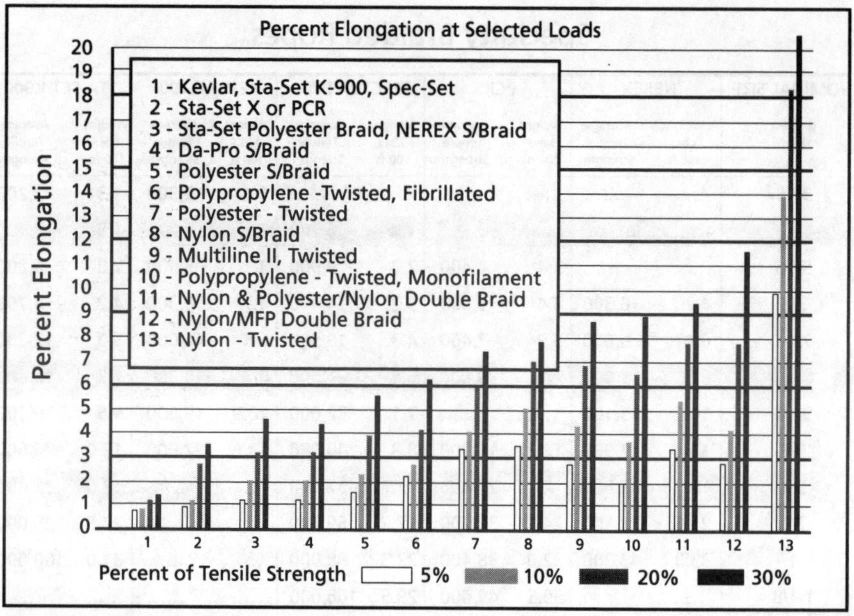

General Information/Rope Safety

New England Ropes takes great care in manufacturing ropes that are of the highest quality. A few common sense rules will assist you in getting the best performance from our products in a safe manner.

Snapback: A serious hazard is created when a line under load parts because it will recoil at a high speed. A person positioned in the recoil path could be seriously injured if struck by the recoiling line. It's the responsibility of the user to know and use the proper techniques for the particular application.

Sunlight: All synthetic fiber ropes will undergo degradation with time when exposed to sunlight. Polypropylene is far more susceptible to UV degradation then polyester or nylon. To prolong the life of your ropes, avoid storing them in direct sunlight.

Chemical: Synthetic fibers have good chemical resistance.However, exposure to harsh chemicals (i.e. strong acids and alkalies) should be avoided.

Damage: Inspect ropes frequently for any signs of damage or wear. Retire any rope that has been cut or is heavily abraded.

Linear Density: Average with maximum 5% more than listed.

Tensile Strengths and Working Loads: As shown in our literature, these strengths are the approximate average for new rope tested under ASTM (D-4268) or Cordage Institute test methods. The tensile strength is the load at which a new rope tested under laboratory conditions can be expected to break. However, to estimate the minimum tensile strength of a new rope, reduce the approximate average by 15%. (Cordage Institute defines minimum tensile strength as two standard deviations below the average tensile strength of the rope). Age, use and the type of termination used including knots will lower tensile strength significantly.

The Cordage Institute specifies that the Safe Working Load of a rope shall be determined by dividing the Minimum Tensile Strength by the Safety Factor. Safety factors range from 5 to 12 for non-critical uses. The working load is a guideline for the use of a rope in good condition for non- critical applications and should be reduced where life, limb, or valuable property are involved, or for exceptional service such as shock, sustained loading, severe vibration, etc.

Stretch Characteristics: desired stretch is determined by the way in which the rope is used. High stretch rope (nylon), with good energy absorption, is preferred for mooring, anchoring and towing, while low stretch ropes (Dacron, Kevlar, Spectra) are preferred for applications where positioning is critical and energy absorption and high stretch is not desired.

(1)

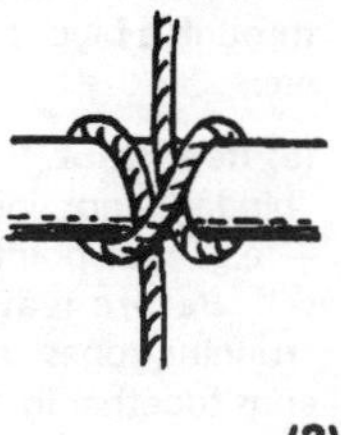
(2)

(3)

(4)

(5)

(6)

(7)

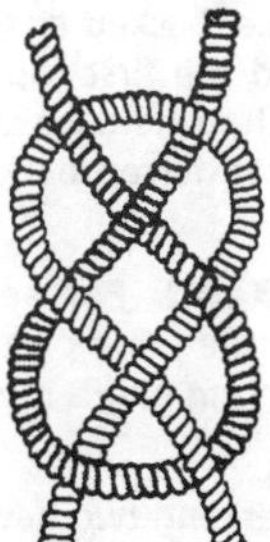
(8)

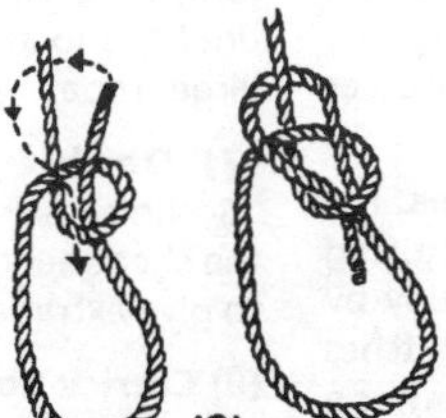
(9)

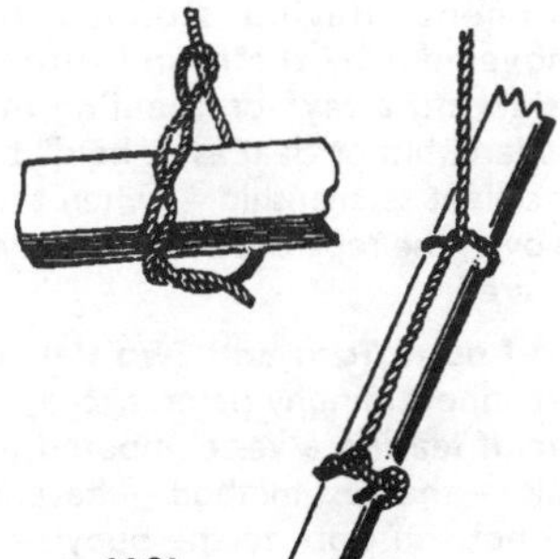
(10)

(11)

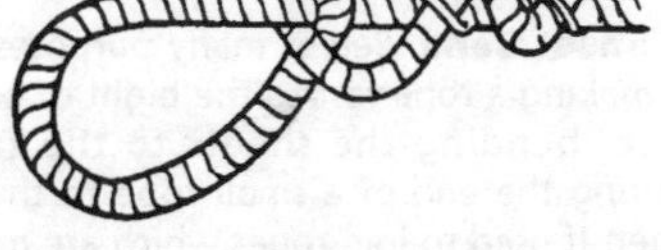
(12)

KNOTS, BENDS AND HITCHES

The following simple bends and hitches are but a few of those used by the professional seaman—they should, however, serve to meet most of the requirements of those working yachts and small boats.

A **Bend** is used to join the ends of two ropes. A **Hitch** secures a rope to another object.

The Round Turn

Although this is only the first movement in securing a rope to a permanent fixture, there is much virtue in a Round Turn not always appreciated by small boat owners. Always remember that a considerable weight can be held with relatively little effort by taking a round turn around the bitts or other secure object. A round turn should always be taken around an open ended protrusion, such as bitts, as this does not necessitate letting go of the rope. When in the act of coming alongside, a round turn or two will take the weight without the danger of jamming.

In emergency, a quick turn round some strong object on board (and the rope then held away tight) will frequently prevent the bow or stern swinging out into the tide at the wrong moment. Having stopped the vessel's movement by the round turn, a judicious "slacking away" or "hauling in" using the bollard, bitt or cleat as a "hold" temporarily is excellent seamanship — when the emergency is over, the rope can be secured or removed as desired.

(1) Round Turn and Two Half Hitches. For securing a dinghy painter to a mooring ring etc. If leaving a vessel moored to a buoy by this — the best method — have loose hitches — not too close to the buoy — and lay the loose end along the standing part of the rope and frap together — it will never come adrift, but is easy to untie.

(2) Clove Hitch. A good hitch for securing a rope at intermediate points. It is not safe with a short end. Difficult to untie after being subjected to heavy strain, especially when wet.

(3) Sheet Bend. Serves many purposes. Used for making a rope fast to the bight of another — i.e. bending the sheets to the sails — securing the end of a small rope to that of a larger. If used to join ropes which are made of different materials, the ends should be seized back or the bend is liable to come adrift. (See also Double Sheet Bend.)

(4) Figure of Eight Knot. To prevent the end of a small rope from accidentally running through a block or the deck lead for jib sheets, etc.

(5) Reef Knot. Has many uses. Is excellent as a "binder" knot, joining the ends of small ropes — e.g. reef points when reefing and furling sail. Before leaving signal haliards or any "running ropes" not in use — always join both ends together in case wind blows them off the cleat and they become unrove. CAUTION: Do not use a reef knot as a bend for tying two ropes together. If the ropes are of different size, or different materials, or one is stiffer than the other, the knot is very liable to capsize.

(6) Rolling Hitch. A most practical knot much used at sea for all purposes. After starting as a clove hitch, an additional hitch is made over the first between this and the standing part of the rope which effectively jams the hitch and prevents sideways pull — the simple form is finished off with a further hitch away from the strain as shown in Fig. 6. Used for securing the tail of a block to a larger rope, hanging off a rope on a stopper, flag swivel sticks, etc. It does not slip or "roll" under normal loading, but if subjected to heavy strain — as when stoppering off a mooring rope — the end (A) which does not carry the load should be "backed and dogged", i.e. backed against the hitch and twisted round the first rope (B) in long lays. The end is then held or stopped until the load can be transferred back to the larger rope.

(7) Double Sheet Bend. For securing "Bosun's Chair" and for the same purposes as the sheet bend. The working end is rove twice to give extra security.

(8) Carrick Bend. For bending two hawsers or wire ropes together. Very secure and unlikely to jam. Each end tucks under/over four times.

(9) Bowline. The most commonly used loop knot. Will never capsize if properly formed. Used to make a loop in the end of a rope without splicing — made quickly and without hesitation when sending small mooring lines ashore.

(10) Timber Hitch. Used for lifting a spar, timber, bale or plank, etc. The turns should always be dogged with the lay of the rope. When used for towing a spar, or to keep a piece of timber pointing in one direction when being lifted, it should be used with a half-hitch as illustrated.

(11) Sheepshank. Used for shortening a rope temporarily. To make more secure, especially if not subjected to a steady pull, the loops should be stopped to the standing part at points a and b.

(12) Lighterman's Hitch. Used by British lightermen to make a towing eye in the end of a barge rope. The lighterman's hitch consists of a loop secured by a half-hitch with two back tucks on the standing part, and will hold as well as any splice.

A few knots known and used correctly and instantly shows a better seaman than one who knows all the names of the lesser used knots, but who is slow or inaccurate in their execution.

ROPE SPLICING

Eye Splice

(1) Unlay the three strands at the end of the rope enough to make at least three tucks — about one turn for each tuck — and form an eye by laying the opened strands on top of the standing part of the rope.

(2) Take the middle end (A, in Fig. 1) and tuck it, from right to left, underneath the nearest strand of the standing part.

(3) Pick up the left end (B, in Fig. 2) and tuck it — again from right to left — under the next strand to the left of the one under which (A) is tucked.

(4) Turn the whole splice over, then take the third end (C) and lead it over to the right of the third strand, so that the third tuck can, again, be made from right to left, as in Fig.3.

(5) There should now be one end coming out from under each strand on the standing part. If two ends come from under the same strand the splice is wrong.

(6) Pull each end tight enough to make a tidy and snug fit. This completes the first round of tucks.

(7) For the second round, take each end over one strand and under the next towards the left. Pull each end tight.

(8) Repeat for the third round. Never use less than three rounds of tucks if the eye is to bear any strain.

(9) If desired, for neatness, the splice can be tapered by adding additional rounds of tucks, first with halved strands and then by halving again before the final round.

Short Splicing

For joining two ropes of the same size together.

(1) Unlay the two ends to be joined—at least one turn for each round of tucks to be made.

(2) Marry these ends together, so that the strands of one rope lay alternately between the strands of the other.

(3) Hold firmly while making tucks. Tucks are made towards the left by passing each end, in turn, over one strand and under the next, in the same manner as described for the eye splice.

(4) If the rope is to bear any strain make at least three rounds of tucks each way.

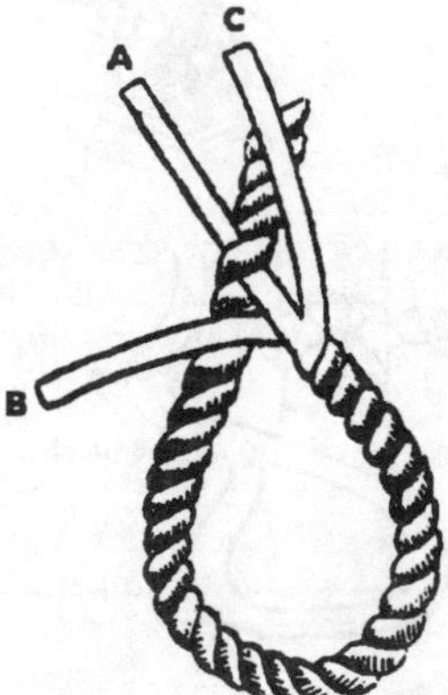

Fig. 1

Fig. 2

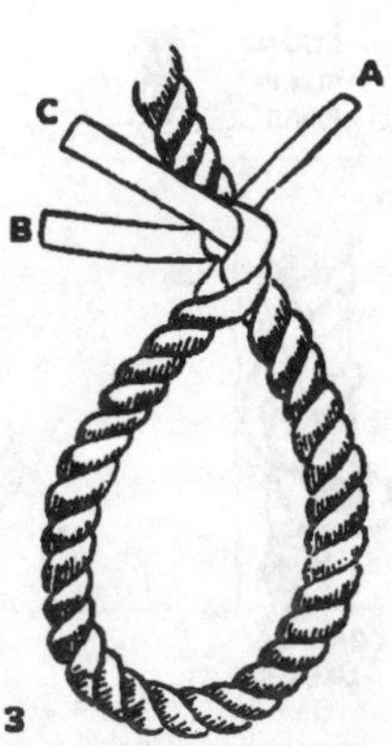

Fig. 3

a

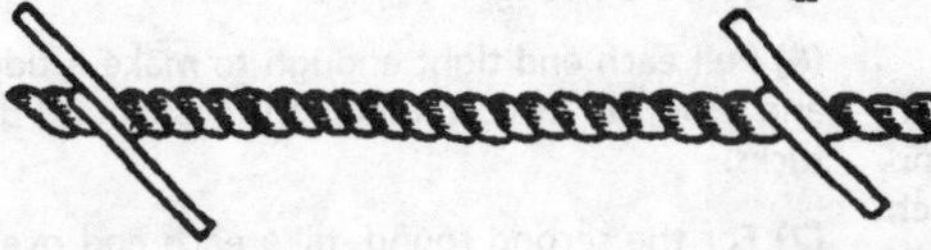

Fig. 4

Long Splice

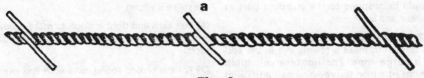

Seldom used in practice but very useful as a temporary measure — i.e. until the rope can be replaced with a new one — for rope which is required to run through a block, because the splice does not thicken it.

(1) Unlay the ends of two ropes to at least four times the distance required for a short splice.

(2) Marry the ends together as though about to begin a short splice.

(3) Select two ends which cross one another from opposite sides, unlay one of them for some length and lay into its place the opposite strand from the other rope until only a short piece is left. Cut off surplus from the end which is unlaid.

(4) Repeat with two more strands but work in the opposite direction.

(5) The third pair of strands (at 'a' in Fig. 4) are left in their original place, so that there are now three pairs of ends. Make an overhand knot with each pair so that the ends follow the lay of the rope and do not cross it.

(6) Pull very tight and then taper off by reducing the yarns in each strand.

Back Splice

Where a rope is not required to run through a block—when whippings are preferable — a back splice may be used to prevent the strands unlaying.

After unlaying the strands for the estimated distance, form a crown by interlacing the

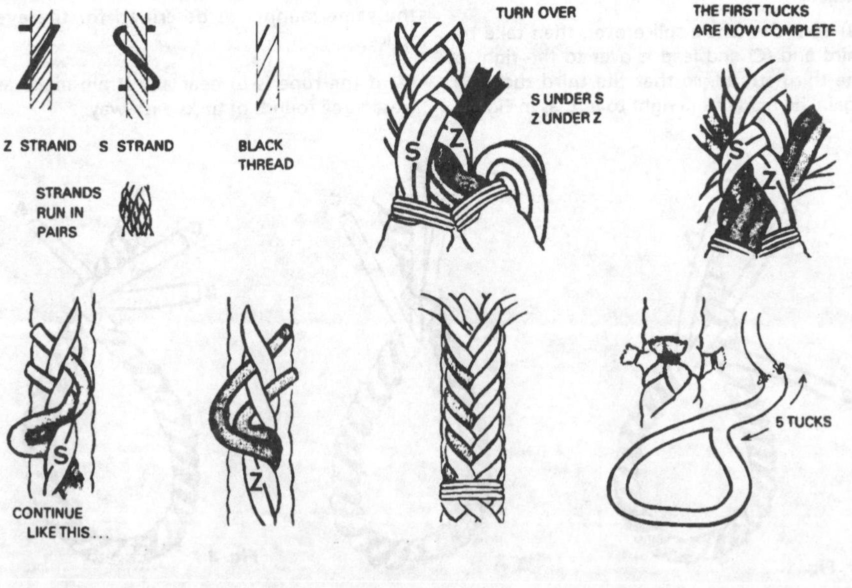

strands at the rope's end. Then tuck the strands "over one and under one" backwards towards the standing part of the rope. This splice is really only of interest with natural fiber ropes. With man-made fibers the rope ends can be fused together by heating.

Eye-Splice—Braided Rope

This double four-part rope is supple and simple to coil in either hand thus making it ideal for anchoring and mooring. The eye splice used is based upon the construction of the rope, which employs both "Z" or right-handed lay strands and "S" or left-handed strands. After whipping or stopping at the point of splice, divide the various Z and S strands as shown and tuck in two pairs front and back of the work. Thereafter the paired strands are divided and tucked separately. Finish by seizing ends as illustrated on previous page.

Sew and Serve Eye Splice—Braided Rope

It is important that stoppings, sewing and finally serving are tight and neat, otherwise the eye splice resulting will be loose and weak. Pass the sail needle right through the rope each time and tug stitch home tightly. Taper the unlaid rope yarns, otherwise it will be impossible to apply a serving to the decreasing diameter of the splice. Set up taut before attempting to serve. Use No. 16 waxed whipping Polyester twine.

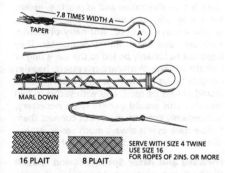

By Courtesy of Marlow Ropes

ROPE WHIPPINGS

Whippings are extensively used in connection with natural fiber ropes to secure the ends from unravelling, but with modern man-made fibers the ends of smaller ropes are usually fused together. There will always, however, be occasions when it is useful to be able to whip the end of a rope or seize an eye or thimble in the middle (e.g. double sheets).

Common Whipping.

(1) Cut off a suitable length of twine and lay one end (D in Fig. 1 opposite) along the end of the rope.

(2) Then take half a dozen or more tight turns around the rope and the twine, working towards the end of rope and against the lay. Pull each turn tight as it is made.

(3) Now lay the other end of twine (BC in Fig. 2) along the rope and over the turns already made.

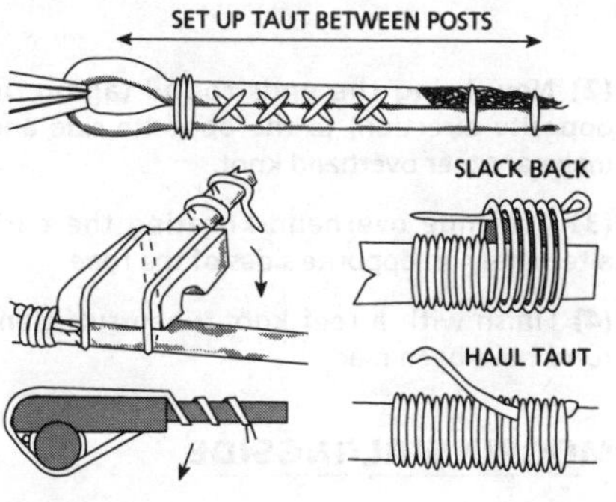

By Courtesy of Marlow Ropes

(4) With part A of the twine, continue to pass turns round over part B.

(5) When the loop remaining at E becomes too small to pass over the rope's end, pull tight on C and cut the end off (Fig. 3).

Palm and Needle Whipping. This is more secure than the common whipping and is very suitable for reef points and all mooring ropes.

(1) Thread a suitable length of twine through a sailmaker's needle.

(2) Pass the needle under one strand and draw through most of the twine.

(3) Take about a dozen or more turns of twine round the rope, working against the lay and pulling each turn well tight as it is made.

(4) Now stitch, by following round between each strand in turn with the needle, as in Fig. 4, and thus tightly frapping the turns in between each strand.

West Country Whipping. Useful when required to whip the bight of a rope.

(1) Place the middle of the twine against the rope, bring the two ends round in opposite directions and make an overhand knot.

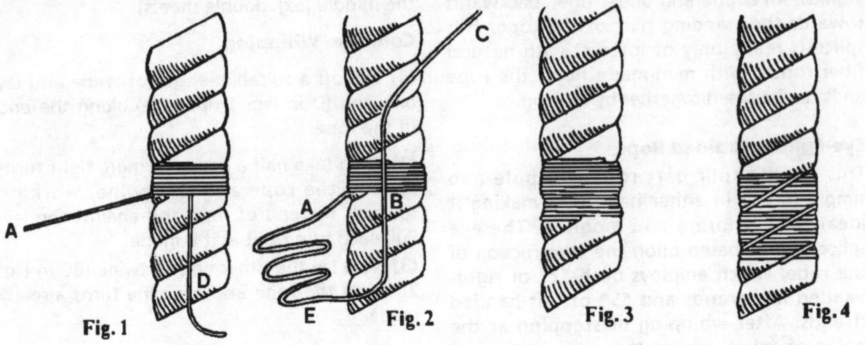

(2) Now bring the ends round (again, in opposite direction) to the opposite side and make another overhand knot.

(3) Continue overhand-knotting the ends alternately on opposite sides of the rope.

(4) Finish with a reef knot when sufficient turns have been made.

MOORING ALONGSIDE

Each year a large percentage of the total damage to yachts occurs when moored alongside a dock.

When approaching the berth, make sure it is clear of overhanging obstructions which can foul the rigging or other parts of the yacht. Look also to see if there are any warning notices on the dock side, or you may return from the shore later to find your stern well jacked up by a sewer pipe, and the tide still falling.

In general, when berthed alongside, the mooring ropes should be positioned as in the diagram below, but circumstances (depending on wind, range of tide, duration of stay, possible movements of other craft, etc.) may demand some modification. It is easier to make a seamanlike job if the function of each rope is understood.

Bow and Stern Lines (1 and 2 see below) should be strong enough to take the main load. They must also be of sufficient length to allow for the *range* of the tide. A rough rule for a range of 15 feet or less is to allow at least three times the range if the ship is berthed at half tide. If moored near High or Low Water the lines should be adjusted later, as required. The bow and stern lines also position the ship alongside the dock and, together with the springs, assist in checking fore and aft surging.

The diagram showing one bow line and one stern is only illustrative and in practice, except for a brief stay at a wharf or pier, two lines would always be used, normally one from each bow and one from either quarter. They need not necessarily be led to the same ring or bollard ashore. With larger vessels, heavier weights being involved, several mooring lines would always be used, and with yachts in bad weather this would generally be necessary, but certainly precautionary. But connect them before dark as it Is always much easier, especially if wind increases during the night.

Forward and After Springs (4 and 3) assist the bow and stern lines in keeping the ship

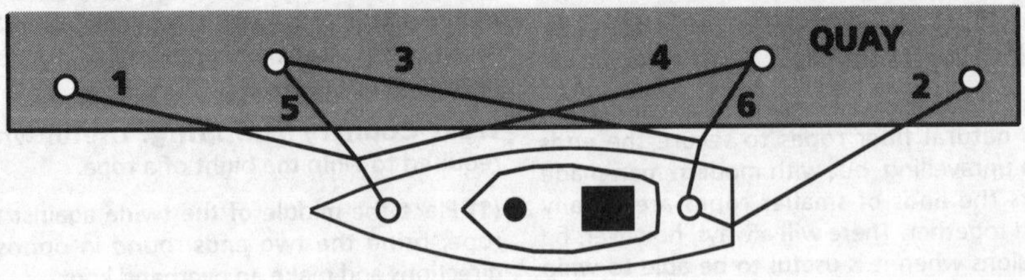

alongside, prevent her from surging fore and aft, and keep the bow and stern from swinging in and out.

Forward and After Breast Ropes (5 and 6). These are seldom necessary with small craft. They are used to hold the ship alongside the dock when boarding or loading, or to limit its distance from the dock. Never leave breast ropes unattended in tidal waters.

Lines which require tending with the rise and fall of the tide should, whenever possible, be made fast so that each one can be tended without disturbing another.

Slip Ropes. Mooring lines are sometimes doubled so that they can be let go from on board. A slip rope is liable to jam when letting go if it has not been passed correctly in the first place—when only ring-bolts are available ashore, it should be passed *down* through a ring which *hangs* at the dock side and *up* through one which *lies* horizontally on top of the dock. When pulling a slip rope on board after letting the end go, haul steadily, don't *jerk*, especially when the loose end is approaching the ring or bollard. A jerk can cause the end to flip round the hauling part and jam. A "slip" rope is only to be used as a temporary measure.

Fenders. Place with the utmost care and, when adjusting for height, bear in mind that the swell from a passing vessel can cause fenders to be toppled inboard if the lanyards are too short.

ANCHORING

Approaching anchorage. Unlash anchor from stowed position and ensure that it is ready for letting go immediately it is required.

Selecting berth. It is the duty of late arrivals to keep clear of vessels already anchored. Allow adequate clearance.

One or two anchors. A vessel moored with one anchor will swing over a much greater area than one moored with two (one upstream and one downstream) and should not be left unattended.

Making a standing or running moor. Stem the tide and motor a little way past the selected berth, drop first anchor and fall back on tide, veering double the amount of chain it is intended to ride to. Drop second anchor and then haul in on first until in the selected position. Shackle second anchor cable to first and veer out until second cable is well below waterline. Vessel should then be lying midway between both anchors. Similarly with a running moor, except that the approach will be made with the tide and the first anchor will be dropped just before the selected berth is reached. Alternatively the second anchor can be laid out with the dinghy—in this case the correct amount of chain is veered with the first anchor—not double the amount.

Depth of water. Let out chain equivalent to at least three times maximum depth or five times if rope is being used. If rope, ensure that it is connected to anchor by two fathoms of chain.

Laying out kedge. Make fast end on board and then take the coil away in dinghy, paying out from there rather than paying out from the yacht. Much easier.

Clearing a fouled anchor. Occasions arise when the anchor becomes fouled by some underwater obstruction, usually a cable or a mooring chain. If the anchor can be hauled up to the surface, a rope can be passed under the obstruction to take the weight while the anchor is being freed, and then slipped. If this is not possible, and assuming that the anchor has been properly buoyed with a buoy rope attached to the crown, it should not prove difficult to trip the anchor by hauling on the buoy rope in the opposite direction to the lay of the main anchor cable. It is important that this main cable should be as slack as possible, possibly by using the vessel's auxiliary engine. If the anchor has not been buoyed remedial action may be a little more difficult.

Considering first the stockless type anchor: it is a comparatively simple matter to slide a small loop of chain, attached to a line, down the anchor cable, so it will come to rest close to the crown of the anchor and the necessary pull can then be exerted.

If, however, it is a fisherman type anchor, freeing may prove a little more difficult as the stock makes it difficult to get the 'retrieving' loop as far as the crown. If, however, the anchor cable is hove up as tightly as possible, it will probably lift the stock off the ground and enable a chain or warp to be dragged under the stock up to the crown. A large bight of chain or weighted rope should be used, preferably towed by two dinghies spaced apart and starting from the downstream side.

Once the loop has engaged with the anchor, the main cable should be slacked away and tension applied by the line in the opposite direction.

Alternatively a large bight of rope suitably weighted, 'middled' over the anchor cable and slid down to the anchor will probably engage the top arm and enable the anchor to be pulled clear, provided that the angle of pull is as near horizontal as possible. In this case the main cable should not be hove in taut when the loop is slid down it.

RIDING TURN ON A WINCH

A problem which occurs sooner or later in most sailing craft is the "riding turn" on a winch. On a sheet winch the result may merely be embarrassing, on a halyard winch it creates a potentially dangerous situation with a sail that cannot be lowered. Fortunately riding turns seem to occur less frequently on halyard winches than on sheet winches.

The cause of the trouble is usually carelessness on the part of the winchman when winching in the sheet or, more likely, when "surging" it to free the sail a little.

When using the normal type of sheet winch, about three turns are laid on the drum, the drum is rotated and as tension increases, the winchman, who is probably also "tailing" the sheet, inadvertently loses control and the sheet momentarily reverses direction. This causes the bottom turn (the one leading from the sail on to the drum) to ride down on to the skirt of the drum where it is then thrown back on to the other turns, jamming them. If the winchman does not spot this but continues winding, it will lock solid.

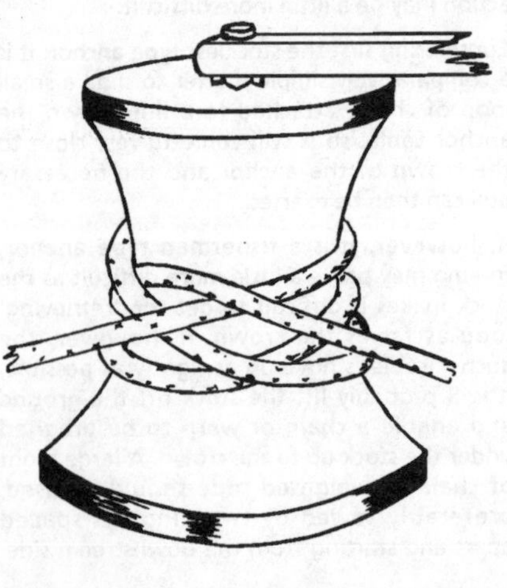

The first step in rectifying the situation is to heave to, thus allowing the crew to concentrate on the problem and also incidentally reducing the tension on the sheet a little. The object of the exercise is to relieve the tension on the sheet so that the riding turn can be sorted out with the aid of a large spike. This can be achieved in several ways. If the headsail is dropped, it may be possible to unhank the tack of the sail thus giving sufficient slack. Assuming that this does not work, it will be necessary to apply tension to the sheet or to the clew of the sail. The latter is usually the easiest alternative. A rope is bent on to the cringle in the clew of the sail and led via a snatchblock to another winch, or a purchase is used, or possibly a Spanish windlass is rigged up. Once the tension has been reduced the riding turn is easily removed.

The halyard winch, however, presents a rather different problem as it will not be possible to attach a rope to the head of the sail to reduce tension in the halyard, and it is unlikely that the tack can be unclipped because of the tension in the sail. If a wire halyard is involved, fix a gripper clip on to the halyard several feet above the winch, place a strop above this, bend a rope on it and lead the rope via a snatchblock to another winch or a purchase. The gripper clip will prevent the strop sliding down the halyard as tension is applied. In the case of a rope halyard, a strop made up of 4 or 5 feet of soft rope can be used. The rope is formed into a loop which is seized on to the halyard well above the winch and each side is passed round the halyard through the opposite side of the loop and back again. This process continues until all slack in the loop is used up when it is in effect plaited round the halyard. A purchase is attached to the bottom end of the strop and as the tension increases the strop grips the halyard. The rope used for the strop should be of smaller diameter than the halyard, otherwise it will not grip effectively.

GETTING ALOFT

At some time during his lifetime the average yachtsman may be faced with the problem of getting to the masthead in difficult circumstances. Perhaps past the first flush of youth, possibly overweight and with only his crew to assist him, the situation looks difficult. Without mast steps (useful but expensive) or a rope ladder long enough to reach the masthead (unlikely to be part of the vessel's equipment), some form of mechanical assistance is required.

A counterweight is probably the most useful approach to the problem. As an example consider the use of five gallon water carriers which will probably be carried on board. Three, filled with water will weigh 125lbs. and will form a useful counterweight to a man weighing 150lbs. The carriers, or some other suitable weight, are attached to one end of the main halyard and the end of a spare halyard is also bent on. The weight is now hauled to the masthead and when it is up the man secures himself in a bosun's chair which is attached to the fall of the halyard. He now proceeds to haul himself up, aided by his wife on deck and the counterweight. His wife then firmly secures the halyard.

Cumbersome and slow perhaps, but it offers the chance of getting aloft when no other assistance is available. It need hardly be mentioned that the person going aloft should be wearing a safety harness to clip on when working.

HEAVING TO

These few notes are not written for the experienced, long range cruising yachtsman who will already have evaluated the respective merits of heaving to, lying a'hull, towing warps and running under bare pole.

The weekend sailor, with a more modest cruising range and who prudently avoids going out in bad weather may not have contemplated the advantages of being able to leave his boat to look after itself for a short period, not necessarily in bad weather. It may be necessary to deal with a little domestic crisis below decks or merely have a peaceful meal in the cockpit, and to do this, knowing that the vessel is quietly looking after itself, is greatly reassuring.

The object is to maintain a steady course at the lowest possible speed and ensure that the vessel's motion is as comfortable as possible. The principle is basically very simple.

The headsail is backed (hauled to windward), the mainsail eased slightly and the tiller lashed a little to leeward—the effect of this is that the main and headsail work against each other, with the result that the vessel fore reaches slowly at probably 60°-65° off the wind and is thus under control, i.e. she does not sheer about but maintains a constant heading.

In practice, however, with modern hulls it may not be quite so simple, particularly with the extreme design of a light displacement hull with narrow fin keel and transom hung rudder. The average cruising yacht, however, should perform adequately once the owner has established the sail trim required. It is well worthwhile trying out the maneuver initially in light winds to see how the vessel performs and then in heavier winds .

Two important points to remember: always bear in mind that although the vessel may be moving very slowly through the water, due to current its speed over the ground may be quite appreciable, so ensure that you have plenty of sea room; secondly, maintain a good look-out at regular intervals.

Remember Rule 5 of the Collision Regulations, the most important one of all.

TOWAGE—YACHTS

Towing or being towed is an eventuality which usually occurs at least once in a lifetime.

As with any emergency that is likely to occur at sea, due consideration should be given to all the possibilities while the vessel is safely on her mooring and the owner is in a contemplative mood.

The ideal arrangement if one is being towed is to use the towed vessel's anchor cable, well secured to a strong cleat, the cable being passed to the towing vessel by means of a heaving line from either vessel. The chain must of course be secured below deck by a lashing and not shackled, in order that it can be slipped immed-iately if necessary. Two advantages of using chain cable are that the weight in the bight reduces snubbing and also that being strongly secured below deck it may not be necessary to secure it to a cleat on deck. If it is not practicable to use the anchor chain and a line is to be used, to what is it to be secured?

In general few modern yachts carry the equivalent of the old time samson post, and while the cleats provided are usually adequate for their particular purpose they may be woefully inadequate to deal with the strain of a tow rope. It is important therefore to consider where and how the towing line should be attached if there are no really adequate cleats or bollards suitably positioned.

Can the tow line be secured round the foot of the mast? If the latter is stepped through the deck the problem is solved. It is important to remember however that although the mast will take the direct strain, the line should also be secured to the deck as close to the stem head as possible. If this is not done the vessel will sheer about in a surprising manner. With the modern mast stepped on deck the situation may be somewhat different, unless it is mounted in a tabernacle where the strain can normally be applied at deck level. If however the mast is merely stepped in a shoe and held in position by the compression of the rigging, further thought is needed. If perhaps due to damage, the rigging is slack, this method should not be used, as a severe jerk on the towline when the vessel is rolling could jerk the mast out of its shoe.

If the stanchions are of reasonable strength and through bolted, then a line secured round several of them and attached to the stem head could be used as the point of attachment for the tow line. This line should be fixed in position before the tow line is secured.

Should the stanchions prove unsuitable it may be necessary to lead a line even farther back, perhaps to the after end of the cabin, remembering that wherever this line leads from it must be secured to the stem head before the tow line is made fast.

Having considered these various aspects, the prudent owner will probably come to the conclusion that the sensible course of action is to bolt a really stout cleat or bollard to the foredeck (with an adequate backing plate under the deck) during fitting out and thus eliminate the major problem if a tow is required.

A good point to consider when being towed is the tow line itself. The legal implications of towage are dealt with under "Notes on Towage and Salvage" in Section 4 – Yachtmaster's Business and from this it will be obvious that one's own line or anchor chain should be passed over to the towing vessel.

Consider now the other side of the picture — that of towing another vessel, and dealing with the point of tow first. If possible the attachment point of the tow line should not be at the stern, although on most yachts it will almost certainly be the only place to secure it. A tug for example has the towing point amidships, a position which permits complete maneuvrability of the towing vessel.

The remarks about cleats on the towed vessel apply equally well to the towing vessel, and although apparently not so important as the cleats at the forward end of the vessel, strong cleats or bitts on the quarters are vital when mooring up in a tidal harbor—the moral is have strong cleats sited wherever a heavy strain is likely to be imposed on the craft.

The towing situation can vary from pulling a vessel off a lee shore in heavy weather to quietly moving a vessel in harbor in calm conditions and obviously the procedure will vary considerably. Considering the first possibility, the most important point is to ensure that the vessel rendering assistance is not herself endangered, either by getting a rope around her prop or running aground and thus creating yet another problem for the rescue authorities. When within a safe distance of the distressed vessel, a line can be floated down attached to an empty water jug, fender etc., and at this point it might be prudent for the rescuing vessel to drop her anchor in case for any reason she becomes unable to maneuver. Having transferred a line, the remainder of the operation is a matter of good seamanship on both vessels, remembering that every situation is different.

If moving another vessel in calm water, especially in harbor, it is usually easier to carry this out with the second vessel lashed alongside the towing craft, properly secured with breast ropes and springs.

GLOSSARY OF NAUTICAL TERMS

ABAFT	Aft of any particular point on the vessel. e.g. abaft the mast – behind the mast.
Abeam	At right angles to the line of the keel.
About	To go about, to change tack.
Aft	Towards the stern of the vessel.
Amidships	Midway between stem and stern.
Apparent wind	The wind felt aboard the boat.
Athwart	From side to side.
Avast	To stop, to hold fast, e.g. avast heaving.
Awash	A vessel, wreck, or shoal so low that water constantly washes over.
Aweigh	Term to indicate that the anchor has broken out of the ground.
BACK	(a) Wind shifting counter clockwise (b) To sheet a headsail out to windward making the bow bear away from the wind.
Backstay	Standing rigging from a masthead, leading aft to take the strain of the mast.
Ballast	Iron or lead placed in bottom of a ship to increase her stability.
Bar	A shoal in the approach to a harbor.
Battens	Thin pieces of wood or plastic set into the leech of the sail to preserve the shape.
Beacon	Aid to navigation, lighted or unlighted, radio or racon, set on the shore or rocks.
Beam	(a) Extreme width of a vessel. (b) Athwartships timber on which the deck is laid.
Beam bearing	Direction of objects when abeam i.e. at right angles to the fore and aft line.
Bearing	Direction of an object expressed in Compass notation.
Bear away	To put the helm up, i.e. keep further away from the wind.
Beating	Sailing towards the direction of the wind by tacking.
Becket	Small rope circle, a simple eye.
Belay	To make a rope fast to a belaying pin or cleat.
Bend	Knot of various kinds.
Bight	Any part of a rope between its ends; also a curve, a cove on a coastline, or in a channel.
Binnacle	The box which houses the Mariner's Compass.
Bitter end	The last part of a cable left around the "bitts" when the rest is overboard.
Bitts	Pair of vertical wood or metal posts fixed on deck with a horizontal cross bar to which ropes may be secured.
Bluff	(a) Steep shore. (b) Full bowed vessel.
Bobstay	A stay for the bowsprit to prevent it lifting; from bowsprit end to stem at waterline.

Bollard	Heavy short post on a wharf or dock to secure ship's mooring lines to.
Bolt rope	A strong rope sewn round the edge of sails to give strength and prevent tearing.
Boom	A spar for many purposes, such as to stretch out the foot of a fore and aft sail.
Boot-top	A band of paint at the waterline between "wind and water".
Bower anchor	Main anchor carried forward in a vessel.
Bow	Forward part of a vessel.
Bowsprit	Heavy spar from deck leading forward from stem head, to which headsails are attached.
Breast line	Ropes forward and aft at right angles to the ship to "breast" into dock.
Bridle	A rope attached to both ends of a boat or object to lift it. Lifting tackle is attached to middle of the rope.
Bring up	To stop, as to come to anchor.
Broach	When running, to accidentally turn and get broadside on to wind and sea.
Bulkheads	Partitions fore and aft or athwartships, forming separate compartments.
Bulwarks	A vessel's topsides that extend above the deck.
Buoy	A float, with distinguishing name, shape, color or light.
Burgee	Pennant (pointed) shaped flag with design indicating the Yacht Club the vessel's owner belongs to.
By the head	Greater draft forward than aft.
By the lee	When running under sail, if the wind blows over the same side as the mainsail.
By the stern	Greater draft aft than forward.
CABLE	(a) 1/10th Nautical mile, (b) Anchor chain.
Capstan	A vertical cylindrical machine for veering or hoisting the anchor chain.
Careen	To heel a vessel over on one side by tackles, to work on her bottom .
Carry way	To continue to move through the water.
Carvel	Edge to edge planking for a vessel's hull.
Caulk	To fill the side or deck seams with oakum or cotton to prevent leaking .
Chain plates	Metal strips fastened outside or inside the hull to take the rigging strain.
Check	To slowly stop a vessel's movement or to slowly ease a rope.
Chine	The fore and aft line of the hull where the bilge turns up towards the topsides of the hull.
Claw off	Working a vessel to windward off a lee shore.
Cleat	A two pronged device for making ropes fast.
Clew	The corner of the sail where the leech meets the foot.
Close-hauled	Sailing close to the wind.
Companion	Ladder in a ship.
Composite	Construction method for a wooden vessel built with metal floors and frames.
Con	To give orders to the helmsman in narrow waters.
Counter	The overhanging portion of a stern.
Course	(a) The direction a vessel steers in. (b) The square sail set from a lower yard.
Cradle	The frame erected round and under a vessel to support her out of the water.
Cringle	Rope round a thimble, worked into a sail.
Crown	(a) Where the arms of an anchor meet the shank. (b) The knot when the strands of a rope are interlocked to start a backsplice.
Crutch	Fitting to support the boom (also Gallows).
DAVIT	Iron crane for hoisting, lowering and holding boats in position in large vessels.
Dead reckoning	The position found by calculation from course steered and distance run.
Deadweight	Total weight of vessel, also known as the displacement.

Deckhead	Underside of a deck. The roof of a ship's cabin.
Deep	Unmarked soundings of the lead line.
Dolphin	A built pile structure for mooring in harbor.
Downhaul	Rope or tackle used to haul down sail or yard.
Down helm	Order to helmsman to put tiller away from wind; up helm is towards wind.
Dowse	(a) To extinguish a light. (b) Lower sail or spar quickly. (c) Spray with water.
Draft	The depth of water occupied by a vessel at any time.
Drogue	A sea anchor – a cone shaped canvas bag to which the vessel lies in heavy weather to keep the bow pointing into the waves, or towed from the stern to slow the speed when running.
EARING	Rope for bending sail or head cringle to a yard, or clew cringle to a boom.
Ebb	The period when the tide falls or flows from the land.
Eddy	Circular motion of the water unconnected with general water movement.
Ensign	The flag, usually carried at the stern, that denotes a vessel's nationality.
Eye of the wind	That point from which the wind is blowing towards the observer.
FAIRLEAD	A fitting for leading a rope over an obstruction to avoid friction.
Fairway	Shipping channel, normally the center of an approach channel.
Fathom	Nautical measurement of depth of six feet or 1.83m.
Fender	Soft rubber or other material to prevent chafe between vessels, or vessel and pier.
Fetch	(a) To make, arrive at a desired point. (b) The distance the wind has from weather shore to ship.
Fiddle	Wooden top, with divisions fitted to cabin table in rough weather.
Flare	The outward spread of a vessel's topsides; also a distress signal.
Fix	A position obtained by taking accurate bearings or by astronomical observation.
Flashing	Navigation light with duration of light less than dark, operating at regular intervals.
Floor	Athwartship structural member fastened to keel and lower ends of frame.
Foot	The lower edge of a sail.
Fore and aft	In line with the keel – lengthways of the ship.
Forward	Towards the bow.
Foul	Opposite to clear, as "foul berth", "foul anchor", "foul bottom".
Frap	To bind ropes together, or to bind a loose sail to prevent it flapping.
Freeboard	The distance from the waterline to the deck outboard edge.
Freshen	Wind freshens when increasing.
Full and bye	Close hauled but with the sails well filled.
Furl	Gathering in sail and securing with gaskets to its spar.
GAFF	The spar to which the head of a fore and aft sail is bent.
Galley	The kitchen of a ship of any size.
Gallows	Frame of wood or metal with rounded top for supporting the boom .
Gimbals	Two concentric rings to hold the compass or stove horizontal at all times.
Go About	To tack.
Goose-neck	A metal fitting for securing a boom to a mast. Allows swing and topping.
Goose-winged	When running and the after mast sail is out on the side opposite to the fore sail.
Ground	(a) A ship touching bottom is said to ground. (b) Ground swell is the long coastal swell.
Gunter	A sliding gunter rig is when the gaff is hoisted vertically, reducing the necessity for a tall mast.
Gunwale	The heavy top rail of a boat.
Guy	A rope or wire used to control a spar or derrick.

HALYARDS	Ropes or tackles used to hoist sails or flags.
Hanks	Strong clip hooks which attach head sails to the mast stays.
Harden up	To bring the vessel closer to the wind.
Hawse pipes	Pipes leading down through the bows through which the anchor cables are led.
Hawser	A heavy rope used for mooring, kedging, lineing, towing or as a temporary anchor line.
Head	Forward in a ship, headsails are those set forward of the foremast.
Head board	A triangular board sewn into the top of a sail, to which the halyard is attached.
Head Sea	Sea from ahead, beam sea is caused by a wind blowing from abeam.
Heads	Toilets in a ship.
Heave the lead	To take soundings with a lead line.
Heave to	A sailing vessel is hove to when a headsail is backed thus reducing the way through the water.
Heaving Line	Light line, knotted on end to throw ashore when berthing, as a messenger for a larger mooring line.
Heel	A list from the upright; the foot of a mast.
Helm	The tiller or wheel.
Hitch	To make a rope fast to a spar or stay, but not to another rope.
Holding ground	The type of bottom for anchor, i.e. good or bad holding ground.
Holiday	An unpainted or unvarnished spot in a vessel.
Hounds band	A band around the mast with securing eyes for attaching the lower stays.
Hull	Structure of a vessel below deck level.
INSHORE	Towards the shore
Irons	A vessel is in irons when caught head to wind and unable to pay off on either tack.
Isophase	Navigation light where duration of light and dark are equal.
JACK-STAY	A bar or rope on which anything travels e.g. a rope leading along the deck, to which safety harnesses may be clipped.
Jack staff	Small staff in the bows from which the jack is flown.
Jib	The triangular sail set as the forward headsail.
Jibe	To allow a fore and aft sail to swing from one side to the other when running.
Jury	After losing mast or rudder, makeshift rig to get the vessel to safety.
KEDGE	A lightweight anchor for kedging or moving the vessel by pulling up to it.
Keel	The fore and aft backbone of a vessel.
King spoke	The spoke of the steering wheel which is upright when the wheel is amidships.
Knot	One nautical mile per hour.
LACING	The long line that secures the sail to a spar through eyelets.
Lapstrake	Planking when one edge overlaps the other lower plank.
Launch	To slide a vessel into the water. A small motor tender.
Lay	To go, i.e. lay aft or lay aloft, lay to (i.e. heave to) lay up, lay a course. The twisting of strands in a rope.
Lazy	An extra such as a lazy painter, i.e. an extra painter.
Leech	The after side of a fore and aft sail, and the outer sides of a square sail.
Lead	The lead weight at the end of the lead line used to find depth of water.
Lee side	The side away from the wind direction.
Lee tide	Tidal stream running with the wind.
Leeward (loo'ard)	Direction away from the wind.
Leeway	The sideways drift of a vessel from her course to leeward, due to wind pressure.
Life line	Line stretched fore and aft for crew to hold on to.

Lift A rope or wire to support a spar, as topping lift.
List When a vessel heels through having greater weight on one side.
Log An instrument for recording the distance run.
Log book The record of events on board a ship, especially navigational.
Loom The reflection on the clouds when the light is still below the horizon; also an oar handle.
Lubber line Line on the inside of a compass bowl indicating the ship's heading.
Luff To keep closer to the wind; forward edge of a sail.

MAKE To attain, i.e. to make harbor. Make fast is to secure. Tides that make increase. Make sail is to set sail.
Marline spike Pointed steel tool for opening strand of rope when splicing.
Marry To fasten two ropes together end to end temporarily, so one can pull the other through the block.
Mast head rig The headstay is rigged to the top of the mast.
Messenger Line run through a single block, used to carry an object, such as another line, aloft.
Midships Order to the helmsman to put the rudder fore and aft.
Miss stays To stay up in the wind when tacking.
Moor To moor is to lie with two anchors down. Vessels are said to moor to a dock when well made fast with several mooring lines.

NEAP TIDES Minimum range of tide, when the moon is in quadrature .
Neaped Of a grounded ship when the tide does not rise high enough to float her.

OCCULTING Navigation light with duration of light more than dark and total eclipse at regular intervals.
Offing Distance from the land.
Overhaul To pull slack into a tackle so there is no strain on any of its parts.

PAY OUT To ease a chain or rope.
Pintle A vertical pin on which the rudder is shipped.
Pitching A ship's movement in a seaway in a fore and aft direction.
Pooped A term to indicate that a heavy sea has come inboard over the stern.
Port The left hand side of a ship looking forward.
Port tack To sail with the wind on the port side.
Porthole Watertight window in the ships side or superstructure for ventilation and light.

RACON Beacon giving characteristic signal when triggered by ship's radar set.
Rake The inclination of the mast in the fore and aft line from the vertical.
Range A line formed when two distant objects are in line, one behind the other.
Ratlines Horizontal ropes as steps affixed to the shrouds to facilitate climbing.
Reach The courses of a sailing vessel between being sailed close hauled and running.
Reefing To reduce sail area by taking in at the reef points.
Round turn To put a turn around a bollard to hold the strain on a rope under tension.
Running rigging Rigging that moves on runs, generally used to control spars and sails.

SAMSON POST Used to secure anchor or tow line.
Scantlings The dimensions of a ship's timbers.
Sheer The rise of a ship's deck towards the bow or stern from amidships.
Sheer strake The upper line of plating or planking on the hull.
Sheet Rope or chain at lower corner of sail for regulating its tension.
Shroud Standing riggng that supports a mast athwartships.
Skeg A fixed vertical fin on the after side of which the rudder is attached.
Slack water Stationary tidal stream.
Slack in stays When a vessel is slow in coming about.

Sole	The floor of a cabin or cockpit.
Sound	To measure the depth of water by lead line or electronic means.
Spring	A mooring rope to prevent a vessel moving fore and aft when tied up alongside a dock, e.g. after spring is attached to the stern of the vessel and led to a bollard on the dock forward of the vessel to prevent it moving astern.
Spring tides	Tides when moon is full or new, when range of tide is greatest.
Stand on	Maintain course.
Standing rigging	Stationary rigging that supports a spar.
Starboard	The right hand side of a ship facing forward.
Starboard tack	With the wind on the starboard side.
Stem	The forward continuation of the keel to which the planking at the fore end of the boat is affixed.
Stern sheets	The platform extending aft from the aftermost thwart.
Stern post	The after continuation of the keel to which the planking at the after end is affixed, or in the case of boats with a transom, the transom.
Stiff	Said of a vessel that is not easily heeled and when heeled returns quickly to the vertical.
Surge	To allow a rope to slip on a power windlass while it is revolving; to allow a rope under tension to slip while on a cleat or bollard.
TABERNACLE	A box-like structure on deck to hold the foot of the mast when this does not run through the deck. Usually opening aft to allow mast to be lowered.
Tackle	A purchase of ropes and blocks.
Taff-rail	A rail around stern of vessel.
Take up	To tighten.
Thwarts	Planks placed across the boat to form seats.
Tiller	Lever for turning the rudder.
Tide rode	Said of an anchored vessel that is lying to the tide rather than the wind.
Toggle	A wooden pin with one end of a line seized to its middle to make fast to an eye.
Transom	The flat stern of a yacht, originally a board to which the after ends of the planking was secured.
Traveller	A metal bar parallel to the deck, running athwartship to allow a sail sheet to be trimmed on either side.
Trick	A period at the wheel.
Tumble home	Where a ship's sides are inclined inwards above the water line.
Turnbuckle	A screw fitting for adjusting the tension of shrouds and stays.
UNDER WAY	When a vessel is not made fast.
Up and down	Vertical, said of the anchor cable.
VANG	A guy for steadying a gaff.
Veer	To ease out a cable. A clockwise shift of the wind.
WARPING	Moving a vessel by means of a hawser.
Weather helm	A boat has weather helm when it has a tendency to turn up into the wind.
Weather side	The side upon which the wind is blowing.
Weather tide	Where the tide is making against the wind.
Wear ship	Changing tacks by turning a ship around before the wind, keeping the sails full (the opposite to tacking).
Weigh	To lift the anchor off the bottom.
Wind rode	Where an anchored vessel is lying to the wind rather than the tide.
Windward	Direction toward the wind.
YARD	A spar suspended from a mast, to spread a sail.
Yaw	When the ship's head is swung by the action of the waves.
Young flood	The first movements in a flood tide.

13

Safety at Sea

Page

SAFETY AT SEA IN SMALL CRAFT

Safety at sea in small craft is not just a matter of carrying a packet of red flares – it is an attitude of mind and this fact should never be forgotten.

It starts with the knowledge that the ship is well found, with adequate gear and equipment and is suitable for the type of passage making that the owner contemplates. Following this should be the knowledge that the vessel is adequately provided with sufficient fuel for main or auxiliary engines and fitted with the necessary spares and equipment to deal with any situations that can be foreseen.

This – very basically deals with the vessel – what of the Skipper and crew?

The Skipper should have sufficient navigational knowledge to be aware of his position at all times and under all conditions, a basically simple requirement but one needing theoretical know-ledge and the ability to put that knowledge to practical use.

He should, in addition, have sufficient knowledge of seamanship, weather forecasting, ship handling and the capabilities of his crew (and himself) to make sound judgements in difficult situations.

Having established that the ship is well-found and the Skipper and crew are competent, consideration should be given to the provision of the accepted "safety equipment.' Apart from obvious items such as personal buoyancy, safety harness, life rafts, etc, there is available an impressive range of equipment designed to assist, directly or indirectly, in avoiding or getting out of, the difficult situation. It is important to remember that all such equipment demands maintenance in some form or other together with the necessary operating knowledge. In difficult circumstances at night, lack of knowledge of the whereabouts of flares or how to operate them, may lead rapidly to a worse situation!

Summing up therefore, safety at sea demands a well found ship and a competent Skipper and crew who do not exceed their limitations. A rescue operation for a small craft at sea is almost invariably due to an error of judgement somewhere along the line and is therefore, an admission of failure to perform adequately under conditions that should have been foreseen.

A final word – probably the greatest danger facing the small yacht at sea, is not being run down by a supertanker, but the everyday risk of man overboard – some ideas on dealing with this situation are included further on in this section.

COAST GUARD SAFETY REQUIREMENTS

This section covers the minimum requirements needed to satisfy United States Coast Guard regulations. Many boaters will want to carry additional items, especially those venturing offshore. At the very least, most boats should carry back-up supplies of flares in case any of them must be used (or in case any fail to work properly).

NOTE: For further Coast Guard regulations see Chapter 4 on Boating Regulations.

To meet U.S.C.G. standards all equipment must be Coast Guard approved. Approved equipment will be labeled as such. There is no prohibition against carrying additional non-approved equipment in addition to the requirements.

PERSONAL FLOTATION DEVICES (PFDs)

PFDs must be Coast Guard approved and in "good and serviceable" condition. They should be of an appropriate size for the wearer and they must be readily accessbile. They should be removed from any plastic or other wrapping. Obviously, they should not be stored in locked or remote lockers. Other gear should not be stored on top of PFDs.

It is important to obtain PFDs designed for small children. Most adult sized flotation devices will not fit a smaller person properly, and in fact may cause the wearer to float in a dangerous position.

All throwable devices must be instantly available. Though not required by law, it is highly advisable to wear a PFD at all times when underway. A point often overlooked is the great danger present in using small dinghies away from the large boat. Small boats are inherently less stable and seaworthy than larger ones. PFDs are also required in your dinghy.

TYPES OF PFD

Type I PFDs are designed as offshore lifejackets. They provide more buoyancy than other types. They are designed to turn unconscious wearers in the water to a face-up position. Type I jackets come in sizes for adults and children. The smaller jackets provide a minimum of 11 pounds of buoyancy, while the larger jackets provide at least 22 pounds of buoyancy.

Type II PFDs are designed as near-shore lifejackets. This type will turn some unconscious wearers to a face-up position in the water. The turning action is not as pronounced as with Type I PFDs. Adult sizes provide at least 15.5 pounds of buoyancy, while children's sizes provide about 11 pounds. Infant sizes provide at least 7 pounds of buoyancy.

Type III PFDs are to be used in near-shore waters when there is a good chance of a quick rescue. Wearers will usually have to turn themselves face-up in the water. You may have to lean back to avoid turning face-down. Type IIIs have the same minimum buoyancy as Type IIs. These jackets come in many types and styles. They are often designed with fashion in mind, as well as safety. Float coats and vest styles can often be worn to provide extra warmth in addition to safety.

Type IV PFDs are throwable devices intended for use in near shore waters. They are not designed to be worn in the water. The most common type is the popular flotation cushion, which is often used in dinghies and small craft. Horseshoe buoys are often found on the stern pulpits of offshore boats. These devices often remain in the sun for long periods, and should be inspected frequently for wear.

Type V PFDs are special use devices designed for particular water activities. They may be carried if used for the approved situation. These devices include deck suits, work vests, board sailing vests and HYBRID PFDs. A typical use is aboard offshore oil platforms where a normal PFD would be too bulky, or too fragile.

HYBRID PFDs are the least bulky of all. They incorporate both inherent buoyancy and inflatable chambers to provide additional buoyancy. They may equal the performance of a Type I, II or III PFD. To be acceptable they must be worn when underway.

PFD REQUIREMENTS

Boats less than 16 feet in length (including canoes and kayaks of any length) must carry at least one Type I, II, III, IV or V PFD for each person on board.

Boats longer than 16 feet must carry at least one Type I, II, III or V PFD for each person on board. In addition, at least one Type IV (Throwable Device) must be carried.

NOTE: If a Type V device is used to count towards requirements it must be worn.

Federal law does not require PFDs on racing shells, rowing skulls or racing kayaks. State laws may vary.

Water skiers are considered to be aboard the vessel and a PFD is required for this person. It is advisable for the skier to wear a PFD designed to withstand the potential impact of a fall at high speed. Some State laws require a skier to wear a PFD.

VISUAL DISTRESS SIGNALS

See Chapter 15 for more information on Distress and Rescue.

Coast Guard Requirements. The requirement to carry visual distress signals became effective January 1, 1981. This regulation requires all United States owned boats, boats on coastal waters, boats on the Great Lakes and boats on U.S. territorial waters to be equipped with visual distress signals.

The only exceptions are during the daytime (sunrise to sunset) for:

(a) Recreational boats less than 16 feet in length

(b) Boats participating in events such as races, regattas or parades

(c) Open sailboats, with no engines and under 26 feet long

(d) Manually propelled boats

These boats will need to carry signals when underway at night.

Non-pyrotechnic devices may be used to meet this requirement. These include a 3 foot square orange distress flag with a black square above a black ball (day use only), and an electric distress light which automatically flashes the international SOS signal (night use only). The international SOS signal is three short flashes, followed by three long flashes, followed by three more short flashes (... --- ...). Flashed four to six times a minutes, this is an unmistakable distress signal, well known to many boaters. These non-pyrotechnic devices must be Coast Guard approved.

Pyrotechnic devices are often used to meet the Coast Guard requirements. Again, all of these devices must be Coast Guard approved, and they must be within their marked service life. The four basic types of pyrotechnic devices are:

(a) Hand held red flares

(b) Orange smoke, hand helf or floating (day use only)

(c) Aerial red meteors, fired from a flare gun or a self-contained launcher

(d)Parachute flares, fired from a flare gun or a self-contained launcher

The aerial flares may be either red or white in color. Red is used as a distress signal, while white is generally considered a practice shot. Boats should carry a minimum of three day/night flares to meet requirements. **Warning:** Some states, and several countries, consider flare guns a firearm. Check with state authorities, or customs officials, before carrying these launchers.

FIRE EXTINGUISHERS

Coast Guard approved fire extinguishers are required on boats where the following conditions exist:

(a) Inboard engines are used

(b) Fuel is stored in closed compartments

(c) Portable fuel tanks are stored in closed compartments

(d) Boats with double bottoms not sealed or filled with flotation material

(e) Closed living spaces

(f) Flammable materials stowed in closed compartments

(g)Permanent fuel tanks, or portable tanks that can't be lifted by those aboard

In practice, most boats with any type of fuel aboard will need to carry at least one fire extinguisher. Most boaters will want to carry several.

Extinguishers are divided into the following classes:

Classes	*Foam*	*Dry CO2*	*Chemical*	*Halon*
B-1	1.25 Gals.	4 lbs	2 lbs	2.5 lbs
B-11	2.5 Gals	15 lbs	10 lbs	10 lbs

All extinguishers must be periodically inspected to make sure they are fully charged and all seals are secure. Pressure gauges should be in the operable range. Generally, any use of an extinguisher means it should be replaced or recharged.

Halon units must be inspected and tagged frequently. Their pressure gauges are not an accurate indicator of the state of charge.

Boats less than 26 feet long must have 1 type B-I.

Boats 26 feet to less than 40 feet long must have at least 2 B-I, or 1 B-II. With an approved fixed system (non-portable, automatic extinguishers), only 1 additional B-I type need be carried.

Boats 40 feet to 65 feet long must carry at least 3 B-I, or 1 B-II and 1B-I. If an approved fixed system is installed, 2 B-I, or 1B-II will meet the portable extinguisher requirement.

VENTILATION

All vessels built after April 25, 1940 which use gasoline are required to be equipped with an approved ventilation system. All compartments where explosive or flammable gasses and vapors may flow should have a ventilation system, unless the compartments are open to the atmosphere.

Boats built after July 31, 1978 should be built to the Coast Guard Ventilation Standard. If your boat meets these regulations there should be the following sign at each ignition switch:

> **Warning:**
>
> **Gasoline vapors can explode. Before starting engine operate blower for at least 4 minutes and check engine compartment bilge for gasoline vapors.**

A natural ventilation system may be used in conjunction with a blower, or by itself. A minimum of one intake duct should be installed so as to extend from the open atmosphere to the lower portion of the bilge.

A minimum of one exhaust duct should extend to a point at least midway to the bilge, or at least below the level of the carburetor air intake.

All owners are responsible for keeping their boats' ventilation systems in operating condition.

BACKFIRE FLAME CONTROL

Gasoline motors installed after April 25, 1940 (except outboards) must be equipped with an acceptable means of backfire flame control. The device must be attached to the air intake with a flametight connection. It must be Coast Guard approved, or comply with SAE J-1928 or UL 1111 standards. It must be marked with the appropriate approval rating.

SOUND PRODUCING DEVICES

Regulations do not specifically require vessels less than 12 meters in length to carry a whistle, horn or bell; however, the navigation rules require sound signals to be produced under certain circumstances. Also, many boats will want to have a horn aboard for negotiating locks and opening bridges. When travelling in fog proper signals must be used.

Vessels 12 meters or more in length are required to carry on board a power whistle, or power horn and a bell.

NAVIGATION LIGHTS

The Navigation Rules in Chapters 1 and 2 cover this subject in detail. We present a short discussion here.

POWER DRIVEN VESSELS

Vessels of less than 7 meters with a top speed of less than 7 knots may show an all around white light and if practicable red and green sidelights.

Vessels of less than 12 meters in length may show red and green side lights (or a combined bow light) and an all around white light from the masthead or a staff at the stern.

Vessels of less than 20 meters in length should show red/green sidelights (or a combined bow light), a white stern light and a white masthead light. Be sure to check the Navigation Rules for proper light characteristics.

SAILING VESSELS

Vessels less than 7 meters may carry a flashlight or lantern to be shown in time to prevent collision.

Vessels less than 20 meters have a variety of options. Very popular is a combined red/green/white masthead (tri-color) light. These have the advantage of less power consumption while being highly visible offshore. Vessels may also show red/green sidelights with a white stern light. The red/green lights may be combined in a single bow fixture. As an option, a masthead all around red may be shown above an all around green in addition to the normal sidelights and stern light.

Sailing vessels under power must show the same lights as a power vessel.

ANCHOR LIGHTS

Vessels at anchor must show an anchor light unless located in a designated anchorage area assigned by the Secretary of Transportation. For vessels less than 50 meters in length the light should be an all around white light visible for two miles. It should be located where it may best be seen.

Many sailboats have masthead anchor lights. It must be kept in mind these are located well above the line of sight of many small coastal vessels likely to be encountered at night. A safer alternative is a light hung a few feet above deck level.

Vessels less than 7 meters in length are not required to display anchor lights unless anchored in or near a narrow channel.

DAY SHAPES

Anchored boats should hange a black ball in the forward part of the vessel. Sailing vessels under power should hang an inverted cone (point down) in the forward part of the vessel.

BLIND ARC FROM THE BRIDGE OF A VESSEL WITH BRIDGE AFT

There is a blind area ahead of and on each bow of any commercial vessel, the larger the vessel the larger the blind area. Simple mathematics will prove the point, but as a general guide line, if you are within a mile of a medium to large vessel i.e. 10,000 to 15,000 tons then you are in the blind arc. Again a simple test is, if you cannot see his bridge then the chances are he cannot see you.

Avoid either remaining in, or crossing the bow within, the blind arc. The actual area of the arc is a function of the size of the vessel, the size of the yacht, the height of eye of the vessel and it's beam. It is the yacht hull that has to be seen, not the mast.

APPLICATION OF COLLISION REGULATIONS

In applying the Navigation Rules the following practical considerations may be of use;

ANY vessel which is of deeper draft than you is "restricted in her ability to maneuver" being restricted to the deeper water, whether in a narrow channel or close to shore, sand banks, etc. and therefore cannot necessarily get out of your way.

Few commercial vessels can maneuver as easily as a yacht so they are also "restricted".

NAVIGATION IN FOG

Basically there is no difference between navigating in fog or daylight but the envelopment of a small craft in dense fog, preventing the navigator from seeing more than a few yards

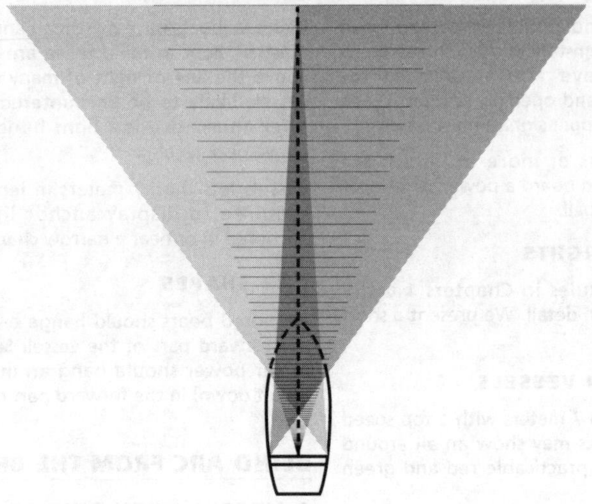

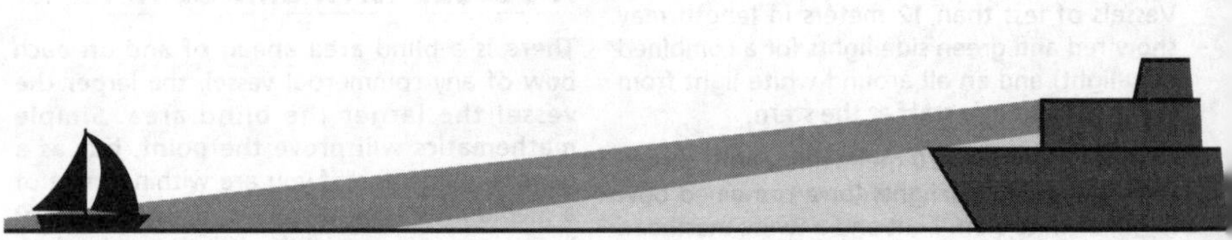

Blind arc under the bow. Doubled if vessel is container or timber carrier.

The Distance/Speed ratio should also be appreciated.

Closing speed	60 kts.	Distance 1 mile.	Meet in 1 minute
Closing speed	30 kts	Distance 1 mile	Meet in 2 minutes
Closing speed	15 kts.	Distance 1 mile	Meet in 4 minutes
Closing speed	7.5kts	Distance 1 mile	Meet in 8 minutes

Which is not a lot of time even at the lower speeds

ahead, has a psychological effect which is quite surprising to those who have not experienced it before. The following checkpoints are suggested as a standard drill in the event of fog:

1. All crew to don safety harness and personal buoyancy and ensure that liferaft is attached to vessel but free to float clear. A man overboard situation in clear weather can be difficult, the same situation in dense fog could easily become catastrophic.

2. Immediately update the position on the chart and then maintain an accurate check at say ½ hour intervals.

3. If under power, immediately reduce speed in order that avoiding action is easily taken if there appears to be imminent danger of collision.

4. Remember to use your fog signal in accordance with the Navigation Rules.

Note: Power vessel making way through the water – 1 prolonged blast ev. 2 min. Power vessel under way but stopped – 2 prolonged blasts with 2 sec. intervals ev. 2 min. Sailing vessel – one prolonged and two short blasts ev. 2 min.

5. When coasting – if possible get out of the shipping lanes into shallow water where there is no possibility of being run down by a large vessel and if circumstances render it advisable, anchor until it is safe to resume passage.

It is doubly important that a radar reflector is hoisted when in fog.

SEA EMERGENCIES

Emergencies inevitably occur at sea (as they do in every other context), but the prudent skipper will make every effort to see that they do not occur as a result of his own carelessness or unpreparedness. Every effort should be made to overcome emergency situations and to plan how best to overcome them if they should occur. What sort of emergencies can happen? What action will be necessary? Are the right spares and equipment carried on board? Have the crew members been properly briefed? Do they know where the flares are stowed? (and do they know how to use them?

These and many other questions should be given serious consideration – tragedies in yachts are fortunately rare, bearing in mind the numbers that put to sea – but those that do happen can usually be traced to carelessness or human error, perhaps even the simple one of neglecting to listen to the weather forecast before departure.

Man overboard

This is one of the most difficult situations that can confront the small craft sailor and one which usually results from someone's carelessness. Every crew member should have a safety harness and it is the skipper's responsibility to ensure that they are worn when weather conditions demand it. Are there adequate attachment points on board and are the crew properly briefed on their location?

There is a general tendency for safety precautions to be rather more casual when rowing out in the dinghy than when underway at sea and it is worthwhile to reflect that among cruising people probably more drowning tragedies occur when rowing out to the parent vessel than when underway in her. Life jackets should always be worn (especially by children) if there is the slightest danger. (Read on for man overboard drill).

Collision at Sea

Fortunately a rare occurrence but nowadays a very real danger in those areas of high density of shipping such as Long Island Sound. A sound knowledge of the Navigation Rules is necessary to evaluate any possible close quarters situation which may arise – can the sound signals in restricted visibility be instantly remembered? Is the vessel on the correct course for crossing a shipping lane? And is the speed adequate? Remember Navigation Rule No. 10 – "a vessel of less than 20m in length or a sailing vessel shall not impede the safe passage of a power driven vessel following a traffic lane". Even outside a traffic lane a large vessel operating in confined waters (which may not appear to be 'confined waters' to a small vessel) may be quite unable to take avoiding action and the responsibility for taking such action then lies squarely with the small vessel. It is important that such action should be taken in good time and is obvious to all vessels involved in the close quarters situation.

Severe Weather

The advent of rough weather should not necessarily be regarded as an emergency. Assuming that the vessel is well found and her crew are prepared, rough weather may pose problems in navigation, but the situation, unless it gets badly out of hand, is not an emergency. The prudent skipper will have reefed down in adequate time, firmly secured all deck gear and have thermos flasks of hot water ready for the preparation of soup later, when conditions in the galley may become difficult. The navigator should ensure that his position on the chart is up to date and consider whether it would be wise to alter course for an alternative destination, bearing in mind the probable conditions to be expected on arrival. For example, certain ports on the New Jersey and Florida coasts can be dangerous for small craft with strong onshore winds.

In severe conditions the skipper may eventually be faced with the alternatives of heaving to, running under bare pole or lying a hull. He should have given careful consideration to these possibilities before the need arises, and will certainly have practised heaving to in moderate conditions and assessed how his boat is likely to behave in more severe conditions. It is of course important to consider how much room there is to leeward when contemplating running off.

Finally remember to take action in good time. A dry, warm and well fed crew can deal much more easily with trouble than can the wet, cold and exhausted crew.

Gas Hazards

Gas explosions in small craft are fortunately rare, and providing certain precautions are taken, should never happen. The installation should be properly carried out and maintained; it is most important to regularly check all flexible connections and always to turn off gas at the cylinder when the cooker is not in use. Inevitably small quantities of gas escape each time the cooker is lit, and being heavier than air sinks down to the bilges where it accumulates. Pumping the bilges daily will evacuate any such accumulation .

Miscellaneous

Engine failure in a well found sailing yacht should not under normal circumstances be regarded as an emergency. If, however, it occurs when the vessel is entering a port with frequent fast moving cross channel ferries entering and leaving, then the situation may become difficult if there is insufficient wind to set sail. It is important to regularly maintain the engine even if only occasionally used, filters should be changed at the appropriate intervals and if no sediment trap is fitted in the fuel line, it would be wise to consider installing one.

Failure due to fuel line trouble should not occur in a well maintained craft. However, a blocked water inlet or worse, a rope round the propeller, can easily occur at any time particularly when in the vicinity of a large port, and the prudent skipper will have considered how he would deal with the situation in the circumstances prevailing at the time. Occasionally with luck, it is possible to clear a rope round the prop by rotating it backwards. Unfortunately the incidence of trash in the sea is a growing problem and the installation of line cutting equipment on the propeller shaft is well worth considering.

On any passage at sea, the anchor, should be very firmly secured, but should always be easily dropped when entering port.

Perhaps fire at sea is the worst emergency which can occur in small craft due to the incredible speed with which it can spread. Fortunately it is the most unusual disaster to occur, but here again thought should be given to dealing with a fire in one's boat (read on for fire precautions). It need hardly be said that personal accidents which may occur ashore within easy reach of medical aid assume a very different complexion when the vessel is perhaps a day or more sailing distance away from medical aid. A working knowledge of first aid and the presence on board of an adequate first aid kit can be a very reassuring factor when dealing with accidents which may occur despite sensible precautions. (See First Aid Chapter 16.)

FIRE PRECAUTIONS IN SMALL VESSELS

Small vessels normally use diesel or gasoline in their main engines and kerosene, alcohol or propane gas for cooking purposes. Each fuel has its own particular hazards, and its own particular virtues.

The flashpoint, i.e. the temperature at which a liquid gives off an inflammable gas, is much higher in diesel and kerosene than it is with gasoline or alcohol. Therefore, the two former fuels are safer under normal working conditions. However, all fuels can become a fire risk if they come into contact with a very hot metal surface like an engine manifold or a hot stove burner.

Fuel tanks, especially for gasoline, should be situated away from the engine and exhaust pipe. The exhaust pipe should be well insulated, and if possible, fireproof themmal insulation placed between it and the fuel tanks. The best solution is to minimize long runs of hot pipe by using a waterlift type of watercooled exhaust. The tank must have a vent pipe extending to deck level, to exhaust any fuel vapor. The fuel piping must be of the best quality, and well secured away from all possibility of chafe. Rigid pipe has a tendency to eventually crack due to vibration. Flexible fuel lines should be inspected frequently, and replaced at regular intervals - before they leak! Armored flexible piping designed for marine use should be used.

Other than an actual spill of gasoline, the greatest danger is an accumulation of explosive vapors in the bilge of the boat. Both gasoline and propane vapors will sink, and every effort should be made to prevent their accumulation. A marine blower (spark proof) should be located in the engine compartment and fuel tank area. The blower should be run for at least 5 minutes before starting your engines. If you have portable gasoline tanks, fill them on the dock, not in your cockpit. A vapor detector can be purchased which will warn of dangerous accumulations. If a proper blower is not installed, a diaphragm type bilge pump can be used to pump vapor from the bilges. Lastly, don't forget your nose - use it after every fill up, and before you start your engines.

Galley installations should be designed with safety in mind. Propane stoves should have automatic flame failure devices on each bumer. These cut off the flow of gas if the fire is blown out for some reason. A solenoid type of switch can be connected directly to the propane tank. When the power is cut off, the flow of propane is cut off. The switch should be in a prominent location, and have a light indicating when it is turned on. The propane tanks should be stored in a vapor tight locker that drains overboard. Spare tanks should also be stored outside the boat. Be careful of deck stored tanks leaking gas that can be carried by a gentle breeze down the companionway.

The piping from the stove to the tanks should be one continuous run if possible. All fittings should be sealed with gas dope, or Teflon tape. Again, rigid pipe (copper) is prone to fracture after long periods of vibration. Many boaters prefer to have one long flexible pipe made up by a gas specialist. This is a very heavy tubing that is extremely resistant to wear, and is not subject to vibration cracking. Of course, all piping must be well secured at frequent intervals.

Alcohol fuel remains popular in the U.S. due to the fact a fire can be extinguished with water. However, alcohol does float on water, so use plenty or you may just spread the flame. A spray bottle of water near the stove is handy both for galley grease fires and as an alcohol fire extinguisher. When lighting an alcohol stove never lean over the burners, as flare ups are common. Extra care must be taken when preheating alcohol or kerosene stoves offshore. The lurching of your boat may send flaming liquid flying about the cabin. If the cook is strapped into the galley with a harness, a very nasty burn is possible. A handy device is a wick that clips onto the burner allowing the preheating liquid to be contained. These wicks are used to preheat pressurized kerosene lamps. Many experienced boaters use a small hand held torch to preheat the burners.

In summary:

1) Keep all compartments where gas can accumulate, clear and well ventilated.

2) Maintain all installations, both gas and liquid fuel, in a good condition - this means regular inspection. It also means inspection of electrical equipment installed in a position where a spark could ignite an accumulation of gas.

3) When filling fuel tanks, ensure that all smoking materials are extinguished and there are no open flames nearby. Know how much fuel you need, to avoid over filling the tank and causing a spill. Always run your bilge blowers after taking on fuel and before starting your engines.

4) Make sure your fire extinguishers are fully charged, inspected to date and in positions where they can be readily found.

FIRE FIGHTING

The following points in connection with fire fighting are intended primarily for small vessels. An officer of a merchant ship is expected to have a good knowledge of fire drill in general and any particular precautions or methods of fire fighting required by a specific type of vessel or cargo.

In case of fire:

1. Alert all on board and tackle the fire, no matter how small as a major incident. A fire can get out of hand with astonishing rapidity. Extinguisher should be aimed at the base or center of the fire where it will probably have the greatest hold.
2. Detail one crew member to alter course or stop the ship so that the wind is prevented from spreading the fire, and to move the life raft to a safe position and ensure it is ready for launching.
3. Close any hatches, ports, etc. that will reduce the draft through the ship.
4. If you can transmit either by radio or visual signalling, inform the nearest ship or shore station of your predicament. It is better to cancel an alarm than to be too late to send one.
5. Launch the dinghy or life raft as soon as it is obvious that it will be required and if a dinghy, make sure that the 'survival kit', i.e. water, flares, etc, is placed aboard.

The above points may be dismissed as painfully obvious and indeed, they are, but they are intended to make the skipper of the small vessel consider his equipment and the general preparedness of himself and his crew to deal with a danger that may confront all of us at some time or other. Finally, again very obvious if water is used successfully to combat a fire – remember to pump the bilges as soon as possible.

MAN OVERBOARD

Sailing is probably one of the safest sports (certainly going to sea is safer than driving along the highway), but there are certain risks which can be evaluated and provision made to deal with them. The greatest of these, and one which in all probability will never happen in the life of the average yachtsman, is "Man Overboard".

The rare chance of it happening, and the rather awe-inspiring problems, tends to induce the 'It won't happen to me' reaction in the average skipper. Probably it will not, but this is no excuse for neglecting seamanlike precautions – if it does happen it can easily prove fatal if the crew members have not practiced their drill – it is the Skipper's responsibility ultimately if an accident happens.

In many of the published articles on the subject the boats carrying out the exercise generally appear to be strongly crewed with three or four men on board. In the following notes it is assumed that the vessel concerned has a man and woman crew, perhaps with two small children – the real life family cruising situation. It is strongly recommended that a 'Man Overboard' exercise should be carried out at reasonable intervals to familiarise all crew members with the problems and their solutions.

It is reasonable to assume that the vessel will have a reliable auxiliary engine and in all probability a VHF radio set, two items which can play an important part in the exercise.

There are three main stages in the M.O.B. Operation. First, stop the vessel and return to the casualty, secondly, secure him alongside and finally, recover him aboard. All three stages must be carried out quickly and effectively. Mental concentration on these three stages will greatly help to discipline and steady the mind during the period when panic can rapidly develop and slow the whole operation down.

The immediate reaction to 'Man Overboard' must be to release the danbuoy (with life buoy attached) from its position on the push pit in order to pinpoint the casualty's position.

There are two generally accepted methods of returning to the casualty – the reach tack reach method and the quick stop method.

The first consists of sailing off on a broad reach for four or five boat lengths, tacking and sailing back on a reciprocal course. When downwind of the casualty tack again, leave the jib backed and fore reach up to the casualty.

The second method, the quick stop method is simple and rapid and tailored to a weak and less experienced crew.

After the danbuoy has been released, tack and leave the jib backed (adjusting the sheets if necessary) to enable the vessel to be fore-reached back to the casualty. After tacking ensure that no ropes are overside and start the auxiliary, furl the jib and motor up-wind to the casualty.

This is one stage where previous exercises in different wind strengths can literally mean the difference between life and death to the casualty.

After the immediate dropping of the danbuoy, and with the vessel heading back to the casualty, the opportunity should be taken to drop astern a 100 foot flotation line attached to the vessel with a lifebuoy at the end. This may prove useful in getting a line to the casualty if difficulties arise when the vessel has been brought back to him. The flotation line and small buoy or lifebuoy should be permanently rigged on the pushpit in such a way that it can be easily released.

The next stage on arrival at the casualty is to secure him alongside. There are various pieces of equipment now available to assist the operation. One type consists of a pole with a stiff plastic loop on the end which can be dropped over the head and shoulders of the casualty. When suitably positioned the loop can be tightened from the inboard end, thus enabling him to be firmly secured alongside. (The construction of a suitable piece of equipment, small enough to stow on board should be within the capability of the average handyman).

The third and final stage of the operation, getting the man aboard, is undoubtedly the most difficult. A useful piece of equipment is a scrambling net. This consists of a strong net six feet by eight feet with four or five inch mesh. This is suspended from the guard wire or stanchion bases and apart from providing a comparatively easy method of scrambling aboard it also enables the crew member to stand in the net and assist the casualty aboard. One occasionally hears references to transom hung boarding ladders being useful – nothing could be less useful if there is a heavy sea

running. Whilst suitable as a bathing ladder in calm conditions, in anything of a seaway the transom will be rising and falling a matter of feet and anyone in the water underneath it would be in a dangerous position. Recovery must be made amidships where the vessel's movement is at a minimum.

At this stage a decision must be made about the use of VHF if this is available. If the casualty is conscious and obviously able, with assistance, to scramble aboard – get him aboard. If however, he is unconscious or there is any doubt about getting him on board, immediately send out a Pan Pan signal giving the vessel's name, position and brief details of emergency, eg. "Pan Pan Yacht XYZ, Position six miles East of Cape May, man overboard, request immediate assistance." It is far better to make a Pan Pan call in good time and then cancel it if recovery is successful than wait until it has proved impossible to recover the casualty. If it is obvious that the crew stand no chance of getting the casualty aboard unaided then a May Day call should be sent immediately.

Assuming that the person is unable to get back on board unaided, some form of mechanical aid is essential. The use of a halyard winch single handed offers no chance of success – the average person without someone to tail

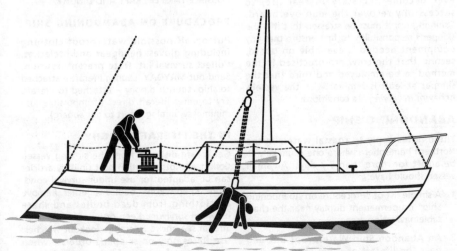

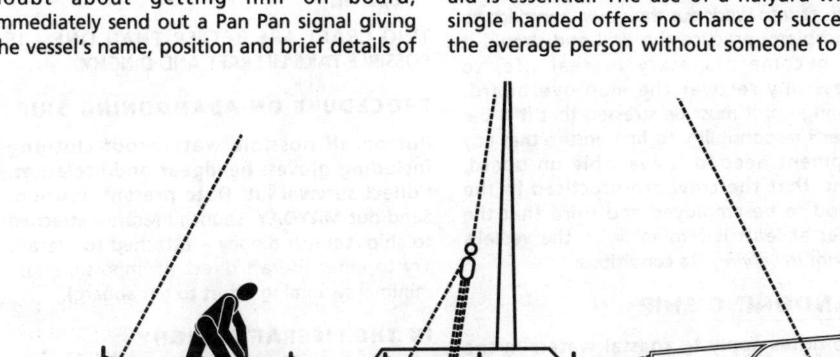

the line would certainly not be able to lift a heavy weight. Additional power must be available and probably the easiest way of providing this is by means of a three-part purchase which can be hoisted up on the main halyard to a predetermined position then used as a tackle to hoist the casualty aboard. This purchase consists of two triple blocks giving the very useful advantage of 4:1. The tackle should be suspended from the main halyard by means of a swivel snap shackle and the tail taken from the tip block via a foresail sheet winch.

Two points to remember, first the point to which the tackle must be hoisted must be determined by trial and error and then carefully noted. Second the stowage of the tackle – inevitably a piece of equipment which may never be used will probably be stowed in some inaccessible position and when required will be found to be a tangled mass of blocks and rope – leading to delays. Probably the best way to stow the gear is in a tight plastic sleeve of sufficient length to allow the tackle to be stowed in it in the fully extended position with a block at each end of the sleeve. This will prevent the rope tangling and ensure that the tackle can be used immediately without having to overrun the turns. The bottom lifeline should always be set up with pelican hooks or lashings so that it can be quickly cut adrift without any trouble, thus enabling a casualty to be rolled aboard without having to be lifted over the top lifeline.

It is hoped that these notes may assist the family crew to work out their own approach to the problem, practice the drill and should it ever become necessary in real life, to successfully recover the man overboard. Summing up, it must be stressed that it is the skipper's responsibility to first ensure that any equipment needed is available on board, second that the crew are practised in the method to be employed and third that the skipper at least is familiar with the vessel's behavior in varying sea conditions.

ABANDONING SHIP

These notes apply to coastal waters in the Northern hemisphere where one is unlikely to be adrift for more than 5-7 days. All small vessels should have:

1. A simple list of "Procedure on Abandoning Ship" on permanent display near the chart table/navigation area.
2. An Abandon Ship Waterproof Box/Bag near the liferaft or cabin entrance. The following suggestions regarding contents, may provide a useful guide:

BASIC SURVIVAL KIT:

1. Container(s) of fresh water (with some air so they float) 2 quarts per person.
2. Flares/rockets/smoke signals
3. "Space" Rescue blanket.
4. Glucose sweets – 500 grammes per person.
5. Flashlight.
6. Compass.
7. Plastic bucket – bailer.
8. 30 feet of line.
9. Emergency radio.

If time allows:

10. Extra warm clothing, sleeping bags, sweaters, etc.
11. First aid box.
12. Ship's Papers, money, passports – kept permanently in plastic folder.
13. Chart(s).
14. Rescue quoit with line.
15. Sheath knife and other tools.
16. Pencils and paper.
17. Food – bread, chocolate, canned food plus opener.

TWO CRAFT ARE BETTER THAN ONE – IF POSSIBLE TAKE LIFERAFT AND DINGHY.

PROCEDURE ON ABANDONING SHIP

Put on all possible waterproof clothing including gloves, headgear and lifejacket. Collect survival kit. Note present position. Send out MAYDAY. Launch liferaft – attached to ship. Launch dinghy – attached to liferaft. Try to enter liferaft direct (if impossible, use minimal swimming effort to get aboard).

IN THE LIFERAFT/DINGHY

Get a safe distance from the sinking vessel. Collect all flotsam – the most unlikely articles can be adapted for use under survival conditions. Keep warm – bodies together. Remove all clothing from dead bodies and share between survivors. Keep dry – especially feet. Stream sea anchor. Arrange lookout watches. Use flares only on skipper's orders – when there is a real chance of being seen. Arrange for collection of rainwater. Ration water to maximum ½ quart per person per day – issued in small doses. Do not drink sea water or urine. If water in short supply only eat sweets from survival rations.

THE WIND CHILL FACTOR

The chart below shows the limitations imposed by winds at low temperatures. Although compiled primarily for use in arctic conditions, it will be of use for those sailing in areas covered by this almanac in winter months.

The point at which the temperature and wind speed intersect on the graph indicates the wind chill factor. The practical implications of the wind chill factors are given below the graph. It must be noted that "proper clothing" means protecting all skin areas from direct wind with sufficient thickness to prevent undue coldness. If clothing becomes wet or frost forms on it, it should be dried as soon as possible.

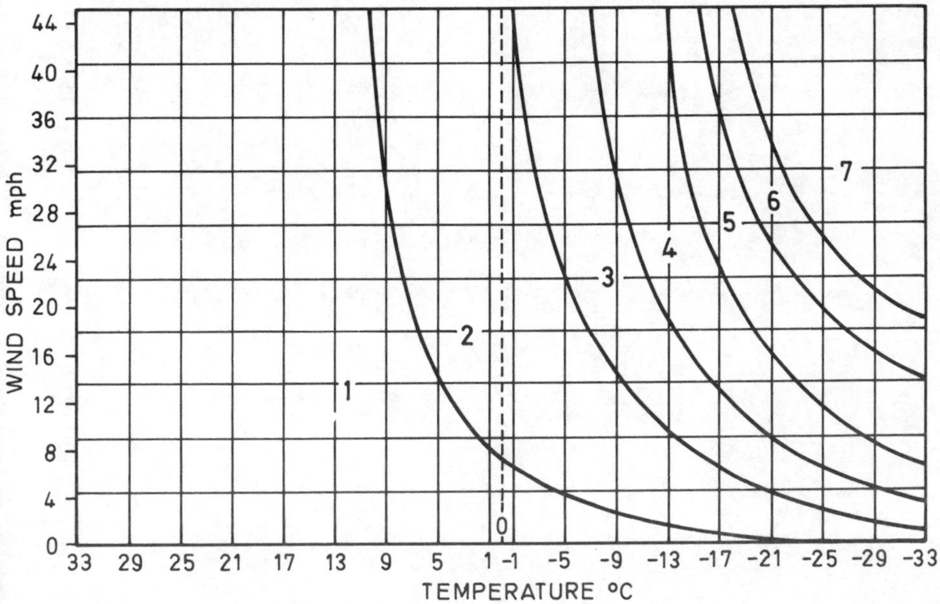

1. Comfortable with normal precautions.
2. Can become uncomfortable on overcast days unless properly clothed.
3. Heavy outer clothing necessary even on clear days.
4. Heavy clothing is mandatory. Unprotected skin will freeze over prolonged period of exposure.
5. Multiple layers of clothing mandatory, especially protection for the face.
6. Proper face protection becomes mandatory. One should not venture on deck alone, exposure must be controlled by careful scheduling.
7. Survival conditions. Crew can become easily fatigued and mutual observation of fellow crew members is mandatory.

14

Emergency Repairs

JURY STEERING

All boats should be fitted with an alternative means of steering in case the rudder, tiller, or wheel is damaged. The simplest form of emergency steering, which was standard issue in ships' lifeboats, was an oar, which could be put into a crutch, oarlock, or strop at the stern, and used in the manner of the Viking ships. When planning a long cruise it is advisable to equip the boat with a long oar or similar, for this purpose. If an oar is not carried, it is worth spending some time in advance working out how a jury steering system is to be set up, if necessary, putting extra fittings on the boat in readiness.

When the rudder or tiller breaks, first stop the boat, by handing all sail or stopping the engines, and then investigate the cause. If the rudder is thrashing around, immediate steps must be taken to control it, or it is likely to damage its gudgeons and pintles. Again there is a lesson to be learned from ship's lifeboats, which had a hole drilled through the outer lower end of the rudder blade through which a line was led from each side of the gunwale and knotted on either side of the hole. This served as an emergency steering system. Yachts will not want to sail around with lines hanging over the stern, but it is worth considering having the hole drilled in the rudder blade at the next re-fit, so that it is there if necessary.

If there is no hole in the rudder, one method of restraining it is to put a rope over the stern, secured on each side of the stern, and haul it tight against the rudder blade. If figure-of-eight knots are put into the rope, the blade will not be able to slip beyond the nearest knots. An alternative is to put lines on each side of a large shackle from which the pin has been removed, and haul the shackle in tight over the aft end of the rudder blade. This method can be used as a rudimentary steering system, provided the shackle can be held in place, by easing on one line as the other is taken up to alter the rudder angle. In a dire situation, even a yachtsman or fisherman anchor can be used to restrain the rudder by putting one line on one arm and another on the cable ring and lowering the anchor down the rudder so that the blade is caught between the shank and arm.

If the tiller has broken, an emergency tiller can be set up by lashing any suitable piece of wood or metal to the rudder head. When the boat has wheel steering, the usual cause of failure is one of the tiller lines. A spare wire, already spliced to fit the system, should be carried, but if it is not, a replacement must be made up on board. With hydraulic steering systems, the usual cause of failure is a leak in the hydraulic pipe lines. If insufficient spare fluid is available, the manual back-up system should be installed. All hydraulic steering systems should have stop valves in the pipe lines and a method of isolating the wheel from the hydraulic rams, so that if the failure is due to some other cause, the wheel can be disconnected.

The most difficult repair is where the rudder stock has broken, as any jury system of steering is going to have to be rigged directly to the rudder blade, and this means using one of the methods described earlier to control the angle of the blade.

Where the entire rudder is lost, it is most unlikely that the modern fin keel and skeg yacht will be able to steer herself by balancing the sails, as was occasionally possible with the older, long keel yachts, or with two-masted boats. However, it may be possible to control direction by setting the jib and hanking a small jib or storm sail to the backstay. The jib will provide power and hold the bow off the wind. By trimming the sheet on the small sail, the boat will tend to come into the wind, by easing the sheet, the boat will pay off. If the boat is fitted with self-steering gear that has an auxiliary rudder, this might just work, but it would be unwise to put too much strain on it, and sail should be reduced to keep the speed down.

The most obvious jury rudder is made up by using a spinnaker pole, or a similar spar, over the stern like a steering oar. The inner end of the pole should be lashed to the backstay, which then acts as a pivot. Two lines should be led from the outer end of the pole, one to each side of the stern, where they pass through a block and then into the cockpit. Experimentation will show whether these lines need to be led to winches or whether they can be pulled and eased manually. If the pole is long enough, it may be possible to lash it to the backstay at a point on its length that

Jury Steering and Jury Rigs are excerpted from *Seamanship* by Robin Knox-Johnston with the permission of Hodder & Stoughton Limited.

allows the inner end of the pole to be operated like a crude tiller, with the fulcrum being at the backstay. However, this is hard work and the lines should be rigged for back-up. The pole on its own will steer the boat as it is moved from side to side (this is how punts are steered), but it will be much more effective if a plank, such as a bunk board, is bolted or lashed to it.

Where the stern of the boat is narrow and the angle of the lines from the spinnaker pole back to the stern is acute, the tension required to pull the pole from side to side is considerable. It can be lessened by widening the angle, and the easiest way to do this is to lash another spinnaker pole square across the stern of the boat, with blocks at each end, and lead the tiller lines through these blocks instead of the ones on the boat's gunwale.

JURY RIGS

Being dismasted is a serious misfortune for a sailing boat, because the rig provides her motive power. Dismasting tends to occur in extremely heavy weather, but could equally be due to the failure of some part of the rigging. In the quest for aerodynamic efficiency some modern racing boats are rigged too lightly, and while modern materials are immensely strong, they are not indestructible. It is important to avoid personal injury when the mast breaks or falls wholesale over the side. One consequence of the loss of the mast in a monohull will be a much quicker motion of the boat, due to the loss of the inertia aloft; this makes remedial work all the more difficult. If you are not far offshore, then it is best to make for port under power once you have sorted out the mess, but if this occasion arises when you are in mid-ocean and beyond the reach of outside help, you must improvise some kind of jury, or temporary, rig. Even if you have large fuel tanks, restoring some sail area will steady the motion of the boat and provide a modicum of sailpower.

If the boat is a ketch, yawl, or schooner and the mainmast breaks, it may be possible to move the other mast into its position. Before my singlehanded circumnavigation I replaced *Suhaili's* wooden mizzen with a lighter aluminum spar, so that if I broke the mainmast, I would have an easier task of moving the mizzen into its place. Provided one mast is left standing, the task of stepping a jury mast in the other position is made much easier because there is already a high point to attach a line to take the jury mast up to a parallel upright position from where tackles can be used on the stays to finish off the job.

Of course, in a ketch or yawl, it may not be necessary to replace a broken mizzen mast, as the boat may sail perfectly well under the sails on the mainmast alone.

In the event that the only mast has broken and been lost, a jury mast will have to be set up from what remains on board, such as the main boom, spinnaker poles, or bowsprit. If a stump of the mast remains, a spar, previously dressed with its shrouds, stays, and halyards, can be lashed upright to this stump.

A reasonable mast can be made by using two spars as sheer legs, and setting up fore and back stays, but this rig is only suited to a square sail, and another spar will be needed as a yard of sorts.

JURY MASTS

When a mast breaks, the first job is to clear the wreckage, and recovering as much usable rigging and bits of the mast as possible as these may come in handy for making a jury rig.

If part or all of the mast has gone overside, it will be attached to the boat by shrouds and stays, so check that it is not endangering the hull of the boat. The next move depends upon the sea state. In anything worse than a small chop, it will be difficult or impossible to haul the mast on board and the wreckage cannot be left lying alongside as it is likely to knock a hole in the hull. If conditions permit, try to recover the sails intact and release all the rigging, but leave a sturdy line attached to a part of the mast or rigging, and then let go. A wooden mast should float clear of the boat; an aluminium one will sink beneath the boat. Either way, the mast should be well clear of the boat but still attached so that it can be recovered to be used as part of the jury rig when the sea conditions improve.

Where the sea conditions are bad, and it is therefore dangerous to try and keep the mast attached, all the wreckage will have to be let go completely, and other items that remain on board must be used to make up the jury rig.

When conditions allow, or if the mast breaks in a reasonable sea, haul the mast in alongside. Start by putting fenders overside between the mast and the hull and lash the mast to the boat to reduce the relative movement between them. Next, remove the rigging by disconnecting it from the mast and then from the deck by undoing the turnbuckles and coil it down. This reduces the weight hanging overside and the load to be heaved on board lessens; it also tidies up the deck and makes working easier.

Hauling the mast on board, unless it is small and light, is not an easy task and so should be tackled methodically. Move the mast fore and aft until its center of gravity is level with the midship section of the boat. Pass strops from the deck, down round the mast and back onto the deck again, and attach tackles to the upper end of the straps to form a simple sling.

If no suitable tackles are available, take a line from the upper part of the strop to a snatch block on deck in line with the strop's position and back to a winch. Alternatively, instead of using a strop, run a line from the winch through a snatch block and then down over the mast and up from beneath the mast to be secured to some strong point on deck.

On a large boat, more than two strops could be used, but on a boat of, say 30 feet in length, two should be sufficient; the strops should be placed between 6 and 10 feet either side of midships, depending on how the hull curves. If the hull is fairly straight, the strops may be farther apart.

Having rigged the tackles, start to take up the weight. If the mast refuses to come up the side easily, the job can be made easier by fitting a temporary ramp, angled down from the deck into the water, up which the mast can slide. Spinnaker poles or the main boom will do for the ramp. Each should be dropped overside between the hull and the mast and then its top end, hauled inboard. This will have the effect of moving the mast upwards and away from the hull. The ramps should be fitted with fore and aft guys so that they cannot slip. Once the ramps are in place, hauling the mast on board with the slings should be a lot easier. Once the mast is aboard, lash it to the deck, and start to work out what materials you have available with which to set up your jury rig.

Mast intact. If the mast is deckstepped and has gone overside only because of rigging failure, then it will probably still be intact. First repair or replace the broken rigging. Even if the only material available is rope, set up temporary rigging replacements with this rope, and make them as tight as possible. The rig is unlikely to be as strong as the original rigging, but it will provide some support, and if reduced sail is subsequently set, it should take the strain.

Mast broken. If the mast has been broken, the first decision is which part of the mast to use for the jury rig. Normally it would be sensible to use the longest remaining section, as more sail could be set, but sometimes it is advisable to use a shorter section because it will be easier to set up, as when, for instance, the top part of the mast is available, as it has halyard sheaves and tangs intact for the rigging.

When a lower section of the mast is to be used and the break is just above a spreader, the spreader level will make a convenient point for the attachment of the fore and backstays. They can either be knotted directly to the mast just above the spreader, or tied off to a strop placed around the mast above the spreaders. Either way, the spreaders will prevent the stays from slipping downwards.

Where the temporary hounds are to be put clear of an obvious point like the spreaders, a jury mast knot will serve to provide good holding points for shrouds and stays. If you are worried that the jury mast knot might slip downwards, you can always put a turk's head around the mast just below the jury mast knot.

Once the temporary hounds are set up, put on shrouds and stays. Blocks will also have to be secured to the hounds to take the temporary headsail and mainsail halyards.

Where the mast has broken close to the deck, leaving a stump, it is usually advisable to leave this stump and lash the jury mast to it. When stepping the mast, make a secure lashing to hold the foot of the jury mast to the bottom of the stump at deck level, and once the mast is upright, lash it to the stump. The best system of lashing is to take at least a dozen tight turns around the two pieces of the spar and finish by frapping the lashing between the two spars and tying it off. If there is space, put more than one such lashing around the spars.

Stepping the mast. There are two alternative methods when restepping the mast. The first is to push the mast forward, its head projecting out over the bow and its heel lashed to hold it at the mast step. Set up two spinnaker poles, or a spinnaker pole and main boom, as sheer legs over the deck, aft of the mast step, and hang a block from the apex of the sheer legs. To avoid damaging the deck, place pieces of wood beneath the heels of the spinnaker poles. Next, put lashings around the bottom of the poles and take them to secure points fore and aft so that the heels cannot slide. Lead a line from the masthead, or a point on the mast that would be the same height as the top of the sheer legs block when the mast is upright, through the block on the sheer legs, and down to a winch on deck. Attach the shrouds and the forestay to their rigging screws and then winch up the mast. The moment it is upright, secure the backstays and then dismantle the sheer legs.

The alternative method, which will almost certainly have to be used if the mast is intact because it will be too long to extend safely over the bows, is to lay the mast on deck with its head over the stern. Rig sheer legs again, just forward of the mast step, and follow the same procedure, but this time it is the forestay that will have to be attached once the mast is upright.

In both systems, all the standing rigging, halyards, running backstays and so on, should be secured to the mast before it is stepped.

Topmast broken. When the upper part of the mast breaks off, leaving a substantial length of the mast still standing, the remaining length can be used to set sail. First remove the wreckage, and if the broken piece of the mast has not already fallen, lower it as gently as possible to the deck. If the break is clean, it may be worth keeping this broken section, as a mast maker might be able to repair the mast, which will be cheaper than buying a new one.

If there are no halyards left below the break, you will have to devise some way of getting aloft to rig temporary stays and halyards. Where there are two lower shrouds, the simplest system is to make ratlines. When the mast has only a single lower shroud, make a ladder by tying off lines between the mast and this shroud. This task may not be easy, as the boat will become stiffer without the extra weight aloft, which reduce her rolling period, making her motion more jerky.

Once it is possible to climb to the top of the broken mast, either put a jury mast knot around the top to attach stays, shrouds, and halyard blocks, or when the break is close above a spreader, attach these to the mast on a strop around the mast just above the spreader.

SPRIT AND GUNTER JURY RIGS

A very handy jury rig can be set up once a mast is stepped, using either the sprit or gunter rigs. The sprit rig is practical when the lower part of the mainsail is intact. Any suitable spar can be lashed roughly in the position of the main boom gooseneck, so that it can rotate a little. Its outer end is then lashed to a suitable point on the leech of the mainsail. The mainsail should be sewn along its new head, and if necessary, a rope should be sewn along this seam to provide extra strength.

The gunter rig is slightly more difficult to set up but will work when the upper part of the mainsail survives and there is more length of mainsail than the mast remaining or the jury mast. The gunter rig is simple to handle and allows a higher sail to be set when the jury mast is short and it is not possible to put parrels on the upper part of the sail because they could not be hoisted above the spreaders.

JURY SAILS

If you are lucky, enough of the mast will remain to allow the mainsail, suitably reefed, to be set. However, if the mainsail is so badly torn that it cannot be repaired, some other sail will have to be set as a mainsail.

On a ketch, this could be the mizzen. On any boat, a jib or staysail can be used and set loose footed, with the clew taken out to the end of the main boom. Where possible, the sail should have its luff secured to the mast, be this its usual luff or its leech if the sail happens to fit better back to front. If the mast track remains, it is a simple job to sew sail slides onto the jury sail. If the track is unusable, it will be necessary to make up parrels to go around the mast; however, this will only work if there are no obstructions, such as spreaders, in the way.

Where it is not possible to make up any form of fore and aft sail, a square sail or a lateen sail may be the only answer. In both cases a spar will be necessary. It is advisable to rig up a halyard for this yard and secure the halyard directly to the pivot point of the yard, or onto slings, so that both the sail and the yard can be lowered easily to the deck when necessary.

If none of the sails left on board will fit as a mainsail, it may be necessary to adapt them for the new rig. No one likes to cut up a perfectly good sail, but there may be no alternative.

DEALING WITH HULL LEAKS

The discovery of a significant quantity of water in the bilges or, worse still, emerging above the floorboards in the cabin naturally leads to one reaction – panic. This is an unhelpful instinct at a time when quick but careful thought and action is required.

FINDING THE SOURCE

While it may initially seem to be a good idea to devote all energies to bailing, this is not the case. Other than switching on any non-automatic bilge pumps and putting spare crew to manual pumps and buckets, the first priority must be to find the source of the water, not always an easy job.

If the water is originating from a hole upwards of 1 inch (25 mm) square below the waterline, there is only a short time available to locate the leak and stem it before the boat sinks or becomes unstable and capsizes.

Is the water fresh or salt? If it is the former and the body of water you are sailing is salt, a domestic supply tank or pipe has split (turn off the domestic electric water pump if fitted), or rainwater has been entering into a compartment in the boat unnoticed over a period of time. In either case, there is no immediate danger. If you are sailing a fresh water body, of course, keep on checking.

Any boat already has a number of holes below the waterline in the form of skin fittings, sea-cocks, instrument transducers, shaft logs, rudder shafts, keel bolts, anode studs, and prop shaft bracket fixings, and these should be suspected before impact damage unless it is obvious that the boat has made contact with something capable of holing it.

Systematically work around all sea-cocks and close all nonessential ones until the leak has been found. Fractured hoses can be difficult to detect. On a boat that is significantly heeled over, sea toilet pipework and submersible bilge pump skin fittings below the heeled waterline could be the source.

If the propeller shaft has been partially or completely pulled out of the boat, ensure the integrity of the rudder and shaft bracket fixings.

Check the cooling water circuit and exhaust on any working engines – the cooling pump is capable of pumping a large quantity of water straight into the bilge via any fractured lines. On powerboats fitted with outdrives, do not forget to look at the transom area in the engine compartment for failure of the rubber bellows sealing the drive to the leg.

If the boat has been taking heavy spray or green water, openings above the waterline such as anchor fittings, hatches, portholes, windows, throughdeck chainplates, and blocked cockpit drains may be suspect.

If no immediate cause is found, hull damage is a possibility, and all internal parts of the hull so far uninspected should be examined as quickly as possible. If furnishings, fixed floors, or interior moldings conspire to hide certain areas, look farther down towards the keel where possible to see if water is flooding from that direction.

TAKING ACTION

Most small craft bilge pump systems can rarely stem the flow of a major leak unaided. Likewise, the proverbial panicked man and bucket is not the savior that popular fable makes him out to be, while manual pumping will quickly tire the operator to below the pump's theoretical maximum capacity.

Once a leak is located, the first course of action is to reduce the volume of the leak to a level that the pumps can easily manage. Time has then been bought to bring about a proper repair if possible, effect a temporary solution sufficient to make port, or in the worst case, commence an orderly call for assistance.

The easiest method of stopping water from flowing through a broken below-waterline skin fitting, sea-cock, hose, or shaft that is completely missing is to drive a round, tapered softwood plug into the hole. Packs of these are available from most major chandleries. To be most effective, suitable-sized examples can be secured near to all skin fittings, with spares carried in a handy locker well above the bilges. Remember that water pressure will try to force these temporary plugs out, so they need to be tended until secured in some way.

Instrument transducers often come with a spare solid plug to fill the hole while the fitting is being cleaned, and these too should be kept in an easily found and accessible place in case of emergencies.

If the hole is uneven, wrapping a rag around a plug may fill the gaps, or forcing cloth alone into place may reduce the flow to manageable levels.

It may seem obvious, but even if it is going to take a relatively short time to locate suitable materials, try to constrict the flow with a hand if possible; a 2-inch (50 mm) hole 30 inches (0.75 m) below the waterline will let in around 40 gallons (180 lts) every minute.

If the propeller shaft has become detached, but is still inside the shaft log, the best solution is to push it back if at all possible, holding it in place with a spare hose clamp until more effective repairs can be effected.

For hull damage, one solution is to rig a collision mat, a cloth (canopy, sail, or even a deflated inflatable without floorboards, for instance) that can be tied over the hole from the outside with ropes secured to the corners. Water pressure holds the cloth against the hull, substantially reducing the flow. Patented devices are also available that work like an umbrella, when pushed through the hole from the inside and opened outside.

In the absence of a collision mat or the time to rig such a device, bunk cushions pressed against the damaged area from the inside will again reduce the flow. These can also be used to reduce water pouring through shattered windows, or failed hatches and portholes.

Aboard a sailboat, changing the tack may reduce the pressure on any damage. Likewise, on fast powerboats the hole may be in a region where, if the boat stays on the plane, the leak is stopped or at least reduced. A change of course or speed on all craft will also assist if the leak is above the waterline. Again, by initially stemming the leak in any way possible, time has been gained to solve the problem.

DISTRESS AND RESCUE

15

DISTRESS & EMERGENCY SIGNALS – EMERGENCY ACTION

INITIATING A CALL

Set the radio to International Distress Frequency 2182 kHz, or Ch. 16 (VHF).

1. First transmit alarm signal (if equipment available) for 30 seconds to 1 minute.

2.THEN transmit distress call

(a) "MAYDAY" spoken 3 times
(b) "THIS IS" (or DE spoken "DELTA ECHO" if language difficulties)
(c) Name of ship spoken three times

3. THEN transmit distress message

(a) Distress signal "MAYDAY"
(b) Name of ship and call sign
(c) Position
(d) Number of crew
(e) Nature of emergency and assistance desired
(f) Any other information that might facilitate rescue and your intentions

4. Acknowledgement will be

(a) Name of ship sending distress call—spoken three times
(b) "THIS IS" (or "DELTA ECHO")
(c) Name or identification of station acknowledging distress call

HOISTING VISUAL SIGNALS

Full details of all distress signals are given in Annex IV of the Collision Regulations (Chapters 1 and 2) but the following ones are most likely to be of use on small vessels (assuming VHF is not available).

By night

(1) Parachute flares
(2) Flaregunl (red flares)
(3) Handheld red flare

By Day

(1) Parachute flares
(2) Orange colored smoke signal
(3) Slowly and repeatedly raising and lowering the arms outstretched to the sides

(4) An article of clothing on an oar

(5) The flag signal "NC" (I am in distress and require immediate assistance)

(6) A square flag having anything resembling a ball above or below it.

Note: If a distress signal is not justified the appropriate International Code signal should be sent by flag or Morse:

"V" I require assistance.
"W" I require medical assistance.

RADIOTELEPHONE, DISTRESS, URGENCY AND SAFETY SIGNALS

RADIOTELEPHONE

All distress and emergency signals should be sent on 2182 kHz 156.8 MHz (Ch. 16 on VHF sets) or on CB channel 09. However, any other frequency may be used at any time if it appears probable that assistance may thereby be obtained more promptly.

Certain of the larger types of radiotelephone sets are equipped with an alarm signal that may be used to precede the actual distress message. An alarm may also be used to precede an urgency Pan Pan signal in cases such as man overboard.

Silence period. Vessels fitted with equipment capable of receiving 2182 kHz should maintain a listening watch during the 3 minute silence period commencing at each hour and half hour.

Types of priority signals. There are three types of priority signals—Mayday, Pan Pan, and Securité (pronounced SAY-CURE-E-TAY).

DISTRESS SIGNALS

A Mayday call or a distress flare may be used only when there is grave and imminent danger to a ship, aircraft, or person and immediate assistance is required.

If for some reason there is an element of doubt about the necessity for sending a Mayday signal, an urgency Pan Pan signal (see on next page) should be sent. This will alert vessels in the vicinity and any Coast guard station within range. In the light of subsequent events the signal can either be cancelled or a Mayday call sent out. In this connection there are two important points to remember. First it is far better to give as much advance warning of trouble as possible, and second, if the situation becomes less urgent and help is no longer required, the distress or urgency signal must be immediately cancelled.

Mayday relay signals. Any vessel hearing a distress call must listen for a short period to see if it is acknowledged by a Coast Guard station. If this does not occur, the vessel that received the Mayday signal must retransmit the signal but preface the distress call with the words Mayday Relay three times followed by the name or call sign of the vessel retransmitting the distress message three times.

Communications control during the distress incident. In Coastal waters the primary responsibility for control of distress incidents lies with the Coast Guard who initiates S.A.R. (Search and Rescue). They will impose silence on all vessels in the vicinity by transmitting the signal SEELONCE MAYDAY, followed by their own name or call-sign. (The signal will be transmitted on the frequency being used to control the incident.) When complete radio silence is no longer necessary, the controlling station will transmit the following message:

MAYDAY
Hello all stations (repeated 3 times)
This is (name of control station)
Name of vessel in distress
PRUDONCE

Essential communications may then be resumed, but it is vital to avoid interference with any signals relating to the mayday incident. When all traffic relating to the incident is concluded, the controlling station will send out a general signal SEELONCE FEENEE, which permits resumption of normal working.

URGENCY SIGNALS

Pan Pan signals The words Pan Pan repeated three times are used when it is necessary to transmit a very urgent message concerning the safety of the ship or some person on board or within sight. It does not imply that the vessel herself is in immediate danger. Examples are cases of injury where urgent medical assistance or advice is required and man overboard when there is doubt about the ability of the vessel to rescue him. Pan Pan signals should, when possible, be addressed to a specific shore station or ship, but if any doubt exists about the nearest shore station, the urgency Pan Pan should be transmitted as a general call.

The urgency signal and message should normally be sent on 2182 kHz or Ch. 16, but if the message itself is long, the urgency signal should be transmitted on the distress frequency together – with a statement that the message will be transmitted on a working frequency. Any vessel hearing an urgency signal must immediately cease transmitting and listen to check whether the urgency signal is acknowledged by a Coast Radio Station. After a period of three minutes, if no acknowledgement is heard, the listening vessel must endeavour to contact a shore station and relay the message.

SAFETY MESSAGES

Securité (pronounced SAY-CURE-E-TAY) repeated three times precedes any important navigational or meteorological warning. The safety signal is sent on a distress frequency, either 2182 kHz or Ch. 16, together with an announcement giving the working channel on which the safety message will be broadcast. Any vessel hearing the safety message must at once cease working on the frequency chosen for the safety message and listen until it is satisfied that it does not concern it.

VHF channel 22A (157·1 MHz) is reserved for communications with the U.S. Coast Guard when the situation does not warrant use of the emergency frequencies. First establish contact on channel 16 (156·8 MHz), then switch to 22A if directed by the radio officer. The coast Guard utilizes other channels when 22A is busy. In certain areas other channels are used for traffic control purposes. Channel 13 (156·650 MHz) is frequently used by the Coast Guard in large harbors such as Norfolk, VA or New York, NY. Channel 67 (156·375 MHz) is used in the New Orleans area for traffic control.

New Bridge-to-Bridge Radiotelephone Regulations require vessels over 20 meters (65·5 feet) to maintain a continuous watch on both channel 16 and 22A. For more information on these regulations see Chapter 4. On portions of the lower Mississippi River, a watch on channels 16 and 67 is mandatory. It may be desirable to transmit safety information on 22A or 67 if channel 16 is unavailable.

EPIRBS

Emergency Position Indicating Radio Beacons (EPIRBs) are designed to alert rescue authorities in emergencies. EPIRBs are made in 6 different classes:

Class A, B and S EPIRBs are the most common aboard cruising oats. Unfortunately, their detection range is limited due to several factors. Satellites must be in line of sight of both the EPIRB and a ground terminal for detection to occur. Due to their basic

Type	*Frequency*	*Description*
Class A	121·5/243MHz	Float free, automatically activated, detectable by aircraft and satellite. Coverage limited.
Class B	121·5/243 MHz	Manually activated version of Class A.
Class C	VHF ch 15/16	Manually activated, operates on maritime channels only, not detectable by satellite.
Class S	121·5/243 MHz	Similar to Class B, except it floats, or is an integral part of a survival craft.
Cat I	406/121·5 MHz	Float free, automatically activated. Detectable by satellite anywhere in the world.
Cat II	406/121·5 MHz	Similar to Cat I, except is manually activated.

design,and frequency congestion, these devices are subject to a high false alarm rate (over 99%); consequently, confirmation is required before search and rescue forces can be deployed. CAUTION: EPIRBs manufactured before October 1988 may have design or construction problems, or may not be detectable by satellite.

Class C EPIRBs are manually activated devices for pleasure craft that do not venture far offshore, or for vessels on the Great Lakes. They transmit a short burst on VHF channel 16, and a longer homing signal on channel 15. A coast station, or other listener, must recognize the brief, recurring tone as an EPIRB. Class C EPIRBs are not recognized outside the United States.

Category I and II EPIRBs transmit on both 406MHz and 121·5 MHz. The 406 MHz signal is received by a satellite transmitter, while the 121·5 MHz signal allows aircraft and rescue vessels to home in on the vessel in distress. The position of a victim can be plotted much more accurately with this system. The signal is also encoded with the vessel's identity. There is no range limitation on this system.

The Coast Guard must certify Category I and II EPIRBs for sale in the U.S. Many commercial vessels are required to carry a Category I transmitter including fishing boats.

Testing EPIRBs. The Coast Guard urges EPIRB owners to periodically examine them for water tightness, battery expiration date and signal presence. FCC rules allow class A, B and S EPIRBs to be turned on briefly (for three audio sweeps, or one second only) during the first five minutes of each hour. Signal presence can be detected by an FM radio tuned to 99·5 MHz, or an AM radio tuned to any vacant frequency and located close to the EPIRB. FCC rules allow class C EPIRBs to be tested within the first five minutes of every hour, for not more than five seconds. Class C EPIRBs can be detected by a marine VHF radio tuned to channel 15 or 16. Category I and II EPIRBs can be tested through their own self test function.

The COSPAS-SARSAT system. This is an international satellite based search and rescue system established by the U.S., the former Soviet Union, Canada and France. It can locate emergency transmissions on the frequencies used by Class A, B, S and Category I and II EPIRBs. the U.S. Coast Guard operates local user terminals designed to receive EPIRB distress calls forwarded from COSPAS-SARSAT satellites.

PYROTECHNIC DISTRESS SIGNALS

All small craft should carry some means of indicating distress and preventing collision at night.

There are internationally recognized ways of indicating distress or risk of collision, using red flares or stars (hand-held, projected, or parachute-suspended) or orange smokes (hand-held or buoyant) for distress and white flares for collision warning.

Distress flares should be used only when there is grave and imminent danger. If not in distress but needing assistance, signal "V" in Morse (· · · –) or hoist flag "V". The distress signals you should carry depends not on the size of your boat, but on the distance from land you are likely to go.

Different types of distress flares are needed to raise the alarm and pin point your position to rescuers. All craft sailing at night should carry white flares to attract the attention of larger vessels when there is risk of collision. Learn how to use your flares and teach your crew, so you will not be caught in distress, possibly at night, trying to read the labels.

COAST GUARD REQUIREMENTS

The requirement to carry visual distress signals became effective January 1, 1981. This regulation requires all United States owned boats, boats on coastal waters, boats on the Great Lakes and boats on U.S. territorial waters be equipped with visual distress signals.

The only exceptions are during the daytime (sunrise to sunset) for:

- Recreational boats less than 16 feet in length
- Boats participating in events such as races, regattas or parades
- Open sailboats, with no engines and under 26 feet long
- Manually propelled boats

These boats still need to carry signals when underway at night.

Non-pyrotechnic devices may be used to meet this requirement. These include a 3 foot square orange distress flag with a black square above a black ball (day use only), and an electric distress light which automatically flashes the international SOS signal (night use only). The international SOS signal is three short flashes, followed by three long flashes, followed by three more short flashes (• • • – – – • • •). Flashed four to six times a minute, this is an unmistakable distress signal, well known to many boaters. These non-pyrotechnic devices must be Coast Guard approved, and they must be within their marked service life. The four basic types of pyrotechnic devices are:

- Hand held red flares
- Orange smoke, hand held or floating (day use only)
- Aerial red meteors, fired from a flare gun or a self-contained launcher
- Parachute flares, fired from a flare gun or a self-contained launcher

The aerial flares may be either red or white in color. Red is used as a distress signal while white is generally considered a practice or warning shot. Boats should carry a minimum of three day/night flares to meet requirements. **Warning:** Some states, and several countries, consider flare guns a firearm. Check with state authorities, or customs officials, before carrying these launchers.

There are many types of flares that meet the minimum requirements for distress signals. Recent tests of flares indicate a great difference in performance among the various types. As with most things, the more you spend, the better the results. The common 12 gauge flare pistol will launch meteors up to about 250 feet. A 25mm gun can launch either meteors, or parachute flares up to 375 feet. Several types of hand held parachute flare launchers can achieve altitudes near 1000 feet. The higher the launch, the greater the range of visibility. Parachute flares may be visible for up to a minute after launch –meteors last only briefly. The further from land you travel, the better your distress signals should be. Always carry more than the minimum required.

SOLAS (Save Our Lives At Sea) approved flares meet very stringent requirements and are preferred for offshore use. There are SOLAS approved devices on the market which may not carry Coast Guard approval. They cannot be used to meet the legal requirements, even though they are excellent distress signals.

Each type of distress signal may come in to play during a rescue. Meteors, or parachute flares could be used to attract attention, either day or night. Hand held flares or orange smoke could be useful in directing rescue vessels to your location. Orange smoke is particularly useful in attracting aircraft during daylight hours.

Great care should always be used with any pyrotechnic device. These items produce a very hot flame, and the ash and slag can cause injury or ignite flammable material. Hand held flares are particularly notorious for dropping red-hot slag all around. If possible, don leather gloves before igniting handheld flares. Always point these devices away from the vessel, and down wind. The Coast Guard recommends firing flares at an angle of about 60 degrees above the horizon in calm winds. As the wind increases you may fire the flare closer to the vertical. Never fire the device straight up – **watch out for masts and rigging above your head!** Look away from the device before firing.

When pyrotechnic devices reach their expiration date, they may no longer be used to meet the Coast Guard requirements. Most boaters will want to keep these expired devices as back-ups to their fresh supply. Always dispose of expired flares properly. Turn them over to the fire department, police, boating officials or the Coast Guard Auxiliary.

Never "test" fire flares without the express permission of the Coast Guard.

SEARCH AND RESCUE

PROCEDURE

Around the coasts of the United States, Puerto Rico and the U.S. Virgin Islands the United States Coast Guard has the responsibility of coordinating search and rescue procedures (SAR) for vessels in distress.

Upon receiving distress calls, all coast radio stations and public correspondence stations will contact the coast Guard immediately. The Coast Guard will request radio silence on the appropriate frequency for all vessels not involved in the emergency. The Coast Guard maintains a continuous watch on the emergency frequencies. The emergency frequencies are channel 16 VHF, 2182 kHz or CB channel 09.

If you hear a distress call, or see a distress signal, you should respond immediately by notifying the nearest Coast Guard station. If you can assist the stricken vessel without endangering yourself, you should. The Federal Boat Safety Act of 1971 contains a "Good Samaritan" clause stating: "Any person . . . who gratuitously and in good faith renders assistance at the scene of a vessel collision, accident, or other casualty without objection of any person assisted, shall not be held liable for any act or omission in providing or arranging salvage, towage, medical treatment, or other assistance where the assisting person acts as an ordinary, reasonably prudent man would have acted under the same or similar circumstances.

If you hear a distress call that the Coast Guard cannot hear, you may have to act as an intermediate relay station. All vessels should immediately clear any channel upon which a distress call is being broadcast. Only respond to the caller if the Coast Guard does not respond.

If the Coast Guard has been informed, they may call upon commercial towage or salvage firms to come to your assistance if there is no immediate threat to the boat or its passengers. The Coast Guard does not maintain a list of approved commercial firms, and they do not inspect any firms to ensure their capabilities. In non-emergency situations the Coast Guard will issue a marine assistance radio broadcast. Commercial firms in the area may respond. It is up to the individual boater to negotiate terms and fees with the commercial firm. The Coast Guard will respond to emergencies.

Distress broadcasts transmitted by EPIRBs may be received by satellite or passing airplanes. All such transmissions are reported to the Coast Guard, If possible, the subject vessel will be contacted by other means. See the section on EPIRBS for more information.

SEA RESCUE BY HELICOPTER

Once the helicopter has become airborne, how soon it locates the vessel and how effective its work can be depends to a large extent on the vessel itself.

LARGE VESSELS

From the air, especially if there is a lot of shipping in the area, it is very difficult for the pilot of a helicopter to pick out the particular ship he is looking for from the many he can see, unless that ship uses a distinctive distress signal that can be clearly seen by him. One such signal is the daylight orange-colored smoke signal. This is very distinct from the air. A well-trained Aldis lamp can also be seen except in very bright sunlight. Display of these signals may mean all the difference between success and failure in the helicopter locating the casualty.

It is essential that the ship's position should be given as accurately as possible if the original distress signal is made by radio. The bearing (mag. or true) and distance from a fixed object, such as headland or lighthouse should be given if possible. The type of ship or yacht, color of sails and hull should be included if time allows, along with brief details of lifesaving equipment, for example liferaft.

Because of their operational limitations, helicopters should not be unnecessarily delayed at the scene of the rescue. Every effort should be made to provide a clear stretch of deck or hatchway and to mark this area with a large letter "H" in white prior to the arrival of the helicopter. A helicopter will approach the ship from astern and hover over the cleared area, heading into wind. In order that the helicopter pilot and crewman may have as large an area of the ship as possible on which to operate consistent with the helicopter remaining heading into the wind, the ship should steam at a constant speed heading 30° to starboard of the prevailing wind direction. If this is not possible the ship should remain stationary head to wind. If these conditions are met the helicopter can lower on to or lift from the clear area, the maximum length of the winch cable being about 200 feet. On no account should the strop on the end of the winch cable, when lowered to the vessel, be secured to any part of the vessel or allowed to become entangled in any rigging or fixtures. If the ship cannot comply with these conditions the helicopter may be able to lift a man from a boat towed astern on a long painter. If the vessel is on fire and making smoke it is of advantage to have the wind two points off the bow. In all cases an indication of wind direction is useful. Pennants and flags are acceptable for this purpose and possible smoke, from the galley funnel, provided that there is not too much smoke.

Helicopters are well practiced in rescuing survivors from either a deck or the sea, the victim, whether on deck or in the water, may be rescued by means of a strop. The crewman is lowered from the helicopter together with the strop which is secured around the victim's back and chest, and both are winched up into the helicopter.

If a victim on a deck is injured to the extent that the use of a strop around his back and chest would aggravate the injury or cause suffering, a crewman is lowered on to the deck with a stretcher. The victim is placed in the stretcher, strapped in in such a manner that it is impossible for him to slip or fall out, and both stretcher and crewman are winched up into the helicopter. If possible, the helicopter will be carrying a doctor who will be lowered to the deck and will assist the victims as necessary.

A yacht in distress may not anticipate a helicopter rescue, particularly in view of the increasing number of inshore rescue boats, but it is always advantageous to be prepared for this type of operation. A yacht, particularly a small one, is not always easily identified from the air. The necessary precautions to ensure easy identification should form part of the normal sea going equipment of every yacht, e.g. sail numbers should be clearly marked, canvas dodgers should be clearly marked with the vessel's name and if the dinghy is carried upside down on the deck, the name should be clearly painted on its bottom.

Failing these precautions a large strip of canvas with the vessel's name should be carried that can be lashed on deck in the event of an emergency.

When the emergency occurs the use of a flare or smoke signal when the helicopter is sighted may materially speed up the rescue. DO NOT FIRE PARACHUTE FLARES WHILE THE HELICOPTER IS EITHER DIRECTLY OVERHEAD OR CLOSE BY. Once it is obvious that rescue is being carried out by this means, a sea anchor, if available, should be streamed in order to reduce drift. Alternatively, the main anchor and cable may be paid out to help reduce surface drift.

It is most important to remember that the helicopter crew will not under any circumstances risk the winching cable becoming entangled with the yacht's mast and rigging. A sailing yacht must therefore prepare for its crew to be picked up from the water a safe distance from the vessel. A life raft or inflatable dinghy should be made ready, and on the approach of the helicopter it should be streamed, complete with crew, on the end of at least a 100 foot warp firmly secured to the parent vessel (unless, of course, there is the danger of the latter foundering). The winchman can then operate in safety, well clear of the yacht and her rigging. In the unfortunate event of the vessel having no life-raft or inflatable dinghy, it will be necessary for the crew to take to the water when the helicopter has located, them. Again, a long warp should be streamed, the crew with life jackets firmly secured can then drift to leeward attached to the warp in a bunch. In the unlikely event of some members of the crew having to be left in the water for an additional period, they will have means of returning to the yacht by means of the warp.

The "pick up" problem does not arise in the case of the small sailing dinghy or the power boat with no mast. In these cases the crew should remain on board unless otherwise instructed by the winchman. Finally, remember that a helicopter cannot remain airborne indefinitely, watch for and carry out the winchman's instructions exactly and immediately.

If from the yacht in trouble it is observed that the helicopter is going to pass by or is on a course that will take it away, continued use should be made of visual distress signals. At the same time, the fact should be reported on the radio to the Coast Guard stating the present bearing and distance of the helicopter. The Coast Guard will pass this information direct to the helicopter.

EXPANDING SQUARE SEARCH

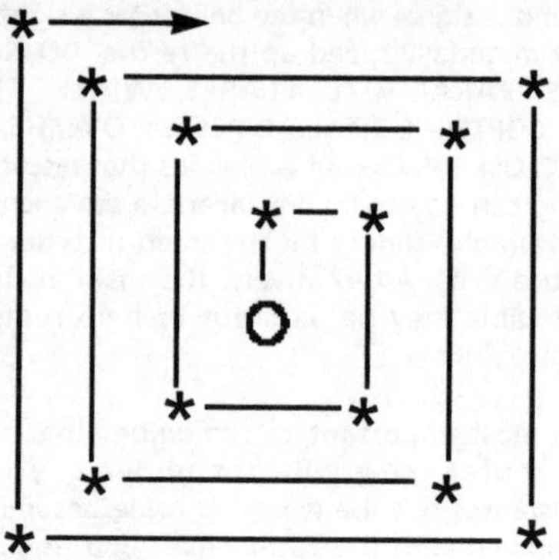

HIGH LINE TECHNIQUE

In very bad weather, it may not be possible to lower the crewman and strop directly onto the deck. In such a case, a rope extension of the winch line may be lowered to the vessel. This should be taken in as the helicopter pays out her wire. Coil down the line on deck clear of snags, but do not make it fast. The helicopter will pay out the full scope of wire and descend, while the ship's crew continue to take in the slack until the winch hook and strop are on board. The victim will then be secured in the strop and, when he or another member of the ship's crew signifies that he is ready, the helicopter will ascend and take in the wire. Pay out the extension rope, keeping enough weight on it to keep it taut, until the end is reached, then cast the end clear of the ship's side; unless further evacuation of crew is intended when, if possible, the end of the line should be retained on board to make recovery of the strop for the next man easier—but do not make the line fast.

Rescue helicopters are fitted with marine VHF and may wish to communicate directly during transfer. Yachts with VHF should monitor Channel 16 (or other channel designated by the Coast Guard) and await instructions.

Remember: Keep clear of the main and tail rotors.

AIRCRAFT SEARCHES AND PATTERNS

In general night visual searches are dependant upon the ability of the survivors to indicate their positions using pyrotechnics, lights, fires, etc. The searching aircraft can only hope to illuminate an accurately defined area i.e., on sighting red flares or flashing lights.

There are several patterns of searches, but the ones most likely to be used for missing craft/persons are the following:

Expanding square search. This procedure begins at a given point and expands in concentric squares. It is used to cover a limited area usually when survivors are known to be in a relatively small area. To execute a square search, the aircraft is flown in such a way as to make good the tracks shown in the diagram that follows.

Note: GREEN flares are used at night only by aircraft to indicate to the survivors that the aircraft is turning. Survivors should, on seeing the flares, wait until the flare has died out and then fire a red flare to indicate their position. When the aircraft fire the green flares, their crews will not look out until the length of time it takes the flare to expire. This is to enable them to retain their night vision.

Track crawl search. The procedure for this search is to fly along the known course from the last known position towards the intended destination and return on a parallel track at the sweep width distance to one side of the original track; then to return parallel to the original track on the other side, again at the sweep width distance.

Note: Green flares will be fired by the aircraft at each turning point and also if the legs are long, at intervals of approximately five minutes. If the aircraft sees a visual aid marking the vessel's, position several green flares will be fired in quick succession.

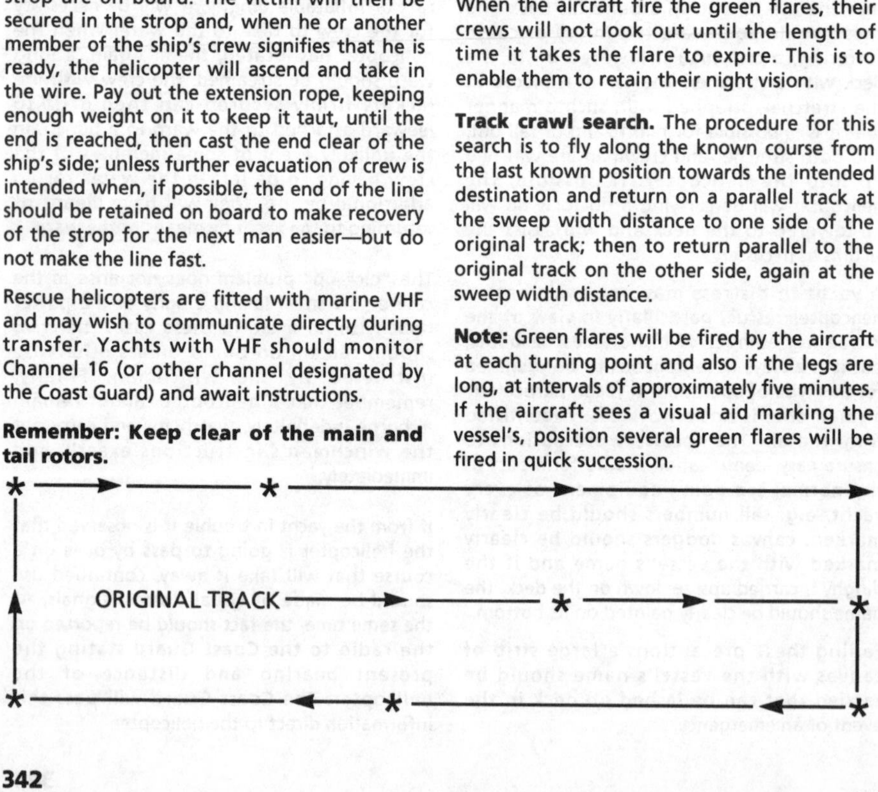

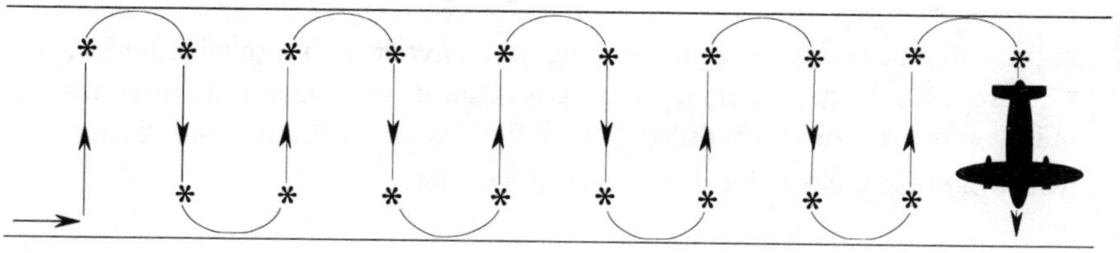

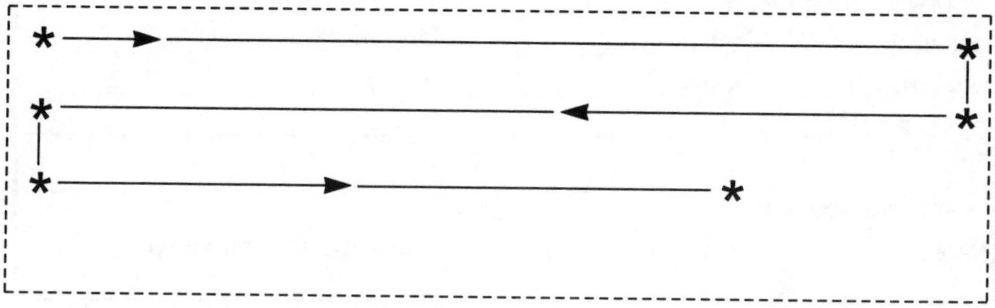

Creeping line ahead search. This procedure is used to search a rectangular area by a single aircraft. The aircraft proceeds to a corner of the search area and flying at the allotted height, sweeps the area, maintaining parallel tracks.

(a) The search area is long and narrow.

(b) The search based on a first priority of the track.

Note: Green flares will be fired by the aircraft at each turning point.

Parallel track search. This procedure is normally used when the search area is large and only the approximate location of the casualty is known. A uniform coverage is desired. The aircraft proceeds to a corner of the search area and flying at the allotted height, sweeps the area maintaining parallel tracks. Successive tracks are flown parallel to each other until the area is covered.

Note: Green flares will be fired along each leg at approximately five minute intervals and also at the turning points.

AIRCRAFT SIGNALS TO SURFACE ASSISTANCE

TO DIRECT VESSELS IN THE VICINITY OF A VESSEL IN DISTRESS TO THE ASSISTANCE OF THE DISTRESSED VESSEL, AIRCRAFT PERFORM THE FOLLOWING MANEUVERS IN SEQUENCE:

1. Aircraft circles the surface assistance at least once.

2. Aircraft crosses the surface assistance course close ahead at low altitude while rocking the wings, or opening and closing the throttle or changing the propeller pitch.

3. Aircraft leads in the direction in which the surface assistance is to be directed.

All three aircraft signals*
Aircraft is directing a surface vessel towards an aircraft or surface vessel in distress.

An aircraft crossing the surface vessel's wake close astern at low altitude while rocking the wings or opening and closing the throttle or changing propeller pitch means the assistance of the surface vessel is no longer required.

*(Repetition of signals have the same meaning.)

FLOAT PLANS

The U.S. Coast Guard no longer accepts float plans from private boaters. However, many marinas and yacht clubs would be happy to assist. At the very least, prudent boaters will inform a friend or relative of their travel plans. Make sure they have a description of your vessel and other information that will make identification easier should the need arise. Be sure to contact those concerned when you are unable to return at the specified time. A sample float plan follows on the next page.

FLOAT PLAN

Complete this page, before going boating and leave it with a reliable person who can be depended upon to notify the Coast Guard or other rescue organization, should you not return as scheduled. Do not file this plan with the Coast Guard.

1. NAME OF PERSON REPORTING AND TELEPHONE NUMBER.

2. DESCRIPTION OF BOAT. TYPE ______

COLOR ______ TRIM ______ REGISTRATION NO. ______

LENGTH ______ NAME ______ MAKE ______

OTHER INFO. ______

3. PERSONS ABOARD

NAME AGE ADDRESS & TELEPHONE NO

______

______

______

4. DO ANY OF THE PERSONS ABOARD HAVE A MEDICAL PROBLEM?

IF SO, WHAT? ______

5. ENGINE TYPE ______ H.P. ______

NO. OF ENGINES FUEL CAPACITY ______

6. SURVIVAL EQUIPMENT: (CHECK AS APPROPRIATE)

PFDS FLARES MIRROR SMOKE SIGNALS FLASHLIGHT FOOD

PADDLES WATER OTHERS ANCHOR RAFT OR DINGY EPIRB

7. RADIO YES/NO TYPE ______

FROM ______ GOING TO ______

EXPECT TO RETURN BY ______ (TIME) AND IN NO EVENT LATER THAN

9. ANY OTHER PERTINENT INFO.

10. AUTOMOBILE LICENSE

TYPE ______ TRAILER LICENSE ______

COLOR AND MAKE OF AUTO

WHERE PARKED ______

11. IF NOT RETURNED BY ______ (TIME) ______

CALL THE COAST GUARD, OR ______ (LOCAL AUTHORITY) ______

12. TELEPHONE NUMBERS ______

______

______

______

LLOYD'S SERVICES FOR OFFSHORE CRUISERS

REPORTING OF YACHTS WHILE OFFSHORE

Yachtsmen intending to undertake long distance voyages and wishing to keep their relatives or families informed of their whereabouts should signal to passing merchant vessels with the international code signal ZD2 (Please report me to Lloyds, London). Such yachts are invited to contact the Lloyd's Intelligence Department, telephone 0260 772277, 2410 in order that the necessary arrangements can be made. Charges are made for any expenses incurred such as telephone calls, postage etc.

In addition, those relatives or friends who feel concerned for the safety of a yacht on a long-distance passage are advised to contact the above number at any time of the day or night.

If the yacht is considered to be outside the British Coastguard area of responsibility Lloyd's will arrange for a general broadcast to shipping in the area or make inquiries of their agents along the vessel's route for later news. A person making an inquiry for an overdue yacht that is considered to be in the British Coastguard area of responsibility will either be given the telephone number of the appropriate Coastguard Liaison Station to contact or Lloyd's will pass the facts direct to that station.

REPORTING YOUR ARRIVAL

If only yachtsmen (and others who put to sea) communicated with their relatives ashore, if only relatives could give worthwhile information about the vessels and their proposed itineraries – such lapses are all too typical when the Coast Guard and others are asked to instigate inquiries.

ALWAYS REPORT ARRIVAL TO SOMEONE AFTER A PASSAGE. Also when delayed or stormbound always telephone details to relatives or business.

STATUTORY DUTIES OF MASTERS IN EMERGENCIES AND COLLISIONS

Under international law the master or person in charge of any vessel shall, so far as he can do so without serious danger to his own vessel, her crew and passengers (if any), render assistance to every person who is found at sea in danger of being lost. If he fails to do so, he is guilty of a midemeanour.

The master of a ship, on receiving at sea a distress signal or information from any source that a vessel or aircraft is in distress, must proceed with all speed to the assistance of the person in distress (informing them, if possible, that he is so doing), unless he is unable, or in the special circumstances of the case considers it unreasonable or unnecessary to do so, or unless he is released from this obligation under certain conditions. If the master of any ship in distress requisitions any ship that has answered his call, it is the duty of the Master of the requisitioned ship to comply with the requisition by continuing to proceed with all speed to the assistance of the persons in distress.

A master is released from the obligation to render assistance as soon as he is informed of the requisition of one or more ships other than his own and that the requisition is being complied with by the ship or ships requisitioned, or if he is informed by the Master of any ship that has reached the persons in distress that assistance is no longer required.

IN CASES OF COLLISION

In every case of collision between two vessels, it shall be the duty of the master or person in charge of each vessel, if and so far as he can do so without danger to his own vessel, crew, and passengers:

(a) to render to the other vessel, her master, crew and passengers such assistance as may be practicable, and may be necessary to save them from any danger caused by the collision, and to stay by the other vessel until he has ascertained that she has no need of further assistance, and also

(b) to give to the master or person in charge of the other vessel the name of his own vessel and of the port to which she belongs and also the names of the ports from which she comes and to which she is bound.

GMDSS – A NEW ERA OF SAFETY AT SEA

Advanced digital communications techniques are heralding a new era of safety for the mariner. These new technologies are making safety equipment easier to use and more affordable than before.

15

With the modern mobile satellite communications terminals that are now available, simply the press of a button alerts the nearest rescue coordination centre (RCC) instantly, wherever you are sailing in the world. Many of these communications systems weigh only a few pounds and can be fitted on even very small yachts.

Having such equipment on board not only helps you during an emergency but also ensures that you are in touch with people on shore however far you are from land and whatever the weather. The facilities available onboard range from data communications to direct-dial telephone, facsimile, telex, and electronic mail and live video and audio broadcasts.

A set of safety regulations is in force, specifying the equipment ships must carry for disaster communications. The regulations form part of the Global Maritime Distress and Safety System (GMDSS) that has been formulated by the International Maritime Organization. These regulations apply to all passenger ships and cargo vessels of 300 gross tonnage or more; ships have until February 1999 to comply with the rules.

What is GMDSS? GMDSS takes advantage of the major technical advances in modern radio and satellite communications. The basic concept of GMDSS is that not only ships in the vicinity of the emergency, but also search and rescue authorities on shore should be alerted instantly to an emergency at sea, so that a rescue operation may be launched without delay.

To achieve this, GMDSS mandates the use of automated communications equipment for rapid and reliable links with shore. In addition, GMDSS provides for the dissemination of maritime safety information warnings. Every ship will be able, irrespective of the area in which it operates, to perform the communications that are essential for the safety of not only the ship itself, but of other ships operating in the same area.

IMO has specified nine principal communications functions that need to be performed by all ships and the equipment that would meet these requirements, depending on the zones in which they operate. These functions are ship-to-shore, shore-to-ship, ship-to-ship distress alerting; search and rescue coordination communications; on-scene communications; transmitting and receiving position signals and maritime safety information; general radiocommunications; and bridge-to-bridge communications.

To specify the communications equipment that must be carried to perform these functions, GMDSS divides the seas into four different operating zones.

GMDSS Global Maritime Distress and Safety System

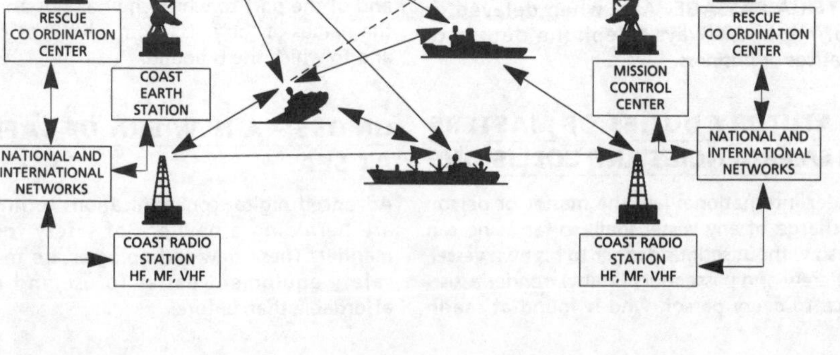

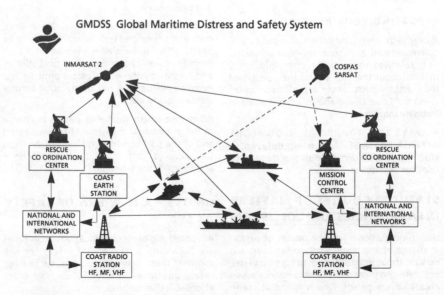

Sea Area A1: An area usually within 20-30 miles from land, within the range of shore-based VHF radio having digital selective calling (DSC) capability.

Sea Area A2: An area excluding A1 but within the range of shore-based MF radio (about 100 miles from shore), having DSC capability.

Sea Area A3: An area excluding A1 and A2 but within the range of services provided by the Inmarsat geostationary satellite system, which covers the whole globe except small areas of navigable water in the polar regions.

Sea Area A4: All other areas outside areas A1, A2, and A3.

GMDSS requires that distress alerts reach a rescue coordination center uncorrupted and without delay; the alerts should pinpoint the tragedy at sea, provide the identity of the ship in distress, the nature of the emergency, and other relevant information. Initiation of an alert should be automatic or by the push of a button.

Proven reliability of satcoms. The geostationary satellite system operated by Inmarsat, the 64-member-country cooperative based in London, offers the most reliable means of communication now available to mariners. It is available 24 hours a day, regardless of weather and atmospheric conditions, and offers clear communications links without fading and interference no matter how far the ship is from shore.

Inmarsat satellite terminals that provide access to the network require no special training to use. All of these terminals have a distress alert facility, often integrated with automatic message generators that give the vessels' position and other vital information.

Ships in distress can use the "Priority 3" channel on these terminals to guarantee automatic top priority over all other messages. No charge is made for use of Inmarsat space segment for:

Distress alerts;

Search and rescue coordination with associate RCCs, including communications subsequent to initial distress alerts relating to the immediate assistance required by a ship that is in grave and imminent danger;

Urgent navigational/meteorological danger reports;

Medical assistance for those caught on a ship in distress.

Added advantages: Inmarsat coverage provides the mariner with the security of trustworthy communications over virtually all of the world's navigable waters, with satellites positioned over four ocean-regions – the Indian, Pacific, and the Atlantic East and West Oceans – arranged to give duplicated, overlapping coverage for most of the world's major shipping areas.

In addition, the Inmarsat system now offers a new emergency position-indicating radio beacon (EPIRB) system, Inmarsat-E, that operates via its satellites. Until now, EPIRBs have been used to transmit distress signals only to the Cospas-Sarsat satellite system. In a distress situation, the free floating EPIRB, which is linked to the ship's electronics system, automatically transmits the ship's identification and position. These beacons can also be activated manually.

A typical transfer time between the activation of the alert and the reception at the nearest rescue coordination center is about 2 minutes.

Satellite communications via Inmarsat thus provide the best answer to GMDSS medium and long-range communications requirements, particularly in sea areas A2 and A3, and the availability of a reliable, round-the-clock communications system for other commercial applications is an added bonus. With an Inmarsat telephone, facsimile or data terminal, you can communicate with the world as you sail — receive electronic "newspapers", the results of the latest races, up-to-date stock market data — and make your journey more enjoyable, more productive and, definitely, safer.

First Aid

16

Page

MEDICAL ADVICE

In case of SERIOUS ILLNESS OR ACCIDENT AT SEA Masters of small vessels can get prompt medical advice by either:

1. RADI0 –Contact nearest shore station OR put out a call 'PAN PAN'

2. DIRECT SIGNALING to other vessels by:
   Flag "W" OR Morse "W" · – – } = I require medical assistance

The principles of first aid are to sustain life and prevent the condition from becoming worse until expert help is available.

ALWAYS KEEP CALM AND REASSURE THE PATIENT.

FIRST-AID BOX

The following suggestions apply to a vessel expecting to be at sea for not more than 72 hours. Dressings and drugs are preferably kept in separate plastic boxes with airtight lids.

DRESSINGS

Sterile nonadhesive dressings
Gauze packs
Cotton wool
Triangular bandage
Elastic bandage
Adhesive bandages
Transparent waterproof adhesive tape
Wound dressings, various sizes

OTHER ITEMS

Airway
Scissors
Assorted safety pins
Disposable syringe and needle (13 gauge)
Reflective blanket ("space" rescue blanket)
Clinical thermometer – Subnormal and normal.
Splinter tweezers

BASIC MEDICINE KIT

Seasickness pills
Pain relievers
Antacid tablets/liquid
Antidiarrhea Tablets
Laxative
Antiseptic cream/lotion
Multivitamins
Eye wash/drops

SUPPLEMENTARY KIT

Sunscreen
Waterproof adhesive plasters
Splints – various sizes
Foot cream/powder

HYPOTHERMIA—EXPOSURE

Cold is dangerous—most people who die following immersion in northern latitudes die from cold injury and not from drowning. Hypothermia is the medical name given to the condition that is often called "exposure".

TREATMENT OF SEVERE HYPOTHERMIA

IF ON RECOVERY FROM THE WATER A BODY FEELS ICE COLD:

1. If unconscious, open airway and check breathing. Complete the ABC of artificial respiration (described opposite) if necessary, and place in recovery position (see p. 6)
2. Remove the outer clothing, and replace any wet clothing with dry.
3. Place victim in sleeping bag, cover with blankets, etc.
4. Place a suitably covered hot-water bottle in left armpit or over breast bone to warm "core" circulation.
5. Give hot drinks and high energy food when conscious.

DO NOT place hot water bottles at extremities as this increases blood flow through the limbs and may result in a dangerous fall in "core temperature".

Note: Never presume that the casualty is dead simply because you cannot detect breathing or a pulse.

Note: It is best to rewarm a victim at the speed cooling took place. Therefore, a person immersed in the sea should be rewarmed rapidly.

PREVENTION OF HYPOTHERMIA

ON BOARD THE EFFECTS OF COLD ARE INSIDIOUS AND MAY AFFECT ANY CREW MEMBER. They are more likely to occur at night, and skippers should be aware of this risk if the temperature drops.

SYMPTOMS:

Victim's skin cold, pale and dry
Body temperature below 95°F
Slowing of physical and mental responses
Irritability or unreasonable behavior
Cramps or shivering
Loss of consciousness
Difficulties with speech or vision

NONE OF THESE WARNINGS SHOULD BE IGNORED

SHOCK

This medical condition accompanies severe injury and illness. The blood circulation fails because blood pressure or volume of blood is reduced, thus failing to supply sufficient oxygen to the vital organs. The condition may prove fatal.

SIGNS AND SYMPTOMS

Skin becomes pale, cold, and clammy.
Victim may feel weak, faint, or giddy.
Pulse is weak and rapid.
Breathing is shallow and fast.
Loss of consciousness is possible.

TREATMENT

1. Treat any serious injury.
2. Lay victim down, keeping head low and turning body to one side.
3. Raise legs, unless fracture of leg suspected. 4. Loosen tight clothing at neck, chest, and waist.
5. Shelter from extremes of temperature – cover with blanket if cold.
6. Monitor condition of pulse, breathing, consciousness.
7. Arrange urgent removal to hospital.

DO NOT give victim anything to eat or drink

DO NOT use hot water bottles.

RESUSCITATION

When a victim is not breathing and his heart is not beating, resuscitation efforts are vital. The general rule is the ABC of resuscitation:

A—Airway

B—Breathing

C—Circulation

AIRWAY

When a victim is unconscious the airway may be blocked or narrowed, making breathing noisy or impossible. Urgent action is needed to open the airway.

1. Lift the victim's chin forward with the index and middle fingers of one hand while pressing the forehead backwards with the other hand. The victim's jaw will lift the tongue forward, clear of the airway.
2. The victim may start to breathe; if so, place in the recovery position.
3. Place your ear above the victim's mouth and nose, look along chest to determine if breathing.
4. Clear the airway of any obstruction, such as food or vomit. Turn head to side, hook two fingers into mouth and sweep out any obstructions.
5. Check if victim is breathing; if so, place in the recovery position (p. 6).

BREATHING

Following checks of the airway, if the victim is found not to be breathing, undertake mouth-to-mouth resuscitation.

1. Open your mouth and take a deep breath, pinch casualty's nostrils with your fingers and support the jaw.
2. Seal your lips around the victim's mouth and blow into the lungs. Watch the chest rise.
3. If chest does not rise, check airway for obstruction.
4. Remove your mouth well away from casualty's and watch his chest fall. Take a deep breath and repeat inflation.
5. After two inflations, check the carotid pulse. If pulse is beating, continue giving inflations at a rate of 12-16 times per minute, until natural breathing is restored.
6. When natural breathing returns, place victim in the recovery position (p. 6).

CIRCULATION

Check the carotid pulse after the first two inflations of the lungs. If it is not present, external chest compression must be performed in conjunction with mouth-to-mouth resuscitation.

1. Lay the victim on his back on a firm surface. Kneel alongside him facing the chest, in line with the heart.
2. Find the junction of the rib margins at the bottom of the breastbone. Place the heel of one hand along the line of the breastbone, two fingers width above this point.
3. Cover this hand with the heel of the other hand and interlock fingers.
4 .Keep arms straight and press down vertically on the lower half of the breastbone.
5. Press down about 2 inches in the average adult, then release pressure. Complete 15 compressions at the rate of 80 compressions per minute.
6. Move to the patient's mouth and give two breaths of mouth-to-mouth resuscitation.
7. Continue with 15 compressions followed by two inflations.
8. Check the pulse after one minute; if pulse present then cease external chest compression, but continue mouth to mouth until breathing returns.
9. If no pulse present, continue with 15 compressions and two inflations. Check pulse every three minutes.

As soon as the pulse returns, stop compressions, but continue with mouth-to-mouth resuscitation until the breathing is restored. Place casualty in recovery position.

RESUSCITATION FOR CHILDREN

The method and rate varies slightly from the adult cycle shown above.

BABIES AND CHILDREN UNDER TWO – For mouth-to-mouth resuscitation, seal your lips around baby's mouth and nose. Gently puff into lungs about 20 breaths per minute.

– For external chest compression, use two fingers only, at rate of 100 times per minute, pressing about half to one inch.

CHILDREN – For mouth-to-mouth resuscitation, seal lips around mouth and nose, gently breathe at 20 times per minute.

– For external compression, use one hand only, pressing one to 1.5 inches at rate of 100 times per minute.

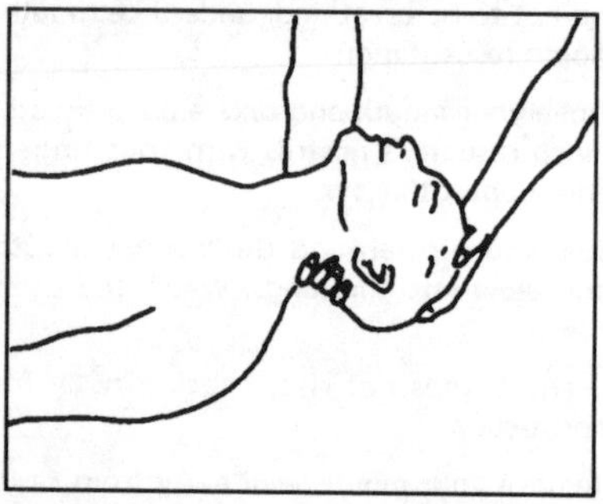

Neck is lifted

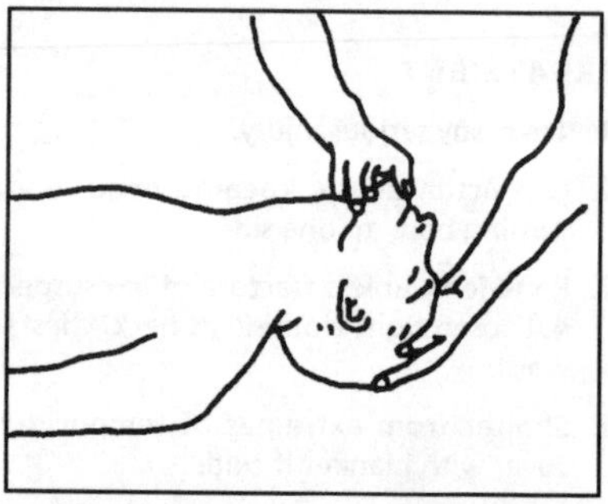

Head is tiled back

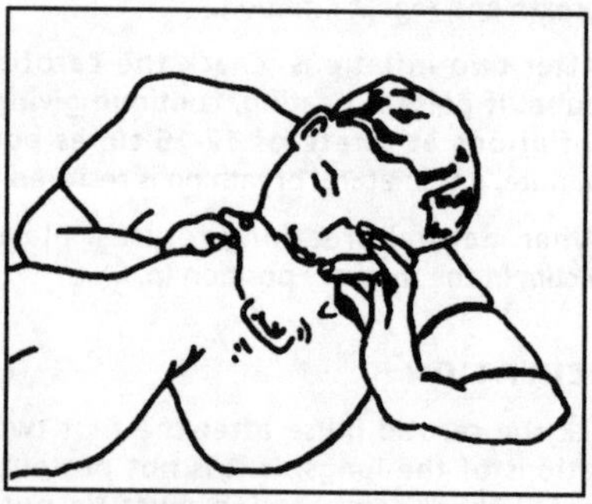

Lungs are inflated via nose or mouth
Chest should be seen to rise

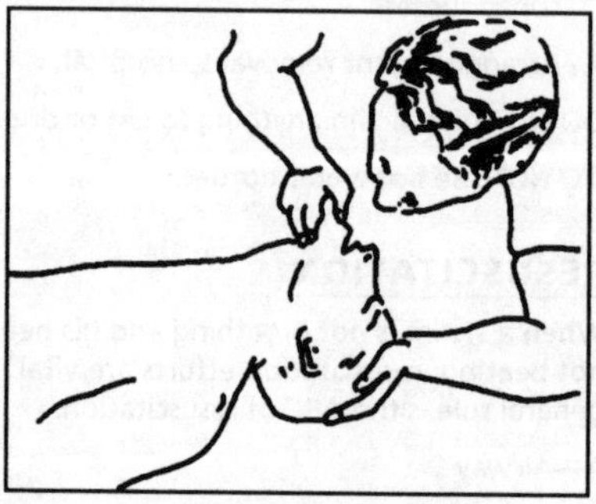

Victim exhales by himself, if necessary, through his mouth. Chest falls

Most people using this head-tilt oral method find in the excitement of the moment that it is not distasteful, but the few who are repulsed by the thought of physical contact with the patient can use a special mask or a simple device with a nylon mouthpiece and valve set in a small plastic sheet. Use of these devices should also reassure any persons worried about the risk of infection from direct mouth-to-mouth contact.

SEASICKNESS

Prevention is much better and easier than cure. Avoid large meals and alcohol before sailing. Keep warm at all times.

Anti-seasickness pills. Take early – at least 1 hour before sailing or at the first indication of deteriorating weather conditions. The best preparations contain Hyoscine in a dose up to 0.6 mgm. which in excess causes a dry mouth. Some people prefer antihistamines but they are more likely to cause drowsiness.Consult the pharmacist or your doctor for suggestions.

Sailors should experiment. Small doses repeated every few hours are often more effective than large doses and cause less side effects.

Start treatment while still feeling 100%. All treatments are much less effective after symptoms have appeared.

Responsibility of a job to do (e.g., taking the helm) will often prevent seasickness, and an observant skipper should consider this when a member of the crew becomes pale or unusually quiet.

Frequent small feeds of dry crackers, dry bread, hot soup, or other foods according to taste should be taken as appropriate with sips of water or tea.

Treatment. Prolonged sickness is dangerous. Mild attacks will respond slowly to the measures outlined above, but more severe attacks will require sedation (by injection if necessary).

Seasick crew should be kept warm in a bunk, if possible near fresh air, and given frequent sips of fluid when awake.

ANY PERSON VOMITING OVER THE SHIP'S SIDE MUST BE ATTACHED BY SAFETY HARNESS OR LINE.

ACCIDENTS

THE ATTENDANT MUST KEEP CALM AND CONSTANTLY REASSURE THE INJURED PERSON.

BURNS AND SCALDS

Principles. If clothing is alight, lay person down to prevent flames reaching facial area, and quench the flames with blanket or cold water. Continue cooling the damaged area for at least 10 minutes with fresh or salt water.

Remove only loose clothing from burnt area. Do not attempt to pull off clothing stuck to skin. Cover lightly with sterile dressing. Keep patient warm. If burns are severe, seek help.

Chemical burns. Remove affected clothing and wash with water. If acid burn, wash with diluted bicarbonate of soda if available. Dry and treat as above.

Electrical burns. Switch off the current. If this is impossible, stand on some dry insulating material such as wood or rubber and try to push the supply away from the patient or the patient's limbs away from the supply with a piece of wood. If the patient is not breathing, clear the airway and start artificial respiration and cardiac massage. Treat burn as above.

CUTS AND BLEEDING

A small quantity of blood can look excessive. Most bleeding can easily be controlled by direct pressure, and the majority of wounds will stop bleeding within 5 or 10 minutes. Apply pressure directly over the wound with a dressing, and bandage firmly. Keep the patient lying down but if possible ELEVATE THE BLEEDING PART. If blood continues to soak through the dressing add gauze pads and bandage firmly. Repeat if necessary. Do not remove the original bandage.

FRACTURES

A fracture is a broken or cracked bone.

Damage to the surrounding tissues and organs may outweigh the importance of the fracture itself.

Symptoms: Pain, Swelling, Deformity, Loss of power, Abnormal movement.

In case of doubt always treat the condition as a fracture.

Bleeding into the surrounding tissues may be severe. If there is excessive swelling do not bandage too tightly as this can stop the circulation to the rest of the limb.

Treatment. Gently correct any deformity if the skin is tightly stretched over the bone or if there is evidence that the circulation is impeded.

Splint the limb using a proper splint, by bandaging to the sound limb or to the trunk or support the limb in a comfortable position with cushions, rolled clothing, etc.

Loosen any clothing that might affect the circulation and watch for signs of constriction – e.g. if the hand or foot below the fracture becomes cold, blue, and swollen, loosen the bandage.

Keep the limb raised above chest height.

Open/Fracture. This is a severe injury in which part of a broken bone pierces the skin. The wound must be covered by a sterile dressing.

If a patient sustains a fracture when in an inaccessible position, it is often better to let him move out of it under his own power if he can.

Once the legs are bandaged together movement of the patient may be very difficult.

SPRAINS

A sprain occurs when the ligaments supporting a joint are damaged, usually by a twist injury of the ankle, wrist, or knee.

Treatment. Apply a pressure bandage by wrapping the joint and the area above and below in a good layer of cotton wool and then bandage firmly, preferably with an elastic bandage. If an arm joint is sprained, support the arm in a sling.

IF IN DOUBT TREAT AS A FRACTURE.

HEAD INJURY

Keep the patient flat and quiet in his bunk if possible. Scalp wounds bleed profusely. Wash with plenty of water and then apply prolonged pressure with a sterile dressing covered by gauze.

Loss of consciousness following a blow on the head suggests concussion. Vomiting or increasing drowsiness are serious signs. Ensure complete rest in the recovery position shown overleaf until seen by a doctor.

Blood or straw-colored fluid seeping from the ear or nose may indicate a fractured skull. Place patient in recovery position with leaking side down to allow fluid to escape. Do not bandage or plug, which could cause a build-up in the skull and pressure on the brain. Immobilize and maintain a check on patient's breathing.

WARNING

If a spinal injury is suspected do NOT place patient in recovery position. Use an airway to maintain respiration and as a means of giving mouth-to-mouth resuscitation. Warn patient to lie still. Soft, solid items such as luggage or padded objects can be placed to prevent movement of head or body.

SYMPTOMS SUGGESTING SERIOUS ILLNESS

Medical help is required urgently in the following situations:

CONTINUOUS SEVERE PAIN IN THE CENTER OF THE CHEST

This suggests a heart attack. The patient should be rested and propped up in his bunk with three or four pillows.

CONTINUOUS SEVERE PAIN IN THE ABDOMEN

If associated with vomiting and shock, this suggests a serious internal disorder such as a perforated bowel. Lay the patient down flat, if acceptable, or with one pillow if more comfortable. Give nothing by mouth. A pillow under the knees may help.

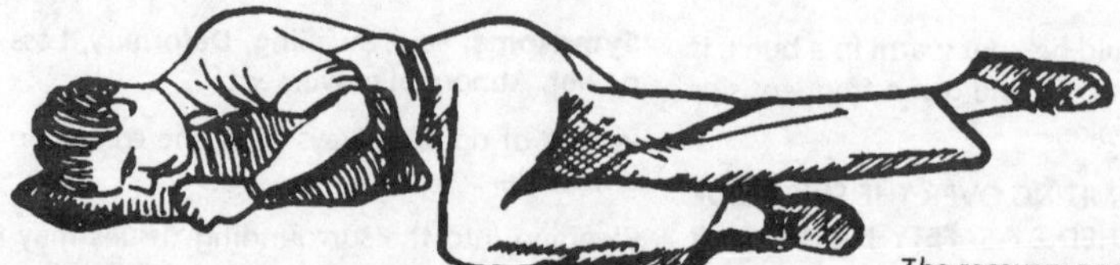

The recovery position.

SICKNESS, PALLOR, SWEATING, AND RAPID BREATHING

This suggests internal bleeding. Confirmation of this may come from the patient vomiting blood or passing black movements. Keep him lying flat with no pillow and as quiet and comfortable as possible.

LOSS OF CONSCIOUSNESS—COMA

This has many causes but is always serious. MAINTAIN A CLEAR AIRWAY.

Treatment. Remove dentures.

Clear the back of the mouth and throat with the finger and wipe away any liquid that has accumulated.

If the patient is not breathing, start artificial respiration.

Once satisfied with the patient's breathing, turn him onto his side with his uppermost knee drawn up to a right angle – the recovery position.

Keep patient's mouth downwards so that any liquid can run out. Loosen all clothing and keep him warm. Give nothing by mouth. Someone should remain with patient to ensure the airway remains clear.

OTHER EMERGENCIES

HEATSTROKE

This is due to high temperature and high humidity.

The patient may collapse suddenly with a high temperaturem – 106°F (41°C) or more, or appear confused and complain of headache or dizziness.

Treatment. Strip the patient. Cover him with sheets or towels soaked in cold water and keep them wet and cold till the patient's temperature is 102°F (39°C). Open all boat ventilators. Cool as rapidly as possible.

FITS, EPILEPSY

Try to prevent the patient from injuring himself. Keep him horizontal.

After the attack, keep him quiet and resting for a few hours.

FAINTING

With the patient sitting, hold his head between his knees, or lay him down and raise legs.

In either case, loosen tight clothing and ensure he can breathe.

NOSE BLEEDS

Sit victim with head well forward.

Have him breathe through his mouth; then pinch soft part of nose.

Bleeding should cease within 10 minutes; if not, continue pressure.

If bleeding persists, seek medical aid.

FOREIGN BODIES IN THE EYE

If the foreign body can be seen beneath the lower lids it can be removed with the moistened corner of a handkerchief. This can also be tried if it can be seen on the white of the eye.

Do not remove anything that adheres to the clear part of the eye.

If the foreign body cannot be seen, it is probably under the top lid.

In this case pulling the top lid over the bottom lid may cause the bottom lashes to sweep it clear.

The patient may try opening and closing his eye with his face in a bowl of clean water.

Should the eye be burned with splashes of caustic chemicals:

Lay the patient down.

Open the eye with your finger.

Wash the eye with large amounts of clean tepid water.

WEIL'S DISEASE – LEPTOSPIROSIS

This is caught through contact with water infected by animal urine. All those using inland waterways are potentially at risk, since the disease can exist on wet vegetation and enters through cuts, grazes, and the mucous membranes of the mouth, nose, and eyes. Take the following simple precautions:

1) Cover any cuts or grazes with waterproof dressings BEFORE sailing.
2) If skin injury occurs during contact with untreated water, wash with clean water, treat with antiseptic, and cover.
3) Avoid immersion and swallowing of untreated water.

4) After water activity, wash hands thoroughly (or shower if immersed) before eating, drinking or smoking.

First symptoms can be confused with flu, – e.g., fever and pain in joints or muscles. If you develop these symptoms after spending time in or by water, tell your doctor immediately. Antibiotics are effective in the early stages of infection, but if left, more serious problems develop.

EMERGENCY CHILDBIRTH

Send for medical aid. If aid is not available, keep calm, and let nature take its course.

Labor may begin with:

1. Backache and regular pains in the abdomen;
2. A "show" of blood-stained mucus; or
3. A gush of water from the birth canal.

Reassure the mother. Get a basket or drawer and blanket ready for baby.

Boil a pair of scissors and three pieces of string about nine inches long for about 15 minutes. These are to cut and tie the cord. Prepare a bed for the mother by covering the mattress with a plastic sheet or newspapers, then a clean sheet. Have a supply of hot water, jugs, and basins available.

Scrub your hands thoroughly and keep crew members with any infection well away.

The first stage of labor, during which the neck of the womb opens, usually lasts several hours. The abdominal pains are usually every 15 to 20 minutes, becoming more frequent as labor progresses.

In the second stage the baby's head descends the birth canal; it may be preceded by a gush of water.

Turn the mother onto her side with her knees drawn up, and cover the top half of her body with a blanket to keep her warm. Encourage her to relax as much as possible when the pains occur. Should a bowel movement appear, wipe it away and wipe the birth canal.

The baby's head will appear, more of it becoming visible with each contraction. At this stage, ask the mother not to bear down, but to try to relax and breathe through her mouth.

Once the baby's head is born, support it with one hand and gently feel if the cord is wrapped around the baby's neck. If it is, ease it gently over the baby's head or shoulders. If a membrane is over the face, remove it.

Do not pull on the baby or the cord. The shoulders are usually born with the next pain; then gently lift baby under its armpits, towards the mother's abdomen.

Immediately attend to the baby's breathing. Hold it upside down, supporting it by the ankles and shoulders. It is slippery so preferably wrap a cloth around the ankles. Wipe the mouth out with a clean handkerchief over your little finger. If the baby does not cry, begin gentle artificial respiration.

When the baby cries, lay it down against its mother's legs, with the head down, to allow any fluid to drain from the mouth.

If there is excessive bleeding, massaging of the lower abdomen will often stimulate the womb to contract.

The afterbirth will be expelled with a pain in about 5 to 15 minutes. Then tie the cord, or tie it if the afterbirth has not been expelled in 15 minutes. Tie one boiled piece of string tightly and firmly about six inches, and the second piece of string about eight inches, from the baby's navel.

Cut the cord between the ligatures. Cover the baby's end of the cord with a sterile dressing and do not apply any antiseptics, etc., to the cord.

Wrap the baby lightly in a blanket and place it in the temporary cot. Inspect the cord for bleeding 10 minutes later, and, if bleeding is suspected, tie another piece of boiled string an inch below the first one.

If the afterbirth has not been expelled, cover the mother's end of the cord with a sterile dressing. Keep the afterbirth for the doctor to inspect.

Wash the mother. Replace the sheets and newspapers with dry ones. Give the mother a hot drink and cookies, and then encourage her to sleep.

SEA SIGNALLING

17

INTERNATIONAL CODE OF SIGNALS

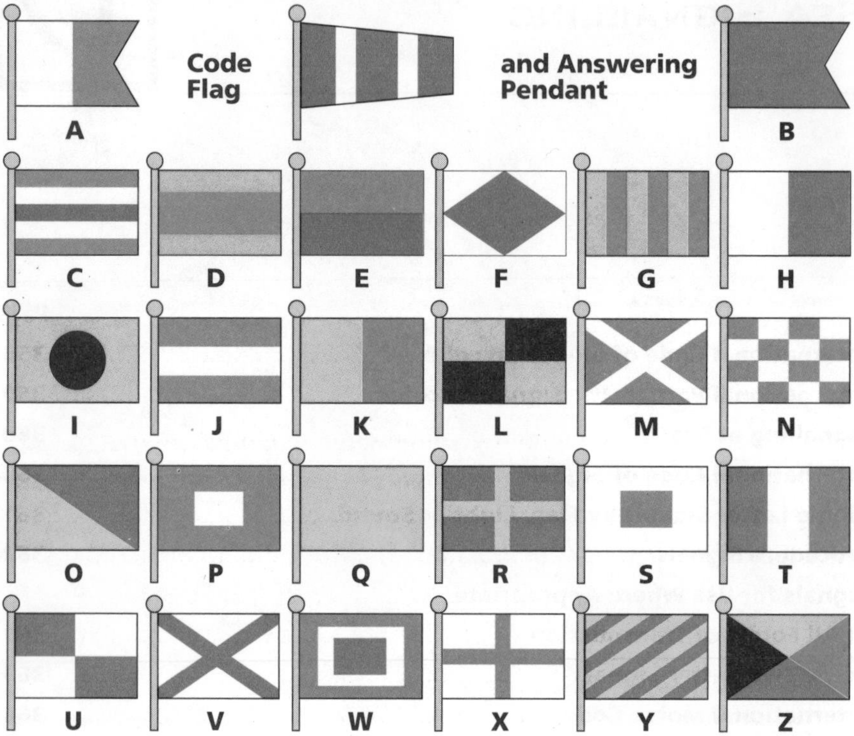

Numeral Pendants

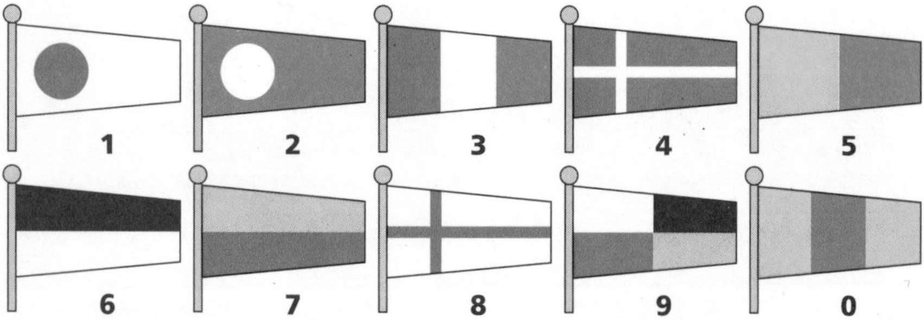

Substitutes

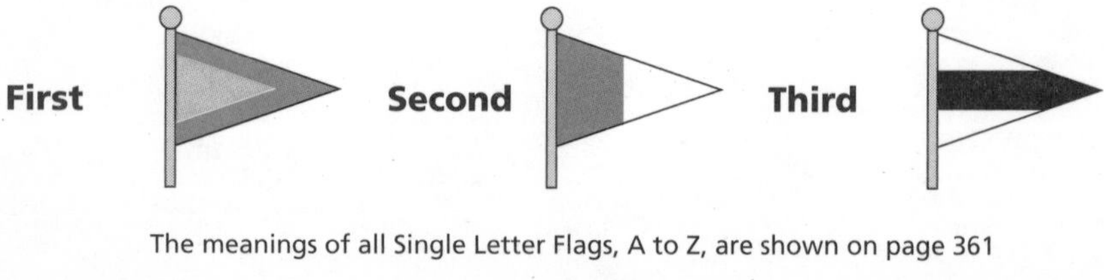

The meanings of all Single Letter Flags, A to Z, are shown on page 361

INTERNATIONAL PORT TRAFFIC SIGNALS

(to be introduced worldwide as circumstances permit)

MAIN MESSAGE

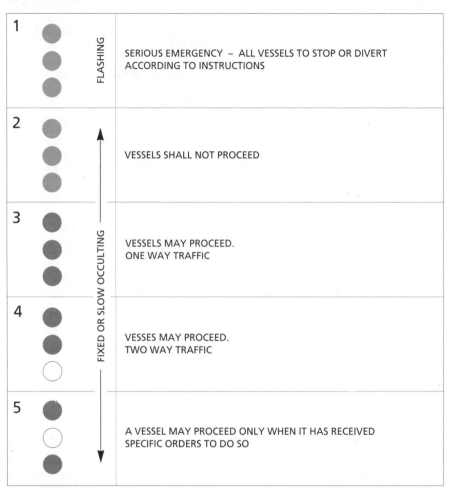

1		FLASHING	SERIOUS EMERGENCY – ALL VESSELS TO STOP OR DIVERT ACCORDING TO INSTRUCTIONS
2		FIXED OR SLOW OCCULTING	VESSELS SHALL NOT PROCEED
3		FIXED OR SLOW OCCULTING	VESSELS MAY PROCEED. ONE WAY TRAFFIC
4		FIXED OR SLOW OCCULTING	VESSES MAY PROCEED. TWO WAY TRAFFIC
5		FIXED OR SLOW OCCULTING	A VESSEL MAY PROCEED ONLY WHEN IT HAS RECEIVED SPECIFIC ORDERS TO DO SO

EXEMPTION SIGNALS AND MESSAGES

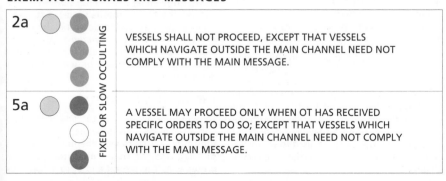

2a	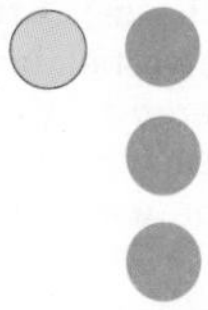	FIXED OR SLOW OCCULTING	VESSELS SHALL NOT PROCEED, EXCEPT THAT VESSELS WHICH NAVIGATE OUTSIDE THE MAIN CHANNEL NEED NOT COMPLY WITH THE MAIN MESSAGE.
5a	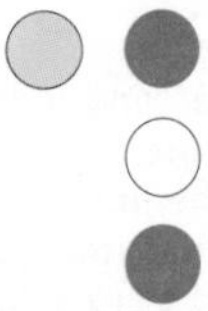	FIXED OR SLOW OCCULTING	A VESSEL MAY PROCEED ONLY WHEN OT HAS RECEIVED SPECIFIC ORDERS TO DO SO; EXCEPT THAT VESSELS WHICH NAVIGATE OUTSIDE THE MAIN CHANNEL NEED NOT COMPLY WITH THE MAIN MESSAGE.

SIGNALLING AT SEA

Signalling at sea in all large vessels is normally carried on by radio, and only when signalling to vessels nearby, or to small vessels, would other means be employed.

Though many small vessels carry VHF radio, the set may be out of order, or special circumstances may warrant the use of visual signalling.

Vessels in sight or hearing of one another may use Sound Signals, Code Flags or Flashing.

DISTRESS SIGNALS BY VESSELS AT SEA

Hardly a day goes by without the ever watchful Coast Guard, or another vessel, sighting a genuine distress signal. Without this signal being given, many vessels would not be rescued, and lives lost needlessly. All seagoing personnel in charge of vessels of every size must know what these signals are, and how to use them. See Chapter 15, Distress and Rescue, for information on distress signals.

CODE FLAGS

All signals are given in one, two or three letter hoists. The International Code of Signals (Pub. 102 from the DMA) is published in the nine most commonly used languages to facilitate communication between crews of different nations. As all urgent or important signals are now made with one or two flags, it is practical for small vessels to carry a few flags for essential distress messages.

FLASHING

Signalling by flashing is carried out by using Morse Code (which is also International). It is necessary to learn the dot-dash sequences and their meanings, and to practice sending and receiving, to be able to talk to any other vessel, up to several miles distant, either day or night. Proficiency at Morse Code is also required for certain Ham, or amateur radio, licenses. Several companies produce practice tapes and flash cards designed to improve your learning curve.

A signalling lamp (also known as the Aldis lamp) is needed for proper Morse Code signalling. It is portable and designed to run on 12 volts. Few pleasure boats carry these items today, so you may have to rely on your boats spotlight, or even a flashlight. Lights are produced with the capability of sending a Mayday signal (SOS) automatically. These may be used to satisfy the Coast Guard distress signal requirement (see Chapter 15).

Aldis lamps are normally held in the crook of the arm and pointed in the desired direction by moving the operator's entire body. Sights are attached to ensure you are pointing the light directly at the target. The usual range is several miles, both day and night. These lamps are very useful for rescue purposes, and even as an ordinary spotlight.

INTERNATIONAL CODE OF SIGNALS

A VESSEL'S IDENTITY

It is often necessary, to inform other vessels of your vessel's name and nationality,for identification purposes.The Ensign ordinarily indicates the nationality of the signalling vessel, but in addition, most registered vessels, warships, and certain other vessels are allotted a combination signal of four flags, the top flag or flags indicating their nationality. For example in British vessels the top flag is either G,M,or 2, in the Netherlands P, in Germany D, while in vessels of the United States of America the top flag is either A, K, N or W. The four flags are always kept bent together on the Bridge for instant use and are known as the vessel's "number". The same four letters or numbers are also the vessel's radio call sign.

THE CODE FLAG AND ANSWERING PENNANT (OR PENDANT)

Known as Code Flag, when flown singly – indicates International Code being used. When used to answer hoists of flags from another vessel it is termed the Answering Pennant.

When any flag hoist is sighted, the Answering Pennant should be hoisted immediately at the "dip" (about half-way up the halliards) and when the Code Book has been consulted and the Signal thoroughly understood, the Answering Pennant is at once hoisted "close up" (at the top of the halliards). After the other vessel has hauled down her hoist the Answering Pennant is lowered to the "dip" again to await another hoist from the other signalling vessel. It may be used also as a decimal point.

THE THREE SUBSTITUTES

To avoid the necessity of carrying more than one set of Flags, Substitutes are used. The first substitute always repeats the uppermost flag of that class of flag which immediately precedes it. The second and third substitutes similarly repeat the second or third flag of that class of flags which immediately precede them. No substitute can be used more than once in a hoist

Example. Longitude 11°11′ = G Numeral 1 first substitute; second substitute; third substitute. Example. MTT = MT second substitute.

SINGLE-LETTER SIGNALS WITH COMPLEMENTS

A (with three numerals)	– AZIMUTH or BEARING
C (with three numerals)	– COURSE
D (with two, four or six numerals)	– DATE
G (with four or five numerals)	– LONGITUDE (last two mins, rest deg.)
K (with one numeral)	– I wish to COMMUNICATE by (Semaphore)
L (with four numerals)	– LATITUDE (first two., deg., rest mins.)
R (with one or more numerals)	– DISTANCE in nautical miles.
S (with one or more numerals)	– SPEED in knots.
T (with four numerals)	– LOCAL TIME (first two hours, rest minutes)
V (with one or more numerals)	– SPEED in kilometers per hour.
Z (with four numerals)	– GMT (first two hours, rest mins.

SINGLE LETTER SIGNALS BY FLAG, LIGHT, OR SOUND

The most important Code signals of all – the single letter signals – consist of Very Urgent signals or those in common use. Seamen should know these by heart, so that there may be no hesitation in acting on them.

The following may be made by any method of signalling, but those marked (*) when made by sound may only be made in compliance with the International Regulations for Preventing Collisions at Sea, Rules 34 and 35.

A • —	I have a diver down; keep well clear at slow speed.
*B — • • •	I am taking in, or discharging, or carrying dangerous goods.
*C — • — •	Yes, affirmative or "The significance of the previous group should be read in the affirmative."
*D — • •	Keep clear of me – I am maneuvering with difficulty.
*E •	I am altering my course to starboard.
F • • — •	I am disabled. Communicate with me.
*G — — •	I require a Pilot. When made by fishing vessels operating in close proximity on the fishing grounds it means: "I am hauling nets."
*H• • • •	I have a Pilot on board.
*I • •	I am altering my course to port.
J • — — —	I am on fire and have a dangerous cargo on board: keep well clear of me
†K — • —	I wish to communicate with you.
L • — • •	You should stop your vessel instantly.
*M — —	My vessel is stopped and making no way through the water.
N — •	No, negative or "The significance of the previous group should be read in the negative." This signal may be given only visually or by sound. For voice or radio transmission the signal should be"No."
O — — —	Man overboard.
P • — — •	In harbor (Blue Peter) hoisted at the foremast head. "All persons should report on board as the vessel is about to proceed to sea. "At sea.It may be used by fishing vessels to mean "my nets have come fast upon an obstruction. "It may also be used as a sound signal to mean "I require a pilot"

Q	– – • –	My vessel is healthy and I request free pratique.
‡R	• – •	
†*S	• • •	I am operating astern propulsion.
*T	–	Keep clear of me I am engaged in pair trawling.
U	• • –	You are running into danger.
V	• • • –	I require assistance.
W	• – –	I require medical assistance.
X	– • • –	Stop carrying out your intentions and watch for my signals.
Y	– • – –	I am dragging my anchor.
*Z	– – • •	I require a tug. When made by fishing vessels operating in close proximity on the fishing grounds it means: "I am shooting nets."

1 • – – – –	6 – • • • •
2 • • – – –	7 – – • • •
3 • • • – –	8 – – – • •
4 • • • • –	9 – – – – •
5 • • • • •	0 – – – – –

†Signals "K" and "S" have special meanings as landing signals for small boats with crews or persons in distress. ‡Single letter Signal R has so far not been allocated a Signal meaning as this already has a meaning in Rule 35 of the Collision Regulations.

PROCEDURE SIGNALS

A bar over the letters composing a signal denotes that the letters are to be made as one symbol.

SIGNALS FOR VOICE TRANSMISSION

Signal	*Pronounced as*	*Meaning*
Interco Code follow(s)	IN-TER-CO	International group(s)
Stop	STOP	Full Stop.
Decimal	DAY-SEE-MAL	Decimal point.
Correction	KOR-REK-SHUN	Cancel my last word or group. The correct word or group follows.

SIGNALS FOR FLASHING-LIGHT TRANSMISSION

AA AA AA etc.	Call for unknown station or general call.
EEEE etc.	Erase signal.
AAA	Full stop or decimal point.
TTTT etc	Answering signal.
T	Word or group received.

SIGNALS FOR FLAGS, RADIO-TELEPHONY AND RADIO-TELEGRAPHY TRANSMISSIONS.

CQ	Call for unknown station(s) or general call to all stations

When this signal is used in voice transmission, it should be pronounced in accordance with the letter-spelling table.

SIGNALS FOR USE WHERE APPROPRIATE IN ALL FORMS OF TRANSMISSION.

AA	"All after ..." (used after the "Repeat signal" (RPT) means "Repeat all after...".
AB	"All before ..." (used after the "Repeat signal" (RPT) means "Repeat all before ..."
AR	Ending signal or End of Transmission or signal.
AS	Waiting signal or period
BN	"All between ... and ..." (used after the "Repeat signal" (RPT)) means "Repeat all between ... and ...".
C	Affirmative – YES or "The significance of the previous group should be read in the affirmative".
CS	"What is the name or identity signal of your vessel (or station)?"
DE	"From ..." (used to precede the name or identity signal of the calling station).
K	"I wish to communicate with you" or "Invitation to transmit".
NO	Negative –NO or "The significance of the previous group should be read in the negative". When used in voice transmission the pronunciation should be "NO".

OK Acknowledging a correct repetition or "It is correct:"

RQ Interrogative, or, "The significance of the previous group should be read as a question".

R "Received" or "I have received your last signal".

RPT Repeat signal "I repeat" or "Repeat what you have sent" or "Repeat what you have received".

WA "Word or group after ..." (used after the "Repeat signal" (RPT) means "Repeat word or group after ... ".

WB "Word or group before ..." (used after the "Repeat signal" (RPT) means "Repeat word or group before .... ".

The procedure signals "C", "NO" and "RQ" cannot be used in conjunction with single letter signals.

SOME TWO LETTER SIGNALS

AC	I am abandoning my vessel.
AN	I need a doctor.
AQ	I have injured/sick person (or number of persons indicated)) to be taken off urgently.
CB	I require immediate assistance.
CK	Assistance is not (or is no longer) required by me (or vessel indicated).
CP	I am (or vessel indicated is) proceeding to your assistance.
DV	I am drifting.
DX	I am sinking (lat...long...if necessary).
ED	Your distress signals are understood.
EL	Repeat the distress position.
FA	Will you give me my position?
FO	I will keep close to you.
GW	Man overboard. Please take action to pick him up (position to be indicated if necessary).
IL	I can only proceed at slow speed.
IT	I am on fire.
JG	I am aground; I am in dangerous situation.

SOME TWO LETTER SIGNALS – Cont.

JH	I am aground; I am not in danger.
JW	I have sprung a leak.
KJ	I am towing a submerged object.
KM	I can take you (or vessel indicated) in tow.
KQ	Prepare to be taken in tow.
KT1	I am sending a towing hawser.
LBI	Towing hawser is fast to chain cable.
NC	I am in distress and require immediate assistance.
NF	You are running into danger.
NG	You are in a dangerous position.
OQ	I am calibrating radio direction finder or adjusting compasses.
PN	You should keep to leeward of me (or vessel indicated).
PP	Keep well clear of me.
QD	I am going ahead.
QI	I am going astern.
QQ	I require health clearance.
QU	Anchoring is prohibited.
RB	I am dragging my anchor.
RU	Keep clear of me. I am maneuvering with difficulty.
TP	Fishing gear has fouled my propeller.
UW	I wish you a pleasant voyage.
UY	I am carrying out exercises – keep clear of me.
XP	I am stopped in thick fog.
YG	You appear not to be complying with the traffic separation scheme.
ZD1	Please report me to Coast Guard New York.
ZD2	Please report me to Lloyds London.
ZM	You should send (or speak) more slowly.
ZS	My vessel is healthy and I request free pratique.
ZV	I believe I have been in an infected area during the last 30 days.
ZW	I require Port Medical Officer.

17

INTERNATIONAL MORSE CODE

Letter	Character	Letter	Character
A	· –	N	– ·
B	– · · ·	O	– – –
C	– · – ·	P	· – – ·
D	– · ·	Q	– – · –
E	·	R	· – ·
F	· · – ·	S	· · ·
G	– – ·	T	–
H	· · · ·	U	· · –
I	· ·	V	· · · –
J	· – – –	W	· – –
K	– · –	X	– · · –
L	· – · ·	Y	– · – –
M	– –	Z	– – · ·
Num'l	**Character**	**Num'l**	**Character**
1	· – – – –	6	– · · · ·
2	· · – – –	7	– – · · ·
3	· · · – –	8	– – – · ·
4	· · · · –	9	– – – – ·
5	· · · · ·	0	– – – – –

Ä (German) = AE (Danish) · – · –
Á or Å (Spanish or Scandinavian) · – – · –
Ch (German or Scandinavian) – – – –
É (French) · · – · ·
Ñ (Spanish) – – · – –
Ö (German) = Ø (Danish) – – – ·
Ü (German) · · – –

IMPORTANT SOUND SIGNALS

Although signalling between vessels may be carried out by whistle or siren using the Morse Code, it is a slow method, and unless in open waters should never be resorted to. Confusion as to any Sound Signals given or its misinterpretation can have most disastrous results, so Sound Signals should be used with the utmost discretion.

On the other hand they should be used decisively and correctly whenever they are required by the Collision Regulations or when the circumstances of the occasion require. The following Sound Signals occur in ordinary Navigation:

FOG SIGNALS BY LIGHTHOUSES, LIGHT VESSELS, BUOYS, ETC.

These cannot of course be memorized – except by Pilots in their own Pilotage area – but should be consulted as required in the annual edition.

SOUND SIGNALS BY YOUR OWN AND OTHER VESSELS IN FOG OR THICK WEATHER

These must be known instinctively as described in the Collision Regulations, Rule 35.

SOUND SIGNALS BY VESSELS MANEUVERING

These are not given in fog, but must be used by vessels maneuvering in sight of other vessels, so must be known without hesitation. See the Collision Regulations, Rule 34.

Note carefully the provision under Rule 34 of the "in doubt " or "wake up" signal of five or more short and rapid blasts.

DISTRESS SIGNALS

Shown fully in Annex IV of the Collision Regulations.

PILOT SIGNALS IN FOG

Pilot vessels waiting to put the Pilot on board sounds four short blasts (· · · ·) as prescribed by Rule 35 of the Collision Regulations.

RIVER APPROACH SIGNAL

A prolonged warning blast by a vessel approaching a bend in a river as described in Rule 9 of the Collision Regulations.

FOG CLOSE QUARTERS WARNING SIGNAL

"R" (· – ·), made by sound signal only, may be used by a vessel at anchor in fog to give warning of her position to an approaching vessel. This signal would be made in addition to her normal sound signal. See Rule 35.

"U" DANGER WARNING SIGNAL

"U" (· · –) should never be neglected – many vessels "standing" towards a sandbank or rocky coast have been saved from disaster by the vigilance of others.

SIGNAL FOR VESSEL TURNING

Although not contained in the Collision Regulations it is the "ordinary practice of seamen" in crowded waterways – to use a special signal for "turning" (either when turning completely round or simply turning athwart the channel) of – four short blasts followed after a very short interval by one short blast if turning to Starboard or two short blasts if turning to Port.

KEEP CLEAR OF ME – I AM MANEUVERING WITH DIFFICULTY

The Sound Signal D (– • •) "keep clear of me – Iam maneuvreing with difficulty" – is a single letter Code Signal, which should be used if necessary in crowded waters.

INTERNATIONAL DIVING FLAG

The International Code Flag A means:

"I HAVE A DIVER DOWN; KEEP WELL CLEAR AT SLOW SPEED"

In the United States, divers commonly show a red flag with a diagonal white stripe. The meaning of this flag is the same as International Code Flag A. The diving flag is frequently seen attached to a float, which in turn is attached to the diver by a tether. As the diver moves below the surface, the warning flag follows along. Unfortunately, this can give the diver a false sense of security – showing the diving flag does not relieve the diver of the responsibility of staying clear of channels and navigation aids. The dive flag should not be flown on a permanent basis, as is seen aboard some dive boats. The flag should only be used when divers are actually in the water.

With the increasing number of underwater swimmers, and diving parties operating along the coasts, and in the harbors, boaters are urged to keep well clear whenever they see the diving flag. Give any vessels flying this flag a very wide berth, and proceed at slow speed. Keep in mind the possibility of floating tethers, lifelines and other temporary obstructions in the vicinity of any divers. Divers near channels should have an observer stationed aboard the dive boat. Mariners are urged to contact the observer if in any doubt as to the location of dive operations.

Flags and Flag Etiquette

18

SOME ENSIGNS AND FLAGS OF THE WORLD

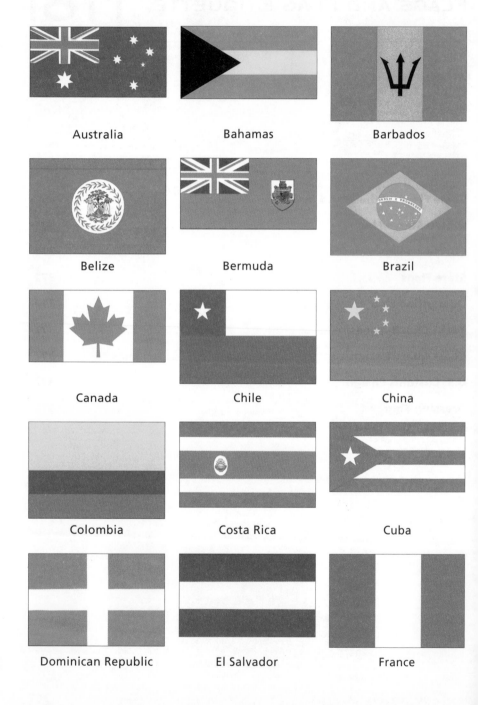

Australia

Bahamas

Barbados

Belize

Bermuda

Brazil

Canada

Chile

China

Colombia

Costa Rica

Cuba

Dominican Republic

El Salvador

France

Germany

Greece

Grenada

Guatemala

Haiti

Honduras

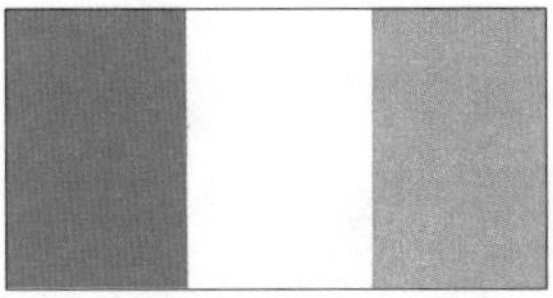

Ireland

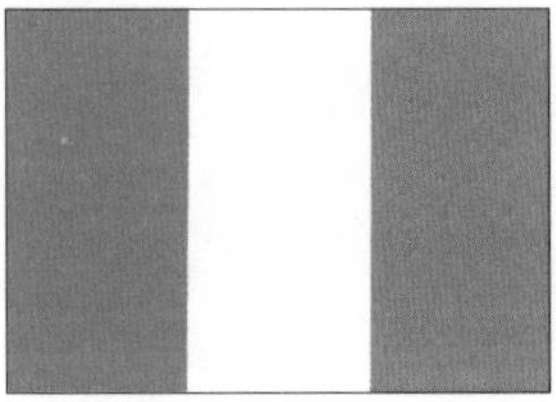

Italy

Jamaica

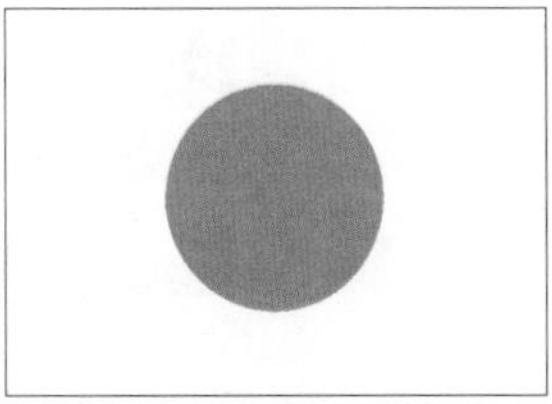

Japan

Liberia

Mexico

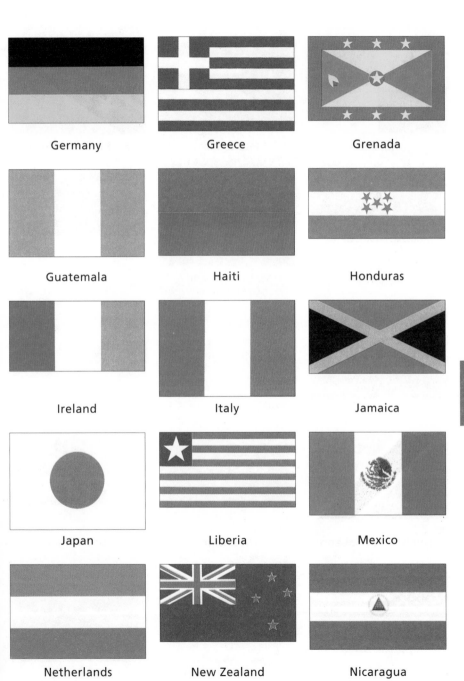

Netherlands

New Zealand

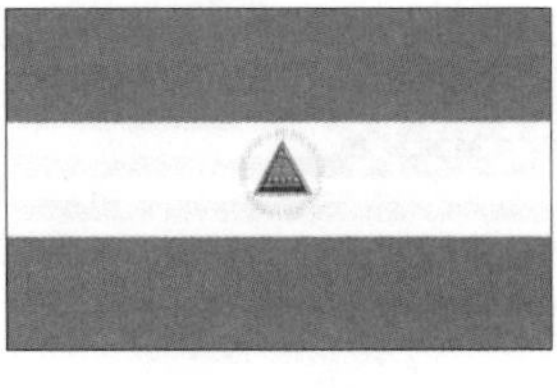

Nicaragua

Panama

Puerto Rico

St. Kitts and Nevis

St. Lucia

St. Vincent and Grenadines

Samoa

Spain

Sweden

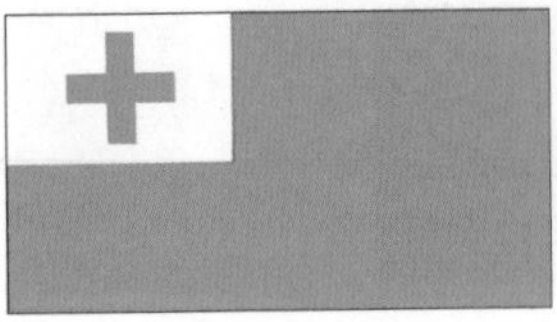

Tonga

Trinidad and Tobago

UK Ensign

United Kingdom

USA

US Virgin Islands

Venezuela

UNITED STATES FLAG

The United States flag is also the United States ensign for use aboard boats of all sizes. This is the same flag as flown ashore. It should normally be flown from a staff at the stern of both power and sail boats. Some power vessels have a mast with a gaff, which is the proper location for the flag. Gaff rigged sailboats may also fly the flag from the aftermost gaff on the boat. Sailboats without a gaff sometimes fly the flag from the leech of the aftermost sail, about 1/3 of the way from the top. Of course this means the flag will be doused when the sail comes down. In this case it is proper to fly the flag from the stern staff while not underway. Some sailboats fly the flag from a backstay in the same manner as a stern staff. You can also fly the flag 1/3 of the distance from the top of the mast as you would a flag attached to the sail.

Some boats fly a special yacht ensign showing a circle of 13 stars on the blue field with a fouled anchor in the center. This flag is proper within the United States, but should not be used in foreign waters.

The appropriate size for the U.S. flag is both a matter of personal taste, and the practical considerations of its location. Obviously, you may want to fly a flag 72 inches long on July 4th, but you may not want to do it on a regular basis. Most flags come in several standard sizes with the horizontal measure being the critical one. As a starting point we offer the following suggested sizes:

BOAT LENGTH IN FEET	HORIZONTAL LENGTH OF FLAG IN INCHES
18 and under	18 inches
19 to 24	24 inches
25 to 30	30 inches
30 to 36	36 inches
36 to 48	48 inches
48 to 60	60 inches

Keep in mind, there are no regulations within the United States requiring any particular size flag, or for that matter, any flag at all (except the Q flag when entering from a foreign port).

In general, the U.S. flag is only flown from sunrise to sunset. In some harbors, yacht clubs routinely fire a cannon at local sunset indicating the proper time to furl your flag. At sea, you only have to fly the national flag when encountering other vessels. It is proper to fly an illuminated flag at night, however few small vessels do so.

The flying of the U.S. flag upside down is understood as a sign of distress, though this is not an official signal.

COURTESY FLAGS

It is proper practice to fly a courtesy flag when sailing in a foreign country. The U.S. flag should still be displayed in its proper place. Generally, it is wise to obtain a selection of flags before leaving the U.S., as these are often hard to find in foreign ports. Many countries have separate flags for use ashore and afloat. In practical terms, few countries will object if the national flag is flown as a courtesy flag. Some countries require the proper flag be flown while in their waters.

The courtesy flag will generally be a small version of the national flag, measuring no more than 18 or 24 inches on the horizontal. It should be flown from the starboard spreader on sailboats, from the starboard side of a tower on a sportfisherman, or from an appropriate antenna or pole on the starboard side of a motor vessel. On two masted boats the flag should fly from the forward mast's starboard spreader. The courtesy flag should fly above other flags in the same location. When first entering a country, it is proper to fly only the yellow Q flag (I request clearance), but many boaters fly both the courtesy flag and the Q flag. Always fly the courtesy flag at the top of the hoist.

STATE FLAGS

Within the United States it is common to fly the state flag appropriate to your home port. Some boaters fly the state flag as a courtesy flag for the state they are traveling through. State flags are flown in the same manner as courtesy ensigns on most boats. State flags may also be flown from the masthead, or on a bow staff. They should not be flown on a stern staff.

QUARANTINE FLAG

When entering a foreign port, or when returning to the United States from a foreign port, the solid yellow Q flag should be flown from the starboard spreader, or appropriate location on the starboard side of a motor vessel. This flag is the International Code Flag for the letter Q. It means, "My vessel is healthy, I request free pratique." In practical terms it alerts the proper authorities your vessel is requesting customs and immigration clearance into the country. It is often necessary to contact the authorities directly on the VHF radio in addition to hoisting the Q flag. In fact, many times you will have to go ashore to call the authorities or visit their offices. Do not assume your Q flag will get an immediate response from the busy officials.

YACHT CLUB BURGEES

It is common for members of yacht clubs to fly their own club burgee. These are often triangular pennants, or sometimes swallowtail pennants. The proper place to fly the burgee is at the highest masthead aboard sailing vessels. Modern boats often have many sensitive instruments, lights and antennas in this location. As a result these club burgees are often flown from the starboard spreader of sailboats. If this location is used, it should not fly above the courtesy ensign when in a foreign port. The position below the port spreader is inferior to the position below the starboard spreader. If you must fly so many flags you need both port and starboard flag hoists, you must decide which flags should be most honored.

The rigging of a masthead burgee requires the flag be attached to a short staff. One end of the halyard is attached near the bottom of the staff, while the other end is attached from six inches to several feet (depending on the length of your staff) higher up. The staff is then hauled up until the upper line dead-ends at the block. Pulling the lower line taught keeps the staff vertical. The staff should be tall enough for the burgee to clear all of the masthead clutter.

On power boats the burgee is usually flown from a bow staff. Power boats with a mast may also fly the burgee from the masthead. If a gaff is present, this is the location of honor and is reserved for the U.S. flag.

COAST GUARD ENSIGN

The United States Coast Guard has their own flag consisting of red and white vertical stripes (16) with the Coast Guard crossed anchors seal on them, a white field in the upper left corner has a "flying eagle" symbol with a shield in the center. This flag is flown day and night by Coast Guard vessels.

Coast Guard Auxiliary vessels participating in official Coast Guard operations may fly an ensign showing the familiar red diagonal stripe on a white background with the crossed anchors seal of the auxiliary in the center. This flag is usually flown from a bow staff, or a masthead position.

U.S. CUSTOMS ENSIGN

The Customs Service has their own ensign which they fly from their vessels. It is similar in appearance to the Coast Guard ensign, but features a larger eagle surrounded by an arc of stars. There are also 16 vertical red and white stripes, but there is no seal on this area.

DRESSING SHIP

It is traditional for boats to "dress ship" when celebrating national holidays or special occasions. The International Signal Flags are used stretched from bow to masthead and down to the stern. On multi-masted vessels they should pass over the masts before descending to the deck. There are several different theories on designing a harmonious pattern for this display. We offer one suggested order as a starting point for your creative desires:

Starting from the stern - E, Q, 3, G, 8, Z, 4, W, 6, P, 1, Code, T, Y, B, X, First Repeater, H, Third Repeater, D, F, Second Repeater, U, A, O, M, R, 2, J, 0 (zero), N, 9, K, 7, V, 5, L, C, S.

A tradition among cruisers is to dress ship with the courtesy flags of the ports visited on a long cruise. This is a fun way to enter your home port after a voyage.

SHIP & BOAT RECOGNITION

19

The following pages are intended only as a simple guide and to stimulate interest in the subject of ship and boat recognition, illustrating some of the wide range of vessels the observer may expect to encounter.

TALL SHIPS

Full Rigged Ship. Sailing vessel with square sails on three or more masts. The few that remain today are used as training vessels.

Barque. Three to five-masted sailing ship, all of them square rigged except the after mast which is fore and aft rigged.

Brig. Two-masted sailing vessel developed from the brigantine and differing from it mainly by being square rigged on both masts.

Brigantine. Two-masted sailing ship, square rigged on the foremast and fore-and-aft rigged the square topsails on the main mast.

Barquentine. Sailing ship with three to five masts, all of them fore-and-aft rigged except the foremast which is square rigged.

Topsail Schooner. Two or more masted vessel, fore-and-aft rigged. The after mast is taller than the foremast which is set with one or more square topsails.

SMALL BOATS

Cape Cod Catboat. single masted fore-and-aft rigged sailing vessel with single gaff mainsail. the mast is stepped near the bow and the boom may overhang the stern. Many have been built as centerboarders, with transom-hung "barn door rudders". Most are under 30 feet in length.

Schooner. Usually double masted fore-and-aft rigged sailing vessels with gaff sails abaft the masts. This example has a marconi sail on the aft mast, and a tipsail set above the gaff main. coastal trading schooners wer built with up to five masts.

Masthead Cutter. Single masted fore-and-aft rigged sailing vessel with running bowsprit, mainsail, and two or more headsails.

Sloop. Single masted fore-and-aft rigged sailing boat with single headsail set from the forestay.

Gaff Cutter. Single masted fore-and-aft rigged sailing craft with two headsails. A gaff yard supports the top edge of an additional topsail.

Yawl. Two-masted fore-and aft rigged sailing vessel similar to the ketch but with a smaller mizzen mast abaft the rudder.

Ketch. Two-masted fore-and-aft rigged sailing ship with mizzen mast situated aft of the main mast but forward of the rudder.

Staysail Schooner. Two-masted fore-and-aft rigged sailing vessel, with mainsail and staysail set between the masts

WARSHIPS

Frigate. Primarily intended for fast escort duties, the frigate is armed with a mixed array of guns, missiles and torpedoes. It can be difficult to distinguish from the destroyer.

Destroyer. A medium-sized fast warship, with an armament of guns, torpedoes, guided missiles and depth charges, noted for its high maneuverability Also used as an escort vessel, providing powerful support in many actions.

Landing Craft. Designed to carry a large number of troops and their vehicles during combined services landing operations. Carries only small arms for defence purposes.

Fleet Service Vessel. An important role is played by these naval support vessels, which carry supplies of oil, fuel, ammunition, spare parts and many other essential items. They are equipped with handling gear and most have a helipad situated aft.

Mine Counter-measure Vessels. The mine-hunter, fitted with sonar equipment, searches for and classifies mines on the seabed, from a distance. The minesweeper is equipped with wires, magnetic cables or acoustic gear to remove and destroy mines from the surface or seabed.

Aircraft Carrier. Easily recognised by its sheer size. Used as a mobile air base at sea, the flat deck extends the length and width of the vessel and serves as a landing strip. Service speed is in excess of 30 knots.

TALL SHIPS

Full Rigged Ship

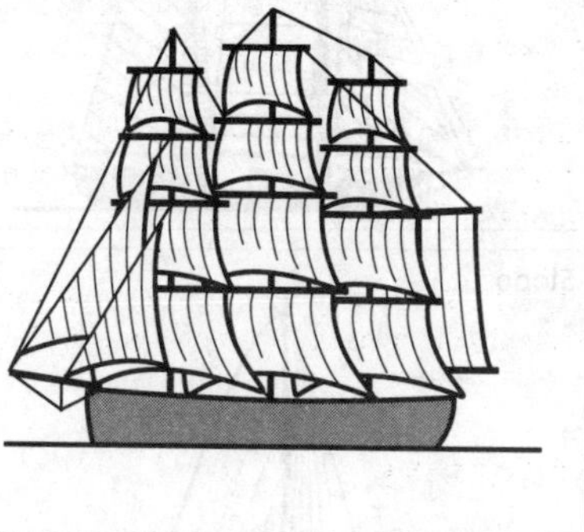

Three Masted Barque

Brig

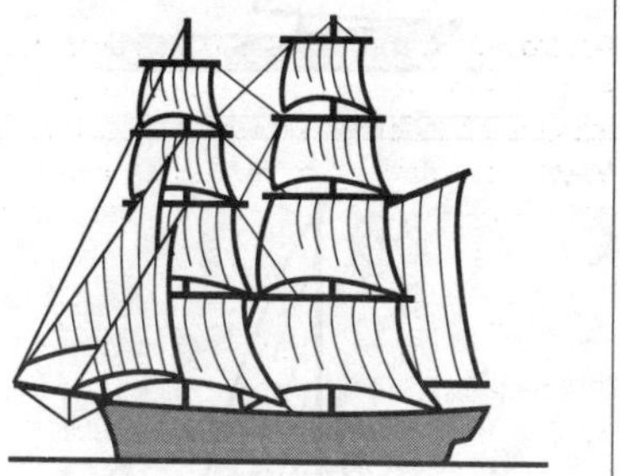

Brianatine

Barquentine

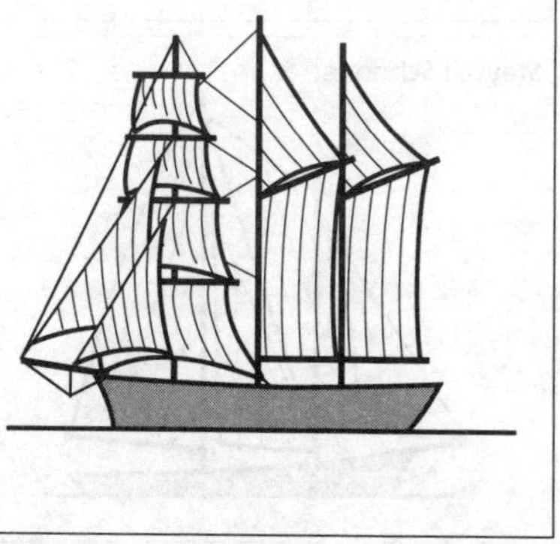

Topsail Schooner

SMALL BOATS

Cape Cod Catboat

Schooner

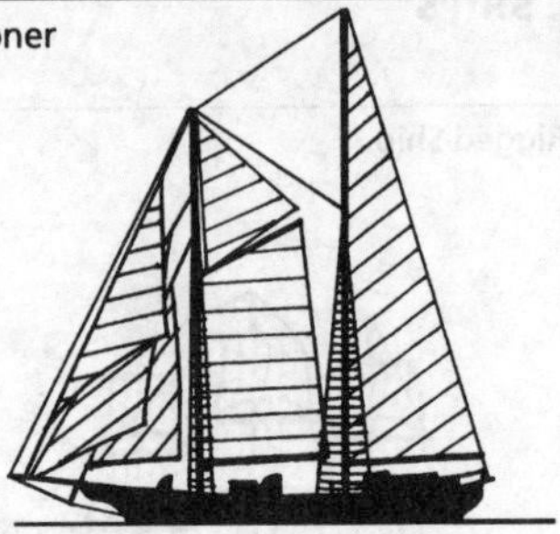

Masthead Cutter

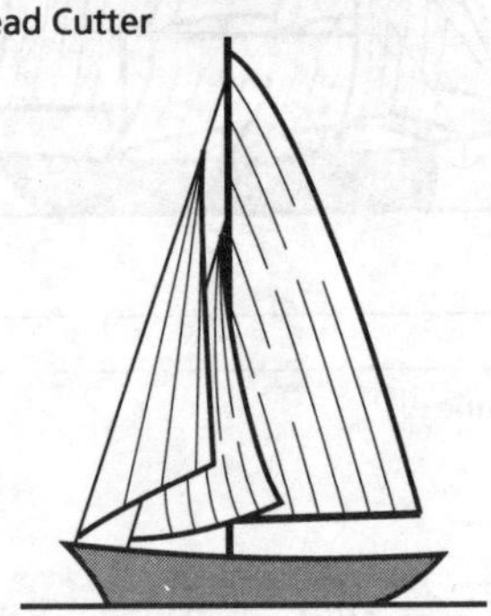

Sloop

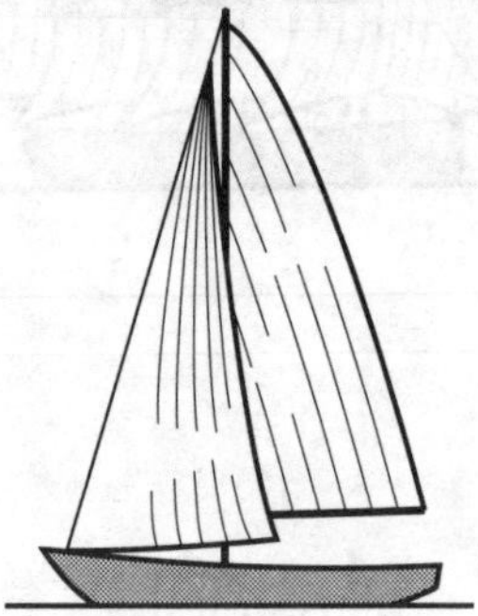

Gaff Cutter

Yawl

Ketch

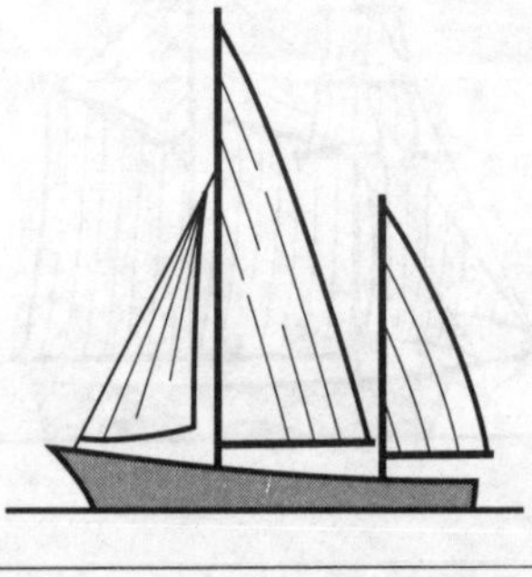

Staysail Schooner

WARSHIPS

Frigate

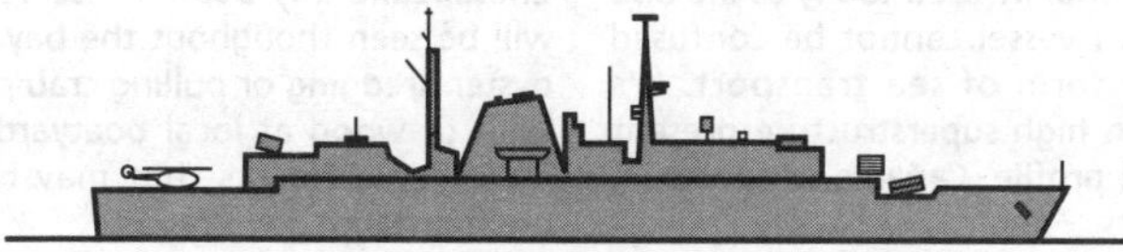

Destroyer

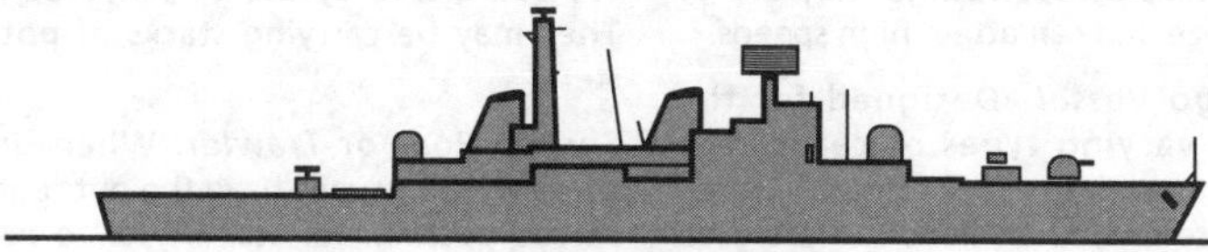

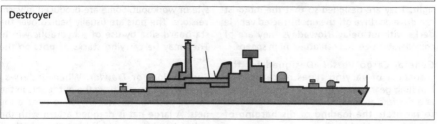

Landing Craft

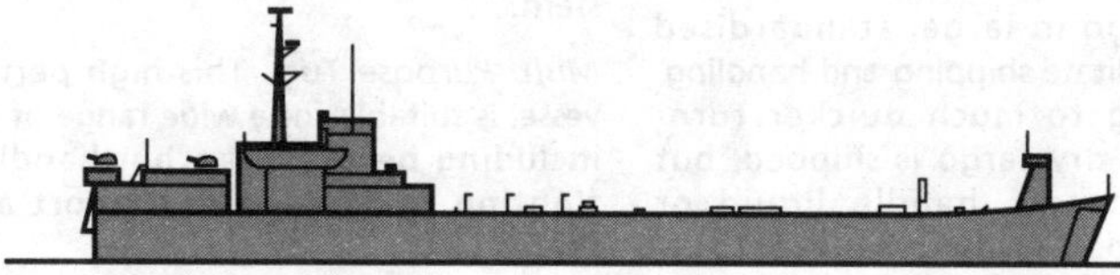

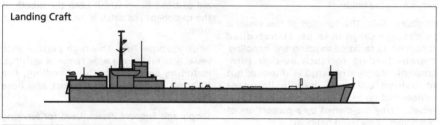

Fleet Service Vessel

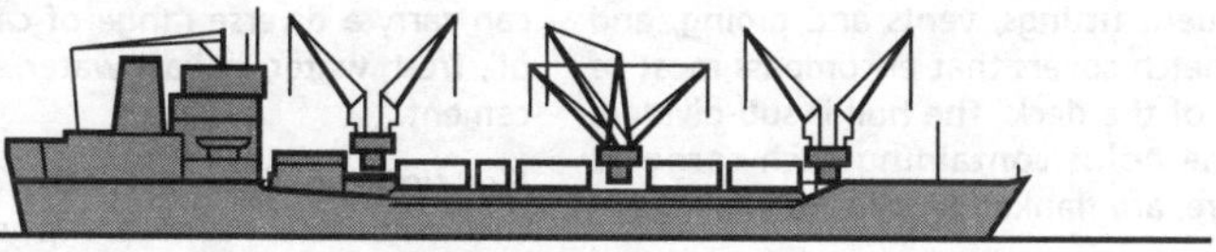

Mine Sweeper

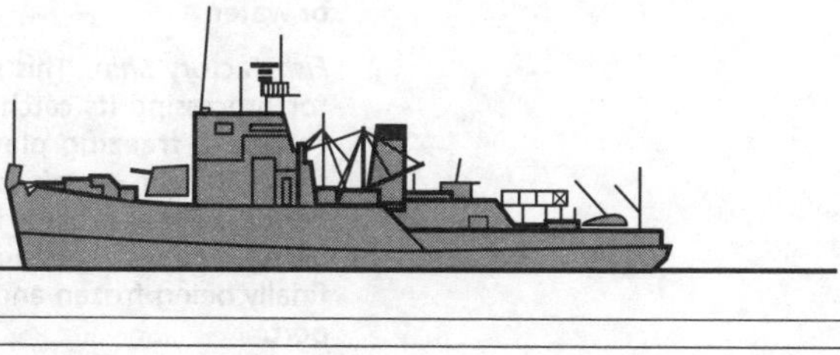

Aircraft Carrier

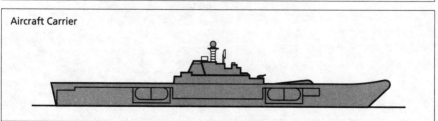

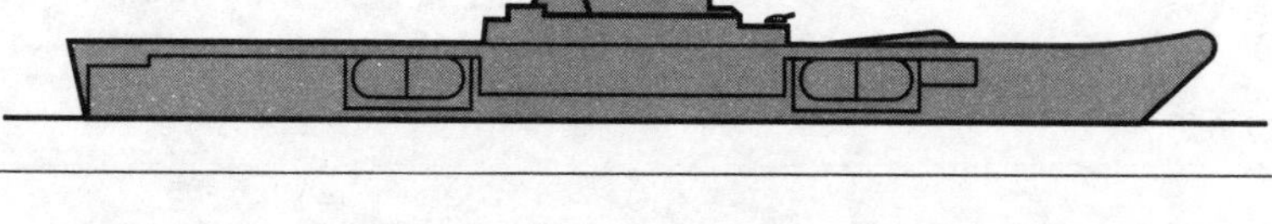

MERCHANT SHIPS

Passenger Liner. Mainly used today as a cruise liner, this type of vessel cannot be confused with any other form of sea transport. It's elegant lines and high superstructure present a very individual profile. Capable of speeds in excess of 20 knots.

Car Ferry. Passenger/car ferries are a familiar sight. They are designed so that the motorist can drive on/drive off the unobstructed vehicle decks without delay. Nowadays they are of considerable size and can attain high speeds.

General Cargo Vessel. Designed for the transport of varying types of cargo, the handling gear is an important feature. Cranes and derricks are carried on deck and are used to facilitate the loading or discharging of cargo from the holds.

Container Ship. The function of this vessel is to package cargo in large, standardised containers to facilitate shipping and handling, thereby leading to much quicker turn-arounds. Mainly dry cargo is shipped, but specialised units can handle liquid or refrigerated cargoes. As these are very costly vessels, many are owned by a consortium of companies, some multi-national.

OBO Carrier. The oil/bulk/ore ship is different from a normal bulk carrier because of its wide range of deck fittings, vents and piping, and the steel hatch covers that encompass most of the width of the deck. The hull is sub-divided, so that the holds containing such cargo as grain or ore, are flanked by oil tanks.

WORK BOATS

Chesapeake Bay Boat. These versatile vessels will be seen thoughout the bay. They may be oyster dredging or pulling crab pots. Many are built of wood at local boatyards. They often have dry exhausts that may be heard at a good distance

Lobster Boat. This is a distinctly New England syle of workboat. Some are produced in yacht versions. The pots are usually hauled over the starboard side by use of a hydraulic winch. They may be carrying stacks of pots on the stern.

Shrimp Boat or Trawler. When underway these vessels usually have the outriggers in the spread position for stability or to handle the nets. A large net is dragged astern with the aid of trawl doors which keep the mouth of the net open. The catch is hauled in over the stern.

Multi-Purpose Tug. This high performance vessel is suitable for a wide range of activities, including berthing, anchor handling, fire fighting, salvage, dive support and hose flushing.

Supply and Support Vessel. Used for servicing oil and gas rig installations and designed to cope with the adverse wind, weather and sea conditions often encountered, these vessels can carry a diverse range of cargoes, e.g. fuel oil, fresh water, ballast water, mud, brine and cement.

Fire fighting Tug. Instantly recognisable by the two fire monitors positioned on a platform above the superstructure. Powerful pumps supply the monitors with either foam or water.

Fish Factory Ship. This ship carries equipment for processing its catch on board including a complete freezing plant, which means that the vessel can remain at sea for much longer periods. Every process is carried out, the fish being cleaned, gutted, filleted etc, before finally being frozen and stored until return to port.

MERCHANT SHIPS

Passenger Liner

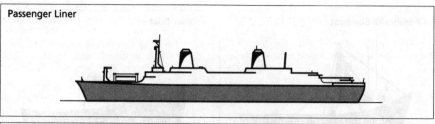

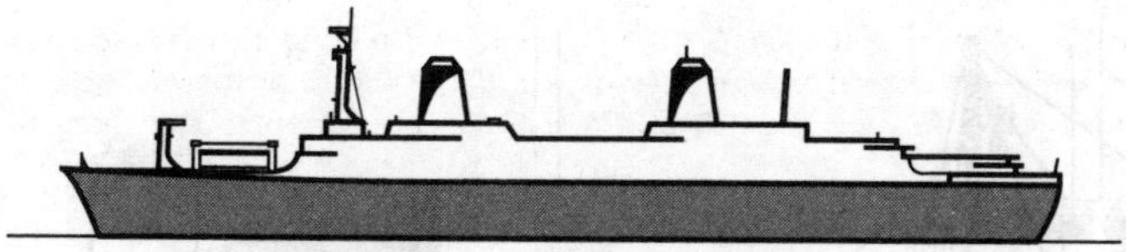

Car Ferry

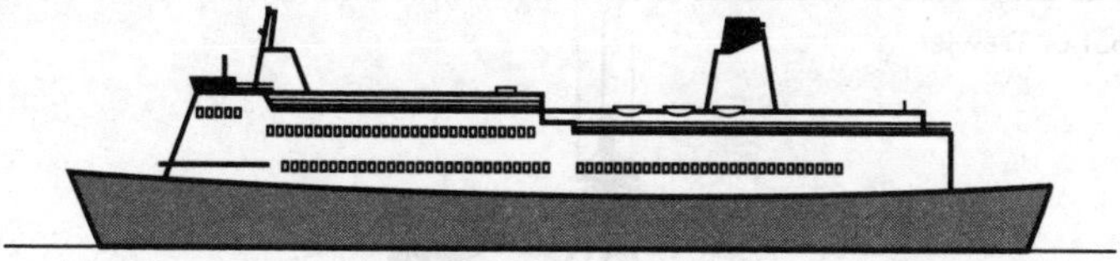

General Cargo Liner

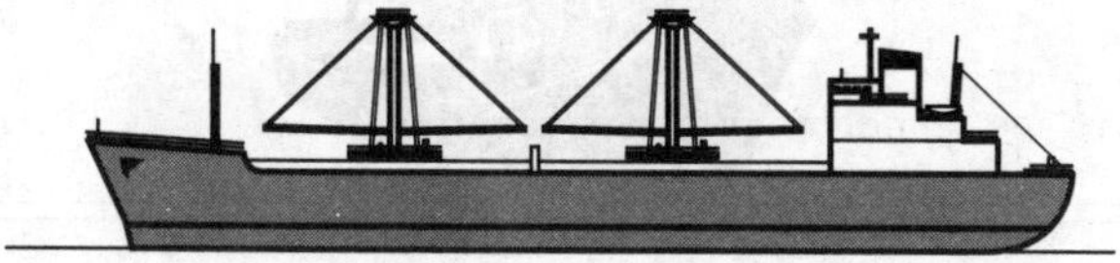

Container Ship

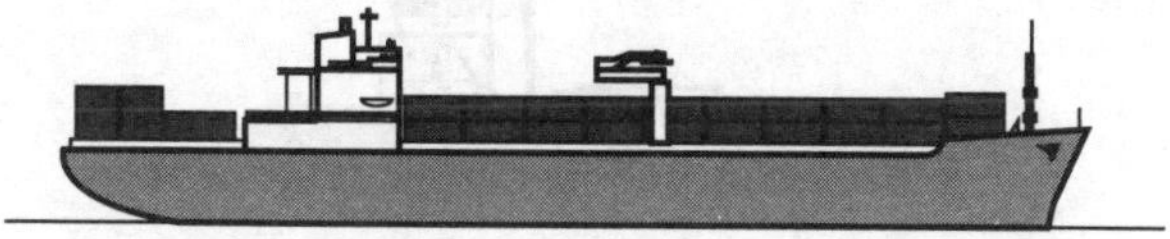

OBO Carrier

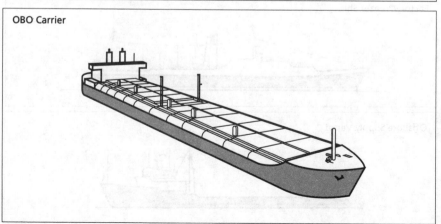

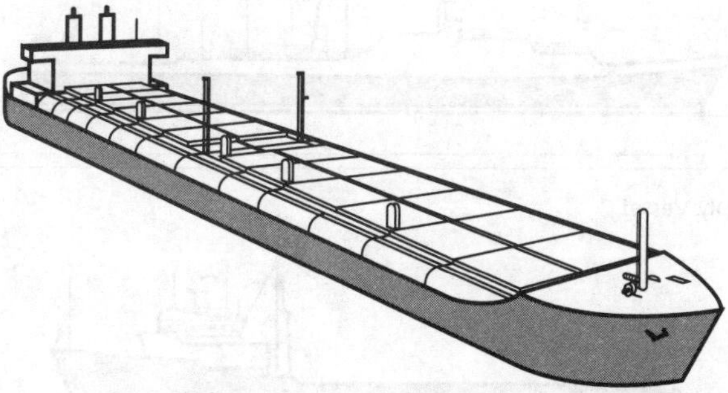

19

WORK BOATS

Chesapeake Bay Boat

Lobster Boat

Shrimp Boat or Trawler

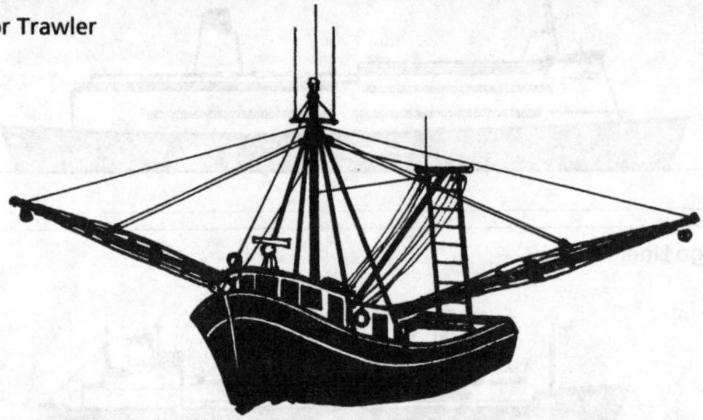

Multi-Purpose Tug

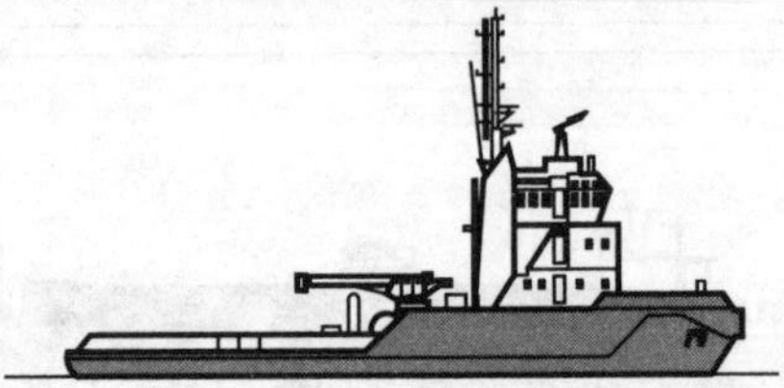

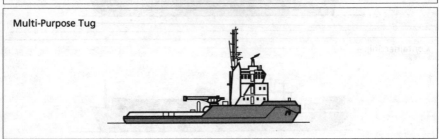

Factory/Freezer Ship

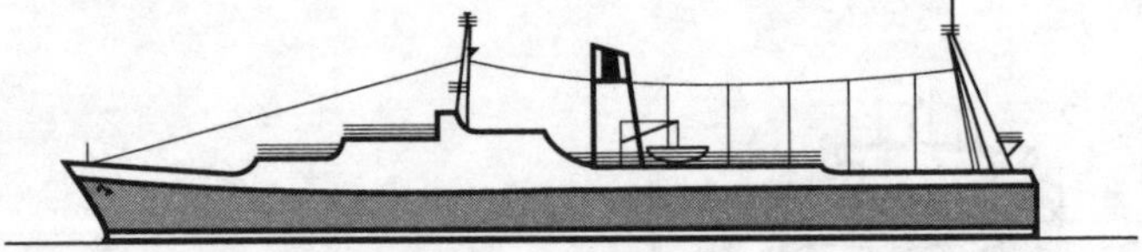

Offshore Supply Vessel

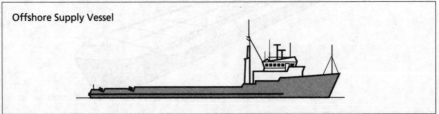

20

Conversions

Page

LINEAR – INTERNATIONAL NAUTICAL MILES, STATUTE MILES AND KILOMETERS

INM	Km	SM	Km	INM	SM	SM	Km	INM
1	1.852	1.15078	**1**	0.53996	0.62137	**1**	1.60934	0.86898
2	3.70	2.30	**2**	1.08	1.24	**2**	3.22	1.74
3	5.56	3.45	**3**	1.62	1.86	**3**	4.83	2.61
4	7.41	4.60	**4**	2.16	2.49	**4**	6.44	3.48
5	9.26	5.75	**5**	2.70	3.11	**5**	8.05	4.34
6	11.11	6.90	**6**	3.24	3.73	**6**	9.66	5.21
7	12.96	8.06	**7**	3.78	4.35	**7**	11.27	6.08
8	14.82	9.21	**8**	4.32	4.97	**8**	12.87	6.95
9	16.67	10.36	**9**	4.86	5.59	**9**	14.48	7.82
10	18.52	11.51	**10**	5.40	6.21	**10**	16.09	8.69
11	20.37	12.66	**11**	5.94	6.84	**11**	17.70	9.56
12	22.22	13.81	**12**	6.48	7.46	**12**	19.31	10.43
13	24.08	14.96	**13**	7.02	8.08	**13**	20.92	11.30
14	25.93	16.11	**14**	7.56	8.70	**14**	22.53	12.17
15	27.78	17.26	**15**	8.10	9.32	**15**	23.14	13.03
16	29.63	18.41	**16**	8.64	9.94	**16**	25.75	13.90
17	31.48	19.56	**17**	9.18	10.56	**17**	27.36	14.77
18	33.34	20.71	**18**	9.72	11.18	**18**	28.97	15.64
19	35.19	21.86	**19**	10.26	11.81	**19**	30.58	16.51
20	37.04	23.02	**20**	10.80	12.43	**20**	32.19	17.38
21	38.89	24.17	**21**	11.34	13.05	**21**	33.80	18.25
22	40.74	25.32	**22**	11.88	13.67	**22**	35.41	19.12
23	42.60	26.47	**23**	12.42	14.29	**23**	37.01	19.99
24	44.45	27.62	**24**	12.96	14.91	**24**	38.62	20.86
25	46.30	28.77	**25**	13.50	15.53	**25**	40.23	21.72
26	48.15	29.92	**26**	14.04	16.16	**26**	41.84	22.59
27	50.00	31.07	**27**	14.58	16.78	**27**	43.45	23.46
28	51.86	32.22	**28**	15.12	17.40	**28**	45.06	24.33
29	53.71	33.37	**29**	15.66	18.02	**29**	46.67	25.20
30	55.56	34.52	**30**	16.20	18.64	**30**	48.28	26.07
31	57.41	35.67	**31**	16.74	19.26	**31**	49.89	26.94
32	59.26	36.82	**32**	17.28	19.88	**32**	51.50	27.81
33	61.12	37.98	**33**	17.82	20.51	**33**	53.11	28.68
34	62.97	39.13	**34**	18.36	21.13	**34**	54.72	29.55
35	64.82	40.28	**35**	18.90	21.75	**35**	56.33	30.41
36	66.67	41.43	**36**	19.44	22.37	**36**	57.94	31.28
37	68.52	42.58	**37**	19.98	22.99	**37**	59.55	32.15
38	70.38	43.73	**38**	20.52	23.61	**38**	61.15	33.02
39	72.23	44.88	**39**	21.06	24.23	**39**	62.76	33.89
40	74.08	46.03	**40**	21.60	24.85	**40**	64.37	34.76
45	83.34	51.79	**45**	24.30	27.96	**45**	72.42	39.10
50	92.60	57.54	**50**	27.00	31.07	**50**	80.47	43.45
55	101.86	63.29	**55**	29.70	34.18	**55**	88.51	47.79
60	111.12	69.05	**60**	32.40	37.28	**60**	96.56	52.14
65	120.38	74.80	**65**	35.10	40.39	**65**	104.61	56.48
70	129.64	80.55	**70**	37.80	43.50	**70**	112.65	60.83
75	138.90	86.31	**75**	40.50	46.60	**75**	120.70	65.17
80	148.16	92.06	**80**	43.20	49.71	**80**	128.75	69.52
85	157.42	97.82	**85**	45.90	52.82	**85**	136.79	73.86
90	166.68	103.57	**90**	48.60	55.92	**90**	144.84	78.21
95	175.94	109.32	**95**	51.30	59.03	**95**	152.89	82.55
100	185.20	115.08	**100**	54.00	62.14	**100**	160.93	86.90

FEET TO METERS

Feet	Meters	Feet	Meters
1	0.30	26	7.92
2	0.61	27	8.23
3	0.91	28	8.53
4	1.22	29	8.84
5	1.52	30	9.14
6	1.83	31	9.45
7	2.13	32	9.75
8	2.44	33	10.06
9	2.74	34	10.36
10	3.05	35	10.67
11	3.35	36	10.97
12	3.66	37	11.28
13	3.96	38	11.58
14	4.27	39	11.89
15	4.57	40	12.19
16	4.88	41	12.50
17	5.18	42	12.80
18	5.49	43	13.11
19	5.79	44	13.41
20	6.10	45	13.72
21	6.40	46	14.02
22	6.71	47	14.33
23	7.01	48	14.63
24	7.32	49	14.94
25	7.62	50	15.24

METERS TO FEET

Meters	Feet	Meters	Feet
1	3.28	26	85.30
2	6.56	27	88.58
3	9.84	28	91.86
4	13.12	29	95.14
5	16.40	30	98.43
6	19.69	31	101.71
7	22.97	32	104.99
8	26.25	33	108.27
9	29.53	34	111.55
10	32.81	35	114.83
11	36.09	36	118.11
12	39.37	37	121.39
13	42.65	38	124.67
14	45.93	39	127.95
15	49.21	40	131.23
16	52.49	41	134.51
17	55.77	42	137.80
18	59.06	43	141.08
19	62.34	44	144.36
20	65.62	45	147.64
21	68.90	46	150.92
22	72.18	47	154.20
23	75.46	48	157.48
24	78.74	49	160.76
25	82.02	50	164.04

FATHOMS TO METERS

Fathoms	Meters	Fathoms	Meters
1	1.83	26	47.55
2	3.66	27	49.38
3	5.49	28	51.21
4	7.32	29	53.04
5	9.14	30	54.86
6	10.97	31	56.69
7	12.80	32	58.52
8	14.63	33	60.35
9	16.46	34	62.18
10	18.29	35	64.00
11	20.12	36	65.84
12	21.95	37	67.67
13	23.77	38	69.49
14	25.60	39	71.32
15	27.43	40	73.15
16	29.26	41	74.98
17	31.09	42	76.81
18	32.92	43	78.64
19	34.75	44	80.47
20	36.58	45	82.30
21	38.40	46	84.12
22	40.23	47	85.95
23	42.06	48	87.78
24	43.89	49	89.61
25	45.72	50	91.44

METERS TO FATHOMS

Metres	Fathoms	Meters	Fathoms
1	0.547	26	14.217
2	1.094	27	14.764
3	1.640	28	15.311
4	2.187	29	15.857
5	2.734	30	16.404
6	3.281	31	16.951
7	3.828	32	17.498
8	4.374	33	18.045
9	4.921	34	18.591
10	5.468	35	19.138
11	6.015	36	19.685
12	6.562	37	20.232
13	7.108	38	20.779
14	7.655	39	21.325
15	8.202	40	21.872
16	8.749	41	22.419
17	9.296	42	22.966
18	9.842	43	23.513
19	10.389	44	24.059
20	10.936	45	24.606
21	11.483	46	25.153
22	12.030	47	25.700
23	12.577	48	26.247
24	13.123	49	26.793
25	13.670	50	27.340

INCHES TO MILIMETERS / **MILIMETERS TO INCHES**

Inches	mm	Inches	mm	mm	Inches	mm	Inches
1	25.40	15	381.00	1	0.0394	15	0.5906
2	50.80	20	508.00	2	0.0787	20	0.7874
3	76.20	25	635.00	3	0.1181	25	0.9843
4	101.60	30	762.00	4	0.1575	30	1.1811
5	127.00	35	889.00	5	0.1969	35	1.3780
10	254.00	40	1016.00	10	0.3937	40	1.5748

10 MILLIETERS = 1 CENTIMETER. 100 CENTIMETERS (1000 MM) = 1 METER = 39.37 INCHES (3.3 FEET)

INCHES TO METERS / **METERS TO INCHES**

Inches	Meters	Inches	Meters	Meters	Inches	Meters	Inches
1	0.0254	7	0.1778	0.1	3.937	0.7	27.559
2	0.0508	8	0.2032	0.2	7.874	0.8	31.496
3	0.0762	9	0.2286	0.3	11.811	0.9	35.433
4	0.1016	10	0.2540	0.4	15.748	1.0	39.370
5	0.1270	11	0.2794	0.5	19.685	1.1	43.307
6	0.1524	12	0.3048	0.6	23.622	1.2	47.244

TO CONVERT METERS TO CENTIMETERS, MOVE DECIMAL POINT TWO PLACES TO THE RIGHT

YARDS TO METERS / **METERS TO YARDS**

Yards	Meters	Yards	Meters	Meters	Yards	Meters	Yards
1	0.91440	6	5.48640	1	1.09361	6	6.56168
2	1.82880	7	6.40080	2	2.18723	7	7.65529
3	2.74320	8	7.31520	3	3.28084	8	8.74891
4	3.65760	9	8.22960	4	4.37445	9	9.84252
5	4.57200	10	9.14400	5	5.46807	10	10.93614

MOVE DECIMAL POINT FOR HIGHER VALUES – e.g. 6,000 METERS = 6,561.68 YARDS

POUNDS TO KILOGRAMS / **KILOGRAMS TO POUNDS**

lb	kg	lb	kg	kg	lb	kg	lb
1	0.454	6	2.722	1	2.205	6	13.228
2	0.907	7	3.175	2	4.409	7	15.432
3	1.361	8	3.629	3	6.614	8	17.637
4	1.814	9	4.082	4	8.818	9	19.842
5	2.268	10	4.536	5	11.023	10	22.046

GALLONS TO LITERS / **LITERS TO GALLONS**

Gallons	Liters	Gallons	Liters	Liters	Gallons	Liters	Gallons
1	3·79	10	37·86	1	0.26	60	15.66
2	7·57	20	75·71	2	0.53	90	23.77
3	11·36	30	113·57	5	1.32	120	39.62
4	15·14	40	151·42	10	2.64	150	39.62
5	18·93	50	189·28	20	5.28	180	47.54

PINTS TO LITERS / **LITERS TO PINTS**

Pints	Liters	Pints	Liters	Liters	Pints	Liters	Pints
1	0·47	6	2·84	1	2.11	6	12.68
2	0·95	7	3·31	2	4.23	7	14.79
3	1·42	8	3·79	5	6.34	8	16.91
4	1·89	9	4·26	10	8.45	9	19.02
5	2·37	10	4·73	20	10.57	10	21.13

SOME USEFUL CONVERSIONS

1 fathom	=	6 feet
1 shackle	=	15 fathoms
1 cable	=	608 ft (approx 100 fathoms)
10 cables	=	1 international nautical mile
1 international nautical mile	=	6076.12 ft = 1.15 statute miles = 1852 m
1 statute mile	=	5280 ft = 1760 yd = 0.87 sea miles

Length

kilometer (km)	=	1093.61yd
meter (m)	=	39.37in
centimeter (cm)	=	0.3937in
millimeter (mm)	=	0.03937in

Area

sq meter (m^2)	=	1.196yd^2
sq centimeter (cm^2)	=	0.1550in^2
sq millimeter (mm^2)	=	0.00155in^2

Volume

cubic meter (m)	=	264 gallons
	=	1000 liters
	=	1.308yd^3
	=	2·11 pints
centiliter (cl)	=	0·34 fl oz
milliliter (ml)	=	0·034 fl oz
1 liter	=	30·272 ounces
1 Imperial gallon	=	4·546 liters
1 Imperial gallon	=	12 U.S. gallons
1 U.S. gallon	=	0·83 Imperial gallons

For **wind speed, temperature and barometer** conversions, see Section 19

OTHER MEASURES

Weight

1 long ton (British) = 2240lb = 1.12 short tons = 1.016 metric ton
1 short ton (USA and Canada) = 20 centals of 100lb each = 2000lb = 0.893 long tons = 0.907 metric tons
1 metric ton = 2204.6lb = 1.1023 short tons = 0.9842 long tons = 1000kg
kilogram (kg) = 2.2046lb
gram (g) = 0.0353oz

Nautical

1 long ton (displacement) = 35cu ft salt water or 36 cu ft fresh water
1 ton (register) = 100 cu ft 1 ton (measurement) = 40 cu ft

Fresh Water

1 cu ft = 7·47 gallons and weighs 62·5 lbs
1 gallon = 3·79 liters and weighs 8·33 lbs
10 British gallons = approx 12 American gallons
1000 liters = 1cu m
1 liter weighs approx 1kg

Salt Water

1 cu ft weighs 64 lb = 31·25 cu ft weighs 1 ton (U.S.)

CONVERSION OF FREQUENCY IN KILOHERTZ TO WAVELENGTH IN METERS
for High Frequency Broadcasting Bands

75 Meter Band		49 Meter Band		41 Meter Band		31 Meter Band		25 Meter Band	
kHz	*Meters*	*kHz*	*Meters*	*kHz*	*Meters*	*kHz*	*Meters*	*kHz*	*Meters*
3900	76.92	5950	50.42	7100	42.25	9500	31.58	11700	25.64
3905	76.82	5955	50.38	7105	42.22	9505	31.56	11705	25.63
3910	76.73	5960	50.34	7110	42.19	9510	31.55	11710	25.62
3915	76.63	5965	50.29	7115	42.16	9515	31.53	11715	25.61
3920	76.53	5970	50.25	7120	42.13	9520	31.51	11720	25.60
3925	76.43	5975	50.21	7125	42.11	9525	31.50	11725	25.59
3930	76.34	5980	50.17	7130	42.08	9530	31.48	11730	25.58
3935	76.24	5985	50.13	7135	42.05	9535	31.46	11735	25.56
3940	76.14	5990	50.08	7140	42.02	9540	31.45	11740	25.55
3945	76.05	5995	50.04	7145	41.99	9545	31.43	11745	25.54
3950	75.95	6000	50.00	7150	41.96	9550	31.41	11750	25.53
3955	75.85	6005	49.96	7155	41.93	9555	31.40	11755	25.52
3960	75.76	6010	49.92	7160	41.90	9560	31.38	11760	25.51
3965	75.66	6015	49.88	7165	41.87	9565	31.36	11765	25.50
3970	75.57	6020	49.83	7170	41.84	9570	31.35	11770	25.49
3975	75.47	6025	49.79	7175	41.81	9575	31.33	11775	25.48
3980	75.38	6030	49.75	7180	41.78	9580	31.32	11780	25.47
3985	75.28	6035	49.71	7185	41.75	9585	31.30	11785	25.46
3990	75.19	6040	49.67	7190	41.72	9590	31.28	11790	25.45
3995	75.09	6045	49.63	7195	41.70	9595	31.27	11795	25.43
4000	75.00	6050	49.59	7200	41.67	9600	31.25	11800	25.42
		6055	49.55	7205	41.64	9605	31.23	11805	25.41
		6060	49.50	7210	41.61	9610	31.22	11810	25.40
		6065	49.46	7215	41.58	9615	31.20	11815	25.39
		6070	49.42	7220	41.55	9620	31.19	11820	25.38
		6075	49.38	7225	41.52	9625	31.17	11825	25.37
		6080	49.34	7230	41.49	9630	31.15	11830	25.36
		6085	49.30	7235	41.47	9635	31.14	11835	25.35
		6090	49.26	7240	41.44	9640	31.12	11840	25.34
		6095	49.22	7245	41.41	9645	31.10	11845	25.33
		6100	49.18	7250	41.38	9650	31.09	11850	25.32
		6105	49.14	7255	41.35	9655	31.07	11855	25.31
		6110	49.10	7260	41.32	9660	31.06	11860	25.30
		6115	49.06	7265	41.29	9665	31.04	11865	25.28
		6120	49.02	7270	41.27	9670	31.02	11870	25.27
		6125	48.98	7275	41.24	9675	31.01	11875	25.26
		6130	48.94	7280	41.21	9680	30.99	11880	25.25
		6135	48.90	7285	41.18	9685	30.98	11885	25.24
		6140	48.86	7290	41.15	9690	30.96	11890	25.23
		6145	48.82	7295	41.12	9695	30.94	11895	25.22
		6150	48.78	7300	41.10	9700	30.93	11900	25.21
		6155	48.74			9705	30.91	11905	25.20
		6160	48.70			9710	30.90	11910	25.19
		6165	48.66			9715	30.88	11915	25.18
		6170	48.62			9720	30.86	11920	25.17
		6175	48.58			9725	30.85	11925	25.16
		6180	48.54			9730	30.83	11930	25.15
		6185	48.50			9735	30.82	11935	25.14
		6190	48.47			9740	30.80	11940	25.13
		6195	48.43			9745	30.79	11945	25.12
		6200	48.39			9750	30.77	11950	25.10
						9755	30.75	11955	25.09
						9760	30.74	11960	25.08
						9765	30.72	11965	25.07
						9770	30.71	11970	25.06
						9775	30.69	11975	25.05

CONVERSION OF FREQUENCY IN KILOHERTZ TO WAVELENGTH IN METERS for High Frequency Broadcasting Bands

19 Meter Band

kHz	*Meters*
15100	19.87
15105	19.86
15100	19.85
15115	19.85
15120	19.84
15125	19.83
15130	19.83
15135	19.82
15140	19.82
15145	19.81
15150	19.80
15155	19.80
15160	19.79
15165	19.78
15170	19.78
15175	19.77
15180	19.76
15185	19.76
15190	19.75
15195	19.74
15200	19.74
15205	19.73
15210	19.72
15215	19.72
15220	19.71
15225	19.70
15230	19.70
15235	19.69
15240	19.69
15245	19.68
15250	19.67
15255	19.67
15260	19.66
15265	19.65
15270	19.65
15275	19.64
15280	19.63
15285	19.63
15290	19.62
15295	19.61
15300	19.61
15305	19.60
15310	19.60
15315	19.59
15320	19.58
15325	19.58
15330	19.57
15335	19.56
15340	19.56
15345	19.55
15350	19.54
15355	19.54
15360	19.53
15365	19.52
15370	19.52
15375	19.51
15380	19.51
15385	19.50
15390	19.49
15395	19.49
15400	19.48
15405	19.47
15410	19.47
15415	19.46
15420	19.46
15420	19.45
15430	19.44
15435	19.44
15440	19.43
15445	19.42
15450	19.42

16 Meter Band

kHz	*Meters*
17700	16.95
17705	16.94
17710	16.94
17715	16.93
17720	16.93
17725	16.93
17730	16.92
17735	16.92
17740	16.91
17745	16.91
17750	16.90
17755	16.90
17760	16.89
17765	16.89
17770	16.88
17775	16.88
17780	16.87
17785	16.87
17790	16.86
17795	16.86
17800	16.85
17805	16.85
17810	16.84
17815	16.84
17820	16.84
17825	16.83
17830	16.83
17835	16.82
17840	16.82
17845	16.81
17850	16.81
17855	16.80
17860	16.80
17865	16.79
17870	16.79
17875	16.78
17880	16.78
17885	16.77
17890	16.77
17895	16.76
17900	16.76

13 Meter Band

kHz	*Meters*
21450	13.99
21455	13.98
21460	13.98
21465	13.98
21470	13.97
21475	13.97
21480	13.97
21485	13.96
21490	13.96
21495	13.96
21500	13.95
21505	13.95
21510	13.95
21515	13.94
21520	13.94
21525	13.94
21530	13.93
21535	13.93
21540	13.93
21545	13.92
21550	13.92
21555	13.92
21560	13.91
21565	13.91
21570	13.91
21575	13.90
21580	13.90
21585	13.90
21590	13.90
21595	13.89
21600	13.89
21605	13.89
21610	13.88
21615	13.88
21620	13.88
21625	13.87
21630	13.87
21635	13.87
21640	13.86
21645	13.86
21650	13.86
21655	13.85
21660	13.85
21665	13.85
21670	13.84
21675	13.84
21680	13.84
21685	13.83
21690	13.83
21695	13.83
21700	13.82
21705	13.82
21710	13.82
21715	13.82
21720	13.81
21725	13.81
21730	13.81
21735	13.80
21740	13.80
21745	13.80
21750	13.79

11 Meter Band

kHz	*Meters*
25600	11.72
25610	11.71
25620	11.71
25630	11.71
25640	11.70
25650	11.70
25660	11.69
25670	11.69
25680	11.68
25690	11.68
25700	11.67
25710	11.67
25720	11.66
25730	11.66
25740	11.66
25750	11.65
25760	11.65
25770	11.64
25780	11.64
25790	11.63
25800	11.63
25810	11.62
25820	11.62
25830	11.61
25840	11.61
25850	11.61
25860	11.60
25870	11.60
25880	11.59
25890	11.59
25900	11.58
25910	11.58
25920	11.57
25930	11.57
25940	11.57
25950	11.56
25960	11.56
25970	11.55
25980	11.55
25990	11.54
26000	11.54
26010	11.53
26020	11.53
26030	11.53
26040	11.52
26050	11.52
26060	11.51
26070	11.51
26080	11.50
26090	11.50
26100	11.49

TEMPERATURE

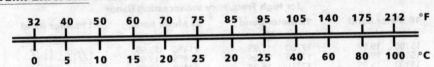

°F	32	40	50	60	70	75	85	95	105	140	175	212
°C	0	5	10	15	20	25	20	25	40	60	80	100

SPEEDS

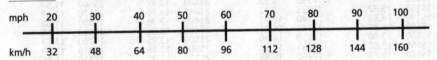

mph	20	30	40	50	60	70	80	90	100
km/h	32	48	64	80	96	112	128	144	160

TIRE PRESSURES

lb/sq in	20	22	24	26	28	30	32	34
kg/sq cm 1	41	1·55	1·69	1·83	1·97	2·11	2·25	2·39

CLOTHING SIZES

Men's Suits and Coats

British	36	38	40	42	44	46	48
American	36	38	40	42	44	46	48
Continental	46	48	50	52	54	56	58

Men's Shirts

British	14	14½	15	15½	16	16½	17
American	14	14½	15	15½	16	16½	17
Continental	36	37	38	39/40	41	42	43

Men's Shoes

British	7	8	9	10	11	12	13
American	7½	8½	9½	10½	11½	12½	13½
Continental	40½	42	43	44½	45½	47	48

Men's Socks

British	9½	10	10½	11	11½	12
American	9½	10	10½	11	11½	12
Continental	39	40	41	42	43	44

Women's Dresses and Suits

British	8	10	12	14	16	18
American	-	8	10	12	14	16
Continental	-	38	40	42	44	46

Women's Shoes

British	4	4½	5	5½	6	7	8
American	5½	6	6½	7	7½	8	8½
Continental	37	37½	38	39	39½	40½	42

Distance Tables

21

ATLANTIC OCEAN DISTANCES
MONTREAL, CANADA, TO PANAMA CANAL ZONE
(Nautical Miles)

Figure at intersection of columns opposite ports in question is the nautical mileage between the two. Example: New York, N. Y., is 1399 nautical miles from San Juan, P. R.

	MONTREAL, CANADA (St. Lambert Lock)	Cabot Strait 47°07·0'N, 60°17·0'W	Gut of Canso (Lock) 45°45·0'N, 61°25·0'W	Portland, Maine 43°39·4'N, 70°14·7'W	Boston, Mass 42°22·0N, 71°03·0'W	NANTUCKET SHOALS 40°30·0'N, 69°25·0'W	NEW YORK, N. Y. 40°42·0'N, 74°01·0'W	Philadelphea, Pa 39°56·8'N, 75°08·3'W	Baltimore, Md 39°16·0'N, 76°34·5'W	CHESAPEAKE BAY ENT 36°56·3'N, 75°58·6'W	Norfolk, Va 36°50·9'N, 75°17·9'W	DIAMOND SHOALS 35°08·0'N, 75°15·0'W	Wilmington, N. C. 34°14·0'N, 77°57·0'W	Charleston. S. C. 32°47·2'N, 79°55·2'W	Savannah, Ga 32°05·0'N, 81°05·7'W	Jacksonville, Fla 30°19·2'N, 81°39·0'W	Key West, Fla 24°33·7'N, 81°48·5'W	STRAITS OF FLORIDA 24°25·0'N, 83°00·0'W	Tampa, Fla 27°56·5'N, 82°26·7'W	Pensacola, Fla 30°24'N, 87°13·0'W	Mobile, Ala 30°42·5'N, 88°02·5'W	NEW ORLEANS, La (via SW Pass) 29°57·0'N, 90°03·7'W	Port Arthur, Tex 29°49·5'N, 93°57·6'W	Galveston, Tex 29°19·0'N, 94°47·0'W	Corpus Christi, Tex 27°48·8', 97°24·0'W	San Juan, P. R. 18°27·8'N, 66°06·7'W	YUCATAN CHANNEL 21°50·0'N, 85°03·0'W	Panama Canal (Atlantic Ent) 9°23·5'N, 79°55·3'W
Cabot Strait	681																											
Gut of Canso (Lock)	717	120																										
Portland, Maine	1276	595	484																									
Boston, Mass	1318	637	526	100																								
NANTUCKET SHOALS	1311	630	519	203	163																							
NEW YORK, N. Y.	1534	853	742	426	386	223																						
Philadelphea, Pa	1682	1001	890	575	535	372	240																					
Baltimore, Md	1838	1157	1046	734	694	531	417	392																				
CHESAPEAKE BAY ENT	1689	1008	896	584	544	361	267	242	150																			
Norfolk, Va	1716	1035	923	611	571	408	294	269	173	27																		
DIAMOND SHOALS	1729	1048	936	628	588	425	345	322	267	117	144																	
Wilmington, N. C.	1948	1267	1155	847	807	644	564	541	486	366	636	219																
Charleston. S. C.	2014	1333	1221	913	873	710	630	607	552	402	429	285	151															
Savannah, Ga	2088	1407	1295	987	947	784	704	681	626	476	503	359	227	102														
Jacksonville, Fla	2172	1491	1379	1071	1031	888	788	765	710	560	587	443	315	197	145													
Key West, Fla	2479	1798	1690	1387	1347	1184	1109	1086	1031	881	908	764	667	572	543	462												
STRAITS OF FLORIDA	2540	1859	1751	1448	1408	1245	1170	1147	1092	942	969	825	728	633	504	523	73											
Tampa, Fla	2772	2091	1983	1680	1640	1477	1402	1379	1324	1174	1201	1057	960	865	836	755	305	232										
Pensacola, Fla	2977	2296	2188	1885	1845	1682	1607	1584	1529	1379	1406	1262	1165	1070	1041	960	510	437	347									
Mobile, Ala	3011	2330	2222	1919	1879	1716	1641	1618	1563	1413	1440	1296	1199	1104	1075	994	544	471	389	89								
NEW ORLEANS, La (via SW Pass)	3080	2399	2291	1988	1948	1785	1710	1687	1632	1482	1509	1365	1268	1173	1144	1063	613	540	502	288	269							
Port Arthur, Tex	3240	2559	2451	2148	2108	1945	1870	1847	1792	1642	1669	1525	1428	1333	1304	1223	773	700	697	504	491	441						
Galveston, Tex	3242	2561	2463	2150	2110	1947	1872	1849	1794	1644	1671	1527	1430	1335	1306	1225	775	702	703	509	496	446	89					
Corpus Christi, Tex	3347	2666	2558	2255	2215	2052	1977	1954	1699	1749	1776	1632	1535	1440	1411	1330	880	807	810	618	605	555	249	207				
San Juan, P. R.	2445	1764	1669	1531	1486	1334	1399	1395	1375	1225	1252	1114	1153	1138	1156	1121	966	1017	1249	1448	1448	1557	1717	1719	1824			
YUCATAN CHANNEL	2730	2049	1937	1629	1589	1426	1346	1323	1268	1118	1145	1001	904	809	780	699	251	192	404	533	562	587	691	696	769	1111		
Panama Canal (Atlantic Ent)	3203	2522	2419	2189	2149	1986	1972	1955	1904	1754	1781	1637	1609	1563	1564	1513	1060	1001	1213	1342	1371	1396	1487	1493	1549	990	809	
PANAMA CANAL, (Pacific Ent) 8°53·0'N, 79°31·0'W	3249	2568	2465	2235	2195	2032	2018	2001	1950	1800	1827	1683	1655	1609	1610	1559	1106	1047	1259	1380	1417	1442	1533	1539	1595	1036	855	46

* Quebec. Canada SUBTRACT 139 MILES

All tabular distances are by outside routes which can be used by the deepest draft vessel that the listed ports can accommodate. Lighter-draft vessels can save considerable mileage by transiting Canso Lock (Canada), the cape Cod Canal (Massachusetts), and the Chesapeake and Delaware Canal (Delaware-Maryland); see the detailed tables. Gulf of Mexico distances are through the Shipping Safety Fairways.

GULF OF MAINE DISTANCES
CALAIS, MAINE, TO CAPE COD, MASS.
(Nautical Miles)

Figure at intersection of columns opposite ports in question is the nautical mileage between the two. Example: Portland, Maine, is 100 nautical miles from Boston, Mass.

Port	Calais, Maine 45°11·4'N, 67°16·7'W	Eastport, Maine 44°54·3'N, 66°59·0'W	Lubec, Maine 44°51·7'N, 67°59·0'W	Machiasport, Maine 44°41·9'N, 67°23·6'W	Jonesport, Maine 44°31·6'N, 67°37·0'W	Bar Harbor, Maine 44°23·5'N, 68°12·0'W	Buck Harbour 44°20·3'N, 68°44·2'W	Stonington, Maine 44°09·2'N, 68°39·8'W	Rockland, Maine 44°06·0'N, 69°05·5'W	Searsport, Maine 44°27·0'N, 68°54·0'W	Bucksport, Maine 44°34·3'N, 68°48·0'W	Bangor, Maine 44°27·0'N, 68°54·0'W	Boothbay Harbor, Maine 43°51·0'N, 69°37·6'W	Wiscasset, Maine 43°59·5'N, 69°40·1'W	Bath, Maine 43°54·5'N, 69°48·7'W	Augusta, Maine 44°18·9'N, 69°46·4'W	Portland, Maine 43°39·4'N, 70°14·7'W	York Harbor, Maine 43°07·9'N, 70°38·6'W	Portsmouth, N. H. 43°04·6'N, 70°44·5'W	Newburyport, Mass. 42°48·6'N, 70°52·4'W	Rockport, Mass. 42°40·0'N, 70°36·5'W	Gloucester, Mass. 42°36·6'N, 70°39·6'W	Salem, Mass. 42°31·3'N, 70°52·5'W	Marblehead, Mass. 42°30·2'N, 70°50·7'W	Lynn, Mass. 42°27·3'N, 70°56·6'W	Boston, Mass. 42°22·0'N, 71°03·0'W	Scituate, Mass. 42°11·9'N, 70°43·5'W	Plymouth, Mass. 41°57·6'N, 70°39·8'W	CAPE COD CANAL E ENT 41°46·8'N, 70°29·0'W	Provincetown, Mass. 42°02·5'N, 70°10·0'W
Eastport	24																													
Lubec	26	3																												
Machiasport	61	46	35																											
Jonesport	66	42	40	20																										
Bar Harbor	98	83	72	52	34																									
Buck Harbour	125	109	98	80	60	39																								
Stonington	118	102	91	73	53	33	16																							
Rockland	145	130	118	100	82	62	22	20																						
Searsport	152	137	126	107	89	70	16	24	23																					
Bucksport	159	145	133	115	96	77	22	30	33	13																				
Bangor	176	162	150	132	113	94	39	47	50	30	17																			
Boothbay Harbor	168	153	142	123	105	86	57	53	42	61	70	87																		
Wiscasset	189	175	162	144	124	105	68	64	62	80	89	106	21																	
Bath	187	173	161	142	122	103	67	63	59	78	86	104	23	30																
Augusta	214	200	188	169	149	130	94	90	86	105	113	131	50	57	27															
Portland	198	183	172	153	135	115	85	81	71	90	98	115	36	44	40	66														
York Harbor	222	208	196	178	159	140	114	109	99	118	126	144	64	72	67	94	43													
Portsmouth	230	216	204	186	167	148	123	119	107	126	135	151	74	82	78	104	56	11												
Newburyport	241	226	215	197	178	159	137	132	118	137	145	162	86	94	89	116	67	25	22											
Rockport	236	221	210	192	173	154	131	126	115	134	143	160	84	92	88	115	66	29	27	16										
Gloucester	245	230	219	200	182	163	138	133	126	145	153	170	95	103	98	125	79	42	40	31	17									
Salem	252	237	226	208	189	170	149	145	133	152	160	177	102	110	105	132	87	49	47	38	24	12								
Marblehead	251	236	225	207	188	169	148	143	132	151	159	176	101	109	104	131	86	48	46	37	23	11	5							
Lynn	261	246	235	217	198	179	157	153	142	161	169	186	110	118	114	141	95	58	56	47	33	22	18	14						
Boston	265	250	239	221	203	184	162	158	147	166	174	191	115	123	119	146	100	63	61	51	37	26	27	19	13					
Scituate	259	244	233	215	196	177	159	155	142	161	169	186	112	120	115	142	97	60	58	48	34	26	24	22	22	21				
Plymouth	268	253	242	224	206	188	174	163	155	174	182	199	125	133	129	156	112	75	73	64	50	43	45	39	40	40	20			
CAPE COD CANAL E ENT	270	225	244	226	209	190	176	165	160	178	187	204	130	139	137	164	118	83	81	72	58	52	53	48	48	52	29	20		
Provincetown	258	243	232	214	197	179	165	155	148	166	175	192	119	127	123	150	107	75	73	63	49	45	49	45	47	49	29	26	22	
NANTUCKET SHOALS 40°30·0'N, 69°25·0'W	312	297	286	271	257	243	237	226	223	242	250	267	207	217	213	240	203	182	180	171	157	155	159	156	159	163	143	144	144	132

Portland Lighted Horn Buoy P (LNB) (43°31·6'N, 70°05·5'W) to Portland 11·3 miles

Each distance is by shortest route that safe navigation permits betweent he two ports concerned. Vessels standing along the coast must make their own adjustments for non-direct routes. For example, the table shows a distance of 214 miles by direct route from Machiasport to Provincetown; the distance via Matinicus Rock and Cape Ann is 235 miles. Distances from Eastport to Machiasport and other ports farther southward are via deep Head Harbor Passage, which is 8 miles farther than via shallow Lubec Channel

COASTWISE DISTANCES
CAPE COD, MASS., TO NEW YORK, N. Y.
(Nautical Miles)

Figure at intersection of columns opposite ports in question is the nautical mileage between the two. Example: New Bedford, Mass., is 74 nautical miles from new London, Conn.

	CAPE COD CANAL E ENT. 41°46·8'N, 70°29·0'W	NANTUCKET SHOALS 40°30·0'N, 70°25·0'W	Nantucket, Mass. 41°17·2'N, 70°05·7'W	Vineyard Haven, Mass. 41°27·3'N, 70°35·8'W	Woods Hole, Mass. 41°31·4'N, 70°40·4'W	New Bedford, Mass. 41°38·1'N, 70°55·1'W	Newport. R. I. 41°29·8'N, 71°19·8'W	Fall River, Mass. 41°42·4'N, 71°09·8'W	Providence. R. I. 41°48·5'N, 71°24·0'W	Great Salt Pond. R. I. 41°11·1'N, 71°34·9'W	Stonington, Conn. 41°19·9'N, 71°54·6'W	New London, Conn. 41°21·4'N, 72°05·4'W	Hartford, Conn. 41°45·0'N, 72°39·0'W	New Haven, Conn. 41°17·4'N, 72°54·5'W	Stratford, Conn. 41°11·3'N, 73°07·3'W	Bridgeport, Conn. 41°10·3'N, 73°10·8'W	South Norwalk, Conn. 41°05·7'N, 73°24·7'W	Stamford, Conn. 41°01·8'N, 73°32·3'W	Montauk, N. Y. 41°02·8'N, 71°57·5'W	Sag Harbor, N. Y. 41°00·2'N, 72°17·7'W	Greenport, N. Y. 41°06·0'N, 72°21·5'W	Port Jefferson, N. Y. 40°57·0'N, 73°04·5'W	MONTAUK POINT, N. Y. 40°42·0'N, 74°01·0'W	NEW YORK, N. Y. 40°42·0', 74°01·0'W	Perth Amboy, N.Y. 40°30·3'N, 74°15·7'W	Elizabethport, N. J. 40°38·8'N, 74°11·2'W
NANTUCKET SHOALS	144																									
Nantucket	69	85																								
Vineyard Haven	43	88	29																							
Woods Hole	22	92	33	7																						
New Bedford	31	111	53	28	15																					
Newport	54	111	71	45	38	38																				
Fall River	69	126	77	51	44	54	16																			
Providence	74	131	91	65	57	58	21	21																		
Great Salt Pond	66	114	80	54	50	48	23	38	43																	
Stonington	77	126	92	67	61	58	34	49	55	19																
New London	89	136	103	77	72	74	48	63	68	29	12															
Hartford	140	187	155	129	125	124	98	113	118	80	66	62														
New Haven	127	171	140	114	109	111	84	100	105	65	52	49	74													
Stratford	132	176	147	121	117	113	90	105	110	72	59	54	81	15												
Bridgeport	138	182	153	127	123	122	95	110	115	78	64	60	86	25	10											
South Norwalk	151	195	166	140	135	135	108	124	129	91	77	73	101	36	26	21										
Stamford	152	196	167	141	136	136	109	125	130	92	79	74	102	37	27	22	11									
Montauk	85	127	99	74	69	66	42	58	63	23	18	20	66	51	56	62	75	76								
Sag Harbor	100	143	114	88	83	81	57	72	77	39	29	27	64	49	54	60	73	74	21							
Greenport	99	142	113	87	82	80	56	71	76	37	28	25	62	47	52	58	71	72	22	11						
Port Jefferson	134	178	149	123	118	118	91	107	112	74	61	56	84	23	15	15	23	24	58	56	54					
MONTAUK POINT	76	113	89	63	59	60	35	51	56	15	19	28	75	62	65	74	84	85	16	32	30	68				
NEW YORK	182	223	196	171	166	166	139	154	159	121	109	104	131	68	57	52	40	33	105	103	102	52	122			
Perth Amboy	202	223	216	191	186	186	159	174	179	141	129	124	151	88	77	72	60	53	125	123	122	72	123	20		
Elizabethport	191	225	206	181	176	176	149	164	169	131	119	114	141	78	67	62	50	43	115	113	112	62	124	10	10	
Port Newark, N. J. 40°41·8'N, 74°09·0'W	193	227	208	183	178	178	151	166	171	133	121	116	143	80	69	64	52	45	117	115	114	64	126	12	15	5

Ambrose Light (40°27·5'N, 73°49·9'W.) to New York (The Battery). 20·7 miles

INSIDE-ROUTE DISTANCES
SOUTH SIDE OF LONG ISLAND
GREENPORT, N. Y., TO EAST ROCKAWAY INLET, N. Y.
(Nautical Miles)

Figure at intersection of columns opposite ports in question is the nautical mileage between the two. Example: Freeport is 61 nautical miles from Shinnecok canal North End

Greenport 41°06·0'N, 72°21·5'W	Sag Harbor 41°00·2'N, 72°71·7'W	Riverside 40°55·0'N, 72°39·4'W	Shinnecock Canal, N. End 40°53·9'N, 72°30·3'W	Shinnecock Inlet 40°50·3'N, 72°28·6'W	Westhampton Beach 40°48·2'N, 72°38·4'W	Moriches Inlet 40°45·8'N, 72°45·3'W	Bellport 40°45·1'N, 72°56·0'W	Patchogue 40°45·5'N, 73°01·2'W	Bay Shore 40°42·8'N, 73°14·2'W	Fire Island Inlet 40°37·8'N, 73°18·6'W	Babylon 40°41·2'N, 73°18·9'W	Amityville 40°39·6'N, 73°24·8'W	Jones Beach 40°36·2'N, 73°30·8'W	Jones Inlet 40°34·4'N, 73°34·9'W	Freeport 40°37·6'N, 73°34·9'W	Long Beach 40°35·7'N, 73°39·4'W	East Rockaway Inlet 40°34·9'N, 73°45·4'W	Rockaway Point 40°32·4'N, 73°56·5'W	NEW YORK (The Battery) 40°42·0'N, 74°01·0'W	Manasquan Inlet, N. J. 40°06·1'N, 74°01·9'W
11																				
21	22																			
16	17	8																		
21	22	13	5																	
28	29	20	12	9																
34	35	26	18	15	7															
42	43	34	26	23	15	11														
48	49	40	32	29	21	17	6													
57	58	49	41	39	30	27	16	13												
62	63	54	46	44	35	32	21	18	9											
61	62	53	45	42	34	30	19	17	5	8										
66	67	58	50	47	39	35	24	22	10	12	6									
72	73	64	56	54	45	42	31	28	17	16	13	7								
76	77	68	60	58	49	45	35	32	21	20	17	11	4							
77	78	69	61	58	49	46	35	32	21	21	18	12	4	4						
80	81	72	64	61	53	49	38	36	24	24	21	15	8	5	6					
85	86	77	69	66	58	54	44	41	29	29	26	20	13	10	11	5				
94	95	86	78	75	67	63	53	50	38	38	35	29	22	19	20	14	9			
107	108	99	91	88	80	76	66	63	51	51	48	42	35	32	33	27	22	13		
116	117	108	100	97	89	85	75	72	60	60	57	51	44	41	42	36	31	27	40	

Ambrose Light (40°27·5'N, 73°49·9'W) to New York (The Battery), 20·7 miles

DISTANCES ON HUDSON RIVER
NEW YORK, N. Y., TO TROY LOCK, N. Y.
(Nautical Miles)

Figure at intersection of columns opposite ports in question is the nautical mileage between the two. Example: Poughkeepsie, N. Y., is 60 nautical miles from Albany, N. Y.

	NEW YORK (The Battery) 40°42·0'N, 74°01·0'W.	Yonkers 40°56·1'N, 73°54·3'W.	Tarrytown 41°04·7'N, 73°52·2'W.	Nyack 41°05·4'N, 73°54·9'W.	Ossining 41°09·6'N, 73°52·3'W.	Haverstraw 41°11·8'N, 73°57·5'W.	Peekskill 41°17·3'N, 73°56·0'W.	West Point 41°23·1'N, 73°57·3'W.	Newburgh 41°30·1'N, 74°00·3'W.	Poughkeepsie 41°42·3'N, 73°56·5'W.	Hyde Park 41°47·3'N, 73°56·9'W.	Kingston 41°55·1'N, 73°59·0'W.	Saugerties 42°04·4'N, 73°56·7'W.	Catskill 42°13·0'N, 73°52·1'W.	Hudson 42°15·3'N, 73°48·1'W.	Athens 42°15·7'N, 73°48·5'W.	Coxsackie 42°21·0'N, 73°47·6'W.	Coeymans 42°28·5'N, 73°47·4'W.	Albany 42°37·9'N, 73°45·3'W.	Rensselaer 42°37·9'N, 73°45·1'W.	Troy 42°43·7'N, 73°41·8'W.	Watervliet 42°43·7'N, 73°41·9'W.
Yonkers	16																					
Tarrytown	24	9																				
Nyack	25	10	2																			
Ossining	29	14	6	6																		
Haverstraw	33	18	9	10	5																	
Peekskill	38	23	15	15	11	6																
West Point	45	29	21	22	17	13	8															
Newburgh	53	37	29	29	25	21	15	8														
Poughkeepsie	66	50	42	43	38	34	29	21	13													
Hyde Park	71	55	47	48	43	39	34	26	18	5												
Kingston	80	64	56	57	52	48	43	35	27	14	9											
Saugerties	89	74	66	66	62	58	52	45	37	24	19	12										
Catskill	99	83	75	75	71	67	61	54	46	33	28	21	11									
Hudson	102	86	78	78	74	70	64	57	49	36	31	24	14	5								
Athens	102	86	78	78	74	70	64	57	49	36	31	24	14	5	1							
Coxsackie	108	93	85	85	80	76	71	63	55	42	37	30	21	11	7	6						
Coeymans	115	100	92	92	88	84	78	70	62	49	44	38	28	19	14	14	7					
Albany	126	110	102	102	98	94	88	81	73	60	55	48	38	29	24	24	18	10				
Rensselaer	126	110	102	102	98	94	88	81	73	60	55	48	38	29	24	24	18	10	0			
Troy	132	116	108	108	104	100	94	87	79	66	61	54	44	35	30	30	24	16	6	6		
Watervliet	132	116	108	108	104	100	94	87	79	66	61	54	44	35	30	30	24	16	6	6	0	
Troy Lock 41°45·1'N, 73°41·1'W	134	118	110	110	106	102	96	89	81	68	63	56	46	37	32	32	26	18	8	8	2	2

COASTWISE DISTANCES
NEW YORK, N. Y., TO CHESAPEAKE BAY ENTRANCE, V. A.
(Nautical Miles)

Figure at intersection of columns opposite ports in question is the nautical mileage between the two. Example: New York, N. Y., is 240 nautical miles from Philadelphia, Pa..

NANTUCKET SHOALS 40°30·0'N, 69°25·0'W;	MONTAUK POINT, N. Y. 41°01·7'N, 71°47·3'W;	NEW YORK, N. Y. 40°42·0'N, 74°01·0'W;	Manasquan Inlet, N. J. 40°06·1'N, 74°01·9'W;	Barnegat Inlet 39°46·0'N, 69°25·0'W;	Atlantic City, N. Y. 39°22·6'N, 74°24·9'W;	Cape May Harbor, N. J. 38°57·1'N, 74°52·6'W;	DELAWARE BAY ENTRANCE 38°50·5'N, 75°03·3'W;	Harbor of Refuge. Del. 38°49·0'N, 75°05·2'W;	CHES. & DEL. CANAL E. ENT. 39°33·8'N, 75°32·8'W;	Wilmington, Del. 39°43·2', 75°31·5'W	Marcus Hook, Pa. 39°48·2', 75°25·2'W	Chester, Pa. 39°50·0', 75°22·0'W	Philedelphia, Pa. 39°56·8', 75°08·3'W	U.S. Steel Basin, Pa. 40°08·2', 74°45·3'W	Trenton, N. J. 40°11·4', 74°45·4'W	Indian River Inlet, Del. 38°36·5', 75°03·6'W	Ocean City, Md. 38°19·6', 75°05·6'W	Chincoteague, Va. 37°56·3', 75°22·8'W	CHESAPEAKE BAY ENT. 36°56·3', 75°58·6'W
113																			
223	122																		
212	117	40																	
221	131	63	22																
242	159	94	52	32															
271	192	128	85	65	37														
285	212	153	97	78	49	16													
285	212	153	98	79	50	17	2												
336	263	204	148	129	100	67	51	52											
347	274	215	159	140	111	78	62	63	11										
353	280	221	165	146	117	84	68	69	17	8									
356	283	224	169	150	121	88	72	73	21	11	3								
372	299	240	184	165	136	103	87	88	36	26	18	15							
395	322	263	207	188	159	126	110	111	59	49	41	38	23						
400	327	268	212	193	164	131	115	116	64	54	46	43	28	5					
285	209	145	105	86	57	24	15	14	66	77	83	86	101	124	129				
295	227	161	121	101	73	40	32	31	83	95	101	104	119	142	147	20			
328	262	201	161	141	113	80	72	71	123	134	140	144	159	182	187	60	41		
381	322	267	219	199	171	141	155	155	206	218	224	227	242	265	270	118	100	69	

Ambrose Light (40°27·5'N, 73°49·9'W) to new York, 20·7 miles.

Five Fathom Bank Lighted Horn Buoy F (38°47·3'N, 74°34·6'W) to Philadelpia, 111 miles.

Delaware Lighted horn Buoy D (38°27·3'N, 74°41·8'W) to Philadelphia, 116 miles.

DISTANCES BY INTRACOASTAL WATERWAY
MANASQUAN INLET, N. J. TO CAPE MAY CANAL, N. J.
(Nautical Miles)

Figure at intersection of columns opposite ports in question is the nautical mileage between the two. Example: Atlantic City N. J., is 13 nautical miles from Ocean City, N. J.

NEW YORK, N. Y. (Ther Battery)* 40°42·0'N, 74°01·0'W.	Shark river Inlet* 40°11·2'N, 74°00·5'W.	Manasquan Inlet* 40°06·1'N, 74°01·9'W.	Bay Head 40°03·8'N, 74°03·1'W.	Mantoloking 40°02·2'N, 74°03·4'W.	Toms River (Town) 39°56·9'N, 74°11·8'W.	Seaside Park 39°55·3'N, 74°05·0'W.	Forked River (town) 39°50·1'N, 74°11·7'W.	Barnegat Inlet 39°46·0'N, 74°06·3'W.	Beach Haven 39°34·0'N, 74°14·8'W.	Atlantic City 39°22·6'N, 74°24·9'W.	Mays Landing 39°26·9'N, 74°43·4'W.	Ocean City 39°17·3'N, 74°34·4'W.	Sea Isle City 39°09·4'N, 74°42·0'W.	Avalon 39°06·6'N, 74°44·0'W.	Stone harbor 39°03·4'N, 74°46·0'W.	Wildwood 39°00·5'N, 74°49·8'W.	Cape May Harbor 38°57·1'N, 74°52·6'W.	Cape May Canal W. Ent. 38°58·0'N, 74°54·0'W.	CHES. & DEL. CANAL E. ENT. 39°33·8'N, 75°32·8'W.
34																			
40	6																		
44	9	4																	
46	11	6	2																
58	23	18	14	12															
54	20	14	10	9	7														
63	29	23	19	17	15	10													
66	32	26	22	20	18	13	8												
79	45	39	35	33	31	26	21	20											
97	62	57	53	51	49	44	39	38	18										
124	90	84	80	79	77	71	66	65	45	30									
108	74	68	64	63	60	55	50	49	29	13	18								
119	85	79	76	74	72	66	61	60	40	25	29	11							
123	89	83	79	77	75	70	65	64	44	28	33	15	4						
128	94	88	85	83	81	75	70	69	49	34	38	20	9	5					
133	99	93	89	88	86	80	75	74	54	39	43	25	14	10	5				
138	103	98	94	92	90	85	80	79	59	43	47	30	18	15	9	5			
142	108	102	98	96	94	89	84	83	63	47	52	34	23	19	14	9	4		
190	156	150	146	144	142	137	132	131	111	95	100	82	71	67	62	57	52	48	

* Outside distances between New York and Manesquan Inlet.

DISTANCES ON DELAWARE BAY AND RIVER
(Nautical Miles)

Figure at intersection of columns opposite ports in question is the nautical mileage between the two. Example: Salem, N. J., is 41 nautical miles form Piladelphia, Pa.

Port	DELAWARE BAY ENT. 38°50·0'N, 75°03·3'W	Roosevelt Inlet, Del. 38°47·7'N, 75°09·4'W	Cape May Canal W. Ent., N. J. 38°58·0'N, 74°58·0'W	St. Jones River Mouth, Del. 39°04·0'N, 75°22·5'W	Mauricetown, N. J 39°17·1'N, 74°59·5'W	Bridgeton, N. J. 39°25·5'N, 75°14·2'W	Smyrna River Mouth, Del 39°22·2'N, 75°30·2'W	Salem, N. J. 39°34·6'N, 75°28·7'W	CHES. & DEL. CANAL E. ENT. 39°33·8', 75°32·8'W	New Castle, Del. 39°39·4'N, 75°33·6'W	Wilmington, Del. 39°43·2'N, 75°31·5'W	Marcus Hook, Pa. 39°48·2'N, 75°25·2'W	Bridgeport, N. J. 39°48·0'N, 75°21·3'W	Chester, Pa. 39°50·0'N, 75°22·0'W	Schuylkill River Mouth, PA 39°52·8'N, 75°11·9'W	Philadelphia, Pa. 39°56·8'N, 75°08·3'W	Burlington, N. J. 40°04·9'N, 74°51·8'W	U.S. Steel Basin, Pa 40°08·2'N, 74°45·3'W	Bordentown, N. J. 40°09·1'N, 74°43·0'W
Roosevelt Inlet, Del.	6																		
Cape May Canal W. Ent., N. J.	9	14																	
St. Jones River Mouth, Del.	20	20	21																
Mauricetown, N. J	33	37	26	30															
Bridgeton, N. J.	51	52	47	35	51														
Smyrna River Mouth, Del	39	40	36	21	39	25													
Salem, N. J.	54	55	51	36	54	39	16												
CHES. & DEL. CANAL E. ENT.	51	52	48	34	51	36	13	5											
New Castle, Del.	58	59	55	40	58	43	20	12	7										
Wilmington, Del.	62	63	59	45	62	47	24	16	11	5									
Marcus Hook, Pa.	68	69	65	51	68	53	30	22	17	12	8								
Bridgeport, N. J.	72	73	69	55	72	57	34	26	21	15	11	4							
Chester, Pa.	72	73	69	55	72	57	34	26	21	15	11	3	6						
Schuylkill River Mouth, PA	80	81	77	63	80	65	42	34	29	23	19	12	14	9					
Philadelphia, Pa.	87	88	84	69	87	72	49	41	36	30	26	18	22	15	7				
Burlington, N. J.	103	104	100	85	103	88	65	57	52	46	42	34	37	31	23	16			
U.S. Steel Basin, Pa	110	111	107	92	110	95	72	64	59	53	49	41	44	38	29	23	7		
Bordentown, N. J.	112	113	109	94	112	97	74	66	61	55	51	43	46	40	31	25	9	2	
Trenton, N. J. 40°11·4'N, 74°45·4'W	115	116	112	97	115	100	77	69	64	58	54	46	49	43	34	28	12	5	4

21

CHESAPEAKE BAY DISTANCES
(Nautical Miles)

Figure at intersection of columns opposite ports in question is the nautical mileage between the two. Example: Washington, D. C., is 155 nautical miles from Annapolis, Md.

CHES. & DEL CANAL E. ENT. 39°33·8'N., 75°32·8'W	Chesapeake City, Md. 39°31·8'N., 75°48·9'W	Havre de Grace, Md. 39°32·7'N., 76°05·0'W	Baltimore, Md. 39°16·0'N., 76°34·5'W	Chestertown, Md. 39°12·4'N., 76°03·8'W	Annapolis, Md. 38°59·0'N., 76°28·6'W	St. Michaels, Md. 38°47·2'N., 76°13·2'W	Cambridge, Md. 38°34·4'N., 76°04·3'W	Solomons, Md. 38°19·2'N., 76°27·4'W	Salisbury, Md. 38°21·9'N, 75°36·3'W	Potomad River Mouth. 37°57·7'N., 76°16·7'W	Washington, D. C. 38°52·4'N., 77°01·4'W	Crisfield, Md. 37°58·6'N., 75°51·9'W	Fredericksburg. Va. 38°17·8'N., 77°27·2'W	Cape Charles, Va. 37°15·9'N., 76°01·4'W	Yorktown, Va. 37°14·4'N., 76°30·5'W	West Point, Va. 37°31·6'N., 76°48·1'W	Newport news, Va. 36°58·0'N., 76°26·0'W	Suffolk, Va. 36°44·3'N., 76°35·0'W	Hopewell, Va 37°19·0'N., 77°16·4'W	Petersburg, Va. 37°14··1'N., 77°24·0'W	Richmond, Va. 37°31·4'N., 77°25·2'W	Norfolk, Va. 36°50·9'N., 76°17·9'W	CHESAPEAKE BAY ENT. 36°56·3'N., 76°58·6'W
13																							
33	20																						
62	49	41																					
78	65	61	45																				
65	52	45	28	40																			
83	70	62	45	59	25																		
98	85	78	60	72	39	36																	
103	90	84	66	78	45	48	39																
143	130	124	107	119	86	89	81	51															
122	109	101	84	96	64	65	58	27	49														
213	200	192	175	187	155	156	149	118	141	96													
134	121	115	98	110	77	80	72	42	43	27	121												
243	230	224	206	219	186	190	182	150	165	125	221	129											
169	156	149	132	146	112	116	107	76	87	50	146	51	122										
192	179	163	155	156	130	126	117	87	100	68	164	64	132	28									
214	201	185	174	178	152	149	140	109	122	90	186	86	154	50	22								
207	194	172	170	167	136	138	129	97	110	86	182	74	143	29	55	63							
209	196	190	172	185	152	156	147	115	128	89	185	92	161	48	55	78	21						
265	252	230	228	225	194	196	187	155	168	144	240	132	201	88	114	122	58	79					
259	246	240	222	235	204	206	197	165	178	137	233	142	211	97	101	123	68	89	10				
284	271	249	247	244	213	215	206	174	187	163	259	151	220	106	132	140	77	98	19	28			
209	196	175	173	170	140	141	132	100	113	89	185	77	146	32	58	66	12	29	70	80	90		
187	174	166	150	162	129	132	123	92	103	67	163	67	136	21	34	56	24	42	82	92	101	27	

DISTANCES ON POTOMAC RIVER
(Nautical Miles)

Figure at intersection of columns opposite ports in question is the nautical mileage between the two. Example: Colonial Beach, Va., is 63 nautical miles from Washington, D. C.

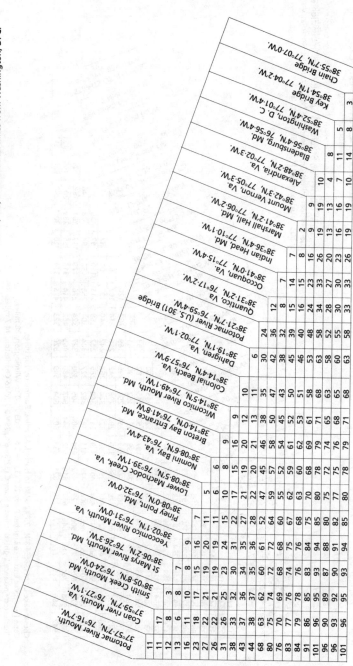

	Potomac River Mouth. 37°57·7'N, 76°16·7'W.	Coan river Mouth, Va. 37°59·7'N, 76°27·1'W.	Smith Creek Mouth, Md. 38°05·8'N, 76°24·0'W.	St Marys River Mouth, Md. 38°06·2'N, 76°26·3'W.	Yeocomico River Mouth, Va. 38°02·1'N, 76°31·0'W.	Piney Point, Md. 38°08·0'N, 76°32·0'W.	Lower Machodoc Creek, Va. 38°08·5'N, 76°39·1'W.	Nomini Bay, Va. 38°08·6'N, 76°43·4'W.	Breton Bay Entrance, Md. 38°14·0'N, 76°41·8'W.	Wicomico River Mouth, Md. 38°14·5'N, 76°49·1'W.	Colonial Beach, Va. 38°14·4'N, 76°57·9'W.	Dahigren, Va. 38°19·1'N, 77°02·1'W.	Potomac River (U.S. 301) Bridge 38°21·7'N, 76°59·4'W.	Quantico, Va 38°31·2'N, 76°17·2'W.	Occoquan, Va. 38°41·0'N, 77°15·4'W.	Indian Head, Md. 38°36·4'N, 77°10·1'W.	Marshall Hall, Md. 38°41·2'N, 77°06·2'W.	Mount Vernon, Va. 38°42·3'N, 77°05·3'W.	Alexandria, Va. 38°48·2'N, 77°02·3'W.	Bladensburg, Md. 38°56·4'N, 76°56·4'W.	Washington, D. C. 38°52·4'N, 77°01·4'W.	Key Bridge 38°54·1'N, 77°04·2'W.
Coan river Mouth, Va.	11																					
Smith Creek Mouth, Md.	11	17																				
St Marys River Mouth, Md.	12	8	3																			
Yeocomico River Mouth, Va.	13	6	8	7																		
Piney Point, Md.	16	11	10	8	9																	
Lower Machodoc Creek, Va.	23	18	17	15	16	7																
Nomini Bay, Va.	27	22	21	19	20	11	5															
Breton Bay Entrance, Md.	26	22	21	19	19	11	6	6														
Wicomico River Mouth, Md.	31	26	25	23	24	15	10	8	9													
Colonial Beach, Va.	38	33	32	30	31	22	17	15	16	9												
Dahigren, Va.	43	37	36	34	35	27	21	19	20	12	10											
Potomac River (U.S. 301) Bridge	44	38	37	35	36	28	22	20	21	13	11	6										
Quantico, Va	68	63	62	60	61	52	47	45	46	38	35	30	24									
Occoquan, Va.	80	75	74	72	72	64	59	57	58	50	47	42	36	12								
Indian Head, Md.	76	70	69	68	68	60	55	52	54	45	43	38	32	8	7							
Marshall Hall, Md.	83	77	76	74	75	67	62	59	61	52	50	45	39	15	14	7						
Mount Vernon, Va.	84	79	78	76	76	68	63	60	62	53	51	46	40	16	15	8	2					
Alexandria, Va.	91	86	85	83	84	75	70	68	69	61	58	53	48	24	23	16	9	9				
Bladensburg, Md.	101	96	95	93	94	85	80	78	79	71	68	63	58	34	33	26	19	19	10			
Washington, D. C.	96	90	89	87	88	80	75	72	74	65	63	58	52	28	27	20	13	13	4	8		
Key Bridge	96	93	92	90	91	82	77	75	76	68	65	60	55	30	30	23	16	16	7	11	5	
Chain Bridge 38°55·7'N, 77°07·0'W.	101	96	95	93	94	85	80	78	79	71	68	63	58	33	33	26	19	19	10	14	8	3

21

COASTWISE DISTANCES
NORFOLK, V. A., TO KEY WEST, FLA.
(Nautical Miles)

Figure at intersection of columns opposite ports in question is the nautical mileage between the two. Example: Norfolk, Va., is 503 nautical miles from Savannah, Ga.

	CHESAPEAKE BAY ENTRACE 36°56·3′N, 75°58·6′W	Norfolk, Va. 46°50·9′N, 76°17·9′W	DIAMOND SHOALS 35°08·0′N, 75°15·0′W	Morehead City, N. C. 34°42·8′N, 76°41·8′W	Southport, N. C. 33°54·8′N, 78°01·0′W	Wilmington, N. C. 34°14·0′N, 77°57·0′W	Georgetown, S. C. 33°21·4′N, 79°16·9′W	Charleston, S. C. 32°47·2′N, 79°55·2′W	Port Royal, S. C. 32°22·3′N, 80°41·6′W	Savannah, Ga. 32°06·0′N, 81°05·7′W	Brunswick, Ga 31°08·0′N, 81°29·7′W	Fernandina Beach, Fla. 30°40·3′N, 81°28·0′W	Jacksonville, Fla. 30°19·2′N, 81°39·0′W	St. Augustine, Fla. 29°53·6′N, 81°18·5′W	Cape Canaveral, Fla 28°24·6′N, 80°36·5′W	Fort Pierce, Fla. 27°27·5′N, 60°19·3′W	Stuart, Fla. 27°12·2′N, 80°15·6′W	Port of Palm Beach, Fla. 26°46·1′N, 80°03·0′W	Port Everglades, Fla. 26°05·6′N, 80°07·0′W	Miami, Fla. 25°47·0′N, 80°11·0′W	Key West, Fla. 24°33·7′N, 81°48·5′W
Norfolk, Va.	27																				
DIAMOND SHOALS	117	144																			
Morehead City, N. C.	222	249	105																		
Southport, N. C.	315	342	198	133																	
Wilmington, N. C.	336	363	219	154	21																
Georgetown, S. C.	365	392	248	184	87	108															
Charleston, S. C.	402	429	285	220	130	151	79														
Port Royal, S. C.	465	492	348	284	191	212	141	90													
Savannah, Ga.	476	503	359	295	206	227	154	102	51												
Brunswick, Ga	527	554	410	346	260	281	210	156	110	104											
Fernandina Beach, Fla.	533	560	416	352	265	286	216	166	120	115	50										
Jacksonville, Fla.	560	587	443	379	294	315	247	197	152	145	82	53									
St. Augustine, Fla.	557	584	440	377	296	317	246	199	157	152	90	61	56								
Cape Canaveral, Fla	612	639	495	438	367	388	324	283	251	251	195	169	167	120							
Fort Pierce, Fla.	647	674	530	476	407	428	368	329	298	298	242	216	214	167	69						
Stuart, Fla.	666	693	549	497	423	444	391	353	324	324	268	242	240	192	91	32					
Port of Palm Beach, Fla.	678	705	561	509	443	464	407	369	341	340	285	262	259	211	110	52	36				
Port Everglades, Fla.	720	747	603	550	485	506	449	411	383	382	327	304	301	253	152	94	78	46			
Miami, Fla.	743	770	626	573	508	529	472	434	406	405	350	327	324	276	175	117	101	68	27		
Key West, Fla.	881	908	764	711	646	667	610	572	544	543	488	465	462	414	313	255	239	207	165	151	
STRAITS OF FLORIDA 24°24·0′N, 83°00·0′W	942	969	825	772	707	728	671	633	605	604	549	526	523	475	374	316	300	267	226	211	73

Chesapeake Light (36°54·3′N, 75°42·8′W) to Norfolk 42 miles; Baltimore, 165 miles.
Cape Fear River Entrance Lighted Buoy 2CF (33°49·5′N, 78°03·7′W) to Wilmington, 28 miles.
Charleston Entrance Lighted Whistle Buoy C (32°39·6′N, 79°40·9′W) to Charleston, 14·7 miles.
Savannah Light (31°57·0′N, 80°41·0′W) to Savannah, 25 miles.
St Johns River Entrance Buoy STJ (30°23·6′N, 81°19·1′W) to Jacksonville, 23 miles.

Each distance is by shortest route that safe navigation permits between the two ports concerned. The navigator must make his own adjustments for non-direct routes selected to run with or avoid the Gulf Stream. For example, the table shows a distance of 561 miles by direct route from Diamond Shoals to Port of Palm Beach; distances via the routes shown is Chapter 3. coast Pilot 4, are: Outer route 572 miles; Gulf Stream route 593 miles; Inner route, 628 miles.

COASTWISE DISTANCES
NORFOLK, V. A., TO KEY WEST, FLA.
(Nautical Miles)

Figure at intersection of columns opposite ports in question is the nautical/statute mileage between the two.
Example: Morehead City, N. C., is 445 nautical miles (512 statute miles) form Fernandina Beach, Fla.

Ports:
- Norfolk, Va. 36°50·9'N, 76°17·9'W
- Elizabeth City, N. C. 36°18·1'N, 76°13·0'W
- Hertford, N. C. 36°11·6'N, 76°28·0'W
- Columbia, N. C. 35°55·0'N, 76°15·4'W
- Edenton, N. C. 36°03·3'N, 76°36·6'W
- Plymouth, N. C. 35°51·8'N, 76°45·6'W
- Manteo, N. C 35°54·6'N, 75°40·2'W
- Belhaven, N. C. 35°32·1'N, 76°37·4'W
- Washington, N. C. 35°32·6'N, 77°03·7'W
- Ocracoke, N. C. 35°06·8'N, 75°59·1'W
- Oriental, N. C. 35°01·5'N, 76°41·8'W
- New Bern, N. C. 35°06·1'N, 77°02·1'W
- Beaufort, N. C. 34°43·1'N, 76°40·2'W
- Morehead City, N. C. 34°42·8'N, 76°41·8'W
- Swansboro, N. C. 34°41·0'N, 77°07·3'W
- Jacksonville, N. C. 34°44·7'N, 77°26·3'W
- Wrightsville, N. C. 34°13·1'N, 77°48·8'W
- Wilmington, N. C. 34°14·0'N, 77°57·0'W
- Southport, N. C. 33°54·8'N, 78°01·0'W
- Little River, S. C. 33°52·2'N, 78°36·6'W
- Bucksport, S. C. 33°39·0'N, 79°05·6'W
- Georgetown, S. C. 33°21·4'N, 79°16·9'W
- McClellanville, S. C. 33°04·7'N, 79°27·6'W
- Charleston, S. C. 32°47·2'N, 79°55·2'W
- Beaufort, S. C. 32°25·6'N, 80°40·2'W
- Savannah, Ga. 32°05·0'N, 81°05·7'W
- Thunderbolt, Ga. 32°01·5'N, 81°02·8'W
- Brunswick, Ga. 31°08·0'N, 81°29·7'W
- Fernandina Beach, Fla. 30°40·3'N, 81°28·0'W

Statute Miles

	Elizabeth City	Hertford	Columbia	Edenton	Plymouth	Manteo	Belhaven	Washington	Ocracoke	Oriental	New Bern	Beaufort, N. C.	Morehead City	Swansboro	Jacksonville	Wrightsville	Wilmington	Southport	Little River	Bucksport	Georgetown	McClellanville	Charleston	Beaufort, S. C.	Savannah	Thunderbolt	Brunswick	Fernandina Beach
Norfolk	89	102	102	113	121	92	138	180	151	184	207	204	205	230	266	283	314	308	344	377	405	430	467	536	585	583	685	717
Elizabeth City		45	45	55	64	45	91	131	105	136	160	154	157	182	217	235	266	260	296	329	358	382	419	488	536	535	636	669
Hertford			30	40	48	53	91	132	112	137	160	158	158	184	219	236	267	261	298	330	358	383	421	489	537	536	638	670
Columbia				29	38	52	90	131	110	136	159	157	157	182	217	235	266	260	296	329	357	382	419	488	536	535	636	669
Edenton					16	62	100	142	120	145	168	166	167	191	227	245	276	270	306	338	366	391	429	497	547	545	647	678
Plymouth						70	109	150	130	154	178	175	175	201	237	254	285	280	315	349	376	402	438	508	556	555	656	688
Manteo							81	121	70	105	127	127	127	152	186	205	236	231	267	299	326	352	388	457	506	505	606	639
Belhaven								45	49	49	72	70	70	96	131	150	181	175	211	243	270	296	334	402	451	450	551	582
Washington									69	64	87	85	85	110	146	163	194	189	224	258	285	311	348	417	465	464	565	597
Ocracoke										47	71	68	68	93	129	147	178	173	208	241	268	293	331	399	449	448	549	580
Oriental											26	25	25	51	86	105	136	130	166	198	226	251	289	357	406	405	506	537
New Bern												44	44	69	105	123	154	148	184	216	245	270	307	376	425	423	525	557
Beaufort, N. C.													3	28	63	81	112	107	143	175	203	229	266	334	383	382	483	514
Morehead City														25	61	79	110	105	140	173	200	226	264	331	381	380	481	512
Swansboro															36	53	64	79	115	147	175	200	238	306	356	353	456	487
Jacksonville																55	86	81	116	148	177	203	239	308	357	356	457	489
Wrightsville																	31	25	61	94	122	147	184	253	302	300	402	434
Wilmington																		24	60	93	121	146	183	252	300	299	402	433
Southport																			36	69	97	122	159	228	276	275	376	409
Little River																				32	61	86	123	192	241	239	341	373
Bucksport																					28	53	91	159	208	206	308	339
Georgetown																						28	64	133	183	181	283	314
McClellanville																							37	106	155	153	255	287
Charleston																								69	120	119	220	251
Beaufort, S. C.																									49	47	150	181
Savannah																										16	117	150
Thunderbolt																											101	133
Brunswick																												40

Nautical Miles

	Norfolk	Elizabeth City	Hertford	Columbia	Edenton	Plymouth	Manteo	Belhaven	Washington	Ocracoke	Oriental	New Bern	Beaufort, N. C.	Morehead City	Swansboro	Jacksonville	Wrightsville	Wilmington	Southport	Little River	Bucksport	Georgetown	McClellanville	Charleston	Beaufort, S. C.	Savannah	Thunderbolt	Brunswick
Elizabeth City	77																											
Hertford	89	39																										
Columbia	89	39	26																									
Edenton	98	48	35	25																								
Plymouth	105	56	42	33	14																							
Manteo	80	39	46	45	54	61																						
Belhaven	120	79	79	78	87	95	70																					
Washington	156	114	115	114	123	130	105	39																				
Ocracoke	131	91	97	96	104	113	61	43	60																			
Oriental	160	118	119	118	126	134	91	43	56	41																		
New Bern	180	139	139	138	146	155	110	63	76	62	23																	
Beaufort, N. C.	177	134	137	136	144	152	110	61	74	59	22	38																
Morehead City	178	136	137	136	145	152	110	61	74	59	22	38	3															
Swansboro	200	158	160	158	166	175	132	83	96	81	44	60	24	22														
Jacksonville	231	189	190	189	197	206	162	114	127	112	75	91	55	53	31													
Wrightsville	246	204	205	204	213	221	178	130	142	128	91	107	70	69	46	48												
Wilmington	273	231	232	231	240	248	205	157	169	155	118	134	97	96	73	75	27											
Southport	268	226	227	226	235	243	201	152	164	150	113	129	93	91	69	70	22	21										
Little River	299	257	259	257	266	274	232	183	195	181	144	160	124	122	100	101	53	52	31									
Bucksport	328	286	287	286	294	303	260	211	224	209	172	188	152	150	128	129	82	81	60	28								
Georgetown	352	311	311	310	318	327	283	235	248	233	196	213	177	174	152	154	106	105	84	53	24							
McClellanville	374	332	333	332	340	349	306	257	270	255	218	235	199	196	174	176	128	127	106	75	46	24						
Charleston	406	364	366	364	373	381	337	290	302	288	251	267	231	229	207	208	160	159	138	107	79	56	32					
Beaufort, S. C.	466	424	425	424	432	441	397	349	362	347	310	327	290	288	266	268	220	219	198	167	138	116	92	60				
Savannah	508	466	467	466	475	483	440	392	404	390	353	369	333	331	309	310	262	261	240	209	181	159	135	104	43			
Thunderbolt	507	465	466	465	474	482	439	391	403	389	352	368	332	330	307	309	261	260	239	208	179	157	133	103	41	14		
Brunswick	595	553	554	553	562	570	527	479	491	477	440	456	420	418	396	397	349	349	327	296	268	246	222	191	130	102	88	
Fernandina Beach	623	581	582	581	589	598	555	506	519	504	467	484	447	445	423	425	377	376	355	324	295	273	249	218	157	130	116	35

* 51 Statute miles via Dismal Swamp Canal
* 44 nautical via Dismal Swamp Canal

21

INSIDE-ROUTE DISTANCES
FERNANDINA BEACH, FLA., TO KEY WEST, FLA
(Nautical Miles)

Figure at intersection of columns opposite ports in question is the nautical/statute mileage between the two.
Example: St. Augustine, Fl., is 271 nautical miles (312 statute miles) from Miami, Fla.

Key West, Fla. 24°33·7'N., 81°48·5'W
Flamingo, Fla. 25°08·5'N., 80°55·4'W
Marathon, Fla 24°42·2'N., 81°06·7'W
Matecumber Harbor, Fla. 24°51·1'N., 80°44·5'W
Travernier, Fla. 25°00·7'N., 80°31·3'W
Miami, Fla. 25°47·0'N., 80°11·0'W
Port Everglades, Fla. 26°05·6'N., 80°07·0'W
Port of Palm Beach, Fla. 26°46·1'N., 80°03·3'W
Jupiter, Fla. 26°56·8'N., 80°05·4'W
Fort Myeres, Fla. 26°38·9'N., 81°52·3'W
Moore haven, Fla. 26°50·0'N., 81°05·3'W
Clewiston, Fla 26°45·6'N., 80°55·2'W
Port Mayaca, Fla. 26°59·1'N., 80°36·8'W
Stuart, Fla. 27°12·2'N., 80°16·6'W
Salerno, Fla. 27°08·8'N., 80°11·6'W
Fort Pierce, Fla. 27°27·5'N., 80°19·3'W
Vero Beach, Fla. 27°39·0'N., 80°22·4'W
Melbourne, Fla.
Eau Gallie, Fla.
Gallie, Fla.
Titusville, Fla.
Cocoa, Fla. 28°21·3'N., 81°43·1'W
New Smyrna Beach, Fla
Daytona Beach, Fla.
Marineland, Fla.
St Augustine, Fla.
Jacksonville, Fla.
Fernandina Beach, Fla.
Norfolk, Va. 36°50·9'N., 76°17·9'W

Statute miles

717	758	778	796	831	846	879	898	915	918	952	966	990	995	1026	1053	1066	1122	1005	1018	1064	1067	1090	1150	1170	1203	1208	1244
	41	60	79	114	130	162	181	198	201	235	249	273	278	310	336	349	406	289	302	348	350	373	435	453	486	491	527
		56	75	109	124	158	176	193	197	230	244	268	274	305	331	344	402	284	297	344	345	368	430	449	481	486	522
			18	53	68	101	120	137	140	174	188	212	217	248	275	288	344	227	241	287	289	312	373	392	425	430	466
				35	51	83	102	119	122	157	170	194	199	230	257	270	327	209	222	269	270	293	356	374	407	412	448
					16	48	67	84	87	121	135	159	165	196	222	235	292	175	188	235	236	259	321	339	372	377	413
						32	52	68	72	106	120	144	150	181	207	220	276	159	173	219	220	243	305	323	356	362	397
							20	36	39	74	87	112	116	147	174	188	244	127	139	186	188	211	273	291	323	329	365
								16	21	54	68	92	98	129	155	168	224	107	121	167	168	191	253	273	304	311	346
									3	38	52	76	81	112	138	152	208	91	104	151	152	175	237	257	288	293	329
										34	47	71	77	108	135	148	205	87	100	147	148	171	234	252	284	290	326
											14	38	44	75	101	114	170	53	67	113	114	137	199	219	250	257	292
												24	30	61	87	100	157	39	53	99	100	123	185	205	236	243	278
													9	40	67	81	137	20	32	79	80	104	166	185	216	222	258
														31	58	70	128	25	38	85	86	109	171	190	222	228	264
															26	40	96	56	69	116	117	141	203	221	253	259	295
																13	70	83	96	143	144	167	229	247	280	285	321
																	56	96	108	155	156	180	242	261	292	298	334
																		152	166	212	213	236	298	318	349	356	390
																			14	60	61	84	146	166	197	204	239
																				47	48	71	133	152	184	190	226
																					1	24	86	106	137	144	178
																						23	85	105	136	142	177
																							62	82	113	120	154
																								22	54	60	96
																									33	40	75
																										39	48
																											84

Nautical Miles

623																											
659	36																										
676	53	49																									
692	69	65	16																								
722	99	95	46	30																							
735	113	108	59	44	14																						
764	141	137	88	72	42	28																					
780	157	153	104	89	58	45	17																				
795	172	168	119	103	73	59	31	14																			
798	175	171	122	106	76	63	34	18	3																		
827	204	200	151	136	105	92	64	47	33	29																	
839	216	212	163	148	117	104	76	59	45	41	12																
860	237	233	184	169	138	125	97	80	66	62	33	21															
865	242	238	189	173	143	130	101	85	70	67	38	26	8														
892	269	265	216	200	170	157	128	112	97	94	65	53	35	27													
915	292	288	239	223	193	180	151	135	120	117	88	76	58	50	23												
926	303	299	250	235	204	191	163	146	132	128	99	87	70	61	34	11											
975	353	349	299	284	254	240	212	195	181	178	148	136	119	111	83	61	49										
873	251	247	197	182	152	138	110	93	79	76	46	34	17	22	49	72	83	132									
885	262	258	209	193	163	150	121	105	90	87	58	46	28	33	60	83	94	144	12								
925	303	299	249	234	204	190	162	145	131	128	98	86	69	74	101	124	135	184	52	41							
927	304	300	251	235	205	191	163	146	132	129	99	87	70	75	102	125	136	185	53	42	1						
947	324	320	271	255	225	211	183	166	152	149	119	107	90	95	122	145	156	205	73	62	21	20					
999	378	374	324	309	279	265	237	220	206	203	173	161	144	149	176	199	210	259	127	116	75	74	54				
1017	394	390	341	325	295	282	253	237	223	219	190	178	161	165	192	215	227	276	144	132	92	91	71	19			
1045	422	418	369	353	323	309	281	264	250	247	217	205	188	193	220	243	254	303	171	160	119	118	98	47	29		
1050	427	423	374	358	328	315	286	270	255	252	223	211	193	198	225	248	259	309	177	165	125	123	104	52	35	34	
1080	458	454	405	389	359	345	317	301	286	283	254	242	224	229	256	279	290	339	207	196	155	154	134	83	65	42	73

DISTANCES ON ST. JOHNS RIVER, FLORIDA
(Nautical Miles)

Figure at intersection of columns opposite ports in question is the nautical mileage between the two. Example: Weleka, Fla., is 66 nautical miles from Jacksonville, Fla.

	St Johns River mouth 30°24·0'N, 81°23·8'W	Mayport 30°23·7'N, 81°25·9'W	Intracoastal Waterway Route 30°23·1'N, 81°27·7'W	Broward River mouth 30°24·6'N, 81°35·7'W	Jacksonville 30°19·2'N, 81°39·0'W	Doctors Lake Inlet 30°08·9'N, 81°41·2'W	Palatka 29°38·6'N, 81°37·6'W	Crescent City 29°25·8'N, 81°30·3'W	Welaka 29°28·8'N, 81°40·5'W	Silver Springs Oklawaha River	Moss Bluff Lock. Oklawaha River	Leesburg. Oklawaha River	Georgetown 29°23·1'N, 81°38·3'W	Astor-Volusia 29°10·0'N, 81°31·4'W	Sanford 28°49·1'N, 81°16·2'W
Mayport	2														
Intracoastal Waterway Route	4	2													
Broward River mouth	12	10	8												
Jacksonville	20	18	16	8											
Doctors Lake Inlet	32	30	28	20	12										
Palatka	68	66	64	56	48	36									
Crescent City	89	87	85	77	69	56	20								
Welaka	86	84	82	74	66	54	18	26							
Silver Springs	136	134	132	124	116	104	68	76	50						
Moss Bluff Lock	145	143	141	133	125	112	76	85	58	14					
Leesburg	162	160	158	150	142	129	94	102	75	31	17				
Georgetown	95	93	91	83	75	62	26	35	8	56	65	82			
Astor-Volusia	109	107	105	97	89	77	41	49	23	71	79	96	14		
Sanford	143	141	139	131	123	111	75	83	57	105	113	131	49	34	
Lake Harney 28°46·8'N, 81°03·2'W	161	159	157	149	141	129	93	101	75	123	131	148	66	52	18

21

GULF OF MEXICO
KEY WEST, FLA., TO PORT BROWNSVILLE, TEX.
(Nautical Miles)

Figure at intersection of columns opposite ports in question is the nautical mileage between the two. Example: Tamp, Fla., is 810 nautical miles from Corpus Christi, Tex.

Port	YUCATAN CHANNEL 21°50·0'N, 85°03·0'W	STRAITS OF FLORIDA 24°25·0'N, 83°00·0'W	Key West, Fla. 24°33·7'N, 81°48·5'W	Port Boca Grande, Fla. 26°43·2'N, 82°15·3'W	St. Petersburg, Fla. 27°46·0'N, 82°37·0'W	Port Tampa, Fla. 27°51·7'N, 82°33·3'W	Tampa, Fla. 27°56·5'N, 82°26·7'W	Port St. Joe, Fla. 29°49·1'N, 85°18·8'W	Panama City, Fla. 30°08·2'N, 85°37·6'W	Pensacola, Fla. 30°24·0'N, 87°13·0'W	Mobile, Ala. 30°42·5'N, 88°02·5'W	Pascagoula, Miss. 30°21·9'N, 88°33·8'W	Gulfport, Miss 30°21·5'N, 89°05·5'W	New Orleans, La (Gulf Outlet)* 29°57·0'N, 90°03·7'W	New Orleans, La (South Pass)* 29°57·0'N, 90°03·7'W	NEW ORLEANS, LA (SW Pass)* 29°57·0'N, 90°03·7'W	Morgan City, La. 29°41·5'N, 91°12·9'W	Lake Charles, La. 30°13·1'N, 93°15·5'W	Port Arthur, Tex. 29°49·5'N, 93°57·6'W	Orange, Tex. 30°05·3'N, 93°43·0'W	Beaumont, Tex. 30°04·7'N, 94°05·2'W	Galveston, Tex. 29°19·0'N, 94°47·0'W	Texas city, Tex. 29°22·7'N, 94°53·2'W	Houston, Tex. 29°45·0'N, 95°17·3'W	Freeport, Tex. 28°56·3'N, 95°20·4'W	Point Comfort, Tex. (Lavaca Bay) 28°38·7'N, 96°33·3'W	La Quinta, Tex. 27°52·6'N, 97°15·7'W	Corpus Christi, Tex. 27°48·8'N, 97°24·0'W	Port Isabel, Tex. 26°03·6'N, 97°12·8'W
STRAITS OF FLORIDA	192																												
Key West, Fla.	251	73																											
Port Boca Grande, Fla.	332	150	223																										
St. Petersburg, Fla.	389	219	292	100																									
Port Tampa, Fla.	399	228	301	109	8																								
Tampa, Fla.	404	232	305	113	18	18																							
Port St. Joe, Fla.	495	369	442	281	240	248	252																						
Panama City, Fla.	506	381	454	294	252	261	265	42																					
Pensacola, Fla.	533	437	510	372	334	343	347	154	139																				
Mobile, Ala.	562	471	544	413	377	386	389	206	193	89																			
Pascagoula, Miss.	554	469	542	414	379	387	392	213	200	94	75																		
Gulfport, Miss	576	492	564	436	401	409	413	235	222	117	98	52																	
New Orleans, La (Gulf Outlet)*	575	513	586	474	444	452	457	288	274	188	170	149	171																
New Orleans, La (South Pass)*	579	524	597	489	459	467	472	308	295	253	236	216	238	–															
NEW ORLEANS, LA (SW Pass)*	587	540	613	512	488	498	502	346	333	288	269	250	271	–	–														
Morgan City, La.	602	581	653	564	539	548	552	397	385	339	324	304	330	304	298	278													
Lake Charles, La.	705	715	789	717	697	706	710	568	558	517	504	484	506	479	472	454	182												
Port Arthur, Tex.	691	700	773	704	684	693	697	565	545	504	491	471	493	466	460	441	190	83											
Orange, Tex.	713	722	795	726	707	715	719	577	567	526	513	493	515	488	482	463	212	105	22										
Beaumont, Tex.	717	726	799	730	710	719	723	581	571	530	517	497	519	492	486	467	216	109	26	27									
Galveston, Tex.	696	702	775	709	690	699	703	562	550	509	496	476	498	471	465	446	235	128	89	111	115								
Texas city, Tex.	702	707	780	714	695	704	708	567	555	514	501	481	503	476	470	451	240	133	94	116	120	9							
Houston, Tex.	740	746	819	752	733	742	746	605	594	553	539	519	542	514	508	490	278	172	132	154	158	47	52						
Freeport, Tex.	717	743	816	747	729	738	742	604	593	552	538	518	540	513	508	489	273	166	126	148	152	84	89	127					
Point Comfort, Tex. (Lavaca Bay)	761	797	870	806	786	795	799	661	649	609	595	575	597	570	564	545	354	248	208	230	234	165	170	209	119				
La Quinta, Tex.	763	802	875	811	792	800	804	666	654	614	600	580	602	575	569	550	390	283	244	266	270	201	206	244	154	112			
Corpus Christi, Tex.	769	807	880	816	797	805	810	671	659	618	605	585	607	580	574	555	395	289	249	271	275	207	212	250	160	117	15		
Port Isabel, Tex.	718	782	855	814	802	810	815	684	673	632	618	598	621	593	588	569	415	376	336	358	362	293	298	337	247	204	137	142	
Port Brownsville, Tex. 25°57·1'N, 97°24·0'W	729	793	866	825	813	822	826	695	684	643	629	609	632	604	599	580	426	387	347	369	373	304	309	348	258	215	148	154	13

* Baton rouge, La. (30°27·0'N, 91°11·7'W) ADD 115 miles.

Entrance lighted whistle buoy (24°27·7'N, 81°48·1'W) to Key West. 6·3 miles.
Entrance buoy T (27°35·3'N, 83°00·7'W) to Tampa. 43 miles.
Entrance buoy 1 (30°16·3'N, 87°17·5'W) to Pensacola. 11·5 miles.
Entrance buoy M (30°08·1'N, 88°03·9'W) to Mobile, 35 miles.
Mississippi River-Gulf Outlet approach buoy NO. (29°26·4'N, 88°56·9'W) to New Orleans. 73 miles.
South Pass entrance buoy 2 (28°58·7'N, 89°06·5'W) to New Orleans, 96 miles.
Southwest Pass entrance buoy SW (28°52·7'N, 89°25·9'W) to New Orleans, 102 miles.
Calcasieu Channel buoy 2B (29°27·3'N, 91°13·4'W) to Lake Charles, 50 miles.

Sabine pass buoy 32 (29°36·9'N, 93°48·3'W) to Port Arthur, 16·6 miles.
Galveston Bay entrance buoy GA (29°08·7'N, 94°25·8'W) to Galveston, 23 miles;
Texas City, 28 miles; houston, 67 miles.
Aransas Pass entrance buoy AP (27°47·6'N, 96°57·4'W) to Corpus Christi, 25 miles.
Brazos Santiago entrance buoy BS (26°03·9'N, 97°06·6'W) to Port Brownsville, 17·5 miles.
All tabular distances are via STRAITS OF FLORIDA, (24°25·0'N, 83°00·0'W), and through the Shipping Safety Fairways. For distances from Key West to west Florida ports via Rebecca Shoal Channel. (24°24·4'N, 82°42·0'W). SUBTRACT 24 miles from Port Boca Grande distance. 17 miles from Tampa Bay distances. 9 miles from Port St. Joe and Panama City distances, and 5 miles form Peensacola distance

COASTWISE AND INSIDE-ROUTE DISTANCES KEY WEST, FLA., TO APALACHICOLA, FLA.

(Nautical Miles)

Figure at intersection of columns opposite ports in question is the nautical mileage between the two. Example: Flamingo is 225 nautical miles from Clearwater.

	Key West, Fla. 24°33·7'N, 81°48·5'W	Marathon. 24°42·2'N, 81°06·7'W	Matecumbe Harbor 24°51·1'N, 80°44·5'W	Flamingo. 24°08·5'N, 80°55·4'W	Cape Sable. 25°09·0'N, 81°11·0'W	Everglades. 25°52·0'N, 81°23·1'W	Naples. 26°08·0'N, 81°47·6'W	Fort Myers. 26°38·9'N, 81°52·3'W	Port Boca Grande. 26°43·2'N, 82°15·3'W	Venice 27°06·7'N, 82°27·8'W	Sarasota. 27°20·0'N, 82°32·9'W	Bradenton. 27°30·0'N, 82°34·4'W	St. Petersburg. 27°46·0'N, 82°37·0'W	Tampa. 27°56·5'N, 82°26·7'W	Clearwater. 27°58·5'N, 82°49·6'W	Tarpon Springs. 28°09·4'N, 82°45·8'W	Cedar Key. 29°08·0'N, 83°01·9'W	St. Marks. 30°09·2'N, 84°12·2'W	Carrabelle. 29°51·0'N, 84°40·0'W
Marathon	42																		
Matecumbe Harbor	65	29																	
Flamingo	70	37	35																
Cape Sable	57	31	32	17															
Everglades	88	80	81	66	49														
Naples	98	100	103	88	71	38													
Fort Myers	134	136	139	124	107	79	44												
Port Boca Grande	144	146	149	134	117	88	54	35											
Venice	172	174	177	162	145	116	82	63	28										
Sarasota	186	189	191	176	159	131	96	78	43	15									
Bradenton	210	213	215	200	183	155	120	102	67	39	25								
St. Petersburg	218	221	224	209	192	163	129	110	75	47	33	22							
Tampa	232	235	237	222	205	177	143	124	89	61	42	36	18						
Clearwater	234	237	240	225	208	179	145	126	91	63	49	38	31	47					
Tarpon Springs	250	253	255	240	223	195	160	142	107	79	65	54	47	63	18				
Cedar Key	310	313	316	301	284	255	221	202	167	139	125	114	107	123	79	68			
St. Marks	387	389	392	377	360	332	297	278	244	216	202	191	164	200	155	145	91		
Carrabelle	389	391	394	379	362	334	299	280	245	218	204	193	186	202	157	147	101	52	
Apalachicola, Fla. 29°43·5'N, 84°58·8'W	406	408	411	396	379	350	316	297	262	234	221	209	202	218	174	164	118	69	25

Routes used in table: Hawk Channel between Marathon and key West; Northwest Channel (Key West) and outside to places between Cape Sable and San Carlos Bay; thece inside to Anclote Keys; and thence outside to St. George Sound. Distances from Everglades nothward are inside via Big Marco River and Gordon Pass.

DISTANCES BY INTRACOASTAL WATERWAY APALACHICOLA, FLA., TO PORT BROWNSVILLE, TEX..

(Nautical and Statute Miles)

Figure at intersection of columns opposite ports in question is the nautical/Statute mileage between the two.
Example: Mobile, Ala., is 398 nautical miles (458 statute miles from Beaumont, Tex.

Statute Miles (upper right) / Nautical Miles (lower left)

Port	Apalachicola	Port St. Joe	Panama City	Fort Walton Beach	Pensacola	Mobile	Pascagoula	Biloxi	Gulfport	New Orleans	Houma	Morgan City	Lake Charles	Orange	Beaumont	Port Arthur	Galveston	Houston	Texas City	Freeport	Port O'Connor	Rockport	Aransas Pass	La Quinta	Corpus Christi	Port Mansfield	Port Isabel	Port Brownsville
Apalachicola, Fla. 29°43·5'N, 84°58·8'W		31	59	129	173	246	255	274	285	348	410	447	604	618	647	640	707	751	708	749	825	877	885	898	905	985	1021	1036
Port St. Joe, Fla. 29°49·1'N, 85°18·8'W	27		41	113	155	230	239	258	268	331	392	430	587	602	629	624	689	734	690	732	809	861	868	881	887	968	1003	1018
Panama City, Fla. 30°08·2'N, 85°37·6'W	51	36		71	114	189	197	216	227	290	351	389	545	560	588	582	648	693	649	690	766	819	826	840	846	926	962	977
Fort Walton Beach, Fla. 30°24·0'N, 86°36·7'W	112	98	62		43	117	127	145	157	219	280	318	474	849	518	511	578	623	579	620	696	748	755	769	774	855	892	907
Pensacola, Fla. 30°24·0'N, 87°13·0'W	150	135	99	37		84	93	112	122	185	246	284	441	456	484	478	544	589	545	587	663	715	722	735	741	822	858	872
Mobile, Ala. 30°41·5'N, 88°02·2'W	214	200	164	102	73		67	85	97	159	220	258	415	429	458	451	518	563	519	560	636	688	696	709	716	796	832	847
Pascagoula, Miss. 30°21·9'N, 88°33·8'W	222	208	171	110	81	58		37	47	110	171	209	366	381	409	403	468	513	470	511	587	640	647	661	666	747	783	797
Biloxi, Miss. 30°23·5'N, 88°52·0'W	238	224	188	126	97	74	32		32	96	157	194	351	366	394	388	453	498	456	496	573	625	632	646	651	732	769	783
Gulfport, Miss. 30°21·4'N, 89°05·6'W	248	233	197	136	106	84	41	28		76	138	175	333	348	375	368	435	480	436	478	554	605	613	626	633	713	749	764
NEW ORLEANS, LA. 29°57·0'N, 90°03·7'W	302	288	252	190	161	138	96	83	66		61	99	255	270	299	292	359	404	360	402	478	529	536	550	556	636	673	688
Houma, La. 29°35·9'N, 90°42·6'W	356	341	305	243	214	191	149	136	120	53		38	194	209	237	231	297	342	299	339	417	468	475	489	495	575	612	626
Morgan City, La. 29°41·3'N, 91°12·7'W	388	374	338	276	247	224	182	169	152	86	33		157	171	200	193	260	305	261	303	379	430	437	451	457	537	574	589
Lake Charles, La. 30°13·1'N, 93°15·5'W	525	510	474	412	383	361	318	305	289	222	169	136		37	66	59	125	170	127	168	244	296	304	316	322	404	440	455
Orange, Tex. 30°04·0'N, 93°43·3'W	537	523	487	425	396	373	331	318	302	235	182	149	32		30	24	90	135	92	132	209	261	268	282	288	368	405	419
Beaumont, Tex. 30°04·6'N, 94°05·2'W	562	547	511	450	421	398	355	342	326	260	206	174	57	26		30	97	142	98	139	215	267	274	288	293	375	411	426
Port Arthur, Tex. 29°49·5'N, 93°57·6'W	556	542	506	444	415	392	350	337	320	254	201	168	51	21	26		67	112	68	109	185	237	244	258	264	345	381	396
Galveston, Tex. 29°18·5'N, 94°48·1'W	614	599	563	502	473	450	407	394	378	312	258	226	109	78	84	58		55	12	46	122	174	182	194	200	281	318	333
Houston, Tex. 29°45·0'N, 95°17·4'W	653	638	602	541	512	489	446	433	417	351	297	265	148	117	123	97	48		55	97	173	224	232	245	252	333	368	383
Texas City, Tex. 29°22·7'N, 94°53·2'W	615	600	564	503	474	451	408	396	379	313	260	227	110	80	85	59	10	48		51	128	180	186	200	206	287	323	338
Freeport, Tex. 28°56·3'N, 95°20·4'W	651	636	600	539	510	487	444	431	415	349	295	263	146	115	121	95	40	84	44		81	132	140	153	160	241	276	291
Port O'Connor, Tex. 28°26·5'N, 96°24·4'W	717	703	666	605	576	553	510	498	481	415	362	329	212	182	187	161	106	150	111	70		52	60	72	78	159	196	211
Rockport, Tex. 28°01·1'N, 97°02·9'W	762	748	712	650	621	598	556	643	526	460	407	374	257	227	232	206	151	195	156	115	45		10	23	30	110	146	161
Aransas Pass, Tex. 27°53·9'N, 97°08·0'W	769	754	718	656	627	605	562	549	533	466	413	380	264	233	238	212	158	202	162	122	52	9		14	20	100	136	151
La Quinta, Tex. 27°52·6'N, 97°15·7'W	780	766	730	668	639	616	574	561	544	578	425	392	275	245	250	224	169	213	174	133	63	20	12		17	98	133	148
Corpus Christi, Tex. 27°48·8'N, 97°24·0'W	786	771	735	673	644	622	579	566	550	483	430	397	280	250	255	229	174	219	179	139	68	26	17	15		102	138	153
Port Mansfield, Tex. 26°33·4'N, 97°25·6'W	856	841	805	743	714	692	649	636	620	553	500	467	351	320	326	300	244	289	249	209	138	96	87	85	89		38	53
Port Isabel, Tex. 26°03·6'N, 97°12·8'W	887	872	836	775	746	723	680	668	651	585	532	499	382	352	357	331	276	320	281	240	170	127	118	116	120	33		15
Port Brownsville, Tex. 25°57·1'N, 97°24·0'W	900	885	849	788	758	736	693	680	664	598	544	512	395	364	370	344	289	333	294	253	183	140	131	129	133	46	13	

PUERTO RICO AND VIRGIN ISLANDS DISTANCES
(Nautical Miles)

Figure at intersection of columns opposite ports in question is the nautical mileage between the two. Example: San Juan, Puerto Rico, is 80 nautical miles form Charlotte Amalie, St. Thomas.

	San Juan, P. R. 18°27·6'N, 66°06·6'W	Farjardo, P. R. 18°20·2'N, 65°37·8'W	Ensenada Honda, P. R. 18°13·8'N, 65°37·4'W	Humacao, P. R. 18°09·9'N, 65°44·6'W	Bahia de Jobos. P. R. 17°57·0'N, 66°13·3'W	Ponce, P. R. 17°58·2'N, 66°37·3'W	Bahia de Tallaboa, P. R. 17°58·9'N, 66°44·6'W	Bahia de Guayanilla, P. R. 17°59·5'N, 66°46·4'W	Bahia de Guanica, P. R. 17°57·5'N, 66°54·5'W	Mayaguez, P. R. 18°13·2'N, 67°09·7'W	Bahia de Aguadilla, P.R. 18°26·0'N, 67°09·6'W	Puerto Arecibo, P. R. 18°28·9'N, 66°42·1'W	Ensenada Honda, Culebra. 18°18·0'N, 65°17·0'W	Isabel Segunda, Vieques. 18°09·2'N, 65°26·7'W	Charlotte Amalie, St. Thomas. V. I. 18°20·0'N, 64°55·5'W	Cruz Bay, St. John. V. I. 18°20·0'N, 64°47·8'W	Road Town, Tortola. B. V. I. 18°25·3'N, 64°37·1'W	Christiansted, St. Croix. V. I. 17°45·0'N, 64°42·0'W	Frederiksted, St. Croix. V. I. 17°42·9'N, 64°53·4'W
Farjardo, P. R.	40																		
Ensenada Honda, P. R.	52	14																	
Humacao, P. R.	59	21	11																
Bahia de Jobos. P. R.	103	65	56	48															
Ponce, P. R.	152*	83	74	65	31														
Bahia de Tallaboa, P. R.	145*	88	79	71	36	13													
Bahia de Guayanilla, P. R.	145*	89	80	72	37	14	5												
Bahia de Guanica, P. R.	138*	99	90	82	47	22	16	15											
Mayaguez, P. R.	92	121	133	131	96	74	67	67	60										
Bahia de Aguadilla, P.R.	74	103	115	123	105	83	76	77	70	23									
Puerto Arecibo, P. R.	43	72	84	92	140	118	112	112	105	58	40								
Ensenada Honda, Culebra.	59	25	25	31	76	93	98	99	109	141	123	92							
Isabel Segunda, Vieques.	55	18	12	17	62	79	85	86	96	136	118	87	15						
Charlotte Amalie, St. Thomas. V. I.	80	46	44	50	93	110	116	117	126	161	144	112	24	33					
Cruz Bay, St. John. V. I.	82	53	51	57	99	116	121	122	132	164	146	115	31	40	11				
Road Town, Tortola. B. V. I.	94	66	65	71	113	131	136	137	147	175	157	126	47	55	24	15			
Christiansted, St. Croix. V. I.	103	68	69	68	101	119	124	125	135	184	166	135	48	54	38	37	42		
Frederiksted, St. Croix. V. I.	96	61	60	58	89	106	111	112	122	171	159	128	42	46	38	39	46	19	
Krause Lagoon, St. Croix. V. I. 17°42·5'N, 64°46·3'W	112	77	72	70	101	117	122	123	133	182	176	144	59	62	54	55	62	35	18

* Via Mona Passage
Limetree Bay, St. Croix, V. I. 1 mi. E of Krause Lagoon

DISTANCES FROM PANAMA
PANAMA, PANAMA

(8°53'00N. 79°31'00W) to:

Junction Points:

Bishop Rock, England (via Mona Passage), 4,388
Cape of Good Hope, Republic of South Africa, 6,466
Fastnet, Republic of Ireland (via Mona Passage), 4,247
Grand Banks South, 2,555
Honshu, Japan, 7,614
Ile d'Ouessant, France (via Mona Passage, 4,374
Montreal, Canada, 3,204
Punta Arenas, Chile, 3,932
Singapore (via San Bernardino Strait), 10,505
Strait of Gibraltar (via Anegada Channel), 4,351
Torres Strait, Australia (via Raine Island entrance), 8,451
Tsugaru Kaikyo, Japan, 8,004
Wilson Promontory, Australia (via Cook Strait), 7,842
Wilson Promontory, Australia (via Foveaux Strait), 7,770
Yucatan Channel, 855

Ports

Abraham Bay, Bahamas, 922
Acajutla, El Salvador, 833
Acapulco, Mexico, 1,426
Almirante, Panama, 198
Amapala, Honduras, 745
Amuay, Venezuela, 678
Angra dos Reis, Brazil, 4,527
Antilla, Cuba, 887
Antofagasta, Chile, 2,140
Apia, Samoa, 5,710
Apra, Guam, 7,988
Arica, Chile, 1,921
Auckland, New Zealand, 6,516
Avarua, Cook Islands, 5,092
Bahia de Samana, Dominican Republic, 1,015
Bahia Blanca, Argentina, 5,776
Bahia de las Calderas, Dominican Republic, 810
Baie Taio-Hae, Marquesas, 3, 826
Bahia Cayo Moa, Cuba, 853
Baltimore, Maryland, U.S.A. (via Windward Passage and Crooked Island Passage), 1,944
Barahona, Dominican Republic, 796
Ba-bers Point, Hawaii, U.S.A. 4,694
Barcelona, Venezuela, 1,014
Belize, Belize, 859
Bikini, Marshalls, 4,915
Boca de Tanamo, Cuba, 869
Bocas del Toro, Panama, 187
Bordeaux, France (via Mona Passage), 4,641
Boston, Massachusetts, U.S.A. (via Crooked Island Passage), 2,200
Bridgeport, Connecticut, U.S.A., 2,118
Bridgetown, Barbados, 1,280
Brisbane, Australia, 7,687
Brunswick, Georgia, U.S.A., 1, 581
Buenaventure, Colombia, 352
Cabedelo, Brazil, 3,149
Caibarien, Cuba, 1,138
Caldera, Chile, 2,302
Caleta Olivia, Argentina, 6,204
Callao, Peru, 1,350
Campeche, Mexico, 1,210
Cap Haitien, Haiti, 860
Cape Town, Republic of South Africa, 6,508
Carmen, Mexico, 1,289
Cartagena, Colombia, 324
Casilda, Cuba, 792
Catia la Mar, Venezuela, 873
Champerico, Guatemala, 954
Charleston, South Carolina, U.S.A., 1,607
Charlotte Amalie, Virgin Islands, 1,072
Charlottetown, Canada, 2,578
Chimbote, Peru, 1,158
Christmas Island, Line Islands, 4,751
Cienfuegos, Cuba, 815
Coatzacoalcos, Mexico, 1,420
Colon, Panama, 44
Comodoro Rivadavia, Argentina, 6,185
Coquimbo, Chile, 2,448
Corinto, Nicaragua, 683
Covenas, Columbia, 308
Dagu, China (via Osumi kaikyo), 9,002
Dagu, China (via Tsugaru Kaikyo), 8,786
Dakar, Senegal, 3,738
Dalian, China (via Osumi Kaikyo), 8,843
Dalian, China (via Tsugaru Kaikyo), 8,627
Dutch Harbor, Alaska, U.S.A., 5,246
Easter Island, Pacific, 2,785
Enderbury Island, Phoenix Islands, 5,599
Eniwetak, Marshall Islands, 7,086
Ensenada, Mexico, 2,791
Esmeraldas, Ecuador, 472
Fanning Island, 4,805
Fort de France, Martinique, 1,202
Fort Liberte, Haiti, 881
Funafuti Island, Tuvalu, 6,217
Galveston, Texas, U.S.A., 1,536
Georgetown, Guyana, 1,558
Colfito, Costa Rica, 334
Conaives, Haiti, 805
Guantanamo, Cuba, 732
Guayaquil, Ecuador, 824
Guaymas, Mexico, 2,370
Guira, Venezuela, 1,200
Gulfport, Mississippi, U.S.A. (northbound),

1,431
Hakodate, Japan, 7,417
Halifax, Canada, 2,338
Hamilton, Bermuda, 1,702
Hilo, Hawaii, U.S.A., 4,527
Ho Chi Minh, Vietnam, 10,017
Hobart, Tasmania, 7,630
Hong Kong, B.C.C., 7,195
Honolulu, Hawaii, U.S.A., 4,685
Iloilo, Philippines, 9,235
Incheon, Republic of South Korea, 8,474
Iquique, Chile, 1,987
Isabel Segunda, Isla de Vieques, 1,060
Jacksonville, Florida, U.S.A., 1,559
Jaluit, Marshall Islands, 6,666
Jarvis Island, 1,173
Johnston Island, 5,359
Kahului, Hawaii, U.S.A., 4,605
Kaneohe Bay, Hawaii, U.S.A., 4,868
Kaunakakai, Hawaii, U.S.A., 4,633
Key West, Florida, U.S.A., 1,108
Kingston, Jamaica, 594
Kobe, Japan, 7,964
Kodiak, Alaska, U.S.A., 4,907
La Ceiba, Honduras, 709
La Guaira, Venezuela, 884
La Libertad, Ecuador, 674
La Libertad, El Salvador, 806
La Palma, Panama, 104
La Romana, Dominican Republic, 889
La Union, El Salvador, 748
Les Cayes, Haiti, 688
Levuka, Fiji Islands, 6,288
Limon, Costa Rica, 234
Los Angeles, California, U.S.A., 2,913
Lota, Chile, 2,825
Lucea, Jamaica, 579
Makassar, Sulawesi (via Selat Sagewin and Selat Salajar), 9,855
Malakal, Palau Islands, 8,674
Manila, Philippines (via Balintang Channel), 9,347
Manila, Philippines (via San Bernardino Strait), 9,370
Manzanillo, Cuba, 732
Mar del Plata, Argentina, 5,543
Maracaibo, Venezuela, 737
Matagorda Bay, Texas, U.S.A., 1,558
Matarani, Peru, 1,790
Mazatlan, Mexico, 2,006
Melbourne, Australia (via Foveaux Strait), 7,928
Midway Island, 5,707
Miller Anchorage, Bahamas, 1,115
Montecristi, Dominican Republic, 881
Monterey, California, U.S.A., 3,165
Montevideo, Uruguary, 5,379
Nagasaki, Japan (east of Honshu), 8,200
Nagasaki, Japan (west of Honshu), 8,299
Naknek, Alaska, U.S.A., 5,604
Nassau, Bahamas (via Windward Passage), 1,210
New Amsterdam, Guyana, 1,581
New Haven, Connecticut, U.S.A., 2,106
New Orleans, Louisiana, U.S.A. (northbound via South Pass), 1,444
New York, New York, U.S.A. (via Windward Passage and Crooked Island Passage), 2,018
Newcastle, Australia, 7,654
Nicaro, Cuba, 881
Nikolayevsk, Soviet Union, (south of Aleutian Islands), 7,293
Nikolayevsk, Soviet Union (via Unimak Passage), 7,296
Nome, Alaska, U.S.A., 5,834
Norfolk, Virginia, U.S.A. (via Windward Passage and Crooked Island Passage), 1,822
Noumea, New Caledonia, 6,982
Nukualofa, Tonga Islands, 5,953
Ocean Island, 6,724
Omura, Japan, 7,766
Oranjestad, Aruba, 661
Osaka, Japan, 7,969
Paamiut (Frederikshaab), Greenland, 3,558
Pago Pago, American Samoa, 5,656
Papeete, French Polynesia, 4,493
Paramaribo, Suriname, 1,691
Paranagua, Brazel, 4,607
Pearl Harbor, Hawaii, U.S.A., 4,692
Pedregal, Panama, 308
Petropavlovsk, Soviet Union, 6,492
Philadeplphia, Pennsylvania, U.S.A. (via Windward Passage and Crooked Island Passage), 1,989
Pisco, Peru, 1,458
Pointe a Pitre, Guadeloupe, 1,211
Ponape, Caroline Islands, 7,321
Ponce, Puerto Rico, 976
Port au Prince, Haiti, 817
Port Antonio, Jamaica, 625
Port Castries, St. Lucia, 1,203
Port Hueneme, California, U.S.A., 2,958
Port Limon, Costa Rica, 218
Port Neward, New Jersey, U.S.A., 2,021
Port Pirie, Australia, 8,467
Port of Spain, Trinidad, 1,202
Portland, Maine, U.S.A. (via Crooked Island Passage), 2,241
Portland, Oregon, U.S.A., 3,869
Porto Alegre, Brazil, 5,148
Prince Rupert, Canada, 4,303
Progreso, Mexico, 1,069
Puerto de Hierro, Venezuela, 1,192
Puerto la Cruz, Venezuela, 1,016
Puerto Armuelles, Panama, 306
Puerto Barrios, Guatemala, 823

Puerto Bolivar, 774
Puerto Cabello, Venezuela, 845
Puerto Cabezas, Nicaragua, 390
Puerto Cortez, Honduras, 776
Puerto Descado, Argentina, 6,222
Puerto Madryn, Argentina, 6,012
Puerto Manati, Cuba, 959
Puerto Montt, Chile, 3,177
Puerto Padre, Cuba, 948
Puerto Sandino, Nicaragua, 649
Puerto Sucre, Venezuela, 1,035
Puerto Vita, Cuba, 915
Punta Cardon, Venezuela, 674
Puntarenas, Costa Rica, 471
Quepos, Costa Rica, 415
Qingdao, China, 8,575
Rabaul, Papua New Guinea, 7,807
Raoul Island, Kermadec ıslands, 6,125
Rio Gallegos, Argentina, 6,455
Rio Haina, Dominican Republic, 845
Roosevelt Roads, Puerto Rico, 1,054
Rotoava, Iles Tuamotu, 4,256
Salaverry, Peru, 1,109
Salina Cruz, Mexico, 1,170
Salvador, Brazil, 3,741
San Antonio, Chile, 2,644
San Diego, California, U.S.A., 2,843
San Felix, Venezuela, 1,535
San Francisco, California, U.S.A., 3,245
San Jose, Guatemala, 886
San Juan del Sur, Nicaragua, 590
San Juan, Peru, 1,590
San Juan, Puerto Rico, 1,036
San Lorenzo, Honduras, 762
Santa Barbara, California, U.S.A., 2,980
Santa Cruz del Sur, Cuba, 731
Santa Maria, Cuba, 814
Santa Rosalia, Mexico, 2,390
Santiago de Cuba, Cuba, 726
Santo Domingo, Dominican Republic, 846
Santos, Brazil, 4,609
Savannah, Georgia, U.S.A. (via Windward Passage and Crooked Island Passage), 1,606
Seattle, Washington, U.S.A., 4,020
Seward, Alaska, U.S.A., 4,916
Shanghai, China (via Osumi Kaikyo), 8,648
Shanghai, China (via Tsugaru Kaikyo), 8,566
Shimonoseki, Japan (east of Honshu), 8,153
Shimonoseki, Japan (west of Honshu), 8,081
Sitka, Alaska, U.S.A., 4,524
Skagway, Alaska, U.S.A., 4,739
St. Georges, Grenada, 1,161
St. John, Canada, 2,361
St. John's, Canada, 2,742
St. Marc, Haiti, 796
Suva, Fiji Islands, 6,325
Swan Island, Honduras, 605
Sweeper Cove, Alaska, U.S.A., 5,586
Sydney, Australia, 7,674
Talara, Peru, 826
Talcahuano, Chile, 2,805
Taltal, Chile, 2,225
Tampico, Mexico, 1,528
Tela, Honduras, 749
Tocopilla, Chile, 2,068
Truk, Caroline Islands, 7,685
Turbo, Colombia, 311
Turiamo, Venezuela, 858
Tuxpan, Mexico, 1,498
Unalakleet, Alaska, U.S.A., 5,967
Valparaiso, Chile, 2,616
Vancouver, Canada, 4,032
Veracruz, Mexico, 1,463
Victoria, Canada, 3,962
Vladivostok, Soviet Union, (north of Aleutian Islands, and La Perouse Strait), 7,757
Vladivostok, Soviet Union, (south of Aleutian Islands, and La Perouse Strait), 7,739
Vladivostok, Soviet Union, (via Tsugaru Kaikyo), 7,833
Vladivostok, Soviet Union, 8,340
Wake Island, 6,673
Washington, D.C., U.S.A., 1,957
Wellington, New Zealand, 6,505
Whittier, Alaska, U.S.A., 4,958
Willemstad, Curacao, 742
Wilmington, North Carolina, U.S.A., 1,656
Weonsan, Demacratic People's Republic of Korea, 8,038
Wotho, Marshall Islands, 4,882
Xiamen, China (via Osumi Kaikyo), 8,943
Xiamen, China (via Tsugaru kaikyo), 8,959
Yokohama, Japan, 7,682
Zamboanga, Philippines, 943

PACIFIC OCEAN DISTANCES
(Nautical Miles)

Figure at intersection of columns opposite ports in question is the nautical mileage between the two.
Example: San Francisco. Calif., is 2,091 nautical miles from Honolulu. Hawaii.

	PANAMA CANAL (Pac. Ent.) 8° 53.0'N., 79° 31.0'W.	San Diego. Calif. 32° 43.0'N., 117° 10.5'W.	Long Beach. Calif. 32° 46.2'N., 118° 13.3'W.	Los Angeles. Calif. 33° 45.0'N., 118° 16.2'W.	San Francisco. Calif. 37° 48.5'N., 122° 24.0'W.	Astoria. Oreg. 46° 11.7'N., 123° 50.0'W.	Portland. Oreg. 45° 33.0'N., 122° 41.7'W.	CAPE FLATTERY. WASH. 48° 26.0'N., 124° 47.0'W.	SWIFTSURE BANK. WASH. 48° 31.0'N., 125° 00.0'W.	Seattle. Wash. 47° 36.2'N., 122° 20.3'W.	Ketchikan. Alaska. 55° 20.5'N., 131° 38.7'W.	Sitka. Alaska. 57° 03.1'N., 135° 20.5'W.	CAPE SPENCER. ALASKA. 58° 10.0'N., 136° 38.3'W.	Port Valdez. Alaska. 61° 06.0'N., 146° 24.0'W.	Seward. Alaska. 60° 06.0'N., 149° 26.0'W.	Anchorage. Alaska. 61° 14.2'N., 149° 53.3'W.	Kodiak. Alaska. 57° 47.1'N., 152° 25.1'W.	UNIMAK PASS. ALASKA. 54° 20.0'N., 164° 45.0'W.	Kuluk Bay. Alaska. 51° 51.6'N., 176° 37.6'W.	Hilo. Hawaii. 19° 44.1'N., 155° 03.5'W.	Kawaihae. Hawaii. 20° 02.3'N., 155° 49.9'W.	Kahului. Hawaii. 20° 54.0'N., 156° 28.2'W.	Honolulu. Hawaii. 21° 18.5'N., 157° 52.3'W.	Pearl Harbor. Hawaii. 21° 20.0'N., 157° 58.3'W.	Nawiliwili. Hawaii. 21° 57.4'N., 159° 21.5'W.	Port Allen. Hawaii. 21° 54.1'N., 159° 35.6'W.
San Diego. Calif. 32° 43.0'N., 117° 10.5'W.	2867																									
Long Beach. Calif. 32° 46.2'N., 118° 13.3'W.	2939	94																								
Los Angeles. Calif. 33° 45.0'N., 118° 16.2'W.	2939	95	3																							
San Francisco. Calif. 37° 48.5'N., 122° 24.0'W.	3270	455	374	371																						
Astoria. Oreg. 46° 11.7'N., 123° 50.0'W.	3803	989	908	904	567																					
Portland. Oreg. 45° 33.0'N., 122° 41.7'W.	3888	1074	992	989	652	85																				
CAPE FLATTERY. WASH. 48° 26.0'N., 124° 47.0'W.	3920	1104	1024	1020	683	153	238																			
SWIFTSURE BANK. WASH. 48° 31.0'N., 125° 00.0'W.	–	–	–	–	–	–	–	10																		
Seattle. Wash. 47° 36.2'N., 122° 20.3'W.	4044	1228	1148	1144	807	278	362	124	134																	
Ketchikan. Alaska. 55° 20.5'N., 131° 38.7'W.	4387	1575	1497	1493	1156	660	745	–	518	659																
Sitka. Alaska. 57° 03.1'N., 135° 20.5'W.	4538	1723	1643	1639	1302	815	900	–	681	815	224															
CAPE SPENCER. ALASKA. 58° 10.0'N., 136° 38.3'W.	4603	1787	1707	1703	1366	883	968	–	739	976	307	85														
Port Valdez. Alaska. 61° 06.0'N., 146° 24.0'W.	4984	2174	2092	2089	1745	1239	1324	–	1100	1234	713	479	400													
Seward. Alaska. 60° 06.0'N., 149° 26.0'W.	4940	2124	2043	2040	1702	1242	1327	–	1100	1234	682	494	422	144												
Anchorage. Alaska. 61° 14.2'N., 149° 53.3'W.	5117	2303	2223	2220	1882	1435	1520	–	1294	1428	892	708	641	385	274											
Kodiak. Alaska. 57° 47.1'N., 152° 25.1'W.	4924	2115	2034	2031	1693	1261	1346	–	1124	1258	742	564	505	280	175	242										
UNIMAK PASS. ALASKA. 54° 20.0'N., 164° 45.0'W.	5228	2412	2331	2328	1990	1626	1711	–	1510	1644	1193	1027	987	761	652	688	505									
Kuluk Bay. Alaska. 51° 51.6'N., 176° 37.6'W.	5604	2806	2725	2722	2403	2071	2156	–	1973	2107	1656	1490	1450	1224	1115	1151	968	463								
Hilo. Hawaii. 19° 44.1'N., 155° 03.5'W.	4527	2175	2143	2140	2019	2214	2299	2260	–	2384	2398	2410	2447	2524	2439	2542	2296	2126	2198							
Kawaihae. Hawaii. 20° 02.3'N., 155° 49.9'W.	4594	2219	2183	2180	2051	2235	2320	2276	–	2400	2405	2412	2445	2513	2432	2535	2289	2110	2164	83						
Kahului. Hawaii. 20° 54.0'N., 156° 28.2'W.	4609	2212	2173	2170	2036	2207	2292	2245	–	2369	2361	2365	2398	2463	2377	2479	2233	2044	2099	121	85					
Honolulu. Hawaii. 21° 18.5'N., 157° 52.3'W.	4685	2278	2236	2233	2091	2246	2331	2285	–	2409	2383	2385	2411	2468	2373	2477	2230	2028	2061	196	140	89				
Pearl Harbor. Hawaii. 21° 20.0'N., 157° 58.3'W.	4690	2283	2241	2238	2096	2251	2336	2290	–	2414	2388	2390	2416	2473	2378	2482	2235	2024	2057	201	145	94	9			
Nawiliwili. Hawaii. 21° 57.4'N., 159° 21.5'W.	4767	2330	2284	2281	2128	2262	2347	2289	–	2413	2368	2361	2388	2429	2332	2440	2184	1963	1989	287	230	181	96	92		
Port Allen. Hawaii. 21° 54.1'N., 159° 35.6'W.	4777	2347	2302	2299	2146	2281	2366	2308	–	2432	2387	2380	2407	2445	2351	2459	2203	1972	1990	297	240	193	106	102	21	
Midway Island. 28° 13.0'N., 177° 22.0'W.	5707	3097	3034	3031	2792	2724	2809	2694	–	2818	2570	2481	2472	2386	2250	2305	2088	1680	1460	1338	1278	1232	1150	1146	1069	1042

HAWAII DISTANCES
(Nautical Miles)

Figure at intersection of columns opposite ports in question is the nautical mileage between the two.
Example: Hilo is 196 nautical miles from Honolulu.

	Hilo. Hawaii. 19° 44.1'N., 155° 03.5'W.	Napoopoo. Hawaii. 19° 28.6'N., 155° 55.3'W.	Kailua. Hawaii. 19° 38.6'N., 156° 00.0'W.	Kawaihae, Hawaii. 20° 02.3'N., 155° 49.9'W.	Mahukona. Hawaii. 20° 11.2'N., 155° 54.2'W.	Hana. Maui. 20° 45.6'N., 155° 59.1'W.	Lahaina (Mala). Maui. 20° 53.5'N., 156°41.5'W.	Kahului. Maui. 20° 54.0'N., 156° 28.2'W.	Kaumalapau. Lanai. 20° 47.4'N., 156° 59.7'W.	Kamalo. Molokai. 21° 02.9'N., 156° 52.7'W.	Kaunakakai. Molokai. 21° 05.1'', 157° 02.0'W.	Haleolono. Molokai. 21° 05.2'N., 157° 15.2'W.	Kalaupapa. Molokai. 21° 11.7'N., 156° 59.3'W.	Honolulu. Oahu. 21° 18.5'N., 157° 52.3'W.	Pearl Harbor. Oahu. 21° 20.0'N., 157° 58.3'W.	Ahukini. Kauai. 21° 59.7'N., 159° 20.1'W.	Nawiliwili. Kauai. 21° 57.4'N., 159° 21.5'W.	Port Allen. Kauai. 21° 54.1'N., 159° 35.6'W.	Waimea. Kauai. 21° 57.4'N., 159° 40.4'W.	Hanalei. Kauai. 22° 12.9'N., 159° 30.1'W.	Nonopapa. Niihau. 21° 52.0'N., 160° 14.1'W.	Midway Island. 28° 13.0'N., 177° 22.0'W.	Johnston Island. 16° 44.6'N., 169° 31.2'W.
Napoopoo	120																						
Kailua	109	11																					
Kawaihae	83	45	34																				
Mahukona	72	50	39	12																			
Hana	85	84	73	48	36																		
Lahaina (Mala)	125	99	88	72	63	57																	
Kahului	121	120	110	85	74	37	27																
Kaumalapau	136	101	91	82	76	72	25	50															
Kamalo	137	112	102	86	77	59	15	30	25														
Kaunakakai	145	120	109	93	85	69	23	39	21	12													
Haleolono	155	124	114	103	95	80	34	50	24	22	13												
Kalaupapa	154	138	127	110	102	70	39	41	54	37	45	33											
Honolulu	196	157	147	140	133	119	73	89	60	61	52	40	53										
Pearl Harbor	201	162	152	145	138	124	78	94	65	66	57	45	58	9									
Ahukini	287	245	236	230	223	210	165	181	151	153	144	132	143	96	92								
Nawiliwili	287	244	235	230	223	210	165	181	151	153	144	132	144	96	92	5							
Port Allen	297	254	245	240	233	220	177	193	161	163	154	142	156	106	102	23	21						
Waimea	303	260	251	246	239	226	182	199	167	169	160	148	162	112	108	29	27	8					
Hanalei	308	266	257	251	244	224	186	194	172	173	164	152	159	116	112	29	32	42	35				
Nonopapa	332	287	278	277	272	262	214	232	199	203	193	181	194	147	143	65	63	45	40	52			
Midway Island	1338	–	–	1278	–	–	–	1232	–	–	–	–	–	1150	1146	–	1069	1042	–	–	–		
Johnston Island	905	–	–	811	–	–	–	796	–	–	–	–	–	725	722	–	668	656	–	–	–	825	
Palmyra Island. 5° 52.5'N., 162° 08.0'W.	959	–	–	928	–	–	–	1010	–	–	–	–	–	959	960	–	986	979	–	–	–	1606	785

PACIFIC COAST
SAN DIEGO, CALIF., TO CAPE FLATTERY, WASH.
(**Nautica**l Miles)

Figure at intersection of columns opposite ports in question is the nautical mileage between the two.
Example: San Francisco. Calif., is 652 nautical miles from Portland, Oreg.

	San Diego. Calif. 32° 43.0′N., 117° 10.5′W.	Newport Beach. Calif. 33° 37.1′N., 117° 55.5′W.	Long Beach. Calif. 32° 46.2′N., 118° 13.3′W.	Los Angeles. Calif. 33° 45.0′N., 118° 16.2′W.	Port Hueneme. Calif. 34° 09.0′N., 119° 12.4′W.	Santa Barbara. Calif. 34° 24.5′N., 119° 41.1′W.	Port San Luis. Calif. 35° 10.4′N., 120° 44.8′W.	Monterey. Calif. 36° 36.5′N., 121° 53.0′W.	San Francisco. Calif. 37° 48.5′N., 122° 24.0′W.	Oakland. Calif. 37° 48.2′N., 122° 19.5′W.	Stockton. Calif. 37° 57.2′N., 121° 18.8′W.	Sacramento. Calif. 38° 33.8′N., 121° 33.0′W.	Eureka. Calif. 40° 47.8′N., 124° 11.2′W.	Crescent City. Calif. 41° 44.5′N., 124° 11.4′W.	Coos Bay. Oreg. 43° 22.4′N., 124° 12.5′W.	Gardiner. Oreg. 43° 43.9′N., 124° 06.8′W.	Florence. Oreg. 43° 58.0′N., 124° 06.3′W.	Newport. Oreg. 44° 37.8′N., 124° 03.1′W.	Depoe Bay. Oreg. 44° 48.6′N., 124° 03.6′W.	Garibaldi. Oreg. 45° 33.3′N., 123° 55.1′W.	Astoria. Oreg. 46° 11.7′N., 123° 50.0′W.	Longview. Wash. 46° 06.3′N., 122° 57.7′W.	Vancouver. Wash. 45° 37.6′N., 122° 41.3′W.	Portland. Oreg. 45° 33.0′N., 122° 41.7′W.	South Bend. Wash. 46° 40.1′N., 123° 47.5′W.	Aberdeen. Wash. 46° 58.4′N., 123° 48.5′W.
Newport Beach	78																								
Long Beach	94	25																							
Los Angeles	95	27	3																						
Port Hueneme	147	81	66	62																					
Santa Barbara	174	108	94	90	29																				
Port San Luis	259	193	179	175	116	91																			
Monterey	370	304	290	266	228	203	121																		
San Francisco	455	389	374	371	312	287	205	96																	
Oakland	458	392	377	374	315	290	208	100	3																
Stockton	526	460	445	442	383	358	276	167	75	78															
Sacramento	530	464	449	446	387	362	280	171	79	82	75														
Eureka	653	587	572	569	510	485	403	294	232	235	303	307													
Crescent City	704	638	624	620	561	537	455	346	283	287	354	358	64												
Coos Bay	817	751	736	733	674	649	567	459	396	399	467	471	180	125											
Gardiner	832	766	751	748	689	664	582	474	411	414	482	486	195	140	42										
Florence	848	782	768	764	706	681	599	490	427	430	496	502	212	156	59	36									
Newport	881	815	800	797	737	713	631	522	459	463	531	534	244	188	92	69	43								
Depoe Bay	891	825	810	807	748	723	641	532	469	473	541	544	254	199	101	78	54	16							
Garibaldi	937	871	857	853	794	770	687	579	516	520	588	591	301	245	150	127	102	63	50						
Astoria	969	922	906	904	845	821	739	630	567	570	639	642	352	296	201	178	153	115	101	58					
Longview	1034	967	953	949	890	866	783	675	612	615	684	687	397	341	246	223	198	160	146	103	45				
Vancouver	1070	1003	988	985	925	901	819	710	647	651	719	722	432	377	281	258	234	196	182	138	80	34			
Portland	1074	1007	992	989	930	905	823	714	652	655	723	727	436	381	285	262	238	200	186	142	85	39	13		
South Bend	1019	953	939	935	876	852	769	661	598	601	670	673	383	327	232	209	184	146	133	90	63	108	143	147	
Aberdeen	1031	965	951	947	888	864	781	673	610	613	682	685	395	339	244	221	196	158	144	102	75	119	155	159	53
CAPE FLATTERY. WASH. 48° 26.0′N., 124° 47.0′W.	1104	1038	1024	1020	961	937	854	746	683	686	755	758	468	411	321	298	273	235	222	179	153	198	234	238	131	117

Entrance buoy SD (32° 37.3′N., 117° 14.7′W.) to San Diego, 8.3 miles.
Entrance buoy LB (32° 42.1′N., 118° 11.0′W.) to Long Beach, 4.9 miles.
Entrance buoy LA (33° 42.0′N., 118° 14.5′W.) to Los Angeles, 3.8 miles.
Entrance buoy SF (37° 45.0′N., 122° 41.5′W.) to San Francisco, 15 miles; Oak!and 18.5 miles; Stockton 87 miles; Sacramento 91 miles.
Humboldt Bay entrance buoy HB (40° 46.4′N., 124° 16.2′W.) to Eureka, 5.5 miles.
Entrance buoy K (43° 22.2′N., 124° 23.0′W.) to Coos Bay (city), 13.3 miles.
Yaquina Bay entrance buoy CR (46° 11.1′N., 124° 11.0′W.) to Astoria, 17.8 miles; Longview 64 miles; Vancouver 98 miles; Portland 103 miles.
Willapa Bay entrance buoy W (46° 42.6′N., 124° 10.8′W.) to South Bend, 19 miles.
Grays Harbor entrance buoy GH (46° 51.9′N., 124° 14.3′W.) to Aberdeen, 21 miles.

SAN FRANCISCO BAY AREA
(Nautical Miles)

Figure at intersection of columns opposite ports in question is the nautical mileage between the two.
Example: Sacramento, California is 74 nautical miles from Napa, California.

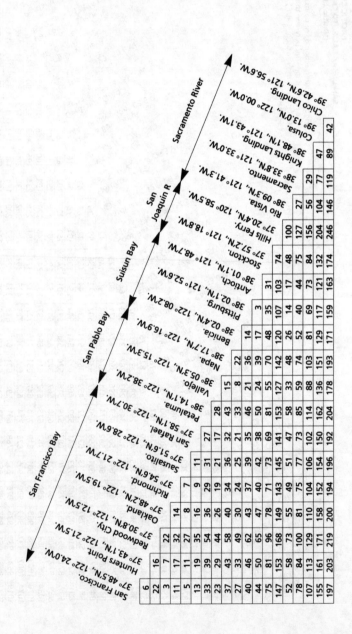

San Francisco Bay – San Pablo Bay – Suisun Bay – San Joaquin R – Sacramento River

	San Francisco. 37° 48.5'N., 122° 24.0'W.	Hunters Point. 37° 43.1'N., 122° 21.5'W.	Redwood City. 37° 30.8'N., 122° 12.5'W.	Oakland. 37° 48.2'N., 122° 19.5'W.	Richmond. 37° 54.6'N., 122° 21.7'W.	Sausalito. 37° 51.6'N., 122° 28.6'W.	San Rafael. 37° 58.1'N., 122° 30.7'W.	Petaluma. 38° 14.1'N., 122° 38.2'W.	Vallejo. 38° 05.3'N., 122° 15.3'W.	Napa. 38° 17.7'N., 122° 16.9'W.	Benicia. 38° 02.4'N., 122° 08.2'W.	Pittsburg. 38° 02.1'N., 121° 52.6'W.	Antioch. 38° 01.1'N., 121° 48.7'W.	Stockton. 37° 57.2'N., 121° 18.8'W.	Hills Ferry. 37° 20.4'N., 120° 58.5'W.	Rio Vista. 38° 09.3'N., 121° 41.3'W.	Sacramento. 38° 33.8'N., 121° 33.0'W.	Knights Landing. 38° 48.1'N., 121° 43.1'W.	Colusa. 39° 13.0'N., 122° 00.0'W.
Hunters Point	6																		
Redwood City	22	16																	
Oakland	3	7	22																
Richmond	11	17	32	14															
Sausalito	5	11	27	8	7														
San Rafael	13	19	35	16	9	11													
Petaluma	33	39	54	36	29	31	27												
Vallejo	23	29	44	26	19	21	17	28											
Napa	37	43	58	40	34	36	32	43	15										
Benicia	27	33	49	30	24	25	21	33	8	22									
Pittsburg	40	46	62	43	37	39	35	46	21	36	14								
Antioch	44	50	65	47	40	42	38	50	24	39	17	3							
Stockton	75	81	96	78	71	73	69	81	55	70	48	35	31						
Hills Ferry	147	153	168	149	143	145	141	153	127	142	120	107	103	74					
Rio Vista	52	58	73	55	49	51	47	58	33	48	26	14	17	48	100				
Sacramento	78	84	100	81	75	77	73	85	59	74	52	40	44	75	127	27			
Knights Landing	107	113	129	110	104	106	102	114	88	103	81	69	73	84	156	56	29		
Colusa	155	161	171	158	152	154	150	162	136	151	129	117	121	132	204	104	77	47	
Chico Landing. 39° 42.6'N., 121° 56.6'W.	197	203	219	200	194	196	192	204	178	193	171	159	163	174	246	146	119	89	42

DISTANCES ON COLUMBIA RIVER SYSTEM

(Nautical Miles)

Figure at intersection of columns opposite ports in question is the nautical/statute mileage between the two.
Example: Astoria, Oreg., is 85 nautical miles (98 statute miles) from Portland, Oreg.

Statute Miles (upper right) — Nautical Miles (lower left)

Columbia River — Willamette River — Snake River

Port	Columbia River Mouth	Ilwaco	Warrenton	Astoria	Longview	St. Helens	Vancouver	Bonneville	Hood River	The Dalles	John Day	Arlington	Umatilla	McNary	Port of Walla Walla	Pasco	Richland	Portland	Oregon City	Salem	Albany	Corvallis	Harrisburg	Ice Harbor Dam	Central Ferry	Lewiston	Johnson Bar landing
Columbia River Mouth, 46° 14.8′N., 124° 05.5′W.		7	13	14	67	86	106	145	170	191	216	242	289	292	318	328	337	112	127	186	221	234	265	335	407	465	556
Ilwaco, Wash., 46° 18.3′N., 124° 02.2′W.	6		14	15	68	87	107	146	171	192	217	243	289	292	318	329	338	113	128	188	222	234	265	336	409	465	557
Warrenton, Oreg., 46° 10.1′N., 123° 55.0′W.	11	12		5	58	77	97	136	161	183	207	232	281	283	308	319	328	102	119	177	212	224	255	326	398	456	547
Astoria, Oreg., 46° 11.7′N., 123° 50.0′W.	12	13	4		52	71	92	131	157	177	203	228	275	277	303	314	323	98	113	171	207	219	250	320	394	450	541
Longview, Wash., 46° 06.3′N., 122° 57.7′W.	58	59	50	45		20	39	78	104	124	150	175	222	224	250	261	270	45	60	120	154	166	197	268	341	397	489
St. Helens, Oreg., 45° 51.7′N., 122° 47.6′W.	75	76	67	62	17		23	63	87	109	135	159	207	209	235	246	255	29	45	104	139	151	182	252	325	392	473
Vancouver, Wash., 45° 37.6′N., 122° 41.3′W.	92	93	84	80	34	20		40	64	86	110	136	184	186	212	222	232	15	30	89	124	136	167	229	302	359	450
Bonneville Lock & Dam, 45° 38.3′N., 121° 56.8′W.	126	127	118	114	68	55	35		25	46	71	97	144	146	171	183	192	54	70	129	163	176	207	189	262	319	410
Hood River (town), Oreg., 45° 43.0′N., 121° 30.0′W.	148	149	140	136	90	76	56	22		21	46	71	119	122	147	158	167	79	94	154	189	200	231	165	237	295	386
The Dalles Lock & Dam, 45° 36.9′N., 121° 08.3′W.	166	167	159	154	108	95	75	40	18		25	51	98	100	125	137	146	100	116	175	211	222	253	143	216	273	364
John Day Lock & Dam, 45° 42.9′N., 120° 41.5′W.	188	189	180	176	130	117	96	62	40	22		25	72	75	100	112	121	125	142	200	235	247	278	117	191	247	338
Arlington, Oreg., 45° 43.6′N., 120° 12.2′W.	210	211	202	196	152	138	118	84	62	40	22		48	51	76	86	96	150	166	224	260	272	303	93	166	223	314
Umatilla, Oreg., 45° 55.4′N., 119° 20.5′W.	251	252	244	239	193	180	160	125	103	85	63	42		2	28	39	48	198	214	273	308	320	351	45	119	175	266
McNary Lock & Dam, 45° 56.4′N., 119° 17.9′W.	254	254	246	241	195	182	162	127	106	87	65	44	2		25	37	46	200	216	275	311	322	353	43	116	173	264
Port of Walla Walla, Wash., 46° 06.0′N., 118° 55.3′W.	276	276	268	263	217	204	184	149	128	109	87	66	24	22		12	21	226	242	300	336	348	379	17	91	147	238
Pasco, Wash., 46° 13.2′N., 119° 05.9′W.	285	286	277	273	227	214	193	159	137	119	97	75	34	32	10		9	237	253	312	346	359	390	14	86	144	235
Richland, Wash., 46° 16.5′N., 119° 16.1′W.	293	294	285	281	235	222	202	167	145	127	105	83	42	40	18	8		246	262	321	356	368	399	23	96	153	244
Portland, Oreg., 45° 33.0′N., 122° 41.7′W.	97	98	89	85	39	25	13	47	69	87	109	130	172	174	196	206	214		16	75	110	122	153	243	316	373	464
Oregon City, Oreg., 45° 21.5′N., 122° 36.5′W.	110	111	103	98	52	39	26	61	82	101	123	144	186	188	210	220	228	14		59	94	106	137	259	331	389	480
Salem, Oreg., 44° 56.2′N., 123° 03.1′W.	162	163	154	149	104	90	77	112	134	152	174	195	237	239	261	271	279	65	51		36	47	78	318	391	448	539
Albany, Oreg., 44° 38.3′N., 123° 06.2′W.	192	193	184	180	134	121	108	142	164	183	204	226	268	270	292	301	309	96	82	31		12	43	353	426	483	574
Corvalis, Oreg., 44° 34.0′N., 123° 15.3′W.	203	203	195	190	144	131	118	153	174	193	215	236	278	280	302	312	320	106	92	41	10		31	365	437	495	586
Harrisburg, Oreg., 44° 16.0′N., 123° 10.2′W.	230	230	222	217	171	158	145	180	201	220	242	263	305	307	329	339	347	133	119	68	37	27		396	468	526	617
Ice Harbor Dam, Wash., 46° 15.1′N., 118° 52.7′W.	291	292	283	278	233	219	199	164	143	124	102	81	39	37	15	12	20	211	225	276	307	317	344		72	130	221
Central Ferry, Wash., 46° 37.6′N., 117° 46.6′W.	354	355	346	342	296	282	262	228	206	188	166	144	103	101	79	75	83	275	288	340	370	380	407	63		58	148
Lewiston, Idaho, 46° 25.1′N., 116° 59.9′W.	404	404	396	391	345	332	312	277	256	237	215	194	152	150	128	125	133	324	338	389	420	430	457	113	50		91
Johnson Bar landing, Idaho, 45° 27.6′N., 116° 33.8′W.	483	484	475	470	425	411	391	356	335	316	294	273	231	229	207	204	212	403	417	468	499	509	536	192	129	79	

DISTANCES IN STRAIT OF JUAN DE FUCA AND STRAIT OF GEORGIA

(Nautical miles)

figure at intersection of columns opposite ports in question is the nautical mileage between the two. Example: Port angeles, Wash., is 69 nautical miles from Seattle, Wash.

CAPE FLATTERY, WASH. 48°26·0'N, 124°47·0'W	SWIFTSURE BANK, WASH. 48°31·0'N, 125°00·0'W	Neah Bay, Wash. 48°22·4'N, 124°36·5'W	Port Angeles, Wash. 48°25·0'N, 123°26·4'W	Victoria, Canada 48°25·0'N, 123°23·5'W	Port Townsend, Wash. 48°06·8'N, 122°45·2'W	Port Ludlow, Wash. 47°55·3'N, 122°41·0'W	Port Gamble, Wash. 47°51·3'N, 122°34·7'W	Everett, Wash. 47°59·3'N, 122°13·2'W	Point Wells, Wash. 47°47·1'N, 122°23·7'W	Seattle, Wash. 47°36·2'N, 122°20·3'W	Eagle Harbor, Wash. 47°37·2'N, 122°30·7'W	Bremerton, Wash 47°33·5'N, 122°38·0'W	Tacoma, Wash. 47°16·0'N, 122°26·0'W	Olympia, Wash. 47°03·1'N, 122°54·3'W	Roche Harbor, Wash. 48°36·6'N, 123°09·1'W	Friday Harbor, Wash. 48°32·2'N, 123°00·9'W	Anacortes, Wash. 48°31·4'N, 122°36·7'W	Bellingham, Wash. 48°45·1'N, 122°29·0'W	Blaine, Wash. 48°59·5'N, 122°45·9'W	Nanaimo, Canada. 49°10·1'N, 123°56·0'W	New Westminster, Canada. 49°12·0'N, 122°54·5'W	Vancouver, Canada. 49°17·4'N, 123°06·6'W
10																						
10	20																					
61	71	54																				
62	71	55	19																			
86	96	79	32	34																		
100	110	93	46	48	16																	
104	114	97	50	53	21	10																
117	127	110	63	66	34	26	28															
111	121	103	56	59	27	19	21	16														
124	134	116	69	72	40	32	34	30	14													
123	133	115	68	71	40	32	34	29	14	8												
131	141	124	77	80	48	40	42	38	23	14	13											
143	153	136	89	91	59	52	53	49	34	25	25	29										
168	178	160	113	115	84	75	78	73	59	50	50	50	34									
83	92	76	36	25	41	54	58	71	64	77	76	85	96	121								
87	96	80	37	30	30	44	48	62	54	67	67	76	86	112	12							
93	102	86	42	36	30	43	47	49	54	66	66	74	86	110	27	18						
108	117	101	54	50	43	57	61	63	68	80	80	88	100	124	37	28	17					
112	121	105	65	55	59	72	76	80	83	95	95	104	115	139	35	37	36	38				
145	154	138	99	89	97	111	115	118	121	134	134	142	154	177	66	69	76	75	55			
139	148	132	93	82	91	105	109	114	116	128	128	137	148	171	60	60	70	71	48	48		
141	150	133	95	83	92	106	110	115	117	129	129	138	149	173	62	62	71	72	48	36	41	

INSIDE - PASSAGE DISTANCES
SEATTLE, WASH. TO CAPE SPENCER, ALASKA
(Nautical Miles)

Figure at intersection of columns opposite ports in question is the nautical mileage between the two.
Example: Ketchikan, Alaska is 220 nautical miles from Juneau, Alaska.

Port	Seattle	Victoria	Dixon Entrance	Hyder	Cape Chacon	Metlakatla	Ketchikan	Craig	Wrangell	Cape Decision	Port Alexander	Petersburg	Sitka	Pelican	Juneau	Haines	Skagway	Gustavus
Seattle. Wash. 47° 36.2'N., 122° 20.3'W.																		
Victoria. Canada. 48° 25.0'N., 123° 28.5'W.	72																	
DIXON ENTRANCE. ALASKA. 54° 28.0'N., 132° 52.0'W.	664	612																
Hyder. Alaska. 55° 54.2'N., 130° 00.6'W.	690	638	169															
Cape Chacon. Alaska. 54° 40.6'N., 131° 59.7'W.	640	588	34	136														
Metlakatla. Alaska. 55° 07.8'N., 131° 34.2'W.	660	608	66	148	32													
Ketchikan. Alaska. 55° 20.5'N., 131° 38.7'W.	659	608	79	144	45	16												
Craig. Alaska. 55° 28.7'N., 133° 09.2'W.	716	664	77	212	76	109	121											
Wrangell. Alaska. 56° 28.2'N., 132° 23.2'W.	749	697	157	234	123	104	89	111										
CAPE DECISION. ALASKA. 55° 59.4'N., 134° 08.1'W.	788	737	126	273	125	143	129	49	75									
Port Alexander. Alaska. 56° 14.8'N., 134° 28.8'W.	812	761	150	297	149	167	153	73	99	24								
Petersburg. Alaska. 56° 48.9'N., 132° 57.8'W.	771	719	180	256	146	126	112	113	40	76	100							
Sitka. Alaska. 57° 03.1'N., 135° 20.5'W.	883	832	221	368	220	238	224	144	170	95	82	159						
Pelican. Alaska. 57° 57.6'N., 136° 13.8'W.	989	937	332	464	331	334	320	255	248	206	186	207	79					
Juneau. Alaska. 58° 17.9'N., 134° 24.7'W.	879	827	288	364	254	235	220	206	148	157	140	108	162	123				
Haines. Alaska. 59° 13.8'N., 135° 26.1'W.	950	898	359	435	325	305	291	253	219	204	186	179	176	136	88			
Skagway. Alaska. 59° 26.8'N., 135° 19.3'W.	962	910	371	447	337	317	303	264	231	215	198	191	187	148	100	14		
Gustavus. Alaska. 58° 23.3'N., 135° 43.6'W.	938	886	290	423	289	293	278	213	208	164	147	166	136	45	82	96	106	
CAPE SPENCER. ALASKA. 58° 10.0'N., 136° 38.3'W.	976	924	319	451	318	321	307	242	235	193	173	195	85	18	110	124	136	32

21

GULF OF ALASKA DISTANCES
(Nautical Miles)

Figure at intersection of columns opposite ports in question is the nautical mileage between the two.
Example: Anchorage is 385 nautical miles from Port Valdez.

	SWIFTSURE BANK. 48° 31.0'N., 125° 00.0'W.	DIXON ENTRANCE. ALASKA. 54° 28.0'N., 132° 52.0'W.	CAPE DECISION. ALASKA. 55° 59.4'N., 134° 08.1'W.	Sitka. Alaska. 57° 03.1'N., 135° 20.5'W.	CAPE SPENCER. ALASKA. 58° 10.0'N., 136° 38.3'W.	Yakutat. 59° 32.9'N., 139° 43.9'W.	Cordova. 60° 33.4'N., 145° 45.3'W.	Port Valdez. 61° 06.0'N., 146° 24.0'W.	Whittier 60° 46.8'N., 148° 39.6'W.	Latouche 60° 03.3'N., 147° 54.1'W.	Seward. 60° 06.0'N., 149° 26.0'W.	Seldovia. 59° 26.5'N., 151° 43.0'W.	Homer. 59° 36.0'N., 151° 24.0'W.	Anchorage. 61° 14.2'N., 149° 53.3'W.	Kodiak. 57° 47.1'N., 152° 25.1'W.	Uyak. 57° 38.6'N., 154° 00.0'W.	Chignik. 56° 17.8'N., 158° 24.0'W.	Unga. 55° 10.6'N., 160° 29.8'W.	False Pass. 54° 51.4'N., 163° 24.0'W.
DIXON ENTRANCE	500																		
CAPE DECISION	588	106																	
Sitka	681	192	95																
CAPE SPENCER	739	259	162	85															
Yakutat	869	402	295	231	141														
Cordova	1093	627	522	472	393	278													
Port Valdez	1100	634	529	479	400	285	78												
Whittier	1113	647	542	492	413	298	96	96											
Latouche	1076	617	525	467	395	286	85	83	64										
Seward	1100	642	553	494	422	312	146	144	125	61									
Seldovia	1167	718	636	580	514	411	260	257	239	172	147								
Homer	1178	729	647	591	525	422	270	267	249	183	158	16							
Anchorage	1294	845	763	708	641	538	387	385	367	300	274	139	143						
Kodiak	1124	687	613	564	505	414	282	280	261	201	175	115	126	242					
Uyak	1200	762	689	628	571	480	339	337	317	254	228	138	149	264	80				
Chignik	1301	874	811	772	717	636	503	501	481	418	392	302	313	428	245	180			
Unga	1394	953	892	865	811	730	597	595	574	511	485	395	406	521	338	273	122		
False Pass	1473	1084	1016	980	926	844	711	709	698	626	600	510	521	636	453	388	236	135	
UNIMAK PASS. 54° 20.0'N., 164° 45.0'W.	1510	1120	1064	1027	987	897	763	761	742	678	652	562	573	688	505	440	289	187	86

BERING SEA AND ARTIC OCEAN DISTANCES
(Nautical Miles)

Figure at intersection of columns opposite ports in question is the nautical mileage betweent he two.
Example: Port Moller is 618 nautical miles from Nome.

	UNIMAK PASS. 54°20·0'N, 164°45·0'W	Dutch harbor. 53°52·7'N, 166°31·8'W	Kuluk Bay. 51°51·6'N, 176°37·6'W	Constantine Harbor. 51°24·0'N, 179°18·1'W	Kiska 51°58·3'N, 177°34·5'W	Alcan Harbor. 52°44·0'N, 174°04·5'W	Massacre Bay. 52°48·9'N, 173°15·6'W	St Paul Island. 57°07·6'N, 170°17·9'W	Port Moller. 55°59·0'N, 160°36·5'W	Meshik 56°56·5'N, 158°49·0'W	Naknek. 58°41·5'N, 157°16·0'W	Dillingham. 59°02·0'N, 158°29·0'W	Platinum. 59°01·5'N, 161°52·0'W	Bethel. 60°49·0'N, 161°47·0'W	Hooper Bay. 61°29·0'N, 166°04·0'W	Apoorn Pass. 63°02·6'N, 163°22·3'W	St. Michael. 63°32·4'N, 161°54·8'W	Unalakleet. 63°53·0'N, 160°50·0'W	Golovnin Bay. 64°22·3'N, 163°06·7'W	Nome. 64°29·0'N, 165°26·0'W	Savoonga. 63°43·0'N, 170°27·0'W	Port Clarence. 65°17·1'N, 166°24·5'W	CAPE PRINCE OF WALES. 65°37·6'N, 168°31·5'W	Deering. 66°06·0'N, 162°44·0'W	Point Hope. 68°21·0'N, 167°18·0'W	Point Lay. 69°48·0'N, 163°08·0'W	Wainwright. 70°40·0'N, 160°00·0'W	Barrow. 71°18·0'N, 156°48·0'W	Barter Island. 70°09·0'N, 143°40·0'W
Dutch harbor.	75																												
Kuluk Bay.	463	407																											
Constantine Harbor.	614	558	175																										
Kiska	672	616	235	79																									
Alcan Harbor.	805	749	368	222	157																								
Massacre Bay.	833	777	396	249	185	33																							
St Paul Island.	254	239	287	501	526	604	632																						
Port Moller.	208	256	627	769	809	920	934	335																					
Meshik	277	325	694	832	871	978	991	381	88																				
Naknek.	377	425	779	912	945	1029	1056	437	198	118																			
Dillingham.	384	432	785	919	951	1036	1062	444	207	130	72																		
Platinum.	307	343	662	789	817	893	921	302	196	179	202	208																	
Bethel.	421	464	776	903	931	1007	1034	415	310	293	315	322	120																
Hooper Bay.	472	485	678	775	783	830	854	304	452	459	486	493	340	454															
Apoorn Pass.	708	721	897	982	981	1015	1037	528	676	684	711	718	565	679	259														
St. Michael.	711	724	900	985	984	1018	1040	529	678	685	712	719	566	680	260	53													
Unalakleet.	737	750	926	1011	1009	1044	1066	555	703	712	738	744	592	706	286	88	35												
Golovnin Bay.	686	699	875	960	958	990	1015	504	652	660	687	693	541	655	235	85	59	66											
Nome.	646	659	835	920	919	950	975	470	618	625	653	659	507	620	200	116	110	126	62										
Savoonga.	642	654	830	915	914	945	970	468	621	628	656	662	510	624	209	229	230	254	197	139									
Port Clarence.	708	720	896	981	980	1013	1036	535	687	695	722	728	576	690	276	228	225	244	179	119	151								
CAPE PRINCE OF WALES.	702	715	891	976	975	1008	1031	529	682	689	717	723	571	685	270	222	219	238	174	114	125	57							
Deering.	900	913	1089	1174	1173	1206	1229	727	880	887	915	921	769	883	468	420	417	436	372	312	323	255	198						
Point Hope.	868	881	1057	1142	1141	1174	1197	695	848	855	883	889	737	850	436	388	385	404	340	279	291	223	166	172					
Point Lay.	998	1011	1187	1272	1271	1304	1327	825	978	985	1012	1019	866	980	566	518	515	534	470	409	420	354	296	302	130				
Wainwright.	1079	1092	1268	1353	1352	1385	1408	906	1059	1066	1094	1100	948	1061	647	599	596	615	551	490	502	435	377	383	211	86			
Barrow.	1155	1167	1343	1428	1427	1460	1483	962	1134	1141	1169	1175	1023	1137	722	674	672	690	626	566	577	510	452	458	286	161	77		
Barter Island.	1428	1440	1616	1701	1700	1733	1756	1255	1407	1414	1442	1448	1296	1410	995	947	945	963	899	839	850	783	725	732	560	434	350	274	
Alaska-Canada Boundary. 69°43·0'N, 141°00·0'W	1490	1503	1678	1763	1762	1795	1819	1317	1469	1477	1507	1513	1358	1472	1058	1010	1007	1025	961	901	912	846	787	794	621	496	412	337	62

Multilanguage Glossary

22

FOUR LANGUAGE GLOSSARY

Translations are given under the following heading:

ENGLISH	FRENCH	SPANISH	DUTCH
1 PROHIBITIONS	Interdictions	Prohibiciones	Verbouwen
2 TYPES OF VESSEL	Types du bateau	Typos de barco	Scheepstypen
3 PARTS OF VESSEL	Parties du bateau	Partes del barco	Scheeps onderdelen
4 MASTS & SPARS	Mâts	Mástiles y palos	Masten
5 RIGGING	Gréement	Aparejo	Tuigage
6 SAILS	Voilure	Velas	Zeilen
7 BELOW DECK	Cabine	Alcázar	Onderdeks
8 NAVIGATION EQUIPMENT	Equipement de navigation	Equipo de navigación	Navigatie uitrusting
9 ENGINES	Moteurs	Motores	Motoren
10 ENGINE ACCESSORIES	Accessoires moteur	Máquina accesorio	Onderdelen van motoren
11 ELECTRICS	Electricité	Electricidad	Elektriciteit
12 FUEL, ETC	Combusitibles	Gazolina	Div brandstoffen
13 METALS	Métaux	Metales	Metalen
14 LIGHTS	Lumières	Luz	Lichten
15 SHIP'S PAPERS	Papiers du bateau	Papeles del barco	Scheepspapieren
16 TOOLS	Outils	Herramientas	Gereedschap
17 CHANDLERY	Ship chandler	Pertrechos	Scheepsbehoeften
18 FOOD	Nourriture	Comida	Proviand
19 SHOPS AND PLACES ASHORE	Boutiques et endroio divers	Tiendas y sitios en tierra	Winkels & plaatsen aan land
20 IN HARBOR	Au port	En el puerto	In de haven
21 FIRST AID	Premiers secours	Primero socorro	Eerste hulp bij ongelukken

---

ENGLISH	FRENCH	SPANISH	DUTCH
1 PROHIBITIONS			
Prohibited area	Zone interdite	Zona prohibida	Verboden gebied
Anchoring prohibited	Defense de mouiller	Fondeadero prohibido	Verboden ankerplaats
Mooring prohibited	Accostage interdite	Amarradero prohibido	Verboden aan te leggen
2 TYPES OF VESSEL (Private)			
Sloop	Sloop	Balandra	Sloep
Cutter	Cotre	Cúter	Kotter
Ketch	Ketch	Queche	Kits
Yawl	Yawl	Yola	Yaw
Schooner	Goélette	Goleta	Schoener
Motor sailer	Bateau mixte	Moto-velero	Motorzeiljacht

ENGLISH	FRENCH	SPANISH	DUTCH
Dinghy	Youyou, prame	Balandro	Jol, bijboot
Launch	Chaloupe	Lancha	Barkas
Motor boat	Bateau a moteur	Motora, bote a motor	Motorboot
Lifeboat	Bateau, canot de sauvetage	Bote salvadidas	Reddingboot
(Commercial)			
Trawler	Chalutier	Pesquero	Stoomtreiler
Tanker	Bateau-citerne	Petrolero	Tankschip
Merchantman	Navire marchand	Buque mercante	Koopvaardijschip
Ferry	Transbordeur, bac	Transbordador	Pont, veerboot
Tug	Remorqueur	Remolcador	Sleepboot
3 PARTS OF VESSEL			
Stem	Étrave	Roda	Voorsteven
Stern	Poupe	Popa	Achtersteven
Forecastle (fo'c's'le)	Gaillard d'avant	Castillo de proa	Vooronder
Fore peak	Pic avant	Pique de proa	Voorpiek
Cabin	Cabine	Camarote	Kajuit
Chain locker	Puits à chaines	Caja de cadenas	Kettingbak
Heads	Toilette	Retrete	W.C.
Galley	Cuisine	Cocina	Kombuis
Chartroom	Salle des cartes	Caseta de derrota	Kaartenkamer
Bunk	Couchette	Litera	Kooi
Pipe cot	Cadre	Catre	Pijkooi
Engine room	Chambre des machines	Cámara de máquinas	Motorruim
Locker	Coffre	Taquilla	Kastje
Bulkhead	Cloison	Mamparo	Schot
Hatch	Écoutille	Escotilla	Luik
Cockpit	Cockpit	Cabina	Kuip
Sail locker	Soute à voiles	Panol de velas	Zeilkooi
Freshwater tank	Reservoir d'eau douce	Tanque de agua potable	Drinkwatertank
Rudder	Gouvernail	Timón	Roer
Propeller	Hélice	Hélice	Schroef
Bilges	Cale	Sentina	Kim
Keel	Quille	Quilla	Kiel
Gunwhale	Plat-bord	Borda, regala	Dolboord
Rubbing strake	Bourrelet de défense	Verduguillo	Berghout
Tiller	Barre	Cana	Helmstok
Stanchions	Chandelier	Candelero	Scepters
Bilge pump	Pompe de cale	Bombas de achique de sentina	Lenspomp
Pulpit	Balcon avant	Pùlpito	Preekstoel
Pushpit	Balcon arrière	Púlpito de popa	Hekstoel
4 MASTS AND SPARS			
Mast	Mât	Palo	Mast
Foremast	Mât de misaine	Trinquete	Fokkemast
Mizzen mast	Mât d'artimon	Palo mesana	Bezaansmast
Boom	Bôme	Botavara	Giek
Bowsprit	Beaupré	Baupres	Boegspriet
Bumpkin	Bout-dehors	Pescante amura trinquette	Papegaaistok
Spinnaker boom	Tangon de spi	Tangon del espinaquer	Nagel-of spinnakerboom
Gaff	Corne	Pico (de vela cangreja)	Gaffel

22

ENGLISH	FRENCH	SPANISH	DUTCH
Spreaders	Barres de flèche	Crucetas	Dwarszaling
Jumper struts	Guignol	Contrete	Knikstagen
Truck	Pomme	Tope (galleta)	Top
Slide	Coulisseau	Corredera	Slede
Roller reefing	Bôme à rouleau	Rizo de catalina	Patentrif
Worm gear	Vis sans fin	Husillo	Worm en wormwiel
Solid	Massif	Macizo	Massief
Hollow	Creux	Hueco	Hol
Derrick	Grue	Pluma de carga	Dirk of Kraanlijn
5 RIGGING (Standing)			
Forestay	Étai avant, étai de trinquette	Estay de proa	Voorstag
Aft stay	Étai arriere	Stay de popa	Achterstag
Shrouds	Haubans	Obenques	Want
Stay	Étai	Estay	Stag
Bob stay	Sous-barbe	Barbiquejo	Waterstag
Backstay	Galhauban	Brandal	Pakstagen
Guy	Retenue	Retenida (Cabo de retenida viento)	Bulletalie
(Running)			
Halyard	Drisse	Driza	Val
Foresail halyard	Drisse de misaine	Driza de trinquetilla	Voorzeil val
Throat halyard	Attache de drisse	Driza de boca	Klauwval
Peak halyard	Drisse de pic	Driza de pico	Piekeval
Burgee halyard	Drisse de guidon	Driza de grimpola	Clubstandaardval
Topping lift	Balancine	Amantillo	Dirk
Main sheet	Écoute de grand voile	Escota mayor	Grootschoot
Foresail sheet	Écoute de Misaine	Trinquetilla (escota de)	Voorzeil of Fokkeschoot
Boom Vary	Hale-bas de bôme	Trapa	Neerhouder
Rope	Cordage	Cabulleria	Touw
Single block	Poule simple	Motón de una cajera	Eenschijfsblok
Double block	Poulie double	Motón de dos cajeras	Tweeschijfsblok
Sheave	Réa	Roldana	Schijf
Shackle	Manille	Grillete	Sluiting
Pin	Goupille	Perno, cabilla	Bout
"D" shackle	Manille Droite	Grillete en D	Harpsluiting
Snap shackle	Manille rapide	Grillete de escape	Patentsluiting
6 SAILS			
Mainsail	Grand voile	Vela mayor	Grootzeil
Foresail	Voile de misaine	Vela trinquete	Voorzeil
Jib	Foc	Foque	Fok
Storm jib	Tourmetin	Foque de capa	Stormfok
Trysail	Voile de cape	Vela de cangrejo	Stormzeil
Genoa	Génois	Foque génova	Genua
Spinnaker	Spinnaker	Espinaquer (foque balón)	Spinnaker
Topsail	Flèche	Gavia	Topzeil
Mizzen sail	Artimon	Mesana	Druil of bezaan
Lugsail	Boile de fortune	Vela al tercio	Emmerzeil

ENGLISH	FRENCH	SPANISH	DUTCH
(Parts of sail)			
Head	Point de drisse	Puno de driza	Top
Tack	Point d'amure	Puno de amura	Hals
Clew	Point d'écoute	Puno de escota	Schoothoorn
Luff	Guidant	Gratil	Voorlijk
Leech	Chute arrière	Apagapenol	Achterlijk
Foot	Bordure	Pujamen	Onderlijk
Roach	Rond échancrure	Alunamiento	Gilling
Peak	Pic	Pico	Piek
Throat	Gorge	Puno de driza	Klauw
Batten pocket	Étui, gaine de latte	Bolsa del sable	Zeillatzak
Batten	Latte	Enjaretado	Zeillat
Cringle	Anneau, patte de bouline	Garruncho de cabo	Grommer
Seam	Couture	Costura	Naad
Sailbag	Sac à voile	Saco de vela	Zeilzak
7 BELOW DECK			
Toilet	Toilette	Retretes	W.C.
Toilet paper	Papier hygiénique	Papel higiénico	Toilet-papier
Towel	Serviette	Toalla	Handdoek
Soap	Savon	Jabón	Zeep
Cabin	Cabine	Camarote	Kajuit
Mattress	Matelas	Colchón	Matras
Sleeping bag	Sac de couchage	Saco de dormir	Slaapzak
Sheet	Drap	Sábana	Laken
Blanket	Couverture	Manta	Wollen deken
Galley	Cuisine	Cocina	Kombuis
Cooker	Cuisinière	Fogón	Kookpan
Frying pan	Poêle à frire	Sartén	Braadpan
Saucepan	Casserole	Cacerola	Steelpan of Stoofpanl
Kettle	Bouilloire	Caldero	Ketel
Tea pot	Théière	Tetera	Theepot
Coffee pot	Cafetière	Cafetera	Koffiepot
Knives	Couteaux	Cuchillos	Messen
Forks	Fourchettes	Tenedores	Vorken
Spoons	Cuillères	Cucharas	Lepels
Can opener	Ouvre-boites	Abrelatas	Blikopener
Corkscrew	Tire-bouchon	Sacacorchos	Kurketrekker
Matches	Allumettes	Cerillas	Lucifers
Dishwashing liquid	Détergent	Detergente	Afwasmiddel
8 NAVIGATION EQUIPMENT			
Chart table	Table à cartes	Planero	Kaartentafel
Chart	Carte marine	Carta Náutica	Zeekaarta
Parallel ruler	Règles parallèles	Regla de paralelas	Parallel Liniaal
Protractor	Rapporteur	Transportador	Gradenboog
Pencil	Crayon	Lápiz	Potlood
Eraser	Gomme	Goma	Vlakgom
Dividers	Pointes sèches	Compas de puntas	Verdeelpasser
Binoculars	Jumelles	Gemelos	Kijker
Compass	Compas	Compás	Kompas
Hand bearing compass	Compas de relèvement	Alidada	Handpeilkompas
Depth sounder	Echosondeur	Sondador acústico	Echolood
Radio receiver	Poste récepteur	Receptor de radio	Radio-ontvangtoestel
Direction finding radio	Récepteur goniométrique	Radio goniómetro	Radiopeiltoestel

ENGLISH	FRENCH	SPANISH	DUTCH
Patent log	Loch enregistreur	Coredera de patente	Patent log
Sextant	Sextant	Sextante	Sextant
9 ENGINES			
Gas engine	Moteur à essence	Motor de gasolina	Benzinemotor
Diesel engine	Moteur diesel	Motor diesel	Dieselmotor
Two-stroke	À deuxtemps	Dos tiempos	Tweetakt
Four-stroke	À quartre temps	Cuatro tiempos	Viertakt
Exhaust pipe	Tuyau déchappement	Tubo de escape	Uitlaatpijp
Gearbox	Boîte de vitesse	Caja de engranajes	Versnelligsbak
Gear lever	Levier des vitesses	Palanca de cambio	Versnellingshendel
Throttle	Accelérateur	Estrangulador	Manette
Clutch	Embrayage	Embrague	Koppeling
Stern tube	Tube d'étambot, arbre	Bocina	Schroefaskoker
Fuel pump	Pompe à combustible	Bomba de alimentación	Brandstofpomp
Carburetor	Carburateur	Carburado	Carburateur
Fuel tank	Réservoir de combustible	Tanque de combustible	Brandstoftank
10 ENGINE ACCESSORIES			
Cylinder head	Culasse	Culata	Cilinderkop
Jointing compound	Pâte à joint	Junta de culata	Vloeibare pakking
Nut	Ecrou	Tuerca	Moer
Bolt	Boulon	Perno	Bout
Washer	Rondelle	Arandela	Ring
Split pin	Coupille fendue	Pasador abierto	Splitpen
Asbestos tape	Ruban d'amiante	Cinta de amianto	Asbestband
Copper pipe	Tuyau de cuivre	Tubo de cobre	Koperpijp
Plastic pipe	Tuyau de plastique	Tubo de plastico	Plastikpijp
11 ELECTRICS			
Voltage	Tension	Voltaje	Spanning
Amp	Ampères	Amperio	Ampère
Spark plug	Bougie	Bujia	Bougie
Dynamo	Dynamo	Dinamo	Dynamo
Magneto	Magnéto	Magneto	Magneet
Dynamo belt	Courroi de dynamo	Correa de dinamo	Dynamo-riem
Battery	Accumulateur	Bateria	Accu
Contact breaker	Interrupteur	Disyuntor	Contactonderbreker
Fuse box	Boîte à fusibles	Caja de fusibles	Zekeringskast
Switch	Commutateur	Interruptor	Schakelaar
Bulb	Ampoule	Bombilla	Lampje
Copper wire	File de cuivre	Cable de cobre	Koperdraad
Distilled water	Eau distillée	Agua destilada	Gedistilleerd water
Solder	Soudure	Soldadura	Soldeer
Flux	Flux	Flux	Smeltmiddel
Insulating tape	Ruban isolant	Cinta aislante	Isolatieband
12 FUEL, ETC			
Gasoline	Essence	Gasolina	Benzine
Kerosene	Pétrole lampant	Petroleo	Petroleum
Diesel oil	Gas-oil	Gasoil	Dieselolie
Alcohol	Alcool à brûler	Alcool desnaturalizado	Spiritus
Lubricating oil	Huile	Aceite de lubricación	Smeerolie

ENGLISH	FRENCH	SPANISH	DUTCH
Two-stroke oil	Huile deux temps	Aceite de motor 2 tiempos	Tweetaktolie
Penetrating oil	Huile penetrante, dégrippant	Aceite penetrante	Kruipolie
Grease	Graisse	Grasa	Vet
13 METALS			
Galvanised iron	Fer galvanisé	Hierro galvanizado	Gegalvaniseerd Ijzer
Stainless steel	Acier inoxydable	Acero inoxidable	Roestvrij staal
Iron	Fer	Hierro	Ijzer
Steel	Acier	Acero	Staal
Copper	Cuivre	Cobre	Koper
Brass	Laiton	Latón	Messing
Aluminum	Aluminium	Aluminio	Aluminium
Bronze	Bronze	Bronce	Brons
14 LIGHTS			
Navigation lights	Feux de bord	Luces de navegación	Navigatie lichten
Mast head light	Fue de téte de mât	Luz del tope de proa	Toplicht
Spreader light	Feu de barre de flèche	Luz de verga	Zalinglicht
Port light	Feu de babord	Luz de babor	Bakboordlicht
Starboard light	Feu de tribord	Luz de estribor	Stuurboordlicht
Stern light	Feu arrière	Luz de alcance	Heklicht
Cabin lamp	Lampe de cabine	Lámpera de camarote	Kajuitlamp
Lamp glass	Verre de lampe	Lámpara de cristal	Lampeglas
Wick	Mèche	Mecha (para engrase)	Kous
15 SHIP'S PAPERS			
Certificate of Registry	Acte de francisation	Patente de Navegación	Zeebrief
Pratique	Libre-pratique	Plática	Verlof tot ontscheping
Ship's Log	Livre de bord	Cuaderno de bitácora	Journaal
Insurance certificate	Certificat d'assurance	Poliza de seguro	Verzekeringsbewijs
Passport	Passeport	Passaporte	Paspoort
Customs clearance	Dédouanement	Despacho de aduana	Bewijs van inklaring door douane
16 TOOLS			
Hammer	Marteau	Martillo	Hamer
Wood chisel	Ciseau à bois	Formón	Beitel
Cold chisel	Ciseau à froid	Cortafrio	Koubeitel
Screwdriver	Tournevis	Destornillador	Schroevedraaier
Spanner	Clé	Llave para tuercas	Sleutel
Adjustable spanner	Clé anglaise	Llave adjustable	Verstelbare sleutel
Saw	Scie	Sierra	Zaag
Hacksaw	Scie à métaux	Sierra para metal	IJzerzaag
Hand drill	Chignolle à main	Taladro de mano	Handboor
File	Lime	Lima	Vijl
Wire cutters	Pinces coupantes	Cortador de alambre	Draadschaar
Pliers	Pinces	Alicates	Buigtang
Wrench	Tourne-à-gauche	Llave de boca	Waterpomptang
17 CHANDLERY			
Burgee	Guidon	Grimpola	Clubstandaard
Ensign	Pavillon	Pabellón	Natie vlag
Courtesy flag	Fanion de courtoisie	Pabellón extranjero	Vreemde natievlag
Q flag	Pavillon Q	Bandera Q	Quarantaine Vlag
Signal flag	Pavillon (alphabetique)	Bandera de senales	Seinvlag

ENGLISH	FRENCH	SPANISH	DUTCH
Anchor	Ancre	Ancla	Anker
Anchor chain	Chaîne d'ancre	Cadena del ancla	Ankerketting
Rope	Cordage	Cabulleria	Touw
Hawser	Cable d'acier	Estacha, amarra	Staaldraad
Synthetic rope	Cordage synthétique	Cabullería sintetica	Synthetisch touw
Nylon rope	Cordage de nylon	Cabullería de nylon	Nylon touw
Dacron	Cordage de Tergal	Cabullería de terylene	Terylene touw
Hemp rope	Cordage de chanvre	Cabullería de canamo	Henneptouw
Fender	Defense	Defensa	Stootkussen
Lifebuoy	Bouée sauvetage	Guindola	Redding boei
Cleat	Taquet	Cornamusa	Klamp
Winch	Winch	Chigre	Lier
Boat hook	Gaffe	Bichero	Pikhaak
Oar	Aviron	Remo	Riem
Fair lead	Chaumard	Guía	Verhaalkam
Eye bolt	Piton de filière	Cáncamo	Oogbout
Paint	Peinture	Pintura	Verf
Varnish	Vernis	Barniz	Lak
Sandpaper	Papier de verre	Papel de lija	Schuurpapier
Foghorn	Corne de brume	Bocina de niebla	Misthoorn
18 FOOD			
Cheese	Fromage	Queso	Kaas
Butter	Beurre	Mantequilla	Boter
Bread	Pain	Pan	Brood
Milk	Lait	Leche	Melk
Jam	Confiture	Compota	Jam
Marmalade	Confiture d'oranges	Marmelada	Marmelade
Mustard	Moutarde	Mostaza	Mosterd
Salt	Sel	Sal	Zout
Pepper	Poivre	Pimienta	Peper
Vinegar	Vinaigre	Vinagre	Azjin
Meat	Viande	Carne	Vlees
Fish	Poisson	Pescado	Vis
Fruit	Fruits	Frutas	Fruit
Vegetables	Légumes	Legumbres	Groenten
Sausages	Saucisses	Embutidos	Worstjes
Ham	Jambon	Jamón	Ham
Beef	Boeuf	Carne de vaca	Rundvlees
Pork	Porc	Carne de cerdo	Varkensvlees
Lamb	Mouton	Carne de cernero	Schapenvlees
Bacon	Lard fumé	Tocino	Spek
Eggs	Oeufs	Huevos	Eieren
Fresh water	Eau douce	Agua dulce	Zoetwater
19 SHOPS AND PLACES ASHORE			
Grocer	Épicier	Tendero de Comestibles	Kruidenier
Greengrocer	Marchand de légumes	Verdulero	Groente handelaar
Butcher	Boucher	Carnicero	Slager
Baker	Boulanger	Panadero	Bakker
Fishmonger	Quincaillerie	Ferretero	Ljzerwarenwinkel
Supermarket	Supermarché	Supermercado	Supermarkt
Market	Marché	Mercado	Markt
Yacht chandler	Fournisseur de marine	Almacén de efectos navales	Scheepsleverancier
Sailmaker	Voilier	Velero	Zeilmakeri

ENGLISH	FRENCH	SPANISH	DUTCH
Garage	Garage	Garaje	Garage
Railway station	Gare	Estación	Station
Bus	Autobus	Autobus	Bus
Post Office	Poste	Correos	Postkantoor
Bank	Banque	Banco	Bank
Pharmacist	Pharmacien	Farmaceútico	Apotheek
Hospital	Hôpital	Hospital	Ziekenhuis
Doctor	Médecin	Medico	Dokter
Dentist	Dentiste	Dentista	Tandarts
20 IN HARBOR			
Harbor	Bassin	Puerto	Haven
Yacht harbor	Bassin pour yachts	Puerto de yates	Jachthaven
Fishing harbor	Port de pêche	Puerto pesquero	Vissershaven
Harbor master	Capitaine de port	Capitan de puerto	Havenmeester
Harbor master's office	Bureau de Capitaine de port	Comandacia de puerto	Havenkantoor
Immigration officer	Agent du service de l'immigration	Oficial de inmigración	Immigratie beamte
Customs office	Bureau de douane	Aduana	Douanekantoor
Prohibited area	Zone interdite	Zona prohibida	Verboden gebied
Anchoring prohibited	Défense de mouiller	Fondeadero prohibido	Verboden ankerplaats
Mooring prohibited	Accostage interdit	Amarradero prohibido	Verboden aan te leggen
Lock	Écluse	Esclusa	Sluis
Canal	Canal	Canal	Kanaal
Mooring place	Point d'accostage	Amarradero	Aanlegplaats
Movable bridge	Pont mobile	Puente móvil	Beweegbare brug
Swing bridge	Pont tourant	Puente giratorio	Draaibrug
Lifting bridge	Pont basculant	Puente levadizo	Hefbrug
Ferry	Bac	Transbordador	Veer
Harbor steps	Éscalier du quai	Escala Real	Haventrappen
21 FIRST AID			
Bandage	Bandage	Venda	Verband
Lint	Pansement	Hilacha	Verbandgaas
Bandaid	Pansement adhésif	Esparadrapo	Kleefpleister
Scissors	Ciseaux	Tijeras	Schaar
Safety pin	Épingle de sûreté	Imperidibles	Veiligheidsspeld
Tweezers	Pince à échardes	Pinzas	Pincet
Thermometer	Thermométre	Termómetro	Thermometer
Disinfectant	Désinfectant	Desinfectante	Desinfecterend-middel
Aspirin tablets	Aspirine	Pastillas de aspirina	Aspirine
Laxative	Laxatif	Laxante	Laxeermiddel
Indigestion tablets	Pillules contre l'indigestion	Pastillas laxantes	Laxeertabletten
Antiseptic cream	Onguent antiseptique	Pomada antiséptica	Antiseptische zalf
Anti-seasickness pills	Remède contre le mal de mer	Pildoras contra el mareo	Pillen tegen zeeziekte
Calamine lotion	Lotion a la calamine	Locion de calamina	Anti-jeuk middel
Wound dressing	Pansement stérilisé	Botiquin para heridas	Noodverband
Stomach upset	Mal à l'estomac	Corte de digestion	Last van de maag

22

ENGLISH	FRENCH	SPANISH	DUTCH

CHART TERMS

ENGLISH	FRENCH	SPANISH	DUTCH
1 Light Characteristics			
F.	Fixe	F.	V.
Oc.	Occ.	Oc.	O.
Iso	Iso	Iso./Isof.	Iso.
Fl.	É	D.	S.
Q	Scint	Ct.	Fl.
IQ	Scint. dis.	Gp. Ct.	Int. Fl.
Al.	Alt.	Alt.	Alt.
Oc.(..)	… Occ.	Gp. Oc. Gr. Oc.	GO.
Fl.(..)	… É	Gp. D.	GS.
Mo	-	Mo	-
FFl	Fixe É	F.D.	V & S
FFl.(..)	Fixe .. É	F. Gp. D./Gp. DyF.	V & GS
2 COMPASS POINTS			
North (N) South (S)	Nord (N) Sud (S)	Norte (N) Sur (S)	Noord (N) Zuid (Z)
East (E) West (W)	Est (E) Ouest (O)	Este, Leste (E) Oeste (W)	Oost (O) West (W))
North East (NE)	Nordé (NE)	Nordeste (NE)	Noord-oost (NO)
North-North East (NNE)	Nord-Nordé (NNE)	Nornordeste (NNE)	Noord-noord-oost (NNO)
North by East	Nord quart Nordé	Norte cuarta al Este (N¼NE)	Noord ten oosten (N-t-O)
3 COLORS			
Black	Noir (n)	Negro (n)	Zwart (Z)
Red	Rouge (r)	Rojo (r)	Rood (R)
Green	Vert (v)	Verde (v)	Groen (Gn)
Yellow	Jaune (j)	Amarillo (am)	Geel (Gl)
White	Blanc (b)	Blanco (b)	Wit (w)
Orange	Orange (org)	Naranja	Oranje (or)
Blue	Bleu (bl)	Azul (az)	Blauw (B)
Brown	Brun	Pardo (p)	Bruin
Violet	Violet (vio)	Violeta	Violet (Vi)
4 RADIO AND AURAL AIDS			
Radiobeacon	Radiophare	Radiofaro	Radiobaken
Diaphone	Diaphone	Diafono	Diafoon
Horn	Nautophone	Nautofono	Nautofoon
Siren	Siène	Sirena	Mistsirene
Reed	Trompette	Bocina	Mistfluit
Explosive	Explosion	Explosivo	Knalsignaal
Bell	Cloche	Campana	Mistklok
Gong	Gong	Gong	Mistgong
Whistle	Sifflet	Silbato	Mistfluit
5 STRUCTURE OR FLOAT			
Dolphin	Duc d'Albe	Dague de Alba	Ducdalf
Light	Feu	Luz	Licht
Lighthouse	Phare	Faro	Lichttoren
Light vessel	Bateau feu	Faro flotanto	Lichtschip
Light float	Feu flottant	Luzflotante	Lichtvlot
Beacon	Balise	Baliza	Baken

ENGLISH	FRENCH	SPANISH	DUTCH
Column	Colonne	Columna	Lantaarnpaal
Dwelling	Maison	Casa	Huis
Framework Tower	Pylone	Armazon	Traliemast
House	Bâtiment	Casa	Huis
Hut	Cabane	Caseta	Huisje
Mast	Mât	Mastil	Mast
Post	Poteau	Poste	Lantaarnpaal
Tower	Tour	Torre	Toren
Mooring buoy	Boueé de corps-mort	Boya de amarre muerto	Meerboei
Buoy	Bouée	Boya	Ton
6 TYPE OF MARKING			
Band	Bande	Fajas horizontales	Horizontaal gestreept
Stripe	Raie	Fajas verticales	Vertikaal gestreept
Chequered	à damier	Damero	Geblokt
Top mark	Voyant	Marea de Tope	Topteken
7 SHAPE			
Round	Circulaire	Redondo	Rond
Conical	Conique	Conico	Kegelvormig
Diamond	Losange	Rombo	Ruitvormig
Square	Carré	Cuadrangular	Vierkant
Triangle	Triangle	Triangulo	Driehoek
8 DESCRIPTION			
Destroyed	Détruit	Destruido	Vernield
Occasional	Feu occasionnel	Ocasional	Facultatief
Temporary	Temporaire	Temporal	Tijdelijk
Extinguished	Éteint	Apagada	Gedoofd
9 TIDE			
High Water	Pleine mer	Pleamar	Hoog water
Low Water	Basse mer	Bajamar	Lagg watery
Flood	Marée montante	Entrante	Vloed
Ebb	Marée decendante	Vaciante	Eb
Stand	Étale	Margen	Stil water
Range	Amplitude	Repunte	Verval
Spring tide	Vive eau	Marea viva	Springtij
Neap tide	Morte eau	Aguas Muertas	Doodtij
Sea level	Niveau	Nivel	Waterstand
Mean	Moyen	Media	Gemiddeld
Current	Courant	Corriente	Stroomt
10 CHART DANGERS			
Sunken rock	Roche subergée	Roca siempre cubierta	Blinde klip
Wreck	Épave	Naufragio (Nauf)	Wrak
Shoal	Haut fond (Ht. Fd.)	Bajo (Bo)	Droogte, ondiepte (Dre.)
Obstruction	Obstruction (Obs.)	Obstrución (Obston.)	Belemmering van de vaart, hindernis (Obstr.)
Overfalls	Remous et clapotis	Escarceos, hileros	Waterrafel
Dries	Assèche	Que vela en bajmar	Droogvallend
Isolated Danger	Danger isolé	Peligro aislado	Losliggend gevaar

ENGLISH	FRENCH	SPANISH	DUTCH
11 WEATHER			
Weather Forecast	Prévions météo	Previsión meteorologica	Weersvoorspelling
Gale	Coup de vent	Duro	Storm
Squall	Grain	Turbonada	Bui
Fog	Brouillard	Niebla	Mist
Mist	Brume légere ou mouillée	Neblina	Nevel
12 DIMENSIONS			
Height	Tirant d'air	Altura	Doorvaarthoogte
Width	Largeur, de large	Ancho, anchura	Breedte
Depth	Profondeur	Fondo, profundidad	Diepte
Draft	Tirant d'eau	Calado	Diepgang

INDEX

D

N

O

P

Q

R

S

T

U

V

W

Y

Z